W9-BNH-983

THE
Versatile Grain
AND THE
Elegant Bean

A Celebration of the World's Most Healthful Foods

Sheryl and Mel London

Illustrated by Kathleen M. Skelly

Simon & Schuster

New York   London   Toronto   Sydney   Tokyo   Singapore

Simon & Schuster
Simon & Schuster Building
Rockefeller Center
1230 Avenue of the Americas
New York, New York 10020

Designed by Richard Oriolo

Manufactured in the United States of America

10 9 8 7 6 5 4 3 2 1

Library of Congress Cataloging-in-Publication Data
London, Mel.
The versatile grain and the elegant bean / by Mel and Sheryl London.
p.   cm.
Includes index.
1. Cookery (Cereals) 2. Cookery (Beans) 3. Grain. 4. Beans.
I. London, Sheryl.   II. Title.
TX808.L65   1992
641.6′31—dc20   91-31857
                                                  CIP

ISBN 0-671-76106-4

Acknowledgments

Until a book is researched, recipes developed, tested, and tasted—kept and enjoyed or discarded because the "evil kitchen gremlins" screwed up the chemistry—until the material is collected, compiled, culled, typed, edited, and retyped, a cookbook is just another vague, vaporous, unfulfilled dream.

Then, suddenly, it's over and that sense of relief is the same that all new parents feel when their baby is shifted from an inside to an outside world. There it is! It's a book!

But no book is ever done alone. There are the esteemed experts who contribute so willingly their wealth of information. There are the people with whom we have consulted, who have given so generously of their time and their advice: the millers, the farmers and the distributors all across the country, the associations and organizations that know so much about grains and about beans, the commissions that always made their members available at the other end of the telephone or through the mail.

We are particularly indebted to Phil Teverow of Dean & DeLuca in New York, possibly one of the most cheerful and knowledgeable of men in the field of the elegant bean. Frank Ford of Arrowhead Mills and the Lundberg Family in California have been old friends for many years now, and both Frank and Harlan Lundberg were most supportive, patiently answering all our questions and opening new doors for us. Our thanks also go to Wayne Carlson of Maskal Forages and Valerie Phipps of the Phipps Ranch, and to Katherine Powis of The Horticultural Society of New York.

And then, of course, comes the really challenging part, the tasting. For just as important to the accuracy of any cookbook is the necessary testing and tasting as well as the critiquing of the recipes.

During the summer months, this was not a problem, for our Fire Island community has a wealth of eager, potential tasters and judges, and tests were delivered to them by bicycle as they came out of the kitchen. But as winter approaches on our island, the families leave and only a few year-round residents remain. With our only store closed, there was no place for fresh supplies and so we returned to the Big Apple and distributed our tests to a fresh supply of "big city" friends and neighbors.

Our thanks therefore go to all who tasted along the way. To our beloved agent, neighbor and friend Madeleine Morel, a special accolade. She refused no test and loved almost everything. To Kathleen Skelly, our best Fire Island tester, whose stunning illustrations are part of this book, we also say thanks. And finally, a bow to our most available, encouraging, patient, loving, understanding and *simpático* editor, Toula Polygalaktos. We have, indeed, been blessed.

For our dear friends
Robert Brascomb
and
Tom Schwab
who are as great together as grains
and beans.

Contents

Contents

Introduction

About ten years ago we published a book that set out to be the "complete" volume on the subject of whole grains and pasta, with some additional information and recipes for legumes or a combination of both. Since we had always been partial to whole grains, fresh vegetables, nonprocessed foods, and to an awareness of a healthful, balanced diet, we spent almost two years in the complex process of creating, testing, tasting (some rejecting), and compiling recipes and information on the subject.

It was ten short years ago, and it was a time when the first reaction to any book about whole grains was bound to bring the comment, "How on earth can you write a whole book about *breakfast?*"

It was a time when now familiar grains such as amaranth, quinoa, and triticale and legumes such as Soldier Beans, azuki, Jacob's Cattle and Christmas limas would bring a blank stare from friends and store clerks alike. Beans were "poor food." Beans were for chili. Millet was for birds. Oats were for "porridge."

Indeed, it was a time when, if unusual grains or beans *were* available, they were only in health food stores. At that time, trying to find any of the overwhelming varieties of grains or legumes such as heirloom beans required an intense and wide-ranging hunt. Added to this, when we finally did find a particular grain, we generally had to grind it down ourselves. We made our own barley grits in a food mill. Rodale's experimental farms gave us amaranth kernels, but we cleaned and pulverized the grain ourselves and we popped it in ingenious Japanese sesame toasters over an open flame atop our kitchen stove.

We learned to make flour from triticale sent to us by our friend Frank Ford at Arrowhead Mills in Texas. Teff was just a name in the dictionary, and even the Ethiopian restaurant in our neighborhood made their *injera* bread not from teff but from Aunt Jemima Pancake Mix! As for quinoa, in spite of its long history dating back to the Incas, it had not yet resurfaced to become a part of our culinary parlance.

In a sense, all of this is quite strange, since much of the world has utilized both grains and legumes as a basic mainstay of its diet, and has done so for thousands of years. Combined in a vast range of diverse and interesting recipes, grains and legumes provide substantial amounts of protein, complex carbohydrates, small amounts of fat, and a range of natural fibers that give the combination extraordinary nutritional vigor. It is no accident that the combination has been the principal food pairing of much of the world.

Almost every national cuisine on every continent has developed a dish that combines the two in what Karen MacNeil in *The Book of Whole Foods* calls a "culinary partnership." The classic example, perhaps, is the basic combination of rice and beans of Latin America *(Moros y Cristianos)*. It has become so ubiquitous and the partnership so intimate that we frequently feel it can be spelled as one word: *ricenbeans!* The Lebanese combine lentils and rice or bulgur in *Mejedrah,* and an ancient Jewish dish called *cholent* is made with barley and lima beans. The Africans blend pigeon peas with rice, the Japanese use azuki beans with their glutinous rice, and the Italian *minestra alla Milanese* combines fresh green beans with risotto. Even more familiar, perhaps, is our Native American *succotash* (lima beans and fresh corn). So this partnership of grains and legumes has always been available to us, if only we cared, and if only we cared to look.

Except for a small segment of the population, Americans generally seemed to consider both grains and legumes as very low on the food chain. Since the price has always been quite moderate (and still is), as recently as ten years ago grains and legumes were both ignored and denigrated as "peasant diet." In that sense, interestingly enough, we were no different from the ancient Romans, who considered dark whole grain breads as fit only for the serfs and the slaves, while the bread made from the refined white flour with all of its nutrition milled out was the bread of the elite.

In addition, both grains and beans have received inaccurate and distorted bad press about their preparation time, another reason for us to reject something nutritious and tasty in an era when "time is of the essence," and we're all so busy that if it can't be microwaved or delivered by messenger, it can't be done at all.

And finally, when we take all of these reasons, valid or not, and add to them the constant marketing/advertising hoopla of the country's purveyors and manufacturers of *processed foods,* it is quite understandable that what may well be the most perfect combination of foods available—at the lowest cost—has been very slow to gain recognition by the vast majority of America's consumers.

Well, to quote a folk song that keeps running through our heads:

The Times They Are A-changin'

Whatever the reasons—possibly because we are better informed, or are paying more attention to our diets, or because we are just getting smarter—we have begun to "rediscover" the value of both grains and legumes. It was the plunderers Pizarro and Cortés and their followers who declared the Incas and the Aztecs "backward," destroying their crops of quinoa and amaranth, both of which had been grown for more than 4,000 years, replacing them with the European staples of barley, rye and wheat.

It is ironic, therefore, that these ancient grains, along with the thousands of varieties of legumes that have been cultivated since antiquity, have now been declared the foods of the future!

And, as so often happens, a revitalized interest in almost anything is bound to see a dramatic rise in the availability of that product. So it has been with whole grains, and certainly, with legumes. Where once the health food store was the only source, both grains and beans are now beginning to appear in supermarkets across the country, as well as in Middle Eastern and Asian specialty food stores, gourmet shops, and other ethnic centers.

We are beginning to see grains and beans that were once rarely found now beginning to proliferate—not only amaranth and triticale and quinoa, but teff, the staple of Ethiopia, Native American blue corn, and a range of beans that we cover later in this book. That range has broadened beyond the familiar lentil or kidney bean to the poetically named anasazi, appaloosa and Spanish tolasana beans. What was once considered "exotic" has taken its place on the supermarket and specialty food shop shelves right next to what we have always thought of as quite ordinary and familiar.

Another sign of the growth and interest in whole grains and legumes has been the menus of chic restaurants. Almost everywhere that we travel today, we find that professional chefs are making certain to include one or more dishes that utilize either whole grains or some variety of legume in combination with meats, fish or poultry, or as a major ingredient in a salad. Over the past few years, the trend seems to be moving toward more bistro food in restaurants and away from the "pretty very small food" of so-called nouvelle cuisine (which many of us will never miss). And, in those bistro dishes, the cuisine almost demands the use of legumes, such as in the classic French cassoulet.

We should add one kind word here about the much-maligned health food stores of years back. At the time, some of them might well have deserved their less-than-wholesome reputation, though many were actually havens for younger people who were light-years ahead of their time in terms of nutrition and the problems with chemically treated products. But, as the world has changed in its attitude toward nutrition and diet, so have the shops that specialize in natural foods. All across the country, health food stores have become an important and varied resource for the home cook. Their range is awesome, and in addition to the fresh organically grown produce, herbs, oils and specialty cereals they provide, they are perfect places in which to find some of the grains and legumes that might not be carried by your local supermarket: buckwheat, barley, millet, rye, basmati and Wehani rice, to name but a very few. In addition, they generally are a perfect source for the variety of *forms* that might be called for in a recipe: groats or grits, meal or flour, cracked or whole grain berries.

There is a final and very important point that we'd like to make. Along with the "rediscovery" of which we spoke, another realization has taken hold in the home kitchens of America: that grains mean more than *breakfast* and that legumes mean much more than chili or "poor food." You will find in this book, for example, that we have used the versatile grain and the elegant bean for every meal of the day, breakfast, lunch, and dinner (and even some between-meal snacks). And we have offered them for everything from appetizers through soups, entrées, side dishes, breads and even some surprising, delectable and tasty desserts.

We hope that we have proven that it is time to discard the myth that the use of whole grains and legumes means *vegetarian* dishes. Certainly, people so inclined will find much to delight them. But, both whole grains and beans can be (and are) used with every category of meat, fish and poultry, at the same time allowing us to reduce the *amounts* of those ingredients while still retaining taste and certainly nutrition. It can become a most successful and joyful alternative way of eating.

Also in the interest of nutrition, taste and an awareness of contemporary culinary demands, we have paid particular attention to the use of sweeteners, fats, and oils and the addition of salt. For variety of taste, we have suggested not only brown and white sugar but also an occasional addition of maple syrup or light honey. As aware of the problems of saturated fats and cholesterol as just about everyone in America is today, you will find that we have used a range of low-cholesterol fats and oils wherever possible, with a great many recipes using canola or corn oil, and Mediterranean dishes that utilize olive oil. You'll also find, on occasion, oriental sesame seed oil is suggested. And as for butter, we have kept it to a minimum, using it only where we thought it important for flavor.

Salt has been covered in another part of the book (see pages 16–17) since this is a subject not easily dealt with in a sentence or two. Some grains require salt *during* cooking; others must be salted *after* cooking and the water in which we cook legumes should *never* be salted before or during cooking. In addition, the *amount* of salt used is really a very personal choice.

As in every one of our cookbooks, each recipe included here has been created and tested by us. Where we have included recipes that have a background of tradition—sort of "the way Grandma used to make it"—we have tried new approaches to those traditional favorites, while still retaining the tastes that we remember. The testing began well over ten years ago and has continued apace right up to the present time.

And, of course, if they were tested, they were also tasted, both by us and by our friends. Some were rejected. The ones that fill the pages that follow were included only after proof that they could meet the standards of flavor and of appearance that would convince our readers and their guests that their own "discovery" of the "rediscovery" was certainly worthwhile.

We hope that you, too, will find what we have found over these many years by adopting a diet that includes both grains and beans. It is—in a phrase that only the Italians could put so poetically—*"modo di vivere"*—a way of life. We know you'll enjoy it.

Sheryl and Mel London
FIRE ISLAND, NEW YORK

THE
Versatile Grain

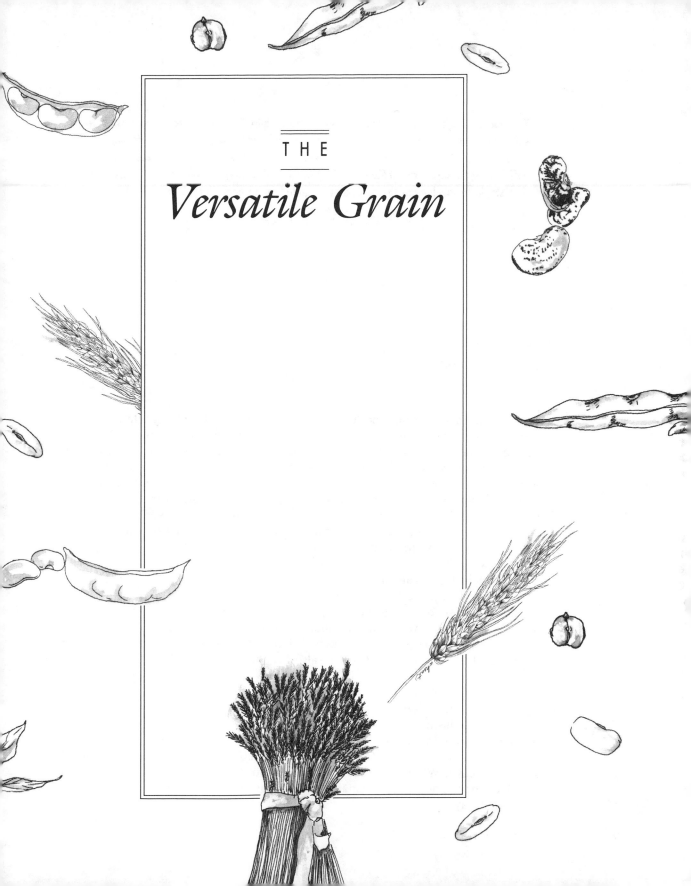

The story...began when the Ice Age was losing its grip. The frozen, iron-hard earth was softening, just enough to support wild grasses and shrubs where the glaciers had retreated...in 10,000 B.C., bromegrass flourished in Kentucky and Kansas, and men pursued buffalo over the sage scrub of Montana....The seeds of [these] wild grasses were harvested as a staple to supplement the buffalo meat grilled on an open fire...

—Adrian Bailey,
The Blessings of Bread

The

Versatile

Grain

and the

Elegant

Bean

2

Tracing the history of grain is not unlike following an adventure story filled with tales of the hunt, survival under the most trying of conditions by small family groups, the changing weather patterns that determined what might be grown and just which cereal grasses might survive until the harvest. As far back as the Neolithic period, the small crop yields were a buffer against starvation, and the villages were centered around the fields of wild wheat (or more probably the grain called spelt, a variety that thrives in poor soil), or of barley or oats. For the wheel had not yet been invented, and when the harvest was over and the fields lay fallow, the entire village moved on to another more promising valley, to plant their seeds once again.

When we read the remarkable and fascinating books that detail the chronicles of grain, such as Reay Tannahill's *Food in History* or the peerless Waverly Root and his *Food,* and we realize that this saga has been a part of our history for so many millennia, we must admit that there is a naggingly malicious part of us that begins to surface. We remember when our own mothers placed the morning hot cereal in front of us and said, with no opportunity for childish rebuttal, "Eat your oatmeal! It's good for you!" Did the mothers of 9000 B.C. also say the very same thing to *their* young ones, possibly calling the oatmeal by whatever they called it in those days: porridge, or possibly pottage or gruel or just plain mush? And if this is so, the most interesting thing about it is that *both* mothers were right! It *is* good for you.

These ties to history are not too farfetched; the Roman Legionnaires were allotted two pounds of grain a day. They roasted it on hot stones or they boiled the grain in water to make a kind of porridge. Then it was cooled and it hardened into a sort of unsweetened cake. When the Romans brought it to the British Isles, it was adopted by the local population and it remains there today, though prepared in a bit more *sophisticated* way.

The continuing saga of this most remarkable and versatile food source has continued uninterrupted on every single continent from the most ancient of times right up until the present. Indeed, no major civilization has ever evolved and thrived *without* growing a basic grain, and even today, more than half the arable land on this earth of ours is devoted to the growing of cereal grasses. And each and every country, each and every grain, has its legends, its history, its traditions, and even its myths and symbolism.

We remember reading some years back about a discovery of an ancient Sudanese people along the banks of the Nile River. They had settled there about fourteen centuries ago, and the archaeologists who unearthed the settlement discovered to their amazement that the bones contained large amounts of the antibiotic tetracycline. Had the doctors of that era known about tetracycline, it would have been no great revelation. But, in this case, the University of Massachusetts research group came up with the theory that the bacteria that manufacture the drug had grown spontaneously in the mud bins of grain—the wheat, the barley and the millet. Not unexpectedly, therefore, they also found that the Sudanese who lived there between the years A.D. 350 and A.D. 550 had a very low rate of infectious disease.

Archaeologists have also discovered silos of maize in their excavations of the Mayan cities. Wheat and barley were found in the ruins of civilizations that date back to Mesopotamia, ancient Greece and the Egypt of the earliest pharaohs. Even frigid Iceland was a cultivator of grain until, about the fourteenth century, the weather turned colder and the staple of the diet became the abundant fish in the surrounding waters. Rice came to Europe with the Saracens, though it had been grown for centuries in China. The Aztecs were growing amaranth and the Incas were cultivating quinoa long before the Spaniards arrived to plunder and to teach them all about "civilization." Grains were not only basic to the diets, they were sometimes the salvation during hard times of famine. In France during the seventeenth century, the universal diet of the peasants was bread and bean soup. The British philosopher John Locke reported that "there was no flesh in the countryside" of France, and that grains and beans were the basic meal.

It is no accident, then, that grains have become a part of tradition and even of veneration, brought right up to the present time here in America as we celebrate our endless wheat fields as "the amber waves of grain." The Roman goddess of agriculture was Ceres, and each year she presided over the festival of Cerealia. In Japan, the god who symbolizes food, well-being and prosperity is known as the Great Grain Spirit. The Incas celebrated maize as the Child of the Sun, the Babylonians worshipped wheat and the Romans kept the masses in check with a combination of "bread and circuses."

The popularity of a particular grain is very much the result of the climate in which it thrives; thus, certain cultures have come to depend upon a specific species as a part of their culinary heritage. The cuisine of a particular area usually reflects its most abundant crops: the sorghum and millet of subtropical China and Africa; the buckwheat of colder Russia; the oats of Scotland and Ireland; the wheat and rye of the Great Plains here in the United States as well as the Canadian prairies and central Russia; the rice of the paddy fields of Texas, the terraced flooded beds of the Philippines and China, and the wet Po Valley of Italy. And, as for corn, it is at home almost all across the Americas and Africa.

Understandably, then, the national dishes of any nation will also reflect their most abundant grain crop: *tsampa* (the barley paste of Tibet), *sushi* (Japan), *oatmeal* (Scotland), *polenta* (Italy), *mealie porridge* (sorghum, millet or maize in Africa), *chapatis* (the wheat of India), *injera* (teff and millet bread of Ethiopia), or *johnnycakes* (white cornmeal and claimed by our Rhode Islanders). Some of these dishes have remained right where they were developed, while others have been successful in making the journey to other regions; possibly oatmeal and sushi are the best examples of well-traveled dishes. However, when Columbus brought back maize from the New World, the Europeans did not take it to their bosoms and they are still not a major producer of the crop, while here in the United States we measure our bounty in the millions of metric tons.

There is one disturbing note to all of this. In spite of its history as a staple and even as the salvation of cultures, in spite of the fact that grains can be (and are) one of the most versatile and nutritious foods, in spite of the fact that our grandmothers and the grandmothers of Europe, Africa, Asia and South America all understood that grains are "good for you," most of this adaptable food source goes directly to feed the animals!

Possibly the reason is not "in spite of" all these things. Possibly it is *because,* here in the West, grains have gotten the historical reputation of feeding the peasant populations during famines, "the poor food syndrome." Possibly it is because we have relegated this remarkable food to a few predictable uses: in breads, cakes, and breakfast cereals. But, the fact still remains that much of what we grow goes to the four-legged population and to the birds.

Oats are for horses. Millet is for the parakeets. Corn is fed to chickens, and a majority of that crop goes to fatten animals, possibly the most inefficient way in which to feed the cattle that will become tomorrow's steaks. We do find that wheat (in dry, temperate zones) and rice (in hot, humid regions) are two major grains that are consumed by human beings. However, as little as *one pound of wheat per year* is consumed directly, the way in which we benefit most from whole grains!

The

Versatile

Grain

and the

Elegant

Bean

4

The Nutrition Pioneers

Certainly there have always been small groups of people who were informed, and who possibly were well ahead of their times. For whatever reasons, they understood that grains were not only healthy and versatile, but were tasty as well. During the first rumblings that heralded a change in America's dietary habits, the food industry was quick to read the handwriting on the wall, sensing a challenge to the establishment, and labeling the counterculture of the sixties as "food neurotics" and "food McCarthyites" (as one well-known fashion magazine did).

Of course, the small group of groundbreakers did contain an element of romanticism and naïveté in their call for a total return to tofu, brown rice and labor-intensive foods. But, somehow, their basic message began to get through, and as Professor Warren Belasco writes in his book *Appetite for Change,* what the food industry first took as a challenge soon became a full-blown panic by the beginning of the seventies. Belasco calls the result "the food wars" and even the government joined in, as then Secretary of Agriculture Earl Butz and allied nutritionists began to attack the *ethics* of these food industry critics.

From the few lone voices of the counterculture, we began to see other signs that people were finally listening. *The Whole Earth Catalog,* first published in 1968, became an almost instant best-seller, followed in turn by other books about nutrition and healthful diets, such as *Fighting the Food Giants* by Paul Stitt and *The Taste of America* by Karen and John Hess. There were speeches and articles by individuals who were once the curmudgeons of our society but who are now considered our food sages: Alice Waters, the late Bob Rodale, Karen and John Hess, Joan Gussow, and Mo Siegel (who founded Celestial Seasonings). Somehow, it finally began to work. We think that somewhere around the end of the 1970s, or possibly at the beginning of the 1980s, the attitude of the *general public* began to change.

By the time we entered the 1990s, every sign showed a new acceptance by a broad range of consumers, many of whom had been raised at the knee of America's packaged, processed food industry and at the counters of the fast food emporiums. Not only was this evident in the realm of whole grains but in other food areas as well. (In spite of George Bush's aversion to it, we note that the per capita consumption of *broccoli* grew over 200 percent in a ten-year period beginning in the mid-seventies!) This era represents the peak of our awareness about saturated fats, about cholesterol and about fiber. Every magazine and most major newspapers have now begun to remind us that the lowly reputation of whole grains has been misunderstood and, thus, should be much improved.

We now begin to find recipes for millet and rye, for oats and Job's tears (a form of barley), for quinoa and for amaranth in all the popular magazines and in the food sections of our newspapers. Perhaps we Americans are beginning to mature in terms of our food choices and our probing for something just a little bit different, for something new, for something to tempt our palates and for something that is, indeed, very good for us. Perhaps we are just beginning to find out some of the things that our elders *instinctively* knew.

We hasten to add one other point about this return to the "comfort foods" of our heritage. The resurgence of grain as a staple would not have happened if it did not also *taste good*. The wide variety of ethnic dishes that have developed all over the world took good advantage of the hearty *flavors* and distinctive tastes inherent in each and every grain, indeed, in each and every *form* of each grain. You'll find, as you go through this book, and as you sample some of the recipes, that we have tried to be true to this concept. It is not by chance that we have called them *versatile grains*.

The

Versatile

Grain

and the

Elegant

Bean

6

The Nutritional Realities

It is quite possible that it is in the area of *nutrition* that grain has been most misunderstood, misquoted and certainly exploited, particularly via the "fads" that have descended upon us through the advertising and marketing techniques of America's food hierarchy.

There was a time not too long ago when the daily newspapers featured photographs of heavyweight champions and long distance runners smiling as they devoured their precontest, well-marbled, thick-cut, blood red, Brobdingnagian-sized slab of steak. Protein was for energy. Saturated animal fat was for endurance. Calories came from animal fat to be burned on the long trek to the finish line or in the boxing ring. During these years of change, we have all noticed that the pictures have given way to athletes eating their last meal for energy—but the chances are that the dish contains *pasta!* There was a time when we were told that *carbohydrates* made us fat. What ever happened to that theory?

It is not protein that your body uses to provide energy in the form of blood sugar glucose. It is the *complex carbohydrates* that do the job, the same form of carbohydrates found in all grains (and in dishes such as pasta), in fruits, vegetables, and in nonfat dairy products. Of course, the body needs its proteins, especially in the early formative years when we are building our body structure and the connective tissues that layer our muscles. We also need more protein after serious illness when there is a need to rebuild muscle tissue. And protein requirements for pregnant or lactating women are much higher. But, for the rest of us, a small amount of grain plus a few ounces of poultry, fish, meat or dairy products—or the addition of legumes—will make the average daily diet quite complete by adding the necessary amino acids.

Enough has been written about the saturated fat in our diet to fill a great many volumes twice the size of this book, but when we compare the nutritional statistics of the average Western diet to one that consists mainly of grains, legumes and moderate portions of meat or dairy products, we begin to see just why it all begins to make sense.

The average fast food hamburger (by whatever name we call it) offers us about 600 calories, mostly in saturated fat. Switching to a batter-fried chicken dinner with all the fixings (mashed potatoes, coleslaw and white rolls) will come somewhere near 850 calories, also astoundingly high in saturated fat. A ten-ounce steak has almost 1,000 calories, 80 percent in fat. And, it is the *fat* that puts the weight on us about twice as fast as either protein or carbohydrates. When we read that a new fast-food emporium appears somewhere at the rate of one every fifteen hours, we are reminded of something the Comte de Volney wrote in another era: "I will venture to say that if a prize were proposed for the scheme of a regimen most calculated to injure the stomach, the teeth, and the health in general, no better could be invented than that of the Americans."

Certainly, saturated fat alone is not the only villain in our diets and health. Heredity has been said to play a part and it probably does. We smoke too much. We work at jobs that create and foster stress, so that food becomes a "sometime thing" taken when we can get it, while eating all the wrong things. We also lay claim to the greatest "sugar fix" in history, with the average individual consuming *over 100 pounds a year!* Sugar, of course, is also a carbohydrate, but what we call a "simple" one. Thus, it is quickly used by the body as a rapid, "pick-me-up" energy source, leaving us even more enervated than before we ate it.

Those who have made an effort to include grains in their diets have learned, as we have, that fiber-rich, complex carbohydrate–filled grains contain much greater amounts of bulk than the foods that we've mentioned earlier. Thus, we are satisfied with smaller portions of each dish, be it appetizer, entrée or dessert. We eat smaller portions. We need less food. One hundred grams of grain will generate only 350 calories, all of it filled with potential energy and no saturated fat.

We have touched on one other value of whole grains, fiber, and it is something that should not go unnoticed. Grains—and fresh fruits and vegetables—are possibly the best source of both soluble and insoluble *fiber* that has yet been found. Soluble fiber helps lower cholesterol levels and stabilize the blood sugar, while insoluble fiber can help with bowel regularity and has been said to reduce the risk of colon cancer by speeding food through the intestines. It is a source of wonder and amusement to us that so much of the food establishment sells the fiber back to us in packages when it is there for us to see and use and eat in its *natural* form, and at a much lower price. If "so many doctors recommend" a commercial fiber laxative, we wonder why they don't just recommend *the whole grain* to begin with!

We are not naive. You may be certain that any new trend in any area of our lives will be followed by an avalanche of new products that will take what we've always had, process it, package it, advertise it, and then sell it back to us at five times the price of the original, perfectly good product. Grains have been no exception. And the food industry has not disappointed us.

The

Versatile

Grain

and the

Elegant

Bean

8

The Nutrition Exploiters:
Building Up the Hype

The first major group to take advantage of the new awareness about the value of whole grains was the breakfast food industry. Little did the pioneer John Harvey Kellogg realize what would transpire when, as a young medical student in the nineteenth century, he begrudged the time and effort it took to prepare the oats, wheat and corn that he bought in bulk. Possibly Kellogg was the first yuppie, for he wrote, "It often occurred to me that it should be possible to purchase cereals at groceries already cooked and ready to eat." Had there been Chinese take-out at that time, the entire history of the industry might be different today!

And so, from his first attempts at what he called Granola, there evolved an industry of ready-to-eat cereals that would eventually bear such euphonious appellations not only of Corn Flakes but Froot Loops, Count Chocula, Cocoa Pebbles and Sugar Pops, possibly the latter being the only one that gave a correct emphasis to a major ingredient in all of them: sugar.

The fact that processing makes these cereals lose most of their vitamins and minerals as the grains are refined seemed to mean nothing to the general public. The fact that chemical preservatives are added to increase shelf life, that protein quality declines and that the basic, original taste of the grain is totally lost has also not seemed to keep the industry from growing into a giant that accounts for nearly *$7 billion* in sales a year at the wholesale level! More incredible, perhaps, is the fact that when a new cereal is introduced, or a new "fad" begins to take hold, it can cost up to $30 million just to develop, test and market the new product.

Cost has never been a factor in making the decision. When new buzzwords began to appear, so did new cereal names—from Kellogg, General Mills, Ralston Purina, Quaker Oats, and lesser-known manufacturers all across the country. To attract the health-conscious adult, advertisers began to inundate us with ways to reduce cholesterol, and add fiber to our diets, and reduce or eliminate sodium and sugar. They renamed the products, increased the price and sold them back to us as "natural" or "light" or "cholesterol-free." With tongue in cheek, Dr. Henry Solomon of the Cornell Medical Center wrote that food labeling was so ludicrous that poison could practically be called healthy if it didn't contain the word "cholesterol." So, sales and profits began to mount, then someone discovered that *oat bran* might well lower cholesterol and profits soared.

All grains are composed of several layers. All come from cereal grasses and are the edible seeds of those grasses. Each kernel has four parts, with an outer hull or husk, generally inedible; this part is removed by methods that vary according to the culture and the tightness of the hull. Wheat, for example, can have the hull removed by threshing, ranging from sophisticated winnowing machines down to the peasant throwing the grains up in a blanket and letting the wind take the chaff. With the hull removed, we still have the whole grain. When we cook it and eat it that way, we derive every bit of nutrition from it that it was meant to give.

The next protective covering on the grain is known as the *bran*. Aside from being rich in vitamins and minerals, it is the prime source of soluble fiber. Under the bran is what we call the *germ,* or the embryo of the seed. When we sprout grains, this is the part that grows, and it's very rich in enzymes, protein, minerals, fat and vitamins. If we polish away both the bran and the germ, we refine the grain to the next layer, the starchy center called the endosperm. Basically, this layer gives us only carbohydrates, as in white flour.

And so, the food industry targeted bran, and specifically oat bran, for someone had come up with the theory that oat bran could reduce cholesterol (but failed to stress the fact that you also had to cut back severely on saturated fat and dietary cholesterol, plus eating fifty grams a day—about half a cup—for six to eight weeks). For two years, the sales of oat bran and oat bran products climbed, and with more than 450 varieties of cereals from which to choose, we were then overwhelmed by another thousand claims that if we bought any of them and ate it we'd live longer, healthier, richer, more productive lives.

There were some doubters, of course. A study that was published in the *New England Journal of Medicine* indicated that oat bran did, indeed, reduce cholesterol, but primarily because *it made people too full to eat fatty foods.* The study concluded that the same effect might be achieved by eating *linguine!*

For two years the hoopla lasted. And then the public began to read the labels more carefully, become rightly cynical about "miracle ingredients" and oat bran *pills* that translated into *fifty* 1,000-milligram pills a day without any guarantee that they even worked. The oat bran muffins of a leading fast food chain actually contained 122 more calories than their Bavarian cream–filled doughnut covered with chocolate frosting! And if fiber was needed, 20 to 35 grams a day from nature's bounty of grains, fruits and vegetables, of what value was a breakfast cereal that promised 2 to 4 grams per one-ounce serving?

With all this, too, sugar was and is still a major ingredient, sometimes masquerading under the aliases of honey or fructose, corn syrup or dextrose. All of the latter provide as many calories as sugar, with the best-selling children's cereals weighing in at over *one tablespoon per serving!*

The sales began to drop and oat bran started to take its place with the Edsel, *Liberty* magazine and Dr. Kellogg's original Granola. Instantly, a new darling of the processed food industry began to surface: *rice bran.*

The most interesting thing about the rice bran phenomenon is that rice bran was unfit for human consumption until just recently. It had a tendency to turn rather rancid very quickly, but modern technology learned how to stabilize it and it then joined the ranks of the latest buzzwords for instant nutrition and the lowering of cholesterol, along with offering the consumer yet another way to include dietary fiber in the diet.

The

Versatile

Grain

and the

Elegant

Bean

10

The New Awareness—
the New Consumer

Has it all been bad? Certainly not. First of all, we think that all the publicity (good and bad), all the advertising (even the hype) and all the newspaper and magazine articles have made the public much more aware of health concerns and the role that whole grains and fiber can play. In addition, there have actually been processed products put on the market that are quite good, that are actually high in fiber and that contain no sugar, sodium or saturated fat. Even the major manufacturers mentioned earlier have made a concerted effort to put whole grain products on the shelves that meet the most stringent criteria and the constant questioning by an ever more sophisticated public. Of course, label reading is still a must, and we note each time we visit our local supermarket that more and more shoppers are carefully scrutinizing the ingredients lists before the product goes into the basket.

Most importantly, perhaps, is the fact that what once was the cry of the counterculture to eliminate preservatives, lower saturated-fat intake and increase dietary fiber has now become the cause of the establishment consumer. The food industry has taken note not only with some of the changes that we've mentioned but also in the areas of substituting vegetable oils for palm, palm kernel and coconut oils and lowering the saturated-fat content of beef. The latter industry still advertises it as "Real Food for Real People," but it also urges moderation in almost everything we eat by cutting down suggested serving sizes not only of beef but of chicken and fish to a modest three-ounce portion. We are beginning to see the demise of the ads that once promoted the "Giant Texas He-Man Steaks" of sixteen ounces or more.

The restaurants that once offered those huge cuts of beef are now featuring lunches that are low in calories, cholesterol and sodium. One of the pioneers, for example, was the famous Four Seasons restaurant in New York; its "Spa Cuisine" was introduced in 1983 and is still going strong today, and we have seen a similar trend all across the country.

And finally, one of the best signs, especially for the authors of a cookbook such as this, is that all of the new awareness, all of the publicity about health and diet, has made the consumer and the home cook realize that there is a world there *outside* of breakfast, especially when it comes to whole grains. There is also a world of ethnic and native dishes that utilizes not only the remarkable fourteen major varieties of grain but a combination of multigrains and a vast assortment of grain *forms* with which to expand our repertoire, while offering both our families and ourselves the most nutritious and the tastiest of diets.

How to Buy Grains

For anyone breaking the bonds of "quick-cooking oatmeal" or "instant grits," the vast selection and choice of grains available these days can be somewhat overwhelming and sometimes very confusing. There are, first of all, the major varieties of grain, many of which are quite interchangeable in recipes. Added to that, each grain can be broken down into a vast array of classifications and forms, all with different properties.

Barley, for example, has more than 200 varieties and the type used for beer is substantially different from the one used for bread or for soup. The rye used for bread is different from the rye used for whiskey. And when it comes to corn, one variety is an ingredient in succotash, yet another is the basic ingredient for tortillas, another for the seasonal, delicious corn on the cob. The movie theater candy counter popcorn or the home version of the same uses yet another type of corn.

Though some packaged grains do give specific instructions about how to prepare them, we have found those guidelines are not always accurate. In addition, not all the *forms* of a particular grain are available commercially packaged, and thus instructions are not readily at hand for the many uses to which that grain form can be put. This is especially true if you purchase your grains from the open sacks at the local health food store or from the covered bins that line the aisles in an array that is quite impressive. Thus, at the beginning of every chapter, we have given the forms of grain that are now available, as well as basic instructions on how to cook everything from grits to groats, from cracked, flaked and popped grains to the flours, meals and sprouts. We have also included a basic recipe for the particular grain, since many grains have different ratios of liquid to grain.

Armed with all of this, here are some general things to look for when you're purchasing grains:

Packaged Grains

We have touched on processed grains earlier in the book, especially in our description of breakfast cereals (see page 9). Keep in mind that any grain that has been processed has also probably lost much of its nutrition in the manufacturing process. It is the raw whole groat or berry that retains much of the nutrition originally put

The

Versatile

Grain

and the

Elegant

Bean

12

there by nature. Keep in mind, too, that the word "natural" means little or nothing these days, for both sugar and salt are included in this category.

You will find that the packaged toasted grain will have a longer shelf life, but much of the mineral and vitamin content will have been lost. And no matter which form of grain you buy, we strongly suggest that you use the amount needed for the recipe and store the remainder as we've suggested later on in this chapter.

Buying Grain in Bulk

We happen to be quite lucky in this area. Within a short five blocks from our New York home, there are at least five stores that carry whole grains in large tempting sacks or in row upon row of pull-out plastic drawers that let us measure out just what we need at the nearby scale. (And at prices that are about one tenth the cost of packaged grains.) They carry marvelous names like Pete's Spice and Angelica's. In other cities across the country, we have seen the same displays in natural food stores. Not only will you find a vast variety of grains by investigating these stores, but you can also buy small amounts rather than the pre-packed eight- or twelve-ounce bags on the supermarket shelves.

However, buying your grain products in bulk can be tricky. When you first enter the store, check to see if the air is dry and not damp or funky, since whole grains have a tendency to develop mold under the latter conditions. If there are bins, are they covered? If you feel that your particular store is not reliable when it comes to storing and keeping their whole grains fresh, it might be time to walk a few more blocks or drive to the next supplier. A busy, active shop is generally a good sign that the grain section has a quick turnover of stock.

Buying Grain by Mail

Even with the wide variety available in our own neighborhood, we still purchase many of our grains by mail from the mills and suppliers around the country. Sometimes this is because the form of grain is just not being carried by our local stores; at other times, we find that we are especially fond of a particular mill because its grains are tastier or handle better than the ones being shipped to our retail outlets. The best example we can give is the hominy grits we use for our hearty winter breakfasts. The grits come from a small mill in Tennessee (Falls Mills in Belvidere), and we order it in five-pound sacks, in spite of the fact that grits are available from five different sources right in our neighborhood.

We have listed some mail order sources at the back of the book, and you'll find that all of them are most gracious and quite willing to ship everything from grits to graham flour. You might also check your local telephone directory for the names of any food cooperatives that might have been formed in your area. Once a mainstay of the counterculture diets of the sixties, many cooperatives have become much more mainstream and now carry a full range of fruits and vegetables, as well as grains.

Cleaning Grains

Most of the packaged grains, especially those from the major suppliers we've mentioned earlier, are quite clean, having been picked over at their source. However, if you purchase your grains in bulk, as we generally do, they have usually been shipped right from the fields or the mills, and in some cases, you'll find tiny bits of chaff, weed seeds or pebbles mixed in the grains. They're easy to see and easy to remove.

First of all: *Don't wash the grains before storing them!* They have a tendency to stick together when they're wet, and they'll get moldy rather quickly if you try to store them. Keep the grains dry; lay them out on a piece of white paper or in a jelly roll pan (the sides of the pan will keep the grain from spilling over onto the counter). Then, under a bright light (with your eyeglasses on if you need them), push the grains aside, bit by bit, removing any particles of foreign matter. Repeat the process once more to make sure you've removed the unwanted bits and pieces.

The

Versatile

Grain

and the

Elegant

Bean

14

Storing Grains

There are really two considerations when it comes to storing your grains for any period of time: temperature and space. Whole grains that are stored under perfect conditions can last an incredibly long time. We remember a story told to us by Paul Hawken, who was president of Erewhon Trading Company, about a farmer in North Dakota who had wheat that was ten years old and still had a 97 percent germination rate. That, along with the archaeological tales of viable grains being found in the ancient tombs of Egypt, lends truth to the statement that proper storage is one of the keys to a long "shelf life."

There are some simple rules for keeping grains fresh and available, without having constantly to make space on the shelves of your cupboards. If you live in a small apartment, as we do, or if storage space is at a premium (which it seems to be for all modern Americans), try to buy your grains in small amounts. Then, store them in one-quart glass jars with tight rubber seals. They make a most colorful decoration in our kitchen, perched atop the highest shelves, with their identifying labels for quick selection.

Grains should always be stored in a dry, cool place, since the germ contains an oil that may eventually turn rancid. Thus, if the shelves of your kitchen are too warm, you may want to refrigerate the grains; they'll keep for months. Of course, our refrigerators offer little space in which to add five or ten jars of grains, so once again we come back to the suggestion that you purchase them in small amounts. No matter how the reliable farms and mills try to keep their storage bins cool, and no matter how close to shipping time the grains are milled or cleaned, you may find that an occasional web or cocoon forms if they're left in too warm a spot, or too humid a kitchen.

A Word About Sprouting and Grinding Grains

Although most grains are now available in all their diverse forms, some of you may want to grind your own grains, or sprout grains and legumes in your own homes, a method that increases the nutritional content substantially. We have included chapters on both, along with tips, instructions and a listing of suppliers of hand and electric mills (see pages 281–285).

About Salt

Everything which inflames one appetite is
likely to arouse the other . . . even salt, in
any but the smallest quantity, is objectionable;
it is such a goad toward carnalism . . .
—Dr. Dio Lewis,
Chastity: or, Our Secret Sins (1874)

Although the current discussions about salt have ignored the good Dr. Lewis's warning, there has been a steady stream of warnings on the subject of salt and hypertension and high blood pressure, sodium overload in processed foods, salt-free diets and solutions, and confessions of "sodium addicts," making it quite unnecessary for us to add our small voices to the flood. However, even though we think that the subject of salt may be very personal, we also feel that it requires a word or two in any book that deals with grains and legumes.

Most processed food and a large majority of restaurant dishes are heavily laden with salt. Indeed, one of the major ingredients in both packages and cans is often salt (read the labels). We have observed our own dinner guests as well as families who are dining out pass the saltshaker around the table *before* they even taste the food that has been put in front of them! Yet, many of those dishes have been salted during the cooking process. A great many well-known chefs adamantly claim that salt has been maligned. Without salt, they say, the dish will lack body; they maintain that salt helps to "tame" hot foods or creates a "taste bridge" for ingredients, or "pulls up" the flavors and makes them "rounder." One well-known West Coast chef claims that he salts his dishes *at every stage.*

On the other hand, some of us who have discarded salt altogether feel that foods such as grains have their own particular flavors and that salt actually masks what the food really tastes like. It brings to mind a statement that we would like to paraphrase a bit: "One person's salt is another person's poison!" Thus, we have tried to do several things in the book that will satisfy both camps.

First of all, we have used many ingredients that provide an excellent way to cut down on salt: fresh herbs (or dried herbs in their absence), citrus (including the pulp

The

Versatile

Grain

and the

Elegant

Bean

16

and the peel of oranges, lemons and limes), as well as fresh vegetables and hot peppers. And, frequently, when we do suggest salt, we can only say *"salt to taste."* This is something we fully understand, since Mel seems to require little or no salt, while Sheryl must have the saltshaker handy and at her side.

There is one critical point when it comes to grains and legumes: *when to use the salt. For grains:* some must be salted *after* cooking (such as amaranth, wheat berries and Wehani brown rice) because salt toughens the outer hull and prevents it from breaking down quickly. *For legumes:* salt is always added *after* they are cooked, since salt added at the beginning will increase your cooking time substantially.

We strongly believe that grains and legumes have their own individual flavors, and what we suggest is that you use a minimal amount of salt if you must, adding more if the taste seems too bland for you. The amounts we have suggested are fairly small. You may want to increase them or eliminate them altogether. But give the natural flavors a chance before you do add salt. As an old friend of ours used to say, "The saltshaker is in your hand."

A recipe is like sheet music. It instructs you on how to get beautiful effects, but you can't fully appreciate a tune until it has been played, or an apple pie until it has been baked.
—Anonymous

SOME GENERAL ADVICE
FOR THE NEW GRAIN COOK

What Pot?

Nonstick—a cleanup blessing. Make sure it has a tight lid so no steam (or very little) can escape. How deep? How wide? A deep pan is best to keep the grains covered with liquid. A wide-bottom pan cooks faster, but needs to be checked more frequently to see if you have the proper amount of water.

Bubble, Bubble, Toil—No Trouble!

Over medium high heat, bring the liquid to a full rolling boil before adding the grain. Add the grain and bring it to a boil again, then cover, reduce the heat to simmer— or use a flame tamer, particularly for electric stoves that don't adjust from high to low immediately.

When Is It Done?

It's done when the grain reaches your personal preference. Some prefer a very soft grain, while others favor a more chewy, toothsome tender bite. However, all the liquid should be absorbed.

While cooking, *don't stir*. Grains bruise easily and tend to get sticky. *Don't peek* while they cook. Steam (moisture) will escape each time the lid is lifted.

If the grain is not to your taste after the liquid has been absorbed, add some boiling water and continue to simmer. Bite test a grain to see if it is done. The underside of a tight pot lid collects moisture, so after cooking, slip a piece of paper towel between the pot and the lid so that the accumulated moisture will be absorbed. Let it stand for five to ten minutes before fluffing with a fork to separate the grains. If some water still remains on the bottom of the pot, just drain it off.

How Much to Cook

Our cooking charts throughout the book are based upon one cup of dry grain, which may yield more cooked grain than some recipes require. We suggest keeping any leftover cooked grain in the freezer for future use as a time and fuel saver. We also find that having cooked grains already on hand makes us use them more frequently in our lunch and dinner recipes.

Amaranth

Amaranthus

Lost Grain of the Aztecs

If we might borrow an amusing comment from food historian Reay Tannahill (*Food in History*), it is unfortunate that Cortés and the Spaniards who discovered Mexico in the sixteenth century were not more concerned with *cooking* than with conquest. Had they been, they might have returned to the Old World with some excellent suggestions about nutrition, about how to prepare maize, and they might also have introduced a remarkable plant that dated back to the Tehuacán cave dwellers more than 8,000 years before.

Unfortunately, the Aztecs practiced cannibalism, and this appalled the Conquistadores, who tortured and executed their own prisoners in the name of Christianity, but who certainly did not *eat* them. A critical part of the Aztec ceremonies was to fashion statues of their war and fire gods from amaranth grain, mixing it either with honey or the sacrificial blood of their victims to form a paste called *zoale*. This was then eaten by the Aztecs or fed to the slaves who were about to be sacrificed.

To history's most bloodthirsty conquerors, this was nothing more than heathen idolatry, a pagan travesty of the Eucharist. And so, among other endeavors that might teach civilization to the Indians, Cortés had Montezuma murdered, the fields of amaranth burned and decreed that anyone in possession of the grain would have both hands cut off.

Prior to all of this, amaranth had been one of the staples in the diet of the Aztecs, a grain so hardy that it grows vigorously under the most adverse conditions, especially in areas that are plagued by drought. Knowing its value, Montezuma is said to have levied annual taxes of amaranth that amounted to somewhere near a quarter million bushels. But, following the crackdown by Cortés, a devastation of the crop that might well be compared with our own "drug war" against coca, amaranth all but disappeared in the Western world, though it does exist in Mexico today as the *alegría* candies, made from popped amaranth and honey.

However, somewhat unnoticed by food historians generally, is the fact that though amaranth might have had its most exciting historical tales woven in Mexico, it has been grown in other parts of the world for centuries. Since both the grain and the leaves are rich sources of nutrition, the plant has been grown in Sri Lanka, India, China, eastern Siberia and the Himalayas, and it is still common in many of those areas as Chinese spinach.

In New Delhi, a confection very much like the Mexican *alegría* is called *laddos,* and among Hindus, popped amaranth grain soaked in milk is the only food allowed on certain festival days. We have read about one method of using amaranth in which it is fermented for the making of beer, while in other parts of Asia, the seeds are parched and milled into flour and then made into a flat bread.

Quite oblivious to all this, the West continued to consider it a "lost" grain until just a few years ago. In 1967, a paper was written by Dr. Jonathan Sauer (then of Stanford University) commenting upon the cultivation of amaranth in India. But it was not until 1973 that some notice was taken of its properties.

Dr. John Robson of the University of Michigan School of Public Health wrote a letter to the late Bob Rodale of Rodale Press detailing his work in famine-stricken areas of Africa. He noticed that the rural people who were eating amaranth and other semiwild plants showed no signs of malnutrition. In conjunction with Rodale's experimental farms at Maxatawney, Pennsylvania, research was started, and it was at that time that we first met amaranth, including it in our earlier book on whole grains.

Nutritionally, it is a most remarkable grain. It is higher in protein than either corn or beans, higher in fiber than wheat, corn, rice or soybeans, rich in vitamins, and it contains the essential amino acid lysine, absent in most other cereal grains. Mixed with wheat, it becomes as complete a protein source as meat or eggs.

It also has marvelous versatility as an ingredient in a range of dishes: breads, salads, candies, pancakes, pilafs or breakfast cereals. (We actually came across a magazine article that recommended a recipe for Amaranth Foo Young! We have, indeed, come a long way.)

The grain cooks easily and quickly, and it always retains its shape. It never gets soft or mushy, the hulls stay firm and chewy and it has an unusual peppery/spicy flavor. It works best in combination with wheat flours since it has a very low gluten content.

The Forms of Amaranth

When we began working with amaranth ten years ago, the only source available to us was from the research facility at Rodale Farms, and even then it was the whole grain, which we and our erstwhile assistant, Tina Gonzalez, had to grind into flour by hand. The few articles that had rediscovered the "lost" Aztec grain were promising that "perhaps one day, it will become more available."

Things have changed tremendously since then. Today, amaranth can be found in several forms, though mostly in health food stores:

The

Versatile

Grain

and the

Elegant

Bean

20

Whole Grain Amaranth. The grain is quite tiny and has been compared in size with millet. The varieties range in color from buff yellow to darker purples and blacks. However, the commercial grains are generally quite pale in color. The grain has an appealing, nutty, almost peppery flavor.

Amaranth Flour. Now quite available across the country in health food stores, milled by several suppliers. It offers a high-quality protein, and when it's mixed with whole wheat flour, the resultant protein balance is close to that recommended for optimum nutrition.

Amaranth Pastas. These can also be found in health food stores. Most are blended with wheat flours.

Commercial Breakfast Cereals. Most of the breakfast cereals sold through health food stores now contain amaranth, sometimes mixed with as many as six other grains to make a substantial, hearty rib-sticking breakfast.

In addition, amaranth grain can be popped and eaten very much like popcorn or used in that form in a range of recipes to add flavor or to lighten the results. The only warning that we might give, however, is that the grain has tremendous keeping power in its natural state, but it turns rancid rather quickly after it's popped. (See below for popping methods.)

Since both the whole grain and the flour are now readily available, we have revised some of our original recipes and have developed some new ones. We feel that, at this point, amaranth has certainly taken its place with the staple grains, coming from the past to stand firmly with the familiar wheat, rye, corn and oats.

How to Pop Amaranth

One cup of amaranth will yield three to four cups of popped amaranth. There are two basic methods by which you can pop amaranth quite easily, depending upon the amount that you need.

For Large Amounts. Use a wok or a heavy skillet. Heat the utensil *while dry* until it is very hot, and then add approximately one tablespoon of the amaranth seeds. A few of the seeds will pop immediately. Use a small pastry brush to keep the seeds moving and to prevent them from burning. When all of the seeds have popped, remove the wok or skillet from the heat and empty the popped seeds into a bowl. Repeat the process until you achieve the desired yield.

For Small Amounts. We use a Japanese sesame seed toaster, which is small and has a removable screen so that the popped seeds don't end up around the kitchen floor. The toaster is available in most Japanese supply shops and is now becoming a part of the regular stock in many kitchen accessory stores. Put one teaspoon of amaranth grain in the toaster, set the screen on top and hold it about two to three inches above the heat source. The seeds will begin to pop in a few seconds.

Popped amaranth has a toasted, nutty flavor.

Amaranth

Grain & Granulation	Amount of Liquid	Cooking Method	Cooking & Standing Time	Approx. Yield	Comments
Whole Grain (1 C. dry)	3 C.	Use nonstick saucepan. In a 3-qt. saucepan, combine water and grain and bring to a boil. Lower heat and simmer, covered.	25 minutes. *No* standing time. Use immediately since grain congeals if left to stand. *Or* press plastic wrap directly on surface of cooked grain to prevent skin from forming. Fork-fluff after standing.	2½ C.	Add salt *after* cooking. Grain has chewy texture and assertive pleasantly almost spicy taste. To rewarm grain, stir in ½ C. boiling water, cover and cook over low heat until warm.

Amaranth, Grilled Eggplant and Green Pepper Salad with Tomato, Cucumber and Feta Cheese

SERVES 8

The eggplant and peppers can be grilled outdoors over coals if you're lucky enough to own a grill and the outdoor space to accommodate it. The version below is for apartment dwellers, who are less fortunate. However, the idea is to achieve a smoky, grilled flavor. The naturally peppery taste of the amaranth strikes just the right note of piquancy and textural contrast in this classic Armenian salad.

Olive oil for brushing pan
2 large eggplants, about 1½ pounds each, stem ends removed and cut in halves lengthwise
1 large green pepper (about ½ pound), cut in half lengthwise and seeded
Coarse salt to taste
⅔ C. cooked amaranth grain (see Chart, opposite page)
1 small red onion, finely minced (about ½ C.)
1 small clove garlic, finely minced (½ tsp.)

1 Tbs. finely minced flat leaf parsley
1 Tbs. finely minced mint
¼ tsp. ground cumin
Salt and freshly ground black pepper to taste
3 Tbs. olive oil
2 Tbs. red wine vinegar
1 Tbs. lemon juice
2–3 plum tomatoes, diced (about 1 C.)
2 Kirby cucumbers or ½ long English cucumber, diced (about 1 C.)
1 oz. feta cheese, crumbled
8 black olives, preferably Kalamata
Sprig mint

Line an 11 × 17-inch jelly roll pan with aluminum foil and brush the surface lightly with olive oil.

Preheat the broiler. Lay the eggplant halves and the green peppers on the prepared pan cut side down. Slip the pan under the broiler on the lowest rack. After about 10 minutes when the skins of the peppers have charred, remove and let cool. Keep the eggplant in the broiler. When the peppers are cool, peel off the skins and cut them into ½-inch squares. There should be about 1 cup.

Grill the eggplants for about 10 minutes more or until the skin is charred. Carefully turn them over and grill for 5 minutes more until soft and lightly browned. Remove from the oven, sprinkle with a bit of coarse salt and turn the eggplants over skin side up. Prop one end of the pan up slightly to drain the eggplants and let cool for about 15 minutes. Now peel off the skin with a small sharp knife, cut the eggplant roughly into cubes and place in a strainer along with the peppers. Put the strainer over a bowl to drain for 10 to 15 minutes more. Then discard the liquid and transfer the eggplant and pepper to a bowl. Add the cooked amaranth and stir well to combine. Then add the onion, garlic, parsley, mint, cumin and the salt and pepper to taste. Stir again and add the olive oil, vinegar, and lemon juice. Gently stir in the tomatoes and cucumber. Cover the bowl and let stand for a minimum of 1 hour for the flavors to meld.

When ready to serve, spoon the mixture onto a large platter. Sprinkle the feta cheese over, stud with the black olives and garnish with the mint. Serve at room temperature along with small leaves of romaine lettuce or wedges of pita bread to act as scoops for the salad.

Savory White Turnip and Amaranth Pancakes

MAKES 14 PANCAKES

The natural sweetness of turnips and the slightly peppery flavor of amaranth are spiked with mustard, orange peel and a haunting whiff of tarragon. Try these pancakes with pork, poultry or grilled duck sausage.

¾ lb. small white turnips, peeled
½ tsp. Dijon-style mustard
2–3 large shallots, finely minced (about
   3 Tbs.)
1 tsp. finely minced orange peel
Pinch dried tarragon, crushed

2 eggs, lightly beaten
¼ C. amaranth flour
Salt and freshly ground black pepper
   to taste
Corn oil for frying

Using the shredder blade of a food processor or a hand grater, shred the turnips and transfer them to a large mixing bowl. Stir in and combine all the remaining ingredients except the corn oil. Using an iron skillet, heat the oil until hot and drop the turnip batter by the tablespoon, flattening each pancake with the back of the spoon. Fry in batches of 4 to 6 at a time until the edges of the pancakes are browned. Turn over and fry the other side. It takes about 3 to 4 minutes for each side. Drain and blot the surface with paper towels and keep them warm in the oven until all the batter is used up.

The

Versatile

Grain

and the

Elegant

Bean

24

Amaranth & Raspberry Muffins
with Oat Streusel

Amaranth and Raspberry Muffins
with Oat Streusel

MAKES 1 DOZEN REGULAR-SIZE MUFFINS
3 DOZEN MINI-SIZE MUFFINS

Who can resist the ruby color and the sweet perfume of the raspberry? And when it's teamed up with the peppery hint of amaranth, the sweetness of the berries is enhanced even more in these easy, unusual muffins.

Oat Streusel

2 Tbs. old-fashioned rolled oats
2 Tbs. all-purpose flour
2 Tbs. light brown sugar
¼ tsp. cinnamon
2 Tbs. butter, at room temperature, cut into pieces

In a small bowl, combine all the dry ingredients. Then, using a pastry blender, work in the butter until the mixture is crumbly. Set aside while you make the muffin batter.

Batter

Butter for greasing muffin pan
½ C. amaranth flour
½ C. whole wheat flour
1 C. all-purpose flour
½ tsp. salt or to taste
½ tsp. baking soda
1 Tbs. baking powder
¼ C. sugar
1 egg, or 2 egg whites
1 C. buttermilk, at room temperature
½ tsp. vanilla extract
⅓ C. canola or corn oil
¾ C. raspberries

Preheat the oven to 400° F. and butter the bottoms only of a 12-cup muffin pan (cup size 2½ inches diameter by 1 inch deep). Unbuttered sides allow the batter to climb and form rounded tops while baking. Add the dry ingredients to a large bowl. Use a whisk to combine them.

To a medium-size bowl, add the egg and beat lightly with a fork. Add the buttermilk, vanilla and oil and beat lightly until combined. Make a well in the center of the dry ingredients and add the liquid all at once. Stir briskly with a fork until the dry ingredients are just moistened. Stir in the raspberries. The batter should look lumpy. Overstirring results in rubbery muffins.

Using a large spoon and a rubber spatula to scrape off the batter, spoon each cup two thirds full and sprinkle about ¾ teaspoon of the streusel on the surface of each muffin. Bake for 20 to 25 minutes until golden and a cake tester inserted in the center comes out clean. Loosen with a knife at once and remove the muffins to a wire rack to cool. Serve warm.

Amaranth, Date and Walnut Bread
with Orange Peel

Ricotta cheese lightly spread on a slice of this warm, sweet, soothingly familiar bread—packed with the nutritious addition of amaranth—makes it perfect for an anytime snack. Prepare it a day in advance so flavors can intensify.

Butter for greasing pan
Flour for dusting pan
8-oz. package pitted dates, cut into pieces (about 1½ C.)
1 C. water
1 tsp. baking soda
1 C. amaranth flour
1 C. whole wheat flour
½ C. all-purpose flour

1 Tbs. baking powder
½ tsp. salt
5 Tbs. soft butter, cut into small pieces
¾ C. sugar
1 Tbs. finely minced orange peel
1 C. coarsely broken toasted walnuts
1 egg, lightly beaten
½ tsp. orange flower water or vanilla extract

Preheat the oven to 300° F. Butter and flour a 9 × 5 ×3-inch loaf pan and set aside. Add the dates and water to a nonstick saucepan, and slowly bring just to the boiling point over medium heat. Remove from the heat and stir in the baking soda, which will foam up. Set aside to cool completely.

In a large bowl, combine all the flour with the baking powder and salt. Using a pastry blender, cut in the butter until the mixture is crumbly in texture. Stir in the sugar, orange peel and walnuts. Add the egg and orange flower water to the date mixture and add to the bowl. Mix thoroughly to form a stiff batter.

Spoon the batter into the prepared pan and smooth the top with a rubber spatula. Bake in the lower part of the oven for about 1 hour and 20 minutes. The loaf should be firm to the touch and should have shrunk slightly from the sides of the pan.

Cool completely in the pan on a wire rack, then turn out and wrap the bread in aluminum foil. The bread will keep well for about a week and it also freezes well.

The

Versatile

Grain

and the

Elegant

Bean

26

Barley

Hordeum

There's More to Barley Than Brew

When the Scottish poet Robert Burns, wrote, ". . . John Barleycorn, thou king o' grain," we must admit that it was really an eighteenth-century paean to malt liquor rather than to bread or soup. And when the colonists first brought the grain to the New World, barley was much more valued for its brewing qualities than for sustenance, and many a long, hard, cold winter must have been spent in blessing the first person who found that the grain could be fermented.

Ironically, this has not changed very much today, for about one third to one half of the crop grown in the United States eventually finds its way into the brewing of beer, while most of the balance of the crop goes to fattening the cows, pigs and other farm animals. We must assume, therefore, that barley has been called "the most important crop of early civilizations" in Asia, Africa and Europe for vastly different reasons.

Barley probably originated in the prehistoric Ethiopian highlands, moving outward on caravan trails and with nomadic tribes into the Indus Valley of Asia and finally becoming a part of almost every civilization, both for sustenance and as a grain of intrinsic value.

As far back as 3500 B.C., the Sumerians used barley as a basis for both a measuring and a monetary system. And in the Babylonian Code of Hammurabi, the grain is also mentioned as a means of simple monetary exchange. Egyptian hieroglyphics that date from as early as 5000 B.C. show the cultivation of the crop, and perhaps one of the most interesting (and possibly apocryphal) stories is one that goes back to that time.

We have read that the ancient Egyptians knew of a way to determine the sex of a pregnant woman's unborn child. The mother-to-be doused barley and wheat with her urine. If the barley sprouted first, the child would be a boy! We hope that the medical profession has taken note that this might well be the first case of amniocentesis in history!

If we delve into the literature and the historical artifacts of almost any ancient culture, barley is a prominent part of the chronicles. In the writings of ancient China around 2800 B.C., the grain is mentioned as one of the five most sacred cultivated crops (the others being rice, millet, soybeans and wheat). It was the major grain of the Greeks, and was a part of the diet of the Romans, Etruscans, Phoenicians and Carthaginians, as well as holding its place as the principal grain of the European continent well into the sixteenth century.

And certainly, the Bible is also filled with tales that make barley a major character. David's army was given rations of barley. One of the plagues of Egypt in Exodus 1 was the storm of hailstones "by which the barley was smitten," and even in the New Testament, the five loaves with which Jesus fed 5,000 people in the miracle of the loaves and the fishes were all made of barley.

Much of the world still uses large amounts of the grain, continuing the long line of its historical heritage; possibly it is only in the United States where it comes as a surprise to find that so little—possibly only 10 percent—goes to help feed the population and to provide a versatile, nutritious addition to our diet.

The Japanese use an ancient form of barley that is now becoming available in our own natural food stores: *hato mugi* or Job's tears *(Coix lacryma-jobi)*. And both the Japanese and the Koreans make an excellent tea called *bori cha* from roasted barley. In Tibet, there is a traditional fermented barley bread that is raised overnight while it spreads out into a large, round shape. Its name reflects the shape: prayer wheel bread. And the Buddhist monks in that country have long been known for their porridge, *tsampa,* which blends barley flour with yak butter and boiling tea. The Chinese, in turn, grind barley flour and mix it with lentils to make a well-balanced, nutritious bread.

In the Western world, barley is generally underutilized, though we do find some barley/wheat flour dark breads in Eastern Europe and in Wales. Poland has been using barley as a side dish instead of rice for centuries. And possibly one use that goes mostly unnoticed outside of England is the barley water cure-all that the British swear by, claiming that it will settle an upset stomach and that drinking it is the secret behind the marvelously smooth, pale skin of British women. In the United States, we generally find it as an occasional pilaf, hot cereal or coffee substitute, and more commonly as a thickener for soups to give body and flavor. Indeed, barley absorbs liquid so thoroughly that a dear friend of ours exclaimed, "Barley *eats* soup!"

The Forms of Barley

Whole Hulled Barley. This is a natural white barley with only the outermost chaff or hull removed. It can be cooked unground, added to soups and casseroles or used as a whole grain cereal.

Unhulled Brown Barley. Used for cooking and for sprouting. It requires presoaking and a long cooking time. For those who would like to try it, it is generally available only in health food stores or by mail order.

The

Versatile

Grain

and the

Elegant

Bean

28

Pearled Barley. This is the most common form found in the United States. Since it has been hulled, most of the vitamin B is lost and milling also reduces the calcium content. However, the protein content remains high, since most of the amino acids are in the germ rather than in the husk. Pearled barley can be used in any of the recipes that are included here, and it is generally available in fine, medium and coarse grains.

Barley Flakes or Rolled Barley. Processed in exactly the same way as rolled oats, barley flakes can be used as a cereal or toasted and used as a thickening agent in soups, stews and baked goods. Because they have been processed, they cook more quickly than the whole grain form. Barley flakes make a chewy breakfast cereal, and they're a nice change from oatmeal on a winter morning. For a delicious treat, try stirring in one-half cup of diced mixed dried fruit for the last five minutes of cooking. Then serve with fresh lowfat milk and a little sugar or honey on the top.

Barley Grits. Whole, hulled barley, toasted and cracked into small pieces. Barley grits are excellent for use as a meat extender in dishes such as meat loaf, or they can be cooked for breakfast in place of hominy grits.

Barley Flour. A finely ground, hulled barley that should be blended with other flours when used in baking, since it has a very low gluten content. The flour can also be used as a thickening agent and it is sometimes recommended for people who are on wheat-restricted diets. At one time we ground our own flour from the unhulled natural barley, but it has now become available in health food stores and through mail order.

Barley Malt. This is a sweet syrup that is somewhat like unsulphured molasses, and in fact, the latter can be substituted for barley malt. It is not quite as sweet as honey. Since very little will be used, store the remainder in a cool place, since warmth may cause it to ferment.

Job's Tears (*Croix lacryma-jobi*). Although a fairly new addition to the cuisine of the Americas, we have already noted that it has a long history in Asia, where it is not only used in cooking but as a restorative tonic. Larger than pearled barley, with a wide brown cleft down one side, Job's tears are not "lost" in dishes like pilafs or in the Flemish Waterzooie (see page 44). Now readily available in health food stores, and in addition to their correct name and *Hato Mugi,* the packages may also be labeled Juno's Tears or River Grain.

Barley

Grain & Granulation	Amount of Liquid	Cooking Method	Cooking & Standing Time	Approx. Yield	Comments
Whole Grain (1 C. dry) —hulled —pearled (medium or fine)	3½ C.	Use nonstick saucepans. Wash and rinse grain several times until final water is clear. Use 3-qt. saucepan and salted water. Bring water to a boil, add grain, return to boil, cover and simmer.	Slip paper towels under pot lid to absorb moisture when standing. Fork-fluff after standing. 30 to 35 minutes. Let stand 10 minutes.	3¼ C.	The hull and bran are removed, plus some germ of pearled barley is polished away. Pearled barley sold in health food stores is slightly darker with a larger grain than supermarket varieties.
—unhulled					*Un*hulled barley is *not* recommended since it never seems to become tender, no matter how long it cooks.
Barley Grits (1 C. dry)	4 C. (½ milk, ½ water)	Use 3-qt. saucepan. Bring milk and water and salt to taste to a boil. Slowly add grain, stirring constantly. Then lower heat and simmer, uncovered, stirring occasionally.	20 minutes.	3⅔ C.	Cooked barley grits are similar in texture to hominy grits and are wonderful in puddings.

Grain & Granulation	Amount of Liquid	Cooking Method	Cooking & Standing Time	Approx. Yield	Comments
Barley Flakes or Rolled Barley (1 C. dry)	3 C.	Use 3-qt. saucepan. Bring salted water to a boil. Slowly stir in grain, return to boil. Lower heat to medium low and cook, uncovered, stirring occasionally.	22 minutes. Cover pot and let stand 5 minutes.	2⅔ C.	Barley flakes are lightly toasted and then rolled in a similar process to oat flakes, adding dried fruit to last 5 minutes of cooking. Served with milk, barley flakes make a nice change for breakfast.

Momma's Barley, Lima Bean and Dried Mushroom Soup

SERVES 6 TO 8

As a child, Sheryl's mother lived in a small village on the Polish-Austrian border during very troubled times. She recalled that the only comfort and one of her most vivid memories was of this favorite soup, which her grandmother had made in vast amounts to feed their large family. Unlike the Polish-Austrian border, this recipe has never changed.

3–4 beef marrow bones, sawed into 2-inch pieces (any chicken backs, necks or chicken parts are a welcome addition as well—see NOTE)
10 C. water
1 large onion
1 large clove garlic
½ C. lima beans, soaked overnight and drained
½ C. fine or medium pearled barley, washed well
1 oz. dried mushrooms, preferably imported from Poland
1 Tbs. rolled oats

½ tsp. paprika
Salt to taste
½ tsp. white pepper or to taste
2 large carrots, quartered
2 large stalks celery with leaves, cut in half crosswise
1 small turnip, peeled
1 small parsnip, peeled
1 parsley root, peeled (see NOTE)
1 medium leek, carefully washed of sand
6 sprigs flat leaf parsley
2–3 sprigs fresh dill

Put the bones and water into a 9-quart (or larger) stockpot. Bring to a boil. Skim the foam from the surface and add the onion, garlic, soaked lima beans and barley. Cover, lower the heat and simmer for 30 minutes.

Meanwhile, cover the mushrooms with boiling water and soak for 20 minutes. Dampen a coffee filter and strain the mushroom liquid through the filter, reserving the liquid. Rinse the mushrooms under cold water, cut them into small pieces and set aside.

Add the oats, paprika, salt and pepper to the pot along with the carrots, celery, turnip, parsnip and parsley root. Cook for 10 minutes more, then add the reserved mushrooms and the strained mushroom liquid, and cook for 30 minutes more.

Meanwhile, tie the leek, parsley and dill together with a piece of white string and add to the pot. Simmer for 45 minutes more. Before serving, lift out and discard the onion, celery, turnip, parsnip and parsley root as well as the herb bouquet and the bones. The soup is even better when it's made the day before and reheated.

NOTE: Although Momma never did it, removing the marrow from the bones before adding them to the pot makes for a leaner soup. Also, if you can't find parsley roots, just add several more sprigs of fresh parsley along with their stems when you make the herb bouquet.

The

Versatile

Grain

and the

Elegant

Bean

32

Tanabour: Armenian Beef, Barley Grits and Yogurt Soup with Mint

SERVES 6 TO 8

This is the "chicken soup" that Armenian mothers serve to their sick. But why wait until you're ill? The soup is fresh-tasting, tangy with yogurt, enriched with egg and laced with soothing, cooling mint.

3 Tbs. olive or canola oil
1 small onion, finely chopped (about ½ C.)
1 large clove garlic, finely minced (1½ tsps.)
½ lb. lean ground beef (optional)
1 tsp. ground cumin
½ tsp. ground allspice
¼ tsp. white pepper
Salt to taste

4–5 scallions, finely sliced (about 1 C.)
1 C. cooked barley grits (see Chart, page 30 and NOTE)
4 C. Chicken Stock, preferably homemade (see page 171)
2 eggs, lightly beaten
3 C. plain yogurt
2 Tbs. finely chopped fresh mint (or 1 Tbs. dried, crushed mint)

In a heavy 4½-quart pot, heat the oil over medium heat. Sauté the onions and garlic until the onions are soft but not brown. Add the ground beef (if you use it), the cumin, allspice and pepper, raise the heat and stir until the meat loses its raw pink color. Season with salt and add the scallions and barley grits, then turn off the heat.

In a large bowl, whisk together the chicken stock, eggs and yogurt, then gradually stir into the pot. Heat it slowly over low heat, stirring with a wooden spoon until the soup has thickened, about 10 minutes. *Do not boil or it will curdle.* Add the mint during the last 5 minutes of cooking. Serve at once.

NOTE: Cooked pearled barley may be substituted for the barley grits if you wish.

Barley, Onion and Chicken Liver Pilaf
with Fresh Sage
SERVES 6 TO 8

This pilaf of barley, onions and chicken livers, scented with fresh sage, is a delightful side dish and a nice change from the ordinary. It is perfect as an accompaniment for any kind of roasted poultry.

1 C. whole pearled or whole hulled barley
4 C. Chicken Stock, preferably homemade (see page 171)
2 Tbs. olive oil
2 large onions, very thinly sliced and separated into rings

8 chicken livers, cut into small pieces
Salt and freshly ground black pepper to taste
4–5 large sage leaves, finely minced
⅛ tsp. paprika

Using a small bowl, wash the barley in cold water, rinsing it several times until the water is clear. Then drain well in a sieve. In a 3-quart saucepan, bring the chicken stock to a boil over medium high heat, then add the barley and stir. When it comes to a boil again, stir, cover, lower the heat and simmer for about 30 minutes or until the barley is tender and the liquid is absorbed. Remove from the heat and let sit for 10 to 15 minutes more to allow the grains to separate.

Meanwhile, heat the olive oil in a large nonstick skillet and add the onions. Cook over medium high heat, stirring occasionally until they are soft and dark in color, about 15 to 20 minutes. Remove the onions with a slotted spoon and stir them into the cooked barley. In the same skillet, cook the chicken livers over medium heat, stirring, for 3 to 4 minutes. Season with salt, pepper and sage and add to the barley and onion mixture.

Return the pilaf to the stove and over low heat just rewarm it until hot. Transfer to a serving dish and sprinkle with paprika.

The

Versatile

Grain

and the

Elegant

Bean

34

Chopped Beef with Barley Grits
and Vegetables

SERVES 6

A new, more healthful twist to America's favorite hamburger—a whole meal chock full of vegetables and whole grains as well as beef. It's a sneaky way to enjoy an increase in fiber and nutrition by using a familiar food as a base.

3 Tbs. olive oil
1 medium carrot, finely minced (about ½ C.)
½ small onion, finely minced (¼ C.)
¼ small red cabbage, finely chopped (1 C.)
1 pound lean ground beef

Salt and freshly ground black pepper to taste
½ cup cooked barley grits (see Chart, page 30)
2 Tbs. finely minced chives
1 egg, lightly beaten

In a nonstick medium-size skillet, heat 1 tablespoon of the oil over medium heat. Add the vegetables and cook, stirring, for 1 minute, then lower the heat to simmer. Cover and cook the vegetables slowly until they are tender. Remove to a bowl, and set aside to cool slightly.

In a medium-size bowl, mix together the ground beef, salt and pepper, cooked barley grits and chives. Stir in the vegetables and the egg and mix well. Wet your hands and form the mixture into 4-ounce balls, then flatten each ball into patties. Add the remaining oil to the same nonstick skillet and cook the patties over high heat for about 4 to 5 minutes on each side. Serve immediately.

Lamb Shanks with Barley, Rosemary, Vegetables and Chick Peas

SERVES 6 TO 8

This hearty lamb and barley stew is based upon the pale-colored Irish lamb stew that was passed on to Mel's mother by a neighbor as they all sat on the steps of their tenement stoop to catch a breath of air on a steamy summer night.

6 lamb shanks, trimmed of fat (weighing about ¾ lb. each), sawed into 3 pieces each
Salt and freshly ground black pepper to taste
2–3 cloves garlic, finely minced (about 2 tsps.)
½ tsp. dried rosemary (or 1 scant Tbs. fresh rosemary)
½ C. whole pearled or whole hulled barley, washed well
1 medium onion, coarsely chopped (¾ C.)
2 stalks celery, quartered
1½ C. water

1 medium-size potato, peeled and cut into 1½-inch chunks
2 small turnips, peeled and quartered
4–5 small carrots, quartered
2 small yams or sweet potatoes, peeled and cut into 1½-inch chunks
¼ lb. string beans, ends trimmed and cut diagonally in half
⅔ C. cooked chick-peas (or canned, rinsed and drained)
½ lb. green peas, shelled or 10½-oz. package thawed frozen peas
Juice of ½ lemon (1 Tbs.)
1 tsp. finely minced lemon peel
2 Tbs. finely minced parsley

Place the pieces of lamb in a large, heavy 7-quart Dutch oven. Sprinkle with salt and pepper and add the garlic, rosemary, barley, onions, celery and water. Bring to a boil over medium high heat, lower the heat and simmer, covered, for 1 hour.

Add the potatoes, turnips, carrots, and yams, and cook for 20 minutes more. Add the string beans and chick-peas and cook for 10 minutes. Add the peas and cook 5 minutes more. Remove from the heat and stir in the lemon juice and lemon peel. Taste for additional salt or pepper, and transfer to a warmed serving dish. Sprinkle the surface with parsley and serve hot.

The

Versatile

Grain

and the

Elegant

Bean

36

Polish Golobki: Barley and Mushroom-stuffed Cabbage Leaves with Sour Cream and Dill Sauce

MAKES 24 CABBAGE ROLLS

A nostalgic ethnic dish that is a part of our American melting-pot heritage. There are many versions of stuffed cabbage from all over the world. Ours is a meatless version.

1 large head green cabbage (about 3–4 lbs.)
2 Tbs. butter
1 medium onion, finely chopped (¾ C.)
¼ lb. mushrooms, finely chopped
1½ C. cooked medium pearled barley (see Chart, page 30)
Juice of ½ lemon (1 Tbs.)

½ tsp. paprika
½ tsp. salt or to taste
¼ tsp. freshly ground black pepper
¼ C. finely minced flat leaf parsley
2 C. hot Beef Stock, preferably homemade (see page 172)
¾ C. sour cream
1 Tbs. finely minced dill

Cut out the core from the cabbage. Boil lots of water in a deep stockpot and place the whole head of cabbage into the boiling water. Parboil for 10 to 15 minutes or until the leaves are soft and pliable. Lift out by inserting a two-prong carving fork into the hole left from coring the cabbage, while supporting the other side of the cabbage with a wide spatula. Drain on paper towels and let cool.

When the cabbage is cooled, carefully separate the leaves and stack together. With a sharp knife, cut an inverted "V" from the tough center part of the cabbage ribs and discard. The leaves will now lie flat. Melt the butter in a nonstick skillet and sauté the onions until wilted. Stir in the mushrooms and cooked barley and cook for 3 minutes. Add the lemon juice, paprika, salt, pepper and parsley and cook for about 1 minute more. Set aside to cool. There should be about 3 cups of filling.

Depending upon the size of the cabbage leaves, spoon about 1 tablespoon of the filling onto the center of each leaf. Fold the sides of the cabbage leaf over the filling first, then roll up from the cut stem end to enclose the filling. Do not roll too tightly or they will expand and burst while cooking.

Place the rolls, seam side down in one layer, in a large skillet or sauté pan with deep sides. Slowly pour the hot beef stock around the rolls, cover and simmer over very low heat for 1 hour and 15 minutes.

Lift out the rolls and place them in one layer on a serving dish and keep warm while preparing the sauce. Pour the remaining liquid into a cup. You will have about ⅓ cup. Strain, wipe out the skillet and return the liquid to it. Then stir in the sour cream and dill. Cook over very low heat, stirring, for 2 minutes. Spoon over the stuffed cabbage rolls and serve at once.

Roti with Hot Chiles, Garlic and Cilantro

MAKES 12 ROTI

Roti are the mainstay of East Indian cuisine. They're made of unleavened dough containing barley flour, potatoes, hot chile, garlic and either cilantro or dill. They're light, yet spicy enough to be satisfyingly filling, and though they're somewhat labor intensive, it's worth the effort because roti cannot be store bought. They're fun to make and they take only 15 minutes to bake. Try them with a cold curried soup.

1 large waxy potato, quartered (about ½ lb.)
1 C. all-purpose flour
¾ C. barley flour
½ tsp. salt or to taste
1 fresh green chile pepper such as serrano, finely minced (about 1 Tbs.)

2 Tbs. finely minced cilantro or dill
1 medium clove garlic, finely minced (1 tsp.)
1½ Tbs. corn or canola oil
2 Tbs. melted butter

In a small saucepan, cook the potatoes in water to cover for about 20 minutes. Cool, then peel and mash with a potato masher.

Transfer the mashed potatoes to a large bowl and combine with the remaining ingredients except the melted butter. Flour your hands and knead the dough right in the bowl until it is no longer sticky. Then gather it into a ball and knead on a lightly floured surface for about 3 minutes or until the dough feels elastic. Cover with a kitchen towel and let it rest for about 15 minutes. Then divide the dough into two parts. Roll each part into a 6-inch-long sausage shape. Cut each part evenly into six pieces, then shape the pieces into balls and cover with a kitchen towel. On a lightly floured surface, roll each ball into an approximate 6-inch circle, using a floured rolling pin. As each roti is rolled, place a piece of waxed paper over it and stack the roti so that they don't stick together and dry out.

Preheat the oven to 200° F. Heat a heavy cast-iron skillet until quite hot. Lower the heat under the skillet to medium high and place one circle into the dry skillet. Cook until the bottom is speckled with brown and the surface bubbles up a bit—about 1½ minutes. Remove the roti, brush with a bit of melted butter and place in an oven-to-table serving dish. Put in the warm oven. Then repeat with the remaining roti and stack in the oven as they are finished, using waxed paper between each one as before. Serve hot.

The

Versatile

Grain

and the

Elegant

Bean

38

Vanilla Barley Pudding with Cinnamon and Tea-poached Plums

SERVES 6

A warm, soothing, intensely vanilla-flavored pudding served with tart poached red plums with the smoky overtones of tea and a hint of sweet, spicy cinnamon.

Vanilla Barley Pudding

1 qt. milk	1 Tbs. butter
2-in. piece of vanilla bean	¼ C. slivered almonds
½ C. sugar	¼ C. heavy cream
Pinch salt	Cinnamon and Tea-poached Plums
1 C. pearled barley, washed well	(see recipe below)
1 tsp. vanilla extract (optional)	

Put the milk into a 3-quart nonstick saucepan. Split the vanilla bean lengthwise and with the point of a sharp knife scrape the tiny black seeds into the milk and then put the pod in as well. Stir in the sugar and salt and bring slowly to a boil. Stir in the barley, cover, but keep the lid slightly ajar. Using a flame tamer to keep the heat as low as possible, simmer for about 40 to 45 minutes or until almost all of the milk is absorbed and the barley is very tender to the bite. Stir it occasionally while cooking. When the pudding is finished cooking, remove the vanilla pod and discard. Taste the mixture to see if more vanilla is needed; this will depend upon the intensity of the vanilla bean. A strong vanilla taste should come through. If not, stir in the vanilla extract, let stand for 5 minutes.

Meanwhile, melt the butter in a small skillet and toast the almonds over low heat until they are golden, about 1 or 2 minutes, stirring or shaking the pan so that the almonds don't burn. Then stir them into the barley mixture. Serve the pudding warm or cold in individual bowls, with some cream poured over the surface. Pass plums to be spooned over pudding.

Cinnamon and Tea-poached Plums

1 C. water	Small stick of cinnamon
2 tea bags, preferably Earl Grey	6 red plums, halved and pitted
⅓ C. sugar	

In a 1½-quart saucepan, boil the water and then steep the tea in it for 5 minutes. Discard the tea bags and add the sugar and cinnamon stick. Bring to a boil and add the plums. Lower the heat, cover and simmer for 3 to 4 minutes, or until the plums are tender but firm. Lift out the plums with a slotted spoon and transfer to a serving dish. Reduce the sauce by boiling for 5 minutes, then strain the sauce over the plums.

Barley Grits, Orange and Carrot Pudding
with Raisins and Toasted Pecans

SERVES 6

Flavored with the sweet spices of cardamom, cloves and scented orange flower water, this unique dessert dotted with shreds of carrot and whole raisins is equal to the ever-popular rice pudding.

4 C. milk
Salt to taste
½ C. sugar
½ C. barley grits
1 large carrot, shredded in a food processor (about 1 C.)
¾ C. raisins (preferably Monukka or Muscat)
1 Tbs. butter

½ tsp. ground cardamom
¼ tsp. ground cloves
2 tsps. orange flower water
1 large navel orange (with peel intact)
12 pecan halves, toasted in 1 tsp. butter
Heavy cream (optional)

In a 3-quart nonstick saucepan, slowly bring the milk, salt and sugar to the boiling point. Gradually add the barley grits, stirring constantly. Then add the shredded carrots, the raisins, butter, cardamom and cloves. Lower the heat and simmer, uncovered, stirring frequently, for 15 minutes or until very thick.

Meanwhile, place the whole orange into a deep saucepan and cover it with water. Bring it to a boil, cover and lower the heat. Simmer for 10 to 15 minutes or until the orange, when tested with the point of a sharp knife, is soft. Drain and discard the water. When the orange is cool enough to handle, cut out and discard the stem end, then quarter the orange. Remove any white pith from the central core of the orange and discard. Cut the orange into smaller pieces and place in the bowl of a food processor. Process until a fine purée is produced. There should be about 1 cup of purée.

Remove the pudding from the heat and stir in the orange flower water and the orange purée into the pudding.

Rinse a 5-cup mold, such as a charlotte mold, with water and keep the mold damp. Spoon the dessert into the mold, cover it with plastic wrap and chill for at least 3 hours or longer. When ready to serve, run a sharp knife around the sides of the mold and invert onto a serving dish. Arrange the toasted pecan halves on the surface like the spokes of a wheel. Cut into wedges to serve, and pass a pitcher of cream at the table if you wish.

The

Versatile

Grain

and the

Elegant

Bean

40

Sweet Barley Flour and Ginger Shortcakes
with Honey-poached Peaches

SERVES 8

Peaches paired with ginger add snap to the natural sweetness of barley flour in these supereasy and quick-to-prepare shortcakes.

Honey-poached Peaches

1½ C. water
¼ C. sugar
⅓ C. honey

1½ Tbs. shredded orange peel, made with a zester tool
4 large ripe, peeled and pitted peaches (about 1½ lbs.), cut into quarters

In a 3-quart saucepan, bring the water, sugar and honey to a boil over medium heat. Lower the heat, add the orange shreds and simmer for 2 minutes. Add the peaches and simmer, uncovered, for 10 minutes, tilting the pan occasionally to pour syrup over the peaches as they cook. Lift the peaches out into a bowl and reduce the syrup to 1½ cups, then pour the syrup over the peaches and cool. Set aside and prepare the shortcakes.

Sweet Barley Flour and Ginger Shortcakes
MAKES 8 SHORTCAKES

1½ C. barley flour
1 C. all-purpose flour
1 Tbs. baking powder
½ tsp. salt or to taste
¼ lb. cold butter, cut into small pieces

½ C. sugar
2 Tbs. finely minced ginger
¾ C. cold milk
Whipped cream and mint leaves

Preheat the oven to 375° F. In a large bowl, add the flours, baking powder, and salt and whisk to blend. Using a pastry blender, cut in the butter until the mixture resembles coarse crumbs. Mix together the sugar and ginger in a small bowl, then add it to the flour and combine. Make a well in the center of the mixture and pour the milk in. Using a fork, pull the dry ingredients toward the center, mixing just until the dough is dampened and the dry ingredients are absorbed. Drop heaping rounded mounds, about 3 tablespoons for each, on an ungreased baking sheet, spacing each mound about 2 inches apart, since they spread while baking.

Bake for 25 minutes or until the tops are slightly golden. Cool on a wire rack for about 10 minutes.

To serve, split the biscuits horizontally with a serrated knife. Spoon some peaches and syrup on the bottom half, replace the top and add a small dollop of whipped cream and a mint leaf if you wish.

Job's Tears

Grain & Granulation	Amount of Liquid	Cooking Method	Cooking & Standing Time	Approx. Yield	Comments
Whole Grain (1 C.)	3 C.	Use nonstick saucepan. Rinse and soak grain overnight and drain. Use 2-qt. saucepan with boiling salted water. Add grain and return to boil. Cover, lower heat and simmer.	Slip paper towels under lid of pot to absorb collected moisture when standing. Fork-fluff after standing. 40 minutes. Let stand 10 minutes.	2½ C.	Overnight soaking cuts down on cooking time by 1 hour and results in a lovely, soft-textured separated grain that is not sticky. It resembles a larger version of barley, but its flavor is very much its own.

Job's Tears with Mushrooms and Parsley

SERVES 6

An old basic favorite with a new twist—using the larger whole grain Job's tears in place of pearled barley. It makes a versatile side dish that complements poultry, meat or fish.

The

Versatile

Grain

and the

Elegant

Bean

3½ C. Beef Stock, preferably homemade (see page 172)
1 C. Job's tears, washed and soaked overnight (see Chart above) (or substitute whole pearled barley)
½ tsp. salt or to taste
3 Tbs. butter

1 large onion, finely chopped (1¼ C.)
1 lb. mushrooms, wiped with damp paper towels and thickly sliced
Juice of ½ lemon (1 Tbs.)
½ tsp. freshly ground black pepper
Salt to taste
¼ C. finely minced flat leaf parsley

Place the beef stock in a 4-quart pot and bring to a boil over medium heat. Slowly add the Job's tears, stirring constantly. When the liquid boils again, cover, lower the heat and simmer about 40 minutes (30 to 35 minutes for pearl barley), or until the liquid is absorbed and the grain is tender. (Bite a few grains to test.) Let rest for 5 minutes.

Meanwhile, heat the butter in a large skillet and sauté the onions over medium low heat until they begin to brown. Stir in the mushrooms and cook, while stirring, for about 5 to 8 minutes. Turn off the heat and add the lemon juice, pepper, and salt, and half the parsley. Stir this mixture into the cooked grain and spoon into a warmed serving dish. Sprinkle the remaining parsley over the top and serve warm.

Job's Tears Baked with Red Kidney Beans, Cheddar Cheese and Cilantro

SERVES 6

A baked grains and beans dish with a firm cheese custard, a layer of onions on the bottom and a south-of-the-border spicing. It makes a fine, light supper or luncheon dish served with crisp, raw vegetables or a green salad for textural contrast.

1 medium-size sweet white onion, thinly sliced and separated into rings	1 C. cooked red kidney beans
1 large clove garlic, finely minced (2 tsps.)	2 C. cooked Job's tears (see Chart, opposite page) or substitute cooked whole pearled barley
1 small jalapeño pepper, seeded and finely minced	½ C. finely minced cilantro
Salt and freshly ground black pepper to taste	1 C. shredded sharp Cheddar cheese (about 3 ozs.)
⅛ tsp. dried oregano	½ tsp. ground cumin
	2 eggs
	1 C. milk

Preheat the oven to 350° F. Generously butter a 2-quart soufflé dish. Place the onion rings on the bottom of the dish, sprinkle with the garlic, jalapeño pepper, salt and pepper and the oregano. In a large bowl, mix together the beans, Job's tears, three quarters of the cilantro, the cheese and cumin and spoon over the onion layer.

Beat the eggs and the milk together with a whisk and pour slowly over all. Bake for about 45 minutes or until firm. Sprinkle the top with the reserved cilantro before serving. Serve hot.

Flemish Waterzooie with Job's Tears

SERVES 8

Waterzooie is a rich, lemony-flavored top-of-the-stove casserole, halfway between a soup and a stew and a complete meal unto itself. Cooked, whole barley can be substituted for the Job's tears, although we prefer the larger grain for its unique, almost beanlike flavor.

2 3–3½-lb. chickens, cut into 8 pieces
1 tsp. salt or to taste
½ tsp. freshly ground black pepper
2 Tbs. butter
1 Tbs. olive oil
3 medium-size leeks, sliced ½ in. thick (about 2½ C.)
3 medium-size carrots, sliced ½ in. thick (about 1½ C.)
3 medium-size stalks celery with leaves, sliced ½ in. thick (about 1 C.)
1 large onion, thinly sliced
6 sprigs flat leaf parsley

4 sprigs thyme
5 whole cloves
¼ tsp. freshly grated nutmeg
4–5 C. hot Chicken Stock, preferably homemade (see page 171)
2 C. cooked Job's tears (see Chart, page 42), or substitute cooked whole pearled barley
3 egg yolks
2 Tbs. heavy cream
Juice of 1 lemon (2 Tbs.)
1 lemon, thinly sliced and seeded (with peel intact)
2 Tbs. finely minced parsley

Dry the chicken pieces well and sprinkle with salt and pepper. Set aside. In a heavy 7-quart Dutch oven, heat the butter and the oil slowly until hot, then make a bed of the leeks, carrots, celery and onions in the bottom of the pot. Tie the parsley, thyme and cloves loosely in a cheesecloth bag for easy removal, and add to the pot. Now add the chicken in one layer and sprinkle with the nutmeg. Cover and cook over medium low heat for 10 minutes, then slowly pour the hot chicken stock over all. Cover again, lower the heat and simmer for about 45 minutes or until the chicken is just tender. Remove the pot from the heat and lift out the chicken to cool.

When the chicken is cool enough to handle, remove and discard the skin and bones, keeping the meat in large chunks. Lift out the cheesecloth bag and discard. Then, in a large 3- or 4-quart oven-to-table casserole, place the Job's tears on the bottom. Lift out the vegetables with a slotted spoon and arrange them evenly on top, then add the chicken. Cover with aluminum foil and keep warm in a low oven while preparing the broth.

Strain the stock into a clean saucepan and heat, but do not boil. In a small bowl, beat the egg yolks and cream with a whisk, then whisk in the lemon juice. Add a ladle full of the hot stock to the egg mixture, whisking constantly. Then slowly whisk the mixture into the stock and stir constantly over the lowest heat possible. Switch the stirring to a wooden spoon so that the soup will not be foamy. When slightly thickened, about 5 minutes, pour it over the chicken and vegetables. Float thin lemon slices on top and sprinkle with the parsley before serving.

The

Versatile

Grain

and the

Elegant

Bean

44

Buckwheat

Fagopyrum, F. esculentum

The Born-Again Grain

When we think of buckwheat, perhaps the most amusing story that comes to mind goes back to a film trip we took, flying from Tokyo to Manila in a jam-packed jet with 317 Japanese business people and our Caucasian film crew of 3. When it was time for lunch, the airline gave a choice of American-style gray "mystery meat" or a Japanese lunch. All 320 passengers opted for the latter.

The main course was soba, the Japanese buckwheat noodles, usually served steaming hot with the addition of small bits of meat or fish. As the lunch was served, a new sound was heard over the steady roar of the jet engines. It was a slurping that grew louder and louder, for as our Japanese seatmate explained, it is perfectly proper to slurp soba in order to cool it on the way to the mouth. We enjoyed ourselves thoroughly, slurping along with the rest of the passengers, putting the long strands of the buckwheat noodles to our lips and then drawing them up loudly until they disappeared. It was fun. It was satisfying. And it was, above all, delicious.

It has been said over and over again, even by our friends, that buckwheat is something that you either love or hate. The Japanese, no doubt, are among its proponents, since there are somewhere around 40,000 soba restaurants in Japan. However, it is yet another of the most underutilized foods in the world, most of it being used for fodder or turned under for "green manure" to improve the soil or grown to attract bees to its startling white blossoms, with the end result being a distinctively flavored honey.

In the United States, about all we can usually recall about buckwheat is the memory of childhood breakfasts that featured stacks of belly-filling pancakes, dark and richly flavored, covered with maple syrup, and eaten as insulation against the long walk to school on a frigid winter morning. Indeed, a dictionary sits on our desk that defines buckwheat as "a food for animals and made into flour for pancakes." Stephen Foster perpetuated its "pancake folklore" in "O Susanna," when he confirmed that it was very popular in the nineteenth-century South: "De buckwheat cake was in her mouth, de tear was in her eye . . ." And Mark Twain, writing about a very disappointing European trip in 1878, promised that he would devour buckwheat pancakes covered with maple syrup, upon his return. In all fairness, it should be reported that on the long list of foods that he missed, he also included soft-shell crabs, fried chicken, Boston baked beans and a one and a half inch-thick Porterhouse steak with butter dripping down its sides!

If, on the other hand, you lay claim to an ethnic background that originated in parts of Asia, Finland, the Tyrol of Austria, northern Italy, Brittany in France, and especially Russia and Middle Europe, then buckwheat is probably quite familiar to you in a variety of dishes that transcend the pancake. In addition, you are probably among those we can number as lovers of buckwheat who cannot understand why someone wouldn't like it at all!

It probably originated in Central Asia, and it's been a staple food in China for a thousand years. It is also not technically a grain, though it has many of the nutritional characteristics and the nutritional structure of grain. Though it carries the word "wheat" as the last part of its name, it really is a cereal *grass* more related to our garden-variety rhubarb than to wheat. Thus it is a perfect food for many people who cannot eat wheat because of allergies. It has high-quality protein in larger quantities than corn, for example, a rich concentration of iron, twice as much B vitamin as wheat, plus calcium, and it grows and matures in only sixty days, usually wherever poor, rocky soil exists. Farmers can thus get two crops a season from buckwheat.

And so we find it in countries like those we've mentioned above, and it has become a part of the long history of those areas. There are several historical versions as to how it got to Europe. Either it was brought there by the Saracens in the fourteenth century or it is called *sarrasin* in French and *grano saraceno* in Italian because it is as dark as the complexions of the Saracens. Whatever the true story, buckwheat became one of the basic ingredients in dishes such as the Russian *kasha,* or it was cooked as a whole grain in a sort of pilaf or a thin porridge made of groats. In northern Italy, there is still a breakfast dish made of buckwheat called *black polenta,* and the *pizzoccheri* of the Italian Valtellina region is a traditional buckwheat pasta. In Brittany, the French developed (and still make) the light buckwheat crêpe called *galettes.*

It was first brought to this country by the Dutch and German settlers and New York State boasted a great many buckwheat fields in those early days. It was they who probably gave it its name, since the Dutch called it *bockweit* and the Germans *buche weisen* or *beech wheat.* They thought that it resembled the beechnut, yet it is nutritionally quite close to wheat. Later on, Jewish immigrants from Central Europe and the Ukraine introduced the buckwheat dishes of their homelands, such as *kasha varnishkes* (kasha with bow tie pasta), which is still popular in ethnic kitchens today.

Somehow, though, the popularity of buckwheat declined in the United States. We actually grew *twenty times* more of the crop in 1866 than we do now, while Russia

The

Versatile

Grain

and the

Elegant

Bean

46

continues to cultivate five times the amount that we do. But slowly this is changing. We have noticed a rebirth of the demand for buckwheat, just as we have noted a new awareness of *all* grains along with beans in home kitchens and in restaurants. Professional chefs are rediscovering the strong and unusual flavors of buckwheat, going past the blinis of Russia and the galettes of Brittany, the pilafs and the pancakes. Some of the top chefs in the country are now offering dishes such as quail with kasha or buckwheat pasta with codfish or scallops or rock shrimp.

And even the pizzoccheri that we mentioned earlier, once denigrated as "peasant food" by the very same people who ate it with gusto, has now begun to appear in restaurants and in packages in specialty food shops. Possibly it is all a rediscovery of our heritage. Possibly we are just becoming smarter and more adventurous about the foods that we choose. We can only urge those who have never tried buckwheat, who have never given it a chance to show its versatility, to try some of the recipes that we've included here.

The Forms of Buckwheat

Basically, there are two forms of buckwheat on the market: *roasted* and *unroasted.* The process of roasting gives it its nutty flavor, dark color and distinctive aroma. Generally, roasted buckwheat is called *kasha,* and since it has a strong flavor, it works best with pork, beef, duck, liver or lamb.

The unroasted white form is called *buckwheat* and it can be used with more delicately flavored foods such as veal or fish. It can also be used in soups, soufflés, and desserts, to stuff vegetables, or as an easily digested cereal for babies or invalids— or for just ordinary people like us who love the special taste of buckwheat!

Currently, Birkett Mills of Penn Yan, New York, is the largest processor and packer of buckwheat in the world and it's sold under the Wolff's label in supermarkets and under the Pocono brand in health food stores. If your local supplier is out of stock, buckwheat can be ordered by mail (see Mail Order Sources, pages 501–506).

Unroasted Buckwheat

Whole Buckwheat Groats. Pale in color and used for stuffings or pilafs or in dishes where the taste of roasted buckwheat would be too assertive.

Creamy Kernel Buckwheat Grits. An almost white cereal, very similar to Cream of Wheat. It is easily digestible and excellent for soufflés and desserts, as well as a perfect cereal for breakfast.

Dark Buckwheat Flour. Ground from the unhulled groat, it is grayish in color with tiny black specks. It is stronger than the light buckwheat flour because it has about 17 percent of the finely milled particles of the hulls. It is usually used alone for pancakes or in combination with wheat flour for baked goods. Since buckwheat is not a true cereal grain, it does not have gluten.

Light Buckwheat Flour. The outside hull is removed before milling. It can be used in baked goods, to thicken sauces, and for pancakes, and it's perfect for more delicate dishes like *ployes* (see page 51). It contains only 7 percent of the dark hull particles.

Unprocessed Buckwheat Seeds. Used for sprouting and planting for soil improvement (green manure) or to grow as a crop. They are now available in health food stores under the Pocono brand.

Roasted Buckwheat (Kasha)

For those with ethnic backgrounds, particularly those originating in Russia and parts of Middle Europe, kasha needs no introduction, for its strong, nutty aroma is quite familiar. For others, it sometimes becomes an acquired taste, and the fact that it has been roasted becomes quite evident the moment the package is opened. It comes in four forms and is generally available in most supermarkets:

Fine: Cooks quickly and is less chewy than the other varieties.
Medium: Good for all-around use.
Coarse: Also good for most purposes. The coarse ground is kasha that has been cracked in large particles.
Whole Grain: Uncracked, and good for pilafs.

The

Versatile

Grain

and the

Elegant

Bean

48

Buckwheat

Grain & Granulation	Amount of Liquid	Cooking Method	Cooking & Standing Time	Approx. Yield	Comments
		Preferred methods recommended by the National Buckwheat Institute.	Put paper towel between lid and pot while standing so excess moisture is absorbed. Fork-fluff after standing.		
Unroasted					
Whole Grain Groats (1 C. dry)	2 C.	Use 10-inch non-stick skillet. Mix grain with lightly beaten egg. Toast in skillet, stirring for 3 minutes to coat the grain with egg and to seal and separate the grain. Add boiling salted water or stock plus 1 tsp. butter. It will splutter up. Cover, lower heat and simmer.	10 to 12 minutes. Let stand 5 minutes.	4 C.	Whole un-roasted buck-wheat is paler in color than kasha, almost an off-white. It also has a more delicate flavor than the roasted buck-wheat.
Creamy Kernel Buck-wheat Grits (½ C. dry)	3 C. (1 C. milk, 2 C. water)	To a 3-qt. sauce-pan, add milk and water. Salt to taste plus small piece of (cont.)	10 to 12 minutes.	2⅓ C.	A bit coarser in texture but similar to Cream of Wheat, with its (cont.)

Buckwheat (cont.)

Grain & Granulation	Amount of Liquid	Cooking Method	Cooking & Standing Time	Approx. Yield	Comments
		butter. Bring to boil, gradually add grain, stirring constantly. Then lower to medium low heat, and cook, uncovered, stirring occasionally toward end of cooking.			own singular flavor. A favorite Soviet breakfast food.
Roasted (Kasha)					
(1 C. dry) —*Whole*	2 C.	Use preferred method (above) for unroasted whole grain for all granulations.	10 to 20 minutes. Let stand 5 minutes.	4 C.	Kasha has a nutty, fragrant, assertive and slightly grassy flavor. It's perfect for those with wheat allergies and it's gluten-free. The choice of the granulation depends upon the final dish.
—*Coarse*	2 C.		10 to 15 minutes. Let stand 5 minutes.	4 C.	
—*Medium*	2 C.		8 to 10 minutes. Let stand 5 minutes.	4 C.	
—*Fine*	2 C.		5 to 6 minutes. Let stand 5 minutes.	4 C.	

Acadian Buckwheat Ployes

MAKES ABOUT 12 PLOYES

Buckwheat is a favored grain of the French-speaking Acadians who settled in the St. John Valley of northernmost Maine. Some Acadians eat these delicately thin buckwheat crêpes at every meal. The cratered surface is perfect to absorb a trickle of maple syrup or fruit preserves, although they are also eaten with a pork and spice mixture called *creton*.

1 C. light buckwheat flour	½ tsp. salt
½ C. all-purpose flour	2 C. warm tap water
1 Tbs. baking powder	

In a medium-size bowl, whisk all the dry ingredients together to combine well. Whisk in the water until the consistency is that of light cream. (You may need a bit more water than the 2 cups, depending upon the absorption of the buckwheat flour or the humidity in your area. Add up to ¼ cup more water if needed.)

Preheat the oven to 200°F. and warm a large oven-to-table shallow dish. Heat a nonstick 8-inch pan over medium high heat until a drop of water dances on the surface. Tear off several sheets of waxed paper and keep them handy on the counter. The waxed paper prevents the crêpes from sticking together when they are stacked.

Pour ¼ cup of the batter into the pan, rotating the pan in a dipping circular motion and working very quickly so that the batter covers the bottom. Cook about 1½ minutes or until the edges of the ployes look dry and curl up slightly. The ployes are cooked on one side only and do not need to be turned over.

Peel off the ployes, holding it by the edges, and place it on a sheet of waxed paper to cool slightly. While the next ployes is cooking, peel the just cooked one off the waxed paper and place it on a fresh sheet of waxed paper in the baking dish in the oven to keep warm. Repeat until the batter is used up and all the ployes are layered between sheets of waxed paper in the oven. Serve them hot, peeling off the ployes from the waxed paper while at the table. Pour syrup or preserves over the ployes, roll up, and eat.

Buckwheat Groats, Garlic and
Sorrel Soup with Fresh Herbs

SERVES 6

Although a whole head of garlic is used in this tart soup, gentle cooking ensures a mild flavor. The influence is from the Georgian region of Russia, where sorrel, buckwheat and garlic marry well.

7 C. Chicken Stock, preferably homemade (see page 171) or half stock, half water
Pinch saffron threads
1 whole large bulb of garlic, peeled, separated into cloves and very coarsely chopped
1 tsp. fresh thyme leaves (or ½ tsp. dried thyme)
1 tsp. finely minced sage
1 Tbs. olive oil

3 whole cloves
½ C. whole buckwheat groats
Salt to taste
¼ tsp. freshly ground black pepper or to taste
2 Tbs. finely minced flat leaf parsley
Juice of 1 large lemon (3 Tbs.)
8–9 large sorrel leaves, with center spine cut out and discarded, finely shredded (1 C.)

In a heavy 4½-quart pot, heat the stock to the boiling point. Add the saffron, lower the heat and simmer for 5 minutes. Add the garlic, thyme, sage, olive oil and cloves and simmer, covered, for 20 minutes or until the garlic is tender. Strain the soup into a bowl pressing the garlic against the strainer with a wooden spoon and scraping the purée from the bottom of the strainer back into the liquid. Discard what remains in the strainer. Return the soup to the pot, add the buckwheat groats, salt and pepper and simmer for 20 minutes more or until the groats are tender. Stir in the parsley, lemon juice and sorrel and simmer for 1 minute more or until the sorrel changes color from bright green to a yellowish green. Serve hot.

The

Versatile

Grain

and the

Elegant

Bean

52

Whole Buckwheat Groats with Lemon,
Red Peppers and Sweet Marjoram

SERVES 6

This lemony pilaf, made with the more delicately flavored unroasted buckwheat rather than roasted kasha with its more imposing flavor, is meant to be served as a side dish or as a stuffing for more delicate fish or chicken dishes.

4 C. cooked whole buckwheat groats (see Chart, page 49)

3 Tbs. butter

1 large clove garlic, finely minced (1½ tsps.)

2 large scallions, thinly sliced (1 C.)

2 large stalks finely chopped celery with leaves (about 1 C.)

1 small sweet red pepper, finely diced (about ⅔ C.)

¼ teaspoon freshly ground black pepper

Salt to taste

1½ Tbs. coarsely chopped fresh sweet marjoram (or 1 tsp. dried marjoram)

1 Tbs. finely minced flat leaf parsley

1 whole lemon

Put the cooked buckwheat in a large bowl and set aside. In a 10-inch skillet, melt the butter and add the garlic, scallions, celery and red pepper. Cook, stirring frequently, for 5 to 8 minutes or until the vegetables are soft but not browned. Then add to the buckwheat and combine with the pepper, salt, marjoram and parsley.

Peel the lemon, mince the peel finely and add 1 teaspoon of the minced peel to the grain and herb mixture. Then peel off and discard the heavy white skin and membrane from the lemon, and using the tip of a knife remove and discard any pits. Cut the lemon sections into very small pieces and toss them with the pilaf.

Use either as a stuffing for chicken or fish, or put into an ovenproof dish, cover with foil and heat in a preheated 350°F. oven for 10 to 15 minutes and serve as a side dish.

Kasha Varnishkes: Whole Kasha Groats
and Bow Tie Pasta

SERVES 6

A classic Eastern European Jewish dish, originally from the Ukraine. It derives its authentic flavors from chicken fat—but canola oil can be used instead, although the flavor will be somewhat dimmed.

2 Tbs. chicken fat or canola oil
1 large or 2 medium onions, coarsely chopped (1¼ C.)
1 egg, lightly beaten
1 C. whole kasha groats
2 C. boiling water

1 Tbs. butter
Salt to taste
¼ tsp. freshly ground black pepper
1½ C. cooked pasta (½ C. uncooked small shells or bow ties)

Heat the chicken fat in a heavy black iron skillet. Add the onions and sauté until browned, stirring occasionally. Transfer the onions to a 5-quart wide-based nonstick Dutch oven, and wipe out the iron skillet with paper towels. In a small bowl, mix together the beaten egg and the kasha. Heat the dry skillet again and when hot, add the kasha/egg mixture, stirring constantly with a wooden spoon, until the grains are sealed and separated.

Heat the Dutch oven with the onions on medium high heat and mix in the kasha. Then slowly add the boiling water. Lower the heat and cover. Cook over very low heat for 25 minutes. Stir in the butter, salt and pepper and then the cooked pasta. Cook for 5 minutes more and remove from the heat.

Let it stand for 5 minutes before spooning it out into a warmed serving platter. Or, prepare the kasha varnishkes well ahead, cover with aluminum foil then rewarm for 15 to 20 minutes in a preheated 325°F. oven.

The

Versatile

Grain

and the

Elegant

Bean

54

Whole Kasha with Mixed Dried Fruit, Walnuts and Herbs

SERVES 6

This pilaf, strongly flavored with generous amounts of fresh herbs, slightly sweetened with tart/sweet dried fruit and crisp walnuts, imparts an added dimension to a stuffing for a crown roast of pork, duck or goose. Also try it mixed with cooked leftover poultry as a warm salad.

2 Tbs. canola oil
1 large onion, finely chopped (1 C.)
3–4 stalks celery with leaves, finely chopped (1½ C.)
2 Tbs. finely minced sage
2 Tbs. thyme leaves
¼ tsp. freshly ground black pepper
Salt to taste

Peel of 1 small lemon, finely minced (1 tsp.)
4 C. cooked whole kasha groats (see Chart, page 50), preferably cooked in chicken stock for extra flavor
1 C. diced mixed dried fruit
½ C. coarsely broken, toasted walnuts

Heat the oil in a large skillet and sauté the onions, stirring occasionally, until wilted. Add the celery, sage, thyme, pepper, and salt and cook, stirring, for 5 minutes more. Stir in the lemon peel and combine with the cooked kasha. Steam the dried fruit in a vegetable steamer to soften and add along with the walnuts. Serve hot as a side dish or use as a stuffing.

Kasha and Onion Turnovers

MAKES ABOUT 24 TURNOVERS

Call them piroshki, as the Russians do, empañadas as the Hispanics do—or *turnovers*, as we do. Whatever you may call them, we call them delicious!

Filling

1 Tbs. melted butter or chicken fat	½ teaspoon salt or to taste
1 large onion, finely chopped (1 C.)	⅛ teaspoon freshly ground black
1 C. cooked medium granulation kasha (see Chart, page 50)	pepper or to taste
	1 Tbs. finely minced parsley

Melt the butter in a heavy 10-inch skillet and sauté the onions over high heat, stirring occasionally until browned. Combine with the cooked kasha, salt, pepper and parsley. Mix well and cool while preparing the dough.

Dough

1 C. all-purpose flour	2 Tbs. ice water
½ tsp. salt or to taste	Butter for greasing baking sheet
¼ lb. soft butter, cut into small pieces	1 egg yolk mixed with 1 tsp. water
2 Tbs. cream cheese	for glaze

In a food processor, place the flour, salt, butter and cheese and process a few strokes until crumbly in texture. Add the ice water and process until a dough forms. Wrap the dough in aluminum foil and chill it for about 30 minutes. Butter a baking sheet and preheat the oven to 375°F. Flour your hands and lightly flour a work surface and a rolling pin. Divide the dough in half, keeping the other half chilled, and roll it out about ⅜ inch thick.

Using the top of a coffee can as a guide, cut the dough into 4-inch circles. Wet the outer edge of each circle and spoon 1 heaping teaspoon of the filling on the circle slightly off-center. Fold the dough over and press the edges with the tines of a fork to seal. Repeat until all of the filling and the dough are used up. As each turnover is made, transfer it with a spatula to the prepared baking sheet. Brush the surface of each turnover with the egg yolk wash and bake for 20 to 25 minutes or until golden brown. Serve hot or warm.

The

Versatile

Grain

and the

Elegant

Bean

56

Chicken and Kasha Terrine with Mushrooms, Red Peppers, Thyme and Rosemary

SERVES 8 to 10

Not as rich as pâté—yet a most unusual terrine, since it has a chicken and grain base. It should be made the day before and served at room temperature as an hors d'oeuvre or part of a buffet.

2 C. finely chopped, boned, skinned, cooked chicken breasts (about 1 lb.)
2 C. cooked fine kasha (see Chart, page 50)
Butter for greasing pan
6 Tbs. butter
2 scallions, finely minced (½ C.)
1 stalk celery, finely minced (½ C.)
1 small red pepper, finely minced (⅔ C.)
1 C. finely chopped mushrooms
2 Tbs. finely minced flat parsley
½ tsp. dried thyme
2 tsps. finely minced fresh rosemary (or ¾ tsp. dried rosemary)
Salt to taste
⅛ tsp. freshly ground black pepper or to taste
⅓ C. all-purpose flour
1 C. hot milk
¼ tsp. Tabasco sauce
1 Tbs. white wine Worcestershire sauce
Pistachio nuts (optional)

In a large bowl, mix the chicken with the kasha and set aside. Butter an 8½ × 4½ × 2½-inch loaf pan or a 6-cup terrine. Preheat the oven to 325°F.

In a 10-inch nonstick skillet, melt 2 tablespoons of the butter and sauté the scallions, celery and red peppers, stirring occasionally, until the vegetables become wilted. Add the mushrooms and stir and cook for 2 more minutes. Combine with the chicken mixture, and the parsley, thyme, rosemary, salt and pepper.

In a 2-quart saucepan, melt remaining 4 tablespoons of butter. Stir in the flour and cook over very low heat, stirring constantly, until the flour loses its raw taste and begins to color slightly. Slowly whisk in the hot milk and continue to whisk until the mixture is very thick. Add the Tabasco and Worcestershire sauce, then combine with the chicken and grain mixture and spoon into the prepared pan. Smooth the surface evenly and press in the pistachio nuts (if used).

Butter a piece of parchment paper to fit the surface and place it, butter side down, over the terrine. Fasten all four corners of the paper by sticking toothpicks into the edges. Bake for 40 minutes. Remove and discard the paper and the toothpicks and let cool on a wire rack. When cooled, cover tightly with aluminum foil and refrigerate it right in the pan.

When ready to serve the next day, loosen and unmold, then turn the terrine right side up so that the pistachios show. Slice thinly with a sharp knife.

Pizzoccheri: Italian Buckwheat Pasta
with Swiss Chard and Potatoes

SERVES 4 TO 6

Dark buckwheat pasta with a rough texture and an earthy hearty flavor is the basis of this classic specialty of the mountainous Valtellina region of Lombardy in northern Italy. The dish is beautiful to behold: nuggets of boiled potatoes nestle in the toast-colored noodles, brightly flecked with shreds of green swiss chard, ruby dicings of red onion and silvery fresh sage in an ivory sauce of melted Taleggio cheese.

3 Tbs. butter	4–6 waxy, new potatoes (½ lb.), peeled and cut in large cubes
1 medium red onion, coarsely diced (about 1 C.)	1 lb. Swiss chard
3–4 large cloves garlic, finely minced (about 1 Tbs.)	½ lb. buckwheat pasta (or ¾-in. tagliatelle or ½-in. fettuce—see NOTE)
2 Tbs. coarsely chopped fresh sage leaves	6 ozs. Taleggio or Fontina cheese, cubed
Salt and freshly ground black pepper to taste	⅓ C. grated Parmesan cheese

In a large 12-inch skillet, melt the butter and sauté the onions and garlic over medium low heat for 5 minutes. Add the sage, salt and pepper and turn off the heat. In a large 9- or 11-quart stockpot or pasta pot, boil a large amount of salted water. Then, using a steamer or colander so that it can be lifted out easily, place the cubed potatoes in the water and cook for 5 to 8 minutes or until tender. Lift out and drain, then add the potatoes to the skillet with the onion mixture. Do not discard the water.

Cut the white stems from the Swiss chard and slice diagonally into ½-inch pieces. Place in the steamer and cook in the same liquid in the stockpot for about 2 minutes. Lift out and drain, then add the stems to the skillet. Shred the leaves into pieces about 1 inch wide, add them to the steamer, and cook in the same pot until wilted, about 2 minutes. Drain and add to the skillet. Bring water to a boil and add the pasta to the same water (no steamer this time) and in vigorously boiling water cook until it is al dente. Drain the pasta in a colander and combine with the other ingredients in the skillet.

Preheat the oven to 400°F. and butter a 3-quart deep oval baking dish. Transfer the contents of the skillet to the baking dish. Stir in the cubes of cheese and sprinkle grated Parmesan on the surface. Bake on the top shelf of the oven for 5 minutes to allow the cheese to melt. Serve at once.

NOTE: Buckwheat pasta is available at specialty shops and natural food stores across the country (see Mail Order Sources).

The

Versatile

Grain

and the

Elegant

Bean

58

Breast of Veal Stuffed with Kasha

SERVES 6

Breast of veal is a flavorful, inexpensive, yet festive cut of meat, done here with a filling that can be prepared in advance. Whole kasha, carrots and onions are tucked into a veal breast that has been marinated overnight in a paste of garlic and paprika.

Kasha Filling

2 Tbs. butter
1 large onion, coarsely chopped (1¼ C.)
Salt to taste, plus ½ tsp. (or to taste)
Freshly ground black pepper to taste
1 large carrot, shredded (1 C.)

2 Tbs. finely minced parsley
1 tsp. finely minced sage
2 eggs
½ C. whole kasha
1 C. water

In a 10-inch nonstick skillet, melt the butter and sauté the onions seasoned with salt and pepper over high heat until browned. Stirring frequently, add the carrots, parsley and sage, transfer the mixture to a bowl and set aside.

In a small bowl, beat the eggs with a whisk until foamy, take off 3 tablespoons of the egg mixture and mix it with the kasha. Set the rest of the egg aside. Using the same skillet, put in the egg-covered kasha and stir over medium high heat until the grains separate. Add the water and ½ teaspoon salt (or to taste) and bring to a boil. Then lower the heat, cover and simmer until the water is absorbed and the grain is tender, about 10 to 15 minutes. Stir the kasha into the onion mixture, along with the remaining egg. Cover tightly and refrigerate overnight.

Breast of Veal

6-lb. lean breast of veal with a pocket cut for stuffing
1 tsp. coarse salt
1 tsp. paprika
¼ tsp. cayenne

4–5 cloves garlic, finely minced (1 Tbs.)
1 large onion, thinly sliced
1 C. Beef Stock, preferably homemade (see page 172), plus additional water if necessary

Place the meat in a shallow pan. In a small bowl, mix together the salt, paprika, cayenne and garlic, then crush into a paste with the back of a wooden spoon. Smear the paste on both sides of the veal, cover tightly with aluminum foil and refrigerate overnight.

When ready to cook, preheat the oven to 350°F., stuff the pocket with the kasha filling and skewer it closed. Place the sliced onion in the bottom of the roasting pan, pour in the beef stock and place the veal, meaty side down, in the pan. Cover it tightly again with foil and roast for 45 minutes. Then remove the foil, raise the oven temperature to 400°F. and roast, basting occasionally and turning it once. Water may be needed for additional basting liquid. Roast for 2 hours or until tender, then cover loosely with foil and let rest for 15 minutes before cutting into serving portions.

Soba: Japanese Buckwheat Noodles
with Smoked Salmon, Cucumber and Shiitake Mushrooms

SERVES 4

Like the American sandwich, soba noodles are the "fast food" of the Japanese for lunch or for a snack. Our version mixes Eastern and Western tastes and ingredients for a cool, refreshing summer salad, picnic or buffet table.

4 large dried Japanese shiitake mushrooms	2 C. soybean sprouts
7 qts. water	1 large English cucumber, cut thinly into 2-in. strips (about 2 C.)
7-oz. package Japanese soba (see NOTE)	4 oz. thinly sliced smoked salmon, cut into ½-in. strips
1 tsp. oriental sesame oil	1 Tbs. coarsely chopped cilantro
2 Tbs. light soy sauce	
4 scallions, sliced diagonally into 1-in. pieces	

Soak the mushrooms in warm water to cover for about 40 minutes. Trim and discard the tough stems. Strain and reserve only ¼ cup of the mushroom liquid for the dressing (recipe follows). Stack the mushrooms one on top of the other and press out and discard any excess liquid. Slice the mushrooms thinly.

Bring 7 quarts of water to a boil in a large pot. Add the soba, stirring constantly with a wooden spoon, and cook about 4 minutes. Drain in a colander and add to a large bowl that is filled with cold water. Swish the soba around and drain again. Return the soba to the bowl and immediately add the sesame oil and the soy sauce. Toss gently with two forks and set aside.

Prepare the dressing. When you are ready to serve, add the mushrooms, scallions, bean sprouts and cucumber to the soba, toss gently with the dressing and spoon onto a large serving platter. Arrange the strips of smoked salmon on top and sprinkle the cilantro over all.

Dressing

2 Tbs. light soy sauce	3 Tbs. canola or safflower oil
2 Tbs. rice vinegar	1 tsp. oriental hot chile oil
½ tsp. sugar	¼ C. reserved liquid from the mushrooms
1 tsp. finely minced lemon peel	
1 tsp. peeled and finely minced fresh ginger	

Combine all the ingredients in a small bowl and blend with a whisk.

NOTE: There are two kinds of soba: the one used in this recipe is a combination of buckwheat with some wheat added. It is, in our opinion, tastier and with a more pleasing texture than the soba with 100 percent buckwheat. The latter is darker in color, stronger in flavor and grainier in texture. However, if you are on a wheat-free diet, use the second type, but cook it for 9 to 10 minutes instead of 4 minutes.

The

Versatile

Grain

and the

Elegant

Bean

Galette de Sarrasin: French Buckwheat Crêpes with Caramelized Apples and Calvados

SERVES 10 TO 12

Friday, for some reason, is traditionally the day for making this classic Brittany specialty. Warm, paper-thin, dinner plate–size buckwheat crêpes are usually served with fizzy, golden, hard apple cider. Our version uses smaller-size crêpes filled with an ambrosial mixture of caramelized apples, pecans and currants with a touch of French Calvados for an altogether glorious dessert.

Caramelized Apples

¼ C. dried currants	½ tsp. cinnamon
2 Tbs. Calvados or applejack	½ C. light brown sugar
4 Tbs. butter	½ C. coarsely broken pecans
6 C. thinly sliced, cored, peeled tart green apples (6–8 apples, depending on size)	⅔ C. heavy cream

In a small cup, soak the currants in the Calvados for 20 minutes. Heat the butter in a 12-inch cast-iron skillet and add the apples and cinnamon. Sauté over high heat, stirring frequently, for 5 minutes, then add 1 tablespoon of the light brown sugar, and continue to sauté until the apples are soft. Stir in the currants and Calvados and the pecans and set aside.

In a 1½-quart nonstick saucepan, combine the cream and the remaining brown sugar and bring slowly to a boil over low heat. Then simmer until thick and amber in color. Pour over the apple mixture and combine. Set aside until the crêpes are prepared.

Buckwheat Crêpes

1 large egg	2 Tbs. all-purpose flour
2 Tbs. melted butter, cooled	½ tsp. salt or to taste
¾ C. milk	Confectioners' sugar (optional)
½ C. light buckwheat flour	

In a medium-size bowl, whisk the egg until frothy. Whisk in the butter and milk. To a small bowl, add both flours along with the salt and with a clean, dry whisk, blend them together. Add the flour to the egg mixture, whisking constantly. Then let the batter rest for 15 minutes.

Heat a nonstick or well-seasoned crêpe pan. Spoon 2 tablespoons of the batter into the pan, rotating the pan as you pour the batter so that a thin layer covers the bottom. Cook for 2 to 3 minutes, until the top looks dry, then turn the crêpe over and cook for 1 minute more. Repeat until all of the batter is used up, stacking the crêpes between aluminum foil and keeping them warm in a low oven as they are being made. When ready to serve, heat the apple mixture slowly, stirring occasionally, until hot. Place a crêpe on each plate, spoon some apple mixture in the center and fold both sides over to enclose the filling. Sprinkle with confectioners' sugar if you wish and serve warm.

French Pear and Hazelnut Buckwheat Torte
with Ginger

SERVES 8

This unusual cake from Brittany is nearly fat-free—the only butter in this cake is that which is used to butter the pan.

Butter for greasing cake pan	**1 tsp. vanilla extract**
½ C. light buckwheat flour	**½ C. coarsely chopped, toasted**
½ C. cake flour	**hazelnuts**
2 tsps. baking powder	**1 lb. ripe Comice pears (about 2**
Pinch salt	**large), peeled, cored and cut into**
1 tsp. ground ginger	**very small pieces, tossed with 1**
2 egg whites plus 1 whole egg	**Tbs. lemon juice**
⅔ C. sugar	**Confectioners' sugar for decoration**

Butter a 9½ × 2-inch round cake pan. Preheat the oven to 350°F. In a large bowl, combine both flours, baking powder, salt and ground ginger, blending with a whisk. Then, sift the mixture twice over a piece of waxed paper and return to the bowl. Set aside.

In the bowl of a food processor, add the egg whites, egg, sugar and vanilla and process until the texture is creamy. Fold gently into the dry ingredients until combined. Then fold in the toasted hazelnuts and the pear/lemon juice mixture. Spoon into the prepared pan and bake for 35 minutes or until a cake tester inserted in the center tests clean. The top should be golden.

Cool in the pan on a wire rack for 25 minutes before unmolding onto a serving plate. Sift the confectioners' sugar over the surface of the cake before serving. Sifting the sugar with a paper doily placed on the cake makes an attractive design. Serve slightly warm.

The

Versatile

Grain

and the

Elegant

Bean

62

Bulgur

Triticum—Wheat

A Grain by Any Other Name . . .

Some years ago, we began to collect the spellings of bulgur, for though it has been a staple grain of Eastern Europe and of the entire Middle East for centuries, no one seems to have settled upon a single way to spell it. Depending upon the country, the local tribe, the maternal grandmother, the misspelling of the cook, bulgur has come down to us in a most erratic combination of letters: bulghur, bulgor, boulgur, bulghar, bulghour, burghul and bourghoul! We're certain that some of our readers have still other kaleidoscopic spellings in their handwritten recipe files, and it somehow reminds us of Eugene Field's delightful verse ("Jest 'Fore Christmas"):

> *Father calls me William,*
> *Sister calls me Will,*
> *Mother calls me Willie, but the*
> *fellers call me Bill!*

Well, no matter what it's called—and in the Old Testament it's called *Arisah*—bulgur is basically whole wheat that's been washed, steamed, the hull removed, parched or dry cooled, then cracked and sifted into its various forms. And though there can't be much to confuse the cook in terms of spelling, one comment should be made about a common myth that seems to persist in spite of what we and other cookbook authors have tried to correct. We came across an item just recently that stated that bulgur was only *cracked wheat* that is sold at inflated prices in the gourmet sections of groceries or in health food stores. Even some of the better-known food writers (who shall remain nameless here) have also passed it off as a twin of its cracked wheat cousin. The myth has continued that one form can be substituted for the other, in spite of the fact that there is a major difference between the two.

The

Versatile

Grain

63

Certainly, both bulgur and what we purchase as cracked wheat are *cracked wheat.* But cracked wheat is *uncooked,* while bulgur has been processed and steamed before cracking, and to the cook that makes all the difference in the world. Preparation time and cooking time are different for the two varieties, and more important, perhaps, is the fact that if we use cracked wheat exactly as we do bulgur, we'd probably feel as if we'd ingested a mouth full of gravel at best and we might well chip a tooth at worst. So, if cracked wheat *is* substituted for bulgur, the cooking time must be adjusted accordingly.

The form of wheat that we call bulgur comes from a very practical historical need. The people of the Middle East, never blessed with a plentiful supply of fuel, tried to find a way to shorten the cooking time of their meals. And so, large amounts of wheat berries were steamed, dried in the sun, then cracked and stored. They then could use small amounts of the bulgur with which to cook, and presoaking (a method that we still use today) would eliminate or shorten the cooking time.

From a nutritional point of view, this was a perfect way to keep the benefits of wheat intact, since the minimal processing barely affects the high protein content, or the amounts of phosphorus, potassium or calcium. The bulgur thus retains the same nutritive value as a complete kernel of wheat.

As with most grains, bulgur has a variety of uses in a range of dishes from appetizers to hors d'oeuvres to soups, side dishes and entrées. And as might be expected, given its heritage, many of them are reflections of the cooking of the Middle East. We have begun to see Arabic and Israeli names appearing on the menus of our local restaurants: *tabbouleh* (bulgur with minced parsley, mint, green onion, tomatoes, cucumbers, olive oil and lemon juice—see page 71), *kibbe* (the national dish of Lebanon—bulgur and lamb—see pages 71, 74) and *mejedrah* (bulgur or rice and lentils—see page 380). The pilafs of Turkey frequently substitute bulgur for rice, and throughout the Middle East, mothers use combinations of bulgur and chick-pea purée and *leban* (sour milk) as a replacement for commercial infant foods.

The Forms of Bulgur

Since bulgur can be made from either red wheat or white wheat, the resultant product will either be fairly dark (red wheat) or have kernels that are pale and golden in color (white wheat). The darker grain is generally found in health food stores, while the lighter bulgur is usually in Middle Eastern food shops or in specialty shops. If the bulgur forms that we've listed below are not available to you, they can also be purchased by mail (see Mail Order Sources, pages 501–506).

#1 *Fine Granulations.* Usually used for making various *kibbe* recipes. It can also be used unsoaked and then baked or fried.

#2 *Medium Granulations.* A good all-purpose granulation usually used for cold salads such as *tabbouleh* and for stuffings.

#3 *Coarse Granulations.* Used for pilafs and for salads, as well as for soups. This granulation has a chewier texture than the others and it retains its shape quite well. It can also be toasted while dry and the liquid poured over it afterward.

The

Versatile

Grain

and the

Elegant

Bean

64

#4 *Whole Bulgur.* Similar in texture to Coarse #3 and can be used interchangeably. Whole bulgur is uncracked.

In the recipes that follow, we have given specific choices for the granulations.

Bulgur

Grain & Granulation	Amount of Liquid	Cooking Method	Cooking & Standing Time	Approx. Yield	Comments
		For all granulations:	Fork-fluff after standing.		
1 C. dry					
#1 Fine	2½ C. boiling water	Pour boiling water over grain and *steep. Do not cook.*	Let stand 15 minutes.	3 C.	To prepare only *1 C.* of presoaked grain, use ⅓ C. dry grain and steep in boiling water for the required amount of time for the selected granulation.
#2 Medium	2½ C. boiling water	After required standing time, line a colander with a man's handkerchief. Gather up the ends and twist to squeeze out excess water. Place in a bowl and fluff with fork, then season with salt.	Let stand 30 minutes.	3 C.	#3 and #4 whole bulgur may also be cooked in 2 C. boiling water for 20 minutes, but the results will be more sticky and will not be usable for recipes in this book. (cont.)

Bulgur (cont.)

Grain & Granulation	Amount of Liquid	Cooking Method	Cooking & Standing Time	Approx. Yield	Comments
#3 Coarse	3 C. boiling water		Let stand 60 minutes.	3 C.	Make certain that, if you purchase the darker-colored bulgur—which is usually *cracked wheat*—it is indeed *precooked* like the more golden-colored bulgur. Cracked wheat requires *cooking,* not steeping!
#4 Whole bulgur #3 and #4 are interchangeable since there is not much difference in granulation.	3 C. boiling water		Let stand 60 minutes.	3 C.	

Bulgur and Lentil Soup
with Mustard Greens

SERVES 6

Whole grains and lentils are cooked with a peppery blend of mustard greens and cayenne to make this soup a satisfying nutritional combination of grains and legumes. It's easy to make and it has a tangy bite.

1 C. green lentils
½ C. dry #4 whole grain bulgur
10 C. water or Beef Stock (preferably homemade, see page 172)
1 large clove garlic
¼ tsp. cayenne
5–6 parsley stems, finely minced (see NOTE)
3 Tbs. oriental sesame oil

2 medium onions, finely chopped (1½ C.)
1 large carrot, shredded (1 C.)
2 C. mustard greens cut in ½-in. chiffonade (spinach or turnip greens can be substituted)
Salt and freshly ground black pepper to taste
2 Tbs. apple cider vinegar

Pick over the lentils and bulgur to remove any foreign matter. Combine them and rinse in a colander. Drain and add to a heavy 6-quart pot, along with the water or beef stock, garlic, cayenne and parsley stems. Bring to a boil, then lower the heat and cover, but leave the lid slightly ajar. Simmer for 1 hour.

Meanwhile heat the oil in a skillet and sauté the onions over low heat, stirring occasionally until they begin to brown, about 10 minutes. Add the onions to the soup after 1 hour, along with the carrots and mustard greens, the salt and pepper. Continue to simmer for 10 more minutes. Then stir in the vinegar just before serving. Serve hot.

NOTE: We prefer the stems from flat leaf parsley for this recipe rather than the leaves because we find that they have more flavor.

The

Versatile

Grain

Butter Pecan, Carrot and Bulgur Pilaf

SERVES 4 TO 6

This healthful side dish can be ready in under 10 minutes, a welcome change from the usual rice or potatoes. Serve it with meat or poultry or as a stuffing for chicken or veal.

3 Tbs. butter
½ C. pecan halves
1 large carrot, shredded (1 C.)
3 C. presoaked #3 coarse bulgur (see Chart, page 66)

½ C. Chicken Stock, preferably homemade (see page 171)
Salt to taste
¼ tsp. freshly ground black pepper
½ tsp. dried tarragon

Melt the butter in a 3-quart nonstick saucepan and add the pecans. Sauté the pecans, shaking the pan frequently for about 2 to 3 minutes. Remove the nuts with a slotted spoon and set aside. In the same pan, add the carrots and stir gently for about 1 minute. Then add the presoaked bulgur, chicken stock, salt and pepper and the tarragon. Cook over medium high heat, stirring occasionally, for about 5 minutes. Transfer to a serving dish and scatter the reserved pecans on top.

The

Versatile

Grain

and the

Elegant

Bean

68

Bulgur and Lamb-covered Indian Eggs
with Cucumber and Radish Raita

SERVES 6

For some unknown reason, before the time of Indian independence, the British colonials referred to this dish as "Scottish eggs." These spicy meat and grain–covered eggs are baked, then cooled with a soothing yogurt sauce. They make a pleasant lunch, first course or, if you double the recipe, a welcome addition to a buffet table.

Cucumber and Radish Raita
MAKES ABOUT 1 CUP

- ¾ C. plain yogurt
- 1 large scallion, finely minced, green top only (2 Tbs.)
- ½ large cucumber, shredded (2 Tbs.)
- 4–6 radishes, shredded (2 Tbs.)
- Salt and pinch white pepper to taste
- Pinch ground cumin

Mix together all the ingredients and allow the flavors to develop in the refrigerator for at least 1 hour or longer.

Indian Eggs

- ½ lb. lean ground lamb
- 1 small onion, grated (about ½ C.)
- 1 small clove garlic, finely minced (1 tsp.)
- ½ C. presoaked #1 fine bulgur (see Chart, page 65)
- 2 Tbs. finely minced parsley
- 1 tsp. finely minced cilantro
- ¼ tsp. Tabasco sauce
- Salt to taste
- 1 wedge lemon (1 tsp. lemon juice)
- ¼ tsp. each ground cumin, powdered ginger, turmeric and ground coriander
- 1 small egg, lightly beaten
- Butter for greasing pan
- 3 hard-cooked eggs
- 2 tsps. butter, cut into small pieces

In a medium-size bowl, mix together the lamb, onions, garlic, bulgur, parsley, cilantro, Tabasco, salt, lemon juice, spices and beaten egg. Preheat the oven to 400°F. and butter a medium-size oven-to-table baking pan. Divide the meat mixture into three equal parts. Wet your hands in cold water and with each part of meat cover each egg to enclose it completely. Place in the prepared baking pan. Dot each "egg" with butter and bake for 20 to 25 minutes. Cool slightly and slice each covered egg in half lengthwise. Spoon some of the raita sauce over each half. Serve at room temperature.

Falafel: Bulgur and Chick-Pea Patties
in Garlic Tahini Sauce

MAKES 18 PATTIES

Throughout the Middle East, falafel is served from street carts. It is usually tucked into a pita bread along with tahini sauce and sometimes marinated cucumbers, tomato, onion and green pepper relish. It's basically a Middle Eastern version of the universal American hamburger.

Garlic Tahini Sauce
MAKES ¾ CUP

1 small clove garlic, finely minced (½ tsp.)
¼ C. tahini (sesame seed paste)
¼ C. plain yogurt
1 Tbs. lemon juice

3 Tbs. cold water
¼ tsp. ground cumin
Salt and freshly ground black pepper to taste

Blend all the ingredients together in a blender or food processor until smooth. Transfer to a bowl and let stand for at least 1 hour for the flavors to meld.

Falafel

1 C. drained, cooked chick-peas
1 C. #1 presoaked fine bulgur
2 cloves garlic, finely minced (about 2 tsp.)
2–3 slices whole wheat bread, soaked in water and squeezed dry (about 1 C.)
Juice of 1 small lemon (2 Tbs.)
1 egg, lightly beaten

1 Tbs. finely minced cilantro
2 Tbs. finely minced parsley
1 tsp. ground cumin
½ tsp. paprika
⅛ tsp. cayenne
Salt and freshly ground black pepper to taste
1 tsp. baking powder
Corn or canola oil for frying

In the bowl of a food processor, process the chick-peas until coarsely chopped, but not puréed. Add all the remaining ingredients except the oil to the food processor and process until blended. The chick-peas will now be more finely chopped. Wet your hands and form the mixture into walnut-size balls. Flatten them slightly and then place them on a waxed paper–lined plate. Chill in the refrigerator, uncovered, for 1 hour.

Heat the oil in a large skillet until very hot but not smoking and fry the falafel in one layer. Turn them once to brown on each side. Drain on paper towels and serve either hot or at room temperature with the sauce in a seperate bowl or tuck a falafel and some sauce into a small pita bread.

The

Versatile

Grain

and the

Elegant

Bean

70

Tabbouleh: Parsley, Mint and Bulgur Salad

SERVES 6

In the Middle East, romaine lettuce is used as a scoop for this lemony, refreshing bulgur salad. A few slices of cucumber are added, then the long leaves of lettuce are partly folded lengthwise and the entire thing is eaten with the fingers.

1 C. presoaked #2 medium bulgur (see Chart, page 65)

1½ C. finely minced flat leaf parsley (about 6 C. loosely packed leaves minced in a food processor)

¼ C. finely minced fresh mint (about ¾ C. loosely packed leaves minced in a food processor)

3 large scallions, finely minced (about ⅔ C.)

¼ tsp. freshly ground black pepper

Salt to taste

¼ tsp. ground cumin

¾ lb. ripe tomatoes, diced in ½-in. cubes (about 2 C.)

Juice of 1 large lemon or more to taste (about 3 Tbs.)

3 Tbs. oil (2 Tbs. canola or safflower oil and 1 Tbs. olive oil)

Romaine lettuce leaves

1 thinly sliced cucumber, either Kirby or long English cucumber

Place the bulgur into a large bowl and add the parsley, mint, scallions, seasonings and tomatoes. Stir gently to combine, then add the lemon juice and stir again. Cover and chill for at least 1 hour to allow the flavors to blend.

Before serving, bring to room temperature. Stir in the oil and correct the seasonings to your taste. A good lemony flavor should be present. On a serving platter, arrange the lettuce like the spokes of a wheel. Mound the salad in the center and scatter the cucumber slices over the lettuce.

Kibbe

—Basic Raw Lamb and Bulgur with Four Variations
—Basic Filling
—Baked "Kibbe on a Tray"
—Filled Boulettes with Three Variations

SERVES 10 TO 12

The national dish in almost every Middle Eastern country—call it *kibbe, kibbey, kibbeh, kibbi, koubbeh* or *kufte, kofte* or *kuftee*, depending upon what part of the area it originates in—is probably prepared in more ways than it is spelled. The base in all of them is fine bulgur and ground lamb. Once you master the basic recipe, the many variations are a snap.

(continued on page 72)

Basic Raw Lamb and Bulgur

2½ lbs. boned leg of lamb from shank
    end, trimmed of all fat and cut into
    cubes (about 4 lbs. with bone in)
1 large onion
1½ C. #1 fine bulgur
1 C. warm tap water
½ tsp. paprika
⅛ tsp. cayenne pepper

1 tsp. salt or to taste
Freshly ground black pepper to taste
¾ tsp. Syrian Mixed Spices (see end
    of recipe) or ½ tsp. allspice and ¼
    tsp. cinnamon
Juice of ½ lemon (1 Tbs.)
3 Tbs. ice water

In the bowl of a food processor, chop the lamb finely in two batches. There will be approximately 5 cups total. Transfer the chopped lamb to a large bowl. Take off 1 cup of the lamb and wrap it, keeping it refrigerated for the Basic Filling recipe, which follows. Place the onion in the food processor and process until very fine. Transfer it to the bowl with the lamb.

Put the bulgur in a small bowl and stir in the cup of warm water. Let the bulgur soak for 15 minutes. It should only be damp enough to allow it to absorb the meat juices when they are combined. (There will be about 4 cups of soaked bulgur.) Then add the soaked bulgur to the large bowl, along with the paprika, cayenne, salt and pepper, the Syrian mixed spices and the lemon juice. Mix to combine, then divide the mixture in half and return one half to the food processor, adding about 1½ tablespoons of the ice water and processing until a smooth mixture is formed.

Repeat in the same manner with the remaining mixture, then wet your hands and knead both batches together in a bowl. Cover the bowl with plastic wrap and set aside for 15 minutes to let the bulgur absorb the meat juices.

Variation #1. This mixture is served raw, similar to steak tartar. To serve six to eight people, use ½ the basic raw recipe. Line a platter with romaine lettuce. Mound the lamb and grain mixture on the lettuce and press a pattern on the surface of the meat by using the tines of a fork. Drizzle with olive oil and surround it with wedges of lemon for sprinkling over the meat. The lettuce leaves are used as a scoop.

Variation #2. To serve six to eight people, use ½ the basic raw recipe. Wet your hands and scoop up about 1 tablespoon of the mixture at a time and roll it into cigarlike shapes. Mix 2 tablespoons parsley and ¼ cup very finely minced scallions. Dip the rolls into the parsley and scallion mixture and then roll them in a small leaf of romaine lettuce to enclose them. Eat them with your fingers.

Variation #3. To serve four to six people, use ¼ of the basic raw recipe. Pinch off olive-size pieces of the raw mixture and poach them in six cups of hot chicken broth over medium heat for 5 minutes. Divide into portions and serve as miniature meat dumplings with the broth.

Variation #4. To serve four to six people, use ½ the basic raw recipe. However, this is *not* a raw mixture. *Kufte kebabs* are grilled over charcoal or broiled in the oven. To prepare *kufte kebabs,* oil six metal skewers and form the basic raw mixture

The

Versatile

Grain

and the

Elegant

Bean

72

into sausage shapes around the skewers. Brush them with melted butter or olive oil and grill or broil them, turning frequently, for about 3 minutes on each side. Slip them off the skewers with a piece of pita bread as a holder.

Basic Filling

This recipe is used in conjunction with the Basic Raw Lamb and Bulgur recipe (above) for Baked "Kibbe on a Tray" and for the Filled Boulettes, which follow.

3 Tbs. butter	1½ tsps. Syrian Mixed Spices (see end
¼ C. pine nuts	of recipe) or 1 tsp. allspice and ½
1 very large onion, finely chopped	tsp. cinnamon
(1 C.)	2 tsps. dried currants
1 C. lean ground lamb (reserved from	Salt and freshly ground black pepper to
the previous recipe)	taste
¼ C. finely minced parsley	

Melt the butter in a medium-size skillet, spoon off the surface foam and discard. Add the pine nuts and toast them, stirring frequently, over low heat until the nuts are tan-colored. Remove with a slotted spoon and set aside. In the same skillet, add the onions and sauté them over medium heat, stirring frequently, for 5 to 8 minutes, or until they *begin* to brown. *Do not brown them.* Add the lamb and stir until it loses its pink color. Stir in the parsley, spices, currants, the reserved pine nuts and the salt and pepper. Let the mixture cool slightly before using.

Baked "Kibbe on a Tray"

SERVES 8 TO 10

Use one entire recipe Basic Raw Lamb and Bulgur and one recipe Basic Filling.

Preheat the oven to 325°F. Liberally butter the bottom and sides of a 9 × 13½ × 2¼-inch rectangular roasting pan. Divide the meat and bulgur mixture into two portions, one slightly larger than the other. With dampened hands, using the large portion first, form it into ¾-inch-thick, large flat patties and line them across the bottom of the pan, placing them very close together. Then, using your fingers, combine the patties until there is one single ¾-inch-thick layer across the bottom of the pan. (It is easier to form the layer this way than to try to make one ¾-inch layer at once.) Smooth the surface.

Spread the basic filling mixture on top. Then flatten the remaining bulgur and lamb mixture by making ½-inch patties, placing them on top and then smoothing and combining them with your fingers so that the entire filling is covered. Using a sharp knife, cut the top layer only, lengthwise, into 2-inch strips. Then cut the layer diagonally 2 inches apart to make diamond shapes.

(continued on page 74)

The

Versatile

Grain

Trickle the surface with 2 tablespoons olive oil or clarified butter and bake for 20 to 25 minutes or until the surface is browned slightly. Remove from the oven and serve by cutting through to the bottom of the pan, following the scored surface markings. Serve hot or at room temperature.

Filled Boulettes

SERVES 10 TO 12

To serve ten to twelve people, use one entire recipe Basic Raw Lamb and Bulgur and one recipe Basic Filling. To serve five to six people, just use half the recipe to make ten to twelve boulettes.

Dampen your hands and scoop up some of the basic raw lamb-bulgur mixture, about the size of a small egg. Form it into a hollow cup, using the thumb and forefinger of the opposite hand to shape the cup. Press the sides to form an even cavity with walls about ½ inch thick. Place about 1 tablespoon of the basic filling into each cavity and, with your fingers, bring the top edge around to seal and enclose the filling. Taper both ends slightly, very much like a football. As you make them, place them on a foil-lined baking sheet. Repeat the process until all are made. There should be about 20 to 24 boulettes. Chill for 30 minutes, uncovered, before cooking in any one of the variations given below:

Variation #1. Poached. Mix 3 cups beef stock with an 8-ounce can of tomato sauce. In a large sauté pan, bring the mixture to a boil, then lower the heat. Let the boulettes simmer for 15 to 20 minutes, turning carefully once during the cooking. Remove the boulettes, reduce the sauce for 5 minutes and pour it over them.

Variation #2. Fried. Heat 2½ to 3 inches corn oil in a large sauté pan to 375°F. on a fat thermometer. Fry the boulettes in several batches, until golden, about 3 to 5 minutes. Drain on paper towels. Keep the boulettes warm in a low oven until all are fried and serve them with wedges of lemon.

Variation #3. Grilled. Brush the boulettes with olive oil and grill them over charcoal or broil them in a preheated oven broiler for 3 minutes on each side until brown. Serve with lemon wedges.

Syrian Mixed Spices

MAKES 1½ TABLESPOONS

2 tsps. ground allspice	½ tsp. ground ginger
1 tsp. finely ground black pepper	⅛ tsp. ground cloves
¾ tsp. ground cinnamon	⅛ tsp. ground cardamom
½ tsp. freshly grated nutmeg	

Combine all the ingredients well and store in a tightly covered jar until ready to use.

The

Versatile

Grain

and the

Elegant

Bean

74

Apple Rum Raisin Cake with Bulgur

SERVES 6

This cake is a prize for apple lovers. It's moist and filled with chopped apples, raisins and fine grain bulgur, then topped with more apple slices under a shimmering glaze.

1 C. dark raisins, preferably Monukka	1 tsp. vanilla extract
2 Tbs. dark rum	1½ C. all-purpose flour
2 tsps. lemon juice	1 tsp. baking powder
3–4 tart green apples such as Granny Smith (about 1¼ lbs.)	½ tsp. baking soda
	½ tsp. salt
Butter for greasing pan	½ tsp. freshly grated nutmeg
Flour for dusting pan	½ tsp. ground cinnamon
⅓ C. soft butter	1 C. presoaked #1 fine bulgur (see Chart, page 65)
¾ C. sugar	
1 egg	½ C. orange marmalade

In a small cup, combine the raisins and rum and set aside. Peel and core the apples and chop two of them coarsely in the bowl of a food processor for about five strokes. Scrape them out into a bowl and mix with 1 teaspoon of the lemon juice. Cut the remaining apple(s) in half, core, and slice paper-thin. Toss with the remaining lemon juice and set aside.

Preheat the oven to 350°F. Butter and flour a 9 × 2½-inch springform cake pan. In the bowl of the food processor, cream the butter and sugar until light and fluffy. Add the egg and vanilla and process until well combined.

In another bowl, add the flour, baking powder, baking soda, salt, nutmeg and cinnamon and beat with a whisk to combine. Add the presoaked bulgur to the bowl of the food processor and then add the dry ingredients. Process until mixed. Using a rubber spatula, transfer the batter to a large bowl and stir in the raisin-rum mixture and the chopped apples. Mix well and scrape into the prepared pan. Place the apple slices lightly overlapping on the surface of the cake and bake for 1 hour or until the cake pulls away from the sides of the pan. Cool on a wire rack for 30 minutes, then remove the sides of the springform, keeping the cake on the base of the pan.

Melt and strain the orange marmalade and brush the glaze over the apples. Serve slightly warm if you wish.

Corn

Zea Mays

A Maze of Amazing Maize

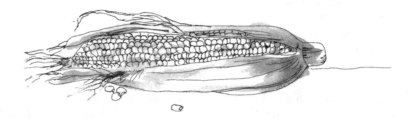

The botanists and the agricultural pundits warn amateur farmers that, if they are going to attempt to grow corn, the fields must be very large so that proper pollination can take place. In spite of this, we decided to ignore the advice, for after having successfully grown squash, lettuce, raspberries, grapes, Swiss chard, tomatoes and sugar snap peas in our tiny Fire Island garden, we set about planting a "crop" of sweet corn—*nine* lonely little seeds in a tiny plot only four by six feet. And we moved back and we watched.

And they grew! First as tiny, green, delicate sprouts, then as increasingly sturdy, slender plants and finally "as high as an elephant's eye," they matured and they flourished in their little plot, against all the expert predictions of doom and failure. By August, each stalk bore the bulging green, silk-laden ears, perfect, healthy, tempting and proud. And, at harvest time, for nine straight days, the same routine took place.

One of us stayed in the kitchen, boiling a large pot of water, while the other one hovered in the garden waiting for word that all was ready, at which time two ears were pulled, shucked on the way up to the kitchen and plunked gently into the pot. The lid was closed, the flame turned off, and the timer set. Of course, we had read, as had everyone, that 90 percent of the sugar in sweet corn turns to starch in only a few hours, and in no way were we going to let even the tiniest bit of the fresh sweet corn taste elude us. And in no way were we disappointed! The homegrown corn tasted as no other corn had ever tasted, and after the ninth day we looked sadly at the barren stalks, shorn of their delicious prizes, leaving us with memories that we can still write about with joy. (See page 83 for our suggested cooking methods for fresh sweet corn.)

The

Versatile

Grain

and the

Elegant

Bean

76

The Americas, of course, have had a love affair with corn. Indeed, if ever there was a native crop indigenous to both continents, it is corn in all its 300 varieties, each for a different use. Throughout history, corn—or maize as it is known in most places— has turned up in a hundred different forms and has provided the base grain for many thousands of dishes. In the Tehuacán Valley in southern Mexico, archaeologists have unearthed somewhere around 23,000 specimens of maize with wild varieties dating back to 5200 B.C. and the cultivated maize to about 3400 B.C.

Though some maize was being grown in China and the Philippines about the sixteenth century, it was basically developed and cultivated by the Indian civilizations in both South and North America. The Andean and Mexican cultures as well as our own Native Americans worshipped maize as a critical crop of survival, and so in the lore of the tribes of the Great Plains, the woodlands and the Great Lakes, among the Shawnees, Zuñi, Navajos, Hopi, Mohawks and Cherokees, we find references to corn as "the Seed of Seeds" or "Sacred Mother" or "Gift of the Gods." To this day, the Pueblo Indians of New Mexico perform the Summer Corn Dance every August, for they say that should they miss even a single year, the earth would become barren, the rains would not fall, children would not be born, the stars would not turn, the tribe and the universe would disintegrate.

Columbus discovered the Arawak Indians growing maize (*mahiz*) in the Caribbean, and there are reports of his amazement at seeing them smoking tobacco that was wrapped in the husks of corn. (There were no reports, however, of corn cob pipes.) And as for the colonists, the crop was a godsend and the Indians taught them to plant corn and to fertilize the fields with the heads and bones of fish. Contemporary documents tell of the months after a crop was planted, when the dogs had one paw tied to their necks so that they couldn't dig up the fermenting skeletons.

Pueblo corn dance

At that time, the mentor for the colonists was an Indian named Squanto, and in 1620 he was given credit for his help and guidance. In fact, until about 1920, there was a variety of corn dubbed *Squantum,* which as far as we can tell has now disappeared. But in a society where there was no way to get milk or dairy products, since cows had not yet arrived from the Old World, the settlers substituted crushed fresh corn mixed with the juice of boiled hickory nuts and chestnuts to use as a heated baby food. Even Henry Wadsworth Longfellow paid tribute to the crop in *Song of Hiawatha* when he wrote that "all around the happy village, stood the maize fields, green and shining."

But, down through modern history, corn has remained typically American. Though Columbus did bring the maize seeds back to Europe, it has not really been

Mitchell Corn Palace

accepted there except in a few minor instances and most of the corn grown on the Continent is still fed to animals. The typical European attitude was perhaps best reflected in a poem we used to recite as kids, "Captain Jinks," written by T. Maclagan at the end of the last century: "I'm Captain Jinks of the Horse Marines, I give my horse good corn and beans . . ." And it has not changed very much over there, with few exceptions such as dishes like *mamaliga* (see page 103) in Eastern Europe (corn-meal mush), sometimes called *Romanian grits,* or the polenta of the Bergamo region of Italy (see page 104).

In the Americas, however, the use of corn has thrived, becoming the largest money crop in the United States and providing the base grain for thousands of dishes. The pioneers who opened the West survived on "hawg and hominy" (salt pork and corn). Cornmeals and corn flours were the basics for dishes that now rank as classics in American cuisine: hasty pudding, Indian pudding, johnnycakes, anadama bread, hoecakes, corn pone and ashcakes, corn chowder and corn porridge—called anything from *samp* to *loblolly* to *mush,* depending upon where you come from. And, of course, there's that good old Southern standby, grits, sometimes embellished in dishes like Louisiana's Grits and Grillades (see page 111).

We certainly can't forget another fine product produced in parts of the South, in which corn has been a most vital ingredient: *corn likker,* brewed in stills both legal and of the moonshine variety. William James Lampton immortalized that particular, ingenious use of corn in his poem *Kentucky,* when he wrote:

The

Versatile

Grain

and the

Elegant

Bean

78

Where the corn is full of kernels
And the colonels full of corn.

The grain has become a part of our language and we don't think twice to label a film or television show as "pure corn" or "corny." And, very much like the Native Americans, we don't hesitate to celebrate corn in our harvest festivals and in the summer cookouts and clam bakes that feature the particularly American delicacy corn on the cob. In Mitchell, South Dakota, the Corn Palace has become an institution, and it has grown into a wonderland of minarets and towers, with an annual redecoration of its exterior with over 2,000 bushels of corn.

The Corn Palace is a startling reminder that so many varieties of corn exist. Nothing on the exterior walls is dyed or colored in any way. The red corn is Bloody Butcher, the speckled corn is Calico or Indian Corn, and the nearly black kernels are usually Blue Flint. About 600,000 tourists make the pilgrimage to Mitchell each year.

If you will bear with us for one more quotation from our eclectic file of poetry, there is one delightful, albeit patriotically overdone stanza in Edna Dean Proctor's "Columbia's Emblem," written at the turn of the century, that pays homage to this most American of grains and it always brings a smile to our faces. She first writes that "The rose may bloom for England" and goes on to eulogize about the lily of France, the shamrock of Ireland, and the thistle in Scotland, concluding with:

But the shield of the great Republic,
The glory of the West,
Shall bear a stalk of the tasseled corn—
The sun's supreme bequest!

We would not dare try to top that one.

A Profile of Corn

From a spiky little weed of 15,000 years back, corn has evolved into a family tree with a hundred different limbs. How we were introduced to a particular form of corn depends upon a variety of factors, the most important of which is probably the *region* of the country in which we grew up. The soft, common *dent corn* was cultivated in the South, while the North grew *flint corn*. As a result, it would be close to heresy to give yellow cornmeal johnnycakes to a Rhode Islander! And if your family was Native American from the Southwest, you knew of *blue corn* long before it surfaced for the rest of us.

These days, of course, most forms of corn are available either in our supermarkets, our health food stores, or certainly by mail order, and no recipe need remain untasted if we so desire.

The Major Types

Sweet Corn. This is the corn-on-the cob variety, as well as the corn that's used for canning and freezing. There are about a hundred different subspecies that bear poetic names like Sweet Sue, Gold Cup, Silver Queen, Platinum Lady and Butter-and-Sugar, and when picked fresh and popped into the pot (see page 83), there's no taste quite like it to the corn aficionado. If you see corn for sale at your roadside farm stand or your local green market, chances are it is this variety.

Field Corn or Dent Corn. This is the corn that is usually dried right in the fields, creating a dent at the top of the kernel, thus its alternate name. Basically, field corn is the commercial variety, with 90 percent used for animal feed, and the rest as processed breakfast foods, cornstarch, corn oils and corn syrups. Any one of about 500 processed products carry "corn" on their list of ingredients, and field corn would probably be the variety.

Indian Corn or Flint Corn. The hard kernels give it its "flint" name, and the multicolored ears are a favorite at the roadside stands during the fall season. We, as many people we know, have ears of Indian corn hanging on a wire in our kitchen, the better to show off their multicolored kernels of blue, red, yellow, black and even orange and purple. Actually, the variety is quite edible when ground.

Blue Corn. Cultivated by the Native Americans of the Southwest, including the Zuñi, Navajo and Hopi tribes, it is sometimes referred to as *Hopi corn* as a result. They grew blue corn for hundreds of years and the dark indigo blue kernels gave a unique color, texture and intense corn flavor to their tribal breads.

Navajo legend explains the origin of blue corn as ". . . all the wise men being one day assembled, a turkey hen came flying from the direction of the morning star and shook from her feathers of an ear of blue corn into the midst of the company." Blue corn was possibly one of the earliest forms of sweet corn cultivated by the settlers.

However, since blue corn is rather difficult to harvest and has a long growing season, the younger generations seemed to have lost interest in continuing the tradition, and as late as 1984, the variety was in danger of becoming extinct, with only 500 acres devoted to the crop in the entire country.

In recent years, there has been a remarkable revival of this sweet and intensely flavored variety, and a host of blue corn products have now become readily available: cornmeal, pancake mix, tortillas, and corn bread. The public, long unaccepting of any but the usual colors, has now begun finally to utilize the blue-gray products from this traditional Native American corn.

The

Versatile

Grain

and the

Elegant

Bean

80

Popcorn. We would be remiss if we omitted one of America's favorite varieties of corn, and indeed popcorn is a very specific and individual crop. Although it has been grown for about 5,000 years and the Incas are known to have used strings of popcorn for their ceremonies, we still string popcorn and cranberries to decorate our Christmas trees. The early settlers popped it as the first breakfast cereal, but the love affair really took hold when the now-famous Orville Redenbacher started developing the modern varieties around 1941. Properly called the "popcorn pioneer," Redenbacher's early experiments gradually led to varieties that can now be popped to forty times their original kernel size!

What makes popcorn unique is that it contains a very hard hull and about 13 to 14 percent internal moisture. With nowhere to go when the kernel is heated, the moisture becomes steam and *voilà!* popcorn for the moviegoers and for the couch potatoes who watch television and VCR programs at home.

Today, in fact, the Popcorn Institute (yes, there *is* a Popcorn Institute) tells us that 70 percent of all popcorn is eaten at home, with about 50 percent in microwave ovens. The overall figures are astounding, especially when we realize that most of the other varieties of corn are consumed by animals. The sales are more than *$2 billion* a year, with every man, woman and child consuming *56 quarts* of popcorn annually. That makes almost *900 million pounds* by the beginning of the nineties and the figure is still going up.

The one mitigating thing about popcorn, though, is that it is probably one of the healthiest of snacks, *if* it's not popped in oil and drenched in butter with a rainfall of salt. Eaten plain, it only has about 30 to 40 calories per cup, while some commercial movie theater popcorn can go as high as 200 calories.

The Forms of Corn

Whole Corn, Dried. Any of the varieties outlined above—white, yellow or blue— used for home grinding into meal or flour or for parching or preparing whole hominy. Whole corn can also be soaked and cooked for use in various dishes when fresh corn is not available.

Cornmeal—Yellow, White or Blue. Cornmeal is usually of medium-fine consistency and the corn germ is retained. The various brands now available differ quite considerably in the performance and the quality of the end product and we have tested many brands, including Indian Head, Erewhon, Goya and Quaker, finding the most consistently good results with Indian Head.

Some cornmeals are "stone-ground" and you may find others labeled "water-ground," though that designation only refers to the power source and not to either stone or metal milling. Whichever product you eventually choose, keep in mind that a good, stone-ground cornmeal does not require the addition of other flours to prevent crumbling. However, since blue cornmeal is more dense than the white or yellow, you will probably have to blend it with equal proportions of flour.

Cornmeal is perfect for use in breads, muffins, griddle cakes, in recipes such as scrapple and in soups. For the north Italian traditional *polenta* (see page 99) either a special cornmeal from Italy should be used or there are some coarse commercial cornmeals (such as Goya) that also work quite well.

Corn Germ. The germ is the central core of the kernel and, as in all grains, is the part where the new plant sprouts or germinates. Ten pounds of corn are needed to provide one pound of germ, and the product is used in exactly the same way that we use wheat germ. It can serve as an extender for meat, can be sprinkled on cereal or yogurt, and can be used in the baking of breads or muffins as well as on salads. It has a popcornlike taste and it's highly perishable. It should be refrigerated after opening. At this time, the only place to find corn germ is in health food stores or it may be available through some mail order sources.

Corn Bran. The bran layer of the kernel, used in exactly the same way as wheat bran or oat bran or rice bran, and it's a good source of soluble fiber.

Whole Hominy. It comes in yellow or white and it's known by various names: *moté, posole, samp* and *nixtamal.* Small kernels of whole, dried amber-colored corn are processed in the same way as whole hominy and are called *chicos.* Whole hominy is also available in cans.

    The process consists of taking the whole corn and treating it with slaked (hydrated) lime or a combination of unslaked lime, calcium carbonate, lye or wood ash. The lime combined with water acts to loosen the hulls and partially "cook" the kernels, while also puffing them up. The corn is then washed to remove the hulls, dried and used for dishes such as soups and stews, or the mote is toasted and then eaten as a snack called *corn nuts.* When it's dried and ground it's called *masa harina,* and it's the only cornmeal that can be used to make *tortillas.* It's found in supermarkets and Hispanic groceries under the Quaker label.

Hominy Grits. Aside from the fact that grits have been the butt of too many jokes and that we never know whether to say, "grits are" or "grits is" (or "grits am"), it's one of our favorite delights and something we look forward to when we're working in the South. Originally developed by Native Americans, they called it "corn without skin" and as far back as 1607, the settlers who came ashore at Jamestown were offered bowls of *rockahominy.*

    Originally made from undegerminated, coarsely ground (preferably stone-ground) white corn, it is now available in both white and yellow forms in fine, medium and coarse grinds—as well as a commercial "instant" brand, which most of us grits connoisseurs disdain. We think true grits should be stone-ground and cooked for a long, long time. Our favorite is mail-ordered to us by a small mill in Tennessee (see Mail Order Sources, pages 501–506).

Corn Flour—Yellow, White or Blue. Corn ground to a finer consistency than cornmeal. It can be used for breading foods, waffles, pancakes, wheat-free pastas and breads. It can also be mixed with wheat flours where gluten is needed for rising.

Cornstarch. In England, just to confuse things a bit, it's called *corn flour.* It's quite familiar to all home cooks, and it's made from a high-starch variety of corn called *indentata.* A finely milled silken powder from the endosperm layer of the grain, it's usually used as a thickening agent for sauces, soups or puddings, but it also has a

The

Versatile

Grain

and the

Elegant

Bean

82

SWEET CORN ON THE COB: A PRIMER

There's no doubt that everyone has his or her special way of preparing corn on the cob. Full pot of water. Half pot of water. Salt. No salt. Sugar. Five minutes. Twelve minutes. Cook until you get nervous! It probably began when the first settlers watched the Indians pick and shuck corn, then throw the ears into pots of boiling water that were placed right alongside the cornfields. In New England, they still say "corn is picked when the cooking water starts to boil" and it is that good advice that we tried to follow when we grew our own tiny crop. Assuming that you, first of all, will find ears of corn picked only hours ago from the nearby field of the local farm—or at worst, corn that has not been sitting around for days and developing starch from the succulent sugars—here are two suggestions that we have found work for us:

Steamed Corn

In a large pot, boil enough water to hold the ears of corn that have been shucked. Add one or two leaves of the inside husk and then add salt when the water comes to a boil. The "no salt" people claim that its addition hardens the kernels but we have not found this to be so.

When the water comes to a boil, place the ears of corn in the water and *turn off the heat,* cover and let sit for nine minutes. The corn will then be ready to eat, but the most important benefit of this method is that you do not have to serve it at once. As you and your guests need another ear of corn (for who can stop at one?), the ones left in the pot will remain hot and will not have cooked any further than the ones that you first ate.

Roasted Corn on a Grill

This is something that we used to do as Boy Scouts and Girl Scouts, and generally we charred the corn to an unrecognizable mess, raw on one side, blackened and incinerated on the other. The trick to roasting corn properly is to peel back the husks, remove most of the tassle silk, then pull the husks back up over the ears and soak them in water for about 30 minutes or more.

Place the grill over the charcoal or wood, leaving only a small space between the corn and the fire. Turn them every few minutes to roast evenly on—all sides. The water that has seeped inside the husks will keep the ears of corn from charring and will steam them evenly as you turn them. Roast for about thirty to forty-five minutes, depending upon how close to the coals they are and how hot the fire is.

long history as a folk medicine, applied to the skin during the "dog days" of summer to ward off prickly heat. It has been appearing in more and more commercial baby powders in place of talc, which has been criticized for some adverse properties.

Puffed Corn. Round, airy, light puffs of corn and, so far as we know, processed only by El Molino and available in health food stores. Puffed corn can be used as a breakfast cereal with fruit and milk, or it can be made into sweet candy snacks.

Popcorn. It's now available in every supermarket in the country, with several companies competing with Orville Redenbacher—General Mills and American Popcorn Company among others. In addition, since popcorn has a particularly nutty flavor, a few small mail order companies have introduced popcorn flour, popcorn pancake mix and popcorn bread mix. They also have a crunchy texture, since they're all made from ground popcorn kernels.

And Lest We Forget. Corn oil, corn syrup and even a range of corn pastas are now available for those of us who have wheat allergies. In Mexico, a black mushroomlike fungus called *corn smut* or *cuitlacoche* is eaten as a delicacy, sautéed in garlic and oil and then used as a stuffing for tortillas, omelettes or crêpes, or as an addition to soups. And just as a final note, corn is the only grain that is eaten as a fresh vegetable.

Corn Breads: A Casual Catalogue

Their names vary. Even the spellings of their names vary. They may be cooked or baked or fried or deep fried. One part of the country (the South) looks with disdain at another part of the country (the North) that actually uses "that yellow stuff" (cornmeal). However, they are all related, for all corn breads are merely variations on a theme, and they all contain combinations of the following ingredients, no matter what their names:

- **Liquid.** Some use sweet milk, some sour milk, others use boiling water, and still others add buttermilk.
- **Shortening.** Take your choice: fat, butter, bacon fat, lard or oil.
- **Flavoring.** Occasionally a bit of sweetening—more in the North than in the South—and usually something salty.
- **Leavening.** Sometimes baking powder or baking soda, or even yeast on rare occasions, plus the addition of eggs.
- **Cornmeal.** Yellow or white or blue.

We will never succeed in clarifying the debate, but here is a general and very casual dictionary of corn breads. If, in your particular section of the country, you use still different names for these breads, let us know through Simon & Schuster and we'll add them in the next edition.

Batter Bread or Skillet Corn Bread. This bread generally contains baking powder and it is usually baked in a cast-iron skillet. It is somewhat firmer in texture than spoon bread (see page 91).

Corn Sticks. Corn bread that is baked in the shape of ears of corn using a special, heavy cast-iron molded pan.

Shingle Bread, Hoecake or Ashcake. This is a classic case of a different name for basically the same bread. It is a stiffer form of batter bread and it has a rich history

The

Versatile

Grain

and the

Elegant

Bean

84

in America. In parts of the South, it was baked in the field on a scoured and greased hoe blade, hence "hoecake." In other parts of the country, it was baked on a new house shingle, in front of an open fire, thus "shingle bread." When this very same batter was baked in the ashes of a fire in a heavy skillet, it became "ashcake."

Johnnycake, Journey Cake, Jonnycake or Shawnee Cake. It was supposedly originated by the Shawnee Indians to be taken on long journeys because of its excellent keeping quality. The Rhode Islanders, on the other hand, claim it as their own, with the people of Newport County claiming an "authentic" recipe made with milk and having a runny consistency, while the South County folks have an "authentic" recipe that uses boiling water with a thicker batter. Kenyon Corn Meal Company now ships the "authentic" johnnycake flour, and it has become available in specialty shops like Dean & DeLuca in New York (see Mail Order Sources, pages 501–506).

Corn Dodgers. Similar to the johnnycake batter, but a bit thicker, the cook shouts "Dodge" if they're tossed in your direction. The batter is shaped into tiny, pinched-off cakes, and then dropped into a heavy, heated cast-iron skillet with bacon fat glazing them while they cook. They're served very crisp and hot. If we take corn dodgers, add an onion, and fry them in the same pan where we've just cooked our fish, *voilà!* We have *hush puppies.*

Corn Pones. These are smaller versions of the corn dodgers, but slightly softer. The mark of the pone is the indentation made by the fingers of the cook who shapes them, sort of a personal imprint.

Hush Puppies. By now, almost everyone is aware of the fact that these classic corn breads got their name from their role as dog pacifiers in the Old South. Pieces of corn bread batter, legend tells us, were pinched off to fry quickly, and then thrown to the howling dogs to keep them quiet while the evening corn bread was baking. Obviously, some smart cook tasted one before throwing it out to the dogs and decided that an error in judgment had been made. Why waste it on the dogs! It's been a Southern specialty for us *people* ever since! Whenever we work in the South, we make certain that the first dinner for our film crew consists of hush puppies and tiny, crisp catfish.

Spoon Bread. An aptly named corn delight since it's eaten with a spoon. More like a pudding than a bread, it contains several eggs to give it a custardy texture.

Tortillas. The basic flat corn bread of Mexico with many variations and as many different names. At one time, we used to make our own tortillas, but it's no longer necessary since several excellent brands are now on the market, both fresh and frozen. We remember with great fondness our very first trip to Mexico in the fifties, hearing the constant "flap-flap" of tortilla dough made of *masa harina* as it was patted flat in the dextrous hands of the village women. In the larger cities, handmade tortillas were gradually replaced by a specially made tortilla press, which in turn has been replaced by *supermercado* brands, made commercially at central bakeries.

Corn

Grain & Granulation	Amount of Liquid	Cooking Method	Cooking & Standing Time	Approx. Yield	Comments
	Use non-stick saucepans for all forms.				
Cornmeal (1 C. dry) (see page 99 for Basic Polenta recipe)	4 C.	No-lump method: Use a 2-qt. saucepan. Boil 3 C. water with salt to taste and whisk 1 C. cold water into cornmeal. Gradually add to boiling water, stirring constantly with whisk. Lower heat and cook, uncovered, over very low heat. Stir frequently with a wooden spoon.	10 minutes.	3¾ C.	

Grain & Granulation	Amount of Liquid	Cooking Method	Cooking & Standing Time	Approx. Yield	Comments
Whole Hominy (*moté* or smaller grain *posole*) (1 C. dry)	6 C. plus additional boiling water as needed.	Soak 3 C. whole grain overnight. Drain. Use a 5-qt. saucepan. Combine grain and fresh un-salted water. Bring to a boil, lower heat and cover. Simmer.	2½ to 3 hours.	8 C.	Add salt 15 minutes before cooking time is completed. **Grain "blooms"** or bursts open when tender. Good "corny" flavor, although long cooking time is needed. Therefore, you may substitute 3 1-lb. cans whole hominy, drained and rinsed to yield about 6 C. Can also be frozen for several months.
Hominy Grits (**coarse granulation**) (1 C. dry) see NOTE below	5 C.	In a 3-qt. sauce-pan, bring salted water to a boil. Slowly add grits, stirring con-stantly with a wooden spoon. When mixture begins to boil again, lower heat and simmer, cov-ered, stirring oc-casionally.	25 to 30 minutes. Let stand 10 minutes.	3 C.	The taste and texture of quick-cooking grits is but the ghost of the real thing. Our personal pref-erence is the coarse granula-tion.

NOTE: The coarse granulation is our preferred grind and all recipes use it. For fine, medium, or instant grits follow package instructions.

Masa Harina and Shrimp Beignets

SERVES 4 TO 6

Crisply fried beignets are made with a paste of shrimp, fresh herbs and fragrant corn flour (masa harina), the same as used for tortillas. Try them as a side dish or an appetizer, or make them very small and spear them on toothpicks for hors d'oeuvres at a cocktail party.

3 C. water	2 Tbs. finely minced parsley
1 C. dry white wine	1 Tbs. fresh thyme leaves
1 bay leaf	⅛ tsp. Tabasco sauce
6 sprigs fresh thyme	Salt to taste
10 sprigs flat leaf parsley	1 C. masa harina (see page 85)
1 lb. medium-size shrimp in shells	1 tsp. baking powder
6 Tbs. softened butter	Corn oil for frying
Juice of 1 large lemon (3 Tbs.)	Lemon wedges
1 Tbs. finely minced chives	

To a 5-quart nonstick Dutch oven, add the water and the wine. Tie the bay leaf and the sprigs of thyme and parsley together with string and add them to the pot. Bring to a boil. Add the shrimp and bring to a boil again. Remove the pot from the heat and let the shrimp stand in the liquid for 5 minutes, then strain and reserve the liquid, discarding the herbs.

When the shrimp are cool enough to handle, peel and devein them. To the bowl of a food processor, add the shrimp, butter, lemon juice, chives, parsley, thyme, Tabasco and salt. Process until the mixture is pastelike in consistency. Scrape the shrimp paste into a bowl, cover and chill for about 40 minutes to blend the flavors. Meanwhile prepare the masa.

In a 2-quart nonstick saucepan, heat 1¼ cups of the reserved shrimp stock to the boiling point, whisk in the masa harina, lower the heat and simmer, whisking constantly, for 2 or 3 minutes or until thick. Transfer to a large mixing bowl, stir in the baking powder and combine with the shrimp paste, beating well with a wooden spoon until smooth. Using 2 tablespoons of the mixture form into oval cakes.

Then, in a heavy iron skillet, heat about ½ inch of the corn oil over high heat and fry the beignets in batches for 2 to 3 minutes on each side until crisp and golden. Drain the beignets on paper towels and keep them warm in a preheated low oven until all are fried. Serve with wedges of lemon to be squeezed over the beignets.

The

Versatile

Grain

and the

Elegant

Bean

88

Cornmeal and Sage Tart
with Chicken Liver Pâté

SERVES 6 TO 8

Warm chicken liver pâté and a crisp sage and onion–flavored cornmeal crust are compatibly married in this appetizer.

Chicken Liver Pâté

2 Tbs. olive oil or melted chicken fat
2 medium-size onions, thinly sliced
½ lb. chicken livers (about 3–4 livers)
1 hard-boiled egg
¼ tsp. freshly ground black pepper
Salt to taste

Heat the oil in a medium-size heavy iron skillet. Add the onions and sauté over medium heat, stirring occasionally, until they are very brown. Lift them out with a slotted spoon and reserve. Increase the heat and add the livers. Sauté quickly for 2 minutes, turn and sauté the other side until the livers lose their pink color. Spoon the onions on top, turn off the heat and let cool for 10 minutes in the skillet. When cool, add the egg to the bowl of a food processor and chop for only a few strokes, then add the liver and onions and process for a few more strokes to form a fairly coarse purée. Season with pepper and salt to taste and set aside.

Cornmeal Crust

Butter for greasing pan
¾ C. yellow stone-ground cornmeal (see page 81)
¼ C. all-purpose flour
1½ tsps. baking powder
½ tsp. salt or to taste
1 egg
½ C. milk
½ small onion, grated (2 Tbs.)
⅛ tsp. freshly ground black pepper
2 Tbs. finely minced sage, plus few extra leaves for garnish
4 Tbs. soft butter, cut into very small pieces

Preheat the oven to 400°F. and butter a 10-inch tart or quiche pan without a removable base. In a small bowl, whisk together the cornmeal, flour, baking powder and salt to blend well. In another, larger bowl, beat together the egg and milk then add the remaining ingredients except the extra sage leaves and beat well. Spoon into the prepared pan and bake for 15 to 18 minutes. Keep oven on at same temperature.

When the cornmeal crust is baked, spread the surface with a layer of the chicken pâté and return it to the oven for 5 minutes to warm. Remove from the oven and decorate the top with fresh sage leaves. Serve warm, cut into wedges.

Corn Bread Ring with Italian Sausage and Pimientos

SERVES 6

A fine-textured corn bread prepared with corn flour rather than the coarser cornmeal. It is baked in a ring mold with a colorful surprise in its interior—whole sausages and bright, red pimientos. The filling can be prepared well in advance and then combined with the batter and baked just 40 minutes before serving.

Sausage Filling

1 lb. Italian sweet sausage (about 6 sausages)

1 large clove garlic, finely minced (1½ tsps.)

½ medium onion, finely minced (2 Tbs.)

Salt and freshly ground pepper to taste

1 Tbs. finely minced flat leaf parsley

1 tsp. finely minced fresh sage (or ½ tsp. dried sage)

⅛ tsp. hot pepper flakes

4 whole pimientos (from a jar or can), rinsed, dried well on paper towels and cut in half

½ C. shredded mozzarella cheese

To a heavy iron skillet, add the sausages and prick them with the point of a knife. Cook slowly on all sides until lightly browned, turning frequently. Remove the sausages with tongs and set aside. Drain all but 1 tablespoon of the accumulated fat and in the same skillet add the garlic, onions, salt and pepper and sauté, stirring frequently until the onions are wilted. Let cool for a few minutes, then stir in the parsley, sage, and hot pepper flakes and set aside. Have the pimientos and mozzarella cheese ready on pieces of waxed paper and prepare the corn bread. (This part of the recipe may be prepared well in advance.)

Corn Bread Ring

Soft butter for greasing mold

2 C. yellow corn flour (see page 82)

1 C. all-purpose flour

2 Tbs. baking powder

1 tsp. salt or to taste

2 C. milk

1 egg, lightly beaten

4 Tbs. butter, melted

Preheat the oven to 425°F. and lavishly butter an ovenproof ring mold 9½ inches in diameter and 2½ inches deep. Prepare the corn bread by first sifting together the dry ingredients into a medium-size bowl. In another small bowl, combine the milk, egg and melted butter. Add the liquid to the dry ingredients, beating to combine well.

Spoon half the corn bread batter into the bottom of the mold. Spoon the onion/garlic mixture over, then arrange the pimientos in a circle on top. Sprinkle with the mozzarella cheese and follow with sausages. Spoon the remaining batter over all and bake for 20 to 25 minutes. Carefully run a sharp knife around the mold and let it stand for 10 to 15 minutes before inverting and unmolding onto a warmed serving platter.

The

Versatile

Grain

and the

Elegant

Bean

90

Double Corn Spoon Bread
with Okra and Tomatoes

SERVES 6

Although spoon bread originated in the colonial South, it is not quite a bread—nor is it a soufflé. Somewhat dense in texture, it is spooned onto a dish very much like a pudding. This West Indian–inspired version is hearty enough for a whole meal when accompanied by a crisp salad. Or serve it as a side dish with grilled chicken.

- 6 oz. okra, stemmed, tips cut off and discarded, then cut ½ inch thick (about 1 C.)
- 1 large plum tomato, diced (½ C.)
- 3 scallions, finely sliced (¾ C.)
- 1 C. corn kernels, either frozen and defrosted or cut from 2 ears fresh corn
- Butter for greasing baking dish
- 1½ C. lowfat milk
- 1 tsp. salt or to taste
- 1 tsp. sugar

- 1 C. stone-ground yellow cornmeal (see page 81)
- 3 Tbs. softened butter
- 1 C. buttermilk, at room temperature
- 3 eggs, separated
- 2 tsps. baking powder
- ½ tsp. baking soda
- 1 Tbs. finely minced fresh sage
- ½ large jalapeño pepper, finely minced (2 tsps.)
- Freshly ground black pepper (optional)

In a medium bowl, combine the okra, tomatoes, scallions and corn and set aside. Preheat the oven to 375°F. and butter a 2-quart baking dish. In a 3-quart nonstick saucepan, heat the milk, salt and sugar to the boiling point. Slowly add the cornmeal and stir with a wooden spoon over medium high heat until the mixture is smooth and thick and leaves the sides of the pan. Transfer to the bowl of a food processor and add the butter. Process a few strokes until incorporated, then add the buttermilk and mix well. Add the egg yolks and process a few strokes, then add the baking powder, baking soda, sage and jalapeño pepper and continue to process until well mixed.

Transfer the mixture to a large bowl and stir in the vegetables. In another deep bowl, beat the egg whites with a beater until stiff. Fold one third of the beaten egg white into the cornmeal mixture, then fold in the remaining beaten egg white. Scrape the mixture into the prepared dish and bake for 35 to 40 minutes or until the top is golden and puffy. Serve at once. Pass the pepper mill for freshly ground pepper at the table if you wish.

Savory Blue Corn Cakes with
Sweet Yellow Corn and Chives

MAKES 1½ DOZEN CAKES

The dark indigo blue corn was originally cultivated by the Native Americans of the Zuñi, Hopi and Navajo tribes in the Southwest. It was central to their culture and to their diet. The grayish-blue flour lends its unique flavor to breads that are used to this day in ceremonies and dance rituals, and we have adapted it here for small, piquant, crisp cakes—a perfect partner with chicken.

¾ C. blue cornmeal (see NOTE)
⅓ C. all-purpose flour
½ tsp. salt or to taste
¼ tsp. freshly ground black pepper
½ tsp. sugar
1 tsp. baking powder
¼ C. finely minced chives

⅔ C. fresh or frozen, defrosted corn kernels
2 eggs, separated
2 Tbs. melted butter, slightly cooled
¼ tsp. Tabasco sauce
½ C. milk
Canola or corn oil for cooking

In a mixing bowl, combine the cornmeal, flour, salt, pepper, sugar, baking powder, chives and corn. In another small bowl, beat the egg yolks with the melted butter, Tabasco and milk, using a wire whisk. Beat until well combined, then beat into the dry mixture. In a deep bowl, beat the egg whites with a dash of salt, using a beater. Beat until stiff, then fold into the batter.

Lightly coat the bottom of a nonstick skillet with the oil and when the skillet is hot, add about 1 tablespoon batter for each corn cake. Cook on one side for about 2 minutes over medium high heat, then turn and cook on the other side until brown. Make several batches until the batter is all used up, keeping the corn cakes warm in the oven while the others are being made. Serve hot.

NOTE: Yellow or white cornmeal can be substituted, but the blue corn has a more intense corn flavor.

The

Versatile

Grain

and the

Elegant

Bean

92

Iron Skillet Buttermilk Corn Bread

SERVES 8

Light and moist, this is one of the easiest and most satisfying quick breads you can make. Try it with a hearty soup or stew, or warm with jam for breakfast. You can also crumble it to make a stuffing for your Thanksgiving turkey.

2 Tbs. butter	1½ tsps. baking soda
2 Tbs. corn oil	1 tsp. salt
1½ C. yellow stone-ground cornmeal (see page 81)	1½ C. buttermilk, at room temperature
1 C. all-purpose flour	1 egg

Preheat the oven to 425°F. Add the butter and oil to a 9-inch cast-iron skillet. When the butter has melted, remove the skillet and take off 4 tablespoons of the butter/oil mixture. Set aside in a small cup.

In a large bowl, combine the cornmeal, flour, baking soda and salt. To a smaller bowl, add the buttermilk and whisk in the egg. Stir in 2 tablespoons of the melted butter/oil mixture, then combine the liquid with the dry ingredients, beating briefly. Spread the mixture in the skillet and bake for 20 to 25 minutes or until a cake tester comes out clean. Pour the remaining butter/oil over the surface. Serve hot or warm.

Corn Flour and Chive Madeleines

MAKES 1 DOZEN MADELEINES

An elegant nibble with a soup or a salad or as an hors d'oeuvre, these airy delicate little morsels are baked in a madeleine mold.

1 Tbs. soft butter for greasing mold	¼ C. all-purpose flour
2 eggs, at room temperature	⅛ tsp. cayenne
¼ tsp. salt	1 tsp. baking powder
1 tsp. sugar	3 Tbs. butter, melted and cooled
¼ C. corn flour (see page 82)	2 Tbs. finely minced chives

Preheat the oven to 375°F. Lavishly butter the cups of a madeleine mold. In a small deep mixing bowl, beat the eggs and salt with an electric hand beater for 5 minutes until very thick. Add the sugar and beat for 1 minute more. Sift both flours with the cayenne and baking powder and gently fold into the egg mixture. Now fold in the melted butter and chives. *(continued on page 94)*

The

Versatile

Grain

93

Spoon a scant tablespoon of the batter into each cup and run a toothpick through the batter to distribute it evenly and to break up any air bubbles. Bake for 8 to 10 minutes, or until the madeleines become golden at the edges. Loosen them with the point of a knife and lift out immediately. Cool slightly on a wire rack and serve while still warm—or rewarm them before serving.

Yellow Corn Pancakes with Blueberries

SERVES 4

These Sunday-morning specials disappear like the proverbial "hot cakes." Select small blueberries so that there are more in each of these light, little, purple polka-dotted pancakes.

1 C. yellow stone-ground cornmeal (see page 81)	½ tsp. baking soda
1 Tbs. all-purpose flour	1 C. blueberries
½ tsp. salt or to taste	1 egg, at room temperature
1 Tbs. sugar	1 C. buttermilk, at room temperature
1 tsp. baking powder	Half butter, half corn oil for frying

To a large bowl, add the dry ingredients, and whisk together to combine. Gently stir in the blueberries and set aside.

In another small bowl, whisk the egg and buttermilk together and combine with the dry ingredients. If the mixture seems too thick, add 1 or 2 more tablespoons of buttermilk. In a nonstick skillet, heat the butter and oil together until hot, then drop the batter by the tablespoonfuls onto the skillet and cook over medium high heat until the edges start to brown. Turn and brown the other side. Keep warm in a low oven until all are made. Serve hot with maple syrup if you wish.

The

Versatile

Grain

and the

Elegant

Bean

94

Parched Corn Green Peppercorn Pones

MAKES 6 PONES

The early settlers adopted the technique of parching—or toasting—corn before grinding it, in order to soften the starches and make them more digestible. The use of parched corn also makes these untraditionally spiced pones crunchy and delectable—with a creamy, soft interior. We think you'll agree that it's well worth the effort to toast and grind the corn.

1 C. parched ground corn (see NOTE) or stone-ground white cornmeal (see page 81)	½ small onion, grated (2 Tbs.)
	1 Tbs. finely minced parsley
	2 Tbs. all-purpose flour
½ C. boiling water	⅓ C. sour cream
¼ tsp. baking soda	3 Tbs. melted butter
¾ tsp. salt or to taste	
1 tsp. drained, rinsed water-packed green peppercorns	

Place the ground corn in a small bowl and pour boiling water over it. Stir to combine. The mixture will be crumbly. Let stand for 20 minutes.

Meanwhile, preheat the oven to 450°F. and place a 10-inch iron skillet in it to heat. Add the baking soda, salt, peppercorns, grated onions, parsley and flour and combine with the ground corn. Then stir in the sour cream and 1 tablespoon of the melted butter. Remove the skillet from the oven and melt the remaining butter in the hot pan to coat the bottom. Using about 2 tablespoons of batter for each one, form six ovals using your hands and squeezing tightly to leave the imprint of your fingers (the mark of a true corn pone.)

Place the pones in the pan and spoon some melted butter over the surface of each. Return the pan to the oven and bake the pones for 20 to 25 minutes. Serve hot.

NOTE: TO PARCH AND GRIND CORN. Using a heavy 10-inch iron skillet, add 1 cup dried white corn and stir over medium heat until it is slightly golden and fragrant. Grind the corn in an electric blender and remove to a bowl. Then return to the blender and grind it again to make sure the texture is even. It should be more grainy than regular commercial stone-ground meal.

New England Johnnycakes

SERVES 4

No one, so far, has ever settled "the great johnnycake controversy." Is it johnnycake or jonnycake or journey cake or Shawnee cake, since the Shawnee Indians also carried them on long journeys? Even the mail order sources we've listed at the back of the book spell their products differently. Did these tempting morsels, indeed, originate on Rhode Island near Newport or in South Carolina, as some claim? And can they be the "real thing" if white flint corn is used, a relative of the original strain of Indian maize that is now obsolete? In the interest of scientific research, of course, we once attended the October Johnnycake Festival in Rhode Island in order to sample them, but the controversy still remains unanswered.

1 C. stone-ground white cornmeal (see page 81), preferably Kenyon's (see Mail Order Sources, pages 501–506)	¾ C. boiling water (or more if needed)
½ tsp. salt or to taste	1 Tbs. soft butter, cut into small pieces
1 tsp. sugar	2 Tbs. cold milk
	Corn oil for frying

Place the cornmeal, salt and sugar in a bowl and whisk to blend. Gradually add the boiling water, stirring with a wooden spoon. Beat in the butter until melted, then add the cold milk. The batter should be very thick.

Heat a thin film of corn oil in a heavy iron skillet until hot but not smoking and drop the batter onto the skillet by tablespoonsful. Lower the heat to medium and bake slowly, about 5 minutes on each side, until crisp and golden on the outside and soft on the inside.

Serve hot, keeping the johnnycakes warm in a preheated low oven until all are made. Try with maple syrup, pork sausages, or as some Rhode Islanders do, with applesauce or creamed codfish or creamed chipped beef.

The

Versatile

Grain

and the

Elegant

Bean

96

Mini Cornmeal and Pumpkin Crêpes
with Cognac and Buttered Pecans

MAKES 3 DOZEN CRÊPES

Tiny sun-colored crêpes with a pumpkin flavor and fragrant toasted pecans are combined to make an autumn dessert or treat for a Sunday brunch.

1 C. yellow stone-ground cornmeal (see page 81)
1 C. all-purpose flour
1 C. sifted confectioners' sugar, plus extra for dusting
1½ tsps. pumpkin pie spice
2 eggs, lightly beaten

1 C. pumpkin purée (use solid-pack canned pumpkin—*not* pumpkin pie filling)
2 Tbs. cognac
3 C. milk
2 Tbs. butter
1 C. coarsely broken pecans

To a large bowl, add the cornmeal, flour, 1 cup sifted confectioners' sugar and pumpkin pie spice and combine with a whisk. In a smaller bowl, whisk together the eggs, pumpkin purée and cognac, then beat them into the dry ingredients. Slowly add the milk, a cup at a time, beating well after each addition to make a smooth batter.

In a small skillet, heat the butter and toast the pecans over medium heat, stirring frequently. Lift them out with a slotted spoon to a bowl and set aside. Heat a nonstick skillet over medium heat. Add 1 tablespoon of batter for each crêpe to the skillet and cook on one side until the surface edges look dry, then turn over and cook on the other side. Cook in several batches and keep the crêpes warm in a preheated low oven until all are made.

To serve, place a few crêpes on a warm plate. Dust the surfaces heavily with sifted confectioners' sugar and scatter the reserved toasted pecans over all.

Gialetti: Venetian Lemon Cornmeal Cookies

MAKES 4 DOZEN 2-INCH COOKIES

In Italian dialect they are called *zaletti* and almost every Venetian household has a recipe for them with some variations. The standards are always yellow cornmeal, from which they take their name, and either currants or raisins.

¾ C. currants or dark raisins
3 Tbs. dark rum
2 Tbs. all-purpose flour, plus 1½ C.
1 C. fine yellow stone-ground
   cornmeal (see page 81)
½ tsp. salt
2 tsps. baking powder

¼ lb. unsalted butter, softened
¾ C. sugar
½ tsp. vanilla extract
1 Tbs. finely minced lemon peel
1 whole egg, plus 1 egg yolk
Butter for greasing baking sheets

Soak the currants in the rum for 30 minutes, stirring a few times to mix. Over a small bowl, drain the currants in a strainer. Most of the rum will have been absorbed, but if any remains, add it to the batter later on. Spread the two tablespoons of flour on a piece of waxed paper, then toss the drained currants in the floured waxed paper and set aside.

In a medium bowl, combine the cornmeal, 1½ cups flour, salt and baking powder, then sift and set aside. In the bowl of a food processor, cream the butter and sugar until light and fluffy. Then add the vanilla and lemon peel and process until combined. Add the egg and egg yolk and combine well. Then add all the dry ingredients and process until well mixed. Add the currants and any remaining rum and process until well combined. The dough will be thick and sticky. Scrape it out into a bowl, cover, and chill for 30 minutes.

Preheat the oven to 375°F. and butter two or three baking sheets. Working with half the dough at a time and keeping the rest chilled, turn it out onto a lightly floured surface and knead four or five times, incorporating a bit of the flour from the surface. Then, with a floured rolling pin, roll out ¼ inch thick and cut with a 2-inch triangle cookie cutter (stars, ovals or round ones can also be used, of course). Place the cookies on the prepared baking sheets about 1 inch apart, since they spread slightly and puff up. Bake for 8 to 10 minutes or until the bottoms of the cookies are golden brown. Cool on the baking sheets for a few minutes before transferring the cookies carefully with a spatula to a wire rack for further cooling. Repeat, rerolling the scraps as well, until all the dough is used up. Stored in an airtight container, they will keep for 1 week.

The

Versatile

Grain

and the

Elegant

Bean

98

Basic Polenta

MAKES ABOUT 12 PIECES

Bergamo in Lombardy and the eastern Veneto of Italy are the regions that are home to polenta. Some of the natives prefer very coarsely milled cornmeal, while Verona uses a bit finer milling and Padua, Venice and Vicenza prefer an even more finely ground cornmeal. An unlined round bottom copper pan called a *pailo* is used for cooking polenta in Italy, and a special wooden board called a *panora* presents the uncut polenta for serving in slices, generally done with a string. In the Valtellina in Lombardy, buckwheat flour or *grano saraceno* is added to the cornmeal, called Polenta Integra.

6½ C. Chicken Stock, preferably homemade (see page 171), or water

1 tsp. salt or to taste (if water is used, adjust salt accordingly)

2 C. polenta cornmeal (see BOX)
Butter, canola oil or olive oil for greasing pan

In a 3-quart nonstick saucepan, bring the stock to a boil over medium high heat. Then pour into a bowl, add salt to taste and, using a whisk, slowly whisk in the polenta. Return the mixture to the saucepan and stir frequently with a wooden spoon over low heat for 20 to 30 minutes. The polenta should peel completely away from the sides of the pot, and it should be thick and creamy, so thick that a wooden spoon placed in the center stands upright for 15 seconds or more.

Lightly grease the bottom of a 7 × 11 × 2-inch pan and turn the polenta out into the pan. Dip a rubber spatula in warm water and smooth the surface. Cover it with plastic wrap and refrigerate it for at least 2 hours, and preferably overnight. When ready to use the polenta in any of the following recipes, cut it into twelve equal pieces approximately 2½ × 2¾ inches. You may also cut diamonds or circles if you wish.

Molino e Frantoio di G. F. Nicoli exports a brand of coarse polenta from Bergamo with an unusually robust flavor, which comes from the drying process. The corn kernels are left on the cob and dried in the sun before being ground into meal. Most other corn is chemically dried in factories before grinding. This same company also exports Polenta Integra, a corn-buckwheat mix. They are both available in gourmet shops around the country or can be ordered by mail from Dean & DeLuca (see Mail Order Sources, pages 501–506).

The most acceptable domestic brand of cornmeal that most closely approximates this Italian export for taste and texture is the Goya brand *coarse-ground* cornmeal, found in most supermarkets.

Polenta Crostini with Prosciutto di Parma
and Fresh Basil

SERVES 6

A rustic appetizer or side dish that everyone seems to love. The polenta, made the day before, is quickly broiled for only 5 minutes on each side.

- 1 recipe Basic Polenta (see page 99), prepared the day before
- 4 Tbs. melted butter
- 4 Tbs. grated Parmesan cheese

- 2 Tbs. finely diced prosciutto di Parma, about 2 oz. (see NOTE)
- 2 Tbs. coarsely chopped basil
- Freshly ground black pepper to taste (optional)

Cut the polenta into 3-inch squares, allowing two per person. Blot dry on paper towels and preheat the broiler. Dip the polenta squares into the melted butter, turning to coat both sides. Place in a flat oven-to-table baking dish, large enough to accommodate the polenta in one layer. Sprinkle with the Parmesan cheese and slip under the broiler for 4 to 5 minutes or until crusty and golden. Sprinkle the tops with prosciutto, basil and pepper. Serve hot.

NOTE: Prosciutto di Parma is more delicate and somewhat less salty than regular prosciutto. However, the regular variety can be used as a substitute.

The

Versatile

Grain

and the

Elegant

Bean

100

Polenta Crostini with Three Cheeses

SERVES 9

Rich, with cheese and cream, this crusty, grilled, rough cornmeal mixture is perfect with any kind of poultry, fish or meat. It is prepared well in advance and then grilled just before serving.

4 Tbs. butter	½ tsp. freshly grated nutmeg
2 medium shallots, finely minced (about 2 Tbs.)	½ C. heavy cream
	½ C. shredded Fontina cheese (about 3 ozs.)
6 C. water	
1 tsp. salt or to taste	½ C. crumbled Gorgonzola cheese
2 C. polenta (see BOX, page 99)	½ C. grated Parmesan cheese
½ tsp. freshly ground black pepper	Butter for greasing baking pan

In a small skillet, melt 2 tablespoons of the butter and sauté the shallots, stirring frequently for about 3 to 5 minutes over medium heat, until they are soft. Set aside.

In a 3-quart nonstick saucepan, boil the water, add the salt and slowly whisk in the polenta so it doesn't lump. Lower the heat to very low. Switch to a wooden spoon and, stirring frequently, cook the polenta for 15 minutes, or until it pulls away from the sides of the pot. Stir in the shallot mixture after about 5 minutes of cooking.

Preheat the oven to 350°F. Remove the polenta from the heat and beat in the black pepper, nutmeg, cream and all the cheeses. Butter a 2½-quart rectangular baking pan and turn the polenta out into it, smoothing the surface with a wooden spoon.

Bake the polenta for 20 minutes. Up to this point, the polenta can be prepared as much as a day in advance. Just refrigerate it, then bring it to room temperature before continuing with the recipe.

When ready to serve, preheat the broiler. Cut the polenta into 2 × 4-inch rectangles, using a knife dipped in water before cutting. Melt the remaining 2 tablespoons of butter. Brush 1 tablespoon on the bottom of an oven-to-table casserole large enough to accommodate the polenta in one layer. Place the polenta in the casserole and brush the other tablespoon of melted butter on the tops. Slip under the broiler about 5 to 6 inches below the source of the heat. When the tops are golden, turn the slices carefully to the other side and brown. Serve at once.

Polenta with Ground Veal, Sage and Green Peas

SERVES 6

Squares of golden, crisply crusted polenta are slipped under the broiler, sprinkled with a touch of Parmesan cheese and butter and surrounded by a robust sauce of veal and sage, which is brightened with sprightly tiny green sweet peas. A totally irresistible combination.

3 ozs. prosciutto, cut into fine dice	Salt and freshly ground black pepper to taste
1 medium red onion	
1 medium carrot	1 recipe Basic Polenta (see page 99), prepared the day before
2 Tbs. coarsely chopped parsley	
2 tsps. olive oil	3 Tbs. butter, melted
1 lb. ground lean veal	2 Tbs. grated Parmesan cheese
10 fresh sage leaves, coarsely chopped	10-oz. package frozen tiny green peas, defrosted
1 C. dry white wine	
3 C. Chicken Stock, preferably homemade (see page 171)	

Put the prosciutto in a medium-size bowl. Process the onion and carrot in the bowl of a food processor and add to the prosciutto along with 1 tablespoon of the parsley. Stir to combine and set aside.

In a large sauté pan, heat the oil and add the veal, stirring until the veal begins to brown. Then add the prosciutto, onion, parsley, carrot mixture and sauté over medium heat for 1 minute, stirring constantly. Turn the heat up to high, stir in the sage and the wine and cook over high heat until the liquid evaporates, about 15 minutes. Stir in the chicken stock and reduce the heat. Simmer, uncovered, for about 45 minutes. Add salt and pepper to taste.

Meanwhile, prepare the polenta. Preheat the broiler. Dip the pieces into the melted butter, turning to coat both sides. Place them in a flat oven-to-table gratin dish. Sprinkle with half the cheese and place in the broiler. Broil for 5 minutes, turn the pieces over, then tilt the pan and baste the tops with the butter from the gratin dish. Sprinkle the remaining cheese on top, return to the oven and broil for 5 minutes more until the surface is brown. Just before serving, stir the peas and the remaining tablespoon of parsley into the veal mixture and heat until hot.

Place two squares of polenta on each plate and spoon the veal sauce around them to serve.

The

Versatile

Grain

and the

Elegant

Bean

102

Mamaliga: Romanian Polenta with Goat's Milk Cheese (Brynza) and Garlic Butter

SERVES 6 TO 8

There is an old saying about *mamaliga,* the rustic Romanian version of the Italian polenta. It's called "The *Mamaliga* Nevers":

- Never cook it in a shiny pot (use a black iron cauldron).
- Never serve it in a dish (it is always served on wood).
- Never cut it with a knife (only with a string).

Probably, in the old peasant kitchens there was *only* a black iron pot, no dishes, and no knife, which is why this saying made its way from generation to generation.

1 recipe Basic Polenta (see page 99)	½ lb. crumbled goat's milk cheese such as Brynza or feta (see NOTE)
6 Tbs. butter	1 Tbs. finely minced parsley
1 large clove garlic, finely minced (1½ tsps.)	Freshly ground black pepper
	1 C. sour cream or plain yogurt

Prepare the polenta according to the basic recipe. However, when it is very thick, rather than putting it into a flat dish, invert the pot at once and let the cornmeal mass fall out onto a large round platter. Keep it warm in a preheated low oven.

In a small saucepan melt the butter with the garlic, but do not allow the garlic to brown. When ready to serve, use a piece of fish line or strong fine string and cut the polenta in half horizontally. Carefully remove the top half with a wide spatula and pour half the garlic butter and half the cheese on the bottom half. Replace the top half and pour the remaining garlic butter and cheese on top. Sprinkle the top with parsley and black pepper and pass the sour cream or yogurt separately at the table to spoon on top of each portion.

NOTE: There is no consistency with either Brynza or feta cheese. At times they are made with goat's milk and sometimes with a combination of cow's and sheep's milk.

Polenta with "Little Birds," Bergamo-Style

SERVES 2 AS A MAIN COURSE
SERVES 4 AS A FIRST COURSE

In Bergamo, polenta used to be served with tiny songbirds that had been trapped in the nets that were tied between trees, a practice that gratefully ended some years ago. They have been replaced by farm-raised quail. These are butterflied and sautéed under weights, a method that only takes 5 to 6 minutes of cooking.

½ recipe Basic Polenta (see page 99), prepared the day before
2 tsps. butter, cut into small pieces
4 quail, weighing 4–5 ozs. each
Freshly ground black pepper to taste
Coarse salt to taste

3 cloves garlic, slivered
4 small sprigs rosemary, plus 4 for garnish
¼ tsp. Tabasco sauce
2 Tbs. olive oil
4 small wedges lemon

Place four pieces of polenta in one layer in a large oven-to-table shallow baking dish. Dot with butter and set aside. Keep in the refrigerator until needed.

Split the quail up the spine with kitchen shears and press flat. Place in another shallow ovenproof dish in one layer. Sprinkle them with fresh pepper and salt. Loosen the breast skin from each quail with your fingers and slip a few slivers of garlic and a sprig of rosemary under the skin. Then coat them evenly with Tabasco and olive oil. Cover with plastic wrap and refrigerate until ready to cook; anywhere from 20 minutes to overnight is fine.

When ready to cook, preheat the broiler and run the polenta under the broiler for 5 minutes or until dappled with brown. Turn the polenta over with a spatula and broil the other side, then turn off the oven and place the pan in the oven to keep warm while cooking the quail.

Heat a large iron skillet, and when hot, place the quail skin side down in one layer. Set another skillet or round baking pan that fits inside the larger skillet over the quail and weight it down with a teakettle filled with water. Sauté over medium high heat for 3 minutes. Remove the teakettle and the pan, turn the quail over with a spatula and replace the weights as before, sautéing for 2 to 3 minutes more. Place one quail on each piece of polenta. Garnish with a sprig of rosemary and a wedge of lemon.

The

Versatile

Grain

and the

Elegant

Bean

104

Polenta with Gorgonzola and
Roasted Red Peppers

SERVES 6 TO 8

Colorful, easy and delicious, the polenta is made the day before. The sauce is simple and very flavorful. Serve it as a main luncheon dish or a side dish for dinner with veal scallops sautéed with capers, parsley and lemon.

Butter for greasing baking dish
1 recipe Basic Polenta (see page 99), prepared the day before and cut into 24 rectangles about 1½ × 3 inches
6 ozs. Gorgonzola cheese, crumbled
½ C. milk
3 Tbs. butter

½ C. heavy cream
Salt and freshly ground black pepper to taste
⅓ C. grated Parmesan cheese
2 medium red peppers, roasted, peeled and seeded, cut into ¼-inch dice (about ¾ C.)
2 Tbs. finely minced parsley

Butter a 3-quart rectangular oven-to-table baking dish and place the slices of polenta in one layer in it. Set aside and preheat the oven to 375°F. To a 3-quart nonstick saucepan, add the Gorgonzola, milk and butter and cook, stirring frequently, over low heat until the cheese has melted and the mixture is smooth. Stir in the cream and continue to simmer for about 1 minute. Add salt and pepper to taste. Spoon the sauce over the polenta and sprinkle with the Parmesan cheese. Bake in the preheated oven for 10 to 15 minutes or until the sauce is bubbly around the edges. Turn up the heat and slip the dish under the broiler for a few minutes to brown the polenta slightly.

Scatter the diced red peppers and the parsley over the surface and serve at once.

Whole Hominy with Spanish Chorizo
and Two Cheeses

SERVES 8

Aglazed pottery cassuela is beautifully suited for serving this peppery rustic Mexican one-dish dinner. It also lends itself to advance preparation and to easy, unhurried entertaining.

Oil or butter for greasing casserole
1 lb. chorizo sausage, sliced ¼ in. thick
3 large cloves garlic
2 large onions (about ¾ lb.)
2 Tbs. olive oil
1 large green pepper, diced (1½ C.)
1 large sweet red pepper, diced (1½ C.)
½ tsp. dried oregano
½ tsp. ground cumin
2 Tbs. coarsely chopped cilantro, plus 1 tablespoon for garnish (about ¼ C. cilantro leaves)

Salt and freshly ground black pepper to taste
6 C. whole white hominy, cooked (see Chart, page 87) or 3 1-lb. cans, drained and rinsed with cold water
⅔ C. light cream or half and half
2 C. shredded sharp Cheddar cheese (about 6 ozs.)
½ lb. Monterey Jack cheese with jalapeño peppers, cut into ½-in. cubes

Oil a 12-inch-wide by 3-inch-deep glazed pottery or other ovenproof casserole and set aside. Sauté the slices of chorizo in a large skillet until they are slightly brown all over. You may need to do this in two batches. Lift out the chorizo when browned and drain on paper towels. Discard the rendered fat from the skillet and wipe with paper towels.

In the bowl of a food processor, finely mince the garlic, then add the onions and pulse for five to six strokes. Heat the olive oil in the skillet over medium heat and sauté the garlic and onions for 5 minutes, stirring occasionally. Then add both green and red peppers and continue to sauté for an additional 5 minutes. Remove the skillet from the heat and add the oregano, cumin, 2 tablespoons cilantro, salt and pepper, along with the reserved chorizo and drained hominy. Stir gently to combine, then add the cream, 1 cup of the Cheddar cheese, reserving the other cup for the top of the casserole, and the cubes of jalapeño Monterey Jack cheese. Stir again to mix well.

At this point, you may transfer the entire mixture to a bowl, cover it with aluminum foil and refrigerate until you wish to bake the casserole. Or preheat the oven to 400°F. and transfer the mixture to the oiled casserole, cover with foil and bake for 20 minutes. Then remove the casserole from the oven, remove and discard the foil and sprinkle the top of the dish with the remaining Cheddar cheese. Return to the oven for 10 more minutes or until the cheese is melted. Scatter the remaining tablespoon of cilantro on the surface before serving. Serve hot from the baking dish.

The

Versatile

Grain

and the

Elegant

Bean

106

Whole Hominy with Fennel Sausage
and Apple Patties

SERVES 6

Tart, sweet apples are enveloped by thin ground pork patties spiced with fennel seed, then layered on top of whole, large kernels of hominy and baked in a creamy Cheddar cheese sauce.

Butter or oil for greasing casserole
2 Tbs. corn oil
1 medium clove garlic, finely minced (1 tsp.)
1 large onion, finely chopped (1 C.)
3½ C. cooked whole hominy (see NOTE and Chart, page 87)
½ C. light cream or half and half
1 C. sharp Cheddar cheese, shredded (about 3 ozs.)

1 lb. Italian fennel sausage, removed from casings
1 egg, lightly beaten
2 Tbs. milk
1 C. soft, whole grain bread crumbs
2 medium-size tart green apples such as Granny Smith
Juice of ½ lemon (2 tsps.)
2 Tbs. finely minced cilantro

Grease a large shallow oven-to-table casserole and set it aside. Heat 2 tablespoons oil in a large skillet and sauté the garlic and onion for 2 to 3 minutes, stirring frequently until wilted. Stir in the hominy and cream and transfer to the prepared casserole. Set aside 2 tablespoons of the shredded Cheddar cheese and sprinkle the remaining cheese over the hominy. Set the casserole aside. Preheat the oven to 400°F.

In a medium-size bowl, combine the sausage meat with the egg, milk and bread crumbs. Wet your hands and form the mixture into twelve balls. Flatten each one between two pieces of waxed paper, making thin patties about 3½ inches in diameter. Set aside.

Peel and core the apples, remove a thin slice from the top and bottom of each apple and discard (or nibble it yourself). Then cut each apple into four slices, cutting across the apple so that each slice has a core hole in the middle. Only six slices of the eight will be used, so again you can nibble the extras. Lay the six apple slices on waxed paper and sprinkle the lemon juice over them. Place each slice of apple between two pork patties, and with wet hands enclose the apple slice completely.

Using a nonstick skillet, quickly brown the six stuffed patties on each side, then lay them over the hominy-cheese mixture. Sprinkle each patty with 1 teaspoon of the reserved cheese. Cover the casserole with aluminum foil and bake in the oven for 25 to 30 minutes, until the cheese is bubbly around the edges. Remove the foil and garnish with cilantro before serving.

NOTE: Canned, drained and rinsed whole hominy (*moté pelado*), either yellow or white, can be used. Two 1-pound cans equal 3½ cups.

Posole: A Stew of Pork, Chicken and Whole Hominy

SERVES 14 TO 16

A traditional Mexican and New Mexican feast-day favorite, served in the Southwest for Christmas Eve—or for any other occasion when there is a large gathering of hungry people.

2½-lb. center-cut rib of pork with bone in	¼ tsp. freshly ground black pepper
2½-lb. whole chicken	¼ tsp. paprika
14 C. water	4 fresh mild chiles such as poblano or pasilla, plus 2 fresh hot jalapeños
1 large onion	2 large tomatoes, coarsely diced (2 C.)
1 bay leaf	
10 whole black peppercorns	14 ozs. dried large whole hominy corn or small whole hominy, soaked overnight and cooked (see Chart, page 87) or
3 Tbs. corn oil	
4 medium onions, coarsely chopped (2 C.)	
3–4 large cloves garlic, finely minced (2 Tbs.)	4 1-lb. cans whole hominy, drained and rinsed in cold water (about 8 C. total)
2 tsps. dried oregano, Greek or Mexican	Salt to taste
1 tsp. dried thyme	¼ C. coarsely chopped cilantro
3 Tbs. flour	

Suggested Garnishes: minced jalapeño chiles, diced tomatoes, radishes, cilantro, minced red onion, tortilla chips or shredded lettuce. You may use one or several if you choose.

Trim the bones from the pork rib, wash and put them into a 7-quart heavy Dutch oven. Cube the meat into 1-inch pieces and refrigerate until needed. Add the whole chicken to the pot, along with the water and the onion. Tie the bay leaf and peppercorns together in a cheesecloth bag and add to the pot. Bring the water to a boil, then lower the heat and simmer for 1 hour.

Meanwhile, in a large skillet, heat 2 tablespoons of the oil and sauté the onions and garlic over medium heat for about 8 to 10 minutes, stirring frequently, until the onions begin to brown. Sprinkle the oregano and thyme over the onions, stir and set aside in a bowl. In the same skillet, heat the remaining tablespoon of oil. Mix the pork cubes with the flour, pepper and paprika and add them to the same skillet. Stir and cook for 10 to 15 minutes over medium high heat until the meat is browned on all sides. Stir in the reserved onion mixture and 2 ladles of the simmering stock. Mix well and turn off the heat while you prepare the chiles.

To prepare fresh chiles, put a wire cake rack over an open flame or under a broiler and char the skins of the chiles, turning them with tongs. Wrap in foil and

The

Versatile

Grain

and the

Elegant

Bean

108

set aside to steam for 5 minutes. Protect your hands with rubber gloves, then scrape off the charred skin, split the chiles open and scrape out the seeds, discarding them along with the stems. Chop what remains in the bowl of a food processor, then stir into the onion/pork mixture. Remove and discard the onion and spice bag from the Dutch oven, lift out the chicken, and when cool enough to handle, discard the skin and bones. Tear the meat into large pieces and set them aside.

Stir the pork, chiles and onion mixture into the stew and simmer for 1 hour more. Then lift out the pork bones, and when they're cool enough to handle, pick off and return to the pot any lean meat scraps from the bones. Discard the bones, add the tomatoes, the hominy, the reserved chicken and salt. Simmer for 30 minutes more with the lid ajar. Stir in the cilantro, then cool and refrigerate overnight to mellow the flavors.

Skim off and discard any surface fat that may have hardened overnight. Reheat, then taste to adjust the seasoning before serving directly from the pot, ladling each portion into large bowls. More oregano, salt or cilantro may be needed. You may pass bowls of crisp tortilla chips and/or any of the additional garnishes you may have selected.

Green Grits and Tomatoes

SERVES 8

A scrumptuous accompaniment for any chicken or pork dish. It may be prepared partially in advance and baked just before serving.

2 C. milk	Salt and freshly ground black pepper to
2 C. water	taste
½ tsp. salt or to taste	Butter for greasing gratin dish
1 C. coarse hominy grits	2 eggs, lightly beaten
4 Tbs. butter	1 C. light cream
⅛ tsp. freshly grated nutmeg	1 C. shredded Gruyère cheese (3 ozs.)
2 zucchini, shredded (about ½ lb.)	4 Tbs. grated Parmesan cheese
½ C. finely minced parsley (about 1½	2–3 small plum tomatoes, very thinly
C. loosely packed leaves)	sliced
3–4 large cloves garlic, finely minced	
(1 Tbs.)	

In a 3-quart nonstick saucepan, bring the milk, water and salt to a boil. Slowly whisk in the hominy grits to prevent lumps. Bring to a boil, then lower the heat, cover and simmer, stirring occasionally with a wooden spoon for about 25 to 30 minutes, until it is thick and the water is absorbed. Beat in the butter and nutmeg, zucchini, parsley, garlic and salt and pepper. Stir and cook for 2 more minutes. You can prepare this recipe up to this point and continue with it 1 hour before serving. Just put the grits mixture in a bowl, cover tightly and refrigerate until needed. It will congeal somewhat, but whisking the mixture will break it up again.

Preheat the oven to 325°F. and butter a 3-quart oven-to-table gratin dish. Whisk in the eggs and cream to the grits mixture, then, using a wooden spoon, add ¾ cup of the shredded Gruyère cheese and 3 tablespoons of the Parmesan, reserving the rest of the cheeses for the top. Transfer the mixture to the prepared baking dish and bake for 45 minutes. Remove the casserole and turn the oven heat to broil.

Lay the sliced tomatoes over the surface, scatter the remaining cheese over them and run under the broiler for a few minutes until the cheese is melted and the surface is dappled and golden. Serve at once.

Hominy Grits Soufflé with Boursin Cheese and Scallions

SERVES 6

A creamy, airy soufflé with fragrant herb and garlic–scented Boursin cheese, scallions and a slight peppery bite. It's wonderful as a side dish with grilled pork sausage or chicken—or alone with a crisp salad for contrasting texture.

Butter to grease soufflé dish
1½ C. milk
1 C. water
Salt to taste
½ C. coarse grits
5-oz. package Boursin cheese, crumbled
3 Tbs. soft butter, cut into small pieces

2 scallions, thinly sliced (about ½ C.)
⅛ tsp. freshly ground black pepper
⅛ tsp. freshly grated nutmeg
½ tsp. Tabasco sauce
4 eggs, separated

The

Versatile

Grain

and the

Elegant

Bean

Preheat the oven to 350°F. and butter a 2½-quart soufflé dish. In a 3-quart nonstick saucepan, bring the milk, water and salt to a boil. Slowly stir in the grits, bring to a boil again, cover and simmer over very low heat, stirring once or twice, for 15 minutes. Stir and let rest, covered, for 5 minutes.

Then, with a wooden spoon, beat in the cheese and butter until incorporated. Take off 1 tablespoon of the scallions for garnish, then stir in the rest of the scallions, black pepper, nutmeg and Tabasco. In a small bowl, beat the egg yolks until frothy and stir them into the grits mixture. In another small bowl, beat the egg whites until they are stiff, using a beater. Fold half the grits mixture into the egg whites with a rubber spatula, then fold in the remaining mixture and spoon it into the prepared soufflé dish.

Bake for 30 to 40 minutes until puffed and golden. Sprinkle with the reserved scallions and serve at once.

Grits and Grillades, New Orleans–Style

SERVES 4

The word "grillades" refers to a braised or "smothered" meat dish composed of very thin slices of veal or, occasionally, beef, with a touch of tomato, peppers and onion. It is invariably paired with hominy grits in this well-known and well-loved Louisiana specialty.

1 lb. lean thin veal scallops (or thin slices of beef sirloin or beef round)	1 stalk celery, finely diced (½ C.)
½ tsp. salt	1 Tbs. fresh thyme leaves
½ tsp. freshly ground black pepper	1 bay leaf
⅛ tsp. cayenne	1 large tomato, peeled and diced (or 14-ounce can Italian plum tomatoes, drained and cubed) (about 1 C.)
3–4 cloves garlic, finely minced (1 Tbs.)	
2 Tbs. olive oil	
1 Tbs. butter	
3 Tbs. all-purpose flour	1½ C. Chicken Stock, preferably homemade (see page 171)
1 large onion, finely chopped (1 C.)	3 C. cooked coarse hominy grits (see chart, page 87)
1 small green pepper, finely diced (⅔ C.)	2 Tbs. finely minced parsley

Pound the meat very thin and cut it into rough 3-inch-square pieces. Dry the meat on paper towels. In a small bowl, combine the salt, both peppers and garlic and smear over the meat. Cover and refrigerate for at least 2 hours or longer to marinate.

Heat the oil and butter in a 12-inch skillet. Coat the meat with the flour. Brown the meat completely over high heat. Remove with tongs and set aside. Lower the heat and, to the same skillet, add the onion, green pepper and celery. Sauté over medium low heat for 5 minutes, stirring occasionally. Then add the thyme, bay leaf, tomatoes and chicken stock and bring to a boil. Lower the heat, cover and simmer for 10 minutes. Place the meat slices in one layer over the sauce. Cover and simmer for 35 to 40 minutes or until the meat is tender when pierced with the tip of a knife. Turn the meat over with tongs every 10 minutes. A thick, rich gravy will form. While the meat is cooking, prepare the grits.

TO SERVE: Pile the grits in the center of a large warm platter. Remove and discard the bay leaf from the meat, then place the grillades around the grits and spoon the gravy over the meat. Garnish with parsley.

Millet

Panicum Miliaceum

Not Strictly for the Birds

The

Versatile

Grain

and the

Elegant

Bean

112

If ever a grain has been subjected to a constantly unfair press, and a staggering amount of misinformation and distortion, or has been totally ignored, it is millet. Unless you are an American pet bird, the chances are that you have continued to ignore any opportunities even to try it. We are not aware of having seen it on any restaurant menu, and very few of our friends have ever sampled it. We found, for example, through the testing of our earlier book about grains and through the two years of creating recipes for this book that the first reaction to the word "millet" is, "Oh yes, I know millet. I feed it to my parakeet!"

Of course, you'll notice that we specifically mentioned *American* birds, for other people around the globe are quite familiar with this remarkable grain, and we are two of its foremost proponents. It is quite possible that millet was the first grain to be cultivated during the Neolithic era, while the first written record goes back to China at about 2800 B.C. The Sumerians, the Etruscans and the Romans ate it, and it was grown in Gaul and is still a major crop of the drier areas of India. Possibly it comes as a surprise to know that millet has served as an alternate for rice for centuries in northern China, Korea and Japan, and about *one third* of the people of the Orient utilize it as an important food source, reaching into the furthest areas of the Himalayas.

And so, it has always remained a mystery to us that millet is so rejected by most Americans—and we suppose that others of the Western world, such as the British, should also be included. Some wag once commented that if you saw millet growing in England, someone has probably just cleaned out the bird cage! That kind of statement along with its constant designation as a "poor man's cereal" has done much to keep it from achieving the prominence that it so richly deserves. (Millet is not alone, by the way. Corn and most legumes have also been dubbed food for poor persons from time to time.)

Millet is one of the most nutritious of grains, easy to digest, and very rich in amino acids, phosphorus and B vitamins, with an iron content that is higher than any grain except for amaranth and quinoa. But we think that its most important claim to fame and the reason it should be looked at most carefully is that it is one of the most outstanding alkaline foods in the worlds, soothing for people on diets recommended for ulcers and colitis.

To this day, it is not only a critical grain for most of Asia, but also for a great part of Africa. In the north of the continent, it's made into a porridge called *tuo zaafi,* while the people of the Sahara Desert use it to make a small flat bread called *taguella.* The Arusha, one of the farmer tribes of the Masai, make beer out of millet, not only for their own consumption but also as an excellent trading product. For a great many years, food writers also included millet as the key ingredient for the Ethiopian bread *injera.* However, only 5 percent of all *injera* is made from millet, with the remainder utilizing a grain that closely resembles it, *teff* (see page 209).

If you look carefully at where millet is grown most successfully, you begin to realize just how hardy it is and how perfect for hot, dry climates. It can lie dormant for weeks during a drought and then, suddenly, with passing rains, it sprouts and is ready for harvest just forty-five days later. It keeps well in storage and is resistant to rotting and insects. If it's kept dry, it has been known to keep for as long as five years. A while back, we read of a botanist in Japan who found some millet seeds at an archaeological dig. They were dated at about 1,500 years old. Kept dry in well-drained volcanic soil for all that time, the seeds were planted and they actually sprouted and produced buds!

Of course, no one doubts these remarkable attributes. But, a good part of the "bad press" of which we speak has a lot to do with reports of its flavor. Some have even called it bitter and we were very much surprised. *We* have found millet to be one of the best-tasting grains, a bit nutlike in flavor, and we use it for every course of a meal, either by itself or in combination with other grains. It's great for stuffing vegetables, poultry or fish, and it's excellent in soups or stews. It also makes a marvelous base for casseroles and serves as a superb whole grain substitute for couscous, if you're allergic to wheat or would like to try a new taste sensation. And finally, we find it quite delicious in custards and desserts.

Yes, it also feeds the birds! But just as with corn and other grains, there are many different varieties of millet, with some writers claiming as many as several thousand. If it makes you feel any better, the millet fed to birds is a special variety of the grain, with a very hard outer hull. We generally use pearl millet, and for the most part, the forms of the grain that we've listed below are found in most natural food stores.

The Forms of Millet

Whole Grain. Always hulled, since the outer layer is indigestible. The resultant grain is tiny and golden.

Millet Meal. A coarsely ground meal used for baked goods and for cereal. It can be purchased already prepared, or it can be ground at home from whole millet, using a home mill or a small electric spice grinder.

Millet Flour. A much finer grind than the millet meal. However, it contains no gluten, and when used in baked goods, it must be combined either with bread flour (white unbleached) or whole wheat flour.

Puffed Millet. Sold in specialty food stores or natural food outlets, it is a whole grain that is puffed under pressure. It's an excellent food for those who want to restrict the portions that they eat while still getting sufficient nourishment, since puffed millet has lots of air. It can also be used in puddings and bread to give them lightness, and it is a perfect breakfast cereal served with milk and fresh fruit.

The

Versatile

Grain

and the

Elegant

Bean

114

Millet

Grain & Granulation	Amount of Liquid	Cooking Method	Cooking & Standing Time	Approx. Yield	Comments
Whole Grain (1 C. dry)	2½ C.	*Method I:* To a 2-qt. saucepan, add 2 teaspoons butter and toast grain for 2 to 3 minutes stirring constantly. You will begin to smell a nutty aroma and hear a slight crackling when grains are toasted. Add boiling salted water, which will bubble up a bit. Stir and return to boiling, cover and cook over very low heat.	25 to 30 minutes. Let stand 10 minutes.	4 C.	This method makes a drier, fluffy, separated grain.
	2½ C.	*Method II:* To a 2-qt. saucepan, add grain slowly to boiling salted water. Return to boil, cover and simmer.	25 to 30 minutes. Let stand 10 minutes.	4 C.	This method produces stickier-textured grains.

Sweet Multicolored Peppers Stuffed with Ground Lamb, Peas, Millet and Mint

SERVES 6

The brightly hued peppers are filled with tiny yellow grains of millet, sweet little green peas, a bit of ground lean lamb and fresh mint. Serve this as a first course or a side dish—the flavors as well as the colors are dazzling.

6 large, thick-walled sweet peppers: 2 red, 2 green and 2 yellow or orange
Olive oil for brushing pan
3 Tbs. olive oil
1¼ C. Chicken Stock, preferably homemade (see page 171)
⅛ tsp. turmeric
Salt to taste
2 tsps. butter
⅓ C. millet
1 C. frozen tiny peas

10 ozs. lean lamb steak, from the leg, cut into cubes and trimmed of all fat and gristle (about 8 ozs. after trimming)
1 small clove garlic, finely minced (½ tsp.)
½ tsp. freshly ground black pepper
1 tsp. lemon juice (1 small wedge lemon)
2 Tbs. finely minced mint, plus 6 small sprigs for garnish

Cut a 1½-inch-diameter circle around the stem end of each pepper, then lift out and discard the stem, core and seeds. Rinse the insides of the peppers and turn them upside down on paper towels to dry. Preheat the oven to 350°F., brush the bottom of an 8 × 11 × 2-inch pan with olive oil and place the peppers upside down in the pan. Brush the skin of the peppers with 2 tablespoons of the olive oil and roast them in the oven for 15 to 20 minutes. Remove from the oven, turn right side up with a pair of tongs and set aside.

Meanwhile, bring the chicken stock and turmeric to a boil in a 1½-quart saucepan. Add salt and 1 teaspoon of the butter, stir in the millet and bring to a boil again. Then lower the heat, cover and simmer very slowly for 20 to 25 minutes, until all liquid is absorbed. Remove from the heat and stir in the frozen peas and the remaining teaspoon of butter. Cover and let it rest for 10 minutes.

In the bowl of a food processor, chop the lamb finely and set aside. In a medium-size nonstick skillet, heat the remaining tablespoon of olive oil and sauté the garlic for a few seconds. Add the chopped lamb and, stirring constantly, sauté until it just begins to lose its pink color. Remove from the heat and stir in salt, pepper, lemon juice and the finely minced mint. Then combine well with the millet and peas.

Fill each pepper to the top with the lamb and millet filling, pressing the filling down gently. You may cover and refrigerate the stuffed peppers at this point and bake them just before serving in an oven, preheated to 350°F. Or, return them to the oven, cover with aluminum foil and bake for 15 to 20 minutes more or until the peppers are tender. Serve, either hot or at room temperature, garnished with sprigs of mint.

The

Versatile

Grain

and the

Elegant

Bean

116

A Torte of Layered Vegetables, Prosciutto and Millet

SERVES 8

The millet and vegetables can be cooked the day before or you may use leftover vegetables. The layers are suspended in a Parmesan and prosciutto custard, scented with oregano, parsley and leeks, a most pleasant contrast of flavors and textures.

2 Tbs. soft butter
½ C. fine dry bread crumbs
1½ C. cooked millet (use Method II, see Chart, page 115)
½ lb. string beans, cooked and coarsely chopped (about 2 C.)
1 small cauliflower, cooked and coarsely chopped (2 C.)
1 lb. asparagus, cooked and coarsely chopped (2 C.)
2 thin leeks, white part only, thinly sliced (1 C.)

1 C. grated Parmesan cheese
2 Tbs. minced parsley
1 Tbs. minced fresh oregano (or 1 tsp. dried Greek oregano)
2 ozs. prosciutto, cut into slivers
5 eggs
¼ tsp. freshly ground black pepper
Salt to taste
3 drops Tabasco sauce
1 C. light cream or half and half
1 Tbs. all-purpose flour
Curly parsley

Preheat the oven to 350°F. Line the bottom of a 2½-quart springform pan with aluminum foil (going up 1 inch on the sides to prevent leakage). Butter the foil evenly and sprinkle with the bread crumbs. Rotate the pan to let the crumbs adhere to the sides and then shake out the excess. Place the millet evenly on the bottom of the pan, then layer each vegetable over the millet in the order given, sprinkling ¼ cup of the cheese and part of the parsley, oregano and prosciutto over each layer.

Then, in a medium-size bowl, beat together the eggs, pepper, salt, Tabasco, cream and flour and slowly pour the mixture over the layered vegetables. Place the pan in another, larger pan and pour 1 inch of boiling water into the bottom of the second pan. Bake for about 50 minutes to 1 hour, or until the center is *almost* set. Remove from the oven and let stand for 10 minutes to firm up the center.

Place on a serving plate and remove the sides of the springform, leaving the base intact. Carefully turn down the edge of aluminum foil and cut it away with a pair of scissors, keeping the foil under the base. Cover the edge with a ring of parsley. If liquid should accumulate on the serving plate, blot it up with paper towels. Serve warm or at room temperature.

Tunisian Chicken and Lamb Tagine
with Millet and Hot Harissa Sauce

SERVES 8 TO 10

Whole millet, which resembles couscous (the semolina flour–based pellets of pasta) to a "T" is used here in a classic Islamic sabbath dish from North Africa. The meat and vegetable selections vary from country to country, and the whim of the cook. The Algerians, for example, use a combination of several meats. Sometimes they add pumpkin and fava beans as vegetables. Try our version, then design your own with either millet or couscous.

2 Tbs. butter	2 large onions, cut into ½-in.-thick slices (about ¾ lb.)
1 Tbs. olive oil	
3-lb. chicken, cut into 10 small pieces	5 small turnips, peeled and cut into halves
½ lb. lean lamb, cut into 1-in. cubes	
1 tsp. finely minced, peeled ginger	4 carrots, cut into 3–4 pieces each
2–3 cloves garlic, finely minced (about 2 tsp.)	3 small zucchini, trimmed and cut into 1½-in. pieces
½ tsp. ground cumin	1 C. cooked chick-peas
¼ tsp. crushed saffron threads	½ C. raisins
¼ tsp. freshly ground black pepper	1 C. small pitted prunes
½ tsp. salt or to taste	1½ lemons, cut into 10 wedges
¼ tsp. ground cinnamon	4 C. cooked millet (use Method I, see Chart, page 115)
¼ tsp. ground cloves	
¼ tsp. freshly grated nutmeg	¼ C. blanched whole almonds, sautéed in 1 tsp. butter
3 C. Chicken Stock, preferably homemade (see page 171)	
Hot Harissa Sauce (see recipe below)	2 Tbs. finely minced parsley

In a 7-quart heavy Dutch oven, heat the butter and the oil. Add the pieces of chicken and lamb. Sprinkle with the ginger, garlic, cumin, saffron, pepper and salt, cinnamon, cloves and nutmeg and sauté over medium high heat until brown all over. Stir occasionally while browning. Then add the chicken stock, bring to a boil, lower the heat to a simmer, cover and cook for 30 minutes. At this point, cook the millet grains and prepare the hot Harissa sauce.

Now, tuck the onions, turnips and carrots around the chicken and the lamb. Tilt the pot and baste the vegetables. Cover and continue to simmer for 20 minutes more. Then add the zucchini, chick-peas, raisins, prunes and lemon wedges. Cover and continue to cook until the zucchini is tender. Do not stir.

To serve, mound the millet in the center of a large platter and sprinkle it with the toasted almonds. Lift out the vegetables and the pieces of chicken and lamb with a slotted spoon and arrange them attractively around the mound of millet. Discard the lemon wedges and garnish with parsley. Add the chick-peas to the millet. Then strain the sauce and return it to a small saucepan and bring to a boil, reserving 2

The

Versatile

Grain

and the

Elegant

Bean

118

tablespoons for the Harissa sauce. Serve the harissa sauce separately in a bowl, to be spooned out at the table.

Hot Harissa Sauce

8 small dried hot red chile peppers
1 clove garlic
¼ tsp. caraway seeds
⅛ ground cumin
⅛ tsp. ground coriander

1 Tbs. olive oil
2 Tbs. sauce from the tagine (see above)
Pinch salt

In a small saucepan, bring the peppers to a boil in water to cover. Let cool, then drain and reserve the liquid. Wearing rubber gloves, split the peppers and discard the seeds. In a small spice grinder or using a mortar and pestle, purée the peppers along with the garlic, caraway, cumin, coriander, olive oil, tagine sauce and salt. Add 1 or more tablespoons of the reserved hot pepper liquid to thin the sauce a bit. Pass the Harissa sauce separately with a warning to use it sparingly. *It is hot!*

NOTE: Harissa can sometimes be found in a tube, imported from France. Try gourmet specialty shops and Middle Eastern shops or check the mail order listings (see pages 501–506).

Fresh Herb and Millet Salad with Tomatoes

SERVES 8

The taste of summer is in every forkful of this verdant grain salad, which relies on lots of fresh herbs and the ripest tomatoes for its sprightly taste.

4 C. cooked millet (use Method I, see Chart, page 115)
⅓ C. finely minced chives
¼ C. finely minced flat leaf parsley
⅓ C. finely minced basil
2 tsps. finely minced marjoram
Salt to taste

Freshly ground black pepper to taste
Juice of ½ large lemon (about 2 Tbs.)
¼ C. olive oil
1 large ripe tomato, skinned and diced (about ½ lb.)
Few black olives (optional)

While the millet is hot, transfer it to a large bowl and combine with the herbs, salt, pepper, lemon juice and oil. Gently stir in the tomatoes. Serve at room temperature, garnished with black olives if you wish.

Hazelnut and Millet Pilaf with Apples and Thyme

SERVES 8 TO 10

A wonderful change from a rice pilaf. Golden, fluffy millet is teamed with toasted hazelnuts for textural contrast, then slightly sweetened with tender apple morsels, a hint of thyme and scallions. A winner with both poultry or any kind of pork.

4 C. cooked whole millet (use
    Method I, see Chart, page 115)
5 ozs. hazelnuts
1 large Delicious apple, peeled, cored
    and diced
Juice of 1 small wedge lemon (1 tsp.)

4 Tbs. butter
6 thin scallions, sliced into ½-in.
    diagonal pieces (1 C.)
1 tsp. dried thyme
1 tsp. salt or to taste
Freshly ground black pepper to taste

Put the cooked millet in a large bowl and set aside. Preheat the oven to 350°F., place the nuts in a pie pan and toast them for 10 to 15 minutes or until their papery skins have cracked. Place the nuts in several layers of paper towels, fold them up to enclose the nuts and rub together with your hands to loosen the skins. A few may cling. Chop the nuts coarsely in the bowl of a food processor and set aside.

Put the apple in a small bowl and toss with the lemon juice. In a large skillet, melt the butter and add the scallions, thyme, and salt and pepper to taste. Sauté over medium high heat, stirring constantly, for 2 minutes. Stir in the chopped nuts, then add the diced apples. Cook, stirring constantly, for 4 to 5 minutes. The apples should be tender but maintain their shape. Stir in the cooked millet. Cook on low heat until warmed through. Transfer to a serving dish or keep warm in a preheated low oven until serving time.

The

Versatile

Grain

and the

Elegant

Bean

120

Puffed Millet Banana Walnut Bread

MAKES 1 LOAF

Two forms of millet are used in this quick, lightly textured bread, and it answers the question about just what to have for breakfast that's nourishing, fast and a change from the usual. Store it, wrapped well, in the refrigerator and then use it for snacks as well.

Butter for greasing pan
2 eggs, separated
1 C. sour cream
¼ C. canola oil
⅓ C. maple syrup
1 tsp. vanilla extract
2 ripe bananas, sliced
1 C. millet flour
½ tsp. salt or to taste

1½ C. all-purpose flour
2 tsps. baking powder
¼ tsp. baking soda
1 tsp. ground cinnamon
¼ tsp. mace
⅛ tsp. ground cloves
½ C. puffed millet
1 C. coarsely broken, toasted walnuts

Preheat the oven to 350°F. and butter a 9¾ × 5¾ × 2¾-inch loaf pan. In the bowl of a food processor, process the egg yolks with the sour cream, oil, maple syrup, vanilla and bananas.

In a large bowl, combine the millet flour, salt, all-purpose flour, baking powder, baking soda, cinnamon, mace and cloves with a whisk to blend well. Stir in the puffed millet, then stir in the egg yolk mixture along with the walnuts with as few strokes as possible.

In a medium-size bowl, beat the egg whites with a beater until stiff, then fold them into the batter. Pour into the prepared pan and bake for 1 hour or until the center tests done with a cake tester. Cool on a wire rack in the pan for 10 to 15 minutes, then remove the bread and let cool further on the rack. Cool completely before slicing.

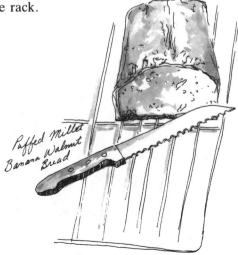

Puffed Millet Banana Walnut Bread

A Dessert Pilaf: Millet, Nuts
and Steamed Dates

SERVES 6

Fluffy and light and a good way of bringing a new touch to your dessert repertoire. In the Middle East, couscous is sometimes used for this dessert pilaf, but we prefer the texture and flavor of millet with the sweetness of the dates.

24	whole dried dates	1½	C. finely ground mixed walnuts and whole almonds (see NOTE), about 6 ozs. total
3	C. cooked millet (use Method I, see Page 115)		
½	tsp. almond extract	⅓	C. light brown sugar
2	Tbs. soft butter, cut into small pieces	1	tsp. ground cinnamon
			Heavy cream (optional)

Steam the dates in a vegetable steamer for 5 minutes and set aside. In a large bowl, mix the hot millet lightly with the almond extract and butter. In another bowl, combine the nuts, brown sugar and cinnamon and toss with the millet using two forks. Lightly mound on a platter and ring the platter with the steamed dates. Serve warm with a pitcher of cream if you wish.

NOTE: Use an electric blender for the nuts. The consistency will be slightly pasty; therefore, crumble the nuts between the palms of your hands in order to distribute evenly when adding them to the millet.

The

Versatile

Grain

and the

Elegant

Bean

122

Millet, Dried Fruit
and Nut Logs with Cognac

MAKES 2 (12-INCH) LOGS

When that sweet-tooth craving takes over your life, nibble without guilt on this candylike but healthful confection.

4 ozs. whole skinned almonds
4 ozs. walnuts
1 C. cooked millet (use Method II, see Chart, page 115)
Peel of 1 small orange, finely minced (about 1 Tbs.)

Safflower or canola oil for oiling blades
4 ozs. dried currants
4 ozs. pitted dates
4 ozs. raisins
4 ozs. dried apricots
1 Tbs. cognac

In the bowl of a food processor, chop together the almonds and walnuts until fine. Transfer the contents to a large bowl and mix with the millet and orange peel. Oil the blades of the food processor with a bland oil such as safflower or canola and add all the dried fruits. Process until the fruits are very fine. Then add the cognac and the millet-nut mixture and process again until well mixed and the mass starts to form into a ball.

Oil your hands well and divide the mixture into two parts. Lay half on waxed paper that has been placed on a work surface and roll and press it into a log shape 12 inches long by 1 inch in diameter. Repeat the process with the remaining mixture. Wrap each log tightly in plastic wrap and keep it at room temperature for 3 days to allow the flavors to blend. Slice the log into ½-inch slices using an oiled knife. The logs will keep for several months, wrapped tightly, in the refrigerator.

Oats

Avena

Discovering "Oat Cuisine"

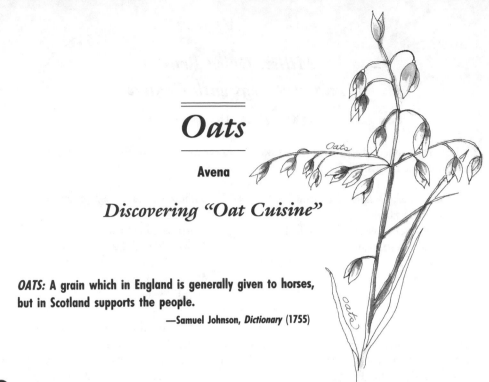

OATS: A grain which in England is generally given to horses, but in Scotland supports the people.

—Samuel Johnson, *Dictionary* (1755)

Old Samuel Johnson might well have been writing for contemporary dictionaries, for as recently as a few years ago, a well-thumbed dictionary on our desk gave a similar definition: "used for making oatmeal and as a food for horses." Certainly, on that count, the unloved oat is in good company with corn, barley and millet. Most of the nutritious grains are used to feed the animals, and in America today about 90 percent of the crop is consumed by our farmyard residents. Too many Americans, alas, still agree with Pliny (we're just not sure if it was the Elder—A.D. 23–79—or the Younger A.D. 61–105) when he wrote that he could not understand how one could eat the same food as animals! (Of course, there are others who say, "How can you eat *animals!*")

That said, it probably all began because oats were originally an unwanted weed, unloved by farmers because the plants usually thrived between rows of wheat and barley. They were unceremoniously pulled up and then burned. Though oats were probably eaten in Neolithic times and during the Bronze Age, they were generally used as a food for the horses of Central Asia or possibly the colder areas of Russia. The roots (no pun intended) are vague, but those who give the origin of oats as the Middle East or Africa are probably incorrect, since the plant thrives best in colder, damper climates, surviving beautifully under conditions that are inhospitable to other grains.

Oats probably came to northern Europe along with the raiders, the merchant caravans, the invaders and the plunderers—along with their horses and the food carried to feed them. The plant proliferated in the colder areas of Europe, such as Scotland, Ireland, Wales, Germany, Denmark and Switzerland. Along the way, it started a "chicken and the egg" conundrum. Since horses were big eaters, the arrival

The

Versatile

Grain

and the

Elegant

Bean

124

of oats made the job of feeding them easier. Thus, the early farmer could have more horses to help with the work. More horses meant larger cultivated fields of wheat and barley—and oats, which then allowed still more horses. In addition, the farmers soon discovered that oats were a great rotation crop.

For all of northern Europe, oats are a part of the culinary heritage. For the Scots, no celebration and no cookbook would be complete without the appearance of oats. *Haggis,* the substantial winter dish steamed in the stomach of a sheep, has the vital addition of oats (and a good shot of Drambuie to give it a kick, we might add), and in the drink called *atholl brose,* the raw oats are soaked in water and then a powerful beverage is made by straining the liquid and using it as a base. It dates from about 1475, and it's mentioned in Sir Walter Scott's *The Heart of Midlothan* and in Robert Louis Stevenson's *Kidnapped.* Perhaps the most charming parts of the Scottish love of oats are the names that pepper the cookbooks of the region, all of them using the grain as a major ingredient: *hodgils, mealie pudding, skirlie, bannocks, cranachan,* and drinks like *stodrum* and *blenshaw.* An old Scottish cookbook calls it "one of the sweetest grains to cook with."

As with the Scots, so with the Welsh and their *brewis* (oatmeal broth) and their *siot* (oatcakes in buttermilk), and with the Swiss and their *muesli,* as well as with the Irish and their marvelous steel-cut oats, a substantial morning starter for the cold, damp, inclement months of winter. Speaking of oatmeal, the Scots consider the use of sugar and milk or cream on the morning cereal as an effete and unnecessary flourish. They put the milk or cream in a separate bowl and then dip each spoonful into it as they eat.

We are not without our ties to oats, of course. The common phrases "feeling one's oats" or "sowing one's wild oats" are quite recognizable and familiar. In Provence, France, the comment that "she gave him his oats" comes from an old tradition in which the suitor of an eligible young woman was encouraged when she sprinkled large amounts of cheese on his oatmeal or rejected when she slipped the oats in his pocket and, in effect, told him to "get lost!" Even though the custom is long gone, the phrase still exists in Provence when a suitor fails in his quest.

The American demand for oats is a recent phenomenon, having much to do with the nutrition-hype that accompanied the promotion of *oat bran* in our diets. Though he wrote it some years back, author and food critic Waverly Root was very clairvoyant when he described oats as a grain that "has progressed from weed to health food." We've covered the oat bran overkill in the section on The Nutrition Exploiters (see page 9).

We would like to add that the grain does have excellent nutritional qualities— protein, B vitamins, calcium and fiber plus unsaturated fats. However, though it is nutritious and one of our favorite grains, it does not offer miracles. Recent studies have determined that it is no more effective in lowering cholesterol than other grains or, indeed, low-fiber wheat flour! We just think that it makes for great, tasty dishes that are not limited to breakfast.

Oats can be used for thickening and enriching soups, for extending meat loaves, for stuffings, pilafs, cakes, breads, muffins, pancakes, granolas and mueslis. The latter dish, by the way, with fruits, nuts and yogurt (see page 130), makes an almost perfect way to start the day as a hearty breakfast. Even if you, as we, can still hear *your* mother shout, "It's cold outside! Eat your oatmeal!" we strongly suggest that you look past its ubiquitous reputation as morning fare and past its major prominence as *porridge.*

In fact, all of this reminiscing about childhood reminds us (and probably you) of the times we were kids and we knew that porridge was something that the British kids ate. And one day, as we grew older, we found out that "oatmeal" correctly refers to *oat flour* and therefore what we called "oatmeal" was indeed porridge, and if you thin down a creamy version by adding milk or cream to rolled oats it becomes "gruel." Another childish fantasy shot down! Here, then, are the forms of oats, all of them correctly designated, we hope.

The Forms of Oats

Whole Oat Groats. These are the untreated, natural, hulled oats, with only the outermost inedible "chaff" or "hull" removed. The basic nutritional value of the grain is thus left intact. Groats can be cooked whole or they can be ground, and they're excellent when mixed with wheat berries. Since they are the entire grain, they take the longest time to cook.

Steel-cut Oats (sometimes called *Scottish Oats* or *Irish Oats*). Natural, unrefined oat groats that have been cut into two or three small pieces for tasty, chewy cereals. They're processed with a small amount of heat by steel blades and therefore they retain most of their B vitamins. They require a fairly long cooking time, but we think they're worth it. However, if they're oven-toasted first (see BOX, opposite page, and Chart, page 128), the cooking time is shortened considerably. They have a good crunch and are generally used for "Scottish-style" recipes such as porridge, oatcakes, griddle cakes, cookies and scones. Cooked steel-cut oats can also be blended with various flours for baking.

Rolled Oats. Large, separate flakes that have first been steamed and then flattened (old-fashioned rolled oats). They're usually used in cereals, cookies, cakes, breads and toppings for fruit crisps. The "quick" or "instant" rolled oats are processed even further and then heat-treated for faster cooking. As a result, they have less nutritive value and we generally avoid them except to make toppings, preferring the "old-fashioned" rolled oats, which only take about five minutes cooking time. In addition, any overprocessed food will generally cost more in your local supermarket.

Oat Bran. The outer covering of the whole oat groat. Though it is certainly healthful, it was the oversold subject of the highly exaggerated marketing campaigns of the past few years. All the other forms of oats also contain some bran. We sometimes use about half a cup of oat bran in some of our home-baked goods, such as breads, to add flavor.

Oat Flour. Finely ground from whole oat groats, with much of the bran remaining. The flour is, therefore, almost as nutritious as the groat itself, and it can be blended with other flours in the baking of bread. However, it has no gluten, so it will not rise

The

Versatile

Grain

and the

Elegant

Bean

126

TOASTING STEEL-CUT OATS

(Irish or Scottish)

Untoasted steel-cut oats take approximately forty minutes to cook. We find that oven-toasting the oats first not only cuts down cooking time to fifteen miutes but also adds a wonderful nutty taste. We usually toast one pound of grain at a time, store it in an airtight container and then use one cup at a time for cooking.

To Toast One Pound of Steel-cut Oats

Preheat the oven to 350°F. Whirl the oats in the bowl of a food processor for a few strokes just to break down the grain a bit. Spread the oats evenly in a 9 × 13 × 2-inch baking dish and toast for twenty minutes, stirring occasionally. Cool and store the oats in an airtight container.

For cooking steel-cut oats, see Chart, page 128.

unless it's mixed with a gluten-rich flour such as unbleached white. The addition of oat flour to home-baked products will also help them to remain fresher for a longer period of time, since the grain has a strong, natural antioxidant. In fact, oats and the derivatives of the grain were used for just that purpose long before the discovery of chemical preservatives. Not only is oat flour excellent in baked goods, imparting a delicate, sweet flavor, but it can also be used as a thickening agent in sauces, soups and stews. Oat flour can be purchased at health food stores or you can make your own by whirling quick oats in an electric blender, then sifting.

Oats

Grain & Granulation	Amount of Liquid	Cooking Method	Cooking & Standing Time	Approx. Yield	Comments
Whole Oat Groats (1 C. dry) (washed & soaked)	2¾ C.	Use nonstick saucepan for all methods. Wash grains and *soak* overnight. Drain. In a 3-qt. saucepan, bring salted water to a boil, stir in soaked grain, return to boil. Cover, lower heat and simmer.	25 minutes. Let stand 10 minutes.	3 C.	Overnight soaking cuts down 35 minutes of cooking time and allows for more even cooking.
Whole Oat Groats (1 C. dry) (washed & unsoaked)			60 minutes. Let stand 10 minutes.		
Steel-cut Oats (Irish or Scottish) (1 C. dry)	3½ C.	This method is only for *toasted* steel-cut oats (see BOX, page 127). In a 3-qt. saucepan, bring salted water to a boil. Slowly add toasted oats while stirring constantly. Return to boil, lower heat to medium low. Cook, uncovered, then cover to let stand.	15 minutes. Let stand 5 minutes.	3 C.	Without toasting, steel-cut oats take 40 to 45 minutes to cook and do not have as nutty a flavor.

Grain & Granulation	Amount of Liquid	Cooking Method	Cooking & Standing Time	Approx. Yield	Comments
Old-Fashioned Rolled Oats (1 C. dry)	2¾ C.	In a 2-qt. saucepan bring salted water to a boil. Stir in oats. Cover and let stand. *Do not cook.*	Let stand 10 minutes.	2½ C.	These are *not* the package instructions. When done this way, the oats are thick, not creamy. If you prefer creamier, more gelatinous oats, follow the package instructions.

Oat and Fresh Tomato Soup with Basil

SERVES 6

A hint of orange peel gives this oat-thickened basil-scented tomato soup an elusive flavor. Lightly cooked, it requires the most luscious tomatoes, found unfortunately only in late summer.

1 C. rolled oats
4 Tbs. butter
1 large onion, chopped (1 C.)
3–4 large cloves garlic, finely minced (1 Tbs.)
2 lbs. ripe tomatoes, peeled and chopped (about 5 C.)

5 C. Chicken Stock, preferably homemade (see page 171)
2 tsps. finely minced orange peel
5–6 large basil leaves, finely minced
Salt and freshly ground black pepper to taste
2 Tbs. finely minced parsley

To a heavy iron skillet, add the oats and toast them over medium low heat, stirring until they turn color, about 5 to 8 minutes. Be careful not to let them burn. Set aside.

In a 7-quart Dutch oven, melt the butter over medium high heat, add the onion and the garlic and sauté for about 5 minutes, stirring, until the onion is wilted. Add the tomatoes and stir for 2 minutes more. Then add the chicken stock and the orange peel and bring to a boil. Lower the heat to medium low and add the basil, reserved oats and salt and pepper. Cover and cook for 8 minutes. Adjust the seasoning and serve hot, sprinkled with parsley.

Swiss Oat Muesli

SERVES 4

We have found most commercial packaged muesli mixtures too tough to chew and very sticky, and yet we love the breakfast combination of oats, fruits and nuts. Our version soaks the oats and dried fruit overnight and adds fresh fruit, nuts and yogurt the next day. It is a completely healthful, lowfat, fiber-rich breakfast—a real comfort food that also tastes very, very good.

1 C. rolled oats	1 tart green apple, with skin
12 pitted dates, cut into small pieces (or you can substitute dried prunes, figs or apricots)	1 C. plain lowfat yogurt
	Light brown sugar (optional)
	1 banana, sliced thinly
¼ tsp. ground cinnamon	12 almonds, walnuts or hazelnuts,
1 C. warm water	coarsely chopped

In a small bowl, combine the oats, dates and cinnamon. Pour water over, stir, cover with foil and soak overnight. Before serving, quarter and core the apple and chop it finely in the bowl of a food processor. Stir it into the oat mixture. Put the mixture into four bowls, top each bowl with ¼ cup yogurt, some brown sugar if you wish, and banana slices. Sprinkle the surface with nuts and serve.

Pineapple Oat Bran Muffins

MAKES 8 MUFFINS

A lowfat, low-cholesterol muffin, high in fiber, and flavored with cinnamon and brown sugar along with tart, sweet, crushed pineapple and orange peel.

Oil for greasing muffin cups	½ tsp. baking soda
8¼-oz. can crushed pineapple	1 tsp. ground cinnamon
1 C. oat bran	1 Tbs. finely minced orange peel
½ C. oat flour	½ C. nonfat plain yogurt
½ C. all-purpose flour	¼ C. canola oil
½ tsp. salt or to taste	1 tsp. vanilla extract
3 Tbs. light brown sugar	2 egg whites, slightly beaten, but not
2 tsps. baking powder	too frothy

Preheat the oven to 400°F. Oil only the bottoms of 8 muffin cups and set aside. Drain the crushed pineapple in a sieve over a bowl, pressing out as much syrup as possible.

The

Versatile

Grain

and the

Elegant

Bean

130

Take off ¼ cup of the syrup and set it aside. Reserve the crushed pineapple.

In a medium-size bowl, whisk together the oat bran, both flours, salt, brown sugar, baking powder, baking soda, cinnamon and orange peel. Set aside. In another bowl, whisk together the yogurt, canola oil, vanilla, reserved pineapple syrup and egg whites. Add the crushed, drained pineapple to this mixture, then add to the dry ingredients all at once, combining with a few swift strokes. *Do not overmix.*

Fill eight muffin cups to the tops with the batter and bake for 15 to 20 minutes or until the edges are slightly golden. Let the muffins rest in the pan about 2 to 3 minutes before loosening them and cooling them on a wire rack. Serve warm.

Yorkshire Potato Oaties with Roquefort Cheese

MAKES ABOUT 24 OATIES

These are untraditional potato oaties. In Yorkshire, they are made with potatoes and oats, but we have added spices, French Roquefort cheese and a bit of grated onion to make these little triangles a delicious side dish for grilled fish, chicken or meat.

1 lb. Idaho baking potatoes, peeled and boiled (about 2 large potatoes)	1 egg, lightly beaten
½ small onion, grated (about ¼ C.)	2 Tbs. milk
4 Tbs. melted butter	2 ozs. Roquefort cheese, crumbled
½ tsp. salt or to taste	½ C. oat flour, plus 2–3 additional tablespoons
Freshly ground black pepper to taste	Butter for greasing griddle
⅛ tsp. freshly ground nutmeg	Additional melted butter (optional)
⅛ tsp. cayenne	

In a large bowl, mash the potatoes along with the onion, melted butter, salt, pepper, nutmeg, cayenne and egg. Heat the milk in a small saucepan, add the Roquefort cheese, stirring constantly to melt it. Combine with the potato mixture and beat in the ½ cup of oat flour. If the dough feels too wet, add more oat flour. Divide the dough into four parts.

Flour your hands and press one part of the dough down on a floured surface until it is ¼ inch thick. Trim the ends and cut parallel horizontal and vertical lines 3 inches apart to form squares, then cut the squares into triangles. Repeat until the remaining dough is used.

Lift the triangles carefully with a spatula to a lightly buttered griddle and cook over medium heat. When the underside is dappled with brown and somewhat dry, turn and brown the other side. Keep them warm in a preheated low oven and serve with additional melted butter if you wish.

Oat and Red Pepper Bread
with Rosemary

MAKES 2 LOAVES

A most unusual, very easy and very delicious bread that is certain to elicit comments and questions from your guests. The red peppers are puréed to give the bread its slight pink color and some are also julienned to show their vivid colors right in each slice.

1 package dry yeast	1 C. oat flour
2 C. warm water, plus 1 Tbs.	2 Tbs. salt
Pinch sugar	¼ tsp. freshly ground black pepper
1½ C. rolled oats	2 Tbs. sugar
5 C. bread flour (see NOTE), plus additional flour as necessary	¼ C. olive oil
2 red peppers (preferably Dutch thick-walled peppers)	2 Tbs. chopped fresh rosemary
	Butter for greasing baking sheet

Put the yeast in a large bowl along with 2 cups warm water. Add the sugar, rolled oats and 1 cup of the bread flour. Mix well with a wooden spoon, cover and let stand in a warm spot for 1 hour. It should bubble up slightly and be spongy in texture.

Meanwhile, prepare the peppers. Roast them on top of the stove or under the broiler until the skins char and blister, turning them frequently. Wrap them in aluminum foil and let them steam for 10 minutes. Then seed the peppers, peel off the skin and blot dry on paper towels. Purée 1 pepper in an electric blender, adding 1 tablespoon of water to keep it liquid. Cut the other pepper into very thin julienne strips. Set the peppers aside.

When the sponge is ready, stir it down with a wooden spoon. Add the oat flour, salt, pepper, sugar, olive oil, rosemary and red pepper purée. Then stir in the strips. Add the remaining bread flour, a cup at a time, stirring as you do so. You may need slightly less or slightly more depending upon the humidity in your area or the altitude at which you are baking. The dough should be firm and slightly wet.

Turn it out onto a lightly floured surface and knead for 8 to 10 minutes, adding more flour if the dough becomes too sticky. Flour your hands frequently to keep the dough workable. Divide the dough in two parts, form round or oval loaves and place them on a buttered baking sheet. Cover with a kitchen towel, put them in a warm spot and let them rise for 1 hour and 30 minutes or until doubled in bulk.

Preheat the oven to 350°F. when the loaves have doubled in size. Take a razor blade and cut a pattern into the top of each loaf to allow the bread to expand as it rises in the oven. Then, using a plant mister, spray the tops with warm water to give it a firmer crust. Bake the breads 45 to 50 minutes or until the loaves sound hollow when tapped on the bottom. Once, about 20 minutes into the baking, spray the tops with water once again. Let cool on wire racks.

The

Versatile

Grain

and the

Elegant

Bean

132

NOTE: Bread flour is a white, hard wheat, usually unbleached flour, that has a higher gluten content than the other all-purpose flours. It works well with low-gluten or no-gluten mixtures such as oat flour.

Whole Oat Groats with Celery, Sage and Thyme

SERVES 6

Fill a crown roast of pork with this lusty, nutty-tasting pilaf, or use it with poultry or pork for a surprisingly delicious side dish.

3 Tbs. butter	2–3 large stalks celery with leaves, finely chopped (1 C.)
3 C. cooked whole oat groats (see Chart, page 128)	Salt and freshly ground black pepper to taste
3 Tbs. olive oil	1 Tbs. finely minced fresh sage (or 1 tsp. dried sage)
1 large onion, finely chopped (1 C.)	½ tsp. dried thyme
1 medium green pepper, finely diced (1 C.)	2 Tbs. finely minced parsley

In a large nonstick skillet, melt the butter and add the cooked groats. Stir and sauté until toasted, about 5 minutes. Transfer to a bowl and set aside. In the same skillet, heat the olive oil, then add the onions and the green pepper. Cook, stirring, for about 3 to 4 minutes, then add all the remaining ingredients except the parsley and the reserved groats. Cook over medium heat, stirring frequently, for 2 to 3 minutes more. Add the groats to the vegetable mixture and heat, stirring occasionally. Serve hot sprinkled with parsley.

Scottish Buttermilk Oat Scones
with Dried Currants

MAKES 8 SCONES

There are Irish scones and English scones—some made with cream, some that contain oat flakes—but only the *Scottish* scones have the crunch of steel-cut toasted oats. They also have a marvelous, nutty aroma, enough to make you plunge into a nostalgic mode for dark afternoons in Scotland, when the scones are served with tea and marmalade in front of a roaring fire.

1 C. steel-cut oats	½ tsp. salt or to taste
1¼ C. buttermilk, at room temperature	⅓ C. dried currants
½ C. oat flour	Butter for greasing baking sheet
½ C. whole wheat flour	4 Tbs. softened butter, cut into small
¼ C. all-purpose flour	pieces
1 tsp. baking soda	1 Tbs. milk
1 tsp. sugar	Cinnamon and sugar for topping
2 tsps. baking powder	

Preheat the oven to 350°F. Place the oats in a pie pan and toast them for 20 minutes, stirring often to toast evenly and not burn. When slightly golden, remove, combine with the buttermilk in a small bowl, and let stand for 20 minutes.

In a large bowl, combine the flours, baking soda, sugar, baking powder, salt and dried currants. Reset the oven to 400°F. and butter a baking sheet. Using a pastry blender, cut the 4 tablespoons butter into the flour until the texture is coarsely crumbled, then stir in the buttermilk/oat mixture until combined. Flour your hands and scoop up the dough, forming it into a ball. Do not overmix. Press the ball of dough directly onto the pan, then press into a ¾-inch-thick circle.

With a sharp floured knife, score the surface, almost to the bottom, making eight wedges. Brush the surface with milk and sprinkle a bit of sugar and cinnamon on top.

Bake for 12 to 15 minutes. Serve hot, cut into wedges and accompany with your favorite fruit preserves, if you wish.

The

Versatile

Grain

and the

Elegant

Bean

134

Toasted Oat and Buttermilk Bread

1 LOAF

A wholesome, tasty, satisfying bread with the nutty flavor of toasted oats. It's also simple enough for a child to make. Toast some for breakfast with your morning cup of coffee.

Butter for greasing baking sheet
1 C. old-fashioned rolled oats, plus some for top
2¼ C. all-purpose flour, plus ¼ C.
2 C. whole wheat flour

1 tsp. baking powder
2 tsps. baking soda
2 tsps. salt
2 C. buttermilk, at room temperature
1 egg, lightly beaten

Butter a baking sheet and set aside. Preheat the oven to 350°F. Put 1 cup of the oats into a pie plate and toast for 10 minutes, then cool. In a large mixing bowl, whisk together the 2¼ cups all-purpose flour, whole wheat flour, baking powder, baking soda, salt and toasted oats. Make a well in the center and add the buttermilk and the egg.

With floured hands, mix the batter until a ball of sticky dough forms. Then flour a work surface with about ¼ cup all-purpose flour and knead the dough for 3 to 5 minutes until a manageable loaf forms. Place the loaf on the prepared baking sheet and press some additional oats on the surface. Dust with flour and bake for 50 minutes or until the bread is lightly brown and sounds hollow when tapped on the bottom. Cool on a wire rack.

Oat Crust and Mixed Berry Tart

MAKES 1 9-INCH TART

The pastry is pressed with the fingers, rather than rolled, to form a nutty crisp base for a darkly vivid mixture of warm soft berries.

Oat Crust

½ C. oat flour	2 Tbs. sugar
⅔ C. all-purpose flour	¼ lb. cold butter, cut into small pieces
¼ C. quick-cooking oats	3 Tbs. cold water
Pinch salt	1 tsp. vanilla extract

Add all the dry ingredients to the bowl of a food processor and process for 1 or 2 pulses to combine. Add the butter and process for about 9 pulses. Add the water mixed with the vanilla and pulse 3 or 4 times, just to combine.

Flour your hands and a piece of aluminum foil. Gather the dough into a ball and flatten it into approximately an 8-inch disk. Wrap the pastry in the foil and chill it in the refrigerator for 1 hour.

After an hour, let the pastry soften at room temperature for about 5 minutes, then turn the disk into a 9-inch tart pan with a removable base. Press the pastry with your fingertips from the center up toward the rim, forming a ridge. Then place in the freezer for 20 minutes.

Preheat the oven to 425°F. Remove the pan from the freezer, line with aluminum foil weighted with pie weights and bake for about 10 minutes. Then remove the foil containing the pie weights, lower the oven temperature to 350°F. and bake for about 5 to 8 minutes more or until the crust is dry and slightly golden. Remove and cool completely in the pan on a wire rack.

Mixed Berry Filling

⅔ C. walnuts, toasted and ground in a blender	1 tsp. lemon juice
2½ C. blueberries	2 Tbs. water
⅔ C. sugar	2 Tbs. cornstarch
¼ tsp. ground cinnamon	1 C. small ripe strawberries
1 tsp. grated orange peel	1 C. raspberries
	Heavy pouring cream (optional)

When the crust has cooled, sprinkle the ground walnuts over the bottom surface and set aside. In a 3-quart nonstick saucepan, mix 2 cups of the blueberries with the sugar, cinnamon, orange peel and lemon juice and bring slowly to a boil, stirring frequently. Combine the water and cornstarch and add to the blueberry mixture. Stir constantly over low heat for 3 to 5 minutes, until thickened. Remove from the heat and gently stir in the remaining blueberries, the strawberries and raspberries. Let cool completely, then spoon the thickened filling over the prepared tart crust.

The

Versatile

Grain

and the

Elegant

Bean

136

Remove the rim of the tart pan, keeping the tart on its base. This should be done just before serving. Serve with a trickle of heavy cream poured from a pitcher at the table after the portions are cut.

Apple and Prune Crumble with Cognac

SERVES 6

A British version of the American crisp. The oat shortbread mixture is "crumbled" over the surface, hence its name. The top is always crisp—which is probably why the name was changed in the early American versions of this homey warm dessert.

Fruit

18 pitted prunes	1 tsp. lemon juice
2 Tbs. cognac	1 tsp. finely minced lemon peel
Butter for greasing baking dish	1 tsp. cinnamon
5 large Granny Smith apples, peeled and thinly sliced (about 8 C.)	⅔ C. light brown sugar

Soak the prunes in the cognac for 1 hour. Preheat the oven to 350°F. and butter a 2-quart baking dish. In a large bowl, toss the apples with the lemon juice, lemon peel, cinnamon and brown sugar, along with the prunes and the cognac. Add to the prepared baking dish.

Oat Crumble Mixture

¼ C. light brown sugar	¼ tsp. vanilla extract
½ C. all-purpose flour	5 Tbs. melted butter
½ C. quick-cooking oats	

Combine the ingredients and let stand for 5 minutes. With your fingers mix to form a crumbly mass, then scatter the crumble over the fruit. Bake for 45 to 50 minutes or until the top is golden brown and the apples are tender. Serve warm with melted vanilla ice cream if you wish.

Oat and Orange Cake with Broiled Icing

SERVES 8 TO 9

Broiled icings are popular with Southern cooks. Here it enhances the sprightly orange taste of this light, yet earthy cake. It is a special favorite of children and yet sophisticated enough for adults.

Cake

Butter for greasing baking pan
⅔ C. boiling water
¾ C. rolled oats
¼ C. soft butter
¾ C. light brown sugar
1 egg
¼ C. frozen orange juice concentrate, thawed but not diluted

½ tsp. vanilla extract
1 C. all-purpose flour
¼ C. oat flour (see page 126)
½ tsp. baking powder
1 tsp. baking soda
½ tsp. cinnamon
Few grains salt

Preheat the oven to 350°F. and butter a 9 × 2-inch round baking pan (or a square 8 × 8 × 2-inch pan). In a small bowl, pour the boiling water over the oats, stir and set aside to cool.

In the bowl of a food processor, cream the butter and brown sugar until light and fluffy. Add the egg and process to incorporate. Add the orange juice concentrate and vanilla and process again until well mixed. To another bowl, add both flours, baking powder, baking soda, cinnamon and salt and whisk to blend. Then add to the food processor a third at a time, along with the oats. Process until well mixed. The batter will be thick.

Scrape into the prepared pan and bake for 35 to 40 minutes or until a cake tester comes out clean when inserted into the center of the cake. Remove the cake from the oven, prepare the icing and raise the oven heat to broil.

Icing

2 Tbs. butter
¼ C. maple syrup
1 Tbs. frozen orange juice concentrate, thawed but not diluted

½ C. flaked coconut
½ C. coarsely chopped walnuts

In a small saucepan, warm the butter and maple syrup. Add the remaining ingredients and spread over the top of the cake. Then, slip the cake under the broiler on the lowest rack and broil for about 2 minutes, watching carefully so that the glaze doesn't burn. Cool slightly before cutting, serving the cake directly from the pan.

The

Versatile

Grain

and the

Elegant

Bean

138

Oat and Nut Orange Florentines

MAKES 5 TO 6 DOZEN

These delicate cookies are filled with candied orange peel, walnuts and oats and then drizzled with chocolate. It's impossible to eat only one.

Butter for greasing baking sheets
1 C. rolled oats
5 Tbs. all-purpose flour
Small pinch baking soda
2 Tbs. very finely minced candied orange peel
½ C. finely chopped walnuts

1 egg
¼ C. maple syrup
⅓ C. mild light honey
1 tsp. vanilla extract
¼ lb. butter, plus 1 Tbs.
¼ C. sugar
3 ozs. semisweet baking chocolate

Preheat the oven to 350°F. Generously butter two baking sheets. Whirl the oats in the bowl of a food processor for a few strokes, then put them into a medium-size bowl. Add the flour, baking soda, candied orange peel and walnuts. Stir to combine and set aside.

In a large bowl, beat the egg, and then add the maple syrup, honey and vanilla. Melt the ¼ pound butter and stir in the sugar until dissolved, then cool and add to the egg mixture. Beat, then add the dry ingredients, combining well.

Drop by the half teaspoon onto the prepared baking sheets, leaving about 2½ inches of space between each cookie, since they will spread while baking. Bake 5 to 8 minutes or until the edges of the cookies are golden.

Loosen all the cookies immediately by using a spatula while they are still soft since they harden very rapidly. Then remove them carefully to a wire rack to cool completely. When they have cooled, melt the chocolate and the remaining 1 tablespoon butter together. Dip a small paring knife into the chocolate and drizzle onto the surface of each cookie, letting the chocolate run off from the tip of the knife. Cool again before storing in an airtight container for a day or two.

Scottish Cranachan with Berries

MAKES 1½ CUPS

Hogmany is Scotland's name for the midnight New Year's celebration and a time for revelry and special foods like this rich, irresistible and easily made cream. Oddly enough, it's made with crunchy toasted steel-cut oats, sugar and Drambuie liqueur. It's traditionally served over fresh berries or as a topping for tarts. If you care to forgo the "booze," try our version or add the liqueur if you prefer.

- ¼ C. steel-cut oats, whirled in a blender
- 1 C. heavy cream
- ¼ C. confectioners' sugar
- 1 Tbs. sour cream
- 2 Tbs. thawed frozen orange juice concentrate, not diluted (or 2 Tbs. Drambuie liqueur)

- Fresh strawberries or raspberries or a combination, allowing about 1 C. per person
- 1 Tbs. finely shredded orange peel, made with a zester tool (optional)

Preheat the oven to 350°F. Place the oats in a pie pan and toast in the oven for about 15 to 20 minutes, stirring often to prevent burning. Remove and set aside to cool.

Whip the cream with a beater until it thickens slightly. Then sift the confectioners' sugar over it 2 tablespoons at a time, beating in between the additions until soft peaks form. The cream should not be completely stiff. Stir in the sour cream and the orange juice concentrate and the oats. Spoon over bowls of berries and top with shreds of orange peel if you wish.

The

Versatile

Grain

and the

Elegant

Bean

140

Quinoa

Chenopodium Quinoa

Mother Grain of the Incas

Possibly one of the most difficult tasks of any food writer is to describe accurately for a reader just what a new food *tastes like.* For years we have heard various dishes—everything from alligator and guinea pig to monkfish and pig's ears—described as a "cross between chicken and lobster"! Thus, it has been fascinating to read the various descriptions of the newly rediscovered Inca grain quinoa. About all that anyone seems to agree upon is that the pronunciation is KEEN-wah. Other than that, we've had a field day trying to pin it down since taste is such a personal thing.

One writer tells us that it's like wild rice and millet, another that it tastes like short grain rice and bulgur, yet another like mustard and millet—or is it like sesame seeds? Or couscous? We will never settle that particular discussion and our own definition of the most remarkable grain is that *it's delicious,* and we strongly suggest that you try it for yourself and make your own decision about its taste.

It originated with the Incas, as amaranth did with the Aztecs and blue corn with the Southwest Native Americans in our own country. All three disappeared until quite recently, at least as far as our own culinary tastes are concerned. Though it has continued to be grown on the altiplano of Peru and Bolivia, as well as in Chile, the acreage has gradually decreased, and until it was "rediscovered" and then brought to Colorado for planting, it had never even been mentioned in books on grains as recently as ten years ago—and that includes our own first book of the subject at about that time.

The Incas, as did the Aztecs, grew a variety of nutritious crops prior to the arrival of the Conquistadores, in this case Pizarro. In addition to quinoa, others have been rediscovered and many have surfaced through specialty mail order resources and in our own neighborhoods. Not only were corn and potatoes grown, but the Incas also cultivated cherimoya, the "custard apple" with a creamy, white flesh, which we first tasted on a flight down to Santiago, Chile, on our way to do a travel documentary.

They grew *pepino dulce,* a small purple and yellow fruit that tastes like honeydew, *arracacha,* a root related to celery and carrots and with a bit of the flavor of roasted chestnuts, and *nuñas,* beans that pop just like popcorn and taste a bit like peanuts (see page 498), and which one food writer described as "vegetarian caviar." But it was quinoa that most disturbed Pizarro, since it was used in the religious ceremonies, and he promptly banned it, making it illegal even to grow a small amount. He decreed that the Indians would henceforth be more "civilized" and in its place he ordered them to grow barley, out of which he made European-style *beer!*

Quinoa is not actually a cereal grain, though it is treated as such, but it is the fruit of an herb in the goosefoot family. It thrives in areas with very little rain, at very high altitudes, in thin cold air, or in hot sun and even in poor soil. Yet, in spite of the adverse conditions under which it grows, it seems to thrive and the plant can grow to as much as six feet in height. There are about 1,800 varieties of quinoa, with a range that covers the entire color wheel: white or pink, orange, green, red, purple or black.

The Aymara Indians on the altiplano of Bolivia still use the entire plant from top to bottom: eaten whole just as rice, or milled into flour, toasted and ground for tortillas or fermented to make a drink called *chicha.* The leaves are eaten as a vegetable or are used to feed the farm animals, the stalks are burned as fuel and we noted with great interest a report from food writer Rebecca Wood that she had seen the wash water from the rinsing of the seeds used as shampoo.

But the most important contribution of quinoa to the world of nutrition is the fact that it is truly a "super grain." It has rightly been called a nutritional powerhouse, and it is probably one of the best sources of protein among all the other cereal grains, containing as much as twice the amount as barley and rice. It is exceptionally high in lysine, an amino acid, as well as in calcium and iron. The Incas called it "the mother grain" and with good reason.

The Forms of Quinoa

A most interesting fact about quinoa from a botanical point of view is that the growing plant has a natural coat that acts as an insect repellant—*saponin.* If the grain is not washed before using it, the saponin tends to be bitter. Some of the quinoa now on the market in health food stores has been prewashed. The Quinoa Corporation, which now grows the grain in Colorado, tells us that they do prewash, and in a letter from David Schnorr, president of the company, which is now based in Torrance, California, he writes:

> However, we do recommend a brief rinsing under running water to remove any of the saponin bitterness. Quinoa can be toasted, but it is not necessary . . . some say that toasting does improve the flavor.

He goes on to say that you may find some tiny black and colored specks scattered within the regular strains. These are called "wild quinoa," and with the exception of

The

Versatile

Grain

and the

Elegant

Bean

142

looking a bit different and not cooking fully, they are no problem and you don't have to spend the time removing them.

We have been purchasing the prerinsed quinoa, and even though David Schnorr recommends that it be briefly rinsed, we have not been doing it and have found the taste quite acceptable. However, there are other varieties now appearing in the marketplace, and we suggest that you read the labels carefully. If they are not prewashed, swish them around in water several times to remove the saponin.

Basically, there are two forms of quinoa now being packaged, plus a range of pastas.

Whole Grain. It cooks completely in about twelve to fifteen minutes. Use it for a side dish in place of rice, or for stuffings, casseroles, even puddings and desserts.

Quinoa Flour. Found in health food stores, it is very low in gluten and thus we don't recommend it for making bread unless it's mixed with other flours such as unbleached white (see Quinoa Glazed Lemon Twist, page 149). It's ideal for allergy-free diets. You can also thicken soups with the flour or use it in your sauces. Stirred into boiling water, it makes a perfect infant cereal.

Quinoa Pastas. The range of pastas is now beginning to increase, both blended with wheat and wheat-free: spaghetti, rotelle, shells, elbows and spaghetti. Most of them are available in health food stores.

Quinoa

Grain & Granulation	Amount of Liquid	Cooking Method	Cooking & Standing Time	Approx. Yield	Comments
Whole Grain (1 C. dry)		All methods, use nonstick sauce-pan.			
	2 C.	*Method I* (see NOTE): Place grain in strainer and rinse several times. In 2-qt. saucepan, bring salted water to a boil. Stir in grain, return to boil, lower heat, cover and simmer.	12 to 15 minutes. Let stand 5 minutes.	3½ C.	A transparent "halo" forms around each tiny grain when cooking is completed.
	2 C.	*Method II:* Do not rinse grain. Use 2-qt. saucepan, toast grain first, stirring constantly over medium heat for 5 minutes. Then add boiling salted water. (It will splutter up.) Lower heat, cover and simmer.	5 minutes toasting. 10 to 12 minutes. Let stand 5 minutes.	3½ C.	

NOTE: The few black seeds found in the grain may not cook completely and may be a bit crunchy. If this is objectionable to you, pick over the dry grain and discard any black seeds before rinsing or toasting.

Roasted Chicken with Quinoa and Mixed Fruit Stuffing

SERVES 8

The complex and intense flavors of the stuffing permeate the chickens as they roast, changing a simple dish into unusual company fare.

Stuffing

YIELDS 5 CUPS

(enough for 2 chickens or 1 small turkey)

¼ lb. fennel pork sausage (1–2 sausages), removed from their casings and crumbled

1 large onion, finely chopped (1 C.)

1 large clove garlic, finely minced (½ tsp.)

1 large tart green apple, peeled and diced (about 1½ C.)

1 medium ripe pear, peeled and diced (about 1 C.)

1 large navel orange

⅔ C. dried currants

⅔ C. coarsely broken, toasted walnuts

1 Tbs. fresh thyme leaves (or 1 tsp. dried thyme)

1 tsp. ground coriander

3 C. cooked quinoa (use Method II, see Chart, opposite page)

2 Tbs. finely minced flat leaf parsley

Salt and freshly ground black pepper to taste

In a large skillet, sauté the crumbled sausage over medium heat until it loses its pink color. Lift out with a slotted spoon and set aside. To the same skillet, add the onions, and garlic and cook, stirring occasionally, for about 5 minutes or until the onions are transparent. Lower the heat, stir in the apples and pears and continue to cook, stirring occasionally.

Remove the peel from the orange with a vegetable peeler and mince it finely. Then peel and discard the white pith from the orange. Cut the orange into pieces and add to the skillet with the remaining ingredients, including the reserved sausage. Stir to combine, then cook for 2 minutes more. Set aside to cool. The stuffing can be prepared ahead and refrigerated. Any leftover stuffing can be frozen.

Chickens

Juice of 1 lemon

2 3-lb. chickens

Salt and freshly ground black pepper to taste

Olive oil for rubbing chickens

2 C. chicken stock for basting

Preheat the oven to 400°F. Squeeze the lemon juice inside and over the chickens. Sprinkle with salt and pepper and stuff each with about 2½ cups of the quinoa stuffing. Skewer cavities of the chickens and place them on a wire rack in a pan, breast side down. Rub a bit of olive oil over the chickens with your hands.

Pour half the stock into the bottom of the pan and roast the chickens for 40 minutes, basting once or twice with the stock and adding more as needed. Turn the chickens over, trickle more olive oil over them and continue to roast and baste for another 35 to 40 minutes.

Remove from the oven and place an aluminum foil tent over the chickens and let them rest for 10 minutes. Place the chickens on a warm serving platter, pour off the drippings into a measuring cup and skim off the surface fat. Reheat the sauce in a small pan and spoon over the chickens before serving.

Quinoa with Sweet and Sour Spiced Red Cabbage and Green Apple

SERVES 10 TO 12

A highly seasoned yet delicate balance of tastes and colors blend to make a lovely dish for vegetarians or a side dish that goes well with pork, poultry or beef.

3 Tbs. olive oil	1 bay leaf
2 large onions, coarsely chopped (1½ C.)	⅛ tsp. ground cloves
2 cloves garlic, crushed	½ tsp. ground ginger
¼ tsp. dried thyme	1 C. dry red wine
½ tsp. ground allspice	¾ C. sweet apple cider
¼ tsp. freshly ground black pepper or to taste	1 large Granny Smith apple, peeled and shredded (about ½ lb.)
2-lb. head red cabbage, coarsely chopped (8 C.)	⅓ C. red wine vinegar
Salt to taste	2 Tbs. mild light honey
⅓ C. dried currants	3½ C. cooked quinoa (use Method II, see Chart, page 144)
½ tsp. whole caraway seeds	2 Tbs. finely minced curly leaf parsley

Heat the olive oil in a 12-inch sauté pan. Add the onions, garlic, thyme, allspice and pepper and sauté over medium high heat for 2 to 3 minutes, stirring frequently, until the onions are translucent. Stir in the cabbage and salt and continue to cook, stirring frequently, until the cabbage is wilted. Stir in the currants, caraway seed, bay leaf, ground cloves and ginger, then add the wine, cider and shredded apple. Cover and simmer for 10 minutes.

Mix the vinegar and honey together and stir into the cabbage. Cover and simmer for 10 more minutes. Then uncover and simmer for 30 minutes or until all the liquid is absorbed. Taste to see if you need additional salt and pepper, more honey or more vinegar. (You may prepare the cabbage the day before to allow the flavors to mellow.)

To serve, spoon the red cabbage in a border on a large serving platter, pile the fluffy quinoa in the center and sprinkle both with the parsley.

The

Versatile

Grain

and the

Elegant

Bean

146

Warm Quinoa Salad with Fennel, Chicken, Prosciutto and Tangerines

SERVES 6 TO 8

A warm, main course salad, in perfect synergism—sweet tangerines and licorice-like fennel, mildly saline prosciutto and delicate fluffy quinoa topped with shreds of sautéed chicken. A true palate teaser.

Orange Vinaigrette
MAKES ½ CUP

3 Tbs. thawed frozen orange juice concentrate, not diluted
1 Tbs. coarse-grain mustard, plus 1 teaspoon
2 Tbs. red wine vinegar

1 Tbs. balsamic vinegar
Salt and freshly ground black pepper to taste
3 Tbs. olive oil

In a small bowl, mix the orange juice and mustard, both vinegars and the salt and pepper, using a whisk. Slowly add the olive oil, whisking constantly. Set the dressing aside while preparing the salad.

Quinoa Salad

10-oz. bulb of fresh fennel, trimmed (save 1 Tbs. fennel fronds for garnish)
1 small lemon, plus 1 wedge lemon
Pinch salt
1 C. slivered, trimmed of fat prosciutto di Parma (about 2 ozs.)
2 Tbs. olive oil

1 lb. skinned, boned chicken breasts, trimmed of fat
Freshly ground black pepper to taste
3½ C. cooked hot quinoa (use Method II, see Chart, page 144)
2–3 scallions, thinly sliced on the diagonal (½ C.)
2 tangerines

Cut the fennel into quarters and put into a 2-quart saucepan. Cover with water and squeeze the juice from the small lemon into the water, also adding the wedge of lemon and a pinch of salt as well. Bring to a boil, then drain and discard the lemon wedge. Run cold water over the fennel and drain well on paper towels. Slice the fennel thinly.

Transfer the fennel to a large bowl and stir in the prosciutto, then set aside. In a medium nonstick skillet, heat the olive oil, blot the chicken breasts with paper towels, season with salt and pepper and sauté for 3 to 5 minutes on each side, or until they are just cooked through. Cool slightly, then cut into ½-inch strips and set aside.

Add the cooked quinoa to the bowl with the fennel and prosciutto and stir in the scallions. With a zester tool, shred enough tangerine peel (about 1 tablespoon) for the garnish and set aside. Then cut off and discard the remaining peel along with the white pith. Using a sharp knife, remove the pits and cut the tangerines into individual sections. Add to the quinoa mixture along with the orange vinaigrette and toss gently to combine.

Pile on a serving platter, place the pieces of chicken around the edge of the platter, scatter the reserved tangerine peel and fennel fronds on top as a garnish. Serve warm.

Quinoa and Yogurt Muffins with Apricot Preserves and Pine Nuts

MAKES 12 MUFFINS

Feather-light, these muffins have tart apricot jam in their middles, along with toasted pine nuts, which adds to the flavor of the quinoa grain. They freeze well and can be rewarmed for whenever you get your "muffin mania."

Butter for greasing muffin pan	1 egg
1 C. quinoa flour	4 Tbs. melted butter, cooled
1 C. all-purpose flour	1 C. plain yogurt
1 tsp. baking soda	¼ C. milk
¼ tsp. salt or to taste	2 Tbs. light mild honey
¼ C. sugar	1 tsp. vanilla extract
½ C. pine nuts	¼ C. apricot preserves

Preheat the oven to 400°F. Butter only the bottoms of a 12-cup muffin pan and set aside. In a large bowl, sift together both flours, the baking soda, salt and sugar. Take off 2 tablespoons of the pine nuts and set aside. Then toast the remaining pine nuts in the oven in a pie pan for 5 minutes, shaking the pan a few times so they don't burn. Cool them slightly, then add to the dry ingredients.

In a smaller bowl, whisk the egg until it's lightly beaten, then whisk in the butter, yogurt, milk, honey and vanilla until thoroughly combined. Make a well in the flour mixture, add the yogurt mixture all at once and swiftly combine with a fork. The batter should be somewhat lumpy.

Spoon 1 tablespoon of the batter into each prepared muffin cup. Then spoon 1 teaspoon of apricot preserves over the batter. Top with another tablespoon of batter and scatter the reserved 2 tablespoons of untoasted pine nuts equally over the tops of each muffin. Bake for 15 to 20 minutes until golden. Test the center with a cake tester, which should be clean on removal. Loosen at once by running a knife around the sides of each muffin. Then remove to cool on a wire rack. Serve slightly warm.

The

Versatile

Grain

and the

Elegant

Bean

148

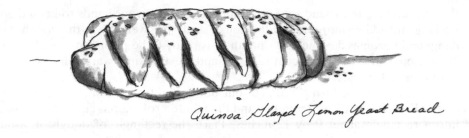

Quinoa Glazed Lemon Yeast Bread

Quinoa Glazed Lemon Twist
(A Sweet Bread)

1 LARGE LOAF

This is a recipe based upon a traditional Swiss sweet bread, but with a twist—the addition of the marvelous taste of quinoa flour. It's a festive bread, just right for luncheon or teatime.

¾ C. milk	2 eggs
¼ lb. unsalted, softened butter (½ C.), plus 1 Tbs. melted butter	Juice of 1 lemon (about 4–5 Tbs.)
⅓ C. sugar	Peel of 1 lemon, minced finely
½ tsp. salt	½ C. quinoa flour
1 ¼-oz. package dry yeast	3–3½ C. all-purpose flour
½ C. warm water	Oil for rising bowl
Pinch sugar	Butter for greasing baking sheet

Glaze

Juice of ½ medium lemon (about 2–3 Tbs.)	2 Tbs. sliced almonds
⅔ C. confectioners' sugar	

In a saucepan, scald the milk and then pour it into a large mixing bowl. Cut up the butter and add it along with the sugar and the salt and let cool to lukewarm.

Put the yeast into a glass, add the warm water and the pinch of sugar. Mix well to dissolve the yeast and let stand for 5 to 10 minutes to proof. The yeast will bubble up after that time. If it doesn't, discard it and use a fresh package.

When the yeast has proofed, stir it into the milk and butter mixture. Then, in a small bowl, beat the eggs with the lemon juice and the minced peel and add to the large bowl.

Now add the flours ½ cup at a time, mixing with a wooden spoon as you do so. When the dough pulls away from the sides of the bowl, turn it out onto a lightly floured surface, and knead for 5 to 8 minutes, flouring your hands to keep them from sticking and adding more flour if the dough seems too wet. When the dough is slightly damp and becomes flexible and smooth, it is ready to be put in an oiled bowl to rise. Turn it once in the bowl to coat it, cover and let stand in a warm place for 1 hour or until doubled in bulk.

When doubled, turn the dough out onto a lightly floured surface and punch it down. Knead about 1 or 2 minutes and then flour a rolling pin and roll out the dough into a rectangle about 9 by 12 inches. Place the rectangle of dough on a buttered baking sheet. Then, dip a sharp knife into flour and cut diagonal slashes (as in the drawing) all the way through to the baking sheet. Using the 1 tablespoon of melted butter, butter the ends of each "finger" before folding them up one by one to overlap and form the final shape of the loaf. Cover lightly with a clean kitchen towel and put in a warm place to double in bulk for a second rising, about 45 minutes.

Preheat the oven to 325°F. Put the loaf in for 10 minutes and then raise the heat to 350°F and bake for 30 to 35 more minutes or until the loaf looks golden brown. Remove from the oven and let the loaf cool on a wire rack for 15 minutes before applying the glaze.

Mix the lemon juice with the confectioners' sugar and apply to the top of the loaf, then set the almonds into the glaze in a decorative manner. Serve warm or at room temperature.

how to braid
Quinoa Glazed Lemon Yeast Bread

The

Versatile

Grain

and the

Elegant

Bean

150

Baked Miniature Pumpkins Filled with Quinoa, Apple and Fig Custard

SERVES 8

Although the tiny saffron-colored pumpkins are in season only from October through January, they cover lots of holidays from Columbus Day to Halloween, Thanksgiving, Christmas and New Year's. When they're filled with a custard of quinoa, dried figs and pecans, they make a more then welcome and very unusual holiday addition to the dessert menu.

8 miniature pumpkins, weighing about ¾ lb. each	¼ tsp. pumpkin pie spice mix
1½ C. milk	1 medium Granny Smith apple, peeled and finely chopped (⅔ C.)
3 eggs	Few drops lemon juice
Pinch salt	6–8 dried figs, finely diced (½ C.)
½ C. light brown sugar	½ C. coarsely broken, toasted pecans
1 tsp. vanilla extract	1 C. heavy cream
1¾ C. cooked quinoa (use Method I, see Chart, page 144)	1 Tbs. fine sugar
	1 tsp. brandy
½ tsp. cinnamon	Fig leaves for plates (optional)

Slice off the stem ends of the pumpkins about 1 inch down, making a lid. Set the lids aside. Scoop out and discard the seeds and the strings from the center, leaving about a ½-inch to ¾-inch wall. Place the pumpkins in one or two shallow baking dishes.

Preheat the oven to 350°F. and boil a kettle of water. In a large mixing bowl, add the milk and the eggs and whisk to combine. Add the salt, sugar and vanilla and whisk again. Then stir in the cooked quinoa and the remaining ingredients except the heavy cream, fine sugar and brandy. Fill each pumpkin with 4 to 5 tablespoons of the filling. Pour 1 inch of boiling water into the bottom of the pans and bake for 45 to 60 minutes. Test the flesh of the pumpkin with the point of a knife to see if they are tender. Remove them from the oven and cool them to lukewarm.

Whip the cream and the fine sugar with a beater until stiff. Then whip in the brandy and set aside.

Serve the pumpkins warm on a fig leaf (if you have access to a fig tree) or on a paper doily. Place the reserved lid on the side of the plate for decoration and spoon some brandied whipped cream on top of each pumpkin.

Miniature Pumpkins filled with Quinoa, Apple è Fig Custard

Quinoa Pasta, Cheese and Fruit Pudding

SERVES 8

Wheat-free quinoa pasta is a blessing for those who are allergic to wheat. This untraditional dessert, based upon a Jewish kugel, made with cheese, custard, apples and raisins, is made with delicate quinoa pasta in place of the traditional noodles.

Butter for greasing baking dish
Salt to taste, plus ¼ tsp.
  6 ozs. quinoa pasta elbows or shells (see NOTE)
  2 Tbs. butter
3-oz. package cream cheese, cut into pieces
  ½ lb. lowfat small curd cottage cheese or ricotta cheese
  ½ C. sour cream

½ C. sugar
3 eggs, separated
1½ tsps. vanilla extract
½ tsp. cinnamon
2 tsps. finely minced lemon peel
2 large Granny Smith apples, peeled, cored and coarsely chopped (2½ C.)
⅓ C. raisins, either dark or golden

Butter a 2-quart baking dish and preheat the oven to 350°F. Boil a large pot of water, add salt to taste and cook the pasta for 5 to 6 minutes. Drain and transfer to a larger bowl and toss with the butter while the pasta is hot. Set aside.

To the bowl of a food processor, add the cream cheese, cottage cheese, sour cream and sugar and process until smooth. Add the egg yolks only, one at a time, and process after each addition. Add the vanilla, cinnamon and lemon peel. Scrape the mixture into the bowl of pasta and stir in the apples and raisins.

In a medium-size bowl, whip the egg whites with a beater, adding the ¼ teaspoon salt and beating until the whites are stiff. Then fold into the cheese-pasta mixture. Spoon into the prepared baking dish and bake for 40 to 45 minutes or until the surface is browned. Let stand for 20 minutes before cutting. Serve warm.

NOTE: Not *all* quinoa pastas are wheat-free. The ones that are wheat-free are pale yellow and are clearly labeled as such. Others are brown and contain wheat. Read the package label carefully.

The

Versatile

Grain

and the

Elegant

Bean

152

Rice

Oryza, O. sativa

The "Bread" of Half the World

As with all travelers, it has always been of special interest to us to see the changes that have taken place in a favorite city or country over a period of years. Through our documentary film work, we have been lucky enough to make many trips to particular locations, finding first that the *physical* look of a city has undergone a "face lift," such as the burgeoning, ever-changing skyline of Hong Kong or downtown Los Angeles. But we also find that changes have taken place in much more subtle ways.

For example, in comparing our first of six trips to Japan back in 1961 to the latest one just two years ago, it was the evolution of *food habits* that caught our attention, at least the surface manifestations. Where once the universal breakfast, even in the larger cities, was a bowl of rice covered with raw egg, pieces of seaweed and dried raw fish with a bowl of miso soup on the side, we noted that menus now include scrambled eggs or toast and marmalade (and probably the best brewed coffee in the world).

Okayu, a Japanese rice porridge version of the Chinese *congee,* has generally been relegated to the countryside inns and as easily digestible food for invalids. In addition, a veritable explosion of fast food palaces has taken place, along with the birth of some very good restaurants that range from French bistro cooking to the fare of the Chinese, Turks, Greeks, Scandinavians, Russians and Americans.

First impressions, of course, are frequently wrong. Thus, if the occasional visitor thinks that the traditions of Japan are being replaced by the Golden Arches or Westernized beyond repair, he or she couldn't be more wrong. For underneath the expansion of Japan into a global host for both tourist and businessperson, along with the natural expansion of all the things that remind them of home, the soul and spirit of the country—as well as its food—is right where it has always been for thousands of years. And it is *rice* that remains the staff of life. And if we speak of rice in Japan, it is *Japanese rice* and no other substitute, for they prefer a short grain, more glutinous variety than our long grain rice.

There are stories, at first thought apocryphal, but later turning out to be true, that Japanese businessmen have actually brought their own rice to the United States in fear of not being able to find it here. (It *is* available.) And with all the changes taking place, with all the innovative introduction of words like "Big Mac" and "Whopper" and "pizza," the Japanese word for *meal* remains the same and probably always will. *Gohan* (han—rice; go—highest reverence) is the word for *cooked rice,* which in turn means *meal,* accompanied by fish or meat or bean curd or vegetables.

All over the countryside, the traveler sees shrines dedicated to Inari, the rice god, and rice is still the offering given to both the Shinto gods and those of Buddhism. In November of 1990, when Prince Akihito became the one hundred and twenty-fifth emperor, following his father, the late Hirohito, he put on a white ceremonial robe, went into a shrine to commune with the spirit of his ancestors and then ate millet and *rice* before coming out just before dawn as the new ruler.

We have used Japan as only a single example, but what we have written might well be the story of most of the world. For in spite of what we think of as "modernization" or "Westernization," the traditional bowl of rice is by far the most important food in the world today. Half of the world's population eats it three times a day, and it is an important and vital component in the dishes of Africa, Asia, South America, and parts of North America and Europe. Where *we* eat bread as a filler, rice in most parts of the world is the *core* of the entire meal.

Americans eat less than 10 pounds of rice per year as compared with the people of the Far East (including Japan), who consume up to *400 pounds per person,* providing half their daily caloric intake. (Parenthetically, we might add that the French, even with their tradition of superb cooking in other areas, eat even less than we do—about 5 pounds per person each year.)

Though we generally associate rice with Asia, and particularly with China, it probably did not originate in that country. Most food historians feel that it was first grown in India about 3000 B.C., though in 1970 some grains of rice were uncovered by a team of archaeologists in Thailand and they've dated them back to abut 3500 B.C. In any case, the crop moved out from Asia and thrived wherever there was abundant water, and where during the growing season the plants could be submerged in from one to eight inches of water. Conditions in the Po Valley of Italy were perfect, just as in the terraces of the Philippines and Indonesia and in the fields of Thailand, and to this day the traveler stands in awe at the breathtaking beauty of the seedlings being planted in their watery beds.

Rice came to the United States at the end of the seventeenth century, when a ship bound for England was blown off course by a severe storm, forcing it to dock at Charleston, South Carolina. In gratitude for the help given by the citizens, the captain of the ship gave the governor of the colony some rice grains, which were duly planted. Today, our rice comes from the Carolinas, Louisiana, Texas and California, and though we grow less than 1 percent of the rice crop of the world, we export about 10 billion pounds each year, nearly 70 percent of what we grow.

The

Versatile

Grain

and the

Elegant

Bean

154

Throughout most of the world, hand labor is still the norm, and we can think of several places where we have stood and watched the planting of seedlings by long rows of farmers and their families, bending either to a singsong rhythm chanted with each stoop of the body, or to the mournful beat of a drum to keep the line moving in a synchronous cadence. Using the ancient methods, it takes about 400 person/days to plant, fertilize and harvest one acre of rice.

Here in the United States, most of our fields are irrigated and then the seeding of the beds is done by *airplane*. The 400 person/days of the rest of the world have been brought down to only *2 days* for the very same tasks. We remember with joy a film that we were producing for the National Council of Farmer Cooperatives, with part of our story being about the rice fields near Sacramento, California.

We stood at one end of a flooded field and watched in childlike wonder as a biplane approached the other end, guided by a young woman on the ground who wildly waved a flag to keep it on its path. As the plane flew over the beginning of the flooded beds, the pilot touched a button and the seed floated down into the water. One quick pass and the first row was done. At that point, the farmer came over to our crew and said quite seriously, "I understand that in Asia they do all this by hand!"

It is interesting to note that rice, for all its universal appeal, is not one of the most nutritious of grains. Though it is low in fat and sodium and high in fiber, it is composed of about 80 percent carbohydrates, with only a small amount of protein, vitamin B_1, phosphorus and potassium. However, when it's combined with other ingredients, such as in the healthful "ricenbeans" (one word) that we've mentioned before and to which we've devoted other recipes in this book, it makes a remarkably economical and nutritious addition to our diets.

Another factor that makes rice worth looking at more than once is the proliferation of the *types* that have begun to become available. Until just recently, with over 7,000 varieties of rice being grown around the world, the major form utilized by Americans has been the long grain white rice, with about 98 percent of all sales in that category and the remaining 2 percent as basic brown rice (see The Basic Forms of Rice, pages 156–157). However, health food stores, specialty shops and even some supermarkets have begun to offer many other interesting varieties: *basmati* rice from India, *sweet glutinous rice* from Japan, *arborio* from Italy and black *Japonica* from Thailand.

Our travels and visits to local ethnic restaurants have begun to make us more aware of the versatility of this popular grain. The *jambalaya* of the Carolinas, the *risengröt* of Scandinavia, the *picadillo* of Cuba and the *paella* of Spain, the *risottos* of Italy, the *rijstafel* of Indonesia, and even the sake of Japan and the *dirty rice* of New Orleans are all "alive and well" in spite of what the philosopher Nietzsche thought. He was quite certain that the eating of rice drove people to opium!

Brown Rice or White Rice?

There is a continuing debate that pits proponents of "white and processed is good" against "brown and natural is poor people's fodder" (or "only for health food nuts") and the subject of rice might be a perfect example of that controversy. And we Americans are not alone.

Of course, when harvested directly from the paddies and the flooded irrigated fields, all rice is "brown," in that it contains the hull (which will be removed), the bran and the germ, and it is exceedingly high in fiber. However, even the Japanese have always considered white rice as the preferred choice, and during World War II, they took their rations of brown rice home, milled it, removed the bran and the embryo buds to convert it to a polished, less nutritious variety. Thus, our own preference for white long grain rice is not at all unusual. In fact, we can trace our own history on the subject back to the era following the Civil War, when the polished white rice in the South gave plantation workers a severe case of beriberi, until someone discovered that the B vitamins could be replaced.

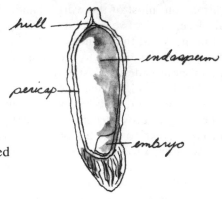

Cross section of a rice kernel

In processing rice to change it from brown to white, machines strip the brown bran layer, leaving a pure carbohydrate white grain. Most of the vitamins, minerals, amino acids, polyunsaturated fats and the fiber are lost.

But we understand only too well that some people just don't like the stronger flavor and the chewier texture of brown rice (just look at the sales figures!) and many of our own recipes utilize white rice as a result. If brown rice is not to your liking, the best solution is to choose the *converted* white rice (which Uncle Ben made famous), since the process of steaming converted rice before milling forces about 70 percent of the nutrients of the bran and germ back into the grain. This includes some of the B vitamins, thiamin, niacin and iron. It also allows the rice to retain about 85 percent of the protein of the original grain. The biggest loss, perhaps, is that most of the fiber is also forfeited.

The Basic Forms of Rice

Long Grain. For either white or brown, long grain rice has the largest kernels. After cooking, the grains remain fluffy and separate, making it perfect for pilafs, salads, poultry stuffings or as a side dish to accompany meat or fish. For brown long grain rice, the hull is removed but the germ and bran are left on the kernel. For white long grain rice, several versions are available on the supermarket shelves:

- **Converted.** Sometimes called "parboiled," converted rice is steamed and pressurized before milling, thus replacing some of the nutrients back into the kernel. This type of rice contains more nutrient value than the two others listed below and is the better choice for the home cook who prefers the white to the brown rice.

The

Versatile

Grain

and the

Elegant

Bean

156

- **Enriched.** Some of the nutrients that are lost in the polishing process are partially replaced in the "enriched" brands.
- **Instant** (or precooked). The rice is partially cooked and then dehydrated. And since it is the least nourishing of all the forms available, most nutritionists pass it off with just two words: *Forget it!* We wholeheartedly agree. In addition, since it is the most highly processed, it also costs more than the other types while giving you the least for your money.

Medium Grain. Brown or white. These are shorter grains than the long grain rice, and they have a better cohesive quality, making them the choice for some pancakes and puddings. Medium grain is not quite as sticky as the short grain rice.

Short Grain. Brown or white. The short grain rice has thicker kernels than the long or medium grain. They are also much softer and they stick together when cooked. Generally, they are used in dishes like risottos (see arborio below), rice balls or croquettes.

Glutinous Rice. A still stickier version of the short grain variety, also known as sweet rice, sticky or waxy rice. The broad, short grains are usually used in the cooking of Southeast Asia for sticky sweets or snacks, as well as for a variety of desserts. It is also the rice used for Japanese sushi.

A Rice Glossary: Some Other Types

In these past few years, much has changed when it comes to our familiarity with rice, over and above the popular white rice and the brown rice of the natural food aficionados. We've even noticed that many Chinese and Japanese restaurants have begun to place signs in their windows and notes on their menus telling their customers that brown rice is available on request.

In addition, through travel, the proliferation of magazine articles on health and nutrition and the growing sophistication of the American public, other rice varieties have become more familiar and more available. Even as this book was being written, still newer varieties began to come to the marketplace. The list continues to grow.

Arborio. The most popular imported name in this category, it is a short grain rice from the Piedmont section of Italy. Each grain has a translucent outer portion and an opaque center. When cooked, it yields a creamy product with an al dente firm-to-the-tooth consistency, and thus it is the prime choice for the Italian risottos. It also has an ability to absorb large amounts of liquid: wine, water or stock. Several other varieties in the same family are now beginning to appear.

Vialone Nano. A smaller kernel than arborio, and currently sold only in Italian specialty markets. It makes a very creamy risotto. Other names that might catch your eye as they become more available are *canaroli* and *tesori*. There is also a California variety called *pearl* that can be used in place of the Italian arborio. A Spanish short grain rice, grown in Valencia and known as *granza,* is now being imported. It is short, very round and quite plump and is used mostly for paellas.

Red Rice or Christmas Rice. This is basically a brown short grain rice and similar in color to Wehani. It is now being grown domestically in California by Lundberg from an Asian strain. It has a russet color and an unusual wild mushroom–like flavor. The special selection Christmas Rice now contains some longer-grained Wehani, but Harlan Lundberg tells us that, in the future, the rice will all be short grain.

Basmati. Named after the tropical basmati blossom of Southeast Asia, it is grown in Iran, India and Pakistan, and is a long grain aromatic variety. Generally, basmati rice is aged for at least a year after harvest in order to develop its full flavor. Some specialty shops also carry *unhulled basmati,* an extra-long-grain variety that is chewier than the hulled rice, and has a taste and texture that we find is a bit like wild rice. There are a few homegrown varieties of aromatic rice that are much milder in flavor: *Texamati.* Grown, of course, in Texas. *Wehani.* A California variety that is reddish-brown. *Wild Pecan Rice.* It has no pecans. However, it is gently milled to retain most of the bran and the taste is evocative of the pecan nut. It was developed by Louisiana State University and it's produced by the oldest rice mill in the United States down in New Iberia.

Popcorn Rice. We came across this long grain rice quite by accident and in our usual cynicism, followed through and said, "Prove it—does it really smell like popcorn when it cooks?" We found that it had been developed by Nelson Jodan at the Louisiana Experimental Station about thirty years ago. It is being grown by Ellis Stansel down in Gueydan, Louisiana (pronounced *Gay*'don) and he sent up a sample of *ten pounds!* It is probably one of the best rice varieties that we've ever worked with or tasted and it handles beautifully. And yes, it does smell just like popcorn when it cooks. We think it may be a distant cousin of basmati, but we won't argue. See the Stansel listing in the section on Mail Order Sources (see pages 501–506).

The

Versatile

Grain

and the

Elegant

Bean

158

Thai Black Rice (Japonica). Though grown in Thailand for centuries, it is among the newest novelty imports to become available to the home cook. Unlike most varieties of long grain rice, the black rice is quite sticky and shiny, and in Thailand it is usually used for making desserts. Another unusual aspect is that its dark color leaches into the cooking water, turning it purple and staining the end product, since the bran coating on this rice is more soluble.

Jasmine White Rice. The jasmine rice is a soft, very white, delicately flavored long grain aromatic rice. It's grown in the southern United States and in Thailand, and it can be substituted for both the domestic and the imported basmati rice.

Wild Rice. Not truly a rice, but the seed of a wild aquatic plant usually found in the Great Lakes section of the United States as well as in Canada. The seeds are hand-gathered, making wild rice much more expensive than the varieties of true rice. We have devoted an entire chapter to wild rice (see page 259).

Some Rice Products: A Catalogue

Since rice is one of the three or four most popular grain forms, it comes as no surprise that not only do new varieties continue to appear, but also that there is a growing catalogue of rice forms and rice products. One of the leaders in this development has been the Lundberg Family Farm in Richvale, California. We've watched with interest as their organic rice farms have flourished and their product line has expanded to include such things as their Wehani rice, Wild Rice Blends, Rizcous, and Red Rice or Christmas Rice.

Other companies have also joined in the marketing steeplechase and both the supermarkets and the natural food stores have begun to offer a vast array of rice cookies and crackers, rice breakfast cereals and processed products. Here, then, is a partial list of what we might call "the standards" plus some of the more unusual:

Rice Bran. The outside brown layer of the rice kernel that contains the bran and a small part of the germ. Its major advantage is that it is very high in dietary fiber (nearly twice that of oat bran), and thus it has begun to be lauded as the next cholesterol buster. However, as they always say, "more research is needed" and nutritionists have found that the benefits of rice bran work with only *some* individuals, with a large amount of bran required to reduce cholesterol. This has not stopped the processed food industry from flooding the marketplace with new snack foods and crackers as well as with exaggerated claims. We withhold judgment, feeling as always, that *all* dietary fiber is good for you, with whatever grain you consume. In calmer times, rice bran can be used in baking cookies or breads or muffins (mixed with wheat flour) or for adding to dishes such as meat loaf.

Rice Bran Oil. At the time of this writing, this is slowly becoming "the new kid on the block." Current studies have been conducted only with monkeys, but they have begun to show that rice bran oil can raise the high-density "good" lipoprotein while reducing the "bad" low-density lipoprotein, thus also reducing the harmful

cholesterol. Just as with rice bran, "more research is needed," but if rice bran oil does turn out to have the same effect in humans as in our primate cousins, the benefits may well be worth the two-tablespoon-dose daily that the scientists are predicting.

Rice Cakes and Rice Crackers. The cakes are generally made from puffed rice while the crackers are baked with rice flour, and for those on wheat- and gluten-free diets, only the rice product is used to make a crispy product. A wide variety is now available and just recently Lundberg Family Farm has developed a *popcorn cake* made of rice (salted or unsalted) that is available in natural food stores.

Rice Cream. Coarsely ground rice, generally used for breakfast cereals or for puddings. If you can't find it premilled and prepacked, you can prepare rice cream in your home blender or spice grinder.

Rice Polish. The flour taken off the rice during the process of making white rice. It also contains small parts of the germ and the bran, with a high content of vitamins, iron and fiber. You can use it in baked goods in very much the same way as corn or wheat germ.

Puffed Rice. The rice is puffed under pressure and then expanded by filling the grains with air. Puffed rice makes an excellent cold breakfast cereal with milk and fresh fruits, as most of our readers have no doubt discovered for themselves, since puffed rice is one of the best-selling commercially packaged cereals in our supermarkets. However, it can also be used for making cakes and candy.

Rice Vinegar. In Japan, rice vinegar is generally used as an accompaniment for sushi and other dishes. The Chinese also use it as a seasoning and it comes in various strengths and colors. You might want to try it for a change the next time you mix a Western-style salad dressing.

The

Versatile

Grain

and the

Elegant

Bean

160

Rice Flakes. Heated and pressed flat under pressure, rice flakes are processed in very much the same way as rolled oats, but they're a bit thicker. They're fine for cooked, hot morning breakfasts in place of rolled oats, and the flakes can also be included in breads and other baked goods.

Rice Flour. Available in white or brown. The flour can be used as a thickener for puddings or in a variety of baked dishes, and since it has no gluten, it's another perfect product for those with wheat allergies. Otherwise, is should be mixed with other gluten flours for baking and cooking. Rice flour has a much silkier texture than the wheat flours.

Rice Meal. The rice is ground and generally mixed with rice cream to make a breakfast cereal.

Rice Noodles. Made from rice flour, the noodles come in various thicknesses. The Chinese use the rice noodles for *mai fun* dishes—wide, flat noodles with beef or pork—while the Malaysians use them for a traditional *laksa*. A thinner variety of rice noodle is the basic ingredient for a wonderfully crisp Thai dish called *mee krob*.

Rice Paper (Banh trang). We first tasted this in Vietnam and you can try them in the Vietnamese restaurants that have now sprung up across the country. They're thin rounds or triangles of dried rice dough and they're soaked and used as wrappers for traditional dishes such as *cha gio*—a Vietnamese version of the Chinese spring roll. The entire roll is wrapped in lettuce with mint and basil leaves and then dipped in a fermented fish sauce called *nuoc cham* that includes chiles and lime juice.

Rice Syrup. An organic brown rice sweetener (produced by the Lundberg Family Farms).

Rice Tea (Toasted). There are two versions: the Japanese (*genmai cha*) and the Chinese (*sao my cha*) and it is usually mixed with an equal amount of green tea (*matsu-cha*) before brewing. It is served hot and has a somewhat nutty flavor.

Rice Wine. As with rice tea, the Chinese and the Japanese both produce it, and you have no doubt sampled the most commonly known Japanese form: *sake* (a tiny, warm or cold beverage with a tremendous kick). The Chinese use rice wine for both cooking and for drinking, while the Japanese have a special sweet form (*mirin*) used for cooking.

Rice at a Glance

Rice Variety	Description	Cooking Method	Cooking & Standing Time	Approx. Yield	Comments
White (1 C. raw) Tested with Carolina brand	Thin, long polished opaque kernels with hull, bran and germ removed, leaving only the endosperm. When cooked, slightly firm, fluffy, dry, separated grains. Bland mild flavor.	Use 2-qt., non-stick saucepan and 2 C. salted water (¼ to ½ tsp. salt), 1 tsp. or 1 Tbs. butter (optional). Bring to boil, stir in rice, return to boil, stir in rice, return to boil, cover and lower heat. Simmer.	15 to 18 minutes. Let stand 5 minutes. Fork-fluff after standing.	3¼ C.	Pilafs, side dishes, casseroles, salads.
Brown (1 C. raw)	Beige and opaque. Hulled, but with bran and germ intact. Contains some green and russet grains. When cooked, texture is chewier and flavor is nuttier and more intense than white rice, but fluffier than short grain brown rice.	Follow same instructions as above, but increase water to 2¼ to 2½ C., since brown rice takes longer to cook.	30 to 45 minutes, depending upon brand and age of rice. Let stand 10 minutes. Fork-fluff after standing.	3¼ C.	This nutritious rice is one that vegetarians prefer, along with short grain brown rice. As an all-purpose rice, it can be used in the same dishes as above.

Rice at a Glance (cont.)

Rice Variety	Description	Cooking Method	Cooking & Standing Time	Approx. Yield	Comments
Converted Rice (1 C. raw) Tested with Uncle Ben's	Although "white," it is slightly tan and transparent, sometimes referred to as "parboiled." It is steamed under pressure before milling, forcing more bran and germ nutrient back into grain. Mild pleasant flavor, slightly sticky texture.	Cook in same manner as above but increase amount of water to 2¼ C.	20 to 22 minutes. Let stand 10 minutes. Fork-fluff after standing.	3¼ C.	Can be used in same dishes as above.
Instant Rice (1 C. raw) Tested with Minute Rice	White grain, slightly puffed. It is partially cooked and then dehydrated. The process makes the rice lose most of its nutrition.	FOLLOW PACKAGE INSTRUCTIONS	FOLLOW PACKAGE INSTRUCTIONS		We do not like the taste or the texture. We do not recommend it.

Rice Variety	Description	Cooking Method	Cooking & Standing Time	Approx. Yield	Comments
Imported White Basmati (1 C. raw) (India, Pakistan)	Aged for 1 year to develop full flavor. Long slender opaque grain, ranging in color from white to tan in raw state. When cooking, mildly fragrant. When cooked, results in very long grains, firm, white and fluffy with separated grains.	Pick over and remove broken grains and foreign matter. *Wash well* and rinse several times. In a 2-qt. saucepan, use 1¾ C. salted water. Butter optional. Follow same instructions as long grain white rice.	18 to 20 minutes. Let stand 5 minutes	3¼ C.	Proper rice to use with Indian and Middle Eastern cuisine. Excellent for pilafs.
Domestic White Basmati (Texmati) (1 C. raw)	Texas-grown, domestic variety, a combination of basmati and long grain American. Creamier color when raw. Fluffier, milder in flavor and aroma than imported basmati.	Does *not* require washing. Use 1¾ C. salted water. Follow same instructions as long grain white rice.	15 to 18 minutes.	3⅓ C.	Use in place of imported basmati for milder-flavored pilafs.

Rice at a Glance (cont.)

Rice Variety	Description	Cooking Method	Cooking & Standing Time	Approx. Yield	Comments
Imported and Domestic Jasmine White Rice (1 C. raw)	Long grain white aromatic. Grown in southern U.S. and Thailand. Long, white, opaque when raw. Soft, very white, delicately mild flavor. Separated grains when cooked.	Does *not* require washing. Use 1¾ C. salted water in 2-qt. saucepan. Follow same instructions as white long grain rice.	18 minutes. Let stand 5 minutes	3¼ C.	Same as basmati rice.
White Popcorn Rice (1 C. raw)	Very white, long grain domestic Louisiana rice. Smells like a movie theater lobby while cooking. White, long, separated grains after cooking. Very flavorful.	Use 2 cups salted water in 2-qt. saucepan. Butter optional. Follow long grain white rice cooking instructions.	15 minutes. Let stand 5 minutes.	4 C.	Excellent. Our favorite for pilafs, salads, casseroles, side dishes.
Wild Pecan Rice (1 C. raw)	Contains no pecans or wild rice. Long grain Louisiana, amber-colored rice containing some of the	Cook same as long grain white rice.	20 minutes. Let stand 5 minutes.	3 C.	Use in place of long grain brown rice when milder flavor is wanted. Good in curries, stuffings (cont.)

Rice Variety	Description	Cooking Method	Cooking & Standing Time	Approx. Yield	Comments
	bran. After cooking, re- sembles brown rice.				and with game.
Brown Bas- mati (1 C. raw)	Light tan grain. Contains bran coat and includes some russet and greenish grain. (See BOX, page 170). After cooking, has more intense flavor than white basmati and is more nourishing.	Wash before cooking. If grain is uneven in size, soak for 1 hour be- fore cooking. Use 2¼ C. salted water in 2-qt. saucepan.	40 minutes. Let stand 5 minutes.	3⅓ C.	Use with highly spiced curries, since flavor is strong and nutty.
Wehani (Brown Rice) (1 C. raw)	Dark russet in color, a Cali- fornia aromatic hybrid. Brown rice crossed with Indian basmati. Very nutty flavor after cooking. Sticky, tooth- some texture.	Rinse well. Use 2½ C. water. *Salt after cooking* or rice will not absorb suffi- cient water.	40 minutes. Let stand 10 minutes.	2⅔ C.	Use in salads for texture and color and slight wild rice flavor.
Black (Japon- ica) Thai Black Rice (1 C. raw)	Long, slightly plump grain with blunt ends. Shaded from black to russet. When cooked, rice is (cont.)	Pick over to clean and wash before cook- ing. Use 1½ C. water in a 2- qt. saucepan. *Salt after cook- ing.*	25 minutes. Let stand 10 minutes.	2 C.	In Asia, it is combined with coconut cream or shredded co- conut for des- serts. Makes (cont.)

Rice Variety	Description	Cooking Method	Cooking & Standing Time	Approx. Yield	Comments
	shiny and indigo-colored. Bran layer is soluble; therefore color leaches into cooking water and food. Smells like grassy new-mown hay. Good flavor, toothsome, slightly glutinous flavor.				a good, dark purple novelty rice pudding.
Wild Rice Technically not a rice. (See Wild Rice chapter, page 259).					
Rice Blends (1 C. raw) There are many blends. We have tested with our favorite "3 Grain Rice Blend," brown basmati, Wehani and (cont.)	A darkly colored, intensely flavored mixture.	Use 2-qt. saucepan, coat rice in 1 Tbs. butter and toast for 2 minutes before adding 2 C. boiling water. Add salt *after* cooking.	40 to 45 minutes. Let stand 10 minutes.	2 C.	Good with mushrooms to accompany strongly flavored game or pork dishes.

Rice Variety	Description	Cooking Method	Cooking & Standing Time	Approx. Yield	Comments
Wild Rice Bits. Experiment with your own choices.					
White Medium Grain (1 C. raw)	Midway in size between short and long. After cooking, has cohesive quality but not quite as sticky as short grain.	Usually imported, so wash first. Cook in same manner as long grain white, but use 2 C. salted water in a 2-qt. saucepan.	18 to 22 minutes. Let stand 5 minutes.	3¼ C.	Use for dishes that require stickier quality, e.g., puddings and molded desserts.
Brown Medium Grain (1 C. raw)	Same size as white, but buff-colored. After cooking, grains are plump and toothsome, and slightly sticky with a nutty flavor.	Rinse grain. Cook in 3-qt. saucepan with 2¼ C. salted water.	40 minutes. Let stand 10 minutes.	3¼ C.	Same uses, but more intensely flavored. Spicing will be needed.
White Short Grain (1 C. raw) Italian arborio, tesori, vialone	Grown in Po Valley in northern Italy. Cooks into creamy yet firm-to-the-tooth risotto.	*See page 173 for special instructions.*			Used for risotto.

Rice at a Glance (cont.)

Rice Variety	Description	Cooking Method	Cooking & Standing Time	Approx. Yield	Comments
Spanish Valencia	Imported from Spain. Almost round in shape. Same properties as Italian short grain rice.	*See page 173 for special instructions.*			Used for paellas and Spanish rice dishes, and for risotto.
California Pearl	Domestic short grain variety. Very absorbent, soft and sticky.	*See page 173 for special instructions.*			Same uses. Interchangeable with those above.
Asian Glutinous or Sweet Rice (1 C. raw)	Imported, slightly opaque white grains. When cooked, they have a delicate, sweet flavor.	Wash and rinse several times before cooking. Then *soak overnight.* Steam cook in 5-qt. Dutch oven using vegetable steamer, or in rice cooker.	Soaking time: overnight. Cook for 20 minutes.	2 C.	All-purpose Japanese rice for sushi and desserts.
Red Rice (1 C. raw) Special Holiday selection called "Christmas Rice"	Basically brown rice with short grain and russet color with bran and germ intact. Grown domestically from Asian strain. Unusual wild mushroom flavor. Chewy texture.	Rinse. Use a 3-qt. saucepan and 2½ C. boiling water. *Do not add salt* until after rice is cooked. Add rice, return to boil. Cover and simmer.	45 minutes. Let stand 10 minutes.	3 C.	Good as side dish with game, such as pheasant or venison. Also good in salads.

Rice at a Glance (cont.)

Rice Variety	Description	Cooking Method	Cooking & Standing Time	Approx. Yield	Comments
Brown Rice (1 C. raw) Regular Short Grain	Transparent, short, oval shape. Shiny and sticky after cooking. Good toothsome nutty flavor.	Rinse grain. Use 3-qt. saucepan and 2¼ C. boiling salted water. Add rice and return to boil. Cover and simmer.	45 minutes. Let stand 10 minutes. (Various brands may vary cooking time.)	3⅓ C.	One of preferred rice varieties for vegetarians.
Glutinous or Sweet Rice	Opaque, oval, short, tan grain. Slightly sweet, strong flavor and very sticky. Tender texture.	See white glutinous rice for instructions. Add additional boiling water as needed for longer cooking time.	60 minutes.	2½ C.	Alternative, with stronger flavor and darker color for Asian dishes and desserts.

Greenish-colored grains, which are sometimes present in brown rice, mean only that there was either a lack of sufficient sunshine in the final ripening stages when the rice was drying or the rice was grown in a nontropical region.

They are perfectly edible, as are the more russet-colored grains also found in brown rice. These are generally grains from which the hull layer has not been totally removed.

Also, brown rice has a shorter shelf life, retaining freshness for about six months, while white rice can be stored indefinitely.

THE STOCK POT

Long before chicken stock came in cans, there used to be a stockpot bubbling away on everyone's stove. It also served the purpose of keeping the winter chill out of the kitchen and it smelled homey and wonderful. It still does. However, it is now found bubbling away primarily in good restaurants and in the homes of those who know that good stock is the structure, the skeleton, the essence and the very soul of flavor in any dish that you prepare.

Although stock and broth are primarily the same thing, a concentrated or boiled-down essence of some kind of meat, poultry or fish and/or bones, vegetables, water and aromatic herbs, the end product is really the beginning of flavor in many bean and grain dishes, particularly with risottos and pilafs.

In a pinch—and a big pinch at that—there are two "store-bought" products that we do suggest, after much personal trial and error:

- Barth's Chicken Nutra-Soup—an instant dehydrated powder, found in health food stores. It contains no salt.
- Swanson's Clear Chicken Broth—a canned product with good flavor, although it does contain salt and monosodium glutamate, as most other canned broths do.

Chicken Stock

MAKES 3 QUARTS

NOTE: *Do not add salt to this stock if you are going to use it for cooking beans.*

- 1 chicken, quartered and trimmed of fat (about 4–5 lbs.)
- 1 lb. chicken wings, backs and other parts
- 4 qts. water
- 2 medium whole onions, or 1 large onion
- 2 medium carrots, cut in halves crosswise
- 1 large leek, green part trimmed and well washed
- 1 clove garlic
- 3 stalks celery with leaves, cut in halves crosswise
- ½ tsp. whole black peppercorns
- 1 tsp. salt (if used)
- 1 bay leaf
- 6 sprigs parsley
- 4 sprigs dill
- 1 sprig thyme
- 2 small parsnips
- 1 small parsley root (optional)

Place the chicken pieces in a large 7- to 9-quart Dutch oven or stockpot. Add the water and bring slowly to a boil. Skim the foam off the surface as it collects. Then add the onions, carrots, leek, garlic, celery, peppercorns and salt. Return to a boil again, then reduce the heat and simmer for 1½ hours, skimming the surface as necessary. Then tie the bay leaf, parsley, dill and thyme together, add them to the pot along with the parsnips and parsley root. Simmer for 1 hour more. Strain into a large container, pressing the solids against the colander to extract as much liquid as possible. The chicken may be skinned and deboned and reserved for other dishes, but discard the vegetables.

Taste for seasoning, then cool and refrigerate or freeze in 1-quart containers for future use.

Beef Stock

Instead of chicken, use 3 pounds of short ribs of beef and 3 to 4 beef marrow bones. All the other ingredients and instructions remain the same.

The

Versatile

Grain

and the

Elegant

Bean

172

RISOTTOS

We were introduced to risotto (to be accurate, the plural would be risotti) during the five years that we had our film office in Rome and we have been fans ever since. Risotto originated in the north of Italy and is always prepared with *arborio* rice or a close relation. It has been called "the pasta of northern Italy" and luckily it has had great success here in the United States and Canada as more and more Italian restaurants have added it to their menus.

An old Italian friend of ours used to say that "risotto follows the seasons" and indeed it does. In spring, it can be made with delicately thin asparagus tips, fava beans or the tiny, sweet *piselli* (peas). Summer makes it perfect for tomato and basil or other herbs. And autumn was one of our favorite seasons, when the *porcini*, those incredible, huge, wild fresh mushrooms, came into the marketplace. Or the paper-thin shavings of white truffles might be added. Then, in winter (or all year long), the risotto can be made with seafood or shellfish.

When you make risotto (risotti) at home, keep in mind that a perfect one requires patience. The principle of the method is to have the rice absorb the stock a little at a time, until the grains swell and a creamy tender union is formed between the rice and the stock. Also remember that the quantity of the stock is *approximate,* since more or less may be needed to achieve the desired result. The idea is to add only a little bit at a time, stir, then allow the liquid to be absorbed. When made in the traditional way, this is a dish that cannot be left unattended on the stove; it must be watched very carefully to achieve the creamy rice texture with grains that are tender but firm, or al dente, to the tooth. (See "The Never-Nevers of Risotto" below.)

The Never-Nevers of Risotto

NEVER rinse the rice before cooking. The essential ingredient for a creamy risotto is the starch coat of the grain.

NEVER use a lightweight pot. Use a heavy pot with a flat bottom and straight sides to ensure even cooking.

NEVER let the cooking stock get cold. Keep it simmering in a separate pot and make sure it's a good, flavorful, preferably homemade stock. See page 171 for a recipe.

NEVER cook risotto too slowly or the texture will be gluey rather than creamy.

NEVER cook it too quickly or the outside will be soft and the inside too firm. Start bite-testing the grains for doneness after about fifteen minutes of cooking.

Basic Risotto with Four Variations
Risotto Milanese:
Saffron and Parmesan Cheese

SERVES 8

An exquisitely simple dish from Milan, which can be made to perfection if a few simple rules are followed. Although it takes individual attention while preparing, it can usually be done in anywhere from 18 to 25 minutes, depending upon the variety and the age of the rice, the shape and size of the pot and the temperature of the broth.

¼ tsp. saffron threads, crushed
½ C. dry white wine
6–7 C. Chicken or Beef Stock, preferably homemade (see pages 171–172)
4 Tbs. soft butter or olive oil
1 large onion, finely minced (1 C.)
2 C. short grain white Italian rice, such as arborio

½ C. grated Parmesan cheese
Salt and freshly ground black pepper to taste
2 Tbs. finely minced parsley (optional)

Steep the saffron threads in the white wine for 10 minutes and set aside. Simmer stock in a separate saucepan. (You may not need all of the liquid.) In a 3-quart nonstick saucepan, slowly melt 3 tablespoons of the butter. When it just begins to bubble, add the onions, stirring constantly with a wooden spoon, and cook until they wilt and just begin to color, about 5 to 8 minutes. Add the rice and stir until the grains are well coated with the butter/onion mixture. This step helps to slow the absorption of the liquid. Stir in about ½ cup of the simmering stock, then the wine and saffron mixture. Stir constantly over medium heat for about 4 minutes, or until the liquid has been completely absorbed. Add another ⅔ cup of the simmering stock and stir until completely absorbed, about 5 to 8 minutes more.

Add simmering stock, using as much of the remaining stock as necessary, reducing the amount with each addition and stirring until the liquid is absorbed. You will need to add less and less liquid toward the end of the cooking time, since the rice will be plumped and will absorb liquid more slowly. After 15 minutes, begin to bite-test a grain of rice. If it is tender, with a slightly firm center, and the rice is creamy but not soupy, the risotto is finished.

Stir in the remaining tablespoon of butter, the Parmesan cheese and the salt and freshly ground pepper. Sprinkle with a bit of parsley if you wish, and serve hot in flat soup plates.

The

Versatile

Grain

and the

Elegant

Bean

174

Follow basic recipe instructions for Risotto Milanese.

Variation #1
Risi e Bisi:
Risotto with Tiny Peas and Prosciutto

Add

1½ C. small fresh green peas (or 10-ounce package frozen small peas, defrosted)
½ C. diced prosciutto di Parma

Add these two ingredients during the last 5 minutes of cooking.

Variation #2
Risotto con Funghi Secchi:
Risotto with Dried Wild Porcini Mushrooms

Add

1 oz. dried porcini mushrooms

Soak porcini mushrooms in warm water to cover for 30 minutes before cooking the risotto. Strain the liquid through a dampened paper coffee filter into a cup to eliminate grit and sand. Rinse the softened mushrooms and cut them into small pieces. Add the mushroom liquid as part of the stock. Then add the mushrooms after 10 minutes of cooking the risotto.

Variation #3
Risotto Primavera:
Risotto with Spring Vegetables

Add

3–4 large shallots, minced (⅔ C.)
¼ C. finely minced basil
¼ C. finely minced flat leaf parsley
8 thin asparagus spears, cut diagonally into 1-in. pieces

2 plum tomatoes, cubed
1 small zucchini, cut into julienne strips

Replace the onion in the original recipe with the minced shallots. Stir the remaining herbs and vegetables into the risotto for the last 8 minutes of cooking. Cook until the vegetables are barely tender.

Variation #4
Risotto con Gamberi:
Risotto with Shrimp

Add

1 lb. small shrimp	1 bay leaf
2 C. boiling water	3 sprigs thyme

Peel and devein the shrimp. Add the shrimp shells to the 2 cups boiling water, along with the bay leaf and the sprigs of thyme. Cover and simmer for 20 minutes. Strain the liquid and discard the shells and herbs. Use this liquid along with the chicken stock. Split the shrimp in half lengthwise and add them to the risotto for the last 3 to 5 minutes of cooking.

The

Versatile

Grain

and the

Elegant

Bean

176

PILAFS

Unlike risotto, pilaf is always prepared with long grain rice and the cooking methods differ substantially. Known throughout India, the Caribbean and the Middle East, the spellings also vary: pilaf, pilaff, pulao, pellao, plove, polo, to mention only a few. In making pilaf, the long grain rice is tossed and toasted in butter until it is completely coated and begins to color. Then boiling stock is added, the pot covered tightly and the rice steamed either on top of the stove or in the oven until all the liquid is absorbed. This allows the grains to become separate and fluffy, but still retain their texture.

Just a few simple additions or variations can create an endless repertoire of delicious recipes.

Basic Long Grain Rice Pilaf

SERVES 6

Butter makes the crisp brown bottom crust that many people prefer in their pilafs. However, cutting down on the butter and substituting some olive oil will appease your conscience and still taste great.

- 5 Tbs. butter (or 3 Tbs. butter and 2 Tbs. olive oil)
- 1 large onion, finely minced (1 C.)
- 1 medium clove garlic, finely minced (1 tsp.)
- 1½ C. long grain rice, either white or brown, or imported basmati rice, white or brown
- 3–4 C. boiling Chicken Stock, preferably homemade (see page 171)
- Salt and freshly ground black pepper to taste

Melt the butter in a heavy shallow 2½- or 3-quart oven-to-table baking pan that can withstand the direct flame of the top of the stove as well as oven heat. Add the onions and garlic and sauté slowly, stirring, over medium low heat for about 2 minutes, or until the onions are translucent. Add the rice and continue to stir for about 2 to 3 minutes more to coat the rice grains with the butter. Raise the heat, add the chicken stock and the salt and pepper and return to boiling.

Cover the baking pan tightly with aluminum foil and reduce the heat as low as possible. Cook 20 to 40 minutes, depending upon the type of rice used (see Chart, pages 162–163). Then remove the foil and test a few grains. Cover with foil again and let the rice stand for 5 minutes before fluffing with a fork. In the Middle East, the rice continues to steam over very low heat until serving time to allow the butter to form a crisp bottom crust. The crust is then scraped from the bottom of the pan and used as a garnish for the surface.

The pilaf can also be baked in a preheated 375° F. oven. Follow the same procedure as for the top-of-the-stove cooking. After the stock comes to a boil, cover with aluminum foil and bake in the oven for about 30 minutes. Remove the foil, fluff with a fork, cover loosely with the foil again and return to the oven with the heat off, until serving time.

Variation #1
Turkish Pilaf with Fine Noodles
and Pine Nuts

Serve with grilled lamb or kufta kabob.

Add

½ **C. vermicelli or cappelini broken   1 Tbs. pine nuts
into small pieces**

Add the vermicelli and the pine nuts to the raw rice and onion mixture and coat them with the butter. Proceed with the basic recipe.

Variation #2
Pilaf with an Herb Bouquet

This is a delicate and excellent pilaf to serve with fish.

Add

1 **bay leaf   3 sprigs flat leaf parsley
3 sprigs thyme**

Tie a string around the herbs for easy removal. Add the bouquet to the rice when the stock is added, and remove and discard it before serving.

**The

Versatile

Grain

and the

Elegant

Bean**

178

Variation #3
Leek and Saffron Pilaf

The white, imported basmati rice is preferable for this pilaf. Try this with poultry.

Add

3 thin leeks, sliced into ½-in. pieces	**1 bay leaf**
½ tsp. crushed saffron threads	**1 Tbs. minced flat leaf parsley**

Instead of the onion in the original recipe, sauté the leeks. Add the crushed saffron threads and bay leaf to the chicken stock, then add to the rice. When cooked, remove and discard the bay leaf and sprinkle with the minced parsley.

Variation #4
Cumin and Sweet Pepper Pilaf

Try this pilaf with a pork roast or grilled sausages.

Add

1 C. finely diced red and green sweet peppers (½ medium red pepper, ½ medium green pepper)
½ tsp. ground cumin

Add the diced peppers to the onion mixture and sauté. Then add the ground cumin to the chicken stock before adding the stock to the rice mixture.

THE PERFECT POT OF RICE

To Wash or Not to Wash. For most domestic brands of rice, there is no need to rinse or wash the grains before cooking, although some cooks prefer to do it anyway. Some time back, white rice was coated with talc, but this was discontinued by order of the Department of Agriculture. However, some imported rice should be rinsed. Put the measured amount in a large bowl and run cold water over the rice, stirring the grains with your fingers or with a wooden spoon. Drain the water and repeat one or two more times. Then drain it well.

Cooking the Rice. Using the instructions in the chart on pages 162–170, put the liquid into a heavy pot with a tight-fitting lid so that no steam can escape. Bring the water to a boil and add salt to your taste, then add the rice. (Some rice must be salted *after* cooking, so read the instructions carefully.) Return to boiling, lower the heat to simmer and cover tightly. We sometimes add a small pat of butter to the liquid to help keep the grains separated. Possibly the most important part of cooking rice is *not to stir it* or to peek and let the steam escape. In a sense, rice breathes as it cooks, and natural channels are formed by the heat, running through the grains as little passages to allow the steam to cook the rice evenly and let the steam escape. If you upset the network by stirring, the rice will not be fluffy and the grains will have a tendency to become gummy and stick together.

After the required cooking time, slip a piece of paper toweling under the pot lid to collect any additional moisture that forms, and let the rice stand for anywhere from five to fifteen minutes (see Chart, pages 162–170). Then, fluff with a fork.

Steamed Glutinous Rice Rolls Filled with
Shrimp, Scallions and Black Sesame Seeds

MAKES 6 LARGE OR 36 SMALL ROLLS

The following recipe is one we frequently make for cocktail parties. It can be prepared well in advance, then reheated for 10 minutes in a vegetable steamer before serving.

½ lb. shrimp, shelled and deveined	¼ tsp. Chinese 5 spice powder (see NOTE)
2 Tbs. tamari (or light soy sauce)	
2 scallions, green part only (about ⅓ C.)	2 C. cooked glutinous (sweet) white rice, cooled slightly (see Chart, page 169)
1 tsp. finely minced ginger	
⅛ tsp. cayenne	1–2 tsps. black sesame seeds

Place the shrimp in a bowl and add the tamari. Marinate for 30 minutes, turning once after 15 minutes. Drain and discard the tamari. Put the shrimp, scallions, ginger, cayenne and 5 spice powder into the bowl of a food processor and process to a pastelike consistency. Cut six 12-inch squares of aluminum foil and set them on a work surface.

Dampen your hands and divide the cooked rice into six equal portions and place a portion on each square of foil. Dampen your fingers to enclose the filling with the rice and make a sausage shape about 4½ inches long by 1½ inches thick. Then roll up the foil and twist the ends to seal them. Place the rolls in a 12-inch skillet and add boiling water to cover. Cover and cook for 30 minutes. Add more boiling water to cover the rolls if necessary.

Lift the packets out with tongs and onto paper towels. Drain and cool for 30 minutes, then open the aluminum foil and, using a wet knife, slice the rolls into ¾-inch-thick slices. Stand the pieces upright and sprinkle with a few black sesame seeds and serve with the following dipping sauce.

Dipping Sauce

¼ C. tamari (soy sauce)	2 tsps. lemon juice
½ tsp. wasabi paste (prepared Japanese horseradish)	Pinch sugar

Stir all the ingredients together and put the sauce into tiny bowls or sake cups.

NOTE: Chinese 5 spice powder is available in oriental specialty shops. It is a ground, sweetly aromatic blend consisting of star anise, cassia bark, fennel seed, whole cloves and anise pepper.

Lettuce and Vegetable Soup with Rice and Saffron (Minestra Alla Milanese)

SERVES 6 TO 8

An especially wonderful soup for dieters or the health conscious, it's a delicately balanced, fresh, clean-tasting dish without any oil or butter in it at all. Best of all, it can be cooked in less than half an hour.

8 C. Chicken Stock, preferably homemade (see page 171)
¼ tsp. saffron threads
⅔ C. Italian short grain white rice such as arborio
½ lb. fresh green beans, ends cut off, and cut into 1½-in. pieces (about 2 C.)
¾ lb. fresh ripe tomatoes, peeled, cut into 1 inch pieces (about 1½ C.)

Salt and freshly ground black pepper to taste
2 medium carrots, sliced paper-thin on the diagonal (1 C.)
1 lb. zucchini, trimmed and cut into 2-in.-long by ½-in.-wide sticks (3 C.)
1 C. fresh or frozen green peas
1 medium head romaine, shredded into ½-in. shreds
Grated Parmesan cheese

In a large heavy pot, bring the chicken stock to a boil along with the saffron. Slowly add the rice, stirring. Then lower the heat and simmer, covered, for 10 minutes. Stir occasionally. Add the green beans, tomatoes, salt and pepper and simmer for about 7 minutes. Add the carrots and zucchini and continue to cook for 5 minutes. The vegetables should be barely tender, so taste them along the way. Stir in the peas and lettuce and continue to cook for an additional 3 minutes. Serve at once, passing grated Parmesan cheese and a pepper mill at the table.

The

Versatile

Grain

and the

Elegant

Bean

182

Old-Fashioned Fresh Herbed Tomato and Rice Soup

SERVES 4 TO 6

An all-time old-fashioned favorite at its best when made with fresh, ripe tomatoes at their seasonal peak, and when fresh herbs have their most pungent flavors. Orange peel and nutmeg are the sweet tastes that just take the edge off the acidity of the tomatoes and help to balance the flavors.

1 Tbs. butter
1 Tbs. olive oil
1 large onion, finely chopped (1 C.)
2½ lbs. ripe tomatoes, peeled and cut in large pieces (about 7–8 tomatoes)
4 C. Chicken Stock, preferably homemade (see page 171)
1 stalk celery, with leaves
4 sprigs thyme
4 sprigs flat leaf parsley
1 bay leaf

1 2-in. strip orange peel
⅔ C. cooked long grain rice, white or brown (see Chart, page 162)
4–5 large basil leaves, finely shredded
Salt and freshly ground black pepper to taste
¼ C. heavy cream
1–2 tsps. honey (optional)
1 Tbs. finely minced flat parsley
1 Tbs. finely minced dill
Few gratings nutmeg

In a heavy 5½-quart Dutch oven, melt the butter and olive oil. Sauté the onions over medium heat until wilted, stirring frequently, for about 5 minutes.

Add the tomatoes and chicken stock and bring to a boil. Tie the celery, thyme, parsley, bay leaf and orange peel together with string and add to the pot. Cover, lower the heat and simmer for 20 minutes. Remove and discard the herb bouquet and transfer the soup in batches to the bowl of a food processor. Purée, returning the soup to the pot after each batch.

Add the cooked rice, basil, salt and pepper and simmer, covered, for 10 more minutes. Stir in the cream and taste. Depending upon the sweetness or the acidity of the tomatoes, stir in some of the honey and taste the soup again to see if the balance is to your taste. Ladle into bowls and sprinkle the surface with some of the parsley, dill and gratings of nutmeg. Serve hot.

Persian Saffron Rice Mold with Chicken, Fruit and Walnuts

SERVES 6

In Iran, *chelo* or plain rice is cooked to accompany kebobs, skewers of grilled chicken, meat or fish. When other ingredients are added to the rice it is then called a *polo*. Like pilaf, a desirable, crisp, golden bottom crust forms during cooking and is known as *dig*, which is then scraped up and spooned over the surface of the rice. These choice crisp morsels have been known to cause squabbles at the table as everyone vies for the crunchy bits.

1 C. boiling water
¼ C. dried currants
6 pitted prunes, cut into small pieces
12 pitted dates, cut into small pieces
6 dried apricots, cut into small pieces
6 dried peaches, cut into small pieces
¼ C. coarsely chopped, toasted walnuts
3 C. cooked long grain white rice, preferably basmati (see Chart, page 164)
¼ lb. butter, melted

¼ tsp. saffron threads, steeped in 1 Tbs. hot water
½ C. plain yogurt
Butter for greasing mold
1 tsp. finely minced lemon peel
1 tsp. allspice
Salt and freshly ground black pepper to taste
2 C. diced, cooked chicken breasts (about 1½ lbs. skinned and boned breasts)

In a bowl, pour boiling water over the dried fruits. Let them steep for 10 minutes, then drain, reserving the liquid. Set aside.

In a separate bowl, mix the walnuts with 2 cups of the cooked rice and set aside. In another bowl, combine the remaining rice with 6 tablespoons of the melted butter, the saffron and the yogurt. Preheat the oven to 400° F. and butter a metal mold, such as a Charlotte mold, that measures 7 × 3 inches. Spoon the saffron rice mixture into the bottom of the prepared mold and pack it down to eliminate air pockets.

To the rice and walnut mixture, add the lemon peel, allspice and salt and pepper and spoon half of this mixture over the saffron rice. Layer half the dried fruit, then half the diced chicken over the mixture. Spoon 1 tablespoon of the reserved fruit liquid and 1 tablespoon of the remaining melted butter over it. Add the rest of the walnut-rice mixture and repeat with the fruit, then the chicken and then the remaining fruit liquid and melted butter. Pack down firmly with a wooden spoon. Cover the top with aluminum foil and bake it on the bottom shelf of the oven for 40 minutes.

Remove from the oven and place the mold on top of the stove over low heat and cook for 5 minutes more to form a golden crust. When ready to serve, place the bottom of the mold in cold water for a few minutes, then invert to unmold onto a serving dish (see NOTE). Scrape any crusty rice from the bottom of the mold and spoon it over the surface.

NOTE: The mound may not be exactly the same shape as the mold. Do not be concerned. Just re-form it with a spatula.

The

Versatile

Grain

and the

Elegant

Bean

184

Yellow Rice, Cuban-Style, with Green Peas, Red Pepper and Black Olives

SERVES 6

Achiote oil brightly colors and flavors this most attractive and simple rice side dish. It enhances almost any kind of chicken, fish or pork main course.

3 Tbs. achiote oil (see NOTE)
2 large shallots, finely minced (¼ C.)
1 small onion, finely minced (¼ C.)
½ small sweet red pepper, finely minced (¼ C.)
1 C. raw long grain white rice

2½ C. hot Chicken Stock, preferably homemade (see page 171)
5 black olives, pitted and sliced, either Alfonso or Kalamata
10-oz. package frozen small green peas, defrosted but uncooked

Heat the oil in a 10-inch skillet and add the shallots, onions and sweet red pepper. Stir and sauté over medium heat for 2 minutes. Add the rice and stir to coat, then sauté for 2 minutes more, stirring. Slowly add the hot stock, bring to a boil, cover, lower the heat and simmer for 15 minutes. Uncover and stir in the olives and peas. Cover again and continue to cook for 2 minutes more or until the liquid is absorbed. Transfer to a warm serving dish.

NOTE: To make achiote oil, combine 1½ tablespoons of achiote seeds (sometimes called annatto) and 3 tablespoons of canola or olive oil in a small skillet. Cook over medium heat for 2 to 3 minutes until the oil is a bright orange. Remove from the heat at once or the color will lighten and the flavor will be lost. Strain out the seeds and discard them. Hispanic and specialty markets carry achiote seeds.

Rice Ring with Mushrooms, Hazelnuts
and Chicken Liver

SERVES 8

The rice ring is composed of different kinds of brown rice, with added wild rice bits, all enhanced with the colors and textures of mushrooms, sage and one chicken liver. It will complement any kind of poultry. Prepare it early in the day, then bake the ring mold right before serving.

4 Tbs. butter
3 large scallions, finely sliced (⅔ C.)
½ lb. mushrooms, finely chopped in the bowl of a food processor
2-oz. chicken liver
Freshly ground black pepper to taste
1 Tbs. finely minced sage
½ C. coarsely chopped hazelnuts

1 C. raw wild rice blend (Lundberg's variety of whole grain brown rices and wild rice bits—see Chart, page 167)
2½ C. hot Chicken Stock or water
Salt to taste
Butter for greasing mold
10-oz. package frozen petite peas
1 tsp. finely minced mint or chervil
¼ C. finely minced flat leaf parsley

In a large skillet, melt 2 tablespoons of the butter, add the scallions and cook, stirring, for 1 minute. Stir in the mushrooms and cook over medium high heat for about 2 to 3 minutes. Then push the mixture to one side and add the chicken liver to the same skillet. Cook, turning it with tongs, for 2 to 3 minutes or until the liver is firm and has lost its pink color. Remove the skillet from the heat. Take out the liver and cut it into tiny pieces and return to the pan. Add the pepper and sage. Stir well and set aside.

In a nonstick 5-quart Dutch oven, melt the remaining butter and add the hazelnuts. Cook and stir over low heat until the nuts begin to turn color. Lift them out with a slotted spoon and stir into the reserved mushroom mixture. To the Dutch oven, add the rice, stirring for a few minutes to coat the grains with the butter. Then add the chicken stock and bring to a boil. Stir in the reserved mushroom mixture, cover and simmer over low heat for about 35 minutes, or until most of the liquid is absorbed. Stir in the salt and adjust the seasoning. (You may prepare to this step well in advance.)

When ready to bake, preheat the oven to 350° F. and generously butter a 6-cup (9-inch) ring mold. Spoon the mixture into the prepared mold, pressing down gently to eliminate any air pockets. (The mold will not be filled to the top.) Cover with aluminum foil and bake for 25 minutes. Let cool for 10 to 15 minutes on a wire rack.

Meanwhile, cook the green peas and mix them either with the mint or chervil. Loosen the edges of the mold with a knife, then invert onto a serving plate. Spoon the cooked peas into the center and garnish with the parsley.

The

Versatile

Grain

and the

Elegant

Bean

186

Saffron Rice with Garlic, Pepper, Pork,
Green Peas and Capers

SERVES 6

This rice and pork dish, with a Spanish accent, is a garlic lover's delight. It simmers on top of the stove and becomes more colorful with each added ingredient. The pork marinates in a pepper and garlic purée for 3 to 4 hours before being cooked with the rice.

Garlic Pepper Pork

2 large cloves garlic
¼ tsp. freshly ground black pepper
⅛ tsp. cayenne
¼ tsp. coarse kosher salt

1 lb. boneless, lean pork tenderloin, thinly sliced ½ in. thick and cut into ½-in. strips

To a small bowl, add the garlic, black pepper, cayenne and salt and mash until a paste is formed. Use either the heel of a knife handle or a mortar and pestle. Mix well with the pork and refrigerate for 3 to 4 hours, stirring once or twice.

Saffron Rice

4 Tbs. olive oil
Garlic Pepper Pork (see above)
1 C. raw long grain converted rice
Salt to taste
2½ C. hot Chicken Stock, preferably homemade (see page 171)
¼ tsp. saffron threads, crushed
1 small bay leaf

⅛ tsp. hot pepper flakes
1½ Tbs. rinsed, drained large capers
1 C. defrosted frozen small green peas (½ 10-oz. package)
1 small roasted red pepper, cut into strips
2 Tbs. finely minced flat parsley
6 wedges lemon

Heat the oil in a 3-quart shallow, heavy oven-to-table casserole. Toss the garlic pepper pork in the hot oil, over medium heat, stirring constantly until the meat loses its color. Add rice and salt and mix with the meat to coat and flavor the grains. Stirring constantly, cook for 2 to 3 minutes. Spoon off 2 tablespoons of the chicken stock into a small cup. Add the saffron to the cup and steep for 5 minutes.

Add the remaining chicken stock to the pork/rice mixture and bring to a boil. Lower the heat and stir in the saffron, bay leaf, hot pepper flakes and capers. Cover tightly with aluminum foil and simmer for about 30 minutes or until most of the liquid is absorbed. Remove the foil, then stir in the peas. Cover again and continue to cook for about 5 minutes more. Remove and discard the bay leaf. Fluff the rice with a fork and stir in the red pepper. Sprinkle with parsley and lay the lemon wedges around the rice, to be squeezed over each portion at the table.

Brown Rice and Onion Purée au Gratin

A favorite side dish with roasted veal, this rice, onion and cheese purée can be prepared early in the day and baked just before serving. It tastes surprisingly like an excellent French onion soup, but with a different consistency.

4 Tbs. butter
1½ lbs. large sweet Bermuda or Vidalia onion, thinly sliced (about 2 large onions)
Salt to taste
⅛ tsp. freshly ground black pepper or to taste
1½ C. cooked short or long grain brown rice, preferably cooked in chicken stock (see Chart, page 171)

Butter for greasing gratin dish
¼ tsp. grated nutmeg
⅛ tsp. cayenne
2 Tbs. dry white wine
¼ C. heavy cream
½ C. shredded Gruyère cheese

In a large skillet, melt 2 tablespoons of the butter and slowly sauté the onions until they are soft and golden. Sprinkle with salt and pepper. Stir in the cooked rice, then purée the onion/rice mixture in batches in the bowl of a food processor and transfer to a large bowl.

Preheat the oven to 400° F. and butter a 2-quart shallow oven-to-table gratin dish. Add the nutmeg, cayenne, wine, cream and 1 tablespoon butter to the purée. Blend and then spoon into the prepared pan. Sprinkle the surface with the cheese and dot with the remaining tablespoon of butter. Bake for 10 to 15 minutes, then turn the oven up to broil and slip under the broiler until the cheese is melted and flecked with brown. Serve at once.

The

Versatile

Grain

and the

Elegant

Bean

188

Green Rice with Snow Peas

SERVES 6

An emerald-colored rice dish that goes particularly well with steamed shrimp, scallops, mussels or clams.

2 Tbs. butter	2½ C. boiling chicken stock or water
4 large shallots, finely minced (¾ C.)	Salt to taste
1 small green pepper, finely minced (½ C.)	¾ C. finely minced flat parsley
1 large clove garlic, finely minced (1½ tsps.)	¼ C. finely minced cilantro
1 C. raw long grain brown rice	⅛ tsp. cayenne
	12 Chinese snow pea pods, blanched for 30 seconds

In a 5-quart nonstick Dutch oven, melt the butter over medium heat and sauté the shallots, green pepper and garlic, stirring, for 3 to 4 minutes. Then add the rice and stir to coat the grains and continue to sauté for another minute or until the vegetables are wilted but not browned. Add the boiling chicken stock and the salt, and return to a boil. Then lower the heat, cover and cook for 35 to 45 minutes or until the rice is tender and almost all the liquid is absorbed. Stir in the parsley, cilantro and cayenne, using a fork to keep the rice fluffy.

Return to the stove, cover and simmer for 2 to 3 minutes more. Remove from the heat and let stand for 10 minutes. Then mound the rice on a platter and place the snow peas around the mound like the spokes of a wheel. Serve hot.

Baked Rice and Herb–Stuffed Tomatoes

SERVES 6

We first tasted this simple dish 20 years ago in Rome at a sidewalk trattoria on the Piazza Navona. We still love it and make it frequently in the summer as a first course or use it alongside roasted meat or fish. We have also made it with leftover risotto and it's delicious that way as well.

6 medium-size ripe tomatoes
1 C. cooked short grain brown rice (see Chart, page 166)
1 large clove garlic, finely minced (1½ tsps.)
2 Tbs. finely minced flat parsley
1 tsp. finely minced fresh oregano leaves (or ½ tsp. dried oregano, preferably Greek)

1 Tbs. finely minced basil
4 Tbs. olive oil
2 tsps. lemon juice
Salt to taste
¼ tsp. freshly ground black pepper
Oil for greasing baking dish
Sprigs curly parsley

Cut a thin slice from the top of each tomato and reserve. Core the centers, scoop out the pulp and juice and chop coarsely. Place in a strainer to drain. To another bowl, add the cooked rice, garlic, parsley, oregano, basil, 2 tablespoons of the olive oil, lemon juice, salt and pepper. Then add the drained tomato pulp and mix well.

Preheat the oven to 400° F. and place the tomato cups in an oiled medium-size shallow oven-to-table baking dish so that they almost touch. Spoon some filling into each tomato cup right to the brim and top with the reserved slices from each tomato. Drizzle the remaining olive oil over the tomatoes and bake for 25 minutes. Cool and serve at room temperature with some of the pan juices spooned over each tomato. Garnish each tomato with a sprig of parsley.

The

Versatile

Grain

and the

Elegant

Bean

190

Suppli al Telefono:
Italian Rice and Mozzarella Croquettes

MAKES 12 CROQUETTES

When the croquettes are pulled apart, the cheese forms strings that closely resemble telephone pole wires—hence the name for this Roman specialty.

3 C. cooked short grain brown rice (see Chart, page 166)
2 eggs, beaten lightly
½ small onion, grated (about 2–3 Tbs.)
Salt to taste
⅛ tsp. freshly ground black pepper or to taste

12 ½-in.-thick slices mozzarella cheese, cut into 2-in.-long strips
¾ C. dry fine bread crumbs
⅓ C. olive oil
⅓ C. corn oil
Lemon wedges

In a large bowl, combine the cooked rice, eggs, onions, salt and pepper. Take 1 tablespoon of the rice mixture and flatten it in the palm of your hand. Lay a strip of cheese in the center and place another tablespoon of rice on top. Roll it into a log shape between the palms of your hands, enclosing the cheese. Put the bread crumbs in a pie plate, then roll the croquette in the crumbs. Repeat with the remaining rice and cheese. Place the croquettes on a waxed-paper-lined plate and chill, uncovered, in the refrigerator for 30 minutes (or longer if you wish to make them well in advance).

When ready to cook, heat both oils in a medium-size skillet until hot and fry 3 croquettes at a time, until brown all over. Drain on paper towels and keep warm in a preheated low oven until all are fried. Serve hot with wedges of lemon to be squeezed over, and pass a pepper mill at the table if you wish.

Seven Vegetable Rice Noodles with
Chile and Sesame Sauce

SERVES 8 TO 10

Sparkling multicolored crackling crisp vegetables are tossed with white hair-thin rice noodles in a zingy hot sauce that is cooled with lime. A dazzling make-ahead dish whose cost belies its opulent presentation.

Chile and Sesame Sauce

Peels of 1–2 large limes, shredded plus juice (¼ C.)	Salt to taste
2 Tbs. rice vinegar	3 Tbs. oriental sesame oil
½ tsp. sugar	1 Tbs. oriental hot chile oil or more to taste

Combine all the ingredients except the lime peels in the bowl of a food processor. Blend well and let stand while preparing the vegetable and rice noodles.

Seven Vegetable Rice Noodles

12 ozs. fine rice noodles (see NOTE)	2–3 scallions, diagonally sliced into 1-in. pieces (¾ C.)
Few drops oriental sesame oil	⅓ C. thinly sliced radishes, stacked and cut into slivers
1½ C. julienne (cut into 1½-in. lengths) cucumber (1 medium English or Kirby cucumber)	1 C. mung bean sprouts, dried on paper towels
1 large carrot, cut into julienne (¾ C.)	1 large fresh jalapeño chile, seeded and finely minced (1 Tbs.)
1 small turnip, peeled and cut into julienne (½ C.)	2 Tbs. finely minced chives or flat leaf Chinese garlic chives
1 small sweet red pepper, slivered (1 C.)	2 tsps. finely minced ginger
1 small sweet green pepper, slivered (1 C.)	½ C. whole cashew nuts
	¼ C. whole cilantro leaves

The

Versatile

Grain

and the

Elegant

Bean

Place the rice noodles in a very large mixing bowl and cover with hot tap water. Let stand for 30 minutes. Drain and toss with a few drops of sesame oil to prevent the noodles from sticking together. Spread the noodles out on a large serving platter and set aside.

In the same mixing bowl, combine all the vegetables, bean sprouts, jalapeño chile, chives and ginger. Spoon the vegetable mixture over the noodles. Pour the dressing on top, and toss gently right on the platter. Scatter the cashew nuts, cilantro leaves and reserved lime peel shreds on top. Cover with plastic wrap and chill, if you wish, until serving time. Then bring to room temperature just before serving.

NOTE: There are two kinds of rice noodles. The ones used here are made from pounded rice flour and resemble long white hairs. They are very thin, opaque and brittle. When briefly deep fried, they become a crisp garnish. The other kind (called rice sticks) is ¼ inch wide and need to be cooked for 5 to 10 minutes, drained, rinsed and drained again.

Brown Basmati Rice Salad with Bitter Greens and Walnut Vinaigrette

SERVES 6

Sweet, tiny green peas and aromatic toothsome brown basmati rice rest on a colorful bed of salad greens. The sweetness of the peas and the perfume of the rice play against the slightly bitter taste of the greens.

1⅓ C. cooked brown basmati rice (see Chart, page 166)

1–2 large shallots, finely minced (2 Tbs.)

1 C. cooked fresh or frozen (10-oz. package) tiny peas

2 Tbs. balsamic vinegar

Juice of ¼ large lemon (1 Tbs.)

Salt and freshly ground black pepper to taste

1 tsp. grainy mustard

⅓ C. walnut oil

10 C. mixed bitter salad greens such as Belgian endive, radicchio, escarole, arugula, mizuna, curly endive

¼ C. coarsely broken toasted walnuts

In a medium-size bowl, mix the cooked rice with the shallots and peas and set aside. In a small bowl, whisk together the vinegar, lemon juice, salt, pepper and mustard until smooth. Slowly whisk in the walnut oil. Stir 2 tablespoons of this dressing into the rice mixture. Put the remaining vinaigrette into the bottom of a large bowl and add the greens. Toss lightly. Distribute the greens evenly among six salad plates. Place some of the rice mixture in the center of each plate and scatter a few walnuts over the top of each salad.

Warm Wehani Rice Salad with Grapes, Pine Nuts and Smoked Turkey

SERVES 6

Wehani is a reddish-brown hybrid rice crossed with aromatic basmati rice that perfumes the air while it cooks. It is teamed here with hickory-smoked turkey, pale green sweet grapes and creamy white pine nuts in a shallot vinaigrette.

Shallot Vinaigrette

Juice of 1 large lemon
¼ tsp. salt
⅛ tsp. freshly ground black pepper
1 tsp. Dijon-style mustard

5 Tbs. canola or safflower oil
1 large shallot, finely minced (1½ Tbs.)

In a small bowl, whisk together the lemon juice, salt, pepper and mustard. Gradually whisk in the oil until blended. Stir in the shallots and set the dressing aside while preparing the salad, allowing the flavors to mellow.

Wehani Rice Salad

2½ C. cooked hot Wehani rice (see Chart, page 166)
1 C. julienne (cut into thin strips) hickory-smoked turkey or smoked chicken (¼ lb.)
1 C. small green or red seedless grapes
3 Tbs. lightly toasted pine nuts

1 C. sliced (in ½-in. diagonals) scallions, green part only (2 large scallions)
¼ tsp. whole fennel seed
Salt and freshly ground black pepper to taste
18 small leaves ruffled-edge leaf lettuce or other soft lettuce

In a large bowl, gently mix all the ingredients together except for the lettuce leaves. Whisk the shallot vinaigrette, pour over and toss gently again. Distribute among six plates, tucking three leaves of lettuce around the edges of each plate. Serve while still warm or at room temperature.

The
Versatile
Grain
and the
Elegant
Bean

194

Swedish Risengröt:
Raspberry and Rice Flour Flummery

SERVES 4

Silky-textured rice flour is mixed with fragrant, ripe berries in a dessert that is typical of the "flummeries," or grain-thickened fruit puddings one finds throughout the north of Europe.

1 pt. fresh raspberries, or 12-oz. package frozen, defrosted raspberries
½ C. fine sugar
2 tsps. lemon juice
1 Tbs. Cointreau or other orange-flavored liqueur

3¼ C. cold water
¼ C. white rice flour (see NOTE)
Few grains salt
2 Tbs. heavy cream
Mint leaves (optional)

Purée the raspberries in the bowl of a food processor, then force them through a sieve, scraping the bottom of the sieve frequently. Transfer to a small bowl and stir in the sugar, lemon juice and Cointreau and set aside. In a medium-size saucepan, bring 3 cups of the water to a boil. Meanwhile, mix the rice flour and the remaining ¼ cold water together in a small bowl. Slowly whisk some of the boiling water into the rice flour paste, then return to the saucepan and whisk into the remaining water. Add the salt and bring to a boil. Stirring constantly, lower the heat and simmer for 3 to 4 minutes, until thick and smooth. Remove from the heat and stir in the purée mixture.

Spoon and scrape into individual glass goblets or dessert bowls, cover with plastic wrap and chill for several hours or overnight. When ready to serve, put the cream in a small flexible plastic bottle with a pointed tip and squeeze two trickles of cream in circles ½ inch apart. Pull the tip of a sharp knife gently through the cream to make an attractive surface sunburst effect. Or serve with a tiny puff of whipped cream and a mint leaf for garnish.

NOTE: Rice flour is sold in natural food stores and in supermarkets (under the Goya label), or it can be ordered from one of the larger mail order houses (see Mail Order Sources, pages 501–506).

Baked Orange Rice Custard with
Dates and Honey

SERVES 6

Paper-thin orange slices float to the top of a honey and orange rice custard—an ambrosial finale for any dinner party.

2 Tbs. soft butter for greasing soufflé dish

1 C. cooked short grain brown or white rice (see Chart, pages 168–169)

1 C. pitted dates, cut in halves

1 navel orange, peeled and with white pith removed, sliced paper-thin to make about 8–9 slices

2 Tbs. mild light-colored honey, plus ⅓ C.

3 C. milk

1 Tbs. finely minced orange peel

1 tsp. vanilla extract

3 eggs, lightly beaten

⅛ tsp. cinnamon

Preheat the oven to 325° F., butter a 1½-cup soufflé dish and boil a kettle of water. Set the dish in a pan large enough to hold boiling water. Spread the cooked rice evenly on the bottom of the prepared dish, then arrange the dates in a layer to cover the rice. Layer the thin orange slices over the dates and trickle 2 tablespoons of the honey over the orange slices. Set aside.

In a 3-quart nonstick saucepan, scald the milk slowly, but do not let it boil. Add the remaining ⅓ cup honey, the orange peel and vanilla extract. Remove from the heat and let cool for 15 minutes. When cooled, whisk the lightly beaten eggs into the milk mixture and very slowly pour over the rice and fruit. The orange slices will float to the top. Place both pans in the oven and pour 1 inch of the boiling water into the larger pan. Bake for 1½ hours or until the center is firm. Dust the surface with cinnamon and serve warm or cold.

The

Versatile

Grain

and the

Elegant

Bean

196

Rye

Secale cereale

*"Rank weeds that every art and care defy . . ."**

During the researching of all our cookbooks, a thought has often occurred to us, "Who was *the first?*" Who was the first person to determine that our domestic mushroom and nearly 40,000 others were edible? Or—who was the first to learn that thirty-two other species of mushrooms bearing such names as "Trumpet of death" were not particularly beneficial to your health? And who finally discovered that "love apples" (tomatoes) were edible or learned that the tapioca plant was poisonous until processed and cooked? And who, indeed, decided that George Crabbe's "rank week"—rye—might not only be edible but darned good eating too.

As with oats, the rye grain started out as a weed and has risen rather rapidly to become the "star" of the European bread world. Unlike the grains that have been grown for millenniums, rye was a rather late bloomer. The Egyptians and the Sumerians did not include it in their range of crops, and the ancient Greeks and Turks labeled it among their more intrusive and obnoxious weeds.

It appeared in Europe about the time of the Middle Ages, and some clever farmer discovered that culling the weed from the midst of the wheat crop was time consuming and frustrating. So he (it probably was a "he") gave up pulling the weed and harvested the rye along with the wheat, ground it into a flour called *maslin* (*miscelin* in French), occasionally mixed it with pea flour, and started it on its way to becoming the choice of cooks and bakers all over the world, and especially in Europe. By the time of the Renaissance, rye was the basic bread of Britain, as well as the countries in the colder areas of the Continent: Scandinavia, Russia, Germany and most countries in Eastern Europe.

*George Crabbe (1754–1832).

Once again, climate and soil conditions have played a role in the proliferation of the grain, for rye is quite hardy, thriving beautifully not only in poor soil but also in temperatures that would freeze most other grain crops. It also tolerates much wetter conditions than the others. One food writer has called it "feisty" and indeed it is. It probably came to North America with the French, who first planted it in seventeenth-century Nova Scotia, while the Dutch and German settlers brought it to America at the same time.

Much of the rye processed in our own country is not quite like the crop that is grown in Europe. Many travelers have returned from the Continent (the authors included) raving about the breads that were served, crusty and dense and with a memorable sour taste. These breads are also generally much darker than our own rye breads. Many are made from unsifted rye flour, while in our own light or medium flour the bran and/or the germ has probably been sifted out. On a recent trip to Eastern Europe we were reintroduced to those remarkable breads, as well as to the true recipes for dishes such as Hungarian Rye and Cabbage Boards (see page 201) and Beet Cabbage and Tomato Borscht with Rye Berries (see page 202).

Rye itself has a strong taste, but the "sour" flavor usually associated with it generally comes from the fact that starters (such as those used in sourdough breads) impart their own taste to the grain. Rye also ferments easily. In Russia, an alcoholic beverage called *kvass* is made from the grain, while most of our own crop is used to continue the tradition of the Western cowboy who used the grain to make rye whiskey, very much the way the Kentuckians learned to utilize corn for something other than a vegetable.

If George Crabbe and the early farmers had nothing but harsh words about rye, at least William Shakespeare *(As You Like It)* saw some romance in the much-maligned grain, when he wrote that "sweet lovers love the spring" and would lie "between the acres of rye."

The Forms of Rye

Though rye is high in protein, it has a very low gluten content. Thus, if you plan to use it in your bread baking, a ratio of about 30 to 40 percent rye to 60 or 70 percent gluten flours (white or whole wheat) should give excellent results. You will also find that rye gives you a sticky dough.

Whole Grain Rye Berries or Groats. The whole grain with only the outer hull removed. Rye berries can be sprouted and used in soups, salads or breads. They can also be used unsprouted for the same dishes or for stews.

Rye Grits. Whole rye cracked into six or eight separate pieces. It is used often as a cereal or can be mixed with other grains or gluten flour for breads. They are generally available in health food stores or can be ordered by mail (see Mail Order Sources, pages 501–506).

Rye Meal. A pumpernickel-type rye, whole ground to the consistency of cornmeal. Blend it with other flours in your baking.

The

Versatile

Grain

and the

Elegant

Bean

198

Rye Flour. Whole ground into a finer consistency than rye meal. It is generally sold as light (or white, with most or all of the bran removed), medium, dark or pumpernickel. Until a few years ago, all forms were available only in health food stores, but the light and medium have begun to appear on supermarket shelves. If you can't find the pumpernickel, it is available by mail (see Mail Order Sources, pages 501–506). Rye flour, when blended with gluten flours, makes excellent bread, sourdough rolls and crackers.

Rye Flakes or Rolled Rye. Groats that are steamed and then pressed or rolled between high-pressure rollers, very much like rolled oats, but with thicker flakes. They can be cooked and eaten as a morning breakfast, or soaked and used to top breads as a nutritious decoration.

Rye

Grain & Granulation	Amount of Liquid	Cooking Method	Cooking & Standing Time	Approx. Yield	Comments
Whole Grain (1 C. dry)	3¼ C.	Pick over grain, rinse and drain. Bring water to boil, without salt, in 2-qt. saucepan. Add grain, return to a boil. Cover, lower heat and simmer.	1 hour. Let stand 10 minutes.	2 C.	*Salt after cooking* and keep grains at room temperature after cooking. Refrigeration toughens the grains.
Rye Grits (1 C. dry)	3½ C.	Bring salted water to boil in 3-qt. saucepan. Gradually add grits, while stirring. Return to a boil, lower heat and simmer, uncovered, stirring occasionally until thick.	35 to 40 minutes.	2⅔ C.	Though a bit thicker than standard grits, makes a good breakfast cereal.
Rye Flakes or Rolled Rye (1 C. dry)	3 C.	Bring salted water to boil in 3-qt. saucepan. Stir in flakes, return to boil, lower heat, cover and simmer.	25 to 30 minutes. Let stand 5 minutes.	2⅔ C.	Same as rye grits.

Hungarian Rye and Cabbage Boards

MAKES 24 BOARDS

Don't sniff at the cabbage,
Don't turn up your nose,
Remember, the cabbage
Is kin to the rose . . .
—Anonymous

This poem was probably written by someone who ate cabbage more frequently than he or she desired. Since this hearty plant grows abundantly in temperate climates and is one of the few fresh vegetables available all year round, it appears in a great many dishes in Middle European cooking, such as in this one from Hungary.

½ small head green cabbage (about 1 lb.)
1 medium-size onion
2 Tbs. butter
1 Tbs. light brown sugar
¼ tsp. paprika
½ tsp. salt or to taste
¼ tsp. freshly ground black pepper

1 C. light rye flour
¾ C. all-purpose flour
1 tsp. baking powder
2 Tbs. soft butter, cut into pieces
2 Tbs. sour cream
1 egg yolk, plus 1 whole egg
Butter for greasing baking sheets
1 tsp. water

Using a shredder blade of a food processor, shred the cabbage and onion very finely. In a large skillet, melt the butter and stir in the brown sugar. Add the cabbage/onion mixture and stir to coat, then simmer, uncovered, for about 25 to 30 minutes, or until browned, stirring occasionally. Add the paprika, salt and pepper and cool in the refrigerator for 20 minutes (or make this well in advance and then cool it.)

To the bowl of a food processor, add both flours and the baking powder and process for a few strokes to combine. Add the butter and process only until the texture is that of coarse crumbs. Then turn the mixture out into a large bowl. Combine the sour cream and the egg yolk and add to the flour mixture, blending in. Add the reserved cabbage mixture and beat well to combine.

With floured hands and a floured work surface, turn the dough out and knead for 5 minutes, adding more flour as necessary. The dough should be slightly damp and soft. Wrap in aluminum foil and chill for 1 hour. Then preheat the oven to 375° F. and butter two or three baking sheets.

Divide the dough into four pieces. Chill the pieces not being used. Flour a piece of waxed paper and a rolling pin and roll the dough out ¼ inch thick. (Dampen the work surface before laying down the waxed paper so it doesn't slide.) Cut the dough into 6 × 2-inch rectangular strips. Carefully peel off the waxed paper and, with a floured spatula, place the pieces on a baking sheet. Repeat until all the dough is used up, rerolling any scraps. Mix the whole egg with the water and brush this glaze on the surface of each strip. Bake for 15 minutes or until golden.

Lift off with a spatula to a wire rack to cool slightly. The boards should be flexible and should be eaten warm—or reheated in a low oven.

The

Versatile

Grain

Beet, Cabbage and Tomato Borscht
with Rye Berries

SERVES 8 TO 10

Sour, sweet and beefy—a classic favorite: a thick Russian soup served with rye berries instead of the traditional kasha.

1¼ lbs. short ribs of beef, bone in and cut into 2-in. pieces

2 medium onions, coarsely chopped (about 1¼ C.)

3 large cloves garlic, coarsely chopped (1 Tbs.)

2-lb. head green cabbage, coarsely chopped (12 C.)

Salt to taste

¼ tsp. paprika

¼ tsp. freshly ground black pepper or to taste

1-lb. can plum tomatoes, with liquid (2½ C.)

2 C. tomato juice

8 C. water

½ C. rye berries, picked over and washed

½ lb. beets, peeled and quartered

1 large bay leaf

1 tsp. fresh oregano (or ½ tsp. dried oregano)

⅛ tsp. ground cloves

Juice of 2 lemons (about ⅓ C.)

3–4 Tbs. sugar or to taste

In a large 7-quart heavy Dutch oven, sear the meat on all sides over medium high heat. Remove the meat with a slotted spoon and set aside. To the same pot, add the onions and garlic and sauté, stirring, for 5 minutes. Then add the cabbage, salt, paprika and pepper and stir and cook for 5 minutes more.

Return the meat to the pot and add the remaining ingredients, except for the cloves, lemon juice and sugar. Bring to a boil, then lower the heat and simmer with the lid slightly ajar, for 2 hours.

Remove and discard the bay leaf. Then mix the cloves, lemon juice and sugar together and stir into the soup. Taste and adjust the seasoning.

The

Versatile

Grain

and the

Elegant

Bean

202

Sweet and Sour Celery with Rye Berries

SERVES 6

The slightly sour rye berries and tender-crisp celery are a delightfully toothsome combination, one that would go well with an intensely flavored fish such as bluefish or with fresh tuna.

10–12 stalks celery, thinly sliced, cut diagonally (about 4 C.)	1 Tbs. butter
1 bay leaf	2 Tbs. sugar
2 whole cloves	3 Tbs. apple cider vinegar
Salt to taste	Freshly ground black pepper to taste
	2 C. cooked rye berries (see Chart, page 200)

In a 2-quart saucepan, bring the celery, water to cover, bay leaf, cloves, and salt to a boil. Lower the heat and simmer for 1 minute, uncovered, until the celery is tender but still crisp. Strain, discarding the bay leaf, cloves and the liquid. Set the celery aside in a bowl.

Wipe out the saucepan, add the butter and stir in the sugar, cooking over medium heat until the butter melts. Add the vinegar and cook for about 1 minute, then return the celery to the pot. Season with the pepper, stir in the cooked rye berries and heat until hot. Taste and adjust the seasoning before serving.

Rye Berries and Parsley Salad with
Kalamata Olives and Pecorino Cheese

SERVES 6

Fresh curly parsley, thought of primarily as a decorative garnish or as a way to give color to a pale dish, is the major complementary focus of this simple and attractive grain salad.

1 Tbs. red wine vinegar
Few drops lemon juice
Salt and freshly ground black pepper to taste
½ tsp. white wine Worcestershire sauce
3 Tbs. olive oil
1 large bunch curly leaf parsley, very coarsely chopped, with no stems (2 C.)

12–14 Kalamata black olives, pitted and slivered (about ½ C.)
2 medium shallots, finely minced (1 heaping Tbs.)
2 C. cooked rye berries (see Chart, page 200)
6 plum tomatoes, thinly sliced
2 Tbs. grated Pecorino-Romano or Parmesan cheese

In a small bowl, whisk together the vinegar, lemon juice, salt, pepper and Worcestershire sauce, then slowly whisk in the olive oil. Set aside.

Process the parsley in the bowl of a food processor for 5 to 6 strokes, until it is coarsely chopped. Transfer to a large bowl. Add the olives, shallots and rye berries. Mix gently, pour the dressing over and mix again. Place the sliced tomatoes on invidivual plates in overlapping slices. Spoon some of the grain and parsley salad in a small mound on the side and sprinkle with some of the grated cheese.

The

Versatile

Grain

and the

Elegant

Bean

204

Rye and Red Onion Focaccia with Thyme

SERVES 6 TO 8
MAKES 1 LOAF

The Italians would proclaim about this traditional bread, *Ha un profumo delizioso!*—it smells delicious! And it tastes good too. Various toppings go well with this puffed-pizzalike bread, but this one uses red onions and thyme. It tastes best when hot from the oven.

Focaccia

¼-oz. package dry yeast	2 Tbs. extra-virgin olive oil, plus
1 C. warm water	1 tsp.
Pinch sugar	1 C. light rye flour
1 tsp. coarse salt or to taste	2 C. all-purpose white flour
Freshly ground black pepper to taste	(approximately)

Pour the yeast into a large glass or a cup, add ¼ cup of the water and the sugar. Let stand for 5 to 10 minutes to proof. If bubbles do not form by that time, discard the yeast and use another, fresher package.

When the yeast has proofed, pour it into a large mixing bowl, add the rest of the water, salt, a few grindings of fresh pepper and 2 tablespoons of the olive oil. Add the rye flour and 1 cup of the white flour, stirring with a wooden spoon. When blended, flour your hands and pour in the balance of the white flour little by little, using your hands to completely blend the dough. If the dough seems damp, you may need a little more white flour. Blend with your hands until the dough is only slightly damp and smooth, then knead right in the bowl for about 5 to 7 minutes. The dough should pull away completely from the bowl and be very easy to handle. If the dough sticks to your fingers, use more flour.

When the dough is kneaded, rub the remaining olive oil over the dough, turning to coat the bottom. Cover the bowl with a clean kitchen towel and place in a warm place to rise until doubled in size, about 1 hour. Prepare the topping.

Red Onion and Thyme Topping

¼ lb. pancetta (salt-cured Italian bacon), cut into tiny cubes	2 large red onions, peeled and sliced into rings (about 1 lb.)
2 Tbs. olive oil	1 tsp. dried thyme

In a small nonstick pan, sauté the pancetta on high heat until very crisp but not burned, about 5 minutes. Remove from the pan with a slotted spoon. To a large skillet, add the olive oil and heat. Add the onions and thyme and the reserved pancetta. Sauté over medium heat stirring occasionally for about 15 minutes or until the onions are very soft and just turning brown. Then remove them with a slotted spoon and set aside.

| 1 Tbs. olive oil | 1 tsp. dried thyme |
| 1 tsp. coarse or kosher salt | |

Preheat the oven to 450° F. Brush a large baking sheet (see **NOTE**) with some of the olive oil. Punch down the dough and turn out onto a lightly floured surface. Stretch, press and pull the dough into a 12-inch circle. Place the circle on the oiled baking sheet. Prick the dough with a fork at about 1-inch intervals. Then brush the dough with the remaining olive oil and sprinkle the top with coarse salt. Distribute the onion mixture on top of the dough, using a wooden spoon to even it out and to press it down gently into the dough. Bake for 15 minutes or until brown around the edges. Slide off onto a wire rack to cool slightly. Sprinkle the top with the thyme by rubbing it between your fingers. Serve hot.

NOTE: If you happen to own a baking stone, you can use it instead of the baking sheet, dusted with white cornmeal.

Dark Raisin Pumpernickel Bread

MAKES 2 LOAVES

This is *not* one of our own recipes. It comes from a woman of many talents—Kathleen Skelly—who not only illustrated this book, but who makes one helluva raisin pumpernickel bread, the best we ever ate. So why compete?

3 ¼-oz. packages dry yeast	3 C. dark rye flour
1½ C. warm water	2½ C. raisins
¾ C. dark molasses	2½–3 C. whole wheat flour
1 tsp. salt	Oil for greasing bowl
¼ C. unsweetened cocoa	Oil for greasing baking sheet
3 Tbs. caraway seeds (optional)	Cornmeal for dusting pan
2 Tbs. vegetable oil	

The

Versatile

Grain

and the

Elegant

Bean

In a large bowl, dissolve the yeast in the warm water. Add the molasses, salt, cocoa, caraway seeds, oil and rye flour and stir until smooth. Add the raisins. Then stir in enough whole wheat flour to make the dough easy to handle. Turn out onto a lightly floured surface, cover and let rest for 15 minutes. Then knead the dough until smooth, about 8 to 10 minutes. If the dough is too sticky, add a bit more whole wheat flour. Place in an oiled bowl, turn to coat, cover with a clean towel and let rise in a warm place until doubled in size, about 1 to 1½ hours.

Punch the dough down, turn out onto a lightly floured surface and knead for 1 to 2 minutes. Then return to the oiled bowl, turn to coat, cover and let rise in a warm place until doubled again, about 45 minutes.

Punch the dough down, turn out onto a lightly floured surface and divide into two equal parts. Press each piece into a flat shape, about 12 inches square. This can be done roughly with your hands or a floured rolling pin. Roll up the squares, jelly roll fashion, and press on the ends to seal them. (Rolling up the dough distributes the raisins more evenly and gives the bread a lovely spiral texture when cut.) Then round out the ends and place both loaves on an oiled baking sheet that has been sprinkled with cornmeal. Cover the loaves and let rise in a warm place until almost doubled in bulk, 45 to 60 minutes.

Preheat the oven to 350° F. Bake the loaves for 30 to 35 minutes, or until they sound hollow when tapped on the bottom. Cool on wire racks.

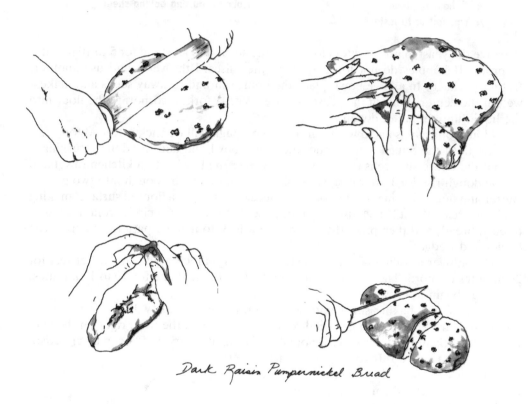

Dark Raisin Pumpernickel Bread

Finnish Rye and
Caraway Flatbread Wheels

MAKES 2 FLATBREADS

In Finland, these flat crunchy breads are traditionally strung on a broom handle and hung to dry until the moisture has evaporated. It is sometimes called "hard tack," and is somewhat like a cracker bread. The Finns break off pieces and use them for open-faced sandwiches.

¼-oz. package dry yeast
1 C. warm water
1 tsp. sugar
2½ C. light rye flour
¾ tsp. salt or to taste

½ tsp. caraway seeds
Oil for greasing bowl
Butter for greasing baking sheet
Flour for dusting baking sheet

Dissolve the yeast in warm water along with the sugar and let stand for 5 to 10 minutes to proof. If bubbles do not form by that time, discard the yeast and use another, fresher package. In a large bowl, place the flour, salt and caraway seeds and make a well in the center. Pour in the yeast mixture. With a fork, incorporate the flour into the liquid until a ball of dough forms.

Flour your hands and a work surface. The dough will be sticky. Knead for a few minutes until the dough feels elastic, then oil a bowl and add the dough, turning it so that the entire surface is coated with oil. Cover the bowl with a kitchen towel and let the dough rise for 1 hour in a warm place. Then divide the dough into two pieces. Butter and flour a baking sheet. Roll each piece of dough on a floured surface, making 8¼-inch circles about ½ inch thick. Cut out and discard a 2-inch circle from the center of each bread, and then prick the bread with a fork to make a pattern of concentric circles and wedges.

Drape over a rolling pin and transfer to the prepared baking sheet. Let rest for 20 minutes or more. Then preheat the oven to 450° F. and bake for 10 to 12 minutes, until they begin to brown.

Slide off the baking sheet onto a wire rack. The breads will be pliable when removed. Turn off the oven heat and return the breads to the oven right on the wire rack. Leave them there for several hours or overnight to dry and become very crisp. Or do as the Finns do. If you live in an area where the humidity is low, string them on a broom handle and suspend them for a few days until they are dry and crisp. Store in an airtight container.

The

Versatile

Grain

and the

Elegant

Bean

208

rye & caraway flat bread wheels

Teff

Eragrostis Tef

Ancient Grain of Ethiopia

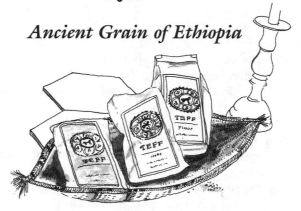

The arrival of teff in this country is really the result of one person's dedication and interest, and it has all happened within the past eight years. Wayne Carlson spent seven years in Ethiopia in the early 1970s, working as a biologist. While he was there, he became familiar with the most common grain of the country, used by the Ethiopians not only for their ubiquitous bread, *injera,* but as a versatile and nutritious grain, especially when combined with legumes, as in many of their native dishes.

Returning to the United States, he started experimenting with teff in his backyard, expanding quickly as the demand by the expatriate Ethiopian community (about 60,000 currently living here) began to grow. Today, with his wife and partner Elizabeth, he harvests over 200 acres under the name of Maskal Forages, Inc., out in Caldwell, Idaho. And little by little the grain has begun to appear outside the Ethiopian community in health food stores, and little by little it has begun to be discovered and accepted by those of us who have never even been to Ethiopia, and could not give details about the daily diet of the country.

As usual, the first reactions here were doubting and cynical. In a telephone conversation with Wayne, he said that the first responses were, "Why would anyone want to grow something that they grow in *Africa?*" And one U.S. Department of Agriculture spokesperson added in classic governmental perception, "The last thing we need is *another* cereal grain!" And as for anyone else even trying to grow it, Wayne says that "no one will grow anything unusual or different unless they know that *someone else* is doing it and marketing it!"

Nonetheless, teff is slowly becoming yet another cereal grain available to the general public, and it happens to be not only nutritious but tasty as well. In a sense, it is all very curious, for teff—like many other grains that have entered our culinary vocabulary—has been around for centuries, if only we had cared to look. And even today, over 35 million people depend upon it and swear by it.

Teff has been described frequently as a "milletlike" grain, and therein lies the confusion, for it is not millet at all. It is probably the most minute grain, taking about 150 seeds to weigh the same as *one* grain of wheat. It is a powerhouse of nutrition, much higher in iron and calcium than wheat, rice, millet or oats, and because it is so tiny, the entire grain must be milled, for there is no way to remove the germ or the husk.

In the Amharic language, teff means "lost," and the description refers to the fact that much of the tiny seed disappears when it's handled and it can't be found if it's dropped on the desert floor (or even in a modern kitchen). Its size has yet another advantage, for in times of crisis, when populations in Ethiopia become nomadic, either through choice or violence, a pocketful of the tiny seed is quite enough to start another crop at the final destination of the family, for it grows well in poor or sandy soils.

The classic use for teff is the traditional Ethiopian bread, *injera.* It is a fermented, very sour bread that measures as much as two feet in diameter and closely resembles a spongy pancake or crêpe. It's made on the concave side of a utensil that looks very much like the Chinese wok. Historians have suggested that *injera* is a direct descendant or relative of other flat breads of the world, probably dating back to the Neolithic period. Teff seeds were found in the ruins of the Dassur Pyramid in Egypt and carbon-dated back to 3359 B.C. Thus, the Indian chapati and *roti,* the Mexican tortilla, the Middle Eastern *markouk* and the traditional Afghan breads are all of similar ancestry.

Frequently, legumes like lentils and garbanzo beans are ground into the *injera* batter to make a more complete amino acid balance, or the legumes are used in the Ethiopian stews (called *Watt* or *Wat*), eaten with the hands, sopping up the meat and the sauce with the *injera.* For many, though, especially in this country, *injera* is an acquired taste with an intense sourness rarely acceptable to the Western palate. As a result, we have not included a recipe for the bread.

The Forms of Teff

Maskal Forages has begun to distribute to health food stores around the country, but they also handle mail order if you can't locate it (see Mail Order Sources, pages 501–506). Teff now comes in three colors: red, brown and white. White is the most delicate and the mildest of the three, and Wayne Carlson notes that even though it's white, it is *not* processed. The red and brown teff have a richer, nuttier flavor.

Whole Grains. Though the Ethiopians would never hear of it, whole grain teff makes a hearty, tasty breakfast cereal. There is no need to presoak the grains, but they should be cooked long enough to make the grains burst open. If they are cooked too short a time, the bran layer will not open and the grain will stay intact.

Teff Flour. The flour is now being sold in health food stores and through mail order, but it can also be made with a home grinder—stone or steel. (If possible, use stone.)

The

Versatile

Grain

and the

Elegant

Bean

You can't grind teff grains in a spice grinder because the grain is much too tiny to mill. See "Grinding Your Own Grains, page 281.

Teff Pasta. Maskal Forages is still experimenting with a line of pasta, and the availability will probably change from time to time. Currently we have tried three kinds:

- 50 percent teff, 50 percent whole wheat
- 50 percent teff, 50 percent semolina
- Wheat-free: 50 percent teff, 50 percent wild rice

Teff

Grain & Granulation	Amount of Liquid	Cooking Method	Cooking & Standing Time	Approx. Yield	Comments
Whole Grain (1 C. dry)	3 C.	*Method I* (toasted): In a 2-qt. saucepan, melt 2 Tbs. butter and toast grain, stirring constantly until you smell a pleasant fragrance. Add boiling salted water. It will sputter. Return to boil, then cover and simmer over *very* low heat, stirring toward end of cooking time.	15 minutes.	3 C.	The grain will be very thick after cooking. When toasted, has a mellow taste and a natural sweetness, plus a crunchy texture, like miniature caviar eggs.
	3 C.	*Method II* (untoasted): In a 2-qt. saucepan, bring salted water to a boil. Slowly add grains, stirring constantly. Return to boil and simmer, covered, stirring toward end of cooking time.	15 minutes.	3 C.	Milder flavor but same texture as above. Can be spooned into nonstick pan and smoothed down, stored in refrigerator until needed and then cut and fried in butter and eaten with maple syrup for an excellent and nutritious breakfast.

Teff Potato and Cheese Biscuits

MAKES 15

Cocoa-colored teff flour and little bursts of cheese give these very tender feather-light biscuits a surprisingly unique, delicious flavor.

6-oz. baking potato such as Idaho or russet, peeled and cut in large pieces
4 Tbs. soft butter
½ C. milk
1¼ C. all-purpose flour

½ C. teff flour
4 tsps. baking powder
¾ tsp. salt or to taste
Scant ¼ tsp. freshly ground black pepper
¾ C. shredded extra-sharp Cheddar cheese

In a small saucepan, cook the potatoes in salted water for 10 minutes. Drain well, add the butter and milk and mash the potatoes in the pan with a potato masher or a fork. Set aside to cool slightly.

Preheat the oven to 425° F. In a medium-size bowl, add the flours, baking powder, salt and pepper and whisk to combine. Stir in the cheese, then add the warm potato mixture and mix lightly with a wooden spoon until a soft dough forms and leaves the sides of the bowl.

Generously flour a work surface and your hands and knead the dough fifteen times, absorbing some of the flour as you knead. Then pat the dough into a ½-inch-thick circle and cut it with a 2-inch floured cookie or biscuit cutter. Or use a glass 2 inches in diameter. Knead in the scraps and continue cutting until all the dough is used up.

Place the biscuits close together on an ungreased 10-inch nonstick cake pan and bake them for about 20 to 25 minutes or until the tops begin to darken slightly. Serve warm.

Savory Vidalia Onion and
Teff Pancakes with Sage

MAKES 14 PANCAKES

Vidalia onions from Georgia—once only available at specialty produce shops—are now found in supermarkets when they come into season from May through August. These sweet delectable onions are a wonderful counterpoint for fresh sage and the unique flavor of the teff in these pancakes, which are crisp on the outside and slightly soft and moist within.

⅓ C. teff flour
½ C. all-purpose flour
2 tsps. baking powder
Pinch sugar
¾ tsp. salt or to taste
¼ tsp. freshly ground black pepper
6–8 large leaves fresh sage, finely minced (about 1 Tbs.)

2 Tbs. finely minced parsley
½ pound Vidalia onions, finely chopped (about 1½ C.)
¼ C. milk, or more
2–3 drops Tabasco sauce
1 tsp. white wine Worcestershire sauce
4–6 Tbs. canola or olive oil

In a medium-size mixing bowl, combine the flours, baking powder, sugar, salt and pepper. Then add the sage, parsley and onions and stir to mix well. In a small cup, mix the milk with the Tabasco and Worcestershire sauce. Add it to the bowl and combine to form a stiff batter. Depending upon the moisture of the onions, a bit more milk may be needed.

In a 10-inch nonstick skillet, heat 2 tablespoons of the oil over medium heat. Drop heaping tablespoonfuls of batter onto the skillet and flatten each with a spatula. Cook for about 2 minutes or until one side is brown, then turn the pancakes over, flatten them again and continue to cook until the other side is brown, about 3 minutes more.

Remove and keep warm in a preheated low oven. Recoat the skillet with 2 tablespoons more of oil for each batch. Serve as a side dish with pork or chicken, or with applesauce as a luncheon dish.

The

Versatile

Grain

and the

Elegant

Bean

214

Teff Pepperoni Bread

MAKES 1 LARGE LOAF

This is yet another bread made with a flour that we seldom, if ever, use. And, we can't imagine why not, for teff has its own natural sweetness and individual taste. The slivers of pepperoni add to both the surprise and to the remarkably good flavor of this bread.

¼-oz. package dry yeast
¼ C. warm water, plus 1 C.
Pinch sugar, plus 1 tsp.
¼ lb. pepperoni
¾ C. cooked whole grain red or brown teff (use Method I, see Chart, page 212)

3½–4 C. all-purpose flour
1½ tsps. salt
2 Tbs. olive oil
Oil for greasing the bowl

Put the yeast into a measuring cup with the ¼ cup of water. Add a pinch of sugar and stir. Let stand for 5 to 10 minutes until the bubbles form. If the yeast does not bubble up, discard and start with a new package.

Cut the pepperoni into very small thin julienne strips, about ½ inch long. Set them aside. Then, in a large bowl, put the teff, 3 cups of the all-purpose flour, the remaining 1 teaspoon sugar, salt and the pepperoni strips. Pour in the yeast mixture and the olive oil. The teff will start out as one large lump, but will magically begin to separate into tiny grains as the procedure continues. Stir the mixture with a wooden spoon.

Slowly add the remaining 1 cup water, stirring as you do so. The dough will be slightly wet. Add part of the remaining white flour very gradually, stirring it in as you do so, then taking over with floured hands. When the dough is still damp but pulls away from the mixing bowl, turn it out onto a lightly floured surface and knead for 5 to 8 minutes, adding flour as you need it and flouring your hands as you do so. Since the teff has liquid in it, the dough will remain slightly damp. When smooth, oil the mixing bowl and place the dough in it, turning once to coat the other side. Then cover with a clean towel and place in a warm place to double in size, about 45 minutes to 1 hour.

When the dough has doubled, turn out onto a lightly floured surface and punch it down, kneading lightly for 2 to 3 minutes. If necessary, add a little more flour to keep the dough from sticking. Butter a 9 × 5 × 3-inch loaf pan and put the dough in it, pressing the dough down to fill the pan completely. Cover the pan with the towel again and put in a warm place. Let rise for about 40 to 45 minutes more, until doubled in size.

Preheat the oven to 375° F. Using a sharp razor blade, slash the top of the dough in two or three diagonals, then with a plant mister spray the dough with warm water to give the crust more crunch. Bake for 45 minutes or until the bottom sounds hollow when tapped. Put the pan on a rack to cool and after about 10 minutes turn the loaf out and continue to cool on the rack. Serve warm or reheat in the oven later on.

Teff Orange Puffs

SERVES 8

An intensely flavored orange sauce forms naturally on the bottom of the baking cups in this light citrus dessert. Long shreds of orange peel add a decorative note.

Butter for greasing custard cups
2 eggs, at room temperature, separated
Pinch cream of tartar
½ C. fine sugar
4 Tbs. soft butter
¼ C. thawed frozen orange juice concentrate, undiluted

1 tsp. vanilla extract
2 Tbs. teff flour
¼ tsp. salt
1 C. milk
Shreds of orange peel, made with a zester tool

Preheat the oven to 325°F. and boil a kettle of water. Butter eight ½-cup custard or soufflé cups and put the cups in a large, shallow pan. Set aside.

In a medium-size deep bowl, beat the egg whites and cream of tartar with a beater until foamy and doubled in volume. Gradually add 2 tablespoons of the sugar, beating until stiff peaks form and the meringue is shiny. Set aside.

In the bowl of a food processor, cream the butter, the remaining sugar and the egg yolks until light and fluffy. Add the orange juice concentrate and vanilla and process until combined. Sift the flour and salt together and add. Then add the milk and process until mixed. The batter will be thin. Gently fold the batter into the meringue and spoon into the prepared cups. Pour boiling water into the pan to a depth of 1 inch. Bake for 30 to 35 minutes or until the tops spring back when lightly pressed with the fingertips.

Remove the cups and place on a wire rack to cool slightly. Then run a knife around the edge of the cups to loosen the puddings. They will shrink a bit as they cool. Invert them on a serving plate, scraping out any sauce that remains on the bottom of the cup and putting it on the surface of the puffs. Scatter a few shreds of orange peel over the tops and serve slightly warm or cold.

The

Versatile

Grain

and the

Elegant

Bean

216

Triticale

Triticum Secale

The Marriage of Wheat and Rye

Any cookbook author worth his or her salt must start out with the pronunciation of the grain: trit-i-*KAY*-lee. Back in the 1960s, it was proclaimed as a possible "super food" to help combat the nutritional needs of the world's exploding population, and a great many articles began to appear both in the technical press and in newspapers across the country about this new miracle grain. In 1975, it was even the subject of a very long speech to the Congress by the late Senator John Tower of Texas, titled "Was Malthus Right?" in which he said in part:

> One of the bright spots in this dreary outlook [He was referring to the Malthus theory (eighteenth century) in which he said that the earth could not produce enough food to feed the indefinite growth of the population.] is the result of work done in my home state, in a small town named Muleshoe.
>
> In Muleshoe, a grain hybrid called triticale is being developed and marketed in bakery products which, I understand, are both tasty and more nutritious than products derived from wheat. Triticale, a cross between wheat and rye, was first produced by a whim of nature . . .

Essentially, the good senator was quite right. As we mentioned, rye was first discovered as a weed that proliferated in the fields of wheat; many of the plants were cross-bred by nature, but the resultant seed was genetically unstable and turned out to be hybrid.

During the 1800s, agronomists and botanists in Europe continued to experiment with the cross between wheat and rye, discovering in their work that the combination was also very protein-rich with a better balance of amino acids than pure wheat, and that it could thrive in much poorer soil than its cousins. Nevertheless, the plant continued to be infertile, and in 1876, botanist A. Stephen Wilson wrote sadly that the plants were totally barren with "not a single kernel having been produced."

In the 1930s, the problem was finally solved. Having studied the sex life of wheat and rye for almost a century, the scientists discovered that the addition of a natural drug (colchicine) would cause the chromosomes to pair (since it takes two to re-create), and *voilà!* triticale became the first human engineered grain in history.

We first discovered it about the time that Mel wrote *Bread Winners* in the late 1970s and we were delighted with its taste and its nutritional value. Through that period, sales of both the whole grain and the flour began to rise and it was again proclaimed "amazing" and a super grain. However, soon after, public acceptance seemed to wane and our friend Frank Ford of Arrowhead Mills told us that, in spite of its qualities, it just didn't seem to catch on, even with cooks who utilized wheat and rye—but would not try a combination.

Interestingly enough, either through a renewed interest in nutrition, or a new generation willing to try something a bit different, triticale seems to be having a revival and we are beginning to discover it again in our favorite health food stores. (It is also available by mail order.) Even some commercial breakfast cereals, such as Barbara's 14 Grains, are including triticale in their mix. And we continue to use it generously in our breads (both berries and flour), in soups, cakes and in pancakes.

Most of all, we love its taste—a bit more flavorful than wheat but not quite as strong as rye. Some have described the taste as "nutlike" or "ryelike," but we think that it has its own distinctive signature, rather mild with a very pleasant and individual aftertaste.

Will triticale be the grain that proves Malthus wrong? It is not for us to predict, for too many "miracle" plants have been the subject of great publicity and expectation, only to find that the public seems to return to their preferred basics of wheat, rice, corn and oats. We think it's worth a try.

The Forms of Triticale

Whole Grain Berries or Groats. Whole berries can also be cracked just like wheat berries to shorten the cooking time, or they can be sprouted for a more nutritious addition to breads or soups. They're also delicious in pilafs.

Triticale Flour. The gluten content of the flour is very low, though it does exist. We find that the best results come with the addition of about 50 percent unbleached white flour (or whole wheat flour) for lightness and ease of kneading and handling. It *will* work by itself, and in any case, most professional bakers suggest that triticale breads be allowed to rise only once, and that kneading be done much more gently than with ordinary dough, since the delicate walls in triticale flour may collapse under rough handling as the gluten develops.

The

Versatile

Grain

and the

Elegant

Bean

218

Triticale

Grain & Granulation	Amount of Liquid	Cooking Method	Cooking & Standing Time	Approx. Yield	Comments
Whole Grain Berries or Groats (1 C. dry)	3 C.	Soak berries overnight in 3 C. water. Drain berries, reserving soaking water. Measure and add enough additional water to make 3 cups. *Do not add salt.* Use a 3-qt. saucepan and bring water to a boil. Add soaked berries and return to boil. Lower heat and simmer.	1 hour 10 minutes. Let stand 5 minutes.	2½ C.	Salt prevents the absorption of liquid. Salt after cooking. The berries will be tender with a slightly pleasant crunch.

Vidalia Onion, Sage and
Olive Triticale Torte

SERVES 6

A savory "upside-down" cake with a buttermilk biscuit dough. The torte is inverted and the top layer is crusty with golden cheese, onions, peppers, olives and a touch of fresh sage. Served with a crisp green salad, it's a complete lunch.

Butter for greasing cake pan
1 small roasted red pepper, cut into 8 thin strips
12 large, black olives, pitted and cut in half (preferably Kalamata or Alfonso olives)
2 Tbs. olive oil
2 large Vidalia onions or sweet Bermuda onions (about ¼ lb.), thinly sliced, but slices kept intact—do not separate into rings
Salt to taste, plus ¾ tsp. (or to taste)

Freshly ground black pepper to taste
2 Tbs. finely shredded fresh sage
1 C. triticale flour
1 C. all-purpose flour
½ tsp. baking soda
¼ tsp. freshly ground black pepper to taste
½ small onion, grated (1 Tbs.)
4 Tbs. butter, cut into small pieces
¾ C. buttermilk
3 oz. shredded Gruyère cheese

Butter a 9½ × 2-inch round nonstick cake pan. Arrange the peppers and olives in a design on the bottom of the pan and set aside. In a large skillet, heat the oil and add the sliced onions. Slowly sauté, turning the onions carefully so they don't separate into rings. When softened, lift out the slices with a spatula and arrange them in overlapping slices over the peppers and olives. Sprinkle the onions with salt, pepper and the sage, then set aside.

Preheat the oven to 400° F. In a medium-size bowl, whisk together the flours, the baking soda, the ¾ teaspoon salt and the pepper. Stir in the grated onion. With a pastry blender, cut in the butter until a coarse, crumbly texture is formed. Stir in the buttermilk and mix to form a dough. Turn the dough out onto a lightly floured surface and, with floured hands, knead for only thirty strokes. Roll or pat the dough into a 9-inch disk and press it gently over the onion layer.

Bake for about 35 minutes. Remove from the oven and cool for 5 minutes on a wire rack. Raise the heat to broil. Invert the torte onto a baking sheet. Scatter the Gruyère cheese over the top and slip the torte under the broiler, watching carefully, until the cheese melts and the top gets slightly golden. Slide the torte onto a serving platter. Cool slightly before cutting it into wedges.

The

Versatile

Grain

and the

Elegant

Bean

220

Dill and Triticale Yeast Bread
with Triticale Berries

MAKES 1 LOAF

Although this bread takes three rises and is time consuming, it does not require your constant individual attention. Mel, the expert bread baker in our family, goes for a walk or a bike ride between rises, then comes back and kneads a bit and leaves for another activity like surf casting off the Fire Island beach. The result: a delicious light bread and a well-exercised mate.

¼-oz. package dry yeast
¼ C. warm water
Pinch sugar
1 Tbs. soft butter, cut into small pieces
1 C. sour cream
1 Tbs. light mild honey
1 egg, beaten
2 Tbs. finely minced onions
2 Tbs. finely minced dill

1 C. triticale flour
1½ C. whole wheat flour
1 C. bread flour
½ tsp. baking soda
½ C. cooked triticale berries (see Chart, page 219) or cooked whole wheat berries (see Chart, page 230)
Oil for greasing bowl
Butter for greasing loaf pan
1 egg white, beaten until foamy
1 tsp. dill seeds

In a small cup, dissolve the yeast in the water. Add the sugar and stir. Let stand for 5 to 10 minutes until the mixture is bubbly. If the yeast does not foam, discard it and start with a new package.

Pour the yeast mixture into a large mixing bowl and add the butter, sour cream, honey, egg, onions and dill and beat well with a wooden spoon. Set aside. Then, to a medium-size bowl, add the flours and the baking soda and whisk to combine. Stir in the cooked triticale berries and add to the liquid ingredients, stirring with a wooden spoon until a dough begins to form. Flour your hands and a work surface, then turn out the dough and knead for 5 to 10 minutes or until it feels elastic. If the dough is too damp, knead in a bit more bread flour. Then oil a large bowl and rotate the dough in the bowl to cover the surface with oil. Cover the bowl with a clean dish towel and put in a warm place to rise for 1 hour.

Turn the dough out onto a floured surface and knead again for 8 to 10 strokes. Return to the bowl again, cover with the towel and put in a warm place for the second rising, about 50 minutes.

Butter a 9 × 5 × 3-inch loaf pan, punch down the dough and shape into a loaf, then put in the pan. Cover the pan with the cloth once again and let rise in a warm place for 30 minutes more. Preheat the oven to 350° F. and bake for 45 to 50 minutes. Remove the loaf from the oven 5 minutes before it is done, and quickly brush the surface with the beaten egg white. Scatter the dill seeds over the surface and return the bread to the oven to complete the baking. Cool on a wire rack for 15 minutes before removing it from the pan. Serve warm or at room temperature. If you freeze the bread, make sure it's wrapped tightly in aluminum foil.

Triticale Carrot Spice Cake with
Maple Walnut Frosting

SERVES 6 TO 8

If you are a carrot cake aficionado you will love the taste of this triticale cake with its hint of rye flavor. It's redolent with sweet spices and just a taste of maple syrup. Although it normally serves six to eight people, *four* of us demolished one right after it was baked!

Cake

Triticale Carrot Cake

Butter for greasing pan
1 C. triticale flour
1 C. all-purpose flour
2 tsps. baking powder
1 tsp. baking soda
Pinch salt
½ tsp. freshly grated nutmeg
½ tsp. ground cloves
2 tsps. cinnamon
½ C. raisins

½ C. coarsely broken, toasted walnuts
¾ C. maple syrup
⅔ C. canola oil
2 eggs
1 tsp. vanilla extract
3–4 carrots, shredded with the shredder blade of a food processor (about 2 C.)
Peel of ½ lemon, finely minced (1 tsp.)

Preheat the oven to 350° F. and butter a 9-inch springform cake pan. In a large bowl, combine the dry ingredients with a whisk. Stir in the raisins and nuts and set aside. In another bowl, whisk together the maple syrup and the oil, then whisk the eggs one at a time until well incorporated. Stir in the vanilla, carrots and the lemon peel, then add the egg mixture to the dry ingredients, beating well with a wooden spoon. Pour and scrape the batter into the prepared pan and bake for 45 to 50 minutes. Test to see if cake is done by inserting a cake tester. If it comes out clean, remove the cake to a wire rack and let it cool completely before removing the sides of the springform pan. Leave the cake on the base. Just before serving, use a wide spatula to loosen and slide the cake off the base onto a serving plate. Frost with the Maple Walnut Frosting.

Maple Walnut Frosting

3-oz. package of softened cream cheese
1 Tbs. soft butter

3 Tbs. maple syrup
2 Tbs. finely chopped, toasted walnuts

In a food processor mix together all the ingredients except the walnuts until smooth. Chill for 15 minutes, then spread *on top* of the cake only. Sprinkle with the chopped nuts, scattering them around the rim of the frosting.

The

Versatile

Grain

and the

Elegant

Bean

222

Wheat

Triticum

Amber Waves of Grain . . .

**Wisdom, Power and Goodness meet
In the bounteous field of wheat.**
—Hannah Flagg Gould (1789–1865), *The Wheatfield*

Very little needs to be said about wheat in order to get some sort of instant recognition of the grain. For, along with corn and rice, it is probably the grain with which most North Americans are most familiar. If ever a quiz show contestant were to be asked about the first thing that comes to mind when "wheat" is mentioned, the almost immediate reaction might well be "America the Beautiful" and the "amber waves of grain" or "wheat is the staff of life." And if asked what is the primary use of wheat, there is no doubt in our minds that the correct answer would be forthcoming: *bread!* For almost all of the wheat grown in North America goes into the milling of unbleached or bleached varieties of white flour.

Wheat is one of the most important food crops in the world today (along with rice), and it is grown in almost every country on earth and in almost every state in the Union. It is so well known, in fact, that it is generally used as the comparative measure of nutrition for other grains by agronomists and botanists (and even these two authors): ". . . compared to wheat." It vies with barley as the oldest cultivated cereal grain, with some food historians dating it back to Iraq about 8,500 years ago. Naturally, along the way it has also been used as a political weapon with wheat sales sometimes dominating the newpaper headlines, and it has exerted a strong influence on history. Also, along the way, it has picked up its share of gods and goddesses, taboos and traditions.

The Greeks worshipped Demeter, the goddess of agriculture, while the Romans had Ceres and the Egyptians their Isis as well as an idol made of unleavened wheat dough that was placed in the area where the wheat was pounded down by the hooves of buffalo, also serving as a fertility symbol. Even today, in Turkey, sheaves of wheat are hung over the doorways to protect the home and to assure health and fertility. In some countries in the Middle East, should a piece of bread fall on the ground, it is picked up at once and kissed, with the perpetrator asking forgiveness of God. And all through Middle Europe, in a tradition that has been carried to this country by immigrants, bread and salt are brought to a new home to ensure good fortune.

On a more practical level, we usually credit the Egyptians of about 6,000 years ago with discovering that wheat breads could be made to rise, though the scientific reasons were forced to wait a few millennia. The starchy endosperm of the wheat berry contains gluten-forming proteins and thus is the perfect vehicle for the properties of yeast. When yeast is added from its natural state in the air or from today's dry or cake yeast, a wheat dough can be made to rise when carbon dioxide gas is produced during the kneading and the elastic gluten expands under the heat. The Egyptians probably made loaves that were quite primitive by today's standards, but it is the same principle that works to give us the puffy loaves that grace the shelves of our bakeries and supermarkets. Since white flour contains most of the starchy endosperm, it thus rises more beautifully than any other flour.

Of course, since the Egyptians had no real idea of just what was taking place, they came up with a solution that preceded the famed San Francisco sourdough starter. Each time they finished the rising and right before baking, they tore off a little piece of the fermented dough and used it in the next batch. And, no fools they, the Egyptians of that time also found a way to use the fermentation for a drink that closely resembled beer.

Our memories of wheat fields closely approximate what anyone who has visited the Great Plains has seen, sometimes by car or train, or flying over the land at 35,000 feet. The fields of wheat seem unending and vast, and indeed they are. And if you have traveled through other parts of the globe, wheat has probably made an indelible mark on your memory as it has on ours, for each culture harvests and prepares the crop for market in its own traditional way. The winnowing (removing the chaff) of the wheat kernels can be done in its most primitive form by throwing the grain up in billowing blankets to let the wind take the residue or by the use of electric fans to do the job, or by the most modern of technologies that process the wheat by the hundreds of tons.

Our most memorable experience came some years ago in Chile, in the foothills of the Andes. Seeing a long, funnel-like cloud of yellow chaff rising above the hilltop, we asked about it and were told that the farmers were winnowing wheat. We walked about two miles to the top of the hill, carrying our camera equipment on our shoulders, and were greeted with a sight that remains indelibly etched in our minds even today. In a large corral, the wheat crop had been unloaded and, followed by two whooping, yelling *huasos* (cowboy farmers), a herd of *wild horses* was running round the circle and stirring up the storm of chaff to let the wind blow it away.

There is a minor postscript to the story. All activity stopped when we were spotted, and we asked if we could film the event for a travel film that we were

The

Versatile

Grain

and the

Elegant

Bean

224

producing. A sly smile crossed the face of one cowboy and he led a horse over to Mel, threw a serape on his shoulders, and stepped back. Yes, they told us, they *would* let us film them, but only if the "gringo" would ride the horse in the corral. Behind the wild horses? Of course. What other way was there? What they didn't know was that Mel had trained on his father's dude ranch and could ride quite well, so followed by one of the cowboys, he whooped into the corral behind the herd, did two or three turns and then swerved out, scared to death. However, the cowboys were true to their word and they spent the rest of the day working for the camera and after introducing us to their wives and women friends even did a *cueca,* the traditional Chilean dance on horseback.

When it comes to the marketing of wheat, there is yet another story to be told. Here in the United States, wheat has become the victim of the most processing, with a resultant draining of the food value found in the original berry. Our almost universal choice of white flour gives us much less protein and calcium than whole wheat, about 74 percent less potassium and an overall loss of from 20 to 30 percent of the natural vitamins and minerals. And that's before the commercial food processors really get hold of it. They take a perfectly healthy wheat berry, remove the germ, excise the bran, shred it, puff it, crush it and then sell it back to us at twice the price or more of the purest and most wholesome form.

We do seem to detect a trend, however, possibly because more and more nutritional information seems to be available to the general public. We think that the average consumer is fast becoming aware of the value of whole grains. Even the commercial food processors are in a race to produce the most healthful wheat cereals and whole grain breads and the proliferation of small bakeries that now sell the dense, dark brown loaves is continuing. In our own downtown New York area, there is a weekly green market that offers the freshest of produce and the vegetable bounty of nearby local farms. Each week we visit and the longest line by far is in front of a truck that brings its whole grain breads from upstate, a wonderful bakery called *Bread Alone,* and the faces of the customers, each one clutching his or her prize of a heavy loaf of bread baked with whole wheat flour, is a delightful sight to see.

The Varieties of Wheat

When we hear the terms *spring wheat* or *winter wheat,* we are referring only to the time of year that the crop is planted. Depending upon the conditions of the climate— months of rainfall, temperature conditions, etc.—the farmers choose the proper time to plant their crops. Actually, though, there are literally thousands of varieties grown around the world (some agronomists count as many as 30,000!), all of them falling into the major categories of spring or winter wheats. Essentially, for the home cook or baker, there are only a very few with which you need to become familiar:

- **Hard Wheat.** Has the highest gluten content and thus is chosen mostly for the baking of bread.
- **Soft Wheat.** Has a higher carbohydrate content than hard wheat and less gluten. Generally it is used for pastries, cookies and cakes.

- **Durum Wheat.** The hard durum wheat represents only a small part of the crop here in the United States and it is used mostly for the production of pastas, since its hard starch granules hold together quite well during cooking. It was the introduction of durum wheat in Europe that made possible not only the pasta but also the hardtack (sea biscuits) that sailors took with them on long journeys. Both the golden-colored semolina flour and couscous are made of durum wheat.

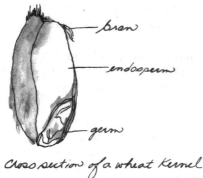

bran

endosperm

germ

Cross section of a wheat kernel

The Forms of Wheat

Whole Grain Wheat Berries. The whole grains of wheat. After soaking, the berries can be cooked and used for pilafs, soups, stews or as a crunchy, healthful addition to home-baked breads. When they're sprouted, wheat berries can be made into croquettes or added to salads or baked goods.

Whole Peeled Wheat Berries. They're sometimes called *frumento* or *grano* in Italian cooking and baking or you may see them as *kutia* in African recipes. They're pale golden in color with only the outer hull removed. They can be used in desserts and cakes or eaten as a pilaf or morning cereal. The peeled berries can also be added to baked goods or soups and they have a gelatinous quality and a delicate flavor when cooled.

Whole Green Wheat Berries. The Germans call them *gruenken* and they're used throughout Middle Europe, as well as in the Middle East, where they're called *frik* or *freeka*. They are the kernels of wheat picked while still unripened and then dried. They have a grassy flavor and are commonly used for casseroles, soups and stews, as well as for pilafs. Green wheat berries can also be ground into flour. They can be found in health food stores or specialty shops or they can be ordered by mail (see Mail Order Sources, pages 501–506). However, be sure to spread the grains out and pick them over to remove foreign matter before using.

Cracked Wheat. Whole wheat berries that have been cracked into coarse or medium granulation. Use them for cereals, casseroles, soups or as a meat extender. Cracked wheat should not be confused with bulgur, which it often is (see below). To identify and distinguish cracked wheat, note that the interior of the uncooked grain is *white*. Bulgur is uniform in color.

Bulgur. Whole wheat that has been washed, steamed, hull removed, then parched or dry-cooled. It is then cracked or sifted into its basic forms. Cracked wheat is uncooked, while bulgur is essentially "precooked" before you use it, so that they are handled quite differently. We have given detailed information about bulgur in its own chapter (see page 63).

The

Versatile

Grain

and the

Elegant

Bean

226

Whole Wheat Grits. The wheat berries are cracked into six or eight pieces, the same process as that used for cracked wheat. However, since the grits are finer, they cook more quickly.

Shredded Whole Wheat. Manufactured commercially in several forms, including large biscuits and small bite-size morsels. In recent years, a form of shredded wheat has been marketed with the addition of bran, and without the use of sugar, a rare occurrence in the world of breakfast cereals.

Whole Unprocessed Pure Bran Flakes. Sometimes called Miller's Bran, it is the outer layer of the hard wheat kernel or berry. It's used to add extra fiber to baked goods or it can be sprinkled on hot or cold cereals. Buy the *unprocessed* variety, since the "ready-to-eat" bran cereals are usually processed.

Wheat Germ. The untreated natural embryo of the wheat berry. It's ready to eat, either raw or toasted, and it can be used for breading poultry, meat or fish, as an extender of meat or for nutritional enhancement in baked goods. Sprinkle some on yogurt or on any cooked or ready-to-eat cereal, put it in candies, cakes, cookies or desserts. Wheat germ must be refrigerated after opening the jar, since the germ contains oils that will quickly turn rancid at room temperature. The best bet is to buy small amounts at a time.

Whole Wheat Flakes or Rolled Wheat. These are wheat berries that are heated and pressed in the same manner as rolled oats, barley, rye or rice. The flakes are quick-cooking and can be used as a cooked cereal or scattered on the surface of baked goods.

Puffed Wheat. The whole wheat berry is heated and then puffed up with air. It is ready to eat as is and requires no cooking. Puffed wheat can be eaten as a breakfast cereal or added to baked goods and candy. Just remember, though, that when you buy wheat in this form, part of your purchase price is going for air and the cost of processing. In addition, the nutritional value is decreased substantially.

Cream of Wheat. Sometimes called *farina*. It is finely ground, hulled wheat that still contains the germ and the endosperm. Only the outer bran layer is missing. Cream of wheat is used as a hot breakfast cereal and for desserts and dumplings.

Wheatina. Sometimes called Bear Mush in various parts of the country, it is a finely ground whole grain cereal that includes the bran.

Wheat Grass. Generally available only in natural food stores and through mail order (see Mail Order Sources, pages 501–506), wheat grass is made from the young wheat plant cut at the moment that the embryo is moving up from the roots through the stalk—about twenty days after sprouting. At that point, it has a high concentration of nutrients, quite similar in quality to green, leafy vegetables. It comes in powder form, and also in tablets or as a seasoning to sprinkle on food. Some natural food stores also serve wheat grass as a juice.

The Wheat Flours

Because of its popularity and its excellent qualities in a broad range of recipes (and especially for bread and cakes), wheat is now being milled into a vast and confusing array of flours. Combinations of hard and soft wheat, specialty flours, whole wheat blends, and several types of the ubiquitous white flour now beckon from the shelves of supermarkets and natural food stores.

White Flour. Basically, white flour is the ground endosperm of the wheat without the bran and the germ. Because of its high gluten content, it is the perfect blend for use with other flours (such as rye) in baked products.

- **Bleached and Unbleached.** Some white flour is bleached to make it even whiter than it is. When using white flour, we prefer the unbleached product, still holding to the theory that the less we tamper with something, the better it's bound to be.
- **All-Purpose Flour.** This is available as bleached or unbleached and is the everyday supermarket paper sack flour. It's a combination of high- and low-gluten flours, and the proportions change depending upon the section of the country in which the flour is milled. When all-purpose flour is sifted several times, it can be used as a substitute for pastry or cake flour.
- **Bread Flour.** This has become quite popular and is a welcome addition to those of us who bake our own bread. Milled from hard, high-gluten wheat, it is usually unbleached. We use it as an addition to whole grain flours to lighten the density of our baked goods.
- **Pastry Flour.** Milled from low-gluten soft wheat, it is of finer texture and is generally used for pastries and cakes. White pastry flour has the bran removed.
- **Cake Flour.** A feather-light flour that is bleached and is used for the baking of cakes. When using it, add two extra tablespoons per cup of cake flour to equal one cup of all-purpose or unbleached flour.
- **Enriched.** Some supermarket brands are sold with an "enriched" label. As always, the milling and processing removes some of the natural ingredients, then to be replaced by the manufacturer. Not one of our favorite selections, only superseded by:
- **Self-Rising Flour.** Since self-rising brands contain baking powder and salt premixed for the consumer, we try to avoid the product. We prefer to have control over the amount of salt that we use in our recipes, and we use only baking powder that does not contain the chemical additive aluminum sulfate.

Whole Wheat Flours. This is a hard wheat flour that retains the bran and germ of the whole wheat berry. However, some commercial supermarket brands do remove some of the germ to increase the shelf life of the flour. Generally, the flour sold in health food stores is stone-ground and does contain the nutrition of the whole berry. Keep in mind, too, that whole wheat flour turns rancid much more quickly than processed white flour, so buy small amounts at a time and keep unused portions in the refrigerator if you have the space. When baked goods are made with 100 percent whole wheat flour, they will not rise quite as high as those made with white flour

The

Versatile

Grain

and the

Elegant

Bean

228

because of the lower gluten content. We occasionally blend whole wheat flour with white unbleached flour to make a perfect compromise.

- **Pastry Flour.** Milled from soft whole wheat and used in the same way as white pastry flour in pies, cookies, cakes, waffles and pancakes. However, with the whole wheat variety, sift the flour twice before measuring and then put the bran left in the strainer back into the flour. This will ensure a lighter product and will keep the flour from packing down.
- **Graham Flour.** Named after its developer, Sylvester Graham, who took whole wheat flour, ground the endosperm very finely and then returned the bran layers to the flour. Graham flour is coarser and flakier than whole wheat flour, though basically they both are in the same immediate family. Occasionally, the commercial graham flours have some of the germ removed for prolonged shelf life.

Semolina Flour. Milled from the endosperm of hard durum wheat, it is not quite white, but more of a buttery-yellow color. Because it has a high protein content and hard starch granules, semolina is perfect for pasta products, allowing them to hold their shape in boiling water and yet be flexible enough to stretch during cooking.

Though pasta is its prime use here, semolina is used in India for a pancake called *dosas,* as well as for vegetable pilafs called *uppmas,* usually served for breakfast. Semolina is also used for making *couscous,* the traditional North African and Middle Eastern dish. Couscous comes in two basic sizes when you buy it from the bulk sacks: fine and medium. There are also prepackaged varieties: *instant,* requiring only soaking, and *quick-cooking,* taking about 5 minutes (see Chart, pages 231–232 for cooking methods).

The Italians have carried semolina to a fine art in the baking of breads and Middle Eastern cooks use it for unusual and delicious desserts.

Wheat

Grain & Granulation	Amount of Liquid	Cooking Method	Cooking & Standing Time	Approx. Yield	Comments
Whole Grain Berries (1 C. dry)	3½ C.	Pick over and toast unwashed berries in a dry skillet until they are fragrant and begin to pop and crackle. Transfer to a bowl and wash, then soak overnight in 3 C. water. Use a 3-qt. saucepan. Drain and re-serve liquid, adding enough to make 3½ C. Bring liquid to a boil. *Do not* add salt until berries are cooked. Add grain, return to boil, cover and simmer.	50 to 60 minutes. Drain off any excess liquid. Let stand 10 minutes.	3 C.	Add salt *after* cooking to help water absorption of grain.
Whole Peeled Wheat Berries (1 C. dry)	3½ C.	Rinse and soak overnight. Drain and use 3-qt. saucepan and lightly salted water. Bring to a boil, add grain, lower heat and simmer covered.	50 to 60 minutes. Let stand 10 minutes.	3 C.	Peeled wheat is more delicately flavored than whole grain. After cooking it is somewhat gelatinous in texture, a de-sirable quality for desserts and soups.

Wheat (cont.)

Grain & Granulation	Amount of Liquid	Cooking Method	Cooking & Standing Time	Approx. Yield	Comments
Cracked Wheat (1 C. dry) Medium Granulation	2⅓ C.	Toast grains in dry skillet 3 to 4 minutes, stirring until there is nutty aroma. In 2-qt. saucepan bring salted water to a boil. Add grain gradually, stirring constantly. It will sputter up. Return to boil, cover and simmer.	15 minutes. Let stand 5 minutes.	2¾ C.	Toasting dry grain before cooking increases nutty flavor. *Fine* granulation is Wheatina. Follow package directions to cook.
Rolled Wheat Flakes (1 C. dry)	3 C.	In 2-qt. saucepan bring salted water to a boil. Add flakes gradually, stirring constantly. Return to boil, cover and simmer.	30 minutes. Let stand 5 minutes.	3 C.	
Semolina Couscous (1 C. dry) *Fine and Medium* (Instant)	1½ C.	Place instant couscous in a bowl, pour boiling chicken stock or salted water over and cover. *Do not cook.*	Let stand covered. Stir in 2 Tbs. soft butter, fluffing with fork as butter melts in order to separate grain. 5 minutes. Let stand 5 minutes.	2¾ C.	Keep covered after fluffing until serving time to prevent drying out the grain.

Grain & Granulation	Amount of Liquid	Cooking Method	Cooking & Standing Time	Approx. Yield	Comments
(1 C. dry) *Medium* (Quick-cooking)	1½ C.	In a 2-qt. saucepan bring salted water or preferably chicken stock plus 2 Tbs. butter to a boil. Stir in couscous gradually. Lower heat and simmer, covered.	Let stand 5 minutes.	2⅔ C.	Our personal preference is the medium granulation, quick-cooking couscous. We think it has better flavor and texture.

Spiced Cracked Wheat Cooked in Apple Juice with Honeyed Apple Slices

SERVES 6

Special, spicy, healthful, Sunday-morning comfort food to go with the newspapers. But then, why wait for Sunday when there are daily newspapers too!

1½ C. dried apple slices
½ C. boiling water
4 Tbs. mild honey
2 Tbs. butter
1 C. cracked wheat, medium granulation

3½ C. apple juice
¾ tsp. ground cinnamon
¼ tsp. ground cardamom
Salt to taste (optional)

Place the dried apples in a small bowl and pour the boiling water over them. Stir in the honey and set aside to steep. Melt the butter in a 3-quart nonstick saucepan, add the cracked wheat and stir to coat with the butter. Toast, stirring constantly, for about 3 to 4 minutes. In a small saucepan, bring the apple juice to a boil. To the cracked wheat, add the boiling apple juice and the spices. It will sputter up. Lower the heat, cover and simmer for 5 to 10 minutes. Remove from the heat and let stand for 5 minutes. Stir in the salt if you wish. Spoon out into individual bowls and top each bowl with some of the honeyed apple slices. Serve hot with a pitcher of milk to pour over if desired.

The

Versatile

Grain

and the

Elegant

Bean

Egyptian Peeled Wheat Berry Chicken
and Chick-Pea Soup

SERVES 8 TO 10

The Egyptian slaves, it is said, built the pyramids on a diet of onions and garlic, which gave them strength and endurance. Filled with grains, beans and chicken, as well as onions and garlic (used unobtrusively), this soup—as most soups and stews— profits from reheating the second day. So make it ahead for the best flavor.

1 C. whole peeled wheat berries, soaked overnight
½ C. dried chick-peas, soaked overnight
Whole 2½-lb. chicken
2 small beef marrow bones, with marrow removed
9 C. water
¼ tsp. turmeric
¾ lb. onions, quartered (2 large onions)

1 large whole clove garlic
2 small turnips, peeled and cut in half
2 stalks celery with leaves
2 small carrots
6 sprigs parsley
½ tsp. whole peppercorns
Salt to taste
1 Tbs. butter
1 tsp. Syrian Mixed Spices (see page 75) or ground allspice

Drain the wheat berries and chick-peas and set aside. To a large, 7-quart heavy Dutch oven, add the chicken, marrow bones and water. Bring to a boil, skim the surface, then lower the heat and add the turmeric, onions, garlic and turnips. Tie the celery, carrots, parsley and peppercorns in a cheesecloth sack for easy removal and tuck into the pot. Simmer, covered, for 1 hour 15 minutes.

Lift out the chicken, marrow bones and bundle of vegetables. Set the chicken aside to cool and discard the bones and the bag of vegetables. Purée the soup and the remaining vegetables in the bowl of a food processor a few batches at a time, returning each batch to the pot. Bring to a boil again, add the soaked chick-peas and the wheat berries, lower the heat and simmer, covered, for 45 minutes to an hour or until the grain and chickpeas are tender. Meanwhile, when the chicken is cool enough to handle, remove the skin and the bones and discard them.

Tear the chicken meat into large pieces and add to the pot. Add salt. In a small skillet, melt the butter and stir in the Syrian mixed spices. Dribble over the soup before serving right from the pot. The spices will float on top, dotting the surface in a polka-dot design. Ladle out into large bowls while the soup is still piping hot.

Triple Wheat Pork and Apple Terrine with Herbs and Spices

SERVES 10 TO 12 AS AN HORS D'OEUVRE
SERVES 6 TO 8 AS A MAIN COURSE

Tiny black flecks of sweet prunes, tart-sweet red apples and fresh green herbs form a mosaic of colors and flavors in this pork terrine.

Oil for greasing terrine
1 slice whole wheat bread, torn into small pieces
½ C. milk
1½ lbs. lean ground pork
¼ C. wheat germ
½ C. cooked cracked wheat (see Chart, page 231)
1 egg, lightly beaten
1 large unpeeled red Delicious apple, finely chopped (¾ C.)

2 medium stalks celery and leaves, finely minced
3 pitted prunes, diced finely
1 large clove garlic, finely minced (1½ tsps.)
¼ tsp. fennel seed
1 Tbs. finely minced sage
2 Tbs. finely minced flat leaf parsley
1 tsp. thyme leaves
⅛ tsp. freshly grated nutmeg
½ tsp. freshly ground black pepper
Salt to taste

Preheat the oven to 350° F. Lightly oil an 8-cup terrine or loaf pan. Place the torn bread in a large mixing bowl and pour the milk over it. Let stand until the bread absorbs the milk. Add the remaining ingredients and mix well to combine using a wooden spoon or your hands. Gently press the mixture into the terrine or loaf pan and bake for 1 hour. Let cool for 15 minutes before inverting onto a serving platter, then carefully turn right side up. Serve hot or warm, sliced thinly, with crisp toasts as an hors d'oeuvre or thick-cut slices as a main dish.

Whole Wheat Stromboli: A Rolled Pizza

SERVES 10 TO 12

The same ingredients that we find in the flat pizza are also in the Stromboli—all except the somewhat thicker, nutty whole wheat crust. Stromboli is also less sloppy to eat. Since it is sliced and eaten with a fork, it somehow acquires a more elegant demeanor—and saves cleaning bills, as anyone who has eaten a dripping slice of pizza can attest to!

The

Versatile

Grain

and the

Elegant

Bean

234

Dough

1 C. warm water	1 C. whole wheat flour
¼-oz. package dry yeast	1¼ C. all-purpose flour
1 tsp. sugar	Oil for greasing baking sheet and
¾ tsp. salt or to taste	waxed paper
2 Tbs. olive oil	

To a large bowl, add the water and the yeast and stir until dissolved. Stir in the sugar, salt and olive oil. In a smaller bowl, combine both flours with a whisk and add to the yeast mixture. Stir with a wooden spoon until a dough forms. Then flour your hands and knead the dough vigorously in the bowl for about twenty strokes. Cover lightly with a kitchen towel and let the dough rest for 15 minutes. Lightly oil a 14 × 17-inch baking sheet. Place a piece of waxed paper on top and lightly oil the waxed paper.

Filling

2 tsps. Dijon-style mustard	1 tsp. dried oregano, preferably Greek
2½ C. shredded mozzarella cheese (about 12 ozs.)	1½ C. diced pepperoni, cooked for 5 minutes (see NOTE) and blotted dry on paper towels
2 large plum tomatoes, coarsely diced (about 1 C.)	⅓ C. grated Parmesan cheese
2 Tbs. coarsely chopped basil	

After the dough has rested, preheat the oven to 400° F. Pat the dough into a rough rectangle. Flour a rolling pin and roll the dough directly onto the waxed papered baking sheet, right to the edges of the sheet. Spread the center part only with the mustard, leaving a border of 1½ inches. Scatter the mozzarella cheese over the mustard. Then follow with the tomatoes, the basil, the oregano and pepperoni. Sprinkle the Parmesan cheese over all.

Brush water on one side of the dough on the long edge and fold the opposite side over the filling. Then, using the waxed paper as an aid, turn over the water-brushed side to enclose the filling. Pinch and press together. Brush the short ends with water, then fold and pinch them in as well. Pull and slide the roll to one side of the baking sheet, using the waxed paper to help. Quickly flip it over so that the seam side is down, then remove the waxed paper.

Bake for 20 to 25 minutes or until the Stromboli is lightly browned. Slide it off onto a long wooden bread board or serving platter. Let cool for 10 to 15 minutes before slicing. The Stromboli freezes well. Just defrost it before reheating in a moderate oven.

NOTE: Although pepperoni is a cooked sausage that is usually eaten as is, we suggest heating and blotting it dry to get rid of excess fat.

Whole Wheat Berries with Wild Mushrooms
and Buttered Toasted Almonds

SERVES 6 TO 8

The fragrance of the forest is in every forkful of the woodsy, earthy mushrooms, teamed in this recipe with puffy, toothsome wheat berries and buttery almonds. It's a side dish that would love to share the same dinner plate with any kind of poultry, fish or veal.

½ oz. dried porcini mushrooms
⅓ C. boiling water
4 Tbs. butter
½ C. sliced almonds
½ lb. mixed fresh wild mushrooms, a combination of any three: chanterelles, morels, shiitake, hedgehog, cremini
½ C. finely minced shallots (about ¼ lb.)

2 cloves garlic, finely minced (1 tsp.)
1 tsp. fresh thyme
Salt and freshly ground black pepper to taste
½ C. beef stock
⅓ C. Madeira wine
3 C. cooked whole wheat berries (see page 230)
2 Tbs. finely minced chives

Put the porcini mushrooms in a cup and pour the boiling water over them. Let stand for 20 minutes. Drain the liquid and mushrooms through a coffee filter into a cup. Squeeze the filter to extract most of the liquid from the mushrooms and reserve the liquid. Remove the mushrooms, cut into small pieces and set aside.

In a 12-inch nonstick skillet, melt 1 tablespoon of the butter. Add the almonds and toast for 1 to 2 minutes, until they just begin to color. Remove with a slotted spoon and set aside.

Wipe the fresh wild mushrooms with a damp paper towel or a soft brush. Trim the tough parts of the stems and slice the mushrooms thickly. Set aside.

Add another tablespoon of the butter to the skillet and sauté the shallots and garlic for 4 to 5 minutes over medium heat, until soft but not browned. Remove to a plate. Melt the remaining butter in the same skillet and add the wild mushrooms. Stirring often, sauté for about 4 minutes, then return the shallots to the wild mushrooms and add the thyme, salt and pepper, the reserved porcini mushrooms and the mushroom liquid. Add the beef stock and the Madeira and bring to a boil. Then cover the skillet and simmer for 8 minutes. Stir in the cooked wheat berries, cover and continue to simmer until the berries are warmed, about 5 to 8 minutes. The berries will absorb the sauce. When ready to serve, gently mix in the reserved almonds, spoon the mixture into a serving dish and garnish with the chives.

The

Versatile

Grain

and the

Elegant

Bean

236

Romanian Cream of Wheat, Chive, Parsley and Tomato Dumplings

MAKES 14 DUMPLINGS

Poached in chicken stock, these lofty and savory little dumplings are exceptionally good as old-fashioned chicken and dumplings or they can be eaten in soup. Prepare them just before cooking, so they puff up and stay up.

- 1 small tomato, finely chopped, drained in a strainer (½ C.)
- 2 Tbs. finely minced chives
- 1 Tbs. finely minced parsley
- 6 C. Chicken Stock, preferably homemade (see page 171)
- ¾ C. milk
- ¼ C. regular Cream of Wheat cereal (*not* instant farina)
- 1 Tbs. butter
- 1 egg, beaten
- Salt to taste
- ⅛ tsp. white pepper

In a small bowl, mix together the tomato, chives and parsley and set aside. In a 5-quart wide-based pot, bring the chicken stock to a boil. In a 2-quart nonstick saucepan, bring the milk to a boil and very slowly add the Cream of Wheat, stirring constantly with a wooden spoon. Lower the heat and stir until quite thick, only a few minutes.

Remove from the heat and stir in the butter. Beat until the butter melts, then add the beaten egg, salt and pepper, and beat again with a wooden spoon. Combine with the tomato and herb mixture.

Wet a teaspoon, scoop up the dumpling batter by the rounded spoonful and push it off with your finger into the simmering stock. Repeat until all the batter is used up. Cover the pot and simmer for 10 minutes. Either lift out the dumplings with a slotted spoon and serve with chicken or serve it right in the poaching stock as a soup course.

Fattoush:
Syrian Whole Wheat Pita Bread Salad

SERVES 6

Although it is eaten year round, this salad is particularly favored in Syria as a Lenten dish. It is also quite similar to the Tuscan *panzanella*, another bread and vegetable salad. Toasted whole wheat pita provides the texture while it absorbs the dressing, and note that the cucumbers are drained before you add them so as not to dilute the flavor.

2 medium-size unpeeled cucumbers, preferably Kirby or English, coarsely diced (about 2 C.)

Salt to taste

2½ medium-size whole wheat pita, lightly toasted and cubed (about 2¼ C.)

3 medium-size tomatoes, cut into ¾-in. pieces (1½ C.)

1 small green pepper, diced (½ C.)

4–5 scallions, thinly sliced (about 1¼ C.)

½ C. finely minced flat leaf parsley

½ C. finely minced mint

1 Tbs. fresh thyme leaves (or 1 tsp. dried thyme)

1 medium clove garlic, finely minced (1 tsp.)

Freshly ground black pepper to taste

⅓ C. fresh lemon juice

⅓ C. olive oil

2 Tbs. crumbled feta cheese or dry goat's milk cheese

In a small bowl, toss the cucumbers with the salt. Transfer to a strainer and drain for 30 minutes. Rinse in cold water and drain again. Set aside. In a large salad bowl, gently combine the pita cubes, tomatoes, green pepper, scallions, parsley, mint, thyme and the drained cucumbers. In a small bowl, mix together the garlic, salt and pepper and the lemon juice. Crush the garlic with the bottom of a knife handle to produce a pasty consistency. Whisk in the olive oil. Pour over the salad and toss to combine. Sprinkle with the cheese and serve at once.

The

Versatile

Grain

and the

Elegant

Bean

238

Whole Wheat Cranberry Orange Walnut
Quick Bread

MAKES 1 LARGE LOAF

The day after baking this bread is the time to slice it, for that is when the flavors have properly intensified. It's perfect with morning coffee, afternoon tea or as a nibble any time of day.

1½ C. cranberries	2½ C. whole wheat flour
½ C. light-colored mild honey	1 Tbs. baking powder
2 large navel oranges	½ tsp. baking soda
1 egg	½ tsp. salt or to taste
4 Tbs. butter, melted and cooled	½ C. coarsely broken, toasted walnuts
Butter for greasing pan	

Coarsely chop the cranberries in the bowl of a food processor. This will take about four pulses. Transfer the cranberries to a small bowl and stir in the honey. Let steep for an hour or until the mixture exudes a liquid.

Meanwhile, peel the zest of both oranges and mince it finely. Set aside. Peel off the white pith from the oranges and discard. Then add the oranges to the food processor, process for three or four pulses, and transfer to the cranberry/honey mixture. Add the egg to the food processor and process until it is well beaten. Add the melted butter and process until combined. Scrape it into the bowl with the cranberry-honey mixture and set aside.

Preheat the oven to 350° F. and butter a 9 × 5 × 3-inch loaf pan. In a large mixing bowl, combine the flour, baking powder, baking soda, salt, walnuts and the reserved, minced orange peel. Add the cranberry mixture to the dry ingredients and combine. Spoon and scrape it into the prepared pan and bake for 50 to 60 minutes or until a cake tester inserted into the center comes out clean. Cool in the pan on a wire rack for 15 minutes, then turn out on the wire rack and continue to cool the loaf completely. Wrap in aluminum foil and eat the following day for the best flavor.

Irish Soda Bread with
Currants and Caraway

MAKES 2 LOAVES

An easy, delicious wholesome bread that takes under an hour from start to finish to prepare and bake. It makes great breakfast toast too.

Butter for greasing baking sheet
Flour for dusting baking sheet
2 C. whole wheat flour
2 C. all-purpose flour
1 tsp. baking soda
2½ tsps. salt or to taste
1 Tbs. sugar

1 Tbs. baking powder
4 Tbs. butter or margarine, cut into
　small pieces
1 C. dried currants
2 tsps. caraway seeds
1 egg
1¾ C. buttermilk, at room temperature

Preheat the oven to 400° F. and butter and flour a 15 × 17-inch baking sheet and set aside. In a large bowl, add the flours, baking soda, salt, sugar and baking powder and whisk to combine. Using a pastry blender, cut the butter into the dry ingredients until it resembles coarse meal. Then stir in the currants and caraway seeds.

In a small bowl, whisk the egg until foamy, add the buttermilk and whisk to combine. Add to the dry ingredients and, with a wooden spoon, mix until a soft dough forms. Flour a work surface generously, and flour your hands. Gather the dough and knead it for 5 minutes on the floured surface until smooth, adding a bit more flour if the dough seems sticky. Divide the dough into two equal parts and shape into round loaves. Slash a cross on the surface with a sharp knife. Place on the prepared baking sheet and bake the bread for about 45 minutes until golden brown or when thumped on the bottom with your hand, it sounds hollow. Cool on a wire rack before serving.

The

Versatile

Grain

and the

Elegant

Bean

240

Greek Christopsomo Bread

MAKES 1 LOAF

A traditional Greek Christmas bread baked with a single almond inside the loaf. Whoever gets the slice with the almond is assured of having good luck in the year to come.

2½–3 C. all-purpose flour
¼-oz. package dry yeast
¾ C. milk
2 Tbs. mild light honey
4 Tbs. butter
½ tsp. salt or to taste
1 egg

Peel of ½ lemon, finely minced (1 tsp.)
Oil for greasing bowl
½ C. golden raisins
½ C. finely chopped, toasted walnuts
1 whole almond (for luck)
Butter for greasing baking sheet

In a large mixing bowl, combine 1 cup of the flour and the yeast. In a small saucepan, heat the milk, honey, butter and salt until just lukewarm. Add to the dry ingredients and mix thoroughly. Add the egg and lemon peel and beat well with a wooden spoon. Add enough of the remaining flour to make a stiff dough. Then turn out onto a lightly floured surface and knead for about 8 to 10 minutes, or until the dough is smooth and elastic.

Lightly oil a large bowl and add the dough, rolling it around in the bowl so that it is covered lightly with the oil. Cover with a kitchen towel and place in a warm place to rise until doubled in bulk, about 45 minutes to 1 hour. Then knead in the raisins, walnuts and almond and let the dough rest, covered lightly, for 10 minutes. Shape it into 1 large round loaf. Butter a baking sheet and place the loaf on it. Cover again with the towel and let rise until almost doubled, about 45 minutes. While the bread is on its last rise, preheat the oven to 375° F.

Bake for 30 minutes or until lightly golden. Cool on a wire rack for 15 to 20 minutes before slicing.

Pastiera di Grana: Peeled Wheat Berry and Ricotta Cheesecake

MAKES 1 9-INCH CAKE

Rich, luscious and perfumed with orange flower water, this dessert is baked only at Easter and Christmastime in Italy. Our version was concocted after some hilarious conversations with Carmelo Borgone, master baker at the venerable, long-established (1894) bakery, Veniero's, in New York's East Village. Carmelo started his recipe with, "You take 600 pounds of ricotta, 20 dozen eggs . . ."

Wheat

¾ C. peeled wheat berries, soaked overnight and drained
3½ C. water
Pinch salt
1 C. milk

1 Tbs. butter
2 Tbs. sugar
1-in. piece of cinnamon stick
2-in. strip lemon peel

In a 3-quart nonstick saucepan, bring the wheat berries, water and salt to a boil. Cover and simmer for 15 minutes, then drain and return the wheat berries to the saucepan. Add the milk, butter, sugar, cinnamon stick and lemon peel. Bring to a boil, then lower the heat and cook, uncovered, stirring frequently, until the milk is absorbed and the wheat berries are plump and tender to the bite, about 45 to 50 minutes. Remove the cinnamon stick and the lemon peel and discard. Cover and set aside to cool. You can prepare the wheat berries a day before and refrigerate.

Pastry Dough

2¼ C. all-purpose flour
¼ C. sugar
Pinch salt
1 tsp. finely minced lemon peel (peel of ½ lemon)
¼ lb. butter, cut into cubes

1 egg yolk (reserve the white for filling—see below)
¼ tsp. vanilla extract
4–5 Tbs. ice water
Butter for greasing springform pan

In the bowl of a food processor, combine the flour, sugar, salt and lemon peel. Add the butter and process for a few strokes. Add the egg yolk and vanilla and process until combined. Then trickle the ice water over and process just until the dough holds together. Turn out the dough onto a floured surface and knead briefly only to combine thoroughly, then wrap in foil and refrigerate for 30 minutes to chill.

Preheat the oven to 400° F. and butter only the sides of a 9 × 2½-inch springform pan. Place one third of the chilled dough on the ungreased bottom of the pan. Cover it with a piece of floured waxed paper, and using your fingers press the dough to fit into the pan. Remove the waxed paper and prick the surface with a fork. Form the remaining dough into a rough rectangle and roll it out with a rolling pin, then cut it

The

Versatile

Grain

and the

Elegant

Bean

242

in half lengthwise. Use both pieces to line the sides of the pan, pressing, patting and stretching the dough to fit and making it adhere to the sides. Press some of the dough into the bottom layer to form a seal to join the base of the pastry. If it tears, it can be patched, so don't worry. But it must be paper-thin to cover the inside completely right up to the top rim of the pan. Then place the pan in the freezer for 10 minutes.

Put into the preheated oven directly from the freezer and bake for 8 to 10 minutes or until the pastry is pale golden. Remove from the oven and cool completely while preparing the filling. This step, too, may be done ahead of time. Lattice strips are sometimes added after the filling, depending upon the region of Italy in which it is made. Our version does not use them.

Filling

4 eggs, separated, plus the reserved egg white from the pastry dough	1 tsp. vanilla extract
½ C. sugar	Peel of 2 oranges, finely minced (about 2 Tbs.)
Pinch salt	¼ C. finely minced candied orange peel
2 lbs. ricotta cheese	2 Tbs. all-purpose flour
Peel of 1 lemon, finely minced (about 1 Tbs.)	2 C. cooked wheat berries (see NOTE)
1 Tbs. orange flower water	Confectioners' sugar for dusting

Preheat the oven to 450° F. In the bowl of a food processor, beat the egg yolks, then add the sugar, salt, and half the cheese. Process until combined. Then add the remaining ingredients except the egg whites. (If the wheat has congealed, break it up with a fork before adding.) Transfer the mixture to a large bowl.

In another bowl, beat the egg whites until stiff. Fold them, half at a time, gently into the cheese mixture and pour into the prepared baked pastry. Place in the preheated oven and bake for 15 minutes. Cover with a tent of foil if the top seems to be browning too quickly. Then reduce the oven heat to 350° F. and bake for 15 minutes more. Reduce the oven temperature once again to 250° F. and, without opening the door, continue to bake for 45 minutes more. Turn off the heat and let the cake remain in the oven for 15 more minutes. Then remove from the oven and cool completely on a wire rack. As the pastiera cools, the center will solidify and will shrink a bit. When completely cool, remove the sides of the springform pan, keeping the cake on the base, and sprinkle the surface with confectioners' sugar.

NOTE: Pale golden wheat berries can be found in Italian specialty shops and health food stores, as well as through some mail order sources (see pages 501–506). The Asti brand canned precooked wheat (*grano cotto*) can also be used.

Currant-Filled Whole Wheat
Eccles Cakes

MAKES 7 CAKES

These are currant-filled sugar and spice–crusted tea cakes from Eccles, a borough in Lancashire, England, and a British treat served warm for breakfast or midafternoon tea or coffee.

Butter for greasing baking sheet
¾ C. whole wheat flour
1 C. all-purpose flour
2½ Tbs. sugar
¼ tsp. salt or to taste
2½ tsps. baking powder
4 Tbs. butter, plus 1 tsp. butter, cut into very tiny pieces

2 eggs, beaten
⅓ C. half and half or light cream
½ tsp. vanilla extract
1 tsp. lemon juice
2 Tbs. plus 2 tsps. dried currants
¼ tsp. ground cinnamon
⅛ tsp. nutmeg
⅛ tsp. ground allspice

Preheat the oven to 450° F. Butter a baking sheet and set aside. In a large bowl, whisk together both flours, 1 tablespoon of the sugar, the salt and baking powder. Using a pastry blender, cut in the 4 tablespoons butter until the mixture is coarse and crumbly. Take off 1 teaspoon of the beaten eggs and set aside. In another bowl, mix the remaining beaten eggs with the half and half (or cream), vanilla and lemon juice. Make a well in the center of the dry ingredients and add the egg/cream mixture, stirring just until blended.

Turn the dough out onto a lightly floured board and knead about fifteen strokes, until the dough is no longer sticky. Roll out to ¾ inch thick and with a 3-inch round cookie cutter (or glass) cut seven circles, rerolling the scraps. Place them about 1½ inches apart on the prepared baking sheet. Poke a well into the center of each circle by using your knuckle, and fill it with about 1½ teaspoons of the currants and a pea-sized dot of the remaining butter. Pinch the opposite edges of the circle together toward the center, enclosing the currants in the dough. (It will pull apart slightly while baking to form an "X" on the surface and reveal the currants.)

Brush the tops with the reserved egg. Mix the remaining 1½ tablespoons of sugar with the cinnamon, nutmeg and allspice and sprinkle the mixture over the tops. Bake in the preheated oven for about 12 minutes or until golden. Serve piping hot.

The

Versatile

Grain

and the

Elegant

Bean

Whole Wheat Bread Pudding with
Rum and Apple Meringue

SERVES 6

The humble bread and butter pudding reaches new heights with a cloud of baked apple meringue resting on a custard, whole wheat base.

1 Tbs. butter for greasing baking dish plus 4 Tbs. soft butter	½ tsp. cinnamon
	¼ tsp. freshly grated nutmeg
4 slices whole wheat bread	1 tsp. vanilla extract
4 egg yolks (reserve the whites)	½ C. dark raisins, preferably Monukka
2 C. milk	or Muscat
½ C. light brown sugar	2 Tbs. dark rum

Preheat the oven to 350° F. Lavishly butter a 1½-quart deep soufflé dish and boil a kettle of water. Spread the remaining butter over the slices of whole wheat bread, then cut the bread into cubes. Place in a small bowl and set aside. In another small bowl, beat the egg yolks with a whisk until they are light. Add the milk, sugar, cinnamon, nutmeg and vanilla and continue to beat until frothy. Add the raisins and the rum and pour over the bread cubes. Let stand until some of the liquid is absorbed by the bread.

Spoon and pour the mixture into the soufflé dish and place in a larger pan. Add enough boiling water to reach 1 to 2 inches up the sides of the soufflé dish. Bake for 1 hour and 10 minutes. During the last 20 minutes of baking time, prepare the apple meringue.

Apple Meringue

4 reserved egg whites (see above)	4 Tbs. sugar
Few grains salt	½ tsp. vanilla extract
¼ tsp. cream of tartar	Peel of ¼ small lemon, finely minced
1 C. unsweetened thick applesauce	(½ tsp.)

In a deep, large bowl, beat the egg whites, salt and cream of tartar with an electric hand beater until very foamy and slightly stiff. Mix the remaining ingredients together and add ½ cup at a time to the egg whites, beating all the while. Continue to beat for 10 minutes or until very stiff. Then spoon large dollops on top of the bread pudding. Return to the oven and continue to bake for about 10 minutes. If the meringue is not golden, slip it under a hot broiler for about 30 seconds. Serve hot or warm.

Whole Wheat Gingerbread Persons with
Citrus and Fresh Ginger

MAKES ABOUT 32 COOKIES

These cookies, flavored with citrus and fresh ginger, appeal to grown-ups as well as children. They are even better the second day after baking—but who can wait?

Whole Wheat Ginger People

⅓ C. light molasses
½ C. apple cider vinegar
¼ lb. soft butter
⅔ C. light brown sugar
Peel of ½ large orange, finely minced
    (1 Tbs.)
Peel of 1 large lemon, finely minced
    (1 Tbs.)
1 Tbs. finely minced, peeled ginger
    (about ¾-in. knob)

1 egg
2 C. whole wheat flour
1½ C. all-purpose flour
1 tsp. cinnamon
¼ tsp. ground cloves
1 tsp. baking soda
¼ tsp. salt

In a small saucepan, slowly heat the molasses to the boiling point. Remove from the heat and stir in the vinegar. Set aside to cool completely. In the bowl of a food processor, cream the butter, then add the sugar and process until light and fluffy. Add the orange and lemon peels and ginger and process until combined. Then add the egg and process again.

In a medium-size bowl, whisk together the flours, cinnamon, cloves, baking soda and salt until combined. Add the cooled molasses mixture alternating with the dry ingredients to the food processor, and process until a very soft dough forms. Scrape out with a floured spatula. Wrap the dough in aluminum foil and refrigerate for 1 hour.

When ready to bake, preheat the oven to 350° F. Line two baking sheets with parchment paper or aluminum foil and set aside. Roll half the dough out on a floured surface to a ¼-inch thickness. Keep the other half of the dough chilled. Cut the persons with a 5½-inch person-shaped cookie cutter, pulling away the dough scraps as you do so (see NOTE). Repeat with the remaining dough and the rerolled scraps until all the dough is used up.

Using a spatula, carefully place the cookies on the prepared baking sheets. Bake 10 to 12 minutes or until golden. Remove at once and cool on a wire rack. When completely cool, store the cookies in an airtight container.

NOTE: Cutting a hole in the top of the cookie before baking will allow you to pull a string through in order to hang them on a Christmas tree.

The

Versatile

Grain

and the

Elegant

Bean

246

Bramborové Knedlíky: Czechoslovakian Semolina and Potato Dumplings

MAKES 14 DUMPLINGS

Serve these delicious dumplings as the Czechs do—with mahogany-skinned crisp roast duckling and sweet and sour red cabbage. It's good with pot roast or the German sauerbraten too.

2 large baking potatoes, peeled and quartered (about 1 lb.)	½ C. fine semolina flour
2 eggs, lightly beaten	½ C. all-purpose flour
Salt to taste, plus ½ tsp. (or to taste)	2 Tbs. melted butter
⅛ tsp. white pepper	Fine dry bread crumbs

In a 1½-quart saucepan, cook the potatoes in boiling salted water to cover for 10 to 15 minutes or until soft. Drain and transfer to a large bowl. Mash the potatoes with a potato masher until smooth, then add the eggs, ½ teaspoon salt and pepper and beat well with a wooden spoon to combine.

In a small bowl, combine both flours with a whisk and add to the potato mixture. Using a wooden spoon, beat to make a stiff, sticky dough. Fill a 12-inch pan with deep sides to within 1 inch from the top with salted water and bring to a boil. Flour your hands well and dust a piece of waxed paper with flour. Using a heaping tablespoon of dough, form it into a ball by rolling it in the palms of your hands, then place each one on the floured waxed paper. Drop the balls into the boiling water, bring the water to a boil once again and cook for 12 to 15 minutes over high heat. After 5 minutes they will start to float to the surface. Loosen any that may stick to the bottom of the pan and stir them around gently so that they cook evenly.

To test for doneness in the center, tear one apart with two forks and taste. Lift them out with a slotted spoon and onto paper towels to blot off excess water. Then transfer them to a serving platter, spoon some of the melted butter over each dumpling and sprinkle them with a few bread crumbs. Pass a pepper mill at the table if you wish.

Hungarian Veal Paprikash with Semolina and Caraway Spaetzle

SERVES 6

While on a trip to Hungary, we wormed this recipe from the chef of a restaurant in Szeged, the home of Hungarian paprika. Even though the quality of the meat was not great, we loved the way it was seasoned. We also watched her make the spaetzle and then duplicated her technique.

Veal Paprikash

- 4 ozs. diced slab or strips bacon, cut into ½-in. pieces
- 2 large onions (¾ lb.), coarsely chopped (about 2 C.)
- 2 large cloves garlic, finely minced (2 tsps.)
- 1 tsp. sweet paprika, plus 1 Tbs.
- ½ tsp. freshly ground black pepper
- ⅛ tsp. cayenne

- 2½ lbs. lean, boneless veal shoulder, cut into 1½-in. cubes
- Salt to taste
- 1½ C. Beef Stock, preferably homemade (see page 172)
- 1½ Tbs. butter
- 2 Tbs. flour
- ¾ C. sour cream
- 2 Tbs. water

In a 10-inch cast-iron skillet, slowly cook the bacon, onions and garlic together over low heat for 25 to 30 minutes, until brown, stirring frequently. Transfer the onion and bacon to a heavy 7-quart Dutch oven.

In a small cup, mix 1 teaspoon of the paprika with the pepper and cayenne and coat the pieces of veal with this mixture. In the same unwashed iron skillet, raise the heat to medium high and quickly brown the meat in batches, turning the pieces frequently for even browning. As the pieces brown, transfer them to the Dutch oven. When all are browned, season with salt. Add the beef stock to the skillet and stir, scraping up any brown bits. Bring to a boil and pour over the meat. Cover the Dutch oven and bring to a boil again, then lower the heat and simmer for 1 hour.

In a small skillet, melt the butter and stir in the flour and the remaining tablespoon of paprika, stirring over low heat until bubbly. Take off a ladle of the sauce from the meat and slowly add it to the skillet, stirring constantly, then return the mixture to the Dutch oven and continue to simmer, stirring occasionally, for 15 minutes more. Keep the veal in the pot and prepare the spaetzle (recipe below).

Then, just before serving, rewarm the veal over low heat, thin the sour cream with the water and stir into the sauce. Continue to simmer over very low heat so the sauce will not curdle. Serve hot and spoon the sauce over the spaetzle.

Semolina Spaetzle with Caraway

- ¾ C. semolina flour
- ¾ C. all-purpose flour
- ¼ tsp. white pepper
- ½ tsp. salt

- ¼ tsp. caraway seeds
- 3 eggs
- ¼ C. milk

The

Versatile

Grain

and the

Elegant

Bean

248

Fill a 12-inch nonstick skillet with salted water and bring to a boil. To a medium-size bowl, add the flours, pepper, salt and caraway and whisk to blend. In another medium-size bowl, beat the eggs with the whisk until light and foamy. Then add the milk to the eggs and slowly add to the dry ingredients, beating well with a wooden spoon. The batter should be very thick.

Scrape the batter into a large measuring cup with a pouring spout. Tilt the cup to guide the batter slowly through the spout and hold it over the boiling water. Using a very sharp knife that is dipped in water between each slice (to keep the batter from sticking), slice off very tiny pea-size pieces of the batter and let them drop into the skillet. When the surface is covered with dough, simmer for 10 minutes. If any stick to the bottom, release them with a spoon so that they float to the top.

Lift the spaetzle out with a slotted spoon, put into a strainer and rinse under cold water. Drain and transfer to a bowl and cover with aluminum foil to keep warm. You will probably need to make the spaetzle in two batches. Just repeat the procedure using the same boiling water.

NOTE: There is a special spaetzle maker tool with large holes to force the batter through. If you have one, use it of course.

Turkish Katayef

SERVES 6

Inspired by a version of Turkish Katayef, usually made with shredded phyllo dough, we tried the same basic ingredients but substituted vermicelli for the phyllo. The resultant dessert is equally delicious, somewhat easier to prepare, and without the loss of classic flavors.

8 ozs. vermicelli, cooked and drained (see NOTE)	½ C. coarsely chopped almonds, with skins
4 Tbs. butter	2 tsps. wheat germ
½ tsp. almond extract	½ tsp. cinnamon
1 tsp. finely minced lemon peel	¾ C. mild light honey
	Soft vanilla ice cream (optional)

Butter an 8-inch square or any other 2-quart baking dish and preheat the oven to 375° F. When the vermicelli is drained and hot, mix it with 2 tablespoons of butter, the almond extract and the lemon peel. Spoon it into the prepared pan and sprinkle the top with the almonds, wheat germ and cinnamon. Trickle the honey over the surface and dot with the remaining butter. Bake it for about 30 to 40 minutes or until the top is slightly brown. Cool on a rack for 15 minutes before cutting it into squares. Serve warm or cold.

In Turkey, clotted cream is usually spooned over the top of each portion, but we tried it with 1 tablespoon of soft vanilla ice cream.

NOTE: Vermicelli are very thin noodles which usually come in nests and are sold in Italian and Middle Eastern specialty shops. (See Mail Order Sources, pages 501–506.)

Semolina, Fennel Seed and
Saffron Yeast Bread

MAKES 1 LOAF

The natural, warm colors of the saffron and the semolina flour give this bread a particularly rich golden tint along with the flavor of licorice-like fennel as an added taste treat for every slice.

¼-oz. package dry yeast	1 Tbs. sugar
¼ C. warm water	1 tsp. coarse or kosher salt
Pinch sugar	1 Tbs. fennel seed, freshly ground in
Pinch saffron threads	a spice grinder
1 Tbs. boiling water	2–2½ C. all-purpose flour
1 C. water	Oil for greasing bowl
1 C. semolina flour	White cornmeal for dusting baking pan

Put the yeast, warm water and sugar in a cup or glass. Stir and let stand for 5 to 10 minutes to proof. The yeast will bubble up. If it doesn't, discard it and try again with a fresh package.

Crumble the saffron threads with your fingers into another cup, add the boiling water and stir. Let stand for 10 minutes to steep. Meanwhile, in a large mixing bowl, put the 1 cup water, the semolina flour, sugar, salt, and ground fennel seed, and mix lightly just to blend. Then, when the saffron has steeped, add it to the dough. Next add the proofed yeast. Add the all-purpose flour a little at a time, blending it in with a wooden spoon. When it begins to feel stiff, use floured hands and knead, while adding flour, until the dough is fairly stiff but resilient and pulls away from the bowl. Turn it out onto a lightly floured surface, and flouring your hands again, knead it for 8 to 10 minutes, adding more all-purpose flour if the dough becomes too sticky. Place the dough in an oiled bowl, turn once to coat, cover it with a clean towel and let it rise in a warm place for 45 minutes to 1 hour or until doubled in size.

Lightly flour a work surface. Turn the dough out, punch it down and knead for 2 to 3 minutes, adding a bit more flour if it's too damp. Spread white cornmeal on a baking sheet, form the dough into a shape (oval or round, it matters not) and place it on the sheet. Cover and let rise for 45 minutes to 1 hour, or until doubled in bulk. About 15 minutes beforehand, preheat the oven to 375° F.

When the dough has risen, use a sharp razor blade to cut a pattern on top to let the dough expand evenly. Use three slashes or a ticktacktoe design. Then with a plant mister spray the top with warm water and put in the oven to bake for 40 minutes. About 20 minutes into the baking, spray the top of the loaf again with warm water and return to the oven. Bake for 40 minutes or until the crust is brown and the bottom sounds hollow when tapped. Let cool on a wire rack. Serve warm or reheat before serving.

The

Versatile

Grain

and the

Elegant

Bean

250

Semolina, Prosciutto and Sweet Marjoram
Black Olive Spoon Bread

MAKES 2 MINI LOAVES

Golden yellow loaves studded with tiny bits of prosciutto and black olives—a bread with the lightness and texture of cake. As the loaves bake, the aroma will transport you to Italy.

Butter for greasing loaf pans
¾ C. fine semolina flour
¾ C. bread flour
2 tsps. baking powder
¼ tsp. freshly ground black pepper
¼ tsp. crushed, dried sweet marjoram
½ C. grated Parmesan cheese

2 Tbs. finely diced prosciutto
(preferably prosciutto di Parma)
Black oil-cured olives, pitted and sliced
(about 2 Tbs.)
3 eggs, separated
¾ C. milk
5 Tbs. butter, melted and cooled

Butter two mini loaf pans, 5¾ × 3 × 2½ inches, or one 8½ × 4½ × 2½-inch bread pan. Preheat the oven to 375° F.

To a large bowl, add the flours, baking powder, pepper, marjoram and Parmesan. Whisk all the dry ingredients to blend. Then add the prosciutto and olives and whisk to distribute.

In a small bowl, whisk together the egg yolks and milk, then add the cooled melted butter. Make a well in the dry ingredients to pour in the egg/butter/milk mixture and beat well with a wooden spoon. Whip the egg whites with a beater until stiff and fold them in with a large rubber spatula. Spoon half the batter into each prepared pan (or all of it into the bread pan) and bake for 30 minutes for the small loaves, 35 to 40 minutes for the larger one, or until the tops are golden.

Remove from the oven, cool for 10 or 15 minutes on a wire rack, then remove from the pans and continue cooling on the rack. Slice and serve slightly warm. The slices can also be toasted lightly.

Egyptian Semolina and Almond Cake with Lemon and Rose Water Syrup

SERVES 8

A rich, sweet almost candylike cake that is perfumed slightly with a hint of rose water in this very Middle Eastern semolina dessert. It's a perfect and satisfying finale, along with a tiny cup of inky black, bitter coffee.

Semolina Cake

1 Tbs. butter for greasing pan	¼ C. water
1 C. semolina flour	1 tsp. vanilla extract
¾ C. sugar	6 Tbs. butter, melted and cooled
Pinch salt	16 whole unskinned almonds

Preheat the oven to 350° F. and butter an 8 × 1½-inch-deep pan and set aside. Reserve any butter that remains. In a medium-size bowl, whisk together the flour, sugar and salt to combine. Add the water, 2 tablespoons at a time, and with a wooden spoon, stir to dampen the flour. Mix the vanilla with the remaining water and add, mixing well. Then beat in the melted, cooled butter, 2 tablespoons at a time, until it's blended well. Spoon the mixture into the pan, spread it out evenly and bake for 40 minutes.

Stir the almonds into the remaining butter left over from buttering the pan, remove the cake and press the almonds into the surface. Arrange them like the spokes of a wheel. Return the cake to the oven and bake for 5 to 10 minutes more or until the edges begin to brown and the center of the cake is firm to the touch. Let cool slightly and, using a sharp knife, cut it into wedges and spoon the syrup, a few tablespoons at a time, over the cake. (Syrup recipe is below and can be made while the cake is baking. The syrup and the cake should be warm.)

Lemon and Rose Water Syrup

½ C. sugar	1 Tbs. lemon juice
¾ C. water	¼ tsp. rose flower water (see NOTE)

In a small, heavy saucepan, combine the sugar, water and lemon juice and cook over moderate heat, stirring constantly, for 2 to 3 minutes or until the sugar dissolves. Then increase the heat to high and bring to a boil. Boil undisturbed for 5 minutes, then remove from the heat and stir in the rose flower water. Set aside to cool slightly before spooning over the cake.

NOTE: Rose flower water can be found in Middle Eastern specialty shops.

The

Versatile

Grain

and the

Elegant

Bean

252

Swiss Semolina and Hazelnut Pudding
with Fresh Blackberries

SERVES 8 TO 10

In the part of Switzerland that borders Italy, semolina is used quite frequently in a variety of dishes. In this recipe, toasted hazelnuts and sweet blackberries complement the smooth, creamy sweet pudding.

4 C. milk
2-in. piece of vanilla bean
2-in. strip orange peel
Few grains salt
⅔ C. fine semolina flour
3 egg yolks
¾ C. sugar

¾ C. hazelnuts, toasted and finely ground in a blender (about ⅔ C. ground)
1 C. heavy cream, chilled
1 Tbs. confectioners' sugar
½ pt. blackberries

To a 3-quart nonstick saucepan, add the milk. Split the vanilla bean lengthwise, scrape the seeds into the milk, add the pod, orange peel and salt. Bring slowly to a boil. Then lift out the orange peel and vanilla pod and discard. Slowly whisk in the semolina, then continue to cook over very low heat, stirring frequently with a wooden spoon until the mixture begins to thicken, about 2 to 3 minutes.

In a medium-size bowl, whisk together the egg yolks and the sugar, then pour one quarter of the semolina into the egg/sugar mixture. Stir well, return to the saucepan and mix together. Continue to cook for 7 to 8 minutes, until thick.

Stir in the ground hazelnuts, remove from the heat and let cool for 20 minutes. In a medium-size chilled bowl, whip the cream and confectioners' sugar with a beater until stiff. Add one third of the cooled semolina mixture to the whipped cream and fold in with a spatula. Then fold this in with the remaining semolina mixture. Spoon the pudding into wine goblets and cover with plastic wrap. Chill until serving time.

Arrange 3 blackberries on top of each dessert just before serving.

Ma'amoul: Lebanese Easter Cakes with
Semolina and Pistachios

MAKES 16 CAKES

Your home will be perfumed with roses while these little nut-filled cakes are baking. Although they taste like a pound of butter has been used in each one, only ⅓ cup of *samna* (clarified butter and bulgur wheat) is used for the entire recipe. The technique for preparing *ma'amoul* reads more complex than it actually is, since they are made in easy stages.

Samna

¼ lb. sweet butter
1 Tbs. fine bulgur wheat

Melt the butter slowly in a small, heavy saucepan. When it starts to foam up, add the bulgur and continue to cook over low heat for 1 minute. Remove and set aside for 30 minutes. Skim off the surface and discard. Then strain through a fine strainer and discard the bulgur. There should be ⅓ cup *samna*.

Semolina Dough

⅓ C. *samna*
1 C. fine semolina flour
½ C. all-purpose flour
Pinch salt

½ C. boiling water
½ tsp. orange flower water (see NOTE)
½ tsp. rose flower water (see NOTE)

Set the prepared *samna* aside. In a medium-size bowl, whisk both flours with the salt to combine. Add the boiling water and beat with a wooden spoon. While beating, add the *samna* and the orange and rose flower waters. Flour your hands well and knead right in the bowl for 2 minutes to combine. The dough will be buttery. Wrap in aluminum foil and set aside at room temperature for 3 hours or overnight.

Pistachio Nut Filling
(MAKES ABOUT ⅔ CUP)

¼ C. sugar
2 ozs. toasted pistachio nuts, finely chopped (about ¼–½ C.)
¾ tsp. cinnamon

Butter for greasing baking sheet
Flour for dusting baking sheet
Confectioners' sugar

Combine the sugar, nuts and cinnamon and set them aside. (If there is some left over after using it, sprinkle the mixture on pancakes.) After the required time to allow the dough to "mellow," flour your hands and unwrap the dough. Knead a few times on the foil wrapping, then flour a knife and cut into sixteen equal pieces. Butter and dust with flour a 14 × 17-inch baking sheet and preheat the oven to 325° F. Flour

The

Versatile

Grain

and the

Elegant

Bean

254

your hands well and form each piece of dough into a ball. Place the ball of dough in the palm of one hand and, using the thumb of the opposite hand, press to form a 2-inch cupped disk. Add about ½ teaspoon of the filling, then pinch the center closed, working toward the ends, to enclose the filling. Then roll lightly into a ball again with your hands and place, smooth side up, on the prepared baking sheet, allowing space between each one. Repeat until all are formed.

Flour a fork and press a cross hatch design on the surface, flattening each cake a bit. The design helps the confectioners' sugar cling to the surface (see NOTE). Bake for 15 to 20 minutes or until the cookies are a very pale golden color. The cookies should be soft, but they become firmer as they cool. Remove with a spatula to a wire rack. While they are hot, dust liberally with confectioners' sugar. When they are cool, dust again with additional confectioners' sugar.

NOTE: Beautiful hand-carved designs cut into a wooden press from Syria are sometimes used to imprint designs on *ma'amoul* (see the Middle Eastern listings in Mail Order Sources, pages 501–506). Rose flower water and orange flower water can be found in Middle Eastern specialty shops.

Ma'amoul mold

Seafood and Couscous Salad Pescara
with Oranges and Red Onions

SERVES 8 TO 10

For luncheons, buffets, as an appetizer or light supper, the combination of seafood with soft, fluffy couscous cooked in a seafood stock, then crisped with red onions, celery and sweet orange, is an irresistible melding of textures and tastes.

1½ C. water	⅓ C. lemon juice
1 C. dry white wine	1 Tbs. white wine vinegar
6 black peppercorns	Freshly ground black pepper to taste
1 bay leaf	Salt to taste
¼ tsp. anise seed	¼ C. finely minced parsley
2 small red whole dried hot chiles such as Japonés	2 Tbs. small nonpareil capers, rinsed and dried on paper towels
1 lb. mussels, scrubbed and debearded	2 tsps. finely minced fresh oregano (or ½ tsp. dried oregano)
½ lb. shrimp, in shell	1 medium red onion, very thinly sliced into rings (about 1 C.)
1 lb. small squid, cleaned	2–3 stalks celery, thinly sliced (1 C.)
½ lb. small scallops or sea scallops sliced horizontally	1 large navel orange, sectioned and cubed (1 C.)
2 C. medium grain quick-cooking couscous	Peel of large orange, finely minced (2 tsps.)
½ C. olive oil	

To a 5-quart Dutch oven, add the water and wine. In a small cheesecloth bag, tie the peppercorns, bay leaf, anise seed and hot chiles and add to the pot. Bring to a boil, cover and simmer for 10 minutes. Raise the heat and add the mussels. Cover and cook for 8 to 10 minutes or until the mussels open. Discard any that don't open. Lift the mussels out with a slotted spoon into a large bowl and when they are cool enough to handle, remove them from their shells and set aside. Return any accumulated liquid to the pot.

Lift out the cheesecloth bag, remove the two hot peppers, cut into tiny pieces and add them to the mussels. Discard the remaining spices. Bring the liquid to a boil again and add the shrimp and squid and cook for 2 minutes. Remove the pot from the heat, lift out the shrimp and squid, add the scallops to the liquid and let them steep without cooking. After 1 or 2 minutes, lift them out and set aside. Shell and devein the shrimp, then cut into small pieces, adding them to the mussels. Cut the squid bodies into thin rings and the tentacles into halves and mix with the other seafood. Add the scallops.

Bring 4 cups of the seafood liquid to a boil again, stir in the couscous, lower the heat and simmer, covered, for 5 minutes. Then let stand for 5 minutes or until the liquid is absorbed. Toss with the olive oil to separate the grains, add to the seafood and toss well. Stir in the lemon juice, vinegar and pepper and taste for salt before

The

Versatile

Grain

and the

Elegant

Bean

256

adding. Then add the parsley, capers, oregano, red onion rings, celery, orange pieces and orange peel. Toss gently, cover the bowl and let marinate in the refrigerator for at least 1 hour. Serve cold or at room temperature in a large shell or a pretty glass bowl.

Couscous and Bulgur Pilaf with Leeks, Carrots, Peas and Chives

SERVES 8

The couscous and bulgur only need to be soaked in a flavorful chicken stock and then combined with lightly sautéed vegetables and fresh chives—a side dish that couldn't be easier to prepare.

¾ C. #2 medium bulgur
2 C. instant medium grain couscous
4 C. boiling Chicken Stock, preferably homemade (see page 171)
4 Tbs. soft butter
4–5 thin leeks, finely chopped, white part plus 1-in. pale green (2 C.)

6 medium carrots, finely chopped (2 C.)
1 C. cooked tiny peas (frozen can be used)
Salt and freshly ground black pepper to taste
3 Tbs. finely minced chives

Place the bulgur in a small bowl and the couscous in a large bowl. Pour 1 cup of the boiling chicken stock over the bulgur and let stand for 15 minutes, or until the liquid is absorbed. Add 2 tablespoons of the butter to the remaining chicken stock and cook until the butter is melted, then pour over the couscous and let stand for 10 minutes until the liquid is absorbed. Now fluff with a fork, add the bulgur and fluff again to combine. Set aside.

In a large skillet, melt the remaining butter. Add the leeks and carrots and sauté over medium heat, stirring frequently, for 5 to 8 minutes, until the leeks are wilted but not brown. Add to the couscous/bulgur mixture. Add the peas and salt and a liberal amount of freshly ground black pepper. Add the chives and toss the mixture with two forks to combine. Transfer to a serving dish and serve hot, or keep warm, covered, in a preheated low oven until ready to serve.

Spiced Couscous with Apricots, Raisins and Pistachio Nuts

SERVES 8

Tongue-tingling fresh ginger and whole dried spices mingle in an exotic blend of softly sweet dried fruit, crunchy whole pistachios and a touch of onion and garlic. Roasted poultry or pork will give this side dish its proper setting.

4 ozs. dried apricots, cut in halves (about ¾ C.)
½ C. raisins, preferably Muscat
1 C. boiling water
3 C. Chicken Stock, preferably homemade (see page 171)
2 tsps. whole cardamom seeds, in their pods
2½-in. stick of cinnamon
2 bay leaves
4 Tbs. butter
2 C. quick-cooking medium grain couscous
1 Tbs. olive oil

2 cloves garlic, finely minced (1 tsp.)
1 medium onion, finely chopped (½ C.)
1-oz. piece of ginger, peeled and finely minced in a food processor (about ¼ C.)
½ tsp. salt or more to taste (depending upon saltiness of chicken stock)
Freshly ground black pepper to taste
Juice of ½ large lemon (2 Tbs.)
¼ C. toasted pistachio nuts
¼ C. finely chopped flat parsley

Put the apricots in a small measuring cup and the raisins in another cup and pour boiling water over each to cover. Let stand for 15 minutes, then strain off the liquid and add to a 2-quart saucepan. Set aside the soaked dried fruits. To the saucepan, add the chicken stock, cardamom, cinnamon stick and bay leaves. Bring to a boil, then lower the heat and simmer for 5 minutes. Strain and discard the spices and return the stock to the same saucepan and, over low heat, stir in the butter until it melts. Stir in the couscous, cover and simmer for 5 minutes, then let sit for 5 minutes.

Meanwhile, heat the olive oil in a small skillet, and add the garlic, onions and minced ginger. Sauté for about 2 to 3 minutes over medium heat, or until the onions are translucent. Stir in the salt and pepper and combine with the couscous, fluffing it with a fork to break up any clumps. Stir in the lemon juice, reserved apricots and raisins, pistachio nuts and parsley. Serve hot or at room temperature.

The

Versatile

Grain

and the

Elegant

Bean

258

Wild Rice

Zizania aquatica

America's Native "Good Berry"

It has been called "the Caviar of Grains" and "the Filet Mignon of Grains" and even *we* dubbed wild rice "the Rolls-Royce of Grains" in our earlier book on the subject. The French explorers who first came across it in the upper Great Lakes region had no idea that it was not a grain at all but an aquatic grass seed and they named it *crazy oats.* But for the Native Americans who lived in the area, it was much much more. They called it *manomin* (or *mahnomen*) after the Menominee tribe—or "good berry" to them, and indeed it was just that to the Ojibways, the Chippewas, Sioux, Fox and Winnebago tribes, as well as to the Menominees, who still live in the area.

During the cold, harsh winters that are typical for the region around Minnesota, the Native Americans learned to survive when game became scarce and thick ice covered the fishing grounds by harvesting and storing the wild rice as their basic food source. And though there are other varieties that are grown in Korea, Burma, Japan and China, they are quite different, and the wild rice that we know here in North America can actually be labeled as a true American crop, and most of it is still grown in Minnesota.

Certainly, as most of us have discovered, wild rice (particularly the premium grade) is a fairly expensive product when we compare it with the grains that are more common or that are grown by using the most modern of agricultural techniques. Much of the harvesting is still done in the old way during what is known as the Native American "rice moon" in September of each year. In earlier days, it was the women who harvested the crop, but today the men share equally in the task. Two people in a birch canoe harvest an allotted section of the flooded lake, one pushing the boat with a long pole, the other pulling the plants down over the gunwale and beating out the grain with two cedar flails. The grain that falls into the water instead of the boat becomes the seed for next year's crop.

Preparing wild rice for market is also a tedious and expensive job, for it takes about three pounds of the seed to get one pound of the product that we eventually see on the supermarket shelves. In the early days, the braves danced on the wild rice in clean, new moccasins in order to loosen the grains from the hulls. And even today the wild rice is put into bags and pounded by hand with clubs. The women of the tribes then winnow the grain by using shallow birch bark trays, tossing the seeds into the air and letting the wind do the rest of the job.

To make matters even more tricky, wild rice is still a difficult crop to grow, vulnerable to the weather. A severe windstorm at harvest time can destroy the entire crop by blowing the seeds into the water before the harvesting boats can make their way among the growing plants. And not only is it a favored food for gourmet cooks but the birds who live in the area also love the seed and they can pick clean an entire area, while insects, disease, bad drainage or high water can all add to the toll.

Of course, there have been changes and improvements. About twenty years ago, some farmers in the Great Lakes region and in California began to grow the crop commercially, but with varying success. In addition, the Native Americans have also instituted some innovative techniques. Airboats are being used for the harvest, and custom-built harvesters skim the laketops, while shipments are made to the vast markets by air. Added to this, there have been some ingenious improvements in parching, hulling and winnowing the wild rice. Yet, the costs remain high, for it still takes three times the amount of grass seed to yield the small packages that seem so high in price at the retail level.

However, there is a fact that many of us seem to forget when we see the sticker price. Depending upon the grade, the cost of wild rice may seem fairly high when we price it per pound. But wild rice *triples* in volume when cooked and one pound can provide *thirty servings* or more. It is a high-fiber food source, rich in proteins, B vitamins and minerals, and it has a very distinctive flavor that has made it the favorite of cooks all over the world. For, after all the technical data and the talk of price, we finally give way to only one measure of judgment: the *flavor.*

Wild rice has a chewy, nutty, smoky flavor that makes it perfect for use as a side dish, as well as for salads, soups and stuffings. It can also be "stretched" by blending it with other forms of rice or with vegetables, poultry, nuts or fruit. However you use it, it will be a vast improvement over the eighteenth-century recipe of a fur trader named Peter Pond, who suggested that we "eat it with Bairs Greas and Sugar . . ."

The Forms of Wild Rice

Giant (Long). This is the super deluxe grade of wild rice, with each grain about one inch long. It is also the most costly of all the grades and is usually reserved for special dishes such as pheasant, quail or venison.

Extra-Fancy (Medium). The most popular grade of wild rice, the grains are of equal size and quality and they're clean and unbroken. This grade is generally used for salads, side dishes and stuffings, and it can also be used interchangeably with the giant grade.

The

Versatile

Grain

and the

Elegant

Bean

260

Select (Short). If appearance is not of primary concern, this grade is perfect, since some grains may be broken or not of uniform length and size. Thus, it is ideal for use in baked goods such as in muffins, in pancakes or in soups and stuffings.

Miscellaneous Grades. There are several other grades, including some that are parboiled or otherwise precooked or processed, and with cooking time thus reduced to as little as five minutes. There are also white and wild rice mixtures now on the supermarket shelves, so that the price seems somewhat reduced. We feel that the three grades that we've listed above are the ones we would strongly recommend for flavor, purity and the best food value. Read the labels carefully, for some may be called "premium" or given another generic name. If the wild rice is packaged in plastic, the easiest way to determine the quality is to look through the window.

Wild Rice

Grain & Granulation	Amount of Liquid	Cooking Method	Cooking & Standing Time	Approx. Yield	Comments
Giant Extra Fancy (6 oz. dry) (Long whole grain 1 in. long.)	4 C.	Pick over and rinse the grain. Add grain to 3-qt. saucepan of boiling, salted water. Return to boil, cover and simmer.	50 to 60 minutes. Drain any excess water. Let stand 10 minutes.	3 C.	When rice is tender, some of the grains will "bloom" or burst open. Bite-test a few before draining. This holds true for all grades.
Medium Grade Extra-Fancy (6 ozs. dry) (About ½-in. uniform size, unbroken grains.)	4 C.	Same as above.	45 to 50 minutes. Drain any excess water. Let stand 10 minutes.	3 C.	
Select Grade (6 ozs. dry) (Not uniform in size. Some broken grains.)	4 C.	Same as above.	45 to 50 minutes. Drain any excess water. Let stand 10 minutes.	3 C.	

NOTE: For 4 ozs. wild rice, use 2¼ C. of water. The yield will be about 2 C. Cook for 45 to 50 minutes and let stand 10 minutes after draining excess water.

Wild and Tame Mushroom Soup with
Wild Rice and Madeira

SERVES 8

Woodsy and earthy mushrooms and wild rice combine exquisitely, as if they were destined to meet in the pot. This delicate yet robust soup is thickened with vegetables and lightened with cream, then enhanced with just a touch of Madeira.

1½ C. warm water
1 oz. dried Japanese shiitake mushrooms
1 lb. fresh cultivated mushrooms
4 Tbs. butter
⅓ C. coarsely chopped shallots (about 2 ozs.)
1 small carrot, diced (½ C.)
1 large stalk celery, diced (½ C.)
¼ lb. peeled diced potatoes (⅔ C.)
¾ tsp. dried thyme

½ tsp. dried marjoram
2 C. cooked wild rice (see Chart, opposite page)
4 C. Chicken Stock, preferably homemade (see page 171)
Salt and freshly ground black pepper to taste
1 Tbs. tomato paste
1 C. light cream
Few drops Tabasco sauce
3 Tbs. Madeira wine
Snipped chives (optional)

In a small bowl, pour the warm water over the dried mushrooms, weighting them down so that the mushrooms are completely submerged and can soak for 30 minutes. Then cut off and discard the tough stems. Squeeze the excess liquid from the mushrooms back into the soaking liquid, then strain the liquid through a dampened coffee filter to get rid of any fine grit. Slice the mushrooms and set them aside along with the liquid.

Wipe the cultivated mushrooms with dampened paper towels, trim off the stems and slice the mushrooms thickly. Set aside.

In a 7-quart Dutch oven, melt the butter and sauté the shallots over medium heat, stirring frequently, for 2 minutes. Add the carrots, celery, potatoes, thyme and marjoram and cook, stirring, for 2 minutes more. Then add both mushrooms and sauté, stirring, for about 5 minutes. Add the cooked rice along with the reserved mushroom liquid and the chicken stock. Bring to a boil, then lower the heat, season with salt and pepper and stir in the tomato paste. Cover and simmer for 30 minutes.

Purée in several batches in a blender or food processor. The soup should not be too smooth. Return the soup to the same pot, stir in the cream and reheat on low heat. Stir in the Tabasco and the Madeira and taste to adjust the salt and pepper. Serve hot, topped with a few snipped chives if you wish.

Acorn Squash Filled with Brussels Sprouts
over Wild Rice and Sausage

SERVES 6

Prepare this dish the night before a Thanksgiving dinner. Just reheat and you can forego the additional vegetables and stuffing for the turkey.

2 medium-size acorn squash, quartered and seeded, steamed 8–10 minutes (about 1½–2 lbs.)

½ lb. very small brussels sprouts, steamed for 5–8 minutes

½ lb. Italian pork sausage, casing removed and crumbled

1 small onion, coarsely chopped (½ C.)

2 C. cooked wild rice (see Chart, page 262)

3–4 fresh sage leaves, finely minced (or ½ tsp. dried sage)

1 tsp. finely minced fresh marjoram (or ½ tsp. dried marjoram)

Salt to taste

⅛ tsp. freshly ground black pepper

1 Tbs. melted butter

1 wedge lemon

Freshly grated nutmeg

Set aside the steamed squash wedges and the steamed brussels sprouts. In a large skillet, sauté the sausage, stirring occasionally, for 5 minutes. Add the onions and cook, stirring, for 10 minutes more. Drain off any accumulated fat and return the skillet to the heat. Stir in the cooked wild rice, sage, marjoram, salt and pepper and spoon the mixture into a shallow 3-quart oven-to-table casserole. Top with the squash. Then fill each squash cavity with some of the brussels sprouts. Drizzle some butter, a few drops of lemon and a few gratings of nutmeg over the vegetables. Cover with foil and refrigerate until ready to serve.

When ready to serve, preheat the oven to 350° F. and heat, covered, for about 15 to 20 minutes.

acorn Squash stuffed with Brussel Sprouts & Wild Rice

The

Versatile

Grain

and the

Elegant

Bean

264

Savory Wild Rice and Apple Pancakes with
Sour Cream and Applesauce

MAKES ABOUT 36 PANCAKES

Savory dinner pancakes spiked with a bit of thyme, apples and earthy flavored wild rice. Try them with any poultry or a roasted ham. They can also be served as a light luncheon dish. Allow three pancakes as a side dish (depending upon appetites) and four to six as a main course.

4 Tbs. butter
2 thin scallions, finely minced (¼ C.)
1 medium tart green apple, peeled, cored and finely diced (1 C.)
½ tsp. dried thyme
⅛ tsp. freshly grated nutmeg
Salt to taste, plus ¼ tsp. salt (or to taste)

Freshly ground black pepper to taste
2 Tbs. coarsely chopped pecans
2 C. all-purpose flour
1 Tbs. baking powder
2 eggs
1¼ C. milk
1½ C. cooked wild rice (see Chart, page 262)

Melt 2 tablespoons of the butter slowly in a 10-inch cast-iron skillet. Add the scallions and apples and sauté, stirring frequently, over low heat for 5 minutes. Add the thyme, nutmeg, salt and pepper and continue to sauté for 5 more minutes, or until the apples are tender. Transfer to a small bowl. Stir in the pecans and set aside. Wipe out the skillet.

Sift the flour, baking powder and salt together onto a piece of aluminum foil. In a large bowl, whisk the eggs until they are light and frothy, then add the milk. Continue to whisk while adding the dry ingredients. Stir in the reserved apple mixture and the cooked rice and beat with a wooden spoon.

Heat about 1 teaspoon of the remaining butter in the iron skillet for each batch of pancakes. Drop them by the tablespoonful and cook over medium high heat until the edges seem dry and the pancakes have a few holes in the surface. Turn over and continue to cook for 2 minutes. Serve hot, keeping the pancakes warm in a preheated oven on low heat until all are cooked. Or, do as many batches as you wish, covering and refrigerating the remaining batter for 2 or 3 days. Serve with the accompanying sauce spooned over each pancake.

Sour Cream Applesauce

8-oz. container sour cream
8-oz. jar of applesauce

Freshly grated nutmeg

Combine the sour cream and applesauce and spoon some over each pancake. Grate some fresh nutmeg over the sauce before serving.

Fennel, Endive and Wild Rice Salad
with Gruyère Cheese

SERVES 6

A lovely year-round luncheon dish, with the addition of a few slices of smoked turkey or grilled salmon to complete it.

2 C. cooked wild rice (see Chart, page 262)

2 endive, thinly sliced, ⅛ in. thick (about 1½ C.)

1 bulb of fennel, cut into ⅛-in.-thick julienne strips (1 C.), reserve 2 Tbs. fennel fronds

3 ozs. Gruyère cheese, cut into julienne strips

¼ C. finely minced chives

2 Tbs. finely minced parsley

½ small roasted sweet red pepper, diced (2 Tbs.)

2 Tbs. lemon juice

1–2 cloves garlic, finely minced (1 tsp.)

1 Tbs. balsamic vinegar

⅓ C. olive oil

Tender leaf lettuce

In a large bowl, gently toss the rice, endive, fennel, cheese, chives, parsley and red pepper. Add the salt and pepper, lemon juice, garlic and vinegar, then drizzle the olive oil over all. Toss again just before serving. Mound the salad on a bed of lettuce leaves, sprinkle with the reserved fennel fronds and serve at room temperature.

Festive Christmas Wild Rice with Red and Green Peppers
and Mushrooms

SERVES 6

An attractive side dish for pork, game or poultry. Or use it as a stuffing for baked chicken breasts.

The

Versatile

Grain

and the

Elegant

Bean

4 Tbs. butter

1 medium onion, coarsely chopped (¾ C.)

1 small green pepper, diced (½ C.)

1 small red pepper, diced (½ C.)

12 medium-size mushrooms, thickly sliced

Salt to taste

¼ tsp. freshly ground black pepper

1 tsp. finely minced lemon peel

2 C. cooked wild rice (see Chart, page 262)

Heat the butter in a large skillet and sauté the onions over medium high heat, stirring constantly for 2 minutes. Add the peppers and mushrooms, salt and pepper and continue to cook, stirring, until the mushrooms give up their liquid and then reabsorb it. Remove from the heat and mix in the lemon peel and cooked rice. Spoon into an oven-to-table casserole. If you wish to prepare it in advance, cover the dish with foil, and when ready to serve, heat in a preheated 350° F. oven for 15 minutes.

Wild Rice with Buttered Pecans and Tangerines

SERVES 6

Try this tangerine-laced wild rice dish with crisply roasted duckling, which has an affinity for orange flavors. You'll find it a refreshing change from the ubiquitous, sweet cloying orange sauces usually served with duck.

2 Tbs. butter
½ C. shelled pecans
3 tangerines
2 C. cooked wild rice (see Chart, page 262)
1 tsp. finely minced, peeled ginger
½ C. finely minced celery leaves, or ¼ C. fresh lovage
1 large scallion, finely minced (¼ C.)
1 Tbs. finely minced parsley
Salt and freshly ground black pepper to taste

Melt the butter in a small skillet and add the pecans. Toast, stirring constantly, until they smell wonderful and begin to color. Set the skillet aside. Peel only the thin rind from two of the tangerines and mince it finely. Then peel all 3 tangerines, pull off any white membrane, and segment them, removing the pits. Combine with the pecans, cooked rice, ginger, celery leaves, scallions, parsley and the salt and pepper. Transfer to a 3-quart oven-to-table dish, cover with aluminum foil and when ready to serve, preheat the oven to 450° F. and bake, covered, for 10 to 15 minutes.

Wild Rice Poultry Stuffing with Apples, Prunes and Toasted Hazelnuts

MAKES 5 TO 6 CUPS

This recipe makes enough stuffing for a 10- to 12-pound turkey, goose or several pheasants. Or you can use it for the center of a festive crown roast of pork. Although we, as many other people, love bread stuffings, we find them extremely filling. This one allows you to leave the holiday table without the usual bloat and semistupor that sets in from overeating the bread stuffings, however delicious they may be.

4 Tbs. butter	Salt and freshly ground black pepper to taste
2 scallions, finely sliced (about ½ C.)	
1 stalk celery, with leaves, finely chopped (½ C.)	1–2 large red apples, unpeeled, cored, and coarsely chopped (2 C.)
½ large green pepper, finely diced (⅓ C.)	¾ C. whole, small pitted prunes
½ C. coarsely chopped mushrooms	⅓ C. coarsely chopped, toasted hazelnuts
1 Tbs. finely minced fresh sage leaves (or 1 tsp. dried sage)	3 C. cooked wild rice (see Chart, page 262)
1 tsp. fresh thyme leaves (or ½ tsp. dried thyme)	

In a large skillet, heat the butter and sauté the scallions over medium heat for 1 minute, stirring constantly. Add the celery, green pepper, mushrooms, sage, thyme and the salt and pepper and sauté for 5 minutes, stirring frequently, until the vegetables are wilted. Remove the skillet from the heat and stir in the apples, prunes, nuts and cooked rice and combine well. Just before roasting, stuff about 4 cups of the mixture into the cavity of the bird, and about 1 cup into the crop. Heat any leftover stuffing separately and serve along with the carved bird.

The
Versatile
Grain
and the
Elegant
Bean

268

Mixed Grains

If You Liked ONE, Would TWO Be Twice as Good?

Up to this point, we have tried to maintain the integrity of the individual grains, so that their specific tastes and their particular nutritional and culinary qualities might become familiar to our readers. However, there are times when the blending of two or more makes for an unusual result—in granolas or pilafs, and certainly in breads, in waffles or in griddle cakes. The innovator, the creator in the kitchen, also has a vast range of legumes with which to experiment in a mingling of grains and beans.

What is the result when we combine millet with cornmeal? Oat and wheat berries? Bulgur with couscous? Barley grits with rice? Once we begin to understand how the individual grains are prepared and used, then the idea of mixing them becomes eminently reasonable, resulting in dishes that meld and complement flavors.

Until just a few years ago, the commercially prepared mixed grains were fairly rare, with companies like Erewhon and Arrowhead Mills offering a few morning cereals (and infant cereals) that blended rice, wheat, oats, barley, triticale, millet, buckwheat, corn—and legumes such as soybeans. But in the last few years, the list has become quite formidable, and though mixed grain products are found almost always in health food stores, the selection has blossomed with new companies offering some of the tastiest and most unusual combinations for both side dishes and for breakfast cereals.

In addition to the Arrowhead Mills and Erewhon products that have been with us for many years, the unusually named Kashi blends a variety of grains and can be eaten either hot as a pilaf or cold as a breakfast cereal mix. Kashi combines *seven* grains plus sesame (and with no salt or sugar). Puffed Kashi has also entered the market in recent years as a competitor on supermarket shelves that are filled with every puffed grain imaginable.

One of our favorites in the commercial sweepstakes is Arrowhead Mill's 7 Grains cereal, a hot cereal that combines all organically grown ingredients. Certainly, any of the new mixed grains are a refreshing change from the morning oatmeal.

But the home cook can also blend grains, using ingenuity, experimentation and the sense of freedom that might well prove that if *one* is good, *two* (or more) might be better. On the following pages, we have offered some of our own suggestions.

Mixed Grains

Grain & Granulation	Amount of Liquid	Cooking Method	Cooking & Standing Time	Approx. Yield	Comments
Kashi (1 C. dry) (7 grains plus sesame)	2¼ C.	In a 3-qt. saucepan bring salted water to a boil. Add grain and cook over *medium* heat, *not low* heat.	25 minutes. Let stand 5 minutes.	2½ C.	A package mixture of 7 slightly hulled grains plus sesame seeds: oats, long grain brown rice, rye, wheat, triticale, buckwheat and barley.
Arrowhead Mill's 7 Grains (1¼ C. dry)	3 C.	In a 3-qt. saucepan, combine water and salt to taste. Add grain and bring to a boil. Lower heat and simmer, uncovered. Stir occasionally.	12 to 15 minutes.	2½ C.	A package mixture of 6 organic grains and one legume: wheat, oats, triticale, millet, corn, buckwheat and soybeans. Our personal breakfast favorite. We also use it in a bread (see page 274).

Mixed Grain Griddle Cakes

MAKES 18 GRIDDLE CAKES

Featherlike, these little griddle cakes seem to rise up and float off the griddle as they bake.

½ C. quick oats (*not* instant)	1 egg
½ C. whole wheat flour	1 C. buttermilk, at room temperature
¼ C. yellow cornmeal	½ C. yogurt
½ tsp. baking soda	2 Tbs. melted and cooled butter
2 tsps. baking powder	1 Tbs. maple syrup, plus additional to
½ teaspoon salt or to taste	pour over

To a large bowl, add the dry ingredients. Whisk together to combine. In a small bowl, beat the egg lightly, then whisk in the remaining liquid ingredients (except the additional maple syrup) and combine with the dry ingredients. Let stand for 15 minutes, then stir it down with a wooden spoon.

Preheat oven to 200° F. Heat a nonstick griddle over medium heat and drop the batter by the tablespoonful, pushing it off with a finger. Bake for 2 to 3 minutes or until the edges are dry. Turn over and continue to bake for 2 to 3 minutes more. Prepare in batches of six griddle cakes each, since they spread somewhat while baking. Keep warm in the preheated oven and serve with the additional maple syrup.

Mixed Grain and Cottage Cheese Muffins

MAKES 1 DOZEN MUFFINS

Since these muffins are not overly sweet, they are most acceptable as a dinner accompaniment. Made with a combination of buckwheat flour, cornmeal and cottage cheese, they are also wonderful with preserves for breakfast.

Butter or oil for greasing muffin pan	½ tsp. baking soda
¼ C. light buckwheat flour	1½ Tbs. sugar
¾ C. all-purpose flour	1 egg
½ C. yellow cornmeal	½ C. small curd lowfat cottage cheese
1 Tbs. baking powder	¾ C. buttermilk
½ tsp. salt	2 Tbs. canola oil

Preheat the oven to 400° F. Butter or oil only the bottoms of a 12-cup muffin pan and set aside. In a large bowl, combine the dry ingredients with a whisk. In a smaller bowl, beat the egg lightly with the whisk, then stir in the cottage cheese, buttermilk and oil. Make a well in the center of the dry ingredients and add the egg mixture all at once. Stir with a fork, just enough to blend the ingredients together. Do not overmix.

Spoon into the muffin cups and bake about 15 to 20 minutes. Loosen the muffins at once, but cool them in the pan on a wire rack for a few minutes before turning them out. Serve hot, or cool, or wrap and freeze the muffins. To reheat, place in a preheated 350° F. oven for 15 minutes and, if frozen, for 25 minutes.

Kashi: Mixed Grain Pilaf with Carrots, Smoked Turkey and Ham

SERVES 6 TO 8

Mixed whole grains are blended with lightly sautéed, shredded carrots, a julienne of smoked turkey and ham and slivers of butter-toasted almonds.

1 Tbs. butter
⅓ C. slivered almonds
2 Tbs. olive oil
1 medium clove garlic, finely minced (1 tsp.)
1 large onion, finely chopped (⅔ C.)
1 C. Kashi or ⅓ C. each whole bulgur, long grain brown rice and whole barley
2 medium carrots, shredded with shredder blade of a food processor (1½ C.)

2½ C. Chicken Stock, preferably homemade (see page 171)
1 tsp. fresh thyme leaves (or ½ tsp. dried thyme)
1 tsp. fresh marjoram (or ½ tsp. dried marjoram)
Salt and freshly ground black pepper to taste
⅔ C. smoked turkey, cut into julienne strips
⅔ C. cooked ham, cut into julienne strips
⅓ C. finely minced flat leaf parsley

In a large, shallow 3-quart oven-to-table casserole, melt the butter and stir in the nuts. Sauté until golden in color. Lift the nuts out with a slotted spoon and reserve. Add the olive oil to the casserole, heat it, then add the garlic and onions and cook, stirring, until the onions are wilted. Add the grains and stir to coat evenly with the oil/garlic/onion mixture. Stir in the carrots, then add the chicken stock, thyme, marjoram, salt and pepper. Bring to a boil. Cover with aluminum foil and lower the heat. Simmer on top of the stove for about 25 to 30 minutes for Kashi, or about 40 minutes for brown rice, barley and whole bulgur mixture, or until the grains are tender and the liquid is absorbed.

Stir in the turkey, ham and parsley. Cover again and let stand for 10 minutes. Before serving, fluff with a fork and scatter the reserved almonds over the top.

The

Versatile

Grain

and the

Elegant

Bean

272

Mixed Grain and Mincemeat Tea Loaf
with Brandy

MAKES 1 LOAF

If you read the labels on a jar of mincemeat, you will see that it includes a large quantity of beef fat or suet. However, this tea loaf, with the same rich, winy flavor of mincemeat, contains only 2 tablespoons of butter in the whole loaf. If you are a cholesterol-watcher, this is quite significant. If you are not, you will still enjoy this healthful, fiber-filled bread.

Vegetarian Mincemeat
(May be made 1 week in advance and refrigerated)

MAKES 2 CUPS

¼ lb. dried apples, coarsely chopped
¼ C. golden raisins
¼ C. dried currants
½ tsp. cinnamon
⅛ tsp. ground cloves
1 tsp. finely minced, peeled ginger

3 Tbs. finely diced, candied orange peel
1 Tbs. finely minced lemon peel
1½ C. apple cider
1 Tbs. brandy
½ C. coarsely broken, toasted walnuts
2 Tbs. soft butter

In a nonstick, wide-base 5-quart Dutch oven, combine all the ingredients except for the brandy, nuts and butter. Bring to a boil, then lower the heat and simmer, uncovered, for 45 minutes to 1 hour, or until the mixture is very thick and the liquid is absorbed. Remove from the heat and stir in the brandy, nuts and butter. Transfer to a container when cool, cover tightly and refrigerate.

Mixed Grain Tea Loaf

Butter for greasing loaf pan
1 C. white cornmeal
1 C. whole wheat flour
1 C. all-purpose flour
½ C. rye flour
½ tsp. salt or to taste

½ tsp. baking soda
2 tsps. baking powder
1½ C. buttermilk, at room temperature
2 C. Vegetarian Mincemeat (recipe above)

Preheat the oven to 350° F. and generously butter a 9 × 5 × 3-inch loaf pan. In a large bowl, add the dry ingredients and whisk to combine. Add the buttermilk and mincemeat and beat well with a wooden spoon. Pour and scrape the dough into the prepared pan. Wet a spatula and smooth the surface. Bake for 1 hour, then cool in the pan on a wire rack for 15 minutes. Remove the loaf from the pan and continue to cool on the rack for 15 minutes more before slicing.

7 Grains Yeast Bread

MAKES 2 LOAVES

This nutritious bread uses a commercial seven-grain product, one of the few times that we have taken this route. The basic ingredient is Arrowhead's 7 Grains cereal, which can be eaten for breakfast or incorporated into any number of dishes that require a mixture of whole grains, such as this easy-to-make yeast bread. Arrowhead's is available in health food stores across the country.

2 ¼-oz. packages dry yeast
¼ C. warm water
Pinch sugar
2½ C. cooked Arrowhead Mill's 7 Grains cereal (see Chart, page 270)
2 C. water
8–9 C. bread flour (see NOTE)

1 Tbs. sugar
2 Tbs. salt
2 Tbs. canola or corn oil
Oil for greasing bowl
Butter for greasing loaf pans
Sesame seeds for topping (optional)

Put the yeast into a small cup or glass and add the warm water. Add a pinch of sugar and stir. Let stand for 5 to 10 minutes to proof, until bubbles form. If the yeast does not proof, discard it and start again with fresh yeast.

Put the cooked grain in a large bowl, add the 2 cups water and the proofed yeast and stir well to separate the grains thoroughly. Then add 2 cups of the bread flour, the sugar, salt and oil. Stir with a wooden spoon, then stir in the balance of the flour a cup at a time. You may need 6 additional cups or more, depending upon the humidity of the area in which you are working. When all the flour is added, the dough should be damp and pull away from the sides of the bowl. Turn out onto a lightly floured surface and flour your hands.

Adding flour if the dough seems damp and sticky, knead for 8 to 10 minutes, keeping your hands floured. The dough will be very pneumatic and should no longer stick to the floured surface. Oil a large bowl and add the dough, turning it once to coat the other side. Cover with a clean towel and put in a warm place to rise until doubled in bulk, about 45 minutes to 1 hour.

When the dough has doubled, turn out onto a floured surface again and punch down, then knead for 1 to 2 minutes. Butter two 9 × 5 ×3-inch loaf pans and divide the dough in two. Put one half in each pan, pressing down to fill the sides. Cover the pans and let stand in a warm place until the dough almost reaches the tops of the pans, about 30 to 45 minutes. About 15 minutes into the second rising, preheat the oven to 375° F.

When the loaves have risen, use a very sharp razor blade to cut several slashes across the tops to allow them to rise evenly in the oven. Spray the tops with water with a plant mister and, if desired, sprinkle with sesame seeds, gently rubbing the seeds into the damp dough by using the tips of your fingers. Bake the loaves for 50 to 55 minutes, spraying the tops once again about 30 minutes into the baking. The breads will rise above the tops of the pans, giving them a most elegant and majestic look. Turn the loaves out and place them on a wire rack to cool. They freeze well.

The

Versatile

Grain

and the

Elegant

Bean

274

NOTE: Bread flour is a high-gluten flour (see page 228), used here because of the bulk of the 7 Grain cereal. All-purpose flour may also be used, but the rise may not be quite as high.

Upside-Down Mixed Grain Skillet Cake with Gingered Pears and Cranberry Glaze

MAKES 1 CAKE

An easy, unusual and delectable cake, baked with a top layer of glazed fruit and served warm. It tastes as good as it smells while it's baking.

Fruit Layer

4 Tbs. butter	1 C. whole cranberries
3 Tbs. sugar	4–5 small Bosc pears, peeled, cored and
3 Tbs. mild honey	coarsely chopped
1 tsp. finely minced, peeled ginger	1 tsp. lemon juice to toss with pears
	so they don't discolor

In a 10-inch cast-iron skillet, slowly melt the butter over low heat. Then add the sugar and honey and stir for 1 minute or until the sugar dissolves. Stir in the ginger. Spread the cranberries evenly in this mixture and remove from the heat. Spoon the chopped pears and lemon juice over the cranberries and set the skillet aside.

Cake

¼ C. yellow corn flour	4 Tbs. soft butter
¼ C. oat flour	½ C. light brown sugar
½ C. whole wheat pastry flour	2 tsps. vanilla extract
1 C. all-purpose flour	2 eggs
Pinch salt	⅔ C. milk
1 Tbs. baking powder	

Preheat the oven to 350° F. In a large bowl, add the flours, salt and baking powder and combine with a whisk. Set aside.

In the bowl of a food processor, process the butter and sugar until creamy, add the vanilla and the eggs, one at a time, and process until the mixture is light. Alternately add one third of the dry ingredients and one third of the milk. Process after each addition until well incorporated. Spoon and scrape the batter evenly over the fruit in the skillet and bake for 45 minutes, or until the center of the cake is done. A cake tester should come out dry. Invert it at once over a serving dish, keeping the skillet on the cake for 10 to 15 minutes before lifting it off. Cool slightly before serving.

Portuguese Broa:
A Corn and Wheat Peasant Bread

MAKES 2 LOAVES

We worked on and off in Portugal some years back, filming the construction of the April Twenty-fifth Bridge over the Tagus River. And we fell in love with the crusty, unusual breads called *Broa,* bringing them home in our luggage after each trip to Lisbon. However, we could never get anyone to part with a recipe that seemed to work, especially since every region had its own secret. The breads in Minho, Beira Litoral and Barcelos were all made differently. We finally discovered that the secret lay in the heat of the brick and stone ovens. This recipe comes from a search made by our friends De and Ele Jackson, who visit once a year when De teaches at the university. It comes from Grandma Lola, and it's as close as we can get to the loaves we once loved so much. It's a great bread to eat with Caldo Verde (see page 468).

Sponge

2 ¼-oz. packages dry yeast
1 C. warm water

1 C. yellow stone-ground cornmeal
1 tsp. sugar

In a large nonmetal mixing bowl, put the yeast, warm water, cornmeal and sugar, and mix well. Cover with a clean towel and put in a warm place to ferment overnight. This will have a sour, yeasty smell the next day.

Bread

Cornmeal sponge (recipe above)
1 C. yellow stone-ground cornmeal
1½ C. warm water
1½ Tbs. salt
1 Tbs. sugar
2 Tbs. corn oil

2–2½ C. bread flour (see page 228)
2 C. whole wheat flour
Oil for greasing bowl
Cornmeal for dusting baking sheet
2 ice cubes

In a large mixing bowl, with a wooden spoon stir together the sponge, the cornmeal, water, salt and sugar. Add the corn oil, stir again, then add 1½ cups of the bread flour. Stirring all the while, add the whole wheat flour 1 cup at a time. The dough will be firm but sticky. When it pulls away from the sides of the bowl, turn out onto a lightly floured surface and knead for 8 to 10 minutes, adding more bread flour as it becomes sticky. Oil a bowl and place the dough in it, turning once to cover the other side. Cover with a clean towel and put in a warm place to double in volume, about 1 hour.

Turn the dough out onto a lightly floured surface, punch down, knead a minute or two and form into two loaves. If the dough seems sticky, add more bread flour. Dust a baking sheet with cornmeal, and place the loaves on the prepared baking sheet, leaving enough room to allow them to expand as they rise. Cover lightly with a towel and let double in size, about 45 minutes.

The

Versatile

Grain

and the

Elegant

Bean

276

About 30 minutes into the second rise, preheat the oven to 425° F. When the breads have risen, use a sharp razor blade to slash the tops in several places or make a cross in the dough, to allow it to rise evenly. Before opening the oven, put the ice cubes in a handy spot. Open the door, put the baking sheet in quickly and throw the cubes on the floor of the oven. Close the door quickly. The steam from the cubes will set the crust and make it firm.

Bake 45 to 50 minutes or until the breads test done by tapping on the bottom and hearing a hollow sound. Cool them on a wire rack.

Sprouting Grains and Legumes

The Magic of Edible Houseplants

Although we have never considered ourselves a part of the generation that demands "instant gratification," there is something about the rapid sprouting of grains and beans that appeals to our wonder and sense of awe when we watch things grow. It is a feeling that is with us when we tend our garden, but it is more intense when we can see the results in just a few short days. From dormant, silent, inert seeds, three to five days (for most sprouts) can bring hundreds of live, nutritious plants to our dining table. We sometimes have from two to four jars of sprouting grains or legumes—wheat, buckwheat, rye, barley, lentils, mung beans—in various stages of growth and we use them in much of our cooking, as well as in our bread baking and salads.

Certainly, we are not nearly the first to discover the wonder and the nutrition of sprouted grains and beans. A Chinese emperor wrote about sprouted mung beans almost 5,000 years ago. And the Sumerians shortly afterward found that barley, when allowed to sprout and ferment, could play a major role in the origins of beer. Through the centuries, before the chemical injections that would delay the natural decaying of foods, bread bakers found that sprouted grains, dried and pounded, kept their loaves frseher than ordinary flour.

Possibly our own familiarity with sprouted berries comes from recent years when no restaurant salad was complete without a scattering of sprouted alfalfa on top. It was during those years, too, that newspaper and magazine articles began to educate all of us about the nutritional values of sprouted grains and beans. Wheat berries, for example, have three times more vitamin E and six times more of some B vitamins

The

Versatile

Grain

and the

Elegant

Bean

278

when they're sprouted. This holds true for protein and vitamin C when we sprout oats and soybeans. As the tiny plants grow, almost every vitamin and mineral multiplies in its nutritional strength. Sprouts are also low in calories and they're tasty when eaten raw. They're easy to digest and, as an added bonus, they're incredibly economical, for as they grow they expand their potential even as they pamper the pocketbook.

Barley, corn and millet increase to twice the volume of the original seeds. Rye and buckwheat give us three times the amount, while wheat and triticale expand to four times the volume. The figures also hold true for legumes, with volume expanding to two to four times the original amount.

Supermarkets across the country are now carrying sprouted soybeans, mung beans, alfalfa and mixed sprouts. However, if you want to try them at home, they're easy to grow and a few simple instructions will suffice. The first morning that you see tiny green shoots bursting from the germ of the berry, you'll join a growing number of home cooks who thrive on the magic of Mother Nature.

The Equipment: What You'll Need

There's no need for elaborate equipment. Although many garden catalogues and mail order companies advertise "sprouters," don't be tempted, for all you need is a large jar, preferably one that is not round, so it will not roll off the kitchen counter. The large-size square mason jars are perfect. For a cover, you'll need a piece of cheesecloth and a strong rubber band with which to fasten the cheesecloth to the mouth of the jar. It's that simple.

Sprouting the Grains or Legumes

1. Spread the grains or legumes out on a large baking sheet or in a large pie pan. Pick over the grains or legumes and remove any foreign matter.
2. Put between one and four tablespoons of the seeds into the jar and fill three-quarters full with lukewarm water. Cover the jar with the cheesecloth and place the rubber band around the mouth to hold it in place. Shake the jar a few times and then drain the water. Fill the jar partially again with fresh lukewarm water and soak overnight *with the jar in an upright position.* The seeds will begin to swell.
3. The next day, drain the water and rinse well, swishing the seeds around in fresh lukewarm water. Repeat two or three times, then drain the water completely.
4. *Place the jar on its side* and keep it in a warm, dark place. (Temperature should be about 70°F.) Repeat the rinsing process two or three times each day. We keep our jars near the sink for easy access and we cover them with a towel, making sure to keep the cheesecloth end open for ventilation.
5. Repeat the process for about three to five days, until the sprouts are developed and about one and a half to two inches long. With most seeds, you will begin to see the results at about the third day. Other seeds may take even less time.

6. When the sprouts are the proper length, place the jar in direct light for the last few hours in order to develop the chlorophyll.
7. Remove the sprouts from the growing jar, place them in a plastic container (uncovered) and refrigerate. They store well for several days, but we suggest that every day they be rinsed under cold water and then returned to the refrigerator.

Some Handy Tips About Sprouting

- When you choose seeds or berries for sprouting, make sure that they are "food store" quality. Seeds that are used for planting may contain chemicals.
- Don't worry about the hulls of the seeds. They provide fiber for your diet.
- Sprouts are kept in darkness until the last few hours because they tend to turn bitter when you grow them in direct light. Put them in direct light only for the last few hours, as suggested in the directions.
- To keep the crop from failing, make sure the water is thoroughly drained each time you rinse the sprouts. We keep our jars at a forty-five-degree angle pointing mouth down in order to drain excess water.
- If, at any time, you see mold or fuzz on the seeds, remove and discard the affected ones.
- After you have measured the amount that you want to sprout, you will probably have some extra seeds left over. These will keep well in a sealed container in a cool, dry place.
- Don't try to accelerate the sprouting process by using hot water or by trying to grow sprouts in a hot place—60°–70°F. is quite perfect.
- If your kitchen is one of those sunny retreats and there is no dark place in which to pamper your crop, you can cover the jar with several layers of a folded towel to keep the sprouts in the dark, but make sure that you leave the cheesecloth-covered end open.

The

Versatile

Grain

and the

Elegant

Bean

280

Grinding Your Own Grains

...The Lure of the Old Mills

There is something about the image of the old water-powered grist mill that tempts us all. Indeed, many of the mills that are listed in our section Mail Order Sources feature just such romantic wooden structures on the banks of a fast-flowing stream, many of them well over 100 years old and still grinding away. Judging by the summer crowds that visit the windmills and the water mills across the country, we are not alone in our feelings. Some years back, in fact, we very nearly bought an old wreck of a mill on the banks of the Little Sugar River in New Hampshire, and the thing that impressed us the most were the original grinding stones that had been left intact on the top floor of the building.

Interestingly enough, the basic principle for grinding grains between stones has remained unchanged over these hundreds of years. The common phrase "keep your nose to the grindstone" comes from the advice given to the miller who leaned forward to see if he could detect the smell of granite coming from the grinding stones, an indication that the adjustment was too close for perfect results.

Today's milling methods and the advent of high-speed rollers, hammer mills and steel-plate mills were developed as an improvement over the old system of slow-turning stones slicing the grains rather than crushing them. But at the same time, though output was increased, the modern mills that operate at such high speeds also overheat and adulterate the flour and the meal. In addition, most commercial methods also remove most of the germ so that the resultant shelf life is increased with a concomitant loss of nutrition and fiber. And—taste!

For many years, then, the only solution was to grind flour ourselves or to get it from one of the mills that continued to use the stone-ground methods. Even then, the range of flours and meals was quite limited—mostly whole wheat flour and corn-meal being offered through the mail, while unusual flours such as amaranth or triticale had to be ground at home. We have found that almost everything is available these days through such suppliers as Arrowhead Mills, Shiloh, Walnut Acres and the hundreds of small mills that offer teff and quinoa, as well as the more common wheat, rye, corn and buckwheat.

This has not stopped some home cooks—and especially many of our bread baker friends—from continuing to grind their own grains at home. Indeed, there may be some of our readers who have heard about it and have always had an urge to try it. Of course, home-ground grains should be used as soon after milling as possible, since there is no such word as "shelf life" when you own your own mill.

Some Grinding Methods

If you do not own a mill and you have no intention of ever buying one, you can grind small amounts in a blender, electric coffee grinder or spice grinder. Food processors, however, do not work very well at all. Softer grains can even be ground in small amounts by using a mortar and pestle.

For people who want to grind larger amounts of grain, there are two basic choices:

Hand Mills. Generally, two basic types of hand mill are available, those with steel grinding burrs and those with stone grinding burrs. Either type will require a fair amount of effort, since the average bread recipe calls for about two and a half pounds of grain, a chore that should take about fifteen to twenty minutes. For an ovenful of bread, it might take most of the day! Although we admit that the idea is romantic, we know very few people in this busy day and age who would tackle the task. Mills range in price from a low end of about $50 to well over $400 with a choice of either stone grinding or steel-blade mills.

Electric Mills. If you choose the stone grinding mill, be sure not to wash the stones after grinding. However, they must be cleaned—a sometimes difficult process—because any residue left on them will turn rancid and affect your future grindings. Steel-bladed mills are easier to clean. Basically, your choice comes down to just how much you want to spend and what kind of grains you'll be milling. Oats, for example, are better with steel, wheat with stone. Electric mills can cost from $150 for a grinding attachment (see below) up to almost $1,000 for the simplest commercial-type electric mills. At this writing, the median price seems to be about $300 to $400.

Before You Buy ... Some Questions to Ask

If you plan to invest in a mill, it pays to approach your selection as you would any expensive piece of equipment or household appliance. We strongly suggest that you investigate thoroughly, and if friends of yours have a home mill, you might want to try it out to see if you really prefer to do your own milling before you use the mail

The

Versatile

Grain

and the

Elegant

Bean

282

order sources for your supplies. One bread baker we know says rather firmly, "I won't even make bread if I can't grind the flour myself!"

- How much grain does the mill grind? How long to grind the flour for one pound? For six?
- How noisy is the mill? Grinding grains can be a noisy process. Unfortunately, it's almost impossible to determine the noise level from the advertising copy.
- Is the mill easy to clean? Are all the parts accessible and easy to take apart—and replace?
- In these days of "battery not included" and kits that have to be assembled at home by a team of geniuses, does the model of your choice come already assembled? Or do you have to assemble it yourself. You may find that it is worth the difference in price to buy a mill that comes ready to grind, especially if you are all thumbs when it comes to using a screwdriver and glue.
- What is the warranty? Are there any other guarantees offered by the manufacturer or distributor?
- If you should need repairs, is there a central repair shop in your area? Shipping costs for the weight of a mill can sometimes be rather high.
- And—speaking of shipping costs—what are they to get the mill from the manufacturer/distributor to you?
- If it's an electric mill, does it have a heavy-duty three-prong plug and wiring to match?

Most of all, keep in mind that you are not buying a mill to save money. It's a lot cheaper to purchase your flour or meal ready-ground. Grinding your own is more in the tradition of "doing your own thing" or "going back to the basics." If it gives you pleasure, then it's well worth it.

Some Grain Mill Manufacturers and Distributors

We've listed below some of the manufacturers of both electric and hand-operated grain mills, some of whom have been in the business for many years. The list is by no means complete, and you will find ads for other mills in the constant stream of catalogues that seem to arrive at your door without end these days. We strongly suggest that you write to them and ask the questions that best suit your purposes. All of them have catalogues or product information sheets as well as price lists and all of them have been quite willing to answer any questions that we've put to them in the past. We're sure that they will be just as helpful to you.

C. S. Bell Company
P. O. Box 291
Tiffin, OH 44883
(419) 448-0791

They make heavy cast-iron mills, including the hand-operated #2 Grist Mill and the #60 Power Mill, which can be hand-operated or attached to an electric motor (purchased separately). The #60 is adjustable for fine or coarse grinding and has interchangeable burrs. They also offer a more expensive power mill, the Milpa, that can grind wet or dry seeds, legumes or grains, and also is adjustable for coarse or fine grinding. The mills can be seen at a range of retail suppliers, including Sears and Southern States Cooperative stores. Send for information and price list.

Country Living Products
14727 Fifty-sixth Avenue N.W.
Stanwood, WA 98292
(206) 652-0671

They manufacture the Country Living Hand Grain Mill, a steel-plated mill that their president, Jack Jenkins, says will grind flour as fine as any stone mill. *East West Journal* (1985) rated it one of the top hand-cranked mills, though it is also convertible to an electric mill because of its V-grooved flywheel. Because of its construction and well-balanced design, it is fairly fast for a small mill and can grind two and a half pounds of flour in about ten minutes. Information is available by mail.

The Grist Milling Company
Retsel Corporation
Box 47
McCammon, ID 83250
(208) 254-3737

Many years ago, we were delighted to find that the founder's name was *Lester*—thus spell his name backward and we have *Retsel*. The company offers several types of grain mills: the Little Ark, a small hand mill, convertible to electric; the Grister Convertible for hand or electric operation; and the more expensive Mil-Rite Grain Mill, the most sophisticated and efficient of the group. Information sheets and price list are available.

In-Tec Equipment Company
Box 123
D. V. Station
Dayton, OH 45406
(513) 276-4077

They offer two unusual grain mills: the first is the top-of-the-line Danish Diamant, which can be hand-operated or attached to an electric motor. Made of cast iron, it has Teflon-coated ball bearings and must be bolted down during use. The second mill is the English-made Atlas #1, a hand-operated mill also made of cast iron, with very few moving parts. Full information is available from In-Tec.

KitchenAid Portable Appliances
701 Main Street
St. Joseph, MI 49085
(616) 982-4500
(800) 422-1230

KitchenAid manufactures a Grain Mill Attachment, model GMA, which can be connected to several models of their mixers. It can be adjusted to grind wheat, rye, rice, corn and other low-moisture grains, varying from flour to very coarse or cracked. If

The

Versatile

Grain

and the

Elegant

Bean

your local appliance or department store doesn't carry the GMA, write for information and price list.

Kuest Enterprises
Box 110
Filer, ID 83328
(208) 326-4084

Bessie and John Kuest have been making the Golden Grain De-Luxe Grinder for about fifteen years. It's electrically operated and it has self-cleaning stones with sharp stainless steel cutting edges to crack the kernel of grain and eliminate wear on the stone. It grinds up to sixty pounds per hour. Kuest also has commercial grinders available. Write for information and prices.

R&R Mill Company Inc.
45 West First North
Smithfield, UT 84335
(801) 563-3333

R&R offers a wide range of grain mills, both hand-operated and electric. All are quite easy to operate. The small, reasonably priced Corona and Corona King mills attach to the countertop for hand operation. They also offer the Mil-Rite Stone Mill and Excalibur Flour Mill, as well as the Bell Power Mill, all electrically operated. Send for their catalogue for further information. It also gives prices.

THE
Elegant Bean

A Gastronomic Renaissance

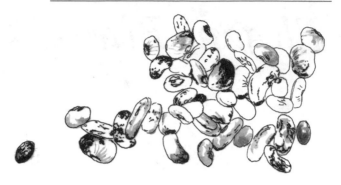

If ever there was a staple food in need of a good public relations campaign, it is the hapless bean—and its more than 10,000 relatives. At least, that has been the case until now. Looked down upon, denigrated by the elitist aristocracy, dubbed with the alias of "poor food" or "poor man's meat," shunned by restaurant chefs, it even carried with it the sarcastic definition that something of no value was "not worth a hill of beans." Even back in the ancient days of the Romans, the philosopher Pythagoras counseled his disciples to *"a fabis abstinete"* or "eat no beans," though in his case it was probably because he truly believed that beans contained the soul of the dead.

The father of the well-known stories, *archy and mehitabel,* Don Marquis, observed that "there will be no beans in the Almost Perfect State." And up until recently, as one food columnist wisely commented, even the mention or discussion of a subject so mundane as *beans* might have drawn nothing but a bored, stifled yawn. But as the nineties dawned, it all changed. Beans were rediscovered. Beans were "in." Beans, once so ignored and vilified, were actually *healthful* for you. Beans were surprisingly versatile. Beans were even *tasty*. From being our poor relations, we watched as beans became *upscale, elegant,* accepted in the very best of "social circles" and with more than a little culinary enthusiasm by the general public, the chefs of the country and the food writers of our daily newspapers and mass circulation magazines.

Along the way, we also discovered that there was more to beans than just plain *beans*. Giving lie to François Rabelais's *(Gargantua and Pantagruel)* description as "looking as like . . . one pea does like another," we found that legumes could be those that came in pods like string beans and snow peas, or shelled fresh like limas, black-eyed peas and green peas, or dried, stored and then soaked to reconstitute

The

Versatile

Grain

and the

Elegant

Bean

288

them like chickpeas, Great Northern, navy and kidney beans. Some are used for animal fodder because they are too coarse for humans, and some are used for humans because they're much too tasty to feed to animals.

We found that beans could be a mosaic of temptation, and they can be fresh or frozen or canned. There are yellow beans, green beans, white beans, purple beans, red, black and wildly patterned beans. Their pods are smooth, fuzzy or irregular, flat, round, straight or curved, long and skinny or shaped just like kidneys. They carry names as simple as pinto or soy or fava or as poetic and imaginative as Tongues of Fire or European Soldiers or Spanish tolasanas. And as their colors and textures and names vary, so do their cooking methods. Chefs and home cooks have begun to discover a new and versatile, inspiring raw material, also learning that beans go with just about everything. And as more and more of us began to recognize all of this, bean sales began to boom.

Phil Teverow, director of new product development and the buyer of beans at New York's Dean & DeLuca, told us that as of this writing, they were selling 100,000 pounds of legumes each year, including heirloom beans and new hybrids, and that he expected an even larger retail sale within the next few years. In Pescadero, California, the Phipps Ranch grows and sells a large variety of heirloom beans right on their property as well as through mail order. Valerie Phipps, co-owner with her husband Tommy, says that "we can't bag them as fast as people buy them!"

With the rapid growth of ethnic restaurants across the country, as well as with the new popularity of bistro food, chefs have begun to include bean dishes on the menus of the most sophisticated and expensive dining establishments. Since beans have always been a key ingredient in almost every cuisine now in favor with the public, it is only natural that we are beginning to see them almost everywhere—in Southwestern, Italian and Thai cooking, French country fare, the menus of the Caribbean, the Middle East, all of Asia, and South and Central America. Someone dubbed this "the Year of the Bean" and the once humble staple has even been paired with the much overused word "gourmet."

The Beneficial Bean

There is probably another important reason that the bean has become an upscale food. We are not only more sophisticated about ethnic cooking these days but we are also better informed about just what is good for us. True, nothing ever became popular just because Mother said to us, *"Eat it! It's good for you!"* Nevertheless, Mother may have had a point when it comes to beans. And we have just begun to listen carefully.

Beans are brimming with soluble fiber, and unlike the hype that accompanied the oat bran craze, beans actually have tremendous versatility in their use with dishes that range from seafood to beef to pork or veal, from pastas to salads, appetizers and desserts. They're an excellent source of protein and iron, they're rich in vitamins, potassium and calcium, very low in fat (and mostly unsaturated at that), and they contain no cholesterol. Though they don't provide all the essential amino acids necessary to make a complete protein, when they're combined with a half cup of whole grains or any other complex carbohydrate, they provide a more complete protein than a hamburger and a serving of french fries with less than half the calories and, certainly, with nowhere near the fat content. A serving of about four ounces of cooked, dry beans contains between 110 and 120 calories, depending upon the variety.

And finally, we should mention something about the cost. When we compare the price of even the most expensive beans to that of the processed foods that fill the supermarket shelves, the *economy* of using legumes in any form becomes quite evident. But possibly the most important thing is that it is not just a passing fancy, and we think that this return to the basic bean is much more than a fad or the "fifteen minutes of fame" for legumes. The growth and acceptance of beans as a contemporary staple food—and an upscale one at that—has been nothing short of phenomenal. The strange thing is that it took so long for it to resurface.

The

Versatile

Grain

and the

Elegant

Bean

290

The Bean Chronicles: Fact and Fancy

Historically, beans have been a critical ingredient in the cuisine of almost every civilization in almost every country around the globe. And, if we were to select just one common term for *all* beans, it might be the word "prehistoric." The American haricot bean dates back about 7,000 years, while the Asian soybean was cultivated more than 4,000 years ago. Favas have been found in Stone Age and Bronze Age archaeological digs, in the ruins of Troy and Rome, as well as in the tombs of ancient Egypt.

As with the history of grains, the bean was critical to the evolution of prehistoric tribes from a hunting society to that of an agricultural one. It took vast areas of land to feed one prehistoric hunter, while that same land planted with beans could feed 5,000 or 6,000 people, with the added advantage of returning nitrogen to the soil to allow for flourishing crops year after year. And so, as Karen MacNeil *(The Book of Whole Foods)* so delightfully put it, "the diet shifted from bison to beans."

Beans were crucial to the survival of the ancient Indians of the Americas, both North and South, and their dried beans frequently saw them through the harsh winters. The Hopi Indians still celebrate an annual bean festival. Beans have also been the staple food of armies and navies from ancient Rome to the modern juggernauts of today, since they store easily and are not very perishable. The good old navy bean got its name as a result of its universal appearance (if not always acceptance) aboard the frigates, battleships and submarines of all the ships at sea. And Teddy Roosevelt once claimed that the battle of San Juan Hill was won on beans!

Along the way, a few areas of the world have also gotten their culinary reputations because of a generous use of beans in their cooking, either because of love for the legumes or simply out of nutritional necessity: hunger. The early explorers of this continent, including Christopher Columbus, sent back a great many of the varieties of beans that had been growing here for so many centuries. In the sixteenth century, the haricot was sent to Italy and was adopted by the early Tuscans as a staple food. The natives then became known as *mangiafagioli*—bean eaters—and the name has stuck to this day.

Our own "beantown"—Boston—is also a part of that heritage, as John Collins Bossidy proclaimed back in 1910:

> And this is good old Boston,
> The home of the bean and the cod . . .

And then he continued with what was to become a famous quip:

> Where the Lowells talk to the Cabots,
> And the Cabots talk only to God.

Actually, the history of beans in the Massachusetts Colony dates as far back as the middle of the seventeenth century, when beans were used for elections each year—white beans for a "yes" vote, black beans for "nay" or an abstention.

Lest our readers think that we are picking on poor old Boston, a city we love dearly, we hasten to add that anything that has been around for 7,000 years is bound to have played a role in folklore, myths, tales of magic, superstitions, as well as with the creation of idols and gods. Possibly you or your grandparents still believe that sleeping in a bean field will certainly lead to madness. Or that dead souls live in the flowers of the broad bean. The miners of England believed that there were more mine disasters when the broad beans bloomed than at any other time.

In Rome, even now, a holiday cake is baked with one fava bean hidden inside and the one who gets the piece with the bean is crowned king (or queen) of the festivities. But if any ancient Chaldeans were around, they might be justly horrified, since they were convinced that someone might be reborn as a fava bean! You might just be eating one of your ancestors.

All of this, of course, has little to do with the major reasons that legumes have been important to the history of cultures. Those who have grown them and have lived with them for centuries have also developed their very own, quite diverse, and sometimes quite healthful cuisines: the Native American succotash, the *tamiya* (bean cake), *ful* (boiled beans) and *ful mudamas* (baked beans) of Egypt, the *cassoulet* of France, *hummus* (chickpeas) of the Middle East, *dal* (lentils and dried peas) of India, the *doufo* and *tofu* (bean curd) of China and Japan, the black-eyed peas and hopping John of our own South, and—dare we say it—the baked beans of Boston.

The

Versatile

Grain

and the

Elegant

Bean

292

Making the Best of the Beans

In the writing of this book, we have, as always, been influenced by our travels as filmmakers and our deep interest in ethnic foods. Thus, many of the recipes that follow have evolved from the traditional ways of cooking, but with a few provisos that have guided us as we've gone along. We know that "old ways" die hard, but our own personal concerns have influenced us to redesign them to meet the standards of nutrition while still maintaining the integrity of the original concepts. Many of our grandmother's recipes gave instructions for the cooking of beans that were quite complex and, in some cases, quite improper in light of what cooks have found out more recently about the nutritional content. Added to that, some of the traditional dishes had inordinate amounts of saturated fat as well as acidic ingredients that made the cooking of beans an all-day affair.

And so, we have kept to the *basics* of each culture. For example, French lentils are not used for dessert traditionally, nor have we even attempted to do so. On the other hand, azuki beans *are* used for exactly that purpose and we have then followed "the rules." However:

- We have updated the recipes to make them conform to contemporary standards of taste and seasoning and, of course, nutrition.
- We have tried to shorten the cooking time for beans through simple techniques of preparation and the selection of the beans themselves.
- Wherever possible, we have combined legumes with grains.
- We have considered the fact that some beans may not be available, though almost every type is now either on the supermarket or specialty shop shelves or can be gotten through mail order. We do believe that the *tastes* vary con-

siderably, but we have suggested substitutes for the less common beans just in case they are not easily obtainable.

• We are very much aware that beans have developed a sometimes unfair (and sometimes fair) reputation for creating flatulence or gas or bloating. We have given some suggestions on page 307 for solving what could be a problem for some people.

There is just one final point that we'd like to make. Given the vast variety of legumes that are now available to us, we fully understand the areas of confusion when confronted with this "bonanza of beans." They are certainly not "looking as like . . . one pea does like another" and we have seen shoppers stand before the fully stacked shelves at Dean & DeLuca in New York, staring in a seemingly hypnotic trance of confusion, admiration or awe. In the concentration that shows in their questioning faces, we can almost hear them say, "They're beautiful, but how do you cook them?" or "What do we serve them with?" and "Do all these beans have *different* flavors?"

And perhaps, in a nutshell, that is exactly what this part of the book is all about!

The

Versatile

Grain

and the

Elegant

Bean

294

How to Buy Beans

If we were to count the blessings that come with the common bean, we might add to its excellent nutrition and wonderful taste the fact that it is a natural product of the earth, and especially with the dried bean, it is maintained in exactly that pristine condition throughout the processing operations—cleaning, sizing, grading—all without washing, and with no chemical treatment to give them "shelf life," with no additives or preservatives to change their taste, their color, or their versatility . . . *or* their nutritional value.

Some years back, in producing a film for the National Council of Farmer Cooperatives, we spoke to farmers across the country who grew beans as a major crop, listened as they told us that good growing weather meant a warm, not too hot sun and adequate moisture from gentle rains or through irrigation. Remarkably, the bean plants develop a strong and mature root system in only a few weeks, with most varieties maturing within a ninety-day cycle. But the comments that struck us most forcibly were the descriptions from farmers who glow as they describe the most beautiful sight they can possibly imagine: a bean field in full flower, for every blossom means an eventual bean.

For the consumer, there are four basic categories of beans that are available quite universally, and each, of course, has its value when it comes to recipe selection, time available to the home cook and, of course, taste and texture:

- **Fresh Shell Beans.** Snow peas, green peas, sugar snaps, string beans, limas, runner beans, yellow wax beans, purple crowder peas, tan and mottled red cranberry beans and black-eyed peas. When they're in season, there's no real substitute.
- **Dried Beans.** With the largest selection of all the categories, in supermarkets, specialty shops and ethnic and natural food stores. They are, of course, the easiest to process, ship and store.

The

Elegant

Bean

- **Frozen Beans.** With some varieties frozen very quickly after harvesting, thus maintaining flavor and nutrition, though losing some textural qualities through freezing and thawing.
- **Canned Beans.** Probably our least favorite form, but quite acceptable under certain conditions and with a few important guidelines.

Pasta, Flakes and Flour

- **Bean Pastas.** Made of mung beans, e.g., *saifun* or cellophane noodles.
- **Bean Flakes.** For purées; partly cooked and rolled such as oats to shorten cooking time. Generally found in health food stores.
- **Bean Flours.** Such as chickpea flour, sometimes called *besan,* and soybean flour.

Buying Dried Beans

As we've mentioned, these are the least processed of all the beans available to the consumer, and they have no preservatives or additives. However, at this time it is unfortunate that the packages that sit on the shelves are not dated to indicate freshness. As a result, the older beans lose moisture over a period of time, making the soaking and cooking time inordinately long. Our favorite beans are what we call "current crop," meaning that they have been planted that spring and harvested in the fall. They are the freshest, most flavorful and have the brightest colors and the best quality. As a result of the freshness, they usually require little soaking time and/or cooking time since their youth fills them with abundant moisture.

Unless a storekeeper actually knows whether or not the beans on his or her shelves are current crop, or at least fairly fresh, there are some tips that might help in making your purchase:

- Learn which stores have heavy traffic so that turnover of stock is continuous. We find that groceries and specialty shops with a large ethnic trade are best. Since beans are important, indeed quite necessary to the cuisines of Latin America and India, the ethnic stores will probably have the freshest supply of such things as pigeon peas and lentils.
- Don't buy unless you can see the beans. See-through packages allow you to note the color, which should be bright. If the color is dull, it indicates that the package has been sitting on a shelf for an overly long time. They will usually stay quite tough no matter how long you cook them, even after extensive soaking.
- Avoid shriveled, cracked or broken beans in a package. This also indicates age.
- Beans should be uniform in size, or else you may run into a cooking/timing problem. The small ones may get soft and overcook, or they may split and dissolve while the larger beans will require additional cooking time.
- Beans that are sold in bulk in burlap sacks are usually cheaper than the su-

The

Versatile

Grain

and the

Elegant

Bean

permarket packaged varieties. However, they may contain more foreign matter and field debris such as twigs, dust or tiny pebbles. In addition, they may get more severe handling during shipment and the seed coats may be cracked. If you do buy in bulk, also check to see that the beans are all approximately the same size.

Buying Frozen Beans . . . Or Freezing Your Own

As we've mentioned, one of the advantages of frozen beans and peas is that they are harvested and then frozen quickly to retain the maximum amount of moisture, nutrition and texture. The freezer compartments of almost every supermarket contain a moderately complete range of fresh shelled beans. We much prefer the frozen string beans to the canned, and we also find that the fresh, tiny young peas that are shelled and frozen give us a time-saving treat all year round. They are actually much sweeter than the older, fresher peas still in their pods—especially after the time it takes to harvest and ship to our local greengrocer. We also find that frozen lima beans, both small and large, along with black-eyed peas, favas and Roman beans keep their texture and flavor quite well.

The one area in which we find some fault is with the frozen sugar snap peas and snow peas, since the freezing process also makes them lose their crisp texture once they're thawed. When fresh, sugar snaps and snow peas need only be blanched with boiling water for less than a minute in order to remove the raw taste, while still retaining flavor and texture. Thus, the freezing process leaves us with a limp, though still tasty vegetable.

If you have a garden and you've discovered, as we have, just how prolific your bean plants can be, you can freeze your own harvest in separate containers and keep them for more than a year. You can also freeze the beans you've already cooked.

Buying Beans in Cans or Jars

When it comes to comparing dried beans with the canned varieties, there is no contest. We're sure you'll agree. However, even though dried beans are far superior in flavor and texture to their sometimes mushier canned cousins, as well as being less costly and providing the most protein for the dollar, the convenience of cooked, canned beans cannot be overlooked when you're pressed for time.

Like all dried beans, canned beans are also processed by many companies under several labels, many of them regional. Thus, we suggest that the first order of business is to select a brand label with a reputation for quality to ensure that they have processed the best of the year's crop. And, though Phil Teverow (of Dean & DeLuca) claims that all canned beans are interchangeable—canned cannellini taste pretty much like canned red pintos or kidneys and all are overcooked—there are still some ways to select adequate substitutes for dried beans. The basic problem, of course, is that you are buying a *can* and the question then becomes, "How do you know what's *in the can?*"

- Experiment. Buy several brands of the same kind of bean in the smallest size available.
- Open the can, drain and rinse the beans. Examine the texture and taste one or two. Then choose your favorite.
- Remember to *read the labels*. Canned products, unlike the natural dried varieties, usually contain additives, preservatives and salt, and occasionally some sugar.

Throughout the book, wherever we have indicated the use of *cooked beans,* if you are pressed for time, canned beans can be used as a substitute, so long as they are drained and rinsed before adding to the recipe.

The

Versatile

Grain

and the

Elegant

Bean

298

How to Store Beans

Dried Beans. We love to store them in airtight glass containers and then line the shelves above our cupboards with a handy decorative and colorful display. Actually, any airtight container will do, and the room should be fairly cool. However, keep in mind that beans do age—just as on the supermarket shelves—and the longer they remain on display, the longer they'll take to reconstitute through soaking, and to soften when they cook.

- Contents of packages bought several months apart *should not be mixed* when storing, since older beans will take longer to cook.

Cooked Beans. Should you cook more beans than you need for a given recipe, they'll keep quite well in the refrigerator for up to three days. They can also be frozen for much longer periods of time.

- Divide your cooked beans in portion sizes or recipe-size containers. If you freeze too many, they'll form an impossible, solid block of beans.
- Cooked beans will keep in the freezer for up to one year.
- The packages of beans from the freezer case at the supermarket will also keep from six months up to one year.
- Bean soups will keep in the freezer for three to six months.

How to Clean Beans

Though most beans that are sold in prepacked bags are usually mechanically cleaned before packaging, we still stick to an old prejudice: Never trust a machine! We think it's still a good idea to pick over the beans, for even in the sanitary confines of the plastic wrap, we have occasionally found stray odds and ends such as weed seed, and even tiny twigs and pebbles that have escaped the machine. And when beans are purchased in bulk, it is absolutely necessary to pick them over before soaking and cooking.

The easiest method is not very time consuming. We find that merely spreading the measured amount of beans in a jelly roll pan (basically, a cookie sheet with sides so that the beans won't spill over onto the counter or floor), and then carefully looking through the beans will do the job in just a few short minutes. Along with any foreign matter or questionable content, also remove and discard any broken bits of beans that you come across.

The

Versatile

Grain

and the

Elegant

Bean

300

To Soak or Not to Soak

Occasionally we come across an article or a chef interview in which a point is made that fresh—current crop—beans need little or no soaking before cooking. We feel, on the other hand, that *all* beans should be soaked after first picking them over. There are several reasons:

- In contrast to high-moisture foods that usually shrink during cooking, dried beans—when soaked and then cooked—will absorb enough moisture to more than double in volume and weight. Soaking helps return the moisture that the beans have lost during drying. Soaking softens them and makes them easier to cook.
- It is quite difficult to determine the age of beans, since packages are not dated, or you may have purchased beans that have been lying on a shelf for some time.
- Soaking helps prevent skins from cracking or bursting while cooking and before they become tender enough to eat.
- After proper soaking, cooking time is reduced by about one half. Prolonged cooking will also cause a loss of vitamins and some minerals.
- Most important of all, soaking helps break down and leach out the indigestible sugars that may cause intestinal gas.
- During soaking, some beans (called "floaters") may rise to the surface. These may be the older beans with little moisture or beans that were harvested prematurely, with the bean shrinking within its seed coat and sometimes trapping dirt. This is the time to easily locate them and discard them. If you find that too many rise to the surface, we suggest finding another supplier.

- The only exceptions to soaking before cooking are split peas and lentils. In addition, some researchers claim that thin-skinned beans, i.e., black-eyed peas, do not require soaking. Our own test trials prove otherwise. We say: Soak!
- Current crop beans—grown in the spring, harvested in late summer or early fall and purchased from a reputable dealer with a fast turnover of product—probably do not require any soaking, but even then, we can never be certain as to freshness. So, once again, we say: Soak! Phil Teverow of Dean & DeLuca adds, "Soaking can't harm the beans in any way. All they will do is absorb the amount of water they can hold, which may be very little if they're very very fresh."

How to Soak—Some Easy Methods and Some Tips

In our trials we used a long (six- to nine-hour) soaking time and a short quick method. We found that there was no discernible difference in the texture and taste of the beans. In addition, all required the same cooking time. Just choose the method that suits you best. You may want to use the longer one—beans that are put up to soak before you go to sleep, then allowed to soak overnight. Or you may want to put them up to soak right before you leave for work, to be ready for cooking that evening for dinner.

Beans usually absorb most of the water they need to rehydrate and swell in about four hours at room temperature. The prime rule for soaking is *always soak in tepid water*. Some books and recipe instructions call for cold water. We disagree, since cold water has a tendency to make the beans tougher.

Before Soaking. Pick over the beans thoroughly, as described on the previous pages. Then put the beans in a strainer, place the strainer in tepid water in a large bowl and swish them around. Some tiny bits may float to the top along with some bean shells. Skim off before pouring off the rest of the water so that they don't mix with the beans again. Repeat the process two or three times in tepid water. Then put the beans in a large bowl and cover with water about four times the volume of the beans.

Long Soaking Method (six to nine hours). This is the traditional "long soak" or "overnight soak" (or what we call the "go to work and come back later soak") that traditional recipes use and it is still quite acceptable. If, for some reason, you find that you have to extend the soaking time for as much as a day or two, just be sure to change the water at least once a day so they don't ferment. Or if you live in a very hot climate, change the water more frequently, particularly if your kitchen is hot. After soaking, drain and discard the soaking water and rinse the beans in tepid water. Then proceed with the recipe instructions.

Short Soaking Method. This is a time saver if you decide at the last moment that beans are to be a part of your menu. Put the picked-over and washed beans in a three-quart saucepan. Add hot tap water to cover the beans by about two to three inches and bring slowly to a boil over medium high heat. Boil for two minutes, then remove the pot from the heat. Cover and let the beans soak for about one hour.

The

Versatile

Grain

and the

Elegant

Bean

Drain off the soaking water. Then rinse the beans in a colander with fresh, tepid water, turning them gently so that all of them are rinsed. Proceed with the recipe instructions.

Some Tips

- Use about four times the volume of water to beans for soaking.
- Never cook beans in the water in which they've been soaking. Soaking leaches out the complex sugars and cooking in the same water will let the beans reabsorb them. The complex sugars may cause the gas that troubles some people.
- *Don't add salt to the soaking water.* Salt will toughen the seed coat and prevent absorption of the water.
- For beans that do not require soaking before they are cooked (split peas, lentils), just rinse them in tepid water, drain and continue with your recipe.
- Some "old wives tales" call for adding baking soda to the soaking water. Avoid it if possible. Baking soda should be used in only the hardest of hard water, since it affects the flavor, destroys the nutrients and makes the beans mushy. That is one of the reasons (in addition to overcooking) that some canned beans have the texture of baby food, since alkalines such as baking soda are used in the processing. Should you live in a hard water area and feel that you must add baking soda, use no more than one-eighth teaspoon to one cup of dry beans.

Cooking the Beans

The cooking time for beans will vary, depending upon several conditions: the variety, size and age of the beans, the hardness of the bean seed coat and of the water and the altitude at which you live. For example, the higher the altitude, the lower the boiling point of water, something that our friends in cities like Denver and Mexico City already know. Thus, an increase in cooking time will be called for. At sea level, the boiling point of water is, of course, 212°F. At 5,000 feet, it drops to 202°F. and at 12,000 feet (La Paz, Bolivia, is a good example) down to 188°F. Thus, not only is cooking time increased, but there is a possibility that you will have to add more liquid. Throughout this section, we have given approximate cooking times for beans (at sea level) and simple charts for cooking each kind of bean are found before every section.

Whether up in the mountains or down near sea level where most of us live, there are some basic tips that we'd like to pass along for the cooking of beans. Luckily, beans are patient creatures that usually do not suffer from being kept waiting or from your taking your time in the preparation and cooking of your recipes, unlike the delicacy and immediacy of a soufflé. While they're cooking, there are other things around the house that can be done.

For Stove-Top Cooking.

- Beans should always be covered with water or *unsalted* stock while cooking. Sometimes aromatic vegetables (such as onions, carrots or celery) and herbs (such as thyme, parsley and oregano) are added for additional flavor.
- Tilt the lid of the pot ever so slightly to prevent boiling over and to allow steam to escape.
- Beans should always be simmered gently so that the skins don't burst.

The

Versatile

Grain

and the

Elegant

Bean

304

- If water level goes down, add boiling water as needed.
- Stir only occasionally—and never bring to a rolling boil or the beans will burst and become mushy.
- Start the beans cooking in *tepid* water—not cold—the same rule that applies to soaking and rinsing.
- If the water should foam, you might want to skim it off just once or twice. Occasionally the foam will coat the beans and make them gritty. However, after just a few skimmings, don't pay attention to the foam. It will sink to the bottom and disappear eventually.
- *Never add salt or anything acidic while the beans are cooking:* tomatoes, vinegar, wine, molasses or citrus juices. Add salt only after the beans are almost tender. And if you're cooking with stock, be certain that it is *unsalted*. If any of these are added before the beans are tender, they will eventually get soft but the cooking time will be greatly increased.
- Keep in mind that the older the beans, the longer they have been stored, the longer the cooking time.
- To test for doneness, bite-taste a few beans, since some may be tender and some may not. They should be tender but not mushy. If they are not the proper consistency, continue to cook and taste them often.
- When cooling, keep the beans in their cooking liquid to prevent them from drying out and so that the skins won't burst or split.
- If you're reheating beans, add a tablespoon or two of water or reserved cooking liquid. As beans cool, they have a tendency to inhale any leftover liquid that may still be there.

Baking Beans.

- Soak the beans overnight, covering them with tepid water about three inches over the volume of the beans.
- Next day, preheat the oven to 325°F. Rinse, drain and place the beans in an ovenproof casserole or bean pot.
- Cover with fresh water to about three inches over the volume of the beans.
- Put the casserole or bean pot on top of the stove, bring to a boil, then cover and place in the center of the oven. Bake forty to sixty minutes or more, depending upon the size and age of the beans. Keep them in their liquid until ready to use.

Pressure Cookers. We have a theory that beans should be watched carefully while they cook and that ingredients should be added along the way. Some people swear by pressure cookers, but we are not too impressed, for once you close the cover and seal it, there is no way to observe just what's going on inside. As we both like to say, "We don't like to cook anything we can't see!" There's no doubt that pressure cookers save time, but they also eliminate any chance for a taste test along the way to keep the beans from overcooking and to allow the addition of seasonings that should be put into the recipe during the cooking process. In addition, foam or bean skins can easily clog the vent of the pressure cooker. We leave the pressure cooker recipes to other books.

And—a Word About Microwaves. Here, too, we firmly believe in traditional, slow cooking, especially when it comes to beans. And here, again, there are several books that give specifics about microwave cooking. Though we do not use a microwave in our kitchen, we have seen a very practical use for them in the *reheating* of bean dishes and bean soups, especially after they've been frozen and stored for future use.

The

Versatile

Grain

and the

Elegant

Bean

306

Abdominal Rumblings . . .
Taking the Rap for a Bad Rep

We would be remiss if we did not comment on a problem, both perceived and real, that accompanies any mention of beans. Whether we call it flatulence or gas or indigestion or discomfort, beans have been the target of a rather undesirable reputation. We remember, as kids, skipping down the city streets to a giggling singsong about, "Beans, beans, the musical fruit . . ." (And giggling even harder as we concluded that "the more you eat, the more you toot!")

It is unfortunate, on the one hand, that beans are healthful and delicious (and quite properly so), while on the other hand, beans are culprits for sometimes embarrassing flatulence for some people. We must add rather quickly that this need not be so, and that there are ways in which to reduce or to eliminate entirely the abdominal rumblings. Interestingly enough, there are other foods that create exactly the same gases and yet they have not been subjected to bad press nor to childhood ditties that make fun of them: broccoli, brussels sprouts, cabbage, oat bran, celery, raisins, raw carrots, milk and even some milk products. All of them—including beans—contain complex sugars called *oligosaccharides,* which the body cannot digest easily. Passing through the small intestine and into the large, they are feasted upon by the bacteria lying in wait in the colon. The by-products are hydrogen, carbon dioxide and other gases, and we have the small beginnings of the problem about which we read so much.

Put very simply, then, if we reduce the complex sugars or eliminate them completely, we also reduce the chance of any flatulence—and possibly also reduce the bad reputation of the poor bean. Basically, the answer lies in the proper soaking and cooking of the beans. For example, by not cooking the beans in the water in which they've been soaked, we can eliminate a great part of the problem, since the complex sugars will be washed down the drain along with the soaking water. True, there may be some small loss of nutrients, but the loss is quite minor.

For cooked, canned beans or those that come in a jar, make sure you rinse them before using. And if you sprout your beans, the oligosaccharides will be almost totally eliminated, along with any resultant flatulence.

One important fact that we have found over the years, which we think you will also discover, is that by making beans a regular part of your diet (just as we recommend that you do with whole grains), your body will eventually adjust to the new nutrition and the problems of flatulence will not remain. Researchers more involved with and more knowledgeable about the subject than we are have found that societies where beans are a daily menu addition do not have the problems of intestinal gas. Just begin with small amounts at first, then increase to normal portions. The more you eat them, the more accustomed your body will become to even the complex sugars that remain.

We also think that traditional cooking techniques as well as the ingredients that were used in years gone by also had something to do with the reputation of the bean. Old-fashioned recipes were laden with enormous amounts of fat, adding not only to our cholesterol count, but serving to keep food in the digestive system much longer, where gases were allowed to form. Thus, the recipes in this book have been designed with pared-down amounts of fat. For example, where ham hocks or bacon are called for, we have cut down the amounts by half or more, while still keeping the flavor, albeit more subtly. Frequently, we have called for Canadian bacon for flavor. We've done the same for sausages, oils and beef bones, all of them added in minimum amounts in recipes that serve from four to ten people. Thus, the amounts of fat per person are quite negligible. It has worked well for us and for our guests.

Essentially, then, we feel that it is a shame to avoid one of the most versatile and healthful additions to the diet because of something that is either a myth for most people or is quite remediable for others. Prepare beans properly, including them frequently in your diet and we think you'll find that it's well worth it. There is really no need to deny yourself this most delicious of foods through fear of bloating!

The

Versatile

Grain

and the

Elegant

Bean

308

Bean Genealogy:
A Complete Guide to the Recipes

Lima Bean & Cabbage Pouches

The bean, being a well-traveled citizen of the world, tracing its family lineage back to the Bronze Age, has been with us long enough to have developed a vast and confusing number of kinsmen, kinswomen and kissing cousins. For the home cook, faced with trying to decipher the bewildering list of close relatives and distant relations, the selection of a particular bean for a recipe has one added enigma: if we look at its *uncooked* state, we have no real idea of what it will *taste* like. And thus, that secret remains locked in until the bean is cooked. What we have tried to do in this most important section of recipes is to unlock some of those doors, to familiarize our readers with *Leguminosae*—the bean family—and to have you feel as we do, that to "know it is to love it." For the more we have learned about this ancient food, the more respect we have developed for the "poor food" that has survived and nourished the world through the ages, finally to become the "elegant" bean of today.

Many of these beans are "heirloom beans," old-fashioned varieties that have been grown for generations on small family farms across the nation. Some are varieties that produce low crop yields and therefore have never been grown on a grand scale. In addition, some heirloom beans have been lost over the centuries for various reasons, have recently been rediscovered and are being grown once again by farmers willing to take the risks of a low-yield crop. Still others, which were originally cultivated by the first European settlers in the United States, have surfaced again through dedicated growers such as the Phipps Ranch in California and the Wannigan Bean Project's work to preserve the heirlooms (now known as Seed Savers Exchange in Missouri). As the heirloom beans began to reappear, their revival was helped tremendously by the support of knowledgeable purveyors, retail outlets and mail order sources, many of whom we have given credit in our acknowledgments for this book.

The heirloom beans are becoming increasingly popular with professional chefs as well as with home cooks, all of whom are responding not only to their colorful names and their unique, attractive and brightly hued appearance, but to their wonderfully sweet taste as well.

But the renaissance has not been limited to the heirloom varieties. Others have surfaced as well. The "hybrid" beans are also becoming increasingly popular, beans that farmers developed for a variety of reasons—to resist scourges such as fungi or insect infestations, as well as those that are particularly beautiful and have their own texture and individual flavor. The appaloosa and the calypso are just two examples of just such work with the hybrids. Others are quite scarce and glamorous, and generally can be found only in specialty food stores or through mail order sources.

And then there are the "imports"—the more common and familiar beans, but still "exotic" since they are known mainly in Europe, the Middle and Far East—such as the Greek *gigandes* or the *ful,* small fava beans of Egypt. But even here, this bean revival has begun to see these varieties appearing in ethnic specialty shops.

We have not ignored, by any means, the familiar supermarket varieties, though depending upon the ethnic group or the region of the country in which you live, almost all of the popular beans also possess aliases. Four people who hail from different parts of the country might refer to the same bean as "black-eyed peas," for example, while another might call them "black-eyed suzies" or "crowder pea" or "brown-eyed pea." To top it all off, the botanist would dub any of them *Vigna sinensis!*

And so, in this section, we have taken into account the fact that gardeners and horticulturists are curious enough to want identification by popular name, Latin family, regional nicknames or aliases (of which there are many that are quite colorful and colloquial). To help both the gardener and the home cook, we have included a drawing in actual size for each variety of bean, as well as a physical description, some information on the characteristics, plus some of the historical journeys that the bean might have taken to eventually get to our kitchen and our cooking pot.

We have also included for each bean some information on the traditional ethnic dishes in which it is used, the special seasonings and flavorings, and in what form the particular bean is available (i.e., fresh in pod, frozen, canned or dried). For each bean we have given a chart of measurements and approximate cooking times. And then, last, but we hope *most,* a range of recipes for each bean, developed with contemporary concerns for health, new techniques and just plain deliciousness.

Indeed, to know them is to love them. And—enjoy them.

The

Versatile

Grain

and the

Elegant

Bean

310

Azuki

Phaseolus angularis

Alias. Adzuki, aduki, adsuki, asuki.

Description. Small, about ¼ inch long, oval shape, russet-colored with a thin white line on the ridge of the bean (the cotyledon). It grows as a bush bean rather than as a vine, with yellow flowers and pods that are up to 5 inches long.

Characteristics. A nutty, light flavor that adapts well to both sweet and savory dishes. The skin is rather thickish.

History. Grown and eaten in China and Japan for thousands of years, where it has been called "the King of Beans." It was brought to America from Japan in 1854 by Admiral Perry.

Traditional Uses. In the Orient, it is eaten dried, fresh or sprouted and sometimes ground into flour. Cooked to a sweet, candied paste, it is served as a confection, and sometimes it is cooked along with glutinous rice to give the rice a festive, pink hue.

Availability. Whole dried, flour, occasionally fresh at ethnic vegetable stands, health food stores, oriental ethnic markets and some supermarkets.

Cooking Chart
Pot: 3 qt.

Type of Bean:	Azuki
Amount:	1 C. dried
Instructions:	Overnight soak (see page 302)
Cooking Time:	30 to 45 minutes
Approx. Yield:	3 C.

Azuki Bean Salad with Cucumber, Watercress and Scallops in a Wasabi Cream

SERVES 4

A warm Japanese-inspired salad of small scallops tossed with hot Japanese horse-radish (wasabi), cooled with a touch of cream and then piled on a bed of watercress, cucumber and sweet azuki beans with a Japanese "vinaigrette."

Wasabi Cream (Prepare first)

1 Tbs. powdered wasabi (Japanese horseradish)	2 Tbs. heavy cream
	½ tsp. lemon juice
1 Tbs. water	Pinch salt

In a small cup, mix the wasabi powder with water to form a paste. Cover and let stand for 10 minutes, then mix with the cream, lemon juice and salt and set aside.

Scallops

¼ C. all-purpose flour	1 lb. bay scallops or Southern calico
Salt and freshly ground black pepper	scallops, dried on paper towels
to taste	2 Tbs. corn oil

Place the flour, salt and pepper in a plastic bag, add the scallops and shake to coat. Remove them from the bag and shake off the excess flour. In a 12-inch skillet, heat the oil until very hot. Add the scallops in one layer and sauté over high heat for 2 minutes. Add the Wasabi Cream, toss to coat and cook for 1 more minute. Transfer to a bowl and set aside.

Beans and Vegetables

2 C. drained, cooked azuki beans (see Chart, page 311)	1½ C. thinly sliced cucumber, stacked and cut into fine julienne
4 C. loosely packed watercress leaves with tough stems removed	2 Tbs. shoyu soy sauce
1–2 scallions, green part only, thinly sliced, cut on the diagonal (about ¼ C.)	2 Tbs. mirin (sweet Japanese rice wine)
	2 Tbs. rice vinegar
	1 tsp. oriental sesame oil
	Few grains cayenne

To a large bowl, add the beans, watercress, scallions and cucumbers. In a small bowl, whisk together the soy, mirin, vinegar, sesame oil and cayenne. Pour over the beans and greens and toss lightly to mix. Spoon onto individual plates and top with a mound of scallops in the wasabi cream.

The

Versatile

Grain

and the

Elegant

Bean

312

Azuki Bean Paste and Sweet Rice Balls with Plum Wine Sauce and Japanese Green Tea

SERVES 10

There are many sweet dishes in Japan that feature azuki beans and many of them are paired with short grain (sweet) glutinous rice. For example, *Shiratama Uji Kintoki* is a dish of shaved ice sweetened with azuki beans nestling underneath. Another dish is made from green tea and balls of chewy pounded rice cakes called *mochi*. *Osekihan*, or red rice, combines *mochi* that is stained pink from the azuki bean cooking liquid and is a special-occasion dish. Our version is an invented one that combines Japanese ingredients put together in a Western fashion. It has a surprisingly clean fresh taste.

1 C. drained, cooked azuki beans (see Chart, page 311)
½ C. superfine sugar
Pinch salt, plus ½ tsp. salt (or to taste)
2 C. water
2 C. glutinous (sweet) white rice, washed and rinsed twice, then soaked overnight or for a minimum of 6 hours, rinsed and drained (see NOTE)

2 tsps. finely minced orange peel, plus a few long shreds of peel, made with a zester tool
1 C. Japanese plum wine
Powdered green tea (*matsu-cha*)

In a 2-quart nonstick saucepan, mix the cooked beans with the sugar and the pinch of salt and bring to a boil, stirring constantly. Press the beans against the side of the pan to crush them, while boiling for 2 to 3 minutes. Transfer to a bowl and set aside to cool.

Wash the saucepan, add the water and ½ teaspoon salt and bring to a boil. Add the soaked rice and return to a boil. Cover the pan and simmer for 20 minutes, then let it stand for 15 minutes to cool. The rice should be very sticky, shiny and slightly warm. Stir in the 2 teaspoons minced orange peel.

Fill a bowl with water to use for dipping your hands. Dampen your hands and place 2 tablespoons of the rice in your palm. Flatten slightly and place ½ teaspoon of the cooked bean mixture in the center and form into a ball, enclosing the filling. As you complete each one, cover with plastic wrap until all the balls are formed. There should be about twenty.

To serve, place two filled rice balls on a small dessert plate. Spoon 1 tablespoon of the plum wine over each, allowing some to trickle on the plate. Sprinkle ¼ teaspoon of green tea over the surface and top with a few reserved shreds of orange peel.

NOTE: The rice for this dish is cooked *in* water rather than steamed *over* water so that the end results in a much more sticky soft texture, necessary for desserts.

The

Elegant

Bean

Azuki Beans with Dried Apples, Honey, Raisins and Cinnamon

SERVES 8 TO 10

Beans with ice cream, you say? Yuk! But don't knock it until you've tried it. Azuki beans are traditionally paired with sweets in Japan, and so we have been inspired to do the same. Here the tiny, sweet red beans are cooked with dried apples, honey, raisins and cinnamon, then, while warm, spooned over vanilla ice cream in an East meets West dessert.

3 C. drained, cooked azuki beans, liquid reserved (see Chart, page 311)

1 C. dried apples, roughly cut into ¾-in. pieces

½ C. black raisins, preferably Monukka or Muscat

¼ C. honey

½ tsp. cinnamon

1 tsp. lemon juice

Vanilla ice cream

Place the cooked beans in a 3-quart nonstick saucepan and set aside. In a small bowl, mix the apples and raisins together and add 1½ cups of the reserved bean liquid. Let stand for 15 minutes, then add to the saucepan along with the honey and cinnamon. Simmer, covered, for about 8 minutes. Stir in the lemon juice and serve warm, spooned over vanilla ice cream. If you reheat the beans and fruit, add ½ cup boiling water to dilute, since most of the liquid will have been absorbed.

The

Versatile

Grain

and the

Elegant

Bean

314

Black Beans

Phaseolus vulgaris

Alias. *Frijoles negros,* turtle beans, Spanish or Mexican black beans, lablab.

Description. Medium size, about ⅝ inch long, oval, slightly squarish shape. They are matte black with a small white line only on the ridge of the bean. The skin is black and the inside is cream colored.

Characteristics. The flavor is earthy, sweet with a hint of mushrooms.

History. Black beans are favored throughout Latin America, South and Central America and the Caribbean, where they originally grew as "New World Beans."

Traditional Uses. They are the basis for Brazil's once-weekly traditional national dish, *feijoada,* as well as Cuban black bean soup with rum and *Moros y Cristianos* (Moors and Christians), a dish of white rice and black beans. They're also found in a great many Mexican dishes.

Availability. Dried and canned in various sizes and processed in several ways. Most supermarkets, specialty stores, health food stores and Hispanic markets carry them.

Cooking Chart

Pot: 3 qt.

Type of Bean:	Black Beans
Amount:	1 C. dried
Instructions:	Overnight soak (see page 302)
Cooking Time:	55 to 60 minutes
Approx. Yield:	2¼ C.
Comments:	The color fades a bit. Cook with lid slightly ajar to avoid boil-overs.

Black Bean Soup with Madeira and Lime

SERVES 10 TO 12

This is a favorite family recipe that has evolved over the years, managing to obtain optimum flavor while lowering fat content. It's a hearty, subtle, yet earthy soup that tastes even better (as most soups and stews do) when made the day before serving it.

2½ C. (1 lb.) black beans, soaked and drained

10 C. water

2 C. chicken or beef stock (unsalted)

1 smoked ham hock (about ½ lb.), or ¼ lb. raw, cured ham such as Smithfield or country ham, cut into ½-in. dice

1 oz. salt pork, tough rind trimmed and discarded, cut into ½-in. dice

3 large onions, coarsely chopped (3 C.)

3 stalks celery, coarsely chopped (1 C.)

2 medium carrots, coarsely chopped (1 C.)

1 Tbs. whole mixed pickling spices, tied in cheesecloth

2 tsps. fresh thyme leaves (or ½ tsp. dried thyme)

2 tsps. finely minced fresh sage (or 1 tsp. dried sage)

¼ tsp. cayenne or more to taste

¼ C. Madeira wine

1 Tbs. tomato paste

2 Tbs. red wine vinegar

2 tsps. light molasses

Salt to taste (optional)

2 hard-cooked eggs (whites only), finely chopped

Paper-thin slices lime

2 Tbs. finely minced parsley

In a 7-quart heavy Dutch oven or a stockpot, bring the beans, water and stock to a boil. Skim off any foam. Lower the heat, cover and simmer for 1 hour. Add the ham hocks, bring to a boil again, then lower the heat and simmer 10 minutes more.

Meanwhile, slowly heat the salt pork in a large skillet so that the fat is rendered. Raise the heat to medium high, add the onions and sauté for 5 minutes, stirring often. Then add the celery and carrots and continue to cook, stirring often, for 5 minutes more. Add the vegetables and the spice bag, stir in the thyme and sage and cook for another hour.

Remove and discard the spice bag and the hock, if used (see NOTE). Purée the soup in batches using a food processor, and return each batch to the pot after puréeing. If the soup is too thick, add more water for the desired consistency. Reheat the soup over low heat, stir in the cayenne, Madeira wine, tomato paste, vinegar and molasses and simmer for 3 minutes more.

Taste for salt and add if necessary. When ready to serve, ladle the soup into serving bowls and sprinkle with some chopped egg white. Float a slice of lime on the surface of each bowl and sprinkle the lime with a pinch of minced parsley.

NOTE: If cured ham is used, purée it with the soup.

The

Versatile

Grain

and the

Elegant

Bean

316

Black Bean Timbale with Cilantro and
Roasted Red Pepper Cream

SERVES 8

A most attractive presentation for a black bean dish with a South-of-the-border accent. Our vegetarian friends love it for its festive, colorful appeal as well as its taste.

Cilantro and Roasted Red Pepper Cream

1 medium roasted red pepper, seeded
2 Tbs. finely minced cilantro
1 small clove garlic, finely minced (½ tsp.)

½ C. sour cream
¼ C. buttermilk
Salt and freshly ground black pepper to taste

Cut one small piece of the red pepper into very fine dice (about 1 tablespoon) and reserve it for the garnish. Cut the remaining pepper into large pieces. Purée in an electric blender, not a food processor, along with the cilantro, garlic, sour cream, buttermilk and the salt and pepper. Scrape the mixture into a small bowl and set aside.

Black Bean Timbale

Butter for greasing mold
2 C. cooked Brazilian-style black beans (see page 315)
3 canned Italian plum tomatoes, drained
1 Tbs. tomato paste
1 small scallion, finely minced (¼ C.)
½ roasted Jalapeño pepper, finely minced (1 tsp.)

2 eggs
1 C. fresh bread crumbs
1 Tbs. sour cream
About 1 Tbs. finely diced roasted red pepper (see above)
1 sprig cilantro

Lavishly butter a 1½-quart mold, such as a Charlotte mold, and preheat the oven to 350°F. Purée the cooked beans, tomatoes, tomato paste, scallions and Jalapeño pepper in the bowl of a food processor until smooth. Add the eggs one at a time and process again, then add the bread crumbs and process until the mixture is smooth.

Spoon into the mold and bake for 1 hour. Let cool in the mold on a wire rack. Then unmold onto the center of a large serving dish. Add the sour cream on top. Scatter the finely diced red pepper over the sour cream and decorate with the sprig of cilantro. Spoon the cilantro and red pepper cream sauce all around the base of the timbale and serve at room temperature.

Hot and Spicy Baked Red Snapper with Black Beans and Cilantro

SERVES 4

Red snapper is a popular fish in the United States and Mexico. In this recipe the fish is marinated in cumin, hot chile and garlic, layered over a bed of black beans and spiked with sherry. It's then topped with tomatoes and roasted yellow peppers in a most Mexican treatment.

4 red snapper fillets (about 1¼ lbs. total)
¾ tsp. hot pepper flakes
1½ tsps. ground cumin
2 large cloves garlic
Salt to taste
5 Tbs. olive oil
3 large cloves garlic, finely minced (about 1 Tbs.)
1 medium onion, finely chopped (½ C.)
2⅔ C. drained, cooked black beans (see Chart, page 315)

Freshly ground black pepper to taste
2 Tbs. dry sherry
2 Tbs. coarsely chopped cilantro, plus extra whole leaves
2 large plum tomatoes, diced (¾ C.)
1 large roasted yellow sweet pepper, peeled and seeded, and cut into 1-in. strips (about ¾ C.)
3 green olives, sliced
Juice of 1 medium lime (3 Tbs.)
1 tsp. dried oregano, preferably Greek

In a flat dish, put the fish in one layer. In a blender, blend the pepper flakes, cumin, garlic, salt and 3 tablespoons of the olive oil to a purée. Spread on the surface of the fish and marinate for 15 minutes. Preheat the oven to 325°F.

In a medium-size skillet, heat the remaining 2 tablespoons olive oil and sauté the minced garlic and onions, stirring frequently for about 3 to 4 minutes until the onions are translucent. Add the beans, salt and pepper, sherry and 2 tablespoons cilantro and stir to combine. Using a large oven-to-table casserole, spoon the beans on the bottom, lay the marinated fish on top. Scatter the tomatoes, yellow pepper and olives on top. Sprinkle with lime juice and then the oregano. Bake for 20 to 25 minutes and test with a skewer to see if it flakes. Garnish with whole cilantro leaves.

The

Versatile

Grain

and the

Elegant

Bean

318

Baked Cuban Black Beans with
Ham Hocks and Rum

SERVES 8 TO 10

Rum and long, slow cooking give these beans their unique flavor. Preparing them 1 or 2 days in advance not only enhances their taste but makes them perfect for a dinner party, since they do not require your constant attention.

1 lb. black beans, picked over, washed and soaked

6 C. tepid water

3 small ham hocks (about 1½ lbs. total)

2 bay leaves

⅓ C. olive oil

3 large cloves garlic, finely minced (2 Tbs.)

2 large sweet Spanish onions, coarsely chopped (3½ C.)

1 large green pepper, finely diced (1¼ C.)

Salt and freshly ground black pepper to taste

¼ tsp. ground cumin

¼ tsp. hot pepper flakes

¼ tsp. cayenne

3 Tbs. red wine vinegar

3 Tbs. dark rum

In a 5-quart nonstick Dutch oven, bring the soaked beans and the water to a boil, lower the heat and simmer for 1 hour or longer, until the beans are tender. Then add the ham hocks and bay leaves and continue to cook for 40 minutes more. Remove the bay leaves and discard them. Remove the ham hocks, let cool and cut out a small piece of lean meat from each hock. Trim off the fat, dice the meat and return to the beans. Drain the beans, saving the liquid for the next part of the recipe.

In a large skillet, heat the oil and sauté the garlic for 30 seconds over medium high heat. Add the onions and green pepper and continue to cook for 5 minutes, stirring occasionally. Season with salt and black pepper. Add the cumin, hot pepper flakes and cayenne and continue to cook, stirring occasionally, for 3 to 5 minutes or just until the onions began to take on color. Stir them into the beans and add 1 cup of the reserved liquid. Continue to cook the beans, uncovered, for 30 to 40 minutes more, adding a bit of additional liquid if they seem dry. Add the vinegar and taste for seasoning. Then cook for 10 minutes more. At this point, if you are serving the dish at once, stir in the rum and serve with hot rice.

If you wish to serve the beans within the next few days, do not add the rum until just before serving. When you plan to serve the beans, bake them in a preheated 350°F. oven, covered, for about 40 minutes or until they are hot. Stir them occasionally and check to see if additional reserved liquid is required. The beans should form a thick sauce but not swim in liquid.

Honey Grilled Chicken with
Mexican Black Bean and Tomatillo Sauce

SERVES 6

The pleasing underlying flavor nuances of astringent tomatillos and serrano peppers in the black bean sauce hit just the right note with grilled sweet honey-glazed chicken tempered with tart lime juice.

Sauce (Makes 1¾ cups)

½ C. dried black beans, soaked and drained, or 1¼ C. cooked beans (see NOTE)
3 C. unsalted chicken stock
2 tomatillos, husked and quartered
1 C. water
2 fresh serrano chiles

¼ small onion, chopped (1 heaping Tbs.)
2 cloves garlic, coarsely chopped (1½ tsps.)
1 Tbs. coarsely chopped cilantro
1 Tbs. olive oil
Salt to taste
2 tsps. lime juice

In a 2-quart nonstick saucepan, bring the beans and 2½ cups of the chicken stock to a boil. Lower the heat and simmer for 1 hour, until the beans are very tender. Add more water if necessary while cooking the beans. Meanwhile, add the tomatillos to a small saucepan along with the water and bring to a boil. Then lower the heat and simmer for 5 minutes. Drain and set aside in a small bowl. Thread the two chiles on a metal skewer and toast over an open flame or under a broiler if stove is electric, turning to scorch the skin, about 1 minute. Enclose in foil for 2 minutes, then stem them, scrape off the skin, discard the seeds and add to the tomatillos. (Wear rubber surgical gloves to prevent the chiles' capsicum oil from burning your hands.)

Add the onions, garlic and cilantro to the tomatillos. When the beans are cooked, add them to the bowl, along with the remaining chicken stock, then purée in a blender. Stir in olive oil and scrape the mixture into a small nonstick saucepan. Prepare the sauce only up to this point. Then while the chicken is grilling, add the salt and simmer the sauce for 3 to 5 minutes, stirring occasionally. Remove from the heat and stir in the lime juice.

Chicken

6 boneless skinned chicken breasts, each weighing 6 ozs.
Juice of 2 limes (about ¼ C.)
¼ tsp. salt or to taste
1 tsp. paprika

2 Tbs. honey
2–3 drops Tabasco sauce
1 large fresh tomato, cut into small cubes and seeded
Few sprigs cilantro

The

Versatile

Grain

and the

Elegant

Bean

Place the chicken in a shallow (nonmetal) pan. Combine the remaining ingredients, except the tomato and cilantro, pour over the chicken and marinate for 15 minutes on each side. Lift the chicken out of the marinade, then broil or charcoal-grill for about 5 minutes on each side or until just cooked through. Discard the marinade.

Serve each grilled chicken breast with 2 tablespoons of sauce spooned over. Scatter a few pieces of tomato over the sauce and garnish with a sprig of cilantro.

NOTE: If canned beans are used, rinse and drain them, add only ½ cup of chicken stock to dilute the sauce, rather than the 3 cups called for in the original recipe.

Black Bean Pancakes with Sour Cream, Red Peppers and Cilantro

SERVES 6

Crisp on the outside and creamy within, this savory blend of black beans with just a touch of Jalapeño chile for bite is lovely with grilled chicken or fish. It's also a good way to use up any leftover black beans.

2 C. cooked black beans (see Chart, page 315)	1 egg, lightly beaten
1 Tbs. tomato paste	Salt and freshly ground black pepper to taste
2 Tbs. finely minced red onion	3 Tbs. yellow cornmeal or masa harina
½ C. fine bread crumbs	Corn oil for frying
½ roasted Jalapeño chile, finely minced (about 1 tsp.)	2 Tbs. sour cream
½ tsp. ground cumin	1½ Tbs. very finely diced red pepper
¼ tsp. dried oregano	Cilantro leaves
1 tsp. balsamic vinegar	

Process the cooked beans in a bowl of a food processor a few strokes, until coarsely chopped. Scrape the beans into a large mixing bowl and add all the ingredients except the cornmeal, corn oil, red pepper, sour cream, red pepper and cilantro leaves. Combine well and divide into six equal parts. Place the cornmeal on waxed paper. Form the mixture into oval cakes and dip in the cornmeal to coat lightly on both sides.

Heat only enough oil to cover the bottom of a large iron skillet. When the oil is hot, carefully lift the pancakes with a spatula and slide them into the pan. Fry for 2 to 3 minutes on each side. Drain on paper towels and transfer to a warm serving dish. Top each bean pancake with 1 teaspoon sour cream, a sprinkling of diced red pepper and 1 or 2 leaves of cilantro.

Gambas al Ajillo: Spanish Garlic Shrimp
with Oregano and Black Beans

SERVES 6

The black beans, scented with cumin, are prepared a day or two in advance and then rewarmed. Oregano and garlic infuse the quickly sautéed shrimp in a robust meld of two strongly flavored elements. Cooked, bland white rice is just the right neutral note to add.

Beans
(Prepare 1 or 2 days in advance)

2 C. black beans, soaked and drained	2 tsps. ground cumin
2 Tbs. Spanish olive oil	¾ lb. smoked ham hock
1 large red onion, coarsely chopped (1 C.)	4½ C. unsalted chicken stock
1 jalapeño chile, seeded and chopped	2 bay leaves
2 large cloves garlic, finely minced (1 Tbs.)	Salt and freshly ground black pepper to taste
1 medium carrot, coarsely chopped (¾ C.)	

In a 3-quart saucepan, cover the beans by 1 inch with fresh tepid water and bring to a boil. Lower the heat and simmer for 20 to 35 minutes. Meanwhile, heat the olive oil in a 5-quart Dutch oven and add the onions, hot chile and garlic. Sauté, stirring, for 1 to 2 minutes. Stir in the carrots and cumin. Add the ham hock and then add the chicken stock and bay leaves and bring to a boil.

Drain the partially cooked beans and discard the cooking liquid. Add the drained beans to the Dutch oven, lower the heat and simmer, covered, 30 minutes more. Add the salt and pepper and continue to simmer for 15 minutes. Then lift out and discard the bay leaves and the ham hock. Drain the beans and return 1 cup of the cooking liquid to the beans. The beans can be refrigerated for 2 days and then reheated. The shrimp take only 3 to 4 minutes to prepare and cook, so make sure that the beans are hot before cooking the shrimp.

Garlic Shrimp

The

Versatile

Grain

and the

Elegant

Bean

2 Tbs. Spanish olive oil	1 tsp. dried oregano, preferably Greek
2 Tbs. butter	Salt to taste
½ tsp. paprika	Freshly ground black pepper to taste
¼ tsp. hot pepper flakes	2 Tbs. dry sherry
3–4 garlic cloves thinly sliced—sliced horizontally (about 1 heaping Tbs.)	Juice of ½ large lemon (2 Tbs.)
1 lb. small shrimp, shelled (about 40 to the lb.)	1 Tbs. coarsely chopped flat leaf parsley

Heat the oil and butter in a large shallow heatproof casserole. Add the paprika, hot pepper flakes and the garlic and sauté over high heat for 1 minute. Add the shrimp, oregano, salt and pepper and sauté for 1 minute. Turn the shrimp over with a spatula and sauté on the other side for 1 minute. Add the sherry and lemon juice and stir for about 30 seconds. Sprinkle with the parsley and serve at once in the same casserole along with the rewarmed black beans.

Moros y Cristianos: Black Beans and Rice with Three Kinds of Peppers

SERVES 8

This dish of black beans and rice dates back to medieval Spain, when the Moors and the Christians were at war.

Beans

1½ C. dried black beans, soaked and drained	1 small stalk celery
1 small onion, stuck with 1 clove	1 bay leaf
1 small carrot	3 sprigs parsley
	Salt to taste

Put the beans in a 3-quart saucepan and cover with fresh tepid water by 2 inches. Add the onion, carrot and celery. Tie the bay leaf and parsley together with a piece of string and add to the pot. Bring to a boil, then simmer, covered, with lid ajar, until tender—about 55 minutes. Lift out and discard the vegetables and herbs. Keep the beans in the liquid. Add the salt. The beans may be done 1 to 2 days in advance, refrigerated and then reheated.

Rice

2 Tbs. olive oil	1½ C. converted long grain rice
1 small onion, finely chopped (½ C.)	3¾ C. hot chicken broth
1 clove garlic, finely minced (1 tsp.)	1 tsp. salt or to taste

In a 5-quart nonstick Dutch oven, heat and oil and add the onions and garlic and sauté over medium heat, stirring, for 1 to 2 minutes. Add the rice and cook, stirring, until transparent, about 3 to 5 minutes. Then add the hot chicken broth and salt and bring to a boil. Lower the heat and simmer for 20 minutes or until the liquid is absorbed. Slip a piece of paper towel between the pot and the lid and let the rice stand for 10 minutes before fluffing with a fork. While the rice is cooking, reheat the beans and prepare the peppers (see below).

Peppers

3 Tbs. olive oil
1 medium onion, sliced thinly and rings separated
1 each large red, green and yellow sweet pepper, cut into 2-in. long by ½-in. wide strips (3½–4 C.)

Salt and freshly ground black pepper to taste
½ tsp. ground cumin
⅛ tsp. cayenne

In a large skillet, heat the oil and add the onions. Stir and sauté for 5 minutes or until the onions are wilted. Add the peppers and the seasonings and continue to sauté, stirring often, for 5 minutes, or until the peppers are tender but still slightly crisp. Set aside.

When ready to serve, mound the rice in the center of a large platter and make a well in the center of the mound. Spoon the peppers into the well. Drain the beans and spoon them around the rice. Serve hot.

Féijão Brasiliero: Roasted Pork Tenderloin with an Orange Campari Sauce and Brazilian-Style Black Beans

SERVES 6

In Brazil, these beans are served either as a side dish or as a part of a *feijoada,* a 2-day labor-intensive multi-ingredient dish with a very high-saturated-fat content, accompanied by manioc (cassava meal), various meats, eggs and oranges. We have attempted in a most humble effort to reinterpret some of the flavors in a less traditional, more contemporary version, with less fat, less fuss and more easily available ingredients.

Brazilian-Style Black Beans (Prepare 1 day in advance)

1½ C. dried black beans, soaked
1 medium-size onion, left whole, plus 1 large onion, coarsely diced (¾ C.)
1 bay leaf
¼ tsp. dried oregano
2–3 Tbs. strong Spanish olive oil
3 large cloves garlic, finely minced (1 Tbs.)

1 tsp. ground cumin
Salt and freshly ground black pepper to taste
¼ C. boiling water, if necessary, plus additional if needed

The

Versatile

Grain

and the

Elegant

Bean

Drain the soaked beans and put them in a 3-quart saucepan. Add fresh tepid water to cover by 2 to 3 inches. Bring to a boil and add the whole onion, bay leaf and oregano. Lower the heat, cover with a lid left slightly ajar and simmer until the beans are very tender, adding more water if needed to keep the beans covered, about 1 hour.

Remove and discard the bay leaf and the whole onion. Drain the beans, reserving any cooking liquid, then return the beans to the pot and set aside. In a large skillet, heat the olive oil and add the diced onions and garlic. Sauté over low heat, stirring occasionally, for 5 minutes, until wilted but not browned. Add the cumin and the salt and pepper and stir in ½ cup of the beans along with some of the bean liquid (or add ¼ cup of boiling water if the bean liquid has been absorbed). Transfer this mixture to the bowl of a food processor and process until a thick purée is formed. Then scrape out and return to the beans in the saucepan and simmer for 15 minutes more. Add additional boiling water if the beans seem too dry. However, they should not be too soupy. There should be only a small amount of liquid in the beans.

Transfer them to a covered bowl and refrigerate until the following day. Rewarm just before the pork tenderloins are finished roasting (see below), adding a bit of additional water and salt if necessary.

Roasted Pork Tenderloin with an Orange Campari Sauce

2 lean pork tenderloins, weighing about ¾–1 lb. each
1 medium clove garlic finely minced (1 tsp.)
⅛ tsp. cayenne
Salt and freshly ground black pepper to taste
1 tsp. paprika
Peel of 1 orange, finely minced (2 Tbs.)

1 tsp. finely minced, peeled ginger
2 Tbs. finely minced flat parsley
⅓ C. orange juice
1 large navel orange, cut into ¾-inch pieces (½ cup orange sections)
¼ C. chicken stock
½ C. campari

Preheat the oven to 350°F. Lightly oil an oven-to-table shallow roasting pan. Add the tenderloins and set them aside. Mix the garlic, cayenne, salt and black pepper, the paprika, orange peel, ginger and parsley together and chop them in a food processor until blended. Spread the mixture on the surface of the pork tenderloins and roast them for 10 minutes. Then mix the orange juice, orange sections, chicken stock and campari together and pour around the meat, spooning a bit of the liquid on top of the pork. Continue to roast for 30 more minutes, basting occasionally.

Pour off the sauce into a small saucepan. Cover the meat loosely with foil to keep warm, and let it rest for 10 minutes. While the meat is resting, reduce the sauce over high heat until it is syrupy, about 8 minutes. To serve, spoon portions of the black beans slightly to the side of a warmed plate, lay thin slices of pork in a semi-circle on the other side and spoon some of the sauce and a few orange slices over the meat. Cooked rice can accompany this dish as well.

Warm Black Bean and Grilled Sea Scallop Salad
with a Basil Chiffonade

SERVES 6

A colorful and filling warm-weather salad. The scallops are marinated and then take only minutes to grill. Just the right kind of fare for lunch or a light dinner at a weekend house.

Beans

3 C. drained, hot cooked black beans (see Chart, page 315)	2 scallions, thinly sliced on the diagonal (½ C.)
1 large ripe tomato, cut into 1-in. pieces (about ¾ lb.)	¼ C. olive oil
1 C. cucumber, either English or Kirby, cut into 1-in. pieces	Salt and freshly ground black pepper to taste
	2 Tbs. red wine vinegar

In a large bowl, gently mix the hot beans with the tomatoes, cucumbers, scallions and olive oil. Add the salt, pepper and vinegar. Mix again, cover and marinate at room temperature for 1 hour. If you wish, after the hour, refrigerate the mixture for several hours, but bring it to room temperature before assembling the salad.

Scallops

¼ tsp. saffron threads	3 Tbs. olive oil
2 tsps. boiling water	Salt and freshly ground black pepper to taste
2 cloves garlic, crushed	
½ bay leaf	1 lb. large sea scallops
Pinch hot pepper flakes	Salad greens—a combination of sweet
1 tsp. dried thyme	romaine and bitter, curly escarole
2 Tbs. dry white wine	4–5 large basil leaves, thinly cut in
1 Tbs. lemon juice	chiffonade

Put the saffron threads in a small cup, spoon the boiling water over them and let steep for 5 minutes. In a small bowl mix together the remaining ingredients, except for the scallops, salad greens and basil, and stir in the saffron and water. Add the scallops and stir, then cover and refrigerate for 1 hour minimum. Stir once while the mixture is marinating.

When ready to cook, lift out and reserve the scallops and discard the marinade. Heat a large heavy nonstick skillet, preferably one with ridges. The scallops can also be grilled on a stove-top grill or on an outdoor grill if you have one. Pan grill for about 2 to 3 minutes on each side, until cooked and opaque. Set aside.

To serve, line one side of a large dinner plate with alternating sweet and bitter greens. Spoon the bean mixture on the other side of the plate. Arrange about five or six scallops over the beans and scatter a few shreds of basil over the surface.

The

Versatile

Grain

and the

Elegant

Bean

326

Black Bean and Fresh Yellow Corn, Avocado and Tomato Salad

SERVES 6 TO 8

A vivid, multicolored salad that would make a lovely presentation on any buffet table. It's equally good as a side dish for grilled red snapper or chicken.

2 C. drained cooked black beans (see Chart, page 315)
1 large ear cooked fresh corn kernels, cut from cob or frozen corn kernels (1 C.)
½ medium or 1 small red onion, finely chopped (½ C.)
Salt and freshly ground black pepper to taste
2–3 medium plum tomatoes, cut into ½-in. cubes (1 C.)

3 Tbs. olive oil
1 heaping Tbs. coarsely chopped cilantro, plus 1 sprig
¼ tsp. Tabasco sauce or more to taste
2 Tbs. red wine vinegar
2 Tbs. lime juice
½ ripe medium avocado, cut into ¾-in. cubes (1 C.)
1 wedge lime

In a large serving bowl, mix the beans with the corn and onions. Season with salt and pepper. Add the tomatoes and olive oil and stir gently to combine. Add the 1 tablespoon cilantro and then the Tabasco, vinegar and lime juice. Stir gently to mix. Add the avocado last and stir again. Let stand at room temperature for 30 minutes to an hour before serving, to allow the flavors to blend. Stir before serving and garnish with the lime wedge and sprig of cilantro.

Black-Eyed Peas

Vigna unguiculata

Alias. Black-eyed Suzies, black-eyed beans, Southern peas, lobia dal, lady peas, cream peas, brown-eyed peas, crowder peas.

Description. Medium size (about ½ inch), creamy white in color, slightly kidney-shaped and plump with an irregular very dark purple circle formed on the ridge (or eye) of the bean.

Characteristics. Thin-skinned, savory and robust, yet with a subtly earthy sweet flavor and a smooth, buttery texture.

History. Since this bean is related to the same species *(Vigna)* as the mung bean and other Chinese legumes, it is thought to have originated in China. From there it probably traveled by sea to Arabic countries and into Africa. It was introduced to the West in about the eighteenth century through the African slave trade and then into our South, where it is grown today. However, well over 90 percent of these beans, when dried, are grown in California and shipped all over the world, along with two subspecies (see below), which are also domestically grown.

Traditional Uses. African and Indian dishes, as well as those from the Caribbean and the Southern United States. They are the basis for the very famous dish of our South, Hopping John (see page 333), a mixture of black-eyed peas and rice. Traditionally, black-eyed peas, eaten on New Year's Day, are supposed to bring luck for the following year. However, the Maine yellow-eyed bean (which belongs to the family *Phaseolus vulgaris*) sometimes alternates with the black-eyes in Southern cooking, which is why we've included them here rather than under the other category.

Availability. Dried, fresh in pod in the summer season, fresh frozen and canned. Most supermarkets and specialty food stores carry them.

Long Beans
(Vigna sesquipedalis)

Alias. Asparagus beans, Chinese long beans, yard long beans, pea beans.

Description. In its pod stage (the form in which it is sold most often), it resembles

The

Versatile

Grain

and the

Elegant

Bean

328

chinese long beans

a very long, pliable string bean, but without the crispness. Its length can run from 18 to 24 inches.

Characteristics. It is a vine-grown annual that thrives in the warm weather and requires lots of water. It is very much like the cowpea, although it has an individually unique flavor, somewhat like asparagus combined with peas.

Traditional Uses. The most popular use of the asparagus bean is for Chinese stir-fry dishes, though it is also used in the cuisine of India as well as in other parts of the Far East and Africa.

Availability. Generally found in the fresh-pod stage in Chinese ethnic markets, and tied in various-size bundles.

Cooking Chart

Pot: 3 qt.

Type of Bean:	Black-Eyed Peas	Maine Yellow-Eyes
Amount:	1 C. dried	1 C. dried
Instructions:	Overnight soak	Overnight soak
Cooking Time:	45 minutes to 1 hour	35 minutes
Approx. Yield:	2 C.	3 C.
Comments:	Cook gently, do not stir too often or tender skins may burst. NOTE: Current-crop black-eyed peas will cook in 20 minutes.	Foams up at first. Very tender skins.

NOTE: Maine yellow-eyes, a Northern bean, and black-eyed peas are placed together in this chart only because they are interchangeable in Southern cooking.

A Vegetable Ragout: Black-Eyed Peas
with Okra, Tomatoes and Corn

SERVES 6 TO 8

All the good flavors of the South, with only a hint of smoky bacon. Bake a hot buttermilk corn bread in an iron skillet (see page 93) and dinner's ready.

1 C. dried black-eyed peas, soaked and drained
4 C. water
1 small whole onion, plus 1 medium onion, coarsely chopped (½ C.)
1 small red whole dried hot chile such as Japonés
1 large bay leaf
Salt to taste

2–3 strips bacon, finely diced (⅓ C.)
28-oz. can plum tomatoes drained and cut into large pieces (2 C.), liquid reserved
1½ C. small whole fresh okra pods, trimmed, or frozen cut okra
1 C. corn kernels, fresh or frozen
Freshly ground black pepper to taste

In a 3-quart saucepan, bring the beans and water to a boil. Skim off the surface foam and add the whole onion, hot chile and bay leaf. Cover, lower the heat and simmer for about 30 minutes or more, until the beans are tender, adding salt during the last few minutes of cooking.

Meanwhile, add the diced bacon to a large skillet and fry until crisp. With a slotted spoon transfer the bacon to a paper towel to drain. Pour off all but 1 tablespoon of the bacon fat. Heat the fat and add the chopped onions, stirring and sautéeing over medium heat for 3 to 4 minutes. Do not let the onions brown. Add the tomatoes and sauté, stirring frequently, for 10 minutes over medium low heat. Stir in the okra and the corn, cover and simmer for 5 minutes.

When the beans are cooked lift out and discard the bay leaf, whole onion and chile. Drain the beans and add them to the skillet. Then add ½ cup of the reserved tomato liquid. Cover and simmer for 5 minutes more. Adjust the seasoning for salt if needed and add freshly ground black pepper. Transfer to a serving dish and sprinkle with the crisp bacon.

The

Versatile

Grain

and the

Elegant

Bean

330

New Year's Day Black-Eyed Peas with Collard Greens and Ham Hock

SERVES 8

In the South, when black-eyed peas are eaten on New Year's Day, it is said to bring good luck for the coming year. Collard greens will bring "health" and the ham hock brings "wealth." A few slices of country ham and red-eyed gravy plus piping hot corn bread are the traditional accompaniments. And—it all tastes just as good up North, too!

2 C. black-eyed peas (or Maine yellow-eyes), soaked and drained	1 stalk celery, finely chopped (½ C.)
4 C. unsalted chicken stock	Freshly ground black pepper to taste
½ tsp. hot pepper flakes	2 tsps. red wine vinegar
1 oz. slab bacon, diced	1 lb. ham hock
1 medium onion, finely chopped (½ C.)	8 C. tightly packed, very coarsely chopped collard greens (about 1 lb. before trimming)
½ large green pepper, finely chopped (½ C.)	Salt to taste

In a 5-quart Dutch oven, bring the beans, chicken stock and hot pepper flakes to a boil. Then lower the heat and simmer for 30 minutes (or more, depending on the age of the beans). They should be almost tender at this point.

Meanwhile, fry the bacon slowly in a 10-inch skillet until crisp. Add the onions, green pepper, celery and black pepper. Stir and sauté for about 5 minutes or until the vegetables begin to color. Then stir them into the beans, along with the vinegar and ham hock. Continue to simmer for 15 minutes, then stir in the collard greens a few cups at a time, so they begin to wilt and fit into the pot. Season with salt and continue to simmer for 30 minutes more, or longer if the beans are not tender.

Remove the ham hock, cool slightly and cut off the lean meat, returning the meat to the pot and discarding the remains. Simmer until heated through before serving. The beans should almost be falling apart, forming a part of the sauce. If the beans are old and need longer cooking, check for additional boiled water as they cook.

Black-Eyed Peas and Vegetable Salad with
Watercress and Walnut Vinaigrette

SERVES 8

The traditional partner for black-eyed peas is bacon. In this recipe, we have not shunned the bacon *flavor,* but we have used lean Canadian bacon instead. Toasted walnuts add the complementary flavor for the tender beans and peppery watercress. Serve it as a first course, a salad, or as a colorful addition to the buffet table.

Walnut Vinaigrette

2 Tbs. red wine vinegar
Salt and freshly ground black pepper
   to taste
2 Tbs. Dijon mustard

⅓ C. walnut oil
3–4 drops Tabasco sauce
2–3 large shallots, finely minced (about
   3 Tbs.)

In a small bowl, whisk the vinegar, salt, pepper and mustard together. Slowly add the walnut oil and Tabasco and mix well. Stir in the shallots and set the vinaigrette aside while preparing the salad to allow the flavors to blend.

Salad

1 C. dried black-eyed peas or Maine
   yellow-eyes or cowpeas, soaked
   and drained
6 thin slices lean Canadian bacon
⅔ C. coarsely broken walnuts
1 large sweet red pepper, cut into
   thin strips 2 in. long (1 C.)

2 small zucchini, stemmed (about
   ½ lb.)
1 bunch watercress, trimmed of
   coarse stems (about 3 C.)

Cook the beans in water to cover by 2 inches, for about 30 minutes or longer. While the beans are simmering, sauté the bacon in a nonstick pan, until it's dappled with brown on both sides. Stack the slices of bacon and cut into dice.

Heat the walnuts in the same skillet until they are toasted. Mix the walnuts gently with the bacon and red pepper and transfer to a large serving bowl. Cut the zucchini into julienne strips about 2 inches long, put them into another bowl and pour boiling water over, blanching for about 1 minute. Drain the beans and, while hot, add them to the serving bowl along with the blanched drained zucchini. Pour the dressing over, mixing gently. When the bean mixture is at room temperature, stir in three quarters of the watercress. Taste for additional salt and pepper. Spoon the salad onto a large platter, scatter the remaining watercress on top and serve at room temperature.

The

Versatile

Grain

and the

Elegant

Bean

332

Black-Eyed Peas and Fresh Snap Green Beans
with Summer Savory

SERVES 6

Our next-door neighbor gave us a wonderful gift from her garden, a stringless variety of snap green beans called Derby. This inspired us to counterpoint them with creamy textured black-eyed peas and summer savory (known as the "bean herb" for its taste affinity for beans).

1 C. dried black-eyed peas, soaked and drained	Salt and freshly ground black pepper to taste
¾ lb. trimmed, fresh snap green beans, cut diagonally into 1-in. pieces (about 2½ C.)	2 Tbs. finely minced chives
	⅛ tsp. hot pepper flakes
3 Tbs. melted butter	1 Tbs. fresh summer savory leaves (or 1 tsp. dried summer savory)
1 Tbs. lemon juice	

In a 3-quart saucepan, cook the black-eyed peas in water to cover by 2 inches. Cook for about 20 to 30 minutes or until they are tender but hold their shape. Drain and rinse under tepid water.

While the black-eyed peas are simmering, place the snap beans in a steamer and steam over boiling water for 5 minutes. Toss them with the hot black-eyed peas, the melted butter and lemon juice. Season with salt and pepper. Gently stir in the chives and the hot pepper flakes. Scatter the summer savory over the surface and serve hot.

Hopping John:
Black-Eyed Peas and Rice

SERVES 8

Hopping John is said to have originated with African slaves on Southern plantations. It is still a Southern favorite to this day, as it is in Africa as well. In Senegal, for example, a dish of black-eyed peas and rice called *chiebou niebe* is made with beef instead of pork for the Muslim population.

2 C. black-eyed peas, soaked and drained	Salt and lots of freshly ground black pepper
1 bay leaf	2½ C. hot cooked long grain white rice (see Chart, page 162)
¼ tsp. hot pepper flakes	Few drops Tabasco sauce
4 ozs. slab bacon, cut into tiny dice (see NOTE)	
2 medium onions, coarsely chopped (about 1 C.)	

To a 5-quart Dutch oven, add the soaked peas, bay leaf, hot pepper flakes and enough tepid water to cover by 1½ inches. Bring to a boil, then lower the heat and simmer for 30 minutes or more, depending upon the age of the beans, until tender.

Meanwhile, in a medium skillet fry the bacon until crisp and golden. Lift the bacon out to drain on paper towels. Pour off all but 3 tablespoons of the bacon fat in the skillet. Add the onions and sauté for about 5 minutes over medium heat, or until the onions are soft and beginning to take on color. Season with salt and pepper, and set the skillet aside.

When the beans are tender, add salt, drain the beans and reserve ⅔ cup of the cooking liquid. Return the beans and the liquid to the pot, add the onions, cover, and simmer for 5 minutes to let the flavors blend. Taste for additional salt and pepper. Stir in the hot cooked rice and heat for 1 to 2 minutes. Stir in the Tabasco sauce and spoon into a serving dish. Top it with the reserved crisp bacon.

NOTE: Some people use salt pork or pig's knuckles in place of the bacon. We tested this recipe using both, as well as cooking the raw rice in the bean liquid, the traditional technique of the South. We found that the rice developed an unpleasant flavor and texture, as far as our personal taste was concerned. Therefore, we combined the cooked rice and beans at the end, and we prefer to use a flavorful bacon in a minimal amount.

Maine Yellow-Eyes with Glazed Bacon: Boston Baked Beans

SERVES 6 TO 8

In Maine, the church suppers are still called "bean hole suppers," and they feature beans baked in a rock-lined pit dug in the earth and cooked for 24 hours. In Boston, the tradition is to sweeten the baked beans with molasses. Almost every region makes adjustments in the seasonings and the sweeteners: in Vermont, maple syrup is used; in Connecticut, they add lots of onions and bay leaf. In the Midwest, tomatoes are included. In Texas, hot chiles are added and instead of a ceramic bean pot they use a big black iron pot, cooking it over an open fire. Our version has honey and brown sugar as a sweetener, plus glazed slab bacon and a touch of vinegar to cut the sweetness.

2 C. Maine yellow-eyes, navy or Great Northern beans, soaked and drained (see NOTE)

6 C. tepid water

8 ozs. slab bacon, dice half and score the other half

1 large onion, coarsely chopped (1 C.)

1 Tbs. dry mustard

½ tsp. freshly ground black pepper

2 tsps. salt or to taste

⅛ tsp. cayenne

¼ C. dark brown sugar

¼ C. honey or molasses

1 Tbs. white wine Worcestershire sauce

3 Tbs. apple cider vinegar

The

Versatile

Grain

and the

Elegant

Bean

334

To a 3-quart saucepan, add the beans and water and bring to a boil. Lower the heat and simmer for 30 minutes, until the beans are almost tender. Drain and reserve the beans and the liquid. (See NOTE.)

In an 8-inch skillet, heat the diced bacon for 4 minutes over low heat. Add the onions and sauté over medium low heat for 5 minutes, stirring frequently until the onion just begins to brown. Set aside.

Preheat the oven to 325°F. and use either a 1½-quart ceramic bean pot or a deep ovenproof casserole. In a small cup, mix the dry mustard, black pepper, salt, cayenne and brown sugar. Stir in the honey, Worcestershire sauce and vinegar. Put half of the bacon/onion mixture into the bottom of the bean pot, then half the beans. Spoon half the honey mixture over the beans, then repeat with another layer. Pour enough of the reserved bean liquid to cover the beans. Place the scored bacon on top. Cover with the lid or with foil and bake for 1 hour. Then remove the cover, increase the heat to 350°F. and bake for 1½ hours more. Check after 1 hour to see if more liquid is needed. During the last half hour of baking, prepare the following glaze and spoon it over the bacon while continuing to bake.

Glaze

2 Tbs. brown sugar

2 tsps. dry sherry

1 tsp. Dijon-style mustard

Combine the ingredients and spoon over the bacon. Serve hot or reheat, covered, in a 325°F. oven until bubbly. Nothing will happen to the beans if they cook for hours. Just make sure that they are covered with liquid at all times.

NOTE: You may also substitute navy beans for the Maine yellow-eyes (which are largely used in New England). However, the initial cooking time will be closer to 45 minutes than 30 minutes.

Chinese Orange Beef with Long Beans
and Peanuts

SERVES 4

If you can't find the long beans at your greengrocer or at a local Chinese market, you may substitute the standard string bean, though we find that they don't impart the same elusive taste and crunchy texture as the originals. The beauty of this recipe is that, after all the KP, it can be prepared in less than fifteen minutes.

½ lb. lean round steak
1 medium clove garlic, minced (about 1 tsp.)
2 Tbs. soy sauce
3 Tbs. dry sherry or Chinese rice wine
1 Tbs. cornstarch
½ tsp. sugar
½ tsp. salt

Peel of 1 orange, made with zester tool (1 Tbs.)
1 lb. Chinese long beans, cut into peanut-size pieces (about 3 C.)
2 Tbs. corn oil
¾ C. unsalted chicken stock
½ C. unsalted peanuts, broken into halves

Semifreeze the beef, or freeze it completely and let it thaw slightly to make it easier to cut. Cut the beef first into ½-inch slices, then into strips and then into pieces about the size of a large peanut.

Place the meat on a flat platter. Whisk together the garlic, soy, sherry and cornstarch. Add the sugar, salt and orange peel and mix well. Then pour this marinade over the beef and let stand for 30 minutes, turning once or twice to coat the meat completely.

Fill a 3-quart saucepan about three-quarters full with water and bring to a boil. When the water is boiling rapidly, add the long bean pieces, bring the water to a boil again and parboil the beans for 3 minutes. Drain the beans and set aside.

Heat a 12-inch nonstick skillet (or Chinese wok) over high heat and add 1 tablespoon of the corn oil. Tip the skillet or wok to cover the surface with the hot oil. Add the beef along with the marinade and quickly stir with a wooden spoon. (If using a skillet, use the wooden spoon. If using a wok, you may use Chinese stir-fry metal tools if you wish.) Stir-fry only until the beef loses its red color, about 30 seconds. Remove quickly to a plate, then add the rest of the corn oil to the same hot skillet. Add the long beans, stirring vigorously for about 10 seconds, then add the chicken stock. Stir once or twice, cover and cook for about 2 minutes. Uncover, add the reserved beef, and mix thoroughly for about 15 seconds. Transfer to a serving platter deep enough to contain it, then top with the peanut halves.

Serve at once, accompanied by a bowl of rice, if you wish.

The

Versatile

Grain

and the

Elegant

Bean

336

Chick-Peas

Cicer arietinum

Alias. *Ceci,* garbanzos, *kali chana, kabuli chana.*

Description. Medium-small in size, about ⅜ inch. Plump and hard, it is one of the most popular bean varieties in Europe and the Western Hemisphere. It is buff-colored with a tiny "beak" at the top. Although *arietinum* translates as "ramlike," since the ancient Romans thought the bean resembled a ram's head with curling horns, we humbly differ in our description. Upon close examination, we think it looks like a "fat chick." In addition to the buff-colored chick-peas, in India there are varieties that range from red to brown to black, all with different names. The varieties called *kali chana* or *kabuli chana* are black on the outside and cream-colored on the inside. When growing in their pods, chick-peas harbor only one or two seeds.

Characteristics. Its flavor is full-bodied, nutty and rich, reminiscent of chestnuts with a bit of crunch. It maintains its shape well after cooking.

History. It is said to have been first cultivated about 5000 A.D. in ancient Mesopotamia, then moved on to the eastern Mediterranean and into India and other parts of Asia. The chick-pea was introduced to Europe through Spain, where it was (and is) called garbanzo. *Ceci* is its Italian alias, from whence came the Roman family name of Cicero.

Traditional Uses. It is widely cultivated, cooked and eaten in various ways in India, where it is ground into a flour called *garam besan.* In the Middle East, one of the two most popular puréed chick-pea dishes is called *hummous* (or hummus), a savory spread made with sesame paste, garlic and lemon—or falafel, made of ground chick-peas and spices, then fried as a fritter. It is sometimes made with dried fava beans as well.

Availability. Dried and canned in various sizes. It is carried in most supermarkets as well as in ethnic specialty stores.

The

Elegant

Bean

```
                      Cooking Chart                          Pot: 3 qt.

Type of Bean:    Chick-peas (supermarket Iberia brand)

    Amount:      1 C. dried

Instructions:    Overnight soak. Discard water after first boil. Use fresh tepid
                 water and proceed.

Cooking Time:    Approximately 1 hour

Approx. Yield:   2 C.

  Comments:      Very foamy. Needs skimming. Chick-peas are one of the cul-
                 prits that can induce intestinal rumblings. The extra step of
                 discarding first boil water will help digestion, if that is a prob-
                 lem.
```

Smoked Salmon Cornucopias Filled with Hummus and Red Caviar

SERVES 8 TO 10

Hummus is treated here in a grand manner, with the purée rolled into cornucopias of smoked salmon, which then wreath a mound of the purée, all crowned with red salmon caviar and fresh dill.

- 3½ **C. drained cooked chick-peas (see Chart, above), or 2 1-lb. cans, rinsed, drained and dried on paper towels**
- 2–3 **large cloves garlic, finely minced (1 Tbs.)**
- ¼ **C. Chicken Stock, preferably homemade (see page 171)**
- ¼ **C. sesame paste (tahini)**

Juice of 1 large lemon (¼ C.)

- ⅛ **tsp. Tabasco sauce**
- ½ **tsp. ground cumin**

Salt and freshly ground black pepper to taste

- ¼ **C. olive oil**
- ⅓ **lb. thinly sliced smoked salmon**
- 1 **Tbs. finely snipped dill, plus several sprigs for garnish**
- 2 **ozs. red salmon caviar**

In the bowl of a food processor, process the chick-peas until roughly puréed. Add the garlic, chicken stock, sesame paste, lemon juice and Tabasco sauce and purée until smooth. Add the cumin, salt and pepper, then pour the olive oil slowly through the feed tube while the machine is on. Spoon and scrape the mixture into a bowl, cover with plastic wrap and let sit at room temperature for at least an hour or longer. Taste to see if more lemon juice, salt or pepper is needed.

The

Versatile

Grain

and the

Elegant

Bean

338

When ready to serve, spoon about 1 tablespoon of the hummus onto a small (3- to 4-inch) slice of smoked salmon and roll it into a cornucopia shape. Spoon the remaining purée in a mound in the center of a serving plate. Sprinkle with some of the snipped dill and scatter a few red caviar eggs over the top. Stand the filled salmon cornucopias upright, leaning them against the mound. Sprinkle the tops of each roll with a bit of snipped dill and add about five caviar eggs to the top. Place the dill sprigs in a wreath around the rim of the plate and serve at room temperature.

Italian Chick-Pea and Ditalini
Pasta Soup with Anchovies

SERVES 6

As with most Italian food, this soup relies upon the freshest and the best-quality ingredients. The tomatoes should be ripe and red, the parsley and rosemary aromatic, the Parmesan cheese of the finest quality Reggiano, and the olive oil extra-virgin.

- ¼ C. olive oil
- 3 large cloves garlic, finely minced (1 heaping Tbs.)
- 6 flat anchovy fillets, rinsed, dried and roughly chopped
- 2 C. cooked chick-peas (see Chart, opposite page)
- 2 C. large cubes tomatoes (about 1 lb.)
- 4 C. Chicken Stock, preferably homemade (see page 171)
- 2 tsps. coarsely chopped rosemary
- ½ C. finely chopped flat leaf parsley, plus 1 Tbs.
- Freshly ground black pepper to taste
- 6 ozs. ditalini pasta, cooked in salt water and drained
- ⅓ C. grated Parmesan cheese

Heat the olive oil in a 4½-quart Dutch oven, stir in the garlic and anchovies and cook over medium high heat, stirring constantly, for 1 minute. Do not let the garlic get brown. Stir in the cooked chick-peas and the tomatoes and cook for 2 minutes. Add the chicken stock and the rosemary and bring to a boil. Then lower the heat and stir in the ½ cup parsley. Simmer for 10 minutes and add the freshly ground black pepper. Add the cooked pasta, cover and simmer for 5 minutes more or until the soup is hot. Serve in bowls with a sprinkling of the cheese and fresh parsley over the top.

Cocido Madrileño with
a Spanish Parsley Garlic Sauce:
Soup, Meat and Vegetables in a Pot

SERVES 8 TO 10

Of Spanish origin, the *cocido* consists of various boiled meats, chick-peas and vegetables scented with aromatic herbs and is traditionally served in two courses. First, the strained broth is served with very fine noodles, followed by the meats and vegetables along with a pungent garlicky sauce. In France, it is *pot-au-feu*, in Italy *bollito misto*, in Catalonia *escudella*, in Venezuela *sancocho*, and an ancient version made without pork and eaten by the Sephardic Jews is called *adafina*. It's a great dish for lots of people for a winter dinner.

1½ C. dried chick-peas, soaked overnight and drained (see Chart, page 338)

12 C. water

2 lbs. lean beef brisket

1 large onion, stuck with 2 whole cloves

6 sprigs flat leaf parsley

2 large garlic cloves

12 whole black peppercorns

1 large bay leaf

3–3½-pound chicken, cut into 8 pieces, including neck and gizzard

½ lb. smoked ham in 1 piece, preferably Serrano or prosciutto

1 stalk celery, cut in half crosswise

2 fat leeks

3 large carrots, cut in half crosswise (¾ lb.)

1 lb. medium-size turnips, peeled

1 lb. small new potatoes, peeled

1 lb. chorizo sausage

Salt and freshly ground black pepper to taste

2-lb. cabbage, cut into 8 wedges

Spanish Parsley Garlic Sauce (see opposite page)

4 ozs. capellini pasta (called *cabellos de ángel* in Spanish), broken into 3-in. pieces

1 Tbs. finely minced parsley

In a 3-quart saucepan, bring the soaked chickpeas with water to cover to a boil. Drain and rinse, then put the chickpeas in an 8- or 9-quart Dutch oven or stockpot. Add the 12 cups of water and the beef brisket and bring to a boil. Skim the surface of foam, then lower the heat. Tie the onion with the cloves, parsley, garlic, peppercorns and bay leaf into a piece of cheesecloth and add it to the pot. Cover and simmer for 1 hour. Add the chicken and the ham and simmer for 45 minutes more. After 20 minutes of cooking, add the celery, leeks, carrots, turnips and potatoes and simmer for the remaining time.

Lift out the cheesecloth bag and discard. Pierce the chorizo with a knife in several places and add it. Then, when the chicken is tender, remove the pieces to a very large serving platter. Season with salt and black pepper and cover with foil to keep warm. Ladle out 1 cup of the stock for the sauce and reserve. Add the cabbage to the pot and cook for 10 to 15 minutes more or until the cabbage is tender but not overcooked.

The

Versatile

Grain

and the

Elegant

Bean

340

While the cabbage is cooking, prepare the Spanish Parsley Garlic Sauce (see recipe below).

When ready to serve, lift out the brisket to a carving board, slice it thinly and place it alongside the chicken. Take out the ham and sausage and arrange on the platter. Spoon a ladleful of stock over the meats so they don't dry out and cover them with foil to keep warm. Place the platter in a preheated low oven.

If your serving platter is large enough (the size of a large turkey platter, for example) the vegetables and chickpeas can also be arranged with the various meats. If not, use another platter and arrange the potatoes, carrots and turnips, cut into quarters, around the platter. With a slotted spoon, lift out the chickpeas and mound them in the center. Season with black pepper and keep warm. Strain the stock, return to the pot and boil. Add the broken pasta and cook at a boil for 5 minutes. Ladle the soup into bowls, sprinkle with some minced parsley, then serve both platters of meat and vegetables with the parsley garlic sauce.

Spanish Parsley Garlic Sauce
MAKES 1¼ CUPS

1 potato, peeled and cut into small cubes (about ½ lb.)
Salt
4 cloves garlic, peeled
1 C. loosely packed flat leaf parsley leaves

2 tsps. white wine vinegar
3 Tbs. olive oil
1 C. reserved stock from cocido (see above)
Salt and freshly ground black pepper to taste

Bring the potatoes and 3 cloves of the garlic to a boil in salted water to cover. Cover and simmer for 10 to 15 minutes, until the potatoes are tender. Chop the remaining clove of raw garlic in the bowl of a food processor. Then add the parsley and process until fine. Drain and discard the water from the potatoes and garlic and add them both to the food processor along with the vinegar. Then slowly add the olive oil through the feeding tube while the processor is on. Add enough of the stock to reach the desired consistency. The sauce should be fairly thick, something like mayonnaise, and as it cools it will become thicker, so you may wish to add all of the stock.

Taste for salt and pepper and spoon into a dish to be passed at the table with the meats and vegetables.

NOTE: If there are any leftovers, including enough stock and parsley sauce, cut the meat and vegetables into bite-size pieces and mix them together for a tasty leftover bonus soup.

Baked Chick-Peas with
Country-Style Spareribs

SERVES 6

Earthy, hearty and substantial is this highly flavored yet simple dish, influenced by the cuisine of the Basque provinces from the rugged Pyrénées that bisect France and Spain.

3 lbs. country-style spareribs (pork loin rib end with bone), trimmed of fat and cut across the bone into 2-in. pieces
1 tsp. powdered hot English-style mustard such as Coleman's
1 tsp. ground cumin
¼ tsp. freshly ground black pepper
Salt to taste
2 Tbs. olive oil
2 medium onions, coarsely chopped (1½ C.)

2–3 cloves garlic, finely minced (1 Tbs.)
1 large carrot, coarsely chopped (½ C.)
1 C. canned Italian plum tomatoes, with juice, cut into chunks
1¾ C. chicken stock
¼ C. coarsely chopped flat leaf parsley
4 C. cooked chick-peas (see Chart, page 338)
¼ C. fine dry bread crumbs

Place the rib pieces in a shallow dish. Combine mustard, cumin, pepper and salt and rub this dry marinade on both sides of the meat. Cover with plastic wrap and leave for a minimum of 2 hours at room temperature or preferably overnight in the refrigerator.

In a large skillet, heat the olive oil over high heat and brown the ribs on all sides. This will probably have to be done in two batches. Preheat the oven to 400°F. Arrange the browned meat in a 3-quart shallow baking dish. Then, in the same skillet, drain off all but 1 tablespoon of the oil. Add the onions, garlic and carrots and sauté over medium heat, stirring and scraping with a wooden spoon any brown bits from the bottom of the skillet. Then stir in the tomatoes and the chicken stock. Bring to a boil, lower the heat and stir in the parsley and cooked chick-peas. Spoon over the ribs in the casserole and sprinkle with the bread crumbs. Bake in the preheated oven for 45 minutes to 1 hour or until the meat is tender and the top is browned. Serve hot. You may also cover, refrigerate and reheat the dish the next day.

The

Versatile

Grain

and the

Elegant

Bean

342

Moroccan Chick-Pea, Carrot and Black Olive Salad
with Cayenne/Cumin Vinaigrette

SERVES 6 TO 8

A hot, spicy dressing brings out the sweetness of the carrots and the chickpeas. Some of the carrots are shredded in a food processor, while some are cut into needle-thin julienne for textural contrast. Serve grilled lamb chops and simply cooked couscous and dinner is ready in 20 minutes.

Cayenne/Cumin Vinaigrette
MAKES ½ CUP

1 medium shallot, finely minced (2 tsps.)
1 small clove garlic, finely minced (½ tsp.)
3 Tbs. red wine vinegar
½ tsp. ground cumin
½ tsp. sweet paprika
¼ tsp. cayenne
Few grindings black pepper
¼ C. olive oil
1 Tbs. coarsely chopped cilantro

To a small bowl, add the shallots, garlic, vinegar, cumin, paprika, cayenne and black pepper and slowly whisk in the olive oil and cilantro.

Salad

2 C. cooked chick-peas (see Chart, page 338)
About 12 Alfonso or Kalamata black olives, slivered (½ C.)
2 large carrots, shredded with shredder blade in a food processor (2 C.)
1 large carrot, cut into thin julienne strips (1 C.)
3 Tbs. coarsely chopped cilantro

Toss all the ingredients except the cilantro lightly with the vinaigrette. Sprinkle with all but a few cilantro leaves and toss again. Pile on a serving platter and garnish with the few remaining cilantro leaves.

Chick-Pea Salad with Capers,
Fresh Haricots Verts and Mixed Herbs

SERVES 4 TO 6

Young French thin and crunchy haricots verts with their fresh verdant taste blend with the chick-peas and sprightly fresh herbs in this summer salad or appetizer. A hint of fresh tomato plus the slightly briny taste of capers complete the balance of flavors.

¼ lb. haricots verts, sliced diagonally in half (about 2–3 in. long)

2 C. drained, cooked chick-peas (see Chart, page 338)

3 scallions, thinly sliced diagonally (about ¾ C.)

1 medium plum tomato, diced (about ½ C.)

1 small clove garlic, finely minced (½ tsp.)

2 Tbs. finely minced parsley

1 Tbs. finely minced chervil

1 tsp. finely minced fresh oregano

1 Tbs. small nonpareil capers, rinsed and drained

⅛ tsp. hot pepper flakes

Salt and freshly ground black pepper to taste

1 Tbs. lemon juice

3 Tbs. tarragon or white wine vinegar

1 tsp. strong Dijon-style mustard

¼ C. olive oil

Boston lettuce leaves or radicchio leaves

Pour boiling water over the haricots verts and let them steep for 2 minutes. Drain and mix with the cooked, drained chick-peas in a medium-size bowl. Add the scallions, tomatoes, garlic, herbs, capers, hot pepper flakes, salt and pepper and toss to combine.

In a small bowl, whisk together the lemon juice, vinegar and mustard, then whisk in the olive oil. Pour the dressing over the salad and mix well. Do not chill. Let stand at room temperature for at least 2 hours before serving. Stir and taste to correct seasoning if needed before spooning the salad on Boston lettuce leaves.

The
Versatile
Grain
and the
Elegant
Bean

344

Cranberry Beans

Phaseolus vulgaris

Alias Romans, *borlotti,* Rosecocos, shellouts or shelly beans, "October beans" (an heirloom bean) and "Tongues of Fire," horticultural beans, *Cargamantos.*

Description. The size (about ½ inch) and the shape (with similar dappled markings) are about the same as the pinto bean. However, the cranberry bean is rounder and more plump and the colors are different: dark tan with a pink cast and wine-colored dappling. The pods resemble the bean itself, with wine-colored stripes on a cream background.

Characteristics. It is much sweeter and more delicate in flavor than the pinto bean, and it loses its markings when it's cooked, becoming a solid color. The bean called Tongues of Fire is an Italian borlotto-type vividly veined bean (called *Lingua di Fuoco* in Italian) and it has a wonderfully fresh flavor. So does the larger, even more brightly hued *Cargamanto.*

History. The cranberry-type beans called Tongues of Fire were grown from a seed variety originally collected from Tierra del Fuego, on the tip of South America, finding their way to Italy, where they (and other borlotto-type beans) are extremely popular.

Traditional Uses. Cranberry beans are used in New England for succotash, either freshly shelled, from the pod, or dried. In Indiana and Ohio, where they call them shellouts or shelly beans, they are cooked with sweet spices, nutmeg and cinnamon. They become tender very easily and absorb aromatic spices and herbs quite well. In Italy, they are eaten fresh from the pod or dried, in a myriad range of pasta dishes, side dishes and soups.

Availability. Dried, and seasonally fresh in their pods.

Cooking Chart

Pot: 3 qt.

Type of Bean:	Dried Cranberry	Tongues of Fire	Cargamantos
Amount:	1 C. dried	1 C. dried	1 C. dried
Instructions:	Tender, skins split easily. Simmer gently.		Take longer cooking time due to tougher skins.
Cooking Time:	40 to 45 minutes	60 minutes	1 hour, 20 minutes
Approx. Yield:	3 C.	2⅔ C.	2⅔ C.
Comments:		Nice beany, meaty taste.	Large, flavorful.

NOTE: *Fresh in pod cranberry beans.* Amount: 2 lbs. fresh in pod equal 2⅔ to 3 C. shelled. Cooking time: 40 minutes. Comments: Colors fade. Approx. Yield: Serves about 8.

Country-Style Cranberry Bean Soup

SERVES 8

Years ago, a fatty, salty pig's foot was used in this old-fashioned soup and then cooked for 3 hours because the salt inhibited the tenderizing of the beans. A less fatty, less salty version cooks in half the time, yet without sacrificing the flavors of the pork and beans, as in this offering.

- 1¼ lbs. boneless country-style spareribs, trimmed of fat and cut into 1-in. cubes
- ¼ tsp. freshly ground black pepper
- 1 large onion, coarsely chopped (1 C.)
- 3 cloves garlic, finely minced (about 1 Tbs.)
- 1 large green or red pepper, diced (1 C.)
- 10 C. water

- 1½ C. dried cranberry beans, soaked and drained
- 1 Tbs. fresh thyme leaves (or 1 tsp. dried thyme)
- 2 Tbs. coarsely chopped parsley
- 1 bay leaf
- 1 small red whole dried hot chile such as Japonés

Salt to taste

Put the meat in a nonstick skillet, sprinkle with the black pepper and sauté over medium heat until brown on all sides. Transfer to a 4- or 5-quart Dutch oven or stockpot. In the same unwashed skillet, sauté the onions over medium heat for 2 minutes. Then add the garlic and cook 1 minute more. Add the peppers and stir, cooking 2 to 3 minutes more. Transfer the mixture to the Dutch oven. Add some of the water to the skillet and stir, cooking and scraping whatever brown bits remain in the skillet. Add to the meat and vegetables along with the remaining water and the beans. Bring to a boil and boil 2 minutes then lower the heat. Add the thyme, parsley, bay leaf and hot pepper. Cover and simmer for 1½ hours, stirring occasionally. Remove and discard the bay leaf and the hot pepper pod. Add salt and more black pepper if needed. Serve hot.

Fresh Cranberry Beans with Italian Sausage, Tomato and Green Fusilli

SERVES 4 TO 6

Fresh cream-colored cranberry beans, veined with red, sit snugly tucked into green fusilli pasta, spiked with an herb-rich light tomato sauce.

- 1 lb. fresh cranberry beans, shelled (about 1½ C.)
- 2 sweet Italian pork sausages, removed from casings and crumbled
- 1 large onion, finely chopped (1 C.)
- 3 cloves garlic, finely chopped (1 Tbs.)
- ⅔ C. dry white wine
- 1 14-oz. can Italian tomatoes, undrained (about 1⅔ C.)
- 1 bay leaf
- 1 tsp. dried oregano, preferably Greek
- 1 tsp finely chopped fresh sage
- ½ tsp. coarsely chopped fresh rosemary
- 4–5 large leaves basil, finely shredded (2 Tbs.)
- 1 tsp. tomato paste
- ¼ tsp. hot pepper flakes
- Salt to taste
- 12 ozs. spinach fusilli pasta
- 2 Tbs. grated Pecorino-Romano or Parmesan cheese
- Freshly ground black pepper to taste
- 1 Tbs. coarsely chopped parsley

In a 3-quart saucepan, put the shelled beans in water to cover and simmer for 35 to 40 minutes, covered, or until the beans are tender. Drain and set the beans aside. In a large 12-inch skillet, sauté the sausages until they lose their color, stirring over medium heat for about 3 minutes. Add the onions and the garlic to the skillet and cook, stirring occasionally, until the onions are wilted. Add the wine and cook for 2 minutes more. Stir in the tomatoes and bring to a boil. Lower the heat and add the bay leaf, oregano, sage, rosemary, basil, tomato paste, hot pepper flakes, the cooked beans, and salt. Stir and simmer, uncovered, while the pasta cooks.

Cook the fusilli in lots of boiling salted water until al dente, about 10 to 12 minutes. Remove and discard the bay leaf from the bean mixture, then drain the pasta and stir into the beans. Transfer to a warm serving dish. Sprinkle grated cheese over the pasta, add black pepper, then scatter the chopped parsley over the top. Serve at once.

The

Versatile

Grain

and the

Elegant

Bean

348

Fagioli Freschi in Umido: Fresh Cranberry Beans with Prosciutto, Rosemary and Tomatoes

SERVES 8 TO 10

When fresh cranberry beans are in season, they offer a very special treat. When they are not available, the dried cranberry beans (or Cargamantos) can be used for this classic Italian bean dish, usually cooked in a wine flask in its native home.

2 lbs. fresh cranberry beans in their pods (about 2–3 C. shelled), or 1½ C. dried cranberry beans, soaked (if you use Cargamantos, see NOTE)	2–3 large shallots, finely minced (2 Tbs.)
	1 small onion, finely minced (⅓ C.)
6 C. tepid water	1 large stalk celery, coarsely diced (½ C.)
¼ C. olive oil	
¼-lb piece of prosciutto di Parma, diced in ¼-in. cubes	1 red whole dried hot chile, such as Japonés
2–3 sprigs fresh rosemary leaves, coarsely chopped (1 Tbs.)	Salt and freshly ground black pepper to taste
2–3 large cloves garlic, finely minced (1 Tbs.)	¼ C. coarsely chopped parsley
	¾ C. dry white wine
	2 C. canned imported Italian plum tomatoes with liquid (cut tomatoes in half)

In a 3-quart saucepan, bring the beans and tepid water to a boil. Cover the pot with the lid slightly ajar and simmer for 40 minutes or until the beans are tender. (If you are using cargamantos, see NOTE below for cooking time.) Add salt the last 5 minutes of cooking.

Meanwhile, prepare the sauce. In a large skillet, heat the oil over medium heat and add the prosciutto and half the rosemary. Cook, stirring, for 30 seconds, then add the garlic, shallots, onions, celery, hot chile, salt and black pepper, and half the parsley. Cook over low to medium heat, stirring occasionally, for 15 minutes. Then raise the heat, add the wine and bring to a boil, cooking it for 3 minutes. Add the tomatoes and their liquid. When the tomatoes boil, lower the heat, cover the skillet and simmer 15 minutes more.

When the beans are tender, turn off the heat and let them remain in their cooking water until the sauce is cooked. Then drain the beans, add them to the tomato mixture and heat, stirring gently once or twice. Stir in the remaining rosemary and parsley. Remove the hot chile pod and serve hot.

NOTE: If you are using Cargamantos instead of fresh or dried cranberry beans, the cooking time will be about 1 hour, 20 minutes instead of 40 minutes.

Lingua di Fuoco Tonnato:
Tongues of Fire Beans with
Fresh Grilled Tuna, Herbs and Spinach

SERVES 8 TO 10

The tuna in this salad is fresh, marinated in an herbal dressing, then grilled and added to lush, fat, tender beans, tomatoes and red onions. It's bordered by dark green, crisp spinach with a sprinkle of pine nuts.

1 C. Tongues of Fire beans or cranberry beans, soaked and drained (see Chart, page 346)	1 Tbs. fresh thyme leaves
	2 tsp. finely minced oregano
	1 Tbs. finely minced flat leaf parsley
1 small onion, stuck with 1 whole clove	¾ C. olive oil
1 small carrot	2 ½-lb. fresh tuna steaks, cut 1 in. thick
1 small stalk celery	½ C. finely diced red onion, plus 4 thin slices (1 medium)
1 bay leaf	
3 sprigs parsley	About 20 cherry tomatoes, cut in quarters, drained (2 C.), or 2–3 large ripe tomatoes, cubed and drained
Salt to taste, plus 1 tsp. (or to taste)	
¼ C. lemon juice, plus 2 Tbs. (about 1½ lemons)	
1 Tbs. red wine vinegar	¾ lb. trimmed, well-washed spinach (about 1 lb. untrimmed)
2 Tbs. coarse-grain mustard	
½ tsp. freshly ground black pepper	2 tsps. pine nuts

To a 3-quart saucepan, add the beans, whole onion and clove, carrot, celery and water to cover by about 3 inches and bring to a boil. Tie the bay leaf and parsley together and add to the pot. Cover and simmer for 1 hour, adding salt to taste during the last 3 minutes of cooking.

Meanwhile, mix the lemon juice, vinegar, mustard, 1 teaspoon salt, pepper and herbs in a small bowl. Slowly whisk in the olive oil. Place the tuna steaks in a shallow glass or ceramic dish and pour ⅓ cup of this dressing over the tuna. Set aside the remainder. Marinate for 30 minutes, turning the tuna once. Then lift out the tuna and broil or grill for 5 minutes on each side, basting frequently with the marinade. Discard the marinade and when the fish is cool enough to handle, break it into large bite-size pieces.

Drain the beans, discard the vegetables and herbs and place the beans in a large bowl to cool. Add the tuna pieces to the beans. Stir in the diced red onion and ⅓ cup of the reserved dressing. Season with salt and pepper and add the drained tomatoes. Stir gently and set aside. In a large mixing bowl, tear the spinach into bite-size pieces and mix it with the sliced red onion and the pine nuts. Toss gently with the remaining ⅓ cup of the dressing. Spoon the spinach around the edges of a very large serving platter. Mound the tuna and beans in the center and serve at room temperature.

The

Versatile

Grain

and the

Elegant

Bean

350

Fava Beans

Vicia faba

Alias. Broad beans, horse beans, *fèves, fabas,* daffa beans, Windsor beans, *grosse bohnen.*

Description. Large, about 1¼ inches long, oval shape, thicker at the bottom end. Where the ridge is split, there is a dark line. The color is light brown.

Characteristics. Creamy texture, nutty flavor. The dried variety is used primarily in this country by ethnic Middle Eastern, Italian, Spanish and Portuguese families. Planted in early spring, fresh favas like to grow in cool weather, doing well in Great Britain, parts of Canada and Long Island in New York State. In California, they are planted in early fall. They grow waist-high, with long, broad, waxy pods.

History. A most ancient bean, traces of the smaller fava's cultivation have been uncovered at archaeological sites dating back to the Bronze Age and the ruins of Troy. It is said to have been a mainstay in the diet of the Egyptian pyramid builders, along with garlic and onions. It was also popular in medieval times, especially in Great Britain. Though it is an "Old World" bean, it has begun to emerge and become more popular in the United States, mostly in the form of fresh shell beans.

Traditional Uses. The dried variety is used primarily by ethnic families when fresh, shelled favas are not available. A Portuguese dish called *Manchoupa* (see page 357) uses the dried beans in a hearty beef and herb stew. The British eat them fresh and use the dried favas for purées.

Availability. The dried variety is available whole in skins or peeled and split and somewhat smaller in size. The dried Egyptian favas, called *ful,* are about the size of small black beans and they vary in color from dark brown to greenish-brown. Fresh shell beans are becoming more available each year at local green markets. Shiny, large, bright green pods open to reveal gleaming green beans resting on their velvety cushions. At the beginning of the season, the young beans can be eaten raw as the Italians do. As they get older and larger, many people prefer to skin them either before or after cooking. Ethnic stores and some supermarkets also sell favas fresh, as well as in cans and jars. Some cans, marked *ful* or *ful medames,* are the cooked version of the smaller, dried Egyptian favas.

NOTE: A rare, acute hereditary enzyme deficiency sometimes causes a blood disorder called favism, actually an allergic reaction only in sensitive people. It affects an enzyme

The

Elegant

Bean

351

found in the hemoglobin, and causes Mediterranean anemia, according to Dr. Heskel Haddad. Favism is caused by inhaling pollen or eating large amounts of fava beans. The disease seems to be limited mostly to men who are of Mediterranean extraction, and only a handful of cases have been recorded in this country, although it seems to be more common in areas such as Sardinia and Calabria in Italy.

Cooking Chart

Pot: 3 qt.

Type of Bean:	Large Split Peeled Favas	Small Whole Egyptian Favas	Large Whole Dried Favas
Amount:	1 C. dried	1 C. dried	1 C. dried
Cooking Time:	15 to 20 minutes	45 to 60 minutes	35 to 40 minutes
Approx. Yield	1⅔ C.	2½ C.	2 C.
Comments:	Very soft. Does not hold its shape. Good for purées.	Tender, skins remain intact.	After soaking, outer skins pull off easily. Some beans split open, some disintegrate to thicken sauce while cooking.

NOTE: *Fresh in pod fava beans.* Amount: 3 lbs. fresh in pod equal 3 C. shelled or 1-lb. can or jar. Cooking Time: Young beans—1 minute. Older beans: 8 to 10 minutes. Approx. Yield: Serves 6. Comments: Use young beans, since large beans need outer skins peeled.

The

Versatile

Grain

and the

Elegant

Bean

352

Split Fava Bean Purée with Dill

Although we tend to think of the fava bean as being indigenous to the Middle East, as well as some parts of Europe such as Italy, Spain and Greece, the British love and eat this earthy flavored bean, which they call "broad beans." This purée, which cooks quite quickly, is done in the British manner with butter and just a smidgeon of cream. We have added lots of dill and a hint of saffron and lemon, making it a marvelous side dish to serve with quickly sautéed salmon.

1½ C. split peeled fava beans, soaked and drained	¼ tsp. saffron threads, crushed
1 medium carrot	2 Tbs. soft butter
1 small stalk celery with leaves	Salt and freshly ground black pepper to taste
1 small onion, stuck with 1 whole clove	2 large shallots, finely chopped (2 Tbs.)
2 large sprigs parsley	2–3 Tbs. heavy cream
3 sprigs thyme	⅓ C. coarsely chopped dill, plus 1 sprig
2 tsps. lemon juice	

To a 3-quart saucepan, add the beans, carrot, celery, onion and clove. Tie the parsley and thyme together and add, along with enough tepid water to cover by about 2 inches. Bring to a boil, then lower the heat and simmer, with lid slightly ajar, for 15 to 20 minutes or until the beans are very soft and have begun to lose their shape. Meanwhile, mix the lemon juice and saffron in a small cup and set aside for 10 minutes.

When the beans are done, lift out the vegetables and herbs and discard them. Drain the beans well, discarding the liquid. Transfer the beans to a medium-size bowl and beat in 1 tablespoon of the butter with a wooden spoon (see NOTE). Then stir in the saffron and lemon juice, and add the salt and pepper.

In a small skillet, heat the remaining butter and sauté the shallots over medium heat, stirring constantly for 2 to 3 minutes or until they are translucent, but not brown. Add to the purée and beat in 2 tablespoons of the cream (1 more tablespoon may be needed if the texture is too dry), then stir in the chopped dill. Taste for salt and pepper. Transfer to an oven-to-table serving dish, cover with aluminum foil and keep warm in a preheated low oven until ready to serve. Garnish with a sprig of dill.

NOTE: This purée is a coarse one. If you prefer a smoother texture, purée it in the bowl of a food processor.

Soupe aux Fèves:
French Cream of Fresh Fava Bean Soup

SERVES 4

A delicate French country soup, served hot or cold and made with bright green fresh fava beans, just a touch of smoky pancetta plus the elusive licorice taste of fresh chervil.

2 lbs. fresh fava beans
1 medium potato, peeled and cut into eighths (about ½ lb.)
2⅔ C. Chicken Stock, preferably homemade (see page 171)
2 ozs. pancetta or bacon, finely minced
1 thin leek, white part only, finely chopped (about ½ C.)

1 medium clove garlic, finely minced (1 tsp.)
½ C. light cream
Salt and freshly ground pepper to taste
3–4 drops Tabasco sauce
1 Tbs. coarsely chopped chervil or parsley

Shell the fava beans. Put them in a 3-quart saucepan along with the potatoes and the chicken stock. Bring to a boil, then cover, lower the heat and simmer gently until the beans and potatoes are very soft, about 30 minutes. Put the beans, potatoes and the stock through a food mill (see NOTE). Then return to the saucepan and keep warm over low heat.

In a small nonstick skillet, sauté together the pancetta, leeks, and garlic over medium heat for 5 minutes, or until the pancetta is brown. Stir occasionally. Then add it to the soup. Stir in the cream, add the salt, pepper and Tabasco and simmer until hot. Ladle into bowls and sprinkle chopped chervil over the surface of each. The soup can also be chilled and served cold.

NOTE: A food mill, rather than a food processor, purées the beans, leaving a residue of the outer skin, thus resulting in a smoother purée.

The

Versatile

Grain

and the

Elegant

Bean

354

Fave alla Campagnola:
Fresh Fava Beans with Parmesan Shards,
Summer Savory and Fresh Fennel

SERVES 4

Although peeling the outer skins of the fava beans may be somewhat labor-intensive, we did not find it at all unpleasant. Two people sitting outdoors, sipping a glass of chilled white wine and peeling away, made it an intimate pleasure.

Salt
2 C. shelled, preferably young fava
   beans (about 2 lbs, see NOTE)
½ C. thinly sliced fennel
2 Tbs. lemon juice
1 tsp. balsamic vinegar
Salt and freshly ground black pepper
   to taste

6 Tbs. olive oil
2 thin scallions, thinly sliced on
   diagonal (½ C.)
1 Tbs. coarsely chopped summer
   savory
Curly endive or red radicchio leaves
1 wedge Parmesan cheese

To a 3-quart saucepan of boiling salted water to cover, add the beans and the fennel and boil for 1 minute. Drain and transfer to a bowl. In another small bowl, whisk together the lemon juice, vinegar, salt and pepper, then whisk in the olive oil until well blended. Pour the mixture over the warm beans and fennel. Stir in the scallions and summer savory. Divide into equal portions on salad plates, each one with a base of a few leaves of curly endive, and top with generous shards of Parmesan cheese, made by scraping a cheese slicer over the Parmesan wedge. Add additional freshly ground black pepper at the table if you wish.

NOTE: If you cannot get young, small fava beans, but only the larger more mature pods, cook them for 8 to 10 minutes rather than 1 minute. And, if the beans are large, peel each bean of its outer skin as well.

Fava Beans Catalan-Style
with Chorizo

SERVES 6

Uncommon and underutilized, the full rich and unique flavor of the fava bean has not yet taken its proper place in American cuisine. We love them and have used them fresh, as whole dried beans, peeled and split for purées and, as in this recipe, canned. Although we usually prefer not to use canned beans, we found these to be pretty tasty and most acceptable.

1 C. cubed, peeled potatoes (about ½ lb.)	½ tsp. dried oregano, preferably Greek
3 C. fresh peeled large fava beans, or 1-lb. can or jar, drained and rinsed (about 3 lbs. if fresh)	Salt and freshly ground black pepper to taste
Salt to taste (optional)	1 bay leaf
1 lb. Spanish chorizo	½ C. dry white wine
2 Tbs. olive oil	2 medium coarsely chopped plum tomatoes, fresh or canned (½ C.)
3 large cloves garlic, finely minced (1 Tbs.)	1 Tbs. coarsely chopped mint
5–6 thin scallions, finely sliced (about ¾ C.)	1 Tbs. coarsely chopped flat leaf parsley

To a 2-quart saucepan, add the potatoes and, if fresh, the fava beans along with salted water to cover. Bring to a boil, cover and simmer for 8 minutes. Drain and set aside in a bowl. If canned fava beans are used, add them to the drained potatoes and transfer them both to a bowl.

Pierce the chorizos in several places with a sharp knife and add them to the same saucepan. Cover with water and bring to a boil, then cover and simmer for 10 minutes. Lift the sausages out with tongs and place on paper towels. Blot them to dry, then slice crosswise into ¼-inch-thick slices and add to the bowl with the beans and the potatoes.

In a 10-inch skillet, heat the olive oil and add the garlic. Sauté, stirring, for 30 seconds, then stir in the scallions, oregano, salt, pepper and bay leaf. Sauté for 2 to 3 minutes until the scallions are wilted, then add the wine and bring to a boil. Stir in the tomatoes and lower the heat. Simmer for 5 minutes, uncovered. Add the bean and sausage mixture and stir gently. Add half the mint and parsley and stir again. Then cover the skillet and simmer for 10 minutes. Remove the bay leaf. Taste and adjust the seasoning. Transfer to a serving platter and sprinkle the remaining mint and parsley over the surface.

NOTE: Scozzaro's Green Broad Beans, either canned or in jars, are fresh, cooked fava beans, not dried beans. They are imported from The Netherlands. Since fresh favas are a bit labor-intensive to shell and peel, these are quite acceptable. (See page 505 for the Oriental Pastry & Grocery Co., which always stocks them.)

The

Versatile

Grain

and the

Elegant

Bean

356

Ful Medames:
Egyptian Fava Beans

SERVES 4 TO 6

*F*ul medames or *Ful mudammas*—another of those regional spelling choices—is one of the most ubiquitous and traditional bean dishes of Egypt, found in almost every restaurant or street stand. It is traditionally baked for hours, but our version takes a lot less time to cook, for the simple reason that it is salted *after* cooking.

1 C. small whole Egyptian fava beans, soaked and drained (see NOTE)	Salt and freshly ground black pepper to taste
4 C. water	Few drops Tabasco sauce
1 lb. lamb ribs or lamb steak cut from the leg or a leftover bone from a leg of lamb	2 hard-boiled eggs, coarsely chopped
4 cloves garlic, peeled	1 small sweet red onion, coarsely chopped (⅓ C.)
2½ tsps. ground cumin	4 small wedges lemon
	Strong fruity olive oil
	2 Tbs. minced cilantro

In a 3-quart saucepan, bring the beans, water, lamb, garlic and cumin to a boil. Lower the heat and cover. Simmer for about 45 to 60 minutes or until the beans are tender. Then add the salt, pepper and Tabasco. When the beans are cooked, lift out the lamb bones and discard. Cut any lean meat off into small pieces and return to the beans.

Drain the beans, reserving 1½ cups of the liquid. Preheat the oven to 325°F and transfer the beans and liquid to a 1½-quart baking dish. Cover and bake for 20 minutes. At the table, serve the beans with separate dishes of chopped egg, chopped red onion, a flask of olive oil and a small dish of cilantro, passing them to be added at will.

NOTE: Although this is a fava bean, it does not cook into the same consistency as the others, remaining shapely after cooking. There is also no substitute for these smaller favas. They can be purchased at Middle Eastern specialty shops (see Mail Order Sources, pages 501–506).

Manchoupa: Portuguese Pot Roast
and Whole Dried Fava Beans

SERVES 8

Apopular dish with the Portuguese community in Martha's Vineyard and Cape Cod, *Manchoupa* is perfect when served on a blustery day. The whole fava beans need to have their tough skins removed before cooking, though in the Middle Eastern countries, the Arab style of eating favas is to bite the end of the skin, squeeze the bean and pop it into the mouth.

3½ lbs. first-cut lean brisket of beef, rump or bottom round	3 medium onions, coarsely chopped (3 C. or about 1 lb.)
2–3 large cloves garlic, finely minced (1 Tbs.)	4 sprigs thyme
1 tsp. sweet paprika	2 sprigs rosemary
¼ tsp. cayenne	1 large bay leaf
1 tsp. coarse salt or to taste	2 C. large chunks, undrained plum tomatoes (use canned Italian plum tomatoes)
2 C. whole dried fava beans	
1 Tbs. olive oil	

Place the meat in a dish, then mix the garlic, paprika, cayenne and salt together in a rough paste and spread it over both sides. Cover with plastic wrap and marinate overnight.

Place the fava beans in a large bowl filled with tepid water and soak overnight. The tough outer skins will loosen and should be peeled off.

In a 3-quart saucepan, place the beans in tepid water to cover and bring to a boil. Drain and discard the water, which will be very foamy. Cover by about 2 inches with fresh tepid water. Bring to a boil again, then lower the heat and simmer, covered, with the lid slightly ajar, for 30 minutes. Drain the beans and set aside.

In a 5-quart heavy casserole, heat the olive oil. Sear the meat on both sides, until very brown, over medium high heat. Remove the meat and set aside. Add the onions to the same casserole and sauté over medium low heat for 5 to 8 minutes, stirring frequently, scraping up any brown bits.

Tie the thyme, rosemary and bay leaf together and add them to the casserole along with the tomatoes. Bring to a boil, then lower the heat and return the meat to the pot. Cover and simmer for 1½ hours. Remove the herbs and discard.

Preheat the oven to 350°F. Remove the meat to a platter. Stir the partially cooked beans into the sauce, then return the meat to the top. Cover and place the casserole in the oven and bake for 1 hour.

To serve, remove the meat and let it rest for 10 minutes, covered loosely with aluminum foil. Slice it into ½-inch-thick slices and arrange them in the center of a shallow ovenproof dish. Spoon the beans and sauce around the meat. Some of the beans will have disintegrated to thicken the sauce, while others will have remained whole. Keep warm in a low oven until serving time, or cool, cover and refrigerate for a day or two.

Reheat in a preheated 350°F oven, adding some additional water if the beans have absorbed the sauce.

The

Versatile

Grain

and the

Elegant

Bean

358

Lentils

Lens esculenta

Their famed shape inspired astronomers and physicists to name their disk-shaped double convex optic glass a "lens," the Latin word for lentil. They've been eaten by man for about 8,000 years in the Middle East, though their exact origin is unknown. Some archaeologists place the beginnings in Turkey, since some of their digs have uncovered the legume. But they have also been found in areas of Iraq, fairly close to the Turkish border.

In predynastic times in Egypt, about 3000 B.C., evidence now shows that the lentil grew and was eaten as a common staple in the diets of the ancient Greeks, Romans, Egyptians and Hebrews, and even today the Middle East is the second-largest consumer of lentils. The honor of being the "greatest lentil consumer" country goes to India, which grows more than fifty varieties. There is even an interesting Parsee dish called *dahnsak,* in which three to nine different kinds of lentils of various flavors, colors and textures are combined. The aim of the dish is to challenge the cook to achieve harmony and proper balance.

Apicius, who wrote the first ancient Roman cookbook more than 2,000 years ago, included a chapter on "pulses" (British for legumes) in which he lists recipes for lentils with mussels (see page 376 for our version), lentils with chestnuts and lentils with spices and herbs, honey and vinegar, as well as a soup of barley, lentils, peas and chickpeas, quite similar to Moroccan Harira (see page 487).

The Old Testament mentions Esau, who sold his birthright to Jacob for a bowl of lentil soup. In fact, it is the French who still refer to lentil soup as *potage Esau.*

Throughout the ages and right up until the present time, lentils have been economical and therefore an available food to the poor, thus shunned by the snobbish who have always wanted to disassociate themselves from what was known as "poor man's meat" with emphasis on the word *poor.* However, for 25 grams of protein, 134 grams of beef would have to be consumed, while 100 grams of lentils contain the same amount, with less cholesterol and more beneficial fiber.

So, for those who are able to judge good food without a high price tag being the criterion of that judgment, the color, texture and flavors of the tiny lens-shaped legumes are once again sparking the imagination of inventive cooks and inspiring them to new recipe possibilities.

The Lentil Mystique

Since there are so many lentil varieties around the world, we have been forced to limit our list to only the most available types. Labels on packages rarely specify the variety of lentil, making it all the more confusing for the consumer. And lentils bought in bulk from sacks only complicate the problem still further, though some knowledgeable storekeepers can often shed light on the nomenclature.

Our chart is compiled for quick complete information on five major varieties that we find are most commonly packaged or sold in bulk.

Some General Guidelines

Lentils do not require soaking, and whether they are whole or skinned and split with the brighter inner color revealed, the cooking time is very short.

Cooked lentils will keep in the refrigerator, tightly covered, for five days, or up to three months if frozen.

A general rule is that one pound of dried lentils will measure two and a quarter cups. After cooking, the amount increases to six cups. A twelve-ounce package of dried lentils will measure one and three-quarter cups and when cooked will yield three cups.

The

Versatile

Grain

and the

Elegant

Bean

360

Cooking Chart

Pot: 3 qt.

Type	Form and Description	Approximate Cooking Times (Do Not Soak Before Cooking!!)	Comments	Availability
Green Lentils **Alias:** large Chilean lentils, lentilles blondes, laird lentil	Flat, disk shape, about ¼ inch, green to golden brown underskin. Domestic. Grown in Northwest.	salad: 20 to 25 minutes side dish: 30 to 40 minutes main dish: 30 to 40 minutes soups/purées: 60 minutes *Yield:* 1 C. dried = 2 C. cooked	Very flavorful	Supermarkets, health food and specialty stores.
Brown Lentils **Alias:** small Chinese, Persian lentils	Smaller than green lentils and more plump. The color is russet brown with skin on. Imported.	salad: 15 to 20 minutes side dish: 25 to 35 minutes main course: 25 to 35 minutes soups/purées: 60 minutes *Yield:* 1 C. dried = 2¼ C. cooked	A bit more defined, earthy taste than green lentils, but can be interchanged with them.	Supermarkets, ethnic, health food and specialty stores.
Whole Red Lentils **Alias:** *chilka masur*	⅛ inch, salmon color with whole skin on. Domestic, grown in Pacific Northwest.	salads: 6 to 8 minutes side dish: 10 minutes main course: 10 minutes soups/purées: 20 minutes *Yield:* 1 C. dried = 2½ C. cooked	Pungeant, turns golden when cooked. Will keep shape if salt or acid (e.g., lemon juice) are added immediately after cooking.	Indian and Middle Eastern specialty stores, supermarkets and health food stores.

Cooking Chart (cont.)

Type	Form and Description	Approximate Cooking Times (Do Not Soak Before Cooking!!)	Comments	Availability
Red Lentils **Alias:** *masur daal*	1/16 inch, flat, peeled and split. Bright red-orange. Imported from Turkey, Egypt, India.	soups/purées: 20 minutes *Yield:* 1 C. dried = 1⅔ C. cooked	Turns golden when cooked. Does not hold its shape. Use only in soups and purées. Foamy at first, but skim the surface before simmering.	Ethnic markets, specialty stores, health food stores and some supermarkets.
French Green Lentils (Le Puy) **Alias:** ponotes	3/16 inch, more plump than flat, with skin on. Drab, olive-green, almost black with mottling and yellow interior. Imported from France.	salads: 20 minutes side dish: 30 minutes main dish: 30 minutes soups/purées: 45 to 60 minutes *Yield:* 1 C. dried = 2¼ C. cooked	Most expensive of all lentils. Firmer and a bit peppery in flavor.	Specialty shops.

The

Versatile

Grain

and the

Elegant

Bean

362

Mercimek Köftesi: Turkish Lentil and Bulgur Rolls with Chopped Vegetable Salad

MAKES 12 ROLLS

The hors d'oeuvres or *meze* served in Turkey and other Middle Eastern countries are similar to the Spanish *tapas*, mini food made to perk up appetites and complement drinks before dinner.

Lentil and Bulgur Rolls

2 C. water
¼ C. dried peeled split red lentils, picked over and washed
Salt to taste
½ C. #1 fine bulgur
2 Tbs. butter

1 large onion, finely chopped (⅔ C.)
1 tsp. ground cumin
1 tsp. paprika
⅛ tsp. cayenne
¼ C. finely minced flat leaf parsley
1 tsp. lemon juice

In a 2-quart saucepan, boil the water, add the lentils and bring to a boil again. Lower the heat, cover, and simmer for 15 minutes. Add salt and stir in the bulgur. Remove from the heat. Cover again and let stand for 30 minutes to absorb the remaining liquid.

Meanwhile, in a medium-size skillet, melt the butter and stir in the onions, cumin, paprika and cayenne. Sauté over low heat, stirring occasionally, for 8 to 10 minutes. Transfer to a bowl. When the bulgur and lentil mixture is ready, add it to the bowl and then add the parsley and lemon juice, beating vigorously with a wooden spoon. Taste for salt and, with wet hands, form the mixture into 2-inch finger-shaped rolls, using a heaping tablespoon for each roll. Arrange the rolls on the outer rim of a platter, cover with plastic wrap and chill while preparing the chopped vegetable salad.

Chopped Vegetable Salad
MAKES 1³/₄ CUPS

1 large tomato, cut into ½-in. dice (1 C.)
½ small red onion, finely diced (⅓ C.)
1 small green pepper, finely diced (½ C.)
Salt and freshly ground black pepper to taste

1 Tbs. red wine vinegar
¼ tsp. ground cumin
¼ tsp. dried mint
2 Tbs. olive oil

In a small bowl, mix the tomatoes, onions and green pepper together gently. Season with salt and pepper. Spoon the vinegar, spices and olive oil over all, and stir gently again. Transfer to a small glass bowl that will fit in the center of the platter on which you've placed the rolls. Serve at room temperature.

Spinach and Sorrel Timbales with
a Curried Red Lentil Sauce

SERVES 4

Tempting and appealing are these sprightly green-tinted timbales surrounded by a thick, spicy and fiery saffron-colored sauce, to be served at room temperature as a first course.

Timbales

¼ lb. sorrel
½ lb. spinach
6 sprigs flat leaf parsley with stems
2 Tbs. butter
1 large clove garlic, finely minced (1 tsp.)
2 scallions, green tops only, coarsely chopped (about ⅓ C.)
1 tsp. lemon juice

1 tsp. white wine Worcestershire sauce
Salt and freshly ground black pepper to taste
Few gratings nutmeg
1 C. half and half or light cream
3 eggs
Butter for greasing molds

Fold the sorrel leaves lengthwise in half and cut out the tough stems. Trim the spinach, wash and dry both greens in a salad spinner and drain them on paper towels, making sure they are very dry. Scatter the parsley sprigs over the greens and set aside.

Preheat the oven to 325° F. and boil a kettle of water. In a nonstick 12-inch skillet, melt the butter, then add the garlic and scallion tops and sauté over low heat for 2 to 3 minutes. Stir in the reserved greens and sauté, stirring constantly for 2 to 3 minutes until they are wilted. Season with lemon juice, Worcestershire sauce, salt, pepper and nutmeg, and mix lightly. Then purée the mixture in an electric blender. There will be about 1 cup of purée. (You can prepare the purée a day in advance if you like.) Set aside.

In a small saucepan, scald the half and half only until bubbles form around the edge. Put the eggs in the bowl of a food processor and blend for a few strokes, then slowly add the scalded cream with the processor running. Then add the purée of greens and blend well. Transfer the mixture to a measuring cup with a spout for easy pouring. Lavishly butter four ½-cup timbale molds or custard cups and pour the mixture not quite to the top of each mold. Cover with aluminum foil and place the molds in a larger pan with deep sides. Pour the boiling water into the pan so that it reaches halfway up the sides of the mold and bake for 35 minutes. Remove the molds from the pan and cool on a wire rack for 20 minutes. While the timbales are baking, prepare the sauce.

The

Versatile

Grain

and the

Elegant

Bean

364

Curried Red Lentil Sauce

1 C. dried, peeled split red lentils, picked over and washed

3 C. water

2 Tbs. olive oil

1 large clove garlic, finely minced (1 tsp.)

1 medium onion, finely minced (¾ C.)

1 tsp. each ground cumin, coriander and turmeric

¼ tsp. each ground cardamom, cayenne and cinnamon

⅛ tsp. ground cloves

Salt and freshly ground black pepper to taste

Sprigs mint (optional)

In a 2-quart saucepan, bring the lentils and water to a boil and then lower the heat. Simmer for 10 minutes. *Do not drain* the cooking liquid. Set the saucepan aside.

In a small skillet, heat the oil and sauté the garlic and onions over medium heat, stirring often for about 5 minutes. Combine the spices in a small bowl and add to the onion mixture. Continue to sauté, stirring, for 1 minute. Then add to the lentils and cooking liquid. Transfer to an electric blender and purée.

When ready to serve, run a thin, sharp knife around the edges of the timbale molds and invert onto serving plates. Spoon the lentil sauce around the base of the plate, garnish with a sprig of mint, if you wish, tucked into the sauce.

NOTE: There will be extra sauce. If you dilute it with chicken stock and serve it topped with minted yogurt, it becomes a silky soup.

Tapenade: Puréed Lentils with
Olives, Anchovies and Capers

MAKES 2 CUPS

A smooth, dark purée from Provence with all the good things from that sunny region in the South of France. It's perfect as an unusual hors d'oeuvre or as a dip for raw vegetable crudités.

¾ C. dried green or brown lentils, picked over and washed
½ C. pitted oil-cured olives
3–4 anchovy fillets, rinsed and drained on paper towels
1 heaping Tbs. nonpareil capers, rinsed and drained on paper towels
2 large cloves garlic, finely minced (about 1 Tbs.)

1 tsp. dried oregano, preferably Greek
Juice of ½ large lemon (2 Tbs.)
2–3 drops Tabasco sauce
¼ C. olive oil
1 Tbs. coarsely chopped parsley

To a 2-quart saucepan, add the lentils with enough tepid water to cover by 2 inches. Bring to a boil, then lower the heat, cover, and simmer until the lentils are very tender, about 30 minutes. Drain and rinse the lentils then drain again. Set aside.

In the bowl of a food processor, chop the olives finely, then add the lentils, anchovies, capers, garlic and oregano, and process until smooth. Add the lemon juice and Tabasco and process for a few more strokes. With the processor running, add the olive oil in a steady stream through the feeding tube, until a thick, creamy purée is formed. Adjust the seasoning, adding more lemon or oil. Place in a mound on a serving dish and scatter parsley on the surface. Serve at room temperature with toasts or thin whole grain crackers.

NOTE: To store in the refrigerator for a few days, put the tapanade in a jar and pour a bit of olive oil over the surface before closing the lid tightly.

The

Versatile

Grain

and the

Elegant

Bean

366

French Lentils with Stellette
Pasta and Mint

SERVES 8

The naturally spicy flavor of these mottled dark green French lentils is sweetened by small cubes of sweet carrots, then cooked in white wine and chicken stock. It is then tossed with tiny star-shaped pasta, a touch of vinegar and some cooling mint to enhance the flavors.

2 Tbs. butter
1 medium onion, finely diced (⅔ C.)
1 thin leek, white part only, well washed, finely diced (⅓ C.)
1 small stalk celery, finely diced (⅓ C.)
1 small carrot, finely diced (⅓ C.)
2½ C. Chicken Stock, preferably homemade (see page 171)
1 C. dry white wine
1 C. dried French green lentils, picked over and washed

Bouquet garni, tied together: 4 sprigs parsley, 4 sprigs fresh thyme, 1 bay leaf
¼ C. tiny-size pasta such as *stellette* (little stars) or *acini di pepe* (peppercorn shaped pasta)
2 Tbs. finely diced prosciutto
Salt and freshly ground black pepper to taste
1 tsp. balsamic or red wine vinegar
1 Tbs. finely minced fresh mint

In a 3-quart saucepan, melt the butter over medium low heat and add the onions, leeks, celery and carrots. Stir occasionally and cook until soft but not brown, about 4 to 5 minutes. Add the chicken stock, white wine and lentils. Bring to a boil, then add the bouquet garni. Reduce the heat, cover the pot with the lid slightly ajar and simmer until the lentils are tender, about 40 minutes (see NOTE). The last 5 minutes, cook the pasta in lots of boiling salted water. Drain and reserve the pasta.

When the lentils are tender, remove and discard the bouquet garni. Stir in the stellette, prosciutto, salt, pepper and vinegar. Spoon onto a serving platter and sprinkle with mint. Serve hot as a side dish or as a warm salad on a bed of *frisé* or radicchio.

NOTE: The addition of wine helps the lentils maintain their shape. However, since it is acidic, it also lengthens the cooking time.

Yemiser Selatta:
Ethiopian Lentil Salad
with Shallots and Hot Chiles

SERVES 4 TO 6

This Ethiopian salad is part of a traditional meal served during Lent and always includes the flat, thin, lacy, soft fermented pancake-like bread *injera,* made of teff flour. It is accompanied by a vegetable mélange called *Atkelt Watt* (or *Atikelt Wat*), a *wat* being a sort of thick stew given its name by its principal ingredients: meat, fish, potatoes, string beans, carrots or beans. *Atkelt* refers to the vegetables.

- 3 large shallots, peeled, sliced thinly lengthwise and then cut into julienne strips (about ⅔ C.)
- 2 Tbs. red wine vinegar
- 1 Tbs. lemon juice
- Small pinch sugar
- 1–2 (depending upon personal preference) long Italian or New Mexico (Anaheim) fresh green chiles, cut into thin julienne 1 in. long by ⅛ in. wide (about 1–2 Tbs.)

- 1 C. dried brown or green lentils, picked over and washed
- ½ tsp. salt or to taste
- Freshly ground black pepper to taste
- 2 Tbs. strong Spanish olive oil
- 1 tsp. finely minced cilantro (optional)

In a small bowl, put the shallots in ice water (include an ice cube) to cover. Let stand for 20 minutes, then drain and blot the shallots dry on paper towels. Wipe out the bowl and return the shallots to it. Add the vinegar, lemon juice and sugar and stir in the hot chile. Let stand while cooking the lentils.

Place the lentils in a 3-quart saucepan and cover with water by 2 to 3 inches. Bring to a boil, then lower the heat and simmer for about 30 to 35 minutes or until the lentils are tender but have kept their shape. Transfer them to a sieve and rinse with hot water. Drain well, place them in a medium-size bowl and gently toss with the salt, pepper and olive oil. Add the shallot/vinegar/chile mixture to the lentils and gently toss again. Sprinkle with cilantro if you wish and let the mixture stand at room temperature for at least 30 minutes to allow the flavors to blend before serving.

The

Versatile

Grain

and the

Elegant

Bean

368

French Lentil and Vegetable Salad with Kielbasa and Chèvre

SERVES 8 AS MAIN COURSE OR 10 AS FIRST COURSE

We frequently serve small portions of this elegant, festive French green lentil salad as a first course. However, larger-portion servings can be used as a main course, for a picnic (since it does not go limp), or a help-yourself buffet table for exactly the same reason—it doesn't wilt.

1½ C. dried French green lentils, picked over and washed
5 C. water
1 small onion, stuck with 1 whole clove
1 small carrot
1 small stalk celery
Bouquet garni, tied in cheesecloth: 3 sprigs flat leaf parsley, 3 sprigs thyme, 1 bay leaf, 4 whole black peppercorns
Salt to taste
3 Tbs. olive oil
1 small clove garlic, finely minced (1 tsp.)
1 medium onion, finely chopped (¾ C.)

1 large stalk celery, finely chopped (½ C.)
1 medium carrot, finely chopped (½ C.)
Juice of ½ medium lemon (1 Tbs.)
2 Tbs. red wine vinegar
6 Tbs. walnut oil
Freshly ground black pepper to taste
1 C. finely diced kielbasa (cut into ½-in. dice—about 4 ozs.)
Lettuce leaves
4 ozs. chèvre, crumbled
2 Tbs. finely minced flat leaf parsley
½ C. tiny black olives such as Niçoise (optional)

In a 5-quart Dutch oven, bring the lentils, water, onion, carrot and celery stalk to a boil. Add the bouquet garni and lower the heat. Simmer for about 20 to 30 minutes, or until the lentils are tender but maintain their shape. Add salt the last few minutes of cooking. Lift out and discard all the vegetables and the bouquet garni. Drain the lentils well, then place them on a triple thickness of paper towels to dry. Transfer to a large bowl and set aside.

Meanwhile, heat the olive oil in a medium-size nonstick skillet, then add the garlic, onions, celery and carrots. Sauté over medium heat for 5 minutes, stirring frequently, then gently stir into the bowl of cooked drained lentils.

To a small bowl, add the lemon juice and vinegar, then whisk in the walnut oil. Pour over the lentils and vegetables. Season with salt and freshly ground black pepper and stir once. Cover tightly with plastic wrap and let it stand for 30 minutes or refrigerate overnight if you wish. But bring to room temperature before adding the remaining ingredients and completing the dish.

Before serving, stir in the kielbasa and adjust the seasoning. Line the serving plates with a few leaves of lettuce. Add the lentil salad and garnish each serving with some of the chèvre, parsley and black olives (if you wish).

The

Elegant

Bean

Faki:
Greek Lentil Soup with Turnip Greens

SERVES 8

An easy-to-make, earthy soup, which profits by cooking it a day or two in advance, giving the lentils a chance to soak up the perfectly blended flavors. Just before serving, the soup is doused with a bit of vinegar and Tabasco sauce.

1½ C. dried green or brown lentils, picked over and washed
8 C. water
2 medium stalks celery, finely diced (½ C.)
1 bay leaf
½ tsp. dried oregano, preferably Greek
3 Tbs. olive oil
2–3 large cloves garlic, finely minced (2 tsps.)
1 medium red onion, finely diced (1 C.)

Salt and freshly ground black pepper to taste
3 Tbs. finely minced parsley
14-oz. can Italian plum tomatoes with liquid
1 lb. trimmed turnip greens or mustard greens or spinach, cut into ½-in. strips
1–2 Tbs. red wine vinegar or more to taste
¼ tsp. Tabasco sauce

In a large pot, bring the lentils, water, celery, bay leaf and oregano to a boil. Lower the heat and simmer, covered with the lid slightly ajar, until the lentils are very tender, about 30 minutes. Remove and discard the bay leaf.

While the soup is cooking, heat the oil in a medium-size skillet and sauté the garlic and onions over low heat until the onions are wilted, about 5 minutes. Add the salt, pepper, parsley and tomatoes, and continue to cook for an additional 5 minutes. Transfer this mixture to the soup when the lentils are tender and cook for 5 minutes. Add the greens and simmer for 10 more minutes (see NOTE).

Remove from the heat and stir in the vinegar and Tabasco. Taste for additional salt and pepper and, if the soup is too thick, add a bit of boiling water. Serve hot.

NOTE: *Before* adding the vinegar and Tabasco, you may refrigerate the soup for 1 or 2 days, then reheat, adding those ingredients just before serving.

The

Versatile

Grain

and the

Elegant

Bean

370

Priest's Soup:
Red Lentils and Rice

SERVES 6 TO 8

This is a thick rice and red lentil soup that dates back to biblical times and is sometimes called Esau's Potage, after the legend of the man who sold his birthright for a bowl of this soup. The Armenians call it *Vartabed Abour* or Priest's Soup, since the story of Esau was told so often by their priests.

- 6 C. Chicken Stock, preferably homemade (see page 171)
- 1 C. dried peeled split small red lentils, picked over and washed
- ¼ C. long grain rice, either white or brown
- 3 medium onions, thinly sliced and separated into rings

- 2 Tbs. finely minced parsley
- Salt to taste
- ⅛ tsp. cayenne
- ¼ tsp. sweet paprika, plus additional for color
- 2 Tbs. olive oil
- 2 Tbs. butter

In a 5-quart Dutch oven, heat 4 cups of the chicken stock to the boiling point. Add the lentils and rice and bring to a boil again, then lower the heat, cover, and simmer for 10 minutes. Add only two of the sliced onions, stir and continue to cook for 20 minutes more. Then add the remaining chicken stock, parsley, salt, cayenne and paprika and continue to cook for 10 minutes more.

Meanwhile, heat the oil and butter in an iron skillet and add the remaining sliced onion. Sauté over medium heat, stirring frequently, until the onion is brown and crisp. Remove and drain on paper towels.

Serve the soup in large bowls with a sprinkling of the brown onions and a few grains of additional paprika for color.

add 6 cups

Lemon Lentils with Curried Shrimp

SERVES 6

This is one of those recipes that is done in stages, with the actual cooking time quite brief. The lentils are made the day before and then reheated The shrimp can also be shelled and the stock prepared the day before as well. The shrimp then cook in under 15 minutes in a delicate curry cream, while the tart, highly spiced lentils are rewarmed. Basmati rice would complete it all.

Lentils

¼ C. corn oil, plus 1 Tbs.
1 medium onion, thinly sliced (¾ C.)
1 lb. dried green or brown lentils, picked over and washed
2 2-in. pieces cinnamon stick
½ tsp. cayenne
¾ Tbs. finely minced, peeled ginger
Peel of 1 large lemon, finely minced (2 tsps.)
3½ C. unsalted Chicken Stock, preferably homemade (see page 171)

2 bay leaves
½ small onion, finely minced (¼ C.)
1 medium clove garlic, finely minced (1 tsp.)
Salt and freshly ground black pepper to taste
Juice of 1 large lemon (1 Tbs.)
3 Tbs. coarsely chopped cilantro

In a 5-quart Dutch oven, heat ¼ cup of the oil and add the sliced onions. Sauté, stirring often, over medium heat until the onions are wilted. Stir in the lentils, cinnamon sticks, cayenne, ginger and lemon peel and cook, stirring often, for about 5 minutes. Add the chicken stock and bay leaves and bring to a boil. Then lower the heat, cover, and simmer for 15 minutes.

Meanwhile, heat the remaining oil in a small skillet. Add the minced onions, garlic, salt and pepper and sauté, stirring occasionally, over low heat until the onions begin to brown slightly. Set aside.

After 15 minutes, when the lentils are partly cooked, remove and discard the cinnamon sticks and bay leaves. Stir in the onion-garlic mixture and the lemon juice and continue to simmer for about 10 to 15 minutes more or until the lentils are tender and still maintain their shape. Add additional stock if the lentils seem dry. Stir in the cilantro. Set the lentils aside while preparing the shrimp, or prepare the lentils the day before, and add a few tablespoons of water when reheating them before serving.

The

Versatile

Grain

and the

Elegant

Bean

372

Shrimp Curry

1½ lbs. large shrimp (about 36)	4 Tbs. butter
2 C. water	4 thick scallions, mince white part
5 whole peppercorns	and green part separately
1 small stalk celery	1 Tbs. curry powder
1 small bay leaf	⅓ C. heavy cream
Few drops white vinegar	Juice of 1 large lime (1 Tbs.)
Salt to taste	Freshly ground black pepper to taste
⅓ C. all-purpose flour	
½ tsp. cayenne	3 Tbs. coarsely chopped cilantro

Peel the shrimp and reserve the shells. Place the shrimp on a plate lined with a paper towel. Cover with plastic wrap and refrigerate until needed. This can be done several hours before.

In a 2-quart saucepan, add the shrimp shells, water, peppercorns, celery, bay leaf and vinegar. Add salt and bring to a boil, then simmer, uncovered, for 15 to 20 minutes. Strain into a measuring cup and set aside. In a plastic bag, mix the flour and cayenne. Take off 1 tablespoon, and set aside. Place the shrimp in the bag and shake to coat them evenly. Shake the shrimp off to remove excess flour and place on a wire rack for 10 minutes to set the coating.

In a 12-inch skillet, heat the butter until very hot. Add the shrimp in one layer and cook over high heat for 1 minute. Turn and sauté another minute. Transfer the shrimp to a plate as they are cooked and set aside. The shrimp should be slightly undercooked.

Reduce the heat to medium and in the same skillet add the white part of the scallions only, reserving the green tops, and sauté, stirring, for 1 minute. Add the curry powder and the reserved tablespoon of cayenne-flour and stir. Add the reserved shrimp stock and bring to a boil. Lower the heat, add the cream and simmer until bubbly. Return the shrimp to the skillet and cook, stirring, for about 1 minute, or until heated through. Add the lime juice and the green scallion tops and adjust the seasoning.

Spoon the shrimp into the center of a large serving platter and surround them with the rewarmed lentils. Garnish with the cilantro.

New Year's Eve Cotechino with
Green Lentils and New Turnips

SERVES 8

In Italy, particularly in the Umbria region where the small, brown delicious Castellucio lentils are grown, this dish is traditionally eaten on New Year's Eve. The *cotechino*, which is available from Italian butchers and specialty stores, is simmered in a flavorful stock, as are the lentils and tiny new turnips. You will probably not wait for New Year's Eve once you've tasted this combination.

2 1-lb. *cotechino* Italian sausage (see NOTE)	2 sprigs parsley
6 C. unsalted beef stock or water	1 large clove garlic
1 small stalk celery	1½ lbs. very small new turnips, peeled
1 small carrot	Salt and freshly ground black pepper to taste
1 medium onion, peeled and halved vertically (don't remove root end or onion will fall apart)	2 C. dried green or brown lentils, picked over and washed
12 whole black peppercorns	1 Tbs. finely minced parsley
2 sprigs thyme (or ½ tsp. dried thyme)	Strong mustard
	Balsamic vinegar or lemon wedges

In a deep stockpot, bring the sausage, beef stock, celery, carrot, onion, peppercorns, thyme, parsley and garlic to a boil. Lower the heat, cover and simmer for 35 minutes. Lift out the sausage and reserve. Strain and reserve the stock and discard the herbs and vegetables. Return the stock and the *cotechini* to the pot, add the turnips and simmer for about 10 minutes or until the turnips are tender but maintain their shape. Remove the turnips to a heatproof dish, season them with salt and pepper and keep warm in a low oven. Lift out the sausage and keep warm, covered with aluminum foil. Bring the stock to a boil, add the lentils and bring to a boil again, then cover and simmer for 40 to 50 minutes or until the lentils are tender and most of the liquid is absorbed. Season liberally with salt and pepper.

To serve, spoon the lentils on one side of a large platter and spoon the turnips on the other side. Slice the *cotechini* into ½-inch-thick slices and arrange in the center of the platter. Sprinkle with parsley and serve warm with strong mustard for the *cotechini* and a few drops of balsamic vinegar or lemon wedges for the lentils.

NOTE: The Modena specialty sausage with the same uncooked mixture is stuffed into a pig's foot; the smaller front foot is called a *zampino*, the larger one, for large families or parties, is called a *zampone*.

The

Versatile

Grain

and the

Elegant

Bean

374

Grilled Lamb Chops with Fresh Herbs
and Lentils with Leeks

SERVES 6

These bistro-style lentils are wonderful teamed with grilled fish or chicken. We pair them here with lamb chops in a tangy herb sauce made with watercress, mint and rosemary.

Lentils

2 C. dried green or brown lentils, picked over and washed

4 C. water

1 large onion stuck with 2 whole cloves

1 large bay leaf

½ tsp. dried marjoram

Salt to taste

2 Tbs. olive oil

3 leeks, trimmed and washed well, finely chopped—use white part and 1 in. of pale green (about 1¼ C.)

1 large clove garlic, finely minced (1 tsp.)

About ½ lb. or 1 large tomato, skinned and cubed (1 C.)

Salt and freshly ground black pepper to taste

2 Tbs. finely minced parsley

In a 3-quart saucepan, combine the lentils and water. Bring to a boil. Add the onion to the pot along with the bay leaf and the marjoram. Cover and simmer for 15 minutes. Add the salt and continue to simmer for 5 minutes more or until the lentils are tender but maintain their shape. Meanwhile, heat the oil in a medium-size skillet, add the leeks and garlic and sauté over medium heat, stirring often, for about 5 minutes, until the leeks are soft but not brown. Stir in the tomatoes, salt and pepper and bring to a boil. Then cover, lower the heat and simmer for 5 minutes more. Set aside.

When the lentils are tender, lift out and discard the onion with cloves and the bay leaf. Drain the lentils and combine with the leek and tomato mixture. Simmer for 2 minutes to heat through. Stir in the parsley and transfer to a serving dish.

You may cover the dish with foil and rewarm it when the lamb chops are ready.

Lamb Chops

3 lbs. rib or loin lamb chops about 1 in. thick, fat trimmed; allow ½ lb. per person—or use lamb steaks cut from the leg

½ C. dry red wine

⅔ C. tightly packed watercress leaves

⅔ C. tightly packed fresh mint leaves

1 Tbs. fresh rosemary leaves

1 large clove garlic

½ tsp. salt or to taste

¼ tsp. freshly ground black pepper

½ tsp. dry hot English mustard such as Coleman's

¼ C. olive oil

In a nonmetal flat casserole or baking dish, marinate the lamb in the red wine for 10 minutes on each side. Meanwhile, add the watercress, mint, rosemary and garlic to the bowl of a food processor and process until very fine. Add the salt, pepper and mustard and process for a few strokes. Then slowly add the olive oil through the feed tube with the processor on until well blended.

Preheat the broiler or grill. Spoon some of the herb sauce on one side of the lamb and broil or grill 2 or 3 inches from the heat source for 3 minutes (for medium rare). Turn the meat over, add the sauce to the other side and broil for 3 more minutes. Serve with the lentils in the center of the plate and the chops around the outer rim.

Poached Mussels and Red Lentil Salad with an Herb and Shallot Vinaigrette

SERVES 8

Shiny black, like patent leather, poached briny mussels are tucked into a bed of lightly cooked, peppery red lentils, which are simmered in the herbed mussel broth for extra flavor.

Herb and Shallot Vinaigrette
MAKES 1 CUP

3–4 large shallots, finely minced (about 3 Tbs.)
1 tsp. fresh thyme leaves
½ tsp. minced fresh rosemary leaves
¼ C. sherry vinegar

¼ tsp. freshly ground black pepper
Salt to taste
1 Tbs. coarse-grain Dijon-style mustard
½ cup olive oil

In a small bowl, whisk together the shallots, herbs, vinegar, pepper, salt and mustard. Slowly add the olive oil, whisking to incorporate, and set aside.

Mussels

4 C. water
3 slices lemon
4 sprigs flat leaf parsley
2 sprigs thyme
2 cloves garlic, smashed

1 large bay leaf
¼ tsp. whole black peppercorns
2 lbs. medium mussels (about 26 to the lb.), scrubbed with a nylon pad and "beards" pulled off

The

Versatile

Grain

and the

Elegant

Bean

376

In a 5-quart Dutch oven, bring the water, lemon, parsley, thyme, garlic, bay leaf and peppercorns to a boil, lower the heat and cover. Simmer for 5 minutes. Raise the heat and add the mussels. Cover the pan and cook until the mussels open, shaking the pan once or twice. The mussels should open in 3 to 4 minutes. Discard any mussels that don't open. Lift the mussels out with a slotted spoon. Strain the liquid, discarding the garlic, herbs, spices and lemon. Reserve the liquid and add enough water to it to make 5 cups. Put the liquid into a 3-quart saucepan.

Lentils

5 C. reserved mussel stock	2 Tbs. small nonpareil capers, rinsed
2 C. whole dried red lentils, picked	and drained
over and washed	½ C. finely minced parsley
Salt to taste	Romaine lettuce leaves

Bring the mussel stock to a boil in the 3-quart saucepan. Stir in the lentils and bring to a boil again. Then lower the heat and simmer, uncovered, just until the color of the lentils lightens, about 5 to 6 minutes. Add salt to taste. The lentils should be tender but firm. Transfer them to a large bowl and gently stir in ⅔ cup of the reserved vinaigrette along with the capers. Let cool before stirring in the parsley. To serve, line a long platter with romaine lettuce leaves. Spoon the slightly warm lentils in the center and arrange the mussels around one side of the platter, tucking some into the lentils. Trickle remaining vinaigrette into the open mussel shells.

Poached Mussels and Red Lentil Salad

French Lentils with
Arabic Lamb Sausage (Merguez)

SERVES 6

A hearty French Moroccan country dish from an area where the Islamic religion forbids the eating of pork. Lightly spiced lamb sausages are baked over a bed of tiny olive-green lentils with a confetti of cubed sweet turnips and carrots. Serve it with rice and a Moroccan salad of oranges and sweet red onion.

1½ C. dried French green lentils, picked over and washed

5 C. unsalted Chicken Stock, preferably homemade (see page 171)

Bouquet garni, tied in cheesecloth: 4 sprigs parsley, 3 sprigs thyme, 1 small onion, stuck with 2 whole cloves, 1 bay leaf, 1 small carrot, 1 small celery stalk

2 Tbs. butter

4–5 large shallots, finely minced (¼ C.)

1 medium carrot, finely diced into ¼ in. cubes (½ C.)

2 medium turnips, peeled and finely diced into ¼-in. cubes (½ C.)

1 tsp. finely minced fresh rosemary

¼ tsp. freshly ground black pepper

Salt to taste

1 lb. *Merguez*, Arabic lamb sausage (see NOTE)

¼ C. fresh bread crumbs

In a 3-quart saucepan, bring the lentils and the chicken stock to a boil. Add the bouquet garni, lower the heat, and with the lid of the pot slightly ajar, simmer for 15 to 20 minutes or until the lentils are tender, but maintain their shape. Lift out and discard the bouquet garni. Drain the lentils and return the liquid only to the saucepan. Over high heat, reduce the liquid until 1 cup remains, about 15 minutes.

Meanwhile, melt the butter in a medium-size skillet and sauté the shallots over medium low heat for 2 minutes, stirring. Add the carrots and turnips and continue to sauté for 2 to 3 minutes more. Add the rosemary, pepper and salt. Stir the vegetables into the lentils along with the reduced liquid. The lentils can be prepared ahead up to this point and refrigerated up to 1 or 2 days.

When ready to serve, preheat the oven to 375°F. and spoon the lentils into a shallow 2-quart oven-to-table baking dish. Add the uncooked sausage in one layer, sprinkle with the bread crumbs and bake for 40 to 45 minutes, until the lentils are bubbling hot and the sausage is browned.

NOTE: Lamb sausages are available in Middle Eastern and specialty food shops.

The

Versatile

Grain

and the

Elegant

Bean

378

Warm Lentil Salad with Fresh Oregano, Vinegared Red Onions and Smoked Turkey

SERVES 4 TO 6

Crisp, sweet-sour red onions with a bit of pungent oregano and the smoky overtones of the turkey slivers, along with soothing warm aromatic lentils, make an easy-to-fix-ahead company lunch.

1 medium red onion, coarsely diced (1 C.)
3 Tbs. red wine vinegar
Small pinch sugar
1 C. dried green or brown lentils, picked over and washed
2 C. water
1 medium carrot, cut in half
1 small stalk celery, cut in half
1 large onion, stuck with 1 whole clove

1 small bay leaf
5 whole peppercorns
4 sprigs parsley
5 sprigs oregano
Salt and freshly ground black pepper to taste
2 Tbs. olive oil
½ lb. smoked turkey, coarsely diced
Romaine lettuce leaves

Mix the red onion with the vinegar and sugar in a small bowl, and let stand, covered, in the refrigerator until ready to use. (If you choose to prepare well in advance, it will keep for several days.)

Add the lentils to a 3-quart nonstick saucepan along with the water, carrot, celery, onion and clove, and bring to a boil. Tie the bay leaf, peppercorns, parsley and 3 sprigs of oregano (reserving the other 2), in a small square of cheesecloth and add to the pot. Simmer for 20 minutes or until the liquid has been absorbed. Remove and discard the vegetables and the cheesecloth bag. Season with salt and pepper. Add the olive oil. Mince the remaining oregano leaves and stir them in along with the turkey.

Transfer to a serving platter lined with romaine lettuce leaves. Spoon the red onion and vinegar mixture over the top. Stir in before serving to keep the onions crisp. Serve warm.

Syrian Rishta: Lentils with Noodles, Onions and Tomatoes

SERVES 6

In Syria, noodles and lentils are spiced in a most unusual way for a Western palate that expects all pasta dishes to contain oregano or basil rather than allspice and coriander. We think you'll find, as we did, that this Middle Eastern combination is rather pleasing and unusual.

2 Tbs. olive oil	¼ tsp. ground cumin
1 large onion, finely chopped (1 C.)	½ tsp. ground allspice
2–3 cloves garlic, finely minced (2 tsps.)	½ tsp. ground coriander
1 C. green or brown lentils, picked over and washed	Salt and freshly ground black pepper to taste
2 C. unsalted chicken stock	8 oz. tagliatelle (¾-in. wide) or fettuce (½-in. wide) noodles or other noodles of similar width (see NOTE)
3 large plum tomatoes, or drained canned Italian plum tomatoes, coarsely chopped (1 C.)	
2 Tbs. tomato paste	1 tsp. lemon juice
¼ tsp. hot pepper flakes	

Heat the oil in a 5-quart nonstick Dutch oven and sauté the onions and garlic over low heat, stirring constantly for 5 minutes or until the onions are soft and begin to brown. Stir in the lentils and add the chicken stock. Bring to a boil, lower the heat, cover and simmer for 15 to 20 minutes. Then stir in the tomatoes, tomato paste, hot pepper flakes, cumin, allspice, coriander, salt and pepper. Simmer for 10 to 15 minutes more or until the lentils are soft but hold their shape.

Meanwhile, boil and drain the pasta. Transfer the lentils and pasta to a large warm serving bowl. Sprinkle with the lemon juice and toss lightly. Serve hot.

NOTE: *Rishta* or "threads" are thin, ribbonlike fresh homemade pasta.

Lebanese Mejedrah: Lentils, Rice and Crisp Fried Sweet Onions

SERVES 8

Every Middle Eastern country serves some form of lentils and grain, sometimes with rice and sometimes with bulgur. We have also seen this dish spelled as *Mujaddara* and *Mejaddarah,* but whatever the spelling, no rice dish is ever served without a crisp, golden crust that forms on the bottom and then is scraped up and either stirred into the rice, or turned out with the lentils onto a serving platter, with the scrapings from the bottom used as a garnish.

The

Versatile

Grain

and the

Elegant

Bean

380

Crisp Fried Sweet Onions

(Prepare and soak the onions 30 minutes before cooking the rice and fry while rice and lentils are cooking.)

3 large, sweet onions such as Washington State Walla Wallas, Georgia Vidalias or sweet red onions
1 qt. milk

2 C. all-purpose flour
½ tsp. salt or to taste
½ tsp. freshly ground black pepper
Corn oil for frying

Peel and slice the onions into ¼-in. slices and separate them into rings. Place them in a large bowl and cover with the milk. Soak, stirring once or twice, for 30 minutes. Meanwhile, mix the flour, salt and pepper together in a large paper bag. Drain and discard the milk and shake the onions in the flour mixture. Heat 1 inch of oil in a heavy iron skillet to about 375°F. on a deep fry thermometer. Fry the flour-coated onions a few at a time until crisp and golden, about 3 minutes. Drain on paper towels, set them aside and keep warm in a low oven.

Lentils and Rice

6 Tbs. butter
1 medium onion, finely chopped (¾ C.)
1 clove garlic, finely minced (1 tsp.)
1½ C. long grain rice, either converted rice or long grain brown or white basmati rice

3–4 C. Chicken Stock (more stock for brown rice), preferably homemade (see page 171)
Salt and freshly ground black pepper to taste
1 C. dried green or brown lentils, picked over and washed

Melt the butter in a heavy 2½-quart shallow casserole. Add the onions and garlic and sauté over medium heat for 1 minute, stirring until the onions are translucent. Stir in the rice and continue to stir until the grains are coated with the butter, about 2 to 3 minutes. Add the stock and the salt and pepper, and bring to a boil over high heat. Cover the casserole tightly with aluminum foil and reduce the heat as low as possible. You may need to place the casserole over two burners on top of the stove to achieve even heat. Cook for 40 minutes and don't peek until the time is up. (Note that cooking times may vary according to the kind of rice used. See Chart, pages 162–164.) Then remove the foil and fluff the rice with a fork, scraping up the bottom crust and stirring it into the rice.

Meanwhile, in a 3-quart saucepan, cover the lentils with water by about 2 inches. Bring to a boil, then cover and simmer until the lentils are tender, about 25 minutes. Drain and rinse the lentils with hot water. Season and stir into the rice when it's finished, and top with the crisp, fried onions. The rice and lentils can be made ahead, covered loosely with foil and kept warm in a preheated low 250° F. oven until serving time. If that is the case, then fry the onions just before serving.

French Lentils with Caramelized Pearl Onions
and Andouille Sausage

SERVES 6 TO 8

The hot cayenne-spiked Cajun sausage contrasts beautifully with sweet and sour tiny crisp pearl onions and the very unique flavor of the French lentils.

1½ C. dried French green lentils, picked over and washed
4 C. water
2 cloves garlic
1 large onion, stuck with 2 whole cloves
1 medium carrot
1 bay leaf
3 sprigs thyme

1½ C. ½-in. cubes andouille sausage (about ½ lb.—parboil for 5 minutes and drain before cutting into cubes—see NOTE)
½ C. olive oil
⅓ C. white wine vinegar
Salt and freshly ground black pepper to taste
1 Tbs. coarse-grain Dijon-style mustard
¼ C. finely minced parsley

In a 3-quart saucepan, bring the lentils, water, garlic, onion and clove and the carrot to a boil. Lower the heat, tie the bay leaf and thyme together with string and add them to the pot. Cover and simmer for 10 minutes. Add the sausage, stir, simmer for about 15 minutes or more, or until the lentils are tender. Lift out and discard the garlic, onion, carrot, bay leaf and thyme.

Drain the lentils in a colander, transfer them to a bowl and stir in the olive oil. Mix the vinegar, salt and pepper with the mustard and stir into the lentil/sausage mixture. Then gently stir in the parsley. Keep warm in a low oven while preparing the caramelized onions or prepare them while the lentils are simmering.

Caramelized Onions

2 Tbs. olive oil
8 ozs. tiny pearl onions, peeled and trimmed
2 Tbs. balsamic or red wine vinegar

1 tsp. tomato paste
2 Tbs. dry white wine
2 Tbs. dried currants
1½ Tbs. sugar

Heat the oil in a nonstick skillet and add the onions. Sauté, stirring frequently, for about 5 minutes over moderately high heat. Mix the vinegar, tomato paste, wine and currants in a small cup and set aside. Sprinkle the sugar over the onions and continue to cook, shaking the pan, for 1 minute more. Add the vinegar mixture and stir, cooking for 2 to 3 minutes, until a thick glaze forms and the onions are tender but slightly crisp. Stir into the lentil/sausage mixture and serve hot or warm.

NOTE: Parboiling removes some of the fat in the sausage.

The

Versatile

Grain

and the

Elegant

Bean

382

Lima Beans

Large Lima Beans
Phaseolus limensis

Alias. Madagascar, Burma, Rangoon, *habas grandes,* Christmas lima beans (an heirloom variety), *fagioli della Nonna* or "Grandma's beans."

Description. Large, ¾ inch to 1 inch long, creamy white with a very slight green tint. The heirloom Christmas lima is larger, about 1 inch to 1¼ inches long, and plumper than the large lima, with a maroon batiklike pattern on a creamy background.

Characteristics. Smooth, creamy, savory, slightly starchy with a distinctive taste. It grows both as a climbing vine or as a bush variety. Many farmers and home gardeners are partial to the Fordhook variety—also known as "potato lima," for its high yield and excellent flavor. A robust grower, although the seeds are slower to form in their pods than the smaller varieties. The Christmas lima is prized for its chestnutlike flavor as well as its beauty.

Small Lima Beans
Phaseolus lunatus

Alias. Baby limas, sieva beans, butter beans, civet beans, and the Dixie speckled butter beans, also known as calico beans or Florida speckled pole limas.

Description. Small, about ½ inch in length, flat, thinner than its larger cousin. The Dixie speckled butter bean is a bit larger (about ⅝ inch) and more plump with a calico pattern of black and cream. The latter is also more resistant to heat and humidity and grows quite well during the "dog days" in the Deep South.

Characteristics. Contrary to popular belief, the small lima bean is *not* a smaller version of the large lima. Note the separate botanical classification. Its texture is more buttery and the thin skins allow it to cook more quickly. It is also more heat and humidity resistant. It grows as a bush bean or as a pole-type bean.

History. Both the large and the small limas are New World Beans, native to the altiplano in Peru, with origins that can be traced back to about A.D. 1500 and christened "lima" after the capital of Peru. The *Christmas lima* is an old-fashioned bean with a low crop yield, which was probably the reason it was forced out of popularity about 70 years ago. However, it is now being resurrected and marketed again, since its flavor is so unique. The sieva beans are smaller and flatter than the Peruvian varieties, but both were brought to Europe by the Spanish explorers. The slave traders introduced them into Africa, where they are still grown as popular legume crops, since they are basically tropical and subtropical beans and do not grow well in cooler climates.

Traditional Uses. Besides its popularity in South and Central America, as well as in Africa, the lima bean was a great favorite with Native Americans, who cooked it in combination with sweet, fresh corn. This then became the popular colonial dish mispronounced as "succotash," from the Native American word *msickquatash.*

Availability. Fresh in the pod, frozen, dried and canned. Can be found in almost all supermarkets and specialty stores.

Cooking Chart
Pot: 3 qt.

Type of Bean:	Large Lima Beans	Christmas Lima Beans	Small Lima Beans (Sieva)	Dixie Speckled Butter Beans
Amount:	1 C. dried	1 C. dried	1 C. dried	1 C. dried
Cooking Time:	45 minutes	60 minutes	50 to 60 minutes	50 to 60 minutes
Approx. Yield:	2 C.	2 C.	3 C.	3 C.
Instructions and Comments:	Cook with lid ajar. Very foamy. Very tender. Some skins slip off after soaking. They may be skimmed off and discarded.	Some skins slip off. Foamy. Cook with lid ajar. Markings fade and beans take on a rosy hue.	Smooth, tender. Creamy liquid forms as some beans disintegrate.	Foamy, cook with lid ajar. Markings fade a bit and beans turn rosy-hued.

NOTE: *Fresh in pod lima beans.* Amount: 2½ to 3 lbs. fresh in pod equal 2 C. shelled. Also available frozen and in cans in various sizes. Cooking time: 10 minutes if beans are young, longer if older. Yield: Serves 4. Comments: Sweet and tender when young, more mealy when past their prime.

The

Versatile

Grain

and the

Elegant

Bean

384

Lima Bean and Savoy Cabbage Pouches

SERVES 9

A mousse of lima bean purée is lightened with egg whites and dotted with pepperoni sausage, filling a pouch made of crinkled cabbage leaves. The pouches are then steamed and tied with chives and sprigs of opal basil. Try it with roast duck, veal or pork, or serve it alone as an appetizer.

Cabbage

2–2½ lb. head savoy cabbage (or use regular cabbage)

Salt (optional)

With a small, sharp knife, cut out the core of the cabbage about 3 inches deep. Boil water in a deep stockpot or pasta pot and add salt if you wish. Place the whole cabbage, core side up, in the boiling water and parboil for about 10 minutes or until the leaves are pliable. Lift out the cabbage by inserting a two-pronged fork into the core side while supporting the other side of the cabbage with a wide spatula. Drain on paper towels. Peel off 9 of the outer leaves. Turn the leaves over and pare away part of the tough outer center spine. They now form a cuplike shape. Set them aside and prepare the beans.

Beans

1 C. dried large lima beans, soaked and drained

4 C. water

3 sprigs parsley

2 sprigs thyme

1 bay leaf

1 small onion, stuck with 1 whole clove

Salt and freshly ground black pepper to taste

1 large clove garlic, finely minced (1½ tsp.)

2 tsps. coarse-grain mustard

2 tsps. lemon juice

12 thin slices pepperoni sausage, finely diced (¼ C.)

3 egg whites

9 chives

9 small sprigs opal basil

In a 3-quart nonstick saucepan, bring the beans and water to a boil. Lower the heat. Tie the parsley, thyme and bay leaf together with a string and add to the saucepan. Add the onion with the clove, cover and simmer for about 40 to 60 minutes with the lid slightly ajar or until the beans are very tender. Skim and discard any skins that float to the surface. Add the salt and pepper in the last 5 minutes of cooking, then lift out the herb bouquet and the clove-studded onion and discard. Drain the beans and add them to the bowl of a food processor along with the garlic, mustard and lemon juice and process until well puréed. Transfer the purée to a bowl, mix in the diced pepperoni and set aside.

In a separate bowl, beat the egg whites with a beater until stiff, then gently fold one third of the bean purée at a time into the beaten egg whites.

Spoon 2 heaping tablespoons of the bean mixture into the center of each cabbage leaf. Gather it together and tie each one with string about 1 inch from the top, forming the pouches. Up to this point, you may prepare this dish well ahead of time. When ready to serve, place the pouches on a steamer rack and steam for 10 minutes. Then lift out, and cut the strings when they've cooled a bit. Tie a chive where the strings had been, cutting the chive ends diagonally and tucking a small sprig of opal basil into the chive knot. Serve warm.

Pink Cream of Lima Bean Soup with Mint and Sugar Snap Peas

SERVES 4 TO 6

Buttery-textured lima beans are paired with sweet, crisp, sugar snap peas for contrast in this rosy-colored soup. It is cooled with a touch of fresh mint and can be served hot or chilled.

1½ C. dried large lima beans, soaked and drained	Salt and freshly ground black pepper to taste
6 C. unsalted chicken stock	2 Tbs. tomato paste
1 small whole carrot	1 tsp. finely minced lemon peel
1 small stalk celery	⅓ C. heavy cream
1 large clove garlic, roughly chopped (1 tsp.)	3–4 drops Tabasco sauce
3 sprigs parsley	1 Tbs. finely minced fresh mint
1 bay leaf	¼ lb. sugar snap or Chinese snow peas, blanched
2 Tbs. butter	
1 large onion, finely chopped (1 C.)	

In a 5-quart Dutch oven, bring the lima beans, chicken stock, carrot, celery and garlic to a boil, with the pot lid slightly ajar. Then lower the heat, tie the parsley and bay leaf together with a piece of string and add to the pot. Simmer, with the pot lid ajar, for 45 minutes or until the lima beans are very tender. Then discard the bouquet of herbs, along with the carrot and celery. Skim and discard any skins that float to the surface.

Meanwhile, melt the butter in a small skillet and add the onions, salt and pepper. Sauté over medium low heat for 10 minutes. Do not let the onions brown. Scoop out a ladle full of broth and add to the onions. Then stir in the tomato paste. Add this mixture to the soup. Add the lemon peel, cream and Tabasco and simmer for 5 minutes.

Just before serving, stir in the mint and taste for additional salt and pepper. Serve the soup hot or chilled with five blanched sugar peas arranged on the surface of each serving like the spokes of a wheel.

The

Versatile

Grain

and the

Elegant

Bean

386

Lima Bean Soup with Kielbasa
and Broccoli Rape

SERVES 8

Tender, creamy large lima beans and slightly bitter broccoli rape are set off with garlicky bites of sausage in a soup that can well be a whole meal.

1 C. dried large lima beans, soaked and drained

8 C. unsalted Beef Stock, preferably homemade (see page 172)

4 Tbs. olive oil

3 large onions, coarsely chopped (about 2 C.)

¾ lb. kielbasa, cut into bite-size pieces

2–3 large tomatoes or equivalent canned Italian tomatoes cut into eighths (about 2 C.)

1½ lbs. broccoli rape, trimmed of tough stems (about ¾ lb. trimmed)

¼–⅛ tsp. hot pepper flakes

Salt to taste

Put the drained lima beans in a 4½-quart heavy-duty Dutch oven along with the beef stock. Bring to a boil, lower the heat and skim off and discard any foam or bean skins that float to the surface. Cover the pot with the lid slightly ajar and simmer for 15 minutes.

Meanwhile, in a large skillet, heat the olive oil and sauté the onions, stirring frequently over medium high heat, for about 8 to 10 minutes or until the onions just become golden. Add them to the beans and continue to simmer for 30 minutes more. Add the kielbasa and tomatoes, bring to a boil, then lower the heat and simmer for 15 more minutes.

Meanwhile, cut the trimmed broccoli rape into a ½-inch chiffonade. Add to the pot, 4 cups at a time, stirring down after each addition. Add the hot pepper flakes and salt and simmer for 30 more minutes. Serve hot or refrigerate and rewarm.

Warm Lima Bean and Ham Salad with Carrots and Honey-Mustard

SERVES 6

Warm, large lima beans are scented with herbs and cubes of sautéed baked ham, then sweetened with carrots, spiked with honey-mustard and green scallions. It makes a hearty winter salad luncheon or a light dinner that takes under 45 minutes to prepare.

1½ C. dried large lima beans, soaked and drained
1 small onion, stuck with 1 whole clove
1 small red dried hot chile such as Japonés
1 tsp. dried thyme
1 tsp. dried oregano, preferably Greek
Salt and freshly ground black pepper to taste

2 Tbs. olive oil
1 lb. baked ham steak, cut into bite-size pieces (about 2 C.)
⅓ C. sherry vinegar
1 heaping Tbs. honey-mustard
3 large carrots (or ½ lb.), shredded (2 C.)
4–5 large scallions, green tops only, diagonally sliced (about ¾ C.)
2 Tbs. canola oil
Few leaves romaine lettuce

To a 3-quart saucepan, add the lima beans, along with the onion and clove, hot chile, thyme, oregano and tepid water to cover by 1½ inches. Bring to boil, then cover the pan with the lid slightly ajar and simmer for about 30 to 40 minutes or until the beans are tender but hold their shape. Season with salt and pepper the last 5 minutes of cooking. Remove and discard the onion and clove and the hot chile.

Meanwhile, in a medium-size skillet, heat the olive oil over medium heat, add the ham and, stirring often, sauté for about 6 to 7 minutes to brown the ham slightly. When the beans are cooked, drain them, put them into a large bowl and add the ham. Do not stir. Return the unwashed skillet to the stove and deglaze the pan with the vinegar. Simmer for 1 minute and stir in the honey-mustard, stirring constantly until dissolved. Then spoon over the ham and beans along with the shredded carrots and the scallions. Pour the canola oil over all, then combine gently. Cooked lima beans are fragile, so too much mixing breaks them up. Serve warm or at room temperature and garnish with a few romaine leaves tucked around the salad.

The

Versatile

Grain

and the

Elegant

Bean

388

Baby Lima Beans with Thirty-Four Garlic Cloves

SERVES 6 TO 8

If you love garlic, you will love these beans! Although they are cooked gently with many cloves of garlic, most of it is discarded and only two cloves are sautéed and added at the end. The gentle cooking greatly tames the garlic. This is a bean dish that would be a delicious choice for a rack or leg of lamb.

2	C. dried baby lima beans, soaked and drained	34	cloves garlic (about 3 ozs. or 1 whole head)
4	whole cloves	1	tsp. salt or to taste
2	medium shallots	2	Tbs. olive oil
2	small red whole dried hot chiles such as Japonés	½	tsp. freshly ground black pepper
1	tsp. dried thyme	½	C. coarsely chopped flat leaf parsley

In a 5-quart nonstick Dutch oven, bring the beans and water to cover by 2 inches to a boil. Skim off any foam, stick two cloves into each of the shallots, and add them to the beans along with the chiles and thyme. Bring to a boil again, cover with the lid slightly ajar and simmer the beans for 30 minutes.

Tie thirty-two of the cloves of garlic in a cheesecloth bag for easy removal later on, and finely mince the remaining two cloves of garlic and set them aside. Add the bag of garlic to the beans and continue to simmer for 25 to 30 minutes. Stir in the salt during the last 5 minutes of cooking. Meanwhile, heat the olive oil in a small skillet, add the minced garlic and sauté over very low heat until the garlic is tender, about 2 to 3 minutes. Do not let the garlic brown or it will be bitter.

When the beans are tender, remove and discard the bag of garlic, the shallots with cloves and the hot chiles. Drain the beans, reserving ½ cup of the liquid, and return the beans to the pot. Stir in the black pepper, the sautéed garlic, the parsley and only enough of the reserved liquid to moisten the beans. Warm the beans gently and spoon into a serving dish, or prepare ahead of time, cover and refrigerate. To reheat the beans, add more of the reserved liquid if the beans seem dry. Taste for additional salt before serving.

Cholent:
Lima Bean, Beef and Barley Stew
SERVES 6

Cholent is a complete "dinner in a dish," commonly served by Jews who strictly follow the religious dictates that forbid cooking on the Saturday sabbath. The *cholent* is usually baked in a heavy earthenware pot and it goes into the oven on Friday at sundown when the sabbath begins, and then cooks slowly for 24 hours until sundown the following day, the end of the sabbath. Obviously, this ancient dish was designed well before the energy crunch. In this speeded-up version, only the beans are soaked overnight and the baking takes under 3 hours.

1 C. large lima beans, soaked and drained	1–2 cloves garlic, coarsely chopped (about 2 tsps.)
3 lbs. beef short ribs	6 C. Chicken Stock, preferably homemade (see page 171)
1 tsp. salt or to taste	½ lb. baking potatoes, peeled and cut into 1-in. cubes (1 C.)
¼ tsp. freshly ground black pepper	
1 tsp. sweet paprika	¾ C. pearl barley, rinsed several times and drained
¼ tsp. ground ginger	
2 Tbs. chicken fat	
About ¾ lb. onions, thinly sliced (3 C.)	

In a 3-quart saucepan, cover the lima beans with tepid water and bring to a boil. Drain, cover again with fresh tepid water and bring to a boil a second time, then lower the heat and simmer for 20 minutes. Skim the bean skins from the surface and discard. Keep the beans in their cooking liquid until needed and set them aside.

Place the beef on a plate. Mix the salt, pepper, paprika and ginger together and spread over the surface of the meat. In a 10-inch cast-iron skillet, heat the chicken fat and brown the meat over medium high heat for about 5 to 8 minutes, turning on all sides. Lift the meat out and transfer it to a 7-quart heavy Dutch oven. Add the onions and garlic to the cast-iron skillet, lower the heat and sauté for 8 to 10 minutes, until the onions are brown and soft. Sprinkle with additional salt and pepper and add to the Dutch oven.

Add 2 cups of the chicken stock to the skillet, bring to a boil, stirring in the brown bits, and pour over the meat and onions in the Dutch oven. Add the potatoes and the barley. Drain the beans, reserving the liquid, and add to the pot. Measure the bean liquid and add enough chicken stock to make 6 cups, reserving any extra stock if needed. Pour over the ingredients in the Dutch oven. Cover and bring to a boil on top of the stove, then lower the heat and simmer for 30 minutes.

Preheat the oven to 300° F., then place the covered pot in the oven and bake for 2½ hours, undisturbed. The consistency should be thick with very little liquid. Check after 1½ hours to see if additional liquid is needed. If so, add ½ cup more chicken stock. Then remove the lid, raise the oven temperature to 500° F. and bake,

The
Versatile
Grain
and the
Elegant
Bean

390

uncovered, for 10 to 15 minutes more, until the surface is browned and a crust has formed. Serve directly from the pot.

NOTE: If you prepare the cholent well in advance, add an additional cup of chicken stock and reheat, covered, in a preheated 300° F. oven for 30 to 40 more minutes or until heated through.

Christmas Lima Beans with Whole Hominy
(An Upscale Succotash)

SERVES 8

This is a succotash you have probably never eaten before. It does have a traditional mixture of corn and beans, but here the chestnutlike flavor of Christmas lima beans is combined with the intense corn taste of whole hominy and then tempered with a bit of cream and perked with Tabasco.

1-lb. can whole white or yellow hominy, drained and rinsed
3 C. cooked Christmas lima beans (or substitute large lima beans—see Chart, page 384)
3 Tbs. butter
1 medium onion, finely chopped (¾ C.)

1 medium green pepper, finely diced (¾ C.)
⅔ C. heavy cream
3–4 drops Tabasco sauce
Salt and freshly ground black pepper to taste

Mix the hominy and cooked beans together gently in a bowl and set aside. Melt the butter slowly in a large skillet, add the onions and sauté for 2 minutes over medium heat. Then add the green pepper. Sauté, stirring occasionally, until wilted, about 10 minutes. Lower the heat, add the cream and Tabasco and heat slowly until the cream bubbles around the edges of the skillet. Do not boil. Season with salt and pepper, and add the reserved hominy and beans. Stir gently, cover and warm over low heat for 10 minutes, stirring occasionally, to coat the beans. Transfer to a shallow serving dish and serve hot.

Dixie Speckled Butter Beans with
Pork Chops and Mustard Greens

SERVES 6

Creamy-textured buttery beans are mixed with sautéed vegetables and slightly bitter mustard greens, then topped with lean pork chops and an onion-apple sauce perked with balsamic vinegar—an amalgam of palate-teasing tastes.

Beans and Mustard Greens

1 C. Dixie speckled butter beans, soaked and drained (or substitute small lima beans)	1 large onion, finely diced (1 C.)
1 bay leaf	1 medium green pepper, finely diced (1 C.)
6 whole peppercorns, tied in cheesecloth	3 stalks celery, finely diced (about 1 C.)
2 strips bacon	1 tsp. sugar
12 C. coarsely chopped, washed but not dried, trimmed mustard greens (about 1 lb.)	2 plum tomatoes, coarsely diced (about ¾ C.)
Pinch hot pepper flakes	Salt and freshly ground black pepper to taste

In a 3-quart saucepan, place the beans, bay leaf and bag of peppercorns with water to cover. Bring to a boil, then lower the heat and simmer for 1 hour with the lid slightly ajar. Add boiling water if necessary in order to keep the beans covered as they cook.

Meanwhile, fry the bacon slowly in a 10-inch nonstick skillet, turning frequently until it is brown and crisp. Drain on paper towels, then crumble and reserve. Pour off most of the bacon fat from the skillet, reserving 2 tablespoons.

Add the mustard greens to the skillet. Stir, add the hot pepper flakes, cover and steam for 5 minutes. Remove the greens to a bowl and set aside. Wipe out the skillet, add and heat 1 tablespoon of the bacon fat, then add the onions, pepper and celery and sauté, stirring occasionally, for 5 to 8 minutes over medium heat until the vegetables begin to brown. Stir in the sugar, tomatoes, salt and pepper. Cover and simmer for 5 minutes. Then transfer the vegetables to a medium-size bowl and set aside.

When the beans are tender, drain them, discard the bay leaf and peppercorns, add salt and stir into the pepper/onion mixture. Taste for seasoning, then spoon into the bottom of a large, shallow oven-to-table casserole. Arrange the greens on top, scatter the crumbled bacon over and set aside.

The

Versatile

Grain

and the

Elegant

Bean

392

Pork Chops

2 lbs. center-cut rib pork chops,
  trimmed of fat (about 6 ozs. per
  chop)
1 Tbs. reserved bacon fat
1 large onion, thinly sliced into rings
  (about 2 C.)

1 large green tart apple, peeled and
  coarsely diced (1 C.)
1 tsp. finely chopped fresh sage
  Salt and freshly ground black
  pepper to taste
1 tsp. balsamic vinegar

Preheat the oven to 350° F. In the same nonstick skillet that you've been using, sear the pork chops on both sides for about 1 minutes per side. As they brown, transfer them in one layer to the casserole. Add the remaining bacon fat to the skillet and sauté the onion rings for 2 minutes. Stir in the apples, sage, salt and pepper. Cover and simmer for 5 minutes until the onion is wilted and the apples are soft. Stir in the vinegar and top each pork chop with about 1 tablespoon of this mixture. Place in the preheated oven and bake for 15 or 20 minutes until the pork is cooked through but not overcooked. In the last 10 minutes of cooking, cover the beans with foil and rewarm in the oven.

Serve each pork chop with some of the beans and mustard greens on the side on warmed dinner plates.

Fresh Baby Lima Beans with Pancetta, Zucchini and Rosemary

SERVES 4 TO 6

We first ate fresh lima beans Neapolitan-style in the little town of Posillipo, near Naples, that became famous because it was the birthplace of Sophia Loren. However, we think the town should be equally famous for its food. But, then again, as Mel says, "Sophia is quite a dish!"

½ **C. finely diced pancetta (Italian unsmoked bacon)**

1 **small clove garlic, finely minced (½ tsp.)**

1 **medium onion, coarsely chopped (¾ C.)**

½ **C. dry white wine**

2–3 **large plum tomatoes, fresh or canned, coarsely diced (1 C.)**

2 **tsps. tomato paste**

Salt and freshly ground black pepper to taste

1⅓ **C. shelled fresh baby lima beans, or 9-oz. package frozen baby limas, partially defrosted**

1 **Tbs. coarsely chopped fresh rosemary leaves**

1 **large or 2 small zucchini, cut into julienne (2 C.)**

1 **Tbs. grated Parmesan cheese**

In a 12-inch skillet, sauté the pancetta slowly for 3 to 4 minutes. Then stir in the garlic and onions and cook over medium low heat for 4 to 5 minutes more. Add the wine, raise the heat and cook until the wine evaporates, about 3 to 4 minutes. Stir in the tomatoes, tomato paste, salt and pepper, lower the heat and simmer for 5 minutes. Add the lima beans and rosemary. Stir, cover and simmer for about 5 minutes. Then add the zucchini and cook until the zucchini is tender but crisp, about 3 to 4 minutes more. Transfer to a serving platter and sprinkle the surface with cheese. Serve hot.

The

Versatile

Grain

and the

Elegant

Bean

394

Mung Beans

Vigna radiata

Alias. Green grams, black grams, split golden grams, *sabat moong* (whole), *moong dal* (hulled).

Description. Small (¼ inch), round-squarish shape. The skin is usually olive-green but some varieties are yellow-brown or black. One variety of black, called *urad* or *kali urad* is found in Africa, the West Indies and Asia, but when it is split and hulled, it becomes cream-colored.

Characteristics. These sweet-flavored pods of the mung bean are eaten as a green vegetable when they're young and tender. The dried beans are also used whole, hulled or split. When hulled, they're a pale yellow, referred to as *moong dal* in India, and when left whole in their hull, *sabat moong,* and their color is green.

History. The mung bean is native to India, where it was first cultivated about 1500 B.C., and then quickly spread to China, where it became a favorite.

Traditional Uses. The people of China and the Philippines favor the use of mung bean sprouts. In India they are puréed and blended with ghee (clarified butter), as well as being ground into flour and used in a variety of dishes. In China and Japan, the starch in the flour is used to make a "pasta" called cellophane or shining noodles, bean threads or *saifun* in Japanese. Sold dry, these translucent gossamer threads must be briefly soaked in hot water before using them—or they can be added dry to cooked soups.

Mung beans can also be sprouted, adding five times more food value, with an added benefit of easier digestion, since the starches found in the beans are broken down into simple sugars during germination. We have given directions for sprouting on page 278.

Availability. Dried whole beans, fresh sprouts in the supermarket produce section, Chinese and Indian markets. Bean thread noodles are usually found in Asian specialty shops.

Cooking Chart

Type of Bean:	Mung Beans	Bean Thread Noodles or Shining Noodles	Mung Bean Sprouts
Amount:	1 C. dried	4-oz. package	1 C.
Cooking Time:	60 minutes	20 minutes	Blanch for 30 seconds and refresh under cold water.
Approx. Yield:	2 C.	4 C.	
Comments:	Foams up at first.		

Vietnamese Mung Bean Thread Noodles with Pork, Shrimp and Fresh Mint

SERVES 4

Hot, sweet, cool and pungent all at once, this dish is attractive to serve and easy to prepare. It's a favorite of ours on warm summer evenings.

Honey Lime Sauce

4 **medium limes**
2 **tsps. light mild honey**

3 **Tbs. light soy sauce**
¼–½ **tsp. dried hot pepper flakes**

Finely mince the peel of 1 lime, cut another lime into wedges for garnish and reserve and squeeze the juice of 3 limes. In a small bowl, mix the lime juice and minced peel, honey, soy sauce and hot pepper flakes and stir until the honey dissolves. Set aside to develop flavor.

Bean Thread Noodles

4 **ozs. uncooked bean thread noodles**
2 **tsps. oriental sesame oil**

Fill a 7-quart pot with water and bring to a boil. Stir in the noodles and shut off the heat. Let the noodles soak for about 20 minutes or until they become transparent.

The

Versatile

Grain

and the

Elegant

Bean

396

Drain in a colander, rinsing them well with cold water. Cut the noodles into 6-inch lengths for easier handling, since they are very slippery when cooked. Transfer them to a large bowl and toss with the oil to prevent them from sticking together. Set aside.

Pork and Shrimp

1 Tbs. corn or peanut oil
½ lb. lean ground pork
1 large clove garlic, finely minced (1½ tsps.)
¼ lb. small whole shrimp, peeled, or large shrimp peeled and cut in half lengthwise

2 scallions, thinly sliced, cut diagonally (½ C.)
6 romaine lettuce leaves, shredded
6–8 sprigs mint

In a 12-inch skillet, heat the oil and add the pork and garlic. Stir constantly over medium high heat for about 3 minutes, until the pork is cooked through. Add the shrimp and cook, stirring constantly, just until the shrimp become opaque, about 30 seconds to 1 minute more. Remove the skillet from the heat and stir in the reserved noodles and the honey-lime sauce and mix well to combine. Spoon onto a large serving platter and scatter the scallions over the surface. Place the shredded lettuce on the outer rim of the platter and tuck in the reserved lime wedges. Pull off the mint leaves and scatter them over all. The lettuce is eaten with the noodles as a crisp and cooling part of the dish.

Mung Bean Sprouts with Bean Curd, Black Beans and Japanese Ginger Sauce

SERVES 4

When it's too hot to cook, try this Japanese-inspired, dramatically attractive salad. Snowy cubes of bean curd are tossed with shiny black beans and needle-thin mung bean sprouts. The fresh, sprightly ginger sauce will perk up the most wilted appetite. It's a good salad to serve with chicken teriyaki.

Japanese Ginger Sauce
MAKES ⅓ CUP

¼ C. Japanese rice vinegar
1 Tbs. mirin (sweet Japanese rice wine)

1 Tbs. sugar
1 Tbs. finely minced ginger

In a small glass or plastic bowl, mix the vinegar, mirin, sugar and ginger and let stand for 15 minutes while preparing the salad.

1½ C. cooked, drained, black beans
(either cook ½ C. dried beans or
use canned beans, rinsed and
drained well)

1 tsp. oriental sesame oil

½ lb. firm bean curd (tofu), dried well
on paper towels and cut into ¾-in.
cubes

1 C. mung bean sprouts, dried well
on paper towels (about ¼ lb.)

1 large mushroom, preferably fresh
shiitake, sliced paper-thin

1 tsp. toasted sesame seeds

1 large scallion, finely sliced, (2 Tbs.)

1 Tbs. coarsely chopped cilantro

In a small bowl, mix the beans with the sesame oil. Spread the beans out on a flat platter and add the bean curd and toss very gently so as not to break the curd. Scatter the bean sprouts over the top, then the sliced mushrooms. Spoon the ginger sauce over all. Then sprinkle on the sesame seeds and scallions and top with the cilantro. Serve cold or at room temperature.

Mung Beans and Potato Curry

SERVES 6

This is a gentle curry made with mild Italian chile instead of the more fiery Indian or Mexican varieties. Try it with *roti*, Indian Barley Flour Bread (see page 38), and a mango chutney for a vegetarian feast.

3 Tbs. butter

1 medium onion, coarsely chopped
(⅔ C.)

1 Tbs. coarsely chopped peeled
ginger

¼ C. raisins

1 tsp. ground coriander

1 tsp. ground turmeric

1 tsp. ground cumin

¼ tsp. ground mace
Salt to taste and a few grinds
black pepper

2 Tbs. finely minced long green
Italian chile (about ¾ of a 3- to
4-in. chile, sometimes called Long
Asian or Fushimi Green)

3–4 large plum tomatoes, fresh or
canned, peeled and cubed roughly
(about 1 C.)

1 C. plain yogurt

12 very small new potatoes, cooked in
salted water and peeled (about 1
lb.)

2 C. cooked mung beans, drained
(see Chart, page 396)

1 Tbs. coarsely chopped cilantro

The

Versatile

Grain

and the

Elegant

Bean

398

Heat the butter in a 12-inch skillet and sauté the onions, ginger and raisins for 5 minutes over low heat, stirring frequently. Stir in the coriander, turmeric, cumin, mace, salt, pepper and chile, and cook for 1 to 2 minutes more. Add the tomatoes and bring to a boil. Then, lower the heat to very low and stir in the yogurt. Simmer, uncovered, over very low heat for 5 minutes. Then add the cooked potatoes and the mung beans and continue to simmer, covered, over very low heat for 10 more minutes, stirring occasionally. Transfer to a serving dish and garnish with cilantro.

Vietnamese Lettuce Bundles with Mung Bean Thread Noodles, Basil and Mint

SERVES 6 TO 8

A fiery hot (for some) or mild sauce (for others) lets you adjust the heat as you wish with additional oriental hot chile oil. Soft leaf lettuce encloses slivers of marinated pork and mung bean threads and a few fresh basil and mint leaves. Double or triple the recipe for an interesting finger food for a buffet.

Sesame and Garlic Hot Sauce

1 small red whole dried hot chile such as Japonés	¼ C. oriental sesame oil
	¼ tsp. sugar
5 Tbs. rice wine vinegar	1 tsp. finely minced lemon peel
5 Tbs. tamari (soy sauce)	2–3 drops hot chile oil
3–4 cloves garlic	

Discard the stem of the chile and place the chile in a blender, blending just enough to crush it. Add the remaining ingredients and blend well. Transfer to a medium-size bowl and set aside.

Pork and Bean Thread Filling

1½ lbs. lean center-cut pork chops with bone	12 large Boston or other soft lettuce leaves
1½ C. water	12 small sprigs mint
8 ozs. mung bean thread noodles	12 medium basil leaves, preferably smaller-leaf French basil
1 tsp. oriental sesame oil	

Cut the meat from the bone of the pork chops, reserving the bones. Trim off the fat and slice the meat into very thin slivers. Set the meat aside. To a medium-size saucepan, add the bones and water, and bring to a boil. Skim the surface, lower the heat and simmer the bones for 20 minutes. Then remove the bones and discard. Add the pork slivers and simmer for 6 to 7 minutes. Transfer the pork slivers with a slotted spoon to the sesame garlic hot sauce, stir and marinate for 30 minutes. Skim and reserve the broth.

In a 7-quart pot, boil a large quantity of water, add the noodles, then turn off the heat and let them soak in the water for 20 minutes or until they are transparent. Then drain well in a colander, cut into 6-inch lengths, put into a large bowl and toss with the sesame oil and ½ cup of the reserved pork broth. Set the noodles aside.

When ready to serve, transfer the pork slivers from the sauce into a bowl, using a slotted spoon and reserving the sauce for dipping.

Lay the lettuce leaves out on a work surface, and spoon 1 or 2 tablespoons of noodles and pork onto each leaf. Top with a few mint leaves and a basil leaf. Roll into bundles, turning in the sides to enclose and lay them, seam side down, on a serving platter. Repeat until the pork is used up. If any noodles are left, serve in separate bowls. Spoon the sauce into very small dishes, one for each person. Add chile oil for those who wish more heat. Dip the lettuce bundles into the sauce, pouring any remaining sauce over the reserved noodles.

The

Versatile

Grain

and the

Elegant

Bean

400

Peanuts

Arachis hypolgaea

Alias. Monkey nuts, groundnuts, *erdnüsse, cacahuètes, maní, ngubba,* goobers, anchics, earth nuts, pindars.

Description. Tan, thin-netted pod, which usually contains two seeds with a papery brownish-red skin, within which rests the oval creamy-tan "nut." The sizes vary—the small Spanish and Valencia nuts are rounder and smaller and are used primarily for peanut butter. The larger oval Virginia variety is usually roasted in the shell or is shelled.

Characteristics. In spite of its unusual growing habits, the peanut looks like the common garden pea when it stands in the fields. But then, after it has flowered and after pollination has taken place, the plant bends down to the earth, where the pods are forced underground and where they finally mature.

History. We probably associate former President Jimmy Carter with the peanut in the United States, since growing it had been a family business in Georgia long before his presidency. In fact, the Democratic delegates to the convention that nominated him carried signs that read, "Make the peanut our national tree!" Well, the peanut does not grow on trees and it's not really a nut, but a legume, as we all probably know.

Although the peanut is over 2,000 years old, it was first introduced by the Portuguese slave traders who brought it to Africa, supposedly from Brazil, where they had found it growing. It took hold to become a cheap, nourishing food crop.

However, long before this time, in ancient Peru pots of peanuts were buried with the dead for sustenance on their long journey into the next world. From Peru, peanuts probably traveled through the trade routes from hot Western Hemisphere countries to the East Indies and the Philippines.

In our own colonies, Thomas Jefferson is known to have grown peanuts during the eighteenth century, but it wasn't until the nineteenth century that the peanut became a leading and important crop in North America.

In the twentieth century, *peanut butter* was promoted at the St. Louis World Fair of 1904 as a health food, and it took off to the delight of generations of children who seemed to have grown up primarily nourished by the stuff. Actually, our Latin American ancestors were mixing ground peanuts with honey many centuries ago, possibly the precursor to our modern peanut butter.

The

Elegant

Bean

Later in this century, George Washington Carver became one of the major promoters of the peanut when he developed more than three hundred different uses for it.

Traditional Uses. In Africa and Indonesia it is used to thicken sauces and soups and the whole peanut is an essential ingredient in Indonesian and Chinese cuisine. One of the primary stews in Africa, for example, is called "groundnut stew."

Peanut oil is another product that is produced on a large scale and used in China, India, Africa and the Americas. Its high smoking point (450° F.) plus the fact that it has 50 percent monounsaturated fat and 30 percent polyunsaturated fat make it a so-called cholesterol lowerer. The peanut itself is high in fat (50 percent) and therefore it easily becomes rancid unless it is closed airtight and refrigerated. Peanuts can be stored this way for 6 months in the shell and 3 months when hulled.

In the United States, the peanut is eaten mostly as a snack food treat and is synonymous with the circus, a visit to the zoo or the ball game. Peanut butter, of course, as we've mentioned above, is also a best-seller, sometimes eaten mixed with sugar as peanut brittle or mixed with popcorn as Cracker Jack or blended in many combinations with chocolate. The nuts are also eaten roasted in oil and "dry-roasted," salted, honey-coated, and unsalted. In the South, where peanuts are grown, they are harvested and immediately boiled in their pods in salted water and sold at roadside stands.

Availability. *Everywhere!!*

THE INTERNATIONAL LEGUME

The Peanut by Any Other Name...

Spanish	*Maní*
French	*Cacahuète*
German	*Erdnuss*
Swedish	*Jordnöt*
Arabic	*Fūl Sūdāni*
Dutch	*Aardnost*
Italian	*Arachide*
Portuguese	*Amendorm*
Russian	*Zemlianoí Orékh*
Japanese	*Rakkasei*
Chinese	*Lu Huo Sheng*

Ham and Peanut Butter Puffs

MAKES 32 PUFFS

A tiny bit of leftover ham makes magic when mixed with peanut butter and egg whites for a quick, unusual hors d'oeuvre.

8 slices thin white bread, crusts trimmed and cut into triangles
½ C. finely chopped baked ham (about 2 ozs.)
½ C. chunky peanut butter

⅛ tsp. Tabasco sauce
¾ tsp. dry hot English mustard
1 Tbs. finely minced fresh chives
2 egg whites

Preheat the oven to 350° F. Place the bread triangles on a baking sheet and set aside. In a small bowl, mix together the ham, peanut butter, Tabasco, mustard and chives with a wooden spoon. In another bowl, beat the egg whites with a beater until stiff, then fold into the ham and peanut butter mixture. Spoon about 1 teaspoon onto each bread triangle and bake for 20 minutes, until crisp. Serve hot.

Indonesian Beef Satay with Peanut and Ginger Hot Sauce

SERVES 6

The master satay chef of Indonesia is the street vendor who carries his kitchen on a shoulder yoke. This "kitchen" is called a *pikulan* and it not only contains all his equipment but also tiny lanterns for night cooking, as well as little tinkling bells to herald his approach. Bite-size, marinated pieces of either beef or pork, shrimp or goat are threaded onto thin disposable bamboo sticks and eaten right off the skewer with a spicy peanut sauce.

Beef

1½ lbs. lean round steak, cut into 1-in. cubes
2 large cloves garlic, finely chopped (about 1 Tbs.)
½ tsp. ground coriander
½ tsp. caraway seeds, ground in a spice or coffee mill
¼ tsp. ground cardamom
2 Tbs. finely grated onion
1 Tbs. dry sherry
¼ tsp. hot pepper flakes

2 Tbs. dark brown sugar
2 Tbs. tamari or light soy sauce
1 Tbs. creamy peanut butter (preferably unsalted)
1 Tbs. lemon juice
1 tsp. finely minced ginger
⅛ tsp. freshly ground black pepper
Peanut and Ginger Hot Sauce (see recipe below)
Hot cooked rice

Thread the cubes of beef on bamboo skewers, allowing four per skewer. Set the skewers into a nonmetal flat dish, such as a gratin dish. Combine the remaining ingredients except the hot sauce and the rice in a small bowl and pour the marinade over the skewers. Cover tightly and refrigerate. After 12 hours, turn the skewers over and spoon the marinade on the other side and continue to marinate for 12 more hours.

When ready to cook, lift the skewers out of the marinade and prepare either a grill or a hibachi. When coals are glowing, grill skewers for 3 to 4 minutes on each side, basting with the marinade. Or place the skewers in a preheated broiler and broil on the top rack, close to the source of heat, for the same amount of time. The meat should be pink in the center and the outside slightly crusty and glazed from the brown sugar. Serve with individual bowls of peanut and ginger hot sauce, which can also be prepared in advance, refrigerated and kept for a month. Accompany the skewers of beef with bowls of hot rice.

Peanut and Ginger Hot Sauce

MAKES 1¼ CUPS

2 thin scallions, finely chopped (about ¼ C.)

2 large cloves garlic, finely chopped (2 tsps.)

1 Tbs. finely chopped ginger

1 Tbs. oriental sesame oil

3 Tbs. tamari or light soy sauce

1 Tbs. mild honey

1½ Tbs. rice wine vinegar

2 tsps. hot chile oil, found in oriental stores and supermarkets

½ C. creamy peanut butter (preferably unsalted)

1 Tbs. canola or peanut oil

⅓ C. hot water, plus additional if desired

Put all the ingredients into a blender and blend until smooth. The sauce will be thick. If you wish to dilute it a bit, add 1 to 2 tablespoons more hot water.

Whole Wheat Peanut Butter and Prune Cookies

MAKES ABOUT 32 COOKIES

These homely nostalgic childhood cookies are made with two kinds of peanut butter, smooth and chunky, with a shiny black prune tucked into the top. They'll remind you of your after-school snack with a glass of milk when you were a kid. Make them when you need the comfort of reminiscing.

The

Versatile

Grain

and the

Elegant

Bean

404

Peanut Butter Cookies

¼ lb. soft butter	1 C. whole wheat flour
½ C. sugar	1 C. all-purpose flour
1 egg	¼ tsp. salt or to taste
1½ tsps. vanilla extract	½ tsp. baking powder
½ C. smooth peanut butter	⅓ C. milk

In the bowl of a food processor, cream the butter and sugar until light and fluffy. Add the egg and vanilla, then the peanut butter and process until well incorporated. In a separate medium-size bowl, whisk together the dry ingredients. Add to the food processor, one third at a time, and mix well. Then add the milk and process until well blended. Turn out onto a piece of foil, wrap and chill for 2 hours. Prepare the topping.

Topping

¼ C. chunky-style peanut butter	1 Tbs. hot water
½ C. light brown sugar	8 pitted prunes, cut into quarters
2 tsps. light corn syrup	

In a small bowl, using a wooden spoon, beat together all the ingredients, except for the prunes, until a thick paste is made. Cover and refrigerate while the cookies chill. Both parts may be made a day or two ahead.

Preheat the oven to 400° F. and lightly butter two baking sheets. Pinch off pieces of the dough and, using your hands, roll them into 1-inch balls. Place on the baking sheets about 2 inches apart and, with your thumb, make a depression in the center of each cookie. If the outer rim cracks too much, just smooth it over a bit with your fingers. Bake for 7 minutes, then remove from the oven. Spoon a scant ½ teaspoon of topping into each depression and gently press one quarter of a prune into the topping. Return the cookies to the oven and continue to bake for 8 to 10 minutes more or until the cookies are lightly golden. Transfer them to a wire rack to cool.

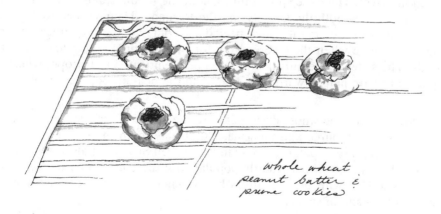

whole wheat peanut butter & prune cookies

Dried Peas

Pisum sativum

Whole Dried Peas

Alias. Dried marrowfats, field peas.

Description. ⅜ to ¼ inch in size, with wrinkled skin, round greenish-gray in color.

Characteristics. Whole dried peas are a fair substitute for fresh shell peas, though they have an earthier sweet flavor rather than the delicate flavor of the fresh. The field pea is the variety that is grown specifically to be used in the dry form.

Split Peas—Green and Yellow

Description. Green split peas are peeled and split in half. They are quite smooth and have a bright green color. Yellow split peas are exactly the same except for the color.

Characteristics. Split peas, both green and yellow, do not maintain their shape when cooked. The yellows also have a more intense, earthy flavor.

History. Dried peas hail from the Middle East and date back to about 6000 B.C. Archaeologists have found them entombed with the mummies that have been unearthed in Egypt. Their use spread throughout the Mediterranean, and they were eaten in this form by both the Greeks and the Romans. Their voyage took them to India, where they were primarily eaten peeled and split and used in purées. In China, a change took place when they were eaten for the first time young and fresh from their pods. The sixteenth century found dried peas cultivated in Europe, where they are reported to have helped ward off a famine in the peasant population of England in 1555.

Traditional Uses. The whole dried peas are the "pease porridge" of our nursery rhymes—cooked to a purée and then mashed. Today, both the green split pea and the yellow split pea are popular not only in the United States but also in Europe and Asia. The yellow variety is particularly popular with the Dutch, Germans and Scandinavians (as well as with their relatives here), where its earthy flavors blend well with smoked ham and in soups.

Availability. Almost everywhere.

The

Versatile

Grain

and the

Elegant

Bean

Fresh Garden Peas

Pisum sativum

Alias. English peas, common garden peas, French peas *(petits pois),* green peas.

Description. 3- to 4-inch pods are split open to reveal five to eight peas of various sizes nesting within (depending upon the state of maturity). In Italy, they are harvested very early, when they are at their smallest and sweetest, and called *piselli*—pure ambrosia. The tiny French variety is called *petits pois* and it is among our favorites.

Sugar Snap Peas

Alias. Mange-tout.

Description. This variety is consumed along with the pod. The pods are more tender than the garden variety, which is grown more for the interior content.

Snow Peas

Alias. Chinese snow peas, *mange-tout.*

Description. A flat, delicate pod with immature "embryo" peas. These are grown and eaten *before* the peas swell the pod.

Characteristics. All of these peas have a fresh, sweet flavor.

History. Fresh peas probably found their way to the French court of Louis XIV through the Chinese silk route to Europe, for it was the Chinese who first grew and ate them fresh. Eventually, they became the rage among the fashionables of the court of the "Sun King."

Traditional uses. They are grown and eaten in myriad ways throughout the world, especially where the climate is temperate.

Availability. Fresh frozen, and fresh in pods. Usually found fresh at farmers' markets and farm stands, especially the sugar snap varieties. Snow peas are carried at Chinese greengrocers and supermarkets as well as specialty markets.

The

Elegant

Bean

407

Cooking Chart

Pot: 3 qt.

Type of Pea:	Whole Dried	Green and Yellow Split Peas	Fresh Garden Peas
Amount:	1 C. dried	1 C. dried	SEE BASIC PREPARATION BELOW
Instructions:	Soak	*Do not* soak	
Cooking Time:	50 to 60 minutes	45 to 60 minutes	
Comments:	For purées or to thicken stews. Distintegrates easily.	For purées or soups and stews. Disintegrates.	

Fresh Garden Peas
(Basic Preparation)

Approximately 3 pounds in pod, shelled, serves four as a side dish. Shell the pods of the garden peas and steam or cook in water until they are tender. Depending upon the size of the peas, the time will vary. For edible podded peas (both sugar snaps and snow peas), snip off their stem ends before cooking and pull off the string that runs the length of the pea. Blanch for 1 minute to take away any raw taste, or wash and eat them raw if you prefer them that way.

The

Versatile

Grain

and the

Elegant

Bean

408

Swedish Yellow Split Pea Soup with Fresh Marjoram and Ham

SERVES 10

Awholesome Midwestern favorite with the Swedish community that originally settled in that region of our country. It is traditionally served with a pot of sweet yellow Swedish mustard on the side.

1 Tbs. olive oil
1½ C. coarsely chopped onion (about ½ lb. or 2 large onions)
2 cloves garlic, finely minced (1 tsp.)
1 small potato, peeled and coarsely chopped (½ C.)
1 C. coarsely chopped carrots (about ¼ lb. or 2 carrots)
2 C. dried yellow split peas (1 lb.), picked over and rinsed well

10 C. water
1 meaty ham bone, or 1-lb. ham steak cut into 2-in. pieces
2 Tbs. coarsely chopped fresh marjoram (or 2 tsps. dried marjoram)
¼ tsp. freshly ground black pepper
Salt to taste
Swedish sweet yellow mustard (optional)

Heat the olive oil in a heavy 7-quart pot. Add the onions and garlic and stir over medium heat for 1 to 2 minutes. Then add the potatoes and carrots and continue to sauté, stirring occasionally, for 3 to 4 minutes more. Add the split peas, water and ham bone and bring to a boil. Boil for 2 minutes and skim the foam from the surface. Lower the heat and add 1 tablespoon of the marjoram and the pepper. Cover and simmer for 1 hour 15 minutes. Remove the ham bone, cut off bite-size pieces of lean ham and return to the pot. Taste for salt and pepper. Garnish with remaining marjoram just before serving and pass the Swedish mustard at the table if you wish.

Erwtensoep: Dutch Green Split Pea Soup
with Rivvels

SERVES 8

A long-simmering thick pea soup without peer and without a ham bone! This one uses beef marrow bones for flavor instead of the expected ham bone. The tiny irregular-shaped golden drop dumplings are a delicious addition.

Soup

3–4 beef marrow bones
1 medium whole onion, cut in half
1 large clove garlic, split
1 large stalk celery, cut in half
2 C. dried green split peas, unsoaked but washed
10 C. water

1 large potato, peeled and cut into 1-in. pieces
1 large carrot, shredded
Salt and freshly ground black pepper to taste
Rivvels

To a 7-quart heavy Dutch oven, add the bones, onion, garlic, celery, split peas and water. Bring to a boil, skim off any foam, then lower the heat and simmer for 1½ hours. Add the potatoes, carrots, salt and pepper and continue to cook for 30 minutes longer. When ready to serve, remove and discard the bones, onion and celery. Serve hot in soup bowls with rivvels.

Rivvels

5–6 Tbs. flour
½ tsp. baking powder
¼ tsp. salt or to taste

1 egg, lightly beaten
2 Tbs. cold water

In a small bowl, whisk together the flour, baking powder and salt to mix. In a cup, mix together the egg and cold water. Add to the dry ingredients and beat well to combine. Using a 5-quart nonstick wide-based pot, fill it three-quarters full with salted water and bring to a boil. Push off half a teaspoon of the dumpling mixture into the boiling water, continuing to measure them off until the mixture is completely used. Cook them over medium high heat for 30 minutes. The rivvels float on the surface of the water when done. Remove with a slotted spoon and add to the soup.

The

Versatile

Grain

and the

Elegant

Bean

410

Ground Beef, Rice and Yellow Split Pea Boulettes with Lemon and Mint

SERVES 6

Clearly Middle Eastern, this assertively spiced dish hails from Lebanon, which has always had a very strong French influence. Instead of bread, the boulettes are bound with short grain brown rice and yellow split peas, which contribute their own very unique flavors.

1 C. water	Salt to taste
¼ C. dried yellow split peas, rinsed	¼ tsp. freshly ground black pepper or to taste
1 C. cooked short grain brown rice	1 egg, beaten
1½ lbs. lean ground beef	1 Tbs. olive oil
4–5 thin scallions, finely minced (¾ C.)	1 Tbs. butter
2 Tbs. grated onion, plus 1 large onion, thinly sliced	1 C. chicken stock
2 Tbs. finely minced fresh dill	2 Tbs. tomato paste
2 Tbs. finely minced parsley	Juice of ½ lemon (1 Tbs.)
¼ tsp. ground turmeric	Few grains sugar
1 tsp. Syrian Mixed Spices (see page 75) or ground allspice	2 sprigs mint, plus sprigs for garnish
	Lemon slices

In a 1½-quart saucepan, bring the water and the split peas to a boil. Then lower the heat, cover and simmer for 20 to 30 minutes or until the split peas are partially cooked. Drain and mix with the cooked rice and set the pot aside to cool slightly.

In a large bowl, mix the beef with the scallions, grated onions, dill, parsley, turmeric, Syrian spices, salt, pepper and egg. Add the rice and split pea mixture and combine. Wet your hands and form this mixture into twelve balls or boulettes, about the size of a medium apple. Place on waxed paper and chill in the refrigerator while preparing the poaching sauce.

In a 12-inch skillet, heat the olive oil and butter and sauté the sliced onions until golden, stirring often. Add the chicken stock. In a small cup, mix the tomato paste, lemon juice and sugar, and add to the skillet. Bring to a boil, add the two mint sprigs, lower the heat and simmer, covered, for 5 minutes. Carefully place the boulettes in one layer into the skillet, cover and simmer gently for 10 minutes. Remove the cover, tilt the pan, and baste the boulettes with the sauce. Cover and simmer again for 20 minutes, basting occasionally.

With a slotted spoon, remove the boulettes to a serving dish. Remove and discard the mint and bring the sauce to a boil, uncovered, for 1 minute to reduce it, stirring constantly. Spoon over the boulettes and garnish with slices of lemon and sprigs of mint.

Whole Dried Pea Purée with Shallots, Herbs and Spices

SERVES 4 TO 6

Long before fresh early spring peas were flash frozen so they might be enjoyed year round, they were dried for winter use. This purée can perhaps be called an adaptation from an old English favorite dating back to our nursery rhyme days. Remember "Pease porridge hot . . ."?

½ lb. whole dried peas, soaked
2½ C. unsalted chicken stock
4 whole cloves
4 large shallots
1 small red whole dried hot chile such as Japonés
½ tsp. dried marjoram

⅛ tsp. dried tarragon
¼ tsp. freshly ground black pepper or to taste
Salt to taste
3 Tbs. soft butter
Freshly grated nutmeg

Drain the soaked peas and put them into a 3-quart nonstick saucepan. Add the chicken stock. Stick a clove into each shallot and add to the saucepan along with the hot chile pod. Bring to a boil, then lower the heat, cover and simmer for 50 to 60 minutes, until the peas are very soft. Turn off the heat, remove and discard the hot chile and the cloves, returning the shallots to the peas. Beat vigorously with a wooden spoon to incorporate the shallots, then stir in the marjoram, tarragon, pepper, salt and butter. Turn the heat on again under the pot and simmer for 5 to 10 minutes more, stirring occasionally. The mixture should be very thick and all the liquid should be absorbed. Taste and correct the seasoning, then grate a bit of nutmeg on the surface. Serve in a shallow casserole with any meat, fish or poultry dish.

The

Versatile

Grain

and the

Elegant

Bean

412

Pigeon Peas

Vigna sinensis

Alias. Gunga peas, longo peas, *gandules,* Congo peas, no-eyed peas, catjang beans.

Description. About ¼ inch long, plump, the shape of a pouch or purse with an elongated eye on the flattish cotyledon. Grayish-yellow in color.

Characteristics. Grows in long, twisted, fuzzy pods and has a pungent flavor. It likes semi-arid tropical conditions, growing well in places like Florida. The pigeon pea is closely related to the cow pea and is botanically in the same classification.

History. Cultivated in Egypt 4,000 years ago, this very old bean was brought to the Southern parts of the United States and the Caribbean by slaves from Africa.

Traditional Uses. Used in combination with rice in many dishes throughout the Hispanic communities of the United States and the Caribbean.

Availability. Dried, canned in various sizes, fresh in the pod where locally grown. Most supermarkets and ethnic stores now carry it.

Cowpeas
Vigna sinensis

Alias. Southern peas, flesh peas, brown crowder or field peas.

Description and Characteristics. They are much smaller in size than the black-eyed peas and have a coffee color.

Availability. Many supermarkets throughout the country stock them.

Cooking Chart

Pot: 3 qt.

Type of bean:	Pigeon Peas	Cowpeas
Amount:	1 C. dry	1C. dried
Instructions:	Overnight soak	Overnight soak
Cooking Time:	1 hour, 30 minutes	30 minutes
Approx. Yield:	3 C.	3 C.
Comments:	Tough skins require long cooking.	Foamy; skim surface.

NOTE: *Canned pigeon peas.* 1-lb. can equals 1½ C. drained. The canned pigeon peas are salty and greener in color.

The

Versatile

Grain

and the

Elegant

Bean

414

Toupin:
A Soup/Stew with Pigeon Peas
SERVES 8

A *toupin*, sometimes called a *daubière* in France, is a tall, narrow pot with a fat base and a narrow funnel top. When soups that are based on dried beans and vegetables are cooked in it, they become thick with a stewlike consistency. If you lack a *toupin* (which most of us lack) use a tall, narrow pot like a stockpot or pasta pot. The depth of the pot influences the cooking chemistry for some reason and the results seem to taste better than the same dish cooked in a regulation wide pot.

3 Tbs. olive oil	2 tsps. dried rosemary
2 medium leeks, with 1-in. green, well washed and thinly sliced (1 C.)	1 tsp. dried thyme
4 cloves garlic, coarsely chopped (1 Tbs. plus 1 tsp.)	2 large tomatoes or 4–5 canned plum tomatoes, cut into large pieces (1½ C.)
3 large shallots, coarsely chopped (⅓ C.)	¼ C. dry white wine
1 large carrot, sliced (⅔ C.)	¼ head savoy cabbage, finely shredded (2 C.)
1 small sweet red pepper, slivered (½ C.)	1 tsp. salt or to taste
½ small rutabaga, peeled and cut into ½-in. dice (2 C.)	½ tsp. freshly ground black pepper
6 C. unsalted chicken stock, plus 2 C. water	Peel of 1 large lemon, finely minced (1 Tbs.)
1½ C. dried pigeon peas, soaked and drained	½ lb. kielbasa or andouille sausage, skinned and sliced ½ in. thick
	3 Tbs. coarsely chopped flat leaf parsley

In a deep 7- or 8-quart narrow stockpot, heat the olive oil, and add the leeks, garlic, shallots and carrots. Cook, stirring, over medium low heat for about 10 minutes, until wilted but not brown. Add the red pepper, rutabaga, chicken stock and water and bring to a boil. Stir in the pigeon peas and return to boiling. Then lower the heat, add the rosemary and thyme and simmer for 45 to 60 minutes or until the beans are almost tender. Then add the tomatoes, wine, cabbage, salt, pepper and lemon peel and continue to simmer for 50 minutes longer with the lid slightly ajar.

While the stew is cooking, sauté the kielbasa slices in a nonstick skillet until they are brown. When the stew has cooked for the allotted time, add the browned sausage slices and 2 tablespoons of the parsley and cook for 10 more minutes. Add the remaining parsley just before serving. Serve directly from the pot.

Arroz con Pollo y Gandules,
Puerto Rican–Style

SERVES 6

Pigeon peas, called *gandules* in Spanish, are used lavishly in Puerto Rico and other Caribbean island dishes. This chicken and rice dish adds green olives, capers, pimiento and a saffron-scented chicken stock for the short grain rice to absorb.

3½-lb. chicken, cut into serving pieces
Coarse salt and freshly ground black
    pepper to taste
½ tsp. dried oregano, preferably
    Greek
¼ C. strongly flavored Spanish olive
    oil
2 large cloves garlic, finely minced
    (1 Tbs.)
2 medium onions, finely chopped
    (1 C.)
2 medium green peppers, cut into
    ½-in. cubes (about 1 C.)
1 bay leaf
2 tsps. sweet paprika
2 C. short grain white rice such as
    Spanish paella rice or arborio
    Italian short grain rice

½ C. dry white wine
¼ tsp. saffron threads
3 C. hot chicken stock
¾ C. coarsely chopped plum tomatoes,
    either fresh or canned and drained
2 Tbs. small nonpareil capers, rinsed
12 green olives, sliced (about ½ C.)
1½ C. cooked pigeon peas (see Chart,
    page 414)
4-oz. jar of pimientos, drained and cut
    into 1-in. long by ½-in. wide strips
    (½ C.)
1 Tbs. coarsely chopped fresh cilantro

Dry the chicken well on paper towels and season with the salt, pepper and dried oregano. Heat the olive oil in a large shallow oven-to-table casserole (at least 15 inches round or oval) and sauté the chicken, skin side down, over medium high heat. Sauté until the chicken is golden brown on all sides, about 15 minutes. Remove the chicken from the casserole to a platter and set aside. Preheat the oven to 325°F.

To the same casserole, add the garlic and onions and stir over medium heat for 1 to 2 minutes. Then add the green pepper and bay leaf. Continue to sauté for 3 to 4 minutes more, until the onions are wilted, but not brown. Stir in the paprika and then add the rice, stirring constantly for about 2 minutes. Season with salt and pepper and add the wine. Add the saffron threads to the hot chicken stock, and add 2 cups of the stock to the rice. Bring to a boil and stir for 1 minute. Then add the tomatoes, capers and olives. Remove and discard the bay leaf and cook the rice on top of the stove over medium heat, stirring occasionally, for about 6 to 7 minutes more or until the rice is no longer soupy but not yet dry. Stir in the cooked pigeon peas and the remaining chicken stock. Arrange the reserved chicken pieces over the rice and place the casserole in the oven, uncovered. Bake for 20 minutes. During the last 5 minutes, scatter the pimientos over the surface and continue to bake. Remove from the oven

The

Versatile

Grain

and the

Elegant

Bean

416

and sprinkle with cilantro, cover tightly with aluminum foil and let sit for 10 minutes. If you prepare the chicken and rice ahead of time, rewarm it, covered, in a medium oven for 15 minutes or until heated through.

Arroz y Gandules ("Ricenbeans")

SERVES 6

Every country on earth weds some sort of bean with rice, so much so that it is generally spoken as one word. This one is a family favorite that comes from Puerto Rico, where Mel's stepmother was born. She always browned the bottom of the rice, and we have followed suit.

3 strips bacon	⅛ tsp. cayenne
1 small onion, coarsely chopped (½ C.)	1 C. long grain white rice
2 cloves garlic, finely minced (1 tsp.)	1⅓ C. cooked pigeon peas, or 1-lb. can, drained and rinsed (see Chart, page 414)
1 medium yellow, orange or red pepper, coarsely diced (1 C.)	2 C. boiling water
½ tsp. dried oregano, preferably Greek or Mexican	1 bay leaf
Salt and freshly ground black pepper to taste	

In a 5-quart nonstick Dutch oven, slowly fry the bacon, turning often until crisp. Drain on paper towels and reserve. To the same pot, add the onions and garlic and sauté over medium heat, stirring often, for 2 minutes. Add the peppers, oregano, salt, pepper and cayenne and sauté for 3 to 4 minutes more, stirring often. Stir in the rice and mix for about 30 seconds. Then stir in the cooked pigeon peas. Add the boiling water, bay leaf and more salt, then bring to a boil. Cover, lower the heat and simmer for 20 minutes. Let stand for 10 minutes. Then uncover the pot and *do not stir*. Heat for 3 to 5 minutes to brown the bottom a bit. Remove the bay leaf and discard. Then fluff with a fork and transfer to a serving dish. Top with the reserved bacon if you wish.

Cowpeas in a Seven Allium Sauce with Grilled Fennel Sausage

SERVES 6

Garlic, shallots, leeks, red onions, scallions, pearl onions and chives are the seven members of the botanical *Allium* tribe. We use all of them to form a sauce for tiny creamy cowpeas.

12 fat cloves garlic, unpeeled
3 large shallots, unpeeled (3 ozs.)
1 Tbs. olive oil
3 sprigs thyme
3 Tbs. butter
1 medium leek, finely chopped, include 1-in. green part (⅔ C.)
1 large red onion, finely chopped (1 C.)
4–5 scallions, finely chopped (about 1 C.)
2 Tbs. finely minced fresh parsley
½ C. light cream

Salt and freshly ground black pepper to taste
12 tiny pearl onions, blanched and peeled
2 tsps. sugar
½ C. dry white wine
¼ C. chicken stock, plus ¼ C. if necessary to reheat
3 C. cooked cowpeas or black-eyed peas (see Chart, page 414)
1 Tbs. red wine vinegar
¾ lb. fennel sausage (about 4)
1 Tbs. finely minced fresh chives

Preheat the oven to 450°F. Place a piece of aluminum foil on a work surface and put the garlic and shallots in the center. Trickle olive oil over both to coat, then add the thyme. Fold the foil to enclose tightly and roast for 40 minutes until the garlic and shallots are soft.

Meanwhile, melt 2 tablespoons of the butter in a medium-size skillet and sauté the leeks, red onions and scallions over very low heat for 20 minutes. Stir frequently and do not brown. Set aside. When the garlic and shallots are cooked, cool, then slip off the skins. Discard the skins and the thyme. Transfer the pulp to a medium-size bowl and mash with a fork.

Return the reserved leek mixture to the heat, stir in the parsley, the garlic and shallot purée and the cream. Season with salt and pepper and turn off the heat.

In a small nonstick skillet, heat the remaining tablespoon of butter, and stir in the pearl onions. Sprinkle with the sugar and sauté over medium high heat for 2 to 3 minutes, shaking the pan often. Add the wine and chicken stock and bring to a boil. Then lower the heat, cover and simmer for 10 to 15 minutes, or until the onions are tender. Stir the onion mixture into the larger skillet, along with the cooked cowpeas and vinegar.

Meanwhile, preheat a grill or an oven broiler, pierce the sausage with a knife in several places and broil, turning frequently to brown evenly. Slice the sausage, tuck the pieces into the beans, and transfer to an oven-to-table serving dish. Sprinkle with the chives and either heat and serve at once, or cover with aluminum foil and heat in the oven just before serving if prepared well in advance. Add ¼ cup of chicken stock or water if the beans are to be reheated later, so they will not be too dry.

The
Versatile
Grain
and the
Elegant
Bean

418

Pink Beans

Phaseolus vulgaris

Alias. Pinquito beans (an heirloom variety).

Description. Smaller and not as square in shape as the pinto, it is also less uniform in size and color. It resembles the shape of the small red bean, with which it is interchangeable in Southwest and Louisiana cuisine.

Characteristics. The pink bean has a sweet, rich, meaty flavor with a slightly mealy texture. Again, it is similar to the pinto bean.

Availability. Dried, in supermarkets and specialty stores. Also available canned.

Cooking Chart   Pot: 3 qt.

Type of Bean:	Pink Beans
Amount:	1 C. dried
Cooking Time:	50 minutes
Approx. Yield:	2¾ C.
Comments:	Some color fades.

Eggplant and Pink Bean Ragout with
Mustard-Glazed Garlic Sausage

SERVES 6

Garlic sausage glazed with a piquant mustard and brown sugar sauce is tucked into the surface of this hearty, chunky stew, perfumed liberally with fresh herbs.

Beans

¼ C. olive oil
3 thin leeks, white part plus 1 in. of green, coarsely chopped (about 1 C.)
2 medium or ½ lb. onions, coarsely chopped (about 1 C.)
2 medium cloves garlic, coarsely chopped (2 tsps.)
1 small green pepper, diced (½ C.)
Salt and freshly ground black pepper to taste
2½ C. peeled fresh ripe tomatoes, cut into chunks, or 1-lb. can plum tomatoes, drained and cut in half

4 C. peeled eggplant (about 1 lb.), cut into 1¼-in. chunks
3 sprigs thyme
3 large fresh sage leaves
1 bay leaf
½ C. dry white wine
¾ C. chicken stock
2⅔ C. cooked pink beans (see Chart, page 419)
2 Tbs. coarsely chopped fresh basil

In a large skillet, heat the olive oil. When hot, add the leeks, onions, garlic and green pepper. Stir, lower the heat and season with salt and pepper. Sauté over medium heat for 5 to 8 minutes, stirring occasionally until the mixture just begins to brown. Stir in the tomatoes and eggplant and simmer, uncovered, for 5 minutes, stirring occasionally.

Tie the thyme, sage and bay leaf together with a string and add to the skillet. Then raise the heat and add the wine, chicken stock and the cooked beans. Bring to a boil, lower the heat and simmer, uncovered, for 20 minutes, stirring occasionally. Remove the herbs and stir in the basil. (Up to this point, the dish can be prepared well in advance, even up to 1 day before.) While the beans are cooking, prepare the sausage.

Mustard-Glazed Garlic Sausage

¾ lb. French garlic sausage or kielbasa, cut into 1-in. pieces and then into quarters
1 C. dry white wine

1 scant tsp. light brown sugar
2 Tbs. coarse-grain mustard
1 Tbs. finely minced fresh parsley

To a heavy skillet, add the sausage and wine. Cook over high heat, stirring occasionally, until most of the wine has evaporated. Stir in the sugar and cook for a few

The

Versatile

Grain

and the

Elegant

Bean

seconds until syrupy. Add the mustard and stir to coat the sausage. Remove from the heat at once and toss with the parsley. Scatter over the surface of the bean ragout. Serve hot.

Pink Beans with Fresh Basil, Tomato and Black Olives

SERVES 6

An assertive fish such as swordfish or bluefish would be just right with these savory beans that are touched with a bit of tomato, warm olives and fine shreds of basil.

1½ C. pink beans, soaked
2 Tbs. olive oil
1 large clove garlic, finely minced (1½ tsps.)
1 medium or large onion, finely chopped (1 C.)
4 C. tepid water
3 sprigs thyme, tied with a string

Salt and freshly ground black pepper to taste
¾ C. diced plum tomatoes (about ¼ lb.)
12 black Kalamata olives, pitted and sliced vertically
½ C. finely chiffonade-cut basil

Drain and rinse the beans, and set aside. In a 3-quart, nonstick saucepan, heat the olive oil and sauté the garlic and onions over medium heat, stirring frequently, for 5 minutes or until wilted but not brown. Stir in the beans and the tepid water and add the thyme. Bring to a boil, then cover, reduce the heat and simmer with the lid slightly ajar for about 50 minutes or until the beans are tender. Check to see if additional water is needed during the last 15 minutes of cooking. Season with salt and pepper, then remove and discard the thyme. Drain the beans, reserving the liquid, and return to the saucepan. Stir in the tomatoes, olives and a little more than half the basil. Add ¼ cup of the reserved liquid and simmer, uncovered, stirring occasionally, for 5 minutes. A bit of thick sauce should form, but the beans should not be soupy. Adjust the amount of liquid for proper consistency. Spoon the beans on to a serving plate and sprinkle the remaining basil over the surface. Serve hot.

Albóndigas with Pink Beans

SERVES 5 TO 6

Through Latin America there is some version of these walnut-size meatballs poached in a broth. We have added a slightly sweetened touch to the meat with fresh mint and raisins, poaching them in a smoky piquant ancho chile broth, and serving them with tender pink beans.

Albóndigas

1¼ lbs. chopped beef or combination of beef and veal	¼ C. finely chopped fresh mint
3 ripe plum tomatoes	¼ C. finely chopped fresh cilantro
1 large scallion, finely minced (¼ C.)	1 Tbs. golden raisins
1 medium clove garlic, finely minced (1 tsp.)	Salt and freshly ground pepper to taste
	2 Tbs. olive oil

Put the meat in a large bowl. Purée the tomatoes in a blender. Add the purée and the other ingredients, except for the olive oil, to the meat. Knead with your hands until incorporated. Add the oil and continue to knead. The mixture should be damp, but not too liquid or too dry. Dampen your hands and form the mixture into walnut-size balls. Refrigerate until cooking time. This step may be prepared well in advance.

Pink Beans

1 C. dried pink beans, soaked, drained and cooked until tender (see Chart, page 419, for cooking time), or 2¾ C. cooked or canned (drained and rinsed) pink beans

Ancho Chile Broth

2 dried ancho or dried pasilla chiles (see NOTE)	2 C. beef stock, preferably unsalted
½ C. warm water	1 medium carrot, finely shredded (1 C.)
3 Tbs. olive oil	¼ tsp. each ground cumin, dried thyme, dried oregano
1 medium onion, finely chopped (¾ C.)	1 small bay leaf
1 medium clove garlic, finely minced (1 tsp.)	Salt and freshly ground pepper to taste

If the chiles are dusty, wipe them clean with paper towels. Toast them for only a few seconds in a cast-iron skillet over medium heat, pressing them down with the back of a wooden spoon until they begin to soften and plump up. *Do not* allow the chiles to get crisp or change color or they will be bitter. Cool, pull off the stems and scrape out the seeds. Tear into pieces and put into a small bowl along with the ½ cup warm

The

Versatile

Grain

and the

Elegant

Bean

422

water. Soak for 1 hour. Blend in a blender along with the soaking liquid and set aside. (This step may be done well in advance.)

In a large skillet, heat the oil and sauté the onions and garlic over low heat until soft but not brown. Stir occasionally for about 5 minutes. Stir in the reserved chile purée, then add the beef stock, stirring constantly. Add the carrots, herbs, bay leaf, salt and pepper. Bring to a boil, then lower the heat to a simmer and add the *albóndigas* in one layer. Simmer, uncovered, for about 5 minutes, then turn over and continue to cook for 3 to 4 minutes more. Transfer with a slotted spoon to a serving dish and keep warm. Remove and discard the bay leaf and raise the heat under the sauce. Reduce and thicken it for about 7 to 8 minutes, then spoon over the *albóndigas*. Serve with the pink beans.

NOTE: The ancho chile is a dried, heart-shaped poblano, which is green when fresh. It is mildly hot, aromatic and very popular in Mexican cuisine.

Pinto Beans

Phaseolus vulgaris

Alias. Mexican strawberries, rattlesnake beans (new hybrid), appaloosa beans (new hybrid).

Description. Slightly smaller than kidney beans (about ⅜ inch to 1 inch long), medium size, squarish oval shape. Light buff-colored background with a freckled pattern in a pinkish-brown color.

Characteristics. Earthy, full-bodied flavor and a mealy texture. They are closely related to red kidney beans.

Rattlesnake Beans

The name of these new hybrid beans is derived from the shape and markings on the pods as well as on the beans themselves. They are of medium size (about ½ inch) and are almost identical in color and pattern to the common pinto. Their squarish blunt shape is what distinguishes them.

Appaloosa Beans

A new hybrid variety that hails from the American Northwest (eastern Washington State and northern Idaho) in the area known as the Palouse. This particular region harbors the largest number of bean growers in the United States, including dry peas and lentils. The Palouse also gave the similarly speckled horse its name of Appaloosa.

Although the beans are from the Northwest, they are particularly well suited to Southwestern fare, as are the pinto beans. Large (¾ inch) thinly shaped beautiful beans, they are creamy white with a black diagonal irregular splotch that distinguishes them.

The

Versatile

Grain

and the

Elegant

Bean

424

History. The common pinto beans are yet another ancient bean that are native to South America. The pintos are from a highly hybridized crop with a long list of heirloom beans that carry colorful names such as the ones above. Pinto means "painted" and the bean takes its name from the pinto horse, which bears similar markings.

Traditional Uses. These beans are common on the tables of most Spanish-speaking countries and are synonymous with our American Southwest cuisine. When they are cooked, the mottled appearance of the pinto fades and it turns a uniform pink and therefore can be used interchangeably with the pink bean or kidney bean.

Availability. The pinto is available most everywhere. The rattlesnake and appaloosa beans are generally found in specialty food stores or through mail order.

Cooking Chart
Pot: 3 qt.

Type of Bean:	Pinto Beans	Rattlesnake Beans	Appaloosa Beans
Amount:	1 C. dried	1 C. dried	1 C. dried
Cooking Time:	45 to 60 minutes	45 to 60 minutes	45 to 50 minutes
Approx. Yield:	2⅔ C.	2½ C.	2½ C.
Comments:	Skim foam from surface.	Tender. Skins split open easily. Cook gently.	Good flavor. However, markings fade.

A WORD ABOUT CHILE POWDER

There are many chile powders on the market, most of which contain cumin, oregano and dehydrated garlic. Sometimes cloves and allspice are also added, as well as salt and occasionally MSG. Many commercial brands are quite popular, even with that range of added ingredients, and if you have no objection to them, we suggest that you continue to use them.

However, we prefer to use the pure ground chile without the additions, especially dehydrated garlic, which we find always has an "off flavor." For convenience, we buy the Pecos Valley Spice brand, distributed by Jane Butel, and the products are available in most specialty shops and department store gourmet shops. It comes in four strengths:

- *Mild* ground California chile
- Hot chile, which is actually *medium hot* southern New Mexico chiles
- Caribe Chile, from northern New Mexico, with a *sweet, hot taste*
- Pequin Quebrado—the *hottest* of the bunch.

Quelites: Pinto Beans with Mild Chiles and Pine Nuts

SERVES 4 TO 6

Quelites, a bean dish from Mexico and our own Southwest, is traditionally made with native wild greens such as lamb's-quarters. Here we have made it with a mixture of more easily available spinach and Swiss chard, steamed and mixed with mildly hot New Mexico (Anaheim) chiles or poblano chiles, then topped with toasted *piñon* (pine nuts), a most beguiling combination of healthful and tasty ingredients.

¼ C. pine nuts
3 Tbs. bacon fat or olive oil
2 cloves garlic, finely minced (1 tsp.)
1 medium onion, finely minced (½ C.)
½ tsp. dried oregano, preferably Mexican or Greek
⅛ tsp. ground coriander
1 tsp. ground cumin
Salt and freshly ground black pepper to taste

2½ C. cooked pinto beans or rattlesnake beans, drained and 1 C. liquid reserved
½ tsp. ground chile powder (see BOX above)
12 C. coarsely chopped greens composed of 1 lb. spinach and ½ lb. Swiss chard

The

Versatile

Grain

and the

Elegant

Bean

426

Toast the pine nuts in a small dry skillet, shaking the pan, until the nuts are light tan in color. Remove the nuts and set aside. In a 12-inch nonstick skillet, heat the bacon fat and slowly sauté the garlic and onions for 3 minutes. Add the oregano, coriander, cumin, salt and pepper and sauté for 3 to 4 more minutes, stirring frequently, until they just begin to color. Stir in the cooked beans along with ½ cup of the bean liquid and the ground chile powder. Cover and simmer for 10 minutes, adding more liquid if the beans seem dry.

Meanwhile, steam the greens in a vegetable steamer and season them with additional salt and pepper if you wish. When ready to serve, stir the greens into the bean mixture and combine gently. Transfer to a serving dish and sprinkle with the toasted pine nuts.

Mexican Grilled Chicken Breasts with Chile Paste and Savory Pinto Beans

SERVES 6

It takes only minutes to grill chicken breasts, which marinate in advance in a mildly hot chile paste. The savory pinto beans can also be prepared well ahead and then rewarmed. Therefore, this is a perfect recipe for an after-work dinner party. Just boil some rice, rewarm the beans, throw the chicken on the grill and clang the dinner bell!

Ancho Chile Paste

MAKES 2 CUPS

5 large mildly hot, dried chiles, such as ancho, New Mexico or pasilla (*chile negro*)

2 C. boiling water

Preheat the oven to 275°F. Place the dried chiles in a single layer on a baking sheet and bake for 5 minutes until the chiles puff up. Remove from the oven, pull off the stems and discard. Split the chiles, scoop out the seeds and discard them. Then tear the chiles in pieces and put in a small bowl. Pour boiling water over and let stand for 30 minutes. Drain and save the liquid. Process the chiles in the bowl of a food processor or in a blender to a purée. Add the liquid and process again to combine. This paste keeps for several weeks tightly covered in a jar, so it's a good idea to make a batch and keep it on hand.

Chicken and Marinade
(Prepare several hours in advance or overnight.)

12 skinless, boneless chicken cutlets (2 per person)

½ C. Ancho Chile Paste (see recipe, page 427)

3–5 cloves garlic, finely minced (2 Tbs.)

Juice of 3 large limes (about 1½ C.)

½ C. olive oil

Salt and freshly ground black pepper to taste

¼ C. finely minced fresh cilantro

Place the chicken in a large flat casserole (not metal) in one layer. Mix the remaining ingredients together and spoon evenly over the chicken. Let the chicken marinate for several hours or overnight, covered tightly, in the refrigerator. Turn the chicken once or twice to coat evenly.

When ready to cook, place the chicken on a prepared charcoal grill close to the source of heat or under a preheated broiler, and grill for 2 to 3 minutes on each side. Then lower the rack in the broiler (or raise it on the grill) and cook until the chicken is just cooked through. Baste with the marinade while grilling to keep the chicken moist. Serve at once with the pinto beans (see below).

Savory Pinto Beans
(The beans may be cooked a day or 2 in advance, salted and left in their liquid and kept in the refrigerator.)

4 C. cooked pinto beans, cooking liquid reserved

2 Tbs. olive oil

1 large clove garlic, finely minced (1 tsp.)

2–3 slices lean Canadian bacon, finely diced (about ½ C.)

1 small onion, finely diced (⅓ C.)

½ large green pepper, finely diced (about ⅓ C.)

1 tsp. chile powder (see BOX, page 426)

Salt and freshly ground black pepper to taste

Take off ⅔ cup of beans and 1½ cups of cooking liquid and set aside. In a large nonstick skillet, heat the oil and add the garlic. Sauté over medium heat, stirring, for about 30 seconds, then add the Canadian bacon. Cook, stirring, for 1 to 2 minutes, then add the onions and green pepper. Stir and sauté until the onions are wilted and just begin to color, about 5 to 8 minutes. Add the reserved ⅔ cup of beans and mash with a potato masher. Then add the 1½ cups of cooking liquid (more may be needed) and bring to a boil. Lower the heat and simmer for 1 minute. Add the chile powder, salt and pepper and stir in the remaining cooked beans. Stir and cook over low heat for about 5 minutes or until the beans are heated and a very thick sauce has formed. If the beans seem too dry, add more liquid. Or, if you plan to reheat the beans, add more of the liquid since the beans have a tendency to absorb it.

The

Versatile

Grain

and the

Elegant

Bean

Appaloosa Beans Provençale with Yellow Peppers and Parsley

SERVES 8

These black and white hybrid beans hail from the Palouse region of eastern Washington and northern Idaho, a big bean-growing area of our country. The conditions and climate in this area are similar to the Provence region of France, hot and dry. So we have combined the two elements: Western American beans with a southern French touch.

4 C. hot, drained, cooked appaloosa beans, or substitute pinto beans (see Chart, page 425)

¼ C. olive oil

1 small red onion, finely diced (⅔ C.)

1 large clove garlic, finely minced (1 tsp.)

3 Tbs. olive paste (*olivada*), or ⅔ C. pitted, sliced Kalamata olives

1 Tbs. nonpareil capers, rinsed and drained on paper towel

1 tsp. Herbes de Provence (see NOTE)

Salt and freshly ground black pepper to taste

⅛ tsp. hot pepper flakes

2 Tbs. red wine vinegar

1 Tbs. lemon juice

1 medium sweet yellow pepper, diced (1 C.)

¼ C. finely minced fresh parsley

Toss the hot beans with the olive oil, then stir in the red onion and garlic. In a small bowl, mix the olive paste with the capers, Herbes de Provence, salt, pepper, hot pepper flakes, red wine vinegar and lemon juice. Pour over the beans and stir gently to combine. Taste to adjust the seasoning, then spoon the mixture out on to a large serving platter. Scatter the yellow peppers and parsley over the surface and serve at room temperature.

NOTE: Herbes de Provence, a dried herb mixture from France, is sold at specialty stores.

Frijoles Borachos con Pico de Gallo:
Drunken Beans with Tomato Salsa

SERVES 6

The beans are cooked in beer with a touch of brown sugar to counterbalance the combination of hot and sweet chiles in this dish. *Pico de Gallo* ("Rooster's Beak") is the Mexican name for freshly made tomato salsa, used these days for everything from a dip for taco chips to perking up the flavor of "Drunken Beans."

- 3 Tbs. olive oil
- 2 cloves garlic, finely minced (about 1 tsp.)
- 1 medium onion, finely minced (⅔ C.)
- 1–2 fresh Anaheim (New Mexico) chiles, seeded and cut into ¼-in. strips
- 1 tsp. dried oregano, preferably Greek
- 1 tsp. ground cumin
- ¼ tsp. ground cloves

- Salt and freshly ground black pepper to taste
- 4 C. drained, cooked pinto beans (see Chart, page 425)
- 1½ C. beer
- 2 Tbs. dark brown sugar
- 1 C. shredded Monterey Jack cheese with jalapeño peppers
- ½ C. shredded Cheddar cheese

In a 10-inch skillet, heat the oil and sauté the garlic for 1 minute. Add the onions, chile, oregano, cumin, cloves, salt and pepper. Sauté over very low heat for 10 minutes, stirring frequently. Add the beans, beer and sugar and simmer for 5 to 8 minutes. Preheat the oven to 300°F. Stir in both cheeses and transfer to a 2-quart oven-to-table casserole and bake for 1 hour. Meanwhile, prepare the sauce, a little of which is spooned over the beans after baking.

Pico de Gallo

MAKES 2 CUPS

- 2 large tomatoes (about 1 lb. total), coarsely diced (2 C.)
- 1 small fresh poblano chile, discard stem and seeds and mince (1 heaping Tbs.)
- ½ fresh Jalapeño chile (or more to taste), discard seeds and stem and finely mince (1 tsp.)

- 1 small clove garlic, finely minced (½ tsp.)
- 1 small red onion, finely minced (⅓ C.)
- ½ C. coarsely chopped fresh cilantro
- 1 Tbs. lime juice
- 1 Tbs. olive oil
- Salt to taste

Prepare as close to serving time as possible, by mixing all the ingredients together in a bowl. If the salsa is made too far in advance it tends to become watery.

The

Versatile

Grain

and the

Elegant

Bean

430

Chili con Carne with Pinto Beans

SERVES 6 TO 8

Opinions about ingredients and cooking methods for chili con carne are extremely individual and fiercely defended. Witness the chili con carne competitions held throughout the Southwest with teams from various states. Some of the controversial methods and ingredients are:

- *always* use an iron pot—*never* use an iron pot
- always used *chopped* beef—only use *diced* beef
- use chile *powder* and *spice mix*—use *pure ground* chiles
- you *must* use tomatoes—*never* use tomatoes
- *always* add the beans—*never* mix in the beans

Since we do not wish to become involved in a typical chile imbroglio, we present our own version, perfected over the years. To each his own!

1 large dried mild red chile, New Mexico Red, also called Colorado or California chile
¼ C. olive oil
2 large onions, coarsely chopped (1½ C.)
3 cloves garlic, finely minced (1 Tbs.)
3 lbs. lean boneless chuck, diced into ½-in. cubes
2 tsps. paprika
1 Tbs. ground cumin
2 tsps. dried oregano, preferably Mexican or Greek
2 Tbs. medium hot ground chile powder (see BOX, page 426)
1 tsp. salt or to taste

35-oz. can Italian plum tomatoes packed in tomato purée
1½ C. unsalted beef broth, boiling
3 Tbs. masa harina (see page 85)
4 C. cooked pinto beans (see Chart, page 425)
1 medium red onion, diced and mixed with 1 Tbs. red wine vinegar for garnish (optional)
Sour cream seasoned with lime juice and salt to taste for garnish (optional)
Shredded Cheddar cheese for garnish (optional)
Coarsely chopped fresh cilantro for garnish (optional)

Split the dried chile, discard the stem and seeds and tear into small pieces. Cover with hot water in a small bowl and steep for 20 minutes. When soft, purée in a blender, scrape out and set aside. In a 7-quart heavy Dutch oven, heat the olive oil, stir in the onions and cook over high heat, stirring constantly, for 1 minute. Add the garlic, stir and sauté for 3 to 4 minutes more until the onions are translucent but not brown. Add the meat and cook over high heat, stirring constantly, until the meat begins to lose color. Sprinkle with paprika, cumin, oregano, chile powder and salt, stir and cook for 5 more minutes. Then add the reserved chile paste and cook for 1 more minute. Stir in the tomatoes and the purée in which they are packed crushing and breaking them up a bit with the back of your wooden spoon. Bring to a boil, then lower the heat and simmer for 15 minutes.

Add the hot beef broth. Sprinkle the masa harina over the surface a bit at a time, stirring constantly as it is added. Simmer for 1½ hours, stirring occasionally. Use a

The

Elegant

Bean

431

flame tamer for slow cooking. Taste and adjust the seasoning. Serve in a deep tureen or earthenware pot. Serve the hot cooked pinto beans in another bowl to be passed at the table. Or, if you wish, prepare a day ahead to allow the flavors to mellow and reheat. Put any or all of the garnishes in separate bowls to pass at the table.

Pintos "Refritos"

SERVES 4 TO 6

Technically "refritos" beans call for frying mashed but already fried beans in large amounts of bacon fat. Since we have always tried to minimize the amount of fat used in our recipes, we are not refrying the pintos in this recipe. Chorizos and 1 ounce of bacon give the beans sufficient flavor. And the cheese and sour cream both contain fat, so why gild the lily?

1 oz. slab bacon, diced	2 tsps. dried oregano, preferably Greek or Mexican
1½ C. coarsely diced chorizo (about ½ lb.)	2 tsps. ground cumin
2 cloves garlic, finely minced (1 tsp.)	4 C. drained, cooked pinto beans or rattlesnake beans, 2 C. liquid reserved (see Chart, page 425)
½ small green pepper, finely minced (¼ C.)	5 ozs. Cheddar cheese, shredded
1 medium onion, finely minced (⅔ C.)	Sour cream
Salt and freshly ground black pepper to taste	Seeded poblano chile, cut into strips
1½ Tbs. ground red mild chile powder (see BOX, page 426)	Cilantro leaves

In a 12-inch nonstick skillet, slowly cook the bacon until it is almost crisp. Add the diced chorizo and cook until the chorizo is browned and the bacon is crisp. Transfer with a slotted spoon to paper towels to drain.

In the same skillet, sauté the garlic for 1 minute, then add the green pepper, onions, salt and pepper and sauté over low heat for 5 minutes. Stir in the ground chile powder, oregano and cumin and continue to cook for 2 minutes more. Add part of the beans to the skillet and ½ cup of the bean liquid and mash the beans with a potato masher. Add the remaining beans and ¾ cup more of the bean liquid and incorporate with the potato masher into a rough purée. Taste for salt and pepper and simmer for 10 to 15 minutes, stirring frequently until very thick. Stir in half the Cheddar cheese, the chorizo and bacon and transfer to a 2-quart shallow oven-to-table casserole. Sprinkle with the remaining cheese and set aside to blend the flavors for about 30 minutes.

When ready to serve, preheat the oven to 325°F. and bake for 20 to 25 minutes until the top is bubbly. Serve with sour cream, roasted mild chile strips and some cilantro to top each portion.

The

Versatile

Grain

and the

Elegant

Bean

432

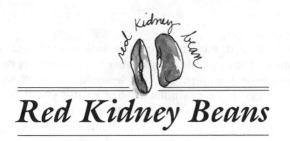

Red Kidney Beans

Phaseolus vulgaris

Alias. Mexican beans, *habichuelas, haricots rouges,* Raj Mah, Spanish Tolasanas.

Description. Medium size (about ½ inch long) and elongated. The bean takes its name from its kidney shape and it comes in two colors: a deep reddish-brown, almost purplish in color, and also a light red, more amber in hue. There is also a *white* kidney bean, referred to as cannellini.

Characteristics. It has a robust, full-bodied flavor and a rich, creamy texture.

History. An ancient cultivar of 7,000 years ago from Southwestern Mexico, where this common be   developed into hundreds of different varieties. Spanish explorers exported it to Europe. The white kidney (cannellini) is used more frequently in Europe.

Traditional Uses. In the West Indies it is cooked with coconut milk, hot chile and herbs. Contrary to popular belief, the large red kidney bean is *not* the bean used for the ubiquitous *chili con carne.* Rather it is the pinto bean or the small red bean.

Spanish Tolasanas

A large, three-quarter-inch mottled red kidney bean, similar to the *ayacotes* bean in Mexico and sometimes referred to as the Prince Bean by growers. It is used for both Spanish and Mexican dishes.

Small Red Beans

Alias habichuelas, *habas pequeños colorados* (meaning "small red beans"). There is also a variety called Red Mexican Bean. The small red bean is about ⅜ inch long, and not quite kidney-shaped, but with the same dark red color. The flavor and other properties are similar to the red kidney, however. This bean is one of the principal ingredients for the classic Southern dish red beans and rice as well as for chili con carne. The Red Mexican Bean is similar in size to the Great Northern bean. The small red bean is a bush bean that does not fall apart easily, but maintains its shape and is therefore very popular with commercial canners and packagers.

Availability. Where locally grown, it can be found fresh in the pod. Otherwise, it is usually found dried in supermarkets, or in cans of various sizes.

Cooking Chart
Pot: 3 qt.

Type of Bean:	Red Kidneys	Spanish Tolasanas	Small Red Beans
Amount:	1 C. dried	1 C. dried	1 C. dried
Cooking Time:	45 to 60 minutes	35 minutes	60 minutes
Approx. Yield:	2¼ C.	2⅔ C.	2⅔ C.
Comments:	Foams up easily. Very tender. Cook with lid ajar to avoid boil-over.	Color fades a bit.	Beans tend to split open if boiled. Simmer gently. Markings and color fade after soaking.

NOTE: *Red canned kidney beans* tend to be packed in a gluelike sauce. Kidney beans are best when freshly cooked.

The

Versatile

Grain

and the

Elegant

Bean

434

Red Bean, Cheese and
Masa Harina Fritters

MAKES 18 TO 20 FRITTERS

Crisp, puffy golden nuggets of red beans blend with the concentrated corn flavor of tortilla flour. They're wonderful to pass at a cocktail party or to serve as an appetizer or side dish.

½ C. masa harina (see page 85)
¼ C. all-purpose flour
½ tsp. baking powder
½ tsp. salt or to taste
⅛ tsp. cayenne
⅛ tsp. ground coriander
½ tsp. ground cumin
½ tsp. dried marjoram
2 eggs, separated
½ C. milk

1 heaping Tbs. finely grated onion
1 C. small red beans, cooked, drained and dried on paper towels (see Chart, opposite page)
1 C. shredded Cheddar cheese (about 3 ozs.)
Corn oil for frying
Sour cream
Cilantro leaves

In a medium-size bowl, whisk together the masa harina, flour, baking powder, salt, cayenne, coriander, cumin and dried marjoram to blend. In another small bowl, beat the egg yolks and milk and stir in the grated onions. Combine well with the dry ingredients, then stir in the beans and cheese. Beat the egg whites until stiff and fold them into the batter. Heat about 1 inch of the corn oil in an iron skillet until hot. Drop the batter by heaping tablespoons into the oil, pushing it off with your finger. Fry the fritters until the edges are brown, about 1 or 2 minutes. Turn over and fry on the other side for another minute or 2. Repeat until the batter is used up. Transfer the finished fritters with a slotted spoon to paper towels to drain, then keep warm in a preheated low oven. Top each fritter with about ½ teaspoon of sour cream and a small cilantro leaf. Serve hot.

Poor Boy Soup with
Red Kidney Beans and Cabbage

SERVES 6

Humble ingredients mark this thrifty, thick country soup from the South, which got its name from a chicken stock made from the unused parts of the chicken: wings, backs and necks, generally left over from the fried chicken Sunday supper.

½ lb. hot Italian sausage, removed from casings

1 Tbs. olive oil, if needed

4 large cloves garlic, finely minced (2 Tbs.)

1 large onion, coarsely chopped (1½ C.)

2 large carrots, coarsely chopped (2 C.)

4 C. coarsely chopped cabbage (about 1 lb.)

½ tsp. dried thyme

½ tsp. dried rosemary

Salt and freshly ground black pepper to taste

2 russet baking potatoes, peeled and cut into 1-in. cubes (about 1 lb.)

4 C. Chicken Stock, preferably homemade (see page 171)

2½ C. drained, cooked kidney beans (see Chart, page 434)

2 ozs. fine capellini or vermicelli noodles, broken into 2-in. pieces

In a heavy 5-quart Dutch oven, sauté the sausage meat over medium heat until it loses its color. If the sausage is fatty, no additional oil will be needed. If not, add the olive oil. Stir in the garlic and sauté, stirring, for 1 minute. Add the onions and cook, stirring, for 3 to 4 minutes. Then add the carrots, cabbage, thyme, rosemary, salt and pepper. Stir occasionally and cook for 5 minutes.

Add the potatoes and chicken stock and bring to a boil. Lower the heat and simmer for 20 to 25 minutes. Stir in the cooked kidney beans and simmer for 5 minutes more. Then add the broken noodles and continue to cook for 5 minutes. Serve at once.

The

Versatile

Grain

and the

Elegant

Bean

436

Gormeh Sabzi:
Iranian Lamb and Kidney Bean Stew
with Spinach and Herbs

SERVES 6

This most unusual stew of lamb and kidney beans simmers on a bed of herbs and spinach and is delicately flavored with lemon and turmeric. Use the natural juices from the stew as a sauce for cooked long grain rice.

2 Tbs. olive oil	1½ lbs. lean lamb, preferably cut from
3 Tbs. butter	leg, cut into ¾-in. cubes
2 large cloves garlic, finely minced	Freshly ground black pepper to taste
(1 Tbs.)	Salt to taste
1-2 medium leeks, white part only,	1½ Tbs. ground turmeric
finely chopped (⅔ C.)	2 C. Chicken Stock, preferably
10 large scallions, thinly sliced (about	homemade (see page 171)
2½ C.)	1 tsp. finely minced lemon peel
1 lb. spinach, well washed, with	2 C. cooked light red kidney beans
stems removed	(see Chart, page 434)
2 C. coarsely chopped flat leaf	Juice of 1 large lemon (¼ C.)
parsley (about ¼ lb.)	Cooked long grain rice (optional)
2 Tbs. snipped fresh dill	

In a 7-quart Dutch oven, heat 1 tablespoon of the olive oil and 1 tablespoon of the butter. Add the garlic and sauté over medium heat for 30 seconds. Add the leeks and scallions and cook for 5 minutes, stirring occasionally, until they are wilted. Add the spinach, parsley and dill and stir constantly for a few minutes, only until the greens are wilted. Set aside.

In a large skillet, heat the remaining butter and oil. Blot the lamb with paper towels so it is very dry. Sprinkle with pepper and add to the skillet a few pieces at a time. Brown the lamb all over, transferring the browned pieces to the Dutch oven as they are browned. Season with salt. Add the turmeric to the same skillet and stir for a few seconds, then add the chicken stock, stirring and scraping any brown bits that cling to the skillet, and bring to a boil.

Strain the liquid over the meat and greens and add the lemon peel. Cover the Dutch oven and bring to a boil. Then lower the heat and simmer for 1 hour. Add the cooked beans and lemon juice and simmer for 15 minutes more. Adjust the seasoning, transfer to a warm platter and serve with cooked long grain rice if you wish.

Baby Clams with Saffron and
Spanish Tolasana Beans

SERVES 4 TO 6

An earthy delicious combination that has all the tastes of Spain. The beans can be cooked well in advance and kept in their cooking liquid until ready to be added to the flavorful, aromatic broth in which the clams are cooked.

Beans

2½ C. Spanish tolasana beans or light red kidney beans, soaked and drained

4 cloves garlic, stuck with toothpicks for easy removal

2 medium onions, each stuck with 1 whole clove (about ¼ lb.)

2 large carrots, cut in half crosswise

4 sprigs parsley

2 large bay leaves

Salt and freshly ground black pepper to taste

To a 5-quart Dutch oven, add the beans, garlic, onions and carrots. Tie the parsley and bay leaves together with string and add. Cover with tepid water to cover by about 2 inches and bring to a boil. Skim any foam from the surface, lower the heat, cover with the lid slightly ajar and simmer for 35 to 40 minutes (45 to 60 minutes for kidney beans) or until the beans are tender. Remove and discard the garlic, onions, carrots and herb bundle. Season with salt and pepper and keep the beans in their liquid so they don't dry out while the clams are prepared.

Clams

¼ C. strong Spanish olive oil

½ small onion, finely minced (2 Tbs.)

3–4 cloves garlic, finely minced (about 1 Tbs.)

¼ tsp. saffron threads, crushed

½ tsp. dried thyme

1 Tbs. sweet paprika

½ C. dry white wine

¼ tsp. hot pepper flakes

2 large plum tomatoes, coarsely diced (1 C.)

3 dozen very small clams, scrubbed and rinsed well

2 Tbs. coarsely chopped flat leaf parsley

Cooked hot rice (optional)

In a 12-inch sauté pan with deep sides, heat the oil and sauté the onions and garlic, stirring constantly over medium high heat until the onion is transparent. Do not let the garlic brown. Stir in the saffron, thyme, paprika, wine, hot pepper flakes and the tomatoes. Bring to a boil, then lower the heat and simmer, covered, for 5 minutes. Raise the heat and add the clams. Cover and cook over high heat, shaking the pan occasionally until the clams open, about 10 to 15 minutes.

When the clams open, remove them with a slotted spoon to a platter, cover with aluminum foil and keep warm. Discard any clams that don't open. Drain the beans

The
Versatile
Grain
and the
Elegant
Bean

438

and add them to the sauté pan, along with half the parsley. Stir gently and simmer, covered, for 5 minutes, or until hot. Adjust the seasoning and transfer the beans to a large shallow, warmed oven-to-table casserole. Stud the surface of the beans with the clams and sprinkle with the remaining parsley. Hot rice can complete the meal if you wish.

Baby Clams with Saffron & Spanish Tolosanos Beans

Red Beans and
"Dirty Rice" Louisiana-Style

SERVES 8

The word "dirty" is an odd one to use when referring to food, yet this Cajun dish prepared with chicken livers, gizzards and lots of pepper, gives the rice its characteristic gray or "dirty" color. The small red beans, although not traditionally mixed into the rice, but generally served separately, are our own touch of color and flavor.

2 Tbs. olive oil
1 Tbs. butter
1 medium onion, finely minced (⅔ C.)
1¼ C. finely minced chicken gizzards with some chicken hearts and livers included (about ¾ lb. total)
1 C. long grain brown rice
2¼ C. Chicken Stock, preferably homemade (see page 171)
Salt to taste

3 Tbs. finely minced scallions, green part only (1 medium scallion)
2 Tbs. finely minced flat leaf parsley
1 medium clove garlic, finely minced (1 tsp.)
¼ tsp. freshly ground black pepper
⅛ tsp. cayenne
⅛ tsp. ground allspice
2¼ C. drained hot cooked small red beans (see Chart, page 434)

Preheat the oven to 350°F. Heat the oil and butter over medium high heat on top of the stove in a large oven-to-table shallow heatproof casserole. Add the onions and sauté for 4 to 5 minutes, stirring often until the onions begin to color. Add the giblets and stir and cook for a few minutes until the pink color is gone. Stir in the rice and cook, while stirring, for about 2 minutes. Add the chicken stock and salt and bring to a boil. Stir in the scallions, parsley, garlic, pepper, cayenne and allspice. Cover the casserole with foil or a lid and transfer to the oven. Bake for 40 minutes, then remove from the oven and let stand for 10 minutes to allow any liquid to be absorbed by the rice. Fluff with a fork and stir in the hot cooked beans. Serve directly from the casserole.

The

Versatile

Grain

and the

Elegant

Bean

440

Warm Red Kidney Bean and Garlic Sausage Salad
with Gruyère and Sweet Pickle Relish

SERVES 6 AS A MAIN COURSE
SERVES 10 TO 12 AS A FIRST COURSE

A first course or a warm summer salad main course. Garlicky sausage, strips of cheese and crunchy vegetables are spiked with hot mustard and served on a tangle of sweet and slightly bitter greens. Perfect fare for wilting summer appetites.

Mustard Vinaigrette
MAKES ⅔ CUP

1½ Tbs. red wine vinegar
1 Tbs. lemon juice
Salt and freshly ground black pepper
    to taste

1–2 drops Tabasco sauce
2 Tbs. coarse-grain hot mustard
6 Tbs. olive oil

In a small bowl, combine the vinegar, lemon juice, salt, pepper, Tabasco sauce and mustard, beating with a wire whisk. Add the olive oil slowly, beating until creamy. Set aside.

Salad

2¼ C. drained, rinsed, cooked red
    kidney beans (see Chart, page 434)
1 small red onion, finely diced (about
    ½ C.)
Salt and freshly ground black pepper
    to taste
1 C. mixed red and green pepper, cut
    into thin strips (1½ in. long)
1 stalk celery, finely diced (about
    ½ C.)
6 ozs. kielbasa or andouille garlic
    sausage, boiled 2 minutes, drained
    and cut into thin strips (about 1 C.)

2 ozs. Gruyère cheese, cut into thin
    julienne 1½ in. long (about ½ C.)
2 Tbs. drained, sweet India pickle
    relish
6 C. torn-up mixed salad greens (such
    as arugula, red leaf lettuce, field
    salad, mizuna Japanese mustard,
    curly endive and romaine) washed
    and dried well
2 Tbs. finely minced fresh parsley

Combine all the ingredients except the salad greens and parsley. Spoon the mustard vinaigrette over and toss gently. To serve as a main course, arrange about 1 cup of the mixed greens around the edge of a serving plate and spoon about 1 cup of the bean mixture in the center. Sprinkle each salad with a bit of minced parsley and serve warm or at room temperature.

Runner Beans

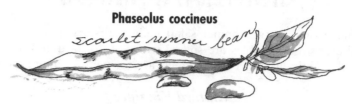

Phaseolus coccineus

scarlet runner bean

Scarlet Runner Beans

Alias. Prizewinners (a Dutch import).

Description. A large bean, between ⅞ inch and 1 inch long, russet red with black heavy mottling near the eye of the bean. The prizewinners have less mottling and only occasional dark spots flecking the base.

Characteristics. The runner bean is another species of the genus *Phaseolus* from the mountainous slopes of the Americas, first cultivated for ornamental purposes. The flowers of the plant, which are also edible and taste like the bean before they mature, are intensely scarlet and known to attract hummingbirds. The pods can be picked young and eaten pod and all (e.g., like string beans), with some left on the plant to mature for drying.

History. Brought to the shores of the British Isles in the seventeenth century as an ornamental and decorative plant because of its beautiful, showy scarlet blossoms. It is now a favorite in both England and the United States, primarily as a food crop for the farmer to dry and sell and for the home gardener both for food and for its beauty.

White Runner Beans

Alias. Alba beans, white Dutch runners.

Description. Slightly smaller than the scarlet runner, about ¾ inch long, it is a creamy colored bean, grown in The Netherlands and preferred there to its scarlet cousin. A new variety called "sweet white runner" has recently been developed as a hybrid and is now available in a limited number of specialty stores.

Traditional Uses. Both scarlet runner and white runner beans are used widely in England and Holland. The sweet white runners taste somewhat like the *gigandes,* a Greek and Spanish import (though about a third larger in size). If scarlet runner beans are not available, a substitute in a pinch would be red kidney beans.

Availability. Sometimes in pods where they are locally grown. In dried form, they can all be found in specialty food shops or ethnic food stores.

The

Versatile

Grain

and the

Elegant

Bean

442

Cooking Chart

Type of Bean:	Scarlet Runner Beans	Prizewinners	White Runner Beans	Gigandes
Amount:	1 C. dried	1 C. dried	1 C. dried	1 C. dried
Cooking Time:	1 hour, 15 minutes	1 hour, 15 minutes	1 hour, 10 minutes	1 hour, 15 minutes.
Approx. Yield:	3 C.	2 C.	3 C.	2½ C.
Comments:	Creamy, sweet center, tougher outer skin.	Full color is retained.	Very sweet flavor, creamy texture.	Sweet flavor. Slightly mealy texture.

Fassolia me Skordalia:
Sweet White Runner Beans or
Greek Gigandes with Skordalia Sauce

SERVES 8 TO 10

This tasty side dish or first course features distinctively flavored very large white beans and a classic Greek sauce redolent with garlic. *Fassolia me Skordalia* is a marriage made in heaven for garlic lovers, and the sauce by itself is marvelous with grilled lamb chops, baked red snapper or just lavished on a piece of good bread.

Beans

2 C. dried sweet white runner beans or Greek dried gigandes beans, soaked and drained (see NOTE)
6 cups water

3 Tbs. olive oil
2 Tbs. finely minced fresh parsley
Salt and freshly ground black pepper to taste

To a 5-quart Dutch oven, add the beans and water and bring to a boil. Lower the heat, cover with the lid slightly ajar and simmer for 1 hour 15 minutes or until the beans are soft, adding salt during the last 5 minutes of cooking. Let them cool slightly in their liquid. Then drain, rinse in hot water, drain again and gently toss while warm with the olive oil, parsley, salt and pepper. Transfer them to a bowl and keep at room temperature or chill for several hours, then bring to room temperature again before serving.

The

Elegant

Bean

Skordalia Sauce

Traditionally, this sauce is made with lots of garlic. However, parboiling the garlic makes a more gentle sauce. Then, adding a bit of fresh garlic to your taste at the very end gives an additional zap to the sauce.

1 peeled waxy new potato, cubed (about ¼ lb.)	½ C. whole shelled and peeled almonds, toasted lightly
Salt	½ tsp. sugar
6 cloves garlic	Juice of 2 large lemons (about ⅓ C.)
4 ozs. (about 4 thick slices) good-tasting white peasant bread with crusts trimmed	2 Tbs. white wine vinegar
	⅔ C. olive oil
	Freshly ground black pepper to taste
	Radicchio leaves

In a small saucepan, cook the potato and 4 cloves of the garlic (reserving 2 cloves), in boiling salted water for 10 minutes or until the potato is soft. Drain and set aside.

Soak the bread in cold water and reserve. In the bowl of a food processor, process the almonds until very fine. Then add the cooked potato and the cooked garlic and process. Dissolve the sugar in the lemon juice and vinegar in a small cup. Drain the bread and, using your hands, squeeze out only half the water. Add the damp bread gradually to the food processor, alternating with the lemon juice mixture and the olive oil. Add the salt and pepper and process until thick and light. Mince the remaining cloves of garlic and add to your taste. Add a bit of cold water if the sauce seems too thick.

To serve, spoon some sauce on a radicchio leaf on the side of a plate and arrange the beans around the sauce. Serve at room temperature.

NOTE: Sweet white runner beans are available through mail order at Dean & DeLuca in New York. Balducci's in New York carries the Greek gigandes, or they may be found at Greek or some Italian groceries or specialty shops (see Mail Order Sources, pages 501–506).

The

Versatile

Grain

and the

Elegant

Bean

444

Gratin of Scarlet Runner Beans Baked with Pasta, Buttered Bread Crumbs and Anchovies

SERVES 6

Large, darkly mottled crimson runner beans are simmered slowly with aromatic vegetables and herbs, then tossed with pasta and topped with bread crumbs mixed with just a touch of anchovy and lots of parsley. Prepare well ahead of time, since the final baking takes just minutes to heat the dish and crisp the top.

1 C. dried scarlet runner beans, soaked and drained (see NOTE)	6 ozs. dried fusilli or penne pasta
1 large whole onion	2 Tbs. olive oil
2 medium carrots, coarsely chopped (⅔ C.)	2–3 cloves garlic, finely minced (2 tsps.)
1 medium stalk of celery with leaves, coarsely chopped (⅓ C.)	½ C. finely minced flat leaf parsley
4½ C. tepid water	Freshly ground black pepper to taste
3 large sprigs flat leaf parsley	Butter for greasing baking dish
3 sprigs thyme	3 Tbs. butter
1 large bay leaf	3 anchovies, rinsed and dried on paper towels
Salt to taste	2 C. fresh bread crumbs

To a 3-quart nonstick saucepan, add the drained beans, onion, carrots, celery and water. Tie the parsley, thyme and bay leaf together with a string and add to the pot. Cover and bring to a boil, then lower the heat and simmer for 1 hour, 15 minutes, adding additional boiled water as needed to keep the beans covered, and salt in the last 5 minutes of cooking.

Meanwhile, bring a large pot of salted water to a boil and cook the pasta until al dente. While the pasta cooks, heat the olive oil in a large skillet and sauté the garlic without browning over medium low heat, stirring for 1 to 2 minutes. Stir in half the parsley. When the pasta is cooked, drain and add to the skillet, stirring it in. Season with pepper and set aside.

When the beans are tender, lift out and discard the onion and the herb bouquet and add salt to taste. Drain and reserve the bean liquid. Stir the beans into the skillet with the pasta. Butter a 2½-quart shallow baking dish and transfer the mixture to the dish. Stir in ⅔ cup of the reserved bean liquid to moisten, then wipe out the skillet. Return the skillet to the stove and melt the 3 tablespoons butter over low heat. Stir in the anchovies and crush them while stirring with a wooden spoon. Add the remaining parsley and stir into the mixture in the baking dish. At this point, you may cover and refrigerate the baking dish. If you do so, put the bread crumbs in a covered bowl and refrigerate them too.

When ready to serve, remove the baking dish from the refrigerator and let it return to room temperature so that the sudden high heat will not shatter it. Preheat the oven to 400°F. Sprinkle the surface of the baking dish with the bread crumbs and bake, uncovered, until the top is brown, about 15 minutes. Serve at once.

NOTE: You may substitute large lima beans for the scarlet runner beans. Check the Chart (see page 384) for cooking time. Since lima beans do not have a dark crimson color like the scarlet runners, substitute spinach pasta for the fusilli or penne in order to get a color contrast.

Warm Gigandes with Fennel, Olives and Red Peppers in a Lemon Mint Vinaigrette

SERVES 8

When cooked, these giant-size creamy-textured beans in a sprightly mint and lemon vinaigrette offer a pleasing contrast to sweet, crisp peppers, vaguely licorice-flavored fennel and slightly briny olives. The combination makes for a good cocktail nibble

1½ **C. dried gigandes beans, sweet white runner beans or large lima beans, soaked and drained**	4–5 **black Kalamata olives, pitted and sliced**
Salt to taste	¼ **C. lemon juice**
½ **small bulb of fennel, thinly sliced (½ C.)**	¼ **C. strongly flavored Spanish olive oil**
½ **small sweet red pepper, thinly sliced (¼ C.)**	**Freshly ground black pepper to taste**
	2 **Tbs. finely minced fresh mint**

The

Versatile

Grain

and the

Elegant

Bean

To a 3-quart saucepan, add the beans with water to cover by 2 to 3 inches and bring to a boil. Lower the heat and simmer until the beans are tender (see Chart, page 443). Add the salt and let the beans stay in the water to cool slightly for about 10 minutes. When the beans have cooled, drain and put them in a medium-size bowl. Add the fennel, red pepper and olives. Put the lemon juice into a small cup and whisk the olive oil into it. Add the black pepper and additional salt if you wish. Stir in the mint and pour the vinaigrette over the warm beans. Stir gently to mix. Serve at once or let stand at room temperature. Stir once again before serving.

Haricots d'Agneau:
Prizewinner Beans with
Lamb, Tomatoes and Fresh Thyme

SERVES 6

A rustic, lusty French farmhouse treat, redolent of fresh thyme.

Beans

1½ C. prizewinner beans (or substitute white cannellini beans), soaked and drained

4 C. water

1 small onion, stuck with 3 whole cloves

1 large carrot

1 bay leaf

3 sprigs fresh thyme

In a 3-quart saucepan, bring the beans, water, vegetables and herbs to a boil, lower the heat and simmer for 1 hour, 15 minutes. Meanwhile, prepare the lamb. (If substituting cannellini beans, see Chart, page 460, for cooking time.)

Lamb

1 Tbs. olive oil

1½ lbs. lean shoulder of lamb, trimmed of fat and cut into 2-in. cubes

¼ tsp. freshly ground black pepper

1 Tbs. flour

1 medium onion, finely chopped (⅔ C.)

2 cloves garlic, finely minced (about 2 tsps.)

Salt to taste

14-oz. can Italian peeled tomatoes, undrained

1 Tbs. tomato paste

1½ C. water

1 bay leaf

1½ Tbs. fresh thyme leaves

Heat the oil in a 10-inch skillet over medium high heat. Sprinkle the meat with pepper and dredge it in the flour. Add the meat to the skillet and brown on all sides. Remove the meat with a slotted spoon to a plate, and add the onions, garlic and salt to the skillet. Stir and cook for 3 minutes. Add the tomatoes, tomato paste and water and return the meat to the skillet. Add the bay leaf and half the thyme leaves. Bring to a boil, cover and lower the heat. Simmer for 1½ hours or until the lamb is tender, stirring occasionally. Then remove and discard the bay leaf.

When the beans are cooked, remove the carrot, cut it into ½-inch dice and add to the lamb. Lift out the onion, bay leaf and thyme sprigs and discard. Drain the beans and combine with the lamb, simmering for 10 more minutes. Transfer to a warm serving dish and sprinkle with the remaining thyme. Serve with rice if you wish.

Soybeans

Glycine max

Alias. Soya beans, *soja, soi,* soypeas.

Description. There are more than 1,000 varieties of soybeans, ranging from the size of a pea to the size of a cherry. They also come in a rainbow of colors: red, black, yellow, brown and green. The most easily available and the most popular in the United States are the yellow ones and the black soybeans, which have a yellow interior. Both are the size and shape of a large pea, about ⅜ of an inch.

Characteristics. Soybeans grow in pods that are covered with a grayish, tawny, fuzzy coat. The pods themselves may range in color from tan to black.

History. The soybean has been cultivated and eaten by the Chinese for thousands of years, probably dating back to 2800 B.C. when its growth was first recorded. However, it did not find its way to nearby Japan until the sixth century and it was not until the seventeenth century that it finally made its way to Europe. As recently as the twentieth century, after World War II, the extraordinary nutritive value of the soybean was first recognized in the United States, and its popularity began to spread among non-Asian Americans. Before that, it was used mostly for animal fodder, with a large proportion of the crop shipped abroad.

Traditional Uses. Of the world's supply of soybeans, 75 percent is grown in the Western Hemisphere, with approximately 55 million tons produced here in the United States alone. Half is harvested for export. It is not a very popular table bean in its whole form, since the flavor is bland and it is the hardest of beans, requiring long soaking and cooking times. Home cooks, particularly, have not embraced the cooked soybean as a table food with the same enthusiasm that industry has.

In the United States, the soybean is used for a vast range of *processed foods,* since its nutritive value is so high. It is found in imitation cheeses and imitation butter (margarine), as well as in imitation hot dogs. It is also found in a plethora of products that are *not* food, e.g., soap, linoleum and plastics, to name but a few.

The

Versatile

Grain

and the

Elegant

Bean

448

There has been a slight change now, however. With the proliferation of Japanese, Chinese and other oriental restaurants, as well as a growing interest in cooking their cuisines at home, we have become more familiar with several soy-based and easily digested table foods, long used by oriental cultures, and have incorporated them into our kitchen larders. For example:

- *Chinese Soy Sauce.* A usually dark and salty sauce made from fermented soybeans and roasted grain such as wheat or barley and hydrochloric acid to break down the soybean. The remains are then mixed with corn syrup, caramel coloring and salt and then diluted with water. It is used as a flavoring in stir frying and other Chinese cooking methods.
- *Shoyu.* A naturally fermented and aged, more mellow soybean product.
- *Tamari.* A wheat-free fermented sauce of soy, salt and water. It is a bit stronger in flavor than shoyu.
- *Miso.* A fermented, concentrated bean paste, made by adding a mold (*koji*) to cooked soybeans, some sort of grain and aging the fermented paste from 6 months to 3 years. Miso is used primarily for making soups, sauces and basic flavoring for Japanese cooking.
- *Tofu.* The custardlike cake made by curdling soy milk in a process similar to that used for cheese. There are two forms of tofu, one of which is firmer in texture since some water is pressed out. The other is soft and custardy. Tofu is neutral enough in taste to take on the flavor of whatever it is cooked with.
- *Tempeh.* Sturdier than tofu and adaptable to many cooking techniques, i.e., grilling, steaming and frying. Tempeh is an ancient fermented food from Indonesia, made with split, cooked soybeans and a funguslike starter to encourage fermentation. It has 50 percent more protein than hamburger and it serves as an excellent meat substitute for people on vegetarian diets.
- *Soy Milk.* A nondairy substitute for those people who are allergic to cow's milk. Although higher in protein than milk, as well as being cholesterol-free, low in fat and sodium and rich in iron, it is lower in calcium and therefore is usually enriched with calcium. This is the milk that is curdled for the making of tofu.
- *Soy Flour.* Usually mixed with other flours for baked goods. It is high in protein (twice that of wheat), and low in carbohydrates. The Japanese frequently use it for confections.
- *Fermented Black Soy Beans.* Strongly flavored, highly salted, and used frequently in Chinese cuisine.
- *Soybean Oil.* Since the soybean is 34 percent oil, it is easily used in the manufacture of margarine and, when it is highly processed, it is included in many supermarket vegetable oils on the shelf.
- *Soybean Sprouts* (see page 278 for sprouting instructions). These 1-inch crisp sprouts appear within 3 to 5 days. However, unlike mung bean sprouts, which can be eaten raw, soybean sprouts must be blanched or cooked for easier digestibility. Sprouting does eliminate any complex sugars that might cause intestinal flatulence (see page 307).

Availability. Fresh "green" soybeans are available shelled from the pod, but usually only in areas in which they are grown. Dried yellow and black soybeans are usually found in health food stores (we find the black ones tastier). Soy milk, soy flour and tempeh are also found in health food stores, but tofu can now be purchased water-packed in your local supermarket as well as in oriental markets. Keep the tofu covered and soaking in water, place in the refrigerator and change the water daily. It will keep for several days.

BASIC PREPARATION

Whole soybeans are more difficult to digest because they contain enzymes that block easy digestion. However, soybeans in the forms used in these recipes have eliminated these enzymes through fermentation. Cooking the whole soybean is also a tedious process and the end result is not really that flavorful. Thus we prefer to use the various other oriental by-product forms of the soybean such as sprouts and tofu.

If you do decide to cook whole soybeans, they need a minimum of twelve hours of soaking, and in hot water it is advisable to change the soaking water once or twice to prevent the bean from souring. Then they take from three to four hours of cooking.

The

Versatile

Grain

and the

Elegant

Bean

450

Napa Cabbage Rolls with Tofu, Spinach and Chicken

SERVES 8 TO 10

Delicately flavored napa cabbage envelopes butterflied chicken breasts that are rolled around a tofu, spinach and shiitake mushroom filling. They are then poached in a mirin-flavored chicken stock, thickened slightly to form a sauce. A light and lovely dish that is made with no fat or oil of any kind, perfect for the diet-watcher.

Filling

3 fresh shiitake mushrooms
½ lb. fresh spinach, trimmed and washed well, then dried and torn into pieces
½ lb. soft tofu, dried on paper towels and cut into large pieces
3–4 scallions, finely minced (½ C.)
1 Tbs. soy sauce
2 tsps. rice vinegar
Salt and freshly ground black pepper to taste
Pinch of cayenne

Cut off the mushroom stems and discard. Wash the mushrooms, dry well on paper towels, add to the bowl of a food processor and chop finely. Add the spinach to the food processor and process until fine. Add the pieces of tofu and process for a few more strokes. Scrape the filling into a bowl and stir in the scallions, soy, vinegar, salt, pepper and cayenne and set aside.

Napa Cabbage

1 large head napa cabbage

Cut off sixteen leaves of the cabbage and add them to boiling water in a large pot. Simmer for 1 minute, then drain and blot on paper towels. Trim off 2 inches of the white part of the cabbage leaves. Dice four of these white pieces and add them to the filling. Discard the rest and set the cabbage leaves aside.

Chicken

2 lbs. chicken breasts, butterflied and pounded thin (there should be 8 thin slices)
¼ C. mirin (sweet Japanese rice wine)
Salt and freshly ground black pepper to taste
2 C. Chicken Stock, preferably homemade (see page 171)
3 Tbs. cold water
1 Tbs. cornstarch

Lay the pieces of chicken in a flat dish. Pour the mirin over them, season with salt and pepper and marinate for 15 minutes. Lift the chicken out and pour the mirin into the chicken stock. Spread some of the filling over the chicken and roll up tightly, then roll again in one cabbage leaf, laying a second leaf over the top in the opposite direction to enclose it. Repeat the process until there are eight rolls. Tie with string so that they don't open while cooking. Into a 5-quart Dutch oven, carefully put the rolls in one layer, placing them tightly against one another. Add the chicken stock and simmer for 20 minutes.

When the chicken rolls are done, use two spoons to remove them to a plate, letting them cool for 5 minutes. Then cut the string and with a sharp knife, cut the rolls into 1-inch slices. Arrange on a platter. Mix the cold water with the cornstarch. Strain the stock, return it to the saucepan and bring to a boil. Slowly stir in the cornstarch mixture and, stirring constantly, cook until the sauce is thickened, about 2 to 3 minutes. Spoon some sauce over the rolls and serve with rice if you wish. Pass any remaining sauce at the table.

Chinese Scallion Pancakes with Soybean Sprouts and Pork

SERVES 4 TO 6

Soybean sprouts are larger and crisper than their more delicate smaller relatives, the mung bean sprouts. These scallion pancakes, sometimes called "doilies" are the same ones (without the scallions) that are used for Peking duck and they are not difficult to make. In fact, the whole recipe takes less time to make than to order and receive delivery from Chinese take-out. And it tastes fresher too.

Chinese Scallion Pancakes (Doilies)
MAKES 12 PANCAKES

1 C. all-purpose flour, sifted	1 scallion, finely minced (1½ Tbs.)
⅛ tsp. salt	Cornstarch for dusting the work
½ C. boiling water	surface
	2 tsps. oriental sesame oil

Put the flour and salt in a medium-size bowl and slowly add the boiling water, mixing with a wooden spoon until a dough forms. Scatter the scallions over the surface of the dough. Sift some cornstarch lightly on a work surface. Gather the dough and knead it for 5 minutes on the surface until smooth and pliable with the scallions well distributed throughout. Invert the bowl over the dough and let rest for 30 minutes. (At this point you can prepare the bean sprout and pork filling if you wish.)

After 30 minutes, sift a bit of additional cornstarch on the work surface and also put some on your hands. Roll the dough with your hands into a 12-inch-long rope. Dip a sharp knife into the cornstarch and cut the rope into 1-inch pieces. Flatten each piece into disks by using the palms of your hands, with each circle about 2½ inches in diameter. Brush the surfaces right to the edges with the sesame oil, then sandwich

The

Versatile

Grain

and the

Elegant

Bean

452

two circles together with the oiled sides in. There will now be 6 pancakes. Roll each double circle thinly (about ¼ inch thick), using a rolling pin. Each circle should now be about 5 inches in diameter.

Heat a nonstick skillet over low heat and cook each pancake individually for 1 minute on each side. As they are finished, gently pull the pancakes apart to form two again. Cover with plastic wrap between each layer and continue the process until you have twelve pancakes. If you wish to make the pancakes well in advance, steam them over boiling water for 10 minutes when you're ready to use them in order to soften and warm them.

Bean Sprout and Pork Filling

½-in. piece ginger, grated (¼ tsp.)
½ clove garlic, grated (about ¼ tsp.)
2 tsps. dry sherry
⅛ tsp. salt
¼ tsp. sugar
2 tsps. soy sauce
1½ tsps. cornstarch
¾ C. lean pork fillet, cut into thin matchstick-shaped pieces (6 ozs. pork—freeze partially for easier slicing)

3 Tbs. corn or peanut oil
¾ lb. soybean sprouts, dried well on paper towels
¼ C. chicken stock
Few cilantro leaves

In a small bowl, combine the ginger, garlic, sherry, salt, sugar, soy sauce and cornstarch. Add the pork and mix to coat. Let stand for 15 minutes, mixing once during that time. Heat a tablespoon of the oil in a large nonstick skillet, until very hot, then add the bean sprouts and stir-fry for 1 minute. Remove the sprouts and reserve.

Add the remaining oil and heat until very hot, then add the pork and stir-fry for 2 minutes. Return the sprouts to the pan, and stir in the chicken stock. Cover, lower the heat and simmer for 1 minute more. Use about 1 tablespoon of the filling for each pancake. Roll and garnish with a cilantro leaf. Allow two to three rolls per person, depending upon appetites.

Tofu with Ginger and Black Sesame Seeds

SERVES 4 TO 8

The firm, bland tofu triangles are a perfect vehicle for soaking up the dark, spicy ginger-scented sauce as they marinate in the refrigerator for 1 to 2 days. Serve them as a light hors d'oeuvre to friends who are on a weight-loss diet.

1 lb. firm tofu (2 square pieces, about ½ lb. each)	2 tsps. oriental sesame oil
1 small clove garlic, finely minced (1 tsp.)	⅛ tsp. hot chile oil
2 tsps. finely minced, peeled ginger	½ tsp. light mild honey
3 Tbs. light soy sauce	1 small scallion, cut on the diagonal, green part only, thinly sliced (1 Tbs.)
2 Tbs. rice vinegar	⅛ tsp. freshly ground black pepper
¼ C. cold water	½ tsp. black sesame seeds

Drain and blot the tofu with paper towels. Cut each square block into quarters, then cut each quarter into triangles. You will have sixteen triangular pieces. Arrange them in an attractive pattern in a shallow dish with sides such as a gratin dish.

In a small bowl, whisk together the garlic, ginger, soy sauce, rice vinegar, water, sesame oil, chile oil and honey. Spoon the mixture over the tofu. Scatter the scallions over all, then sprinkle with pepper and sesame seeds. Cover with plastic wrap and marinate in the refrigerator for 1 to 2 days. Tilt the dish occasionally and spoon some of the sauce over the surface. Serve chilled or at room temperature.

The

Versatile

Grain

and the

Elegant

Bean

454

The "White Bean" Family

Phaseolus vulgaris

Alias. Haricot beans—and covering the mature dried seed of various pod beans listed below. It is a large family.

Great Northern Beans

Medium size, about ½ inch long, flattish, slight kidney shape and bright white color.

Steuben Yellow-Eye Beans

Flatter "eye" beans and probably the original beans used for Boston baked beans. They are white with an amber eye that covers half the surface of the beans.

Swedish Brown Beans

Not really a white bean, but their cooking properties are similar to the beans listed above and thus we have included them here. They are hardy bush beans, light brown in color, and have adapted well to Northern climes. They were introduced into the Midwestern plains states by Scandinavian immigrants about 100 years ago and thus might fall under the category of "imported" beans rather than New World.

Navy Beans

Small (¼ inch), plumpish, oval white beans. Some packagers do not differentiate between navy beans and pea beans or even Great Northern beans, and thus there may be several varieties in one package.

Pea Beans

Alias small whites or California beans. These are very small, about half the size of navy beans and are interchangeable with them.

Jacob's Cattle Beans

Alias coach dogs or Dalmatian beans, and sometimes referred to by growers as Trout beans. They are heirloom beans that are kidney-shaped, grown in New England since the colonial days. Jacob's Cattle beans are long (⅝ inch) beans that are slim, creamy white with a large, dark maroon-colored splotch and tiny satellite freckles of the same color.

Anasazi Beans

Named after the Navajo word meaning "ancient ones." The Indians of the American Southwest and Mexico still grow and treasure these beans from Colorado, generally

The

Versatile

Grain

and the

Elegant

Bean

456

believed to be the descendants of the Jacob's Cattle bean, which they closely resemble. The anasazi beans are a bit smaller (about ½ inch long) and more plump, although the colors and the patterns are quite similar, but without the freckles.

Cannellini Beans

Alias, white kidney beans, *haricots blancs, fasolia, fagioli*. They are white, oval, kidney-shaped beans with a tough seed coat and a smooth texture. They were originally cultivated in South America, but are associated with and extremely popular in central Italy, Greece and France.

Soldier Beans

Alias red-eye beans, they are a cool-area heirloom variety that is grown in Maine and in other parts of the country as well. They are distinguished by the splashes of color in the shape of a soldier's silhouette at the eye or hilum. They are chalk white and kidney-shaped, about ⅝ inch long, and a handsome and interesting addition to the white bean family.

Marrow Beans

The roundest of the white beans, about ½ inch in size, and with a lovely unctuous flavor.

China Yellow Beans

Alias sulphur beans because of their color. In spite of their name, they are not from China but traditional to Maine. They possess a silky soft texture and a mellow flavor.

French Navy Beans

Alias *cocos blancs* in France, they are heirloom beans that are white, plump, about ⅜ inch in size, with a slightly green undertone produced by pale veining. The beans have a unique baconlike flavor and a silken texture and are quite delicious.

Calypso Beans

Round, plump, about ½ inch long, they are an absolutely beautiful hybrid bean and a most dramatic-looking newcomer. Half white, half black, plus the addition of one black polka dot for emphasis, this unique and novel bean looks as though the ancient Chinese yin and yang symbol of harmony had been imprinted on its surface.

Flageolets

Called the "Rolls-Royce of Beans" they originated in the Americas but were developed in France in the 1800s. They are medium-size (about ½ inch), kidney-shaped and a pale, pale green. They are actually the immature kidney-shaped pod beans that are removed from their pods when they are very young rather than after they have reached maturity. Consequently, they still carry their delicate pale green color. Flageolets are cultivated mostly in France and Italy, after which we transport them right back to where they originated. Their transportation costs probably make them the most expensive of all beans.

Pod Beans

Alias String beans, snap beans, green beans, yellow wax beans. This group is usually eaten in the pod and they are sometimes called *fillet beans*. The French call them

The

Versatile

Grain

and the

Elegant

Bean

458

haricots verts and the Germans dub them *Buschbohnen*. The pod beans grow either as pole beans or bush beans and they require careful care and a fast growing season, along with frequent picking, to harvest them at their most delicate, stringless best. These beans are usually sold fresh in season, as well as frozen and in cans (which we dislike intensely!).

History. Along with lima beans, red kidneys, pinto beans and black beans, all of these beans are "New World" beans, (with the exception of the Swedish brown beans), meaning that they were growing in the Western Hemisphere long before the European explorers came to our shores. Sometimes they are called haricot beans, supposedly mispronounced from the Aztec word *ayacotl* by the Conquistadores and the other adventurers who came to the New World from Europe.

It was their practice to send home seeds of all the new foods they encountered, and by doing so they changed the direction of European gastronomy. The same pattern was followed as exploration expanded into various parts of the United States, Mexico, and Central and South America where some beans were found growing wild both as tall climbing plants and low bush varieties, some of which were eaten pods and all (such as the familiar string bean). Each climate also yielded different varieties, from the dry, hot Pueblo region to the damp, colder climates of the temperate Northeast. The pods were allowed to mature and dry on the vine, providing winter supplies for the explorers, while some others were sent back home.

The white kidney beans (or cannellini beans) were sent back to Italy during the sixteenth century and then became a major crop in Tuscany. In France, the first plantings of these haricot beans began in the eighteenth century near the town of Soissons, where a local variety exists and is known by the name Soisson bean.

Traditional uses. It depends upon the regional popularity and ethnic preferences. For example, one dish evolved from the Pilgrims, who watched the Native Americans bake beans with deer fat in clay vessels that were buried in a hole lined with hot stones and left overnight to bake. From those lessons baked bean dishes evolved that were slowly cooked in the oven or a pit (bean hole), along with mustard, pork fat and some sort of sweetening such as brown sugar, maple sugar or molasses.

green bean

Availability. Dried, fresh in the pod, frozen. They are carried in most supermarkets, ethnic specialty and gourmet food stores. Some are available through mail order (see Mail Order sources, pages 501–506).

Cooking Chart

Type of Bean:	Cannellini (White Kidney)	Pea Beans (Small Whites)	Soldier Beans	Steuben Yellow-Eye Beans	Jacob's Cattle Beans
Amount:	1 C. dried	1 C. dried	1 C. dried	1 C. dried	1 C. dried
Approx. Cooking Time:	45 minutes	1 hour	25 minutes	30 minutes	35 minutes
Approx. Yield:	2½ C.	2½ C.	2½ C.	2 C.	2⅔ C.
Comments:				Markings remain but not defined.	Thin skinned. Foamy, needs skimming. Color fades a bit when cooking.

Type of Bean:	Marrow Beans	Calypso Beans	Navy Beans	Great Northern Beans	Swedish Brown Beans
Amount:	1 C. dried	1 C. dried	1 C. dried	1 C. dried	1 C. dried
Approx. Cooking Time:	1 hour, 15 minutes	30 minutes	45 to 60 minutes	45 minutes	45 to 60 minutes
Approx. Yield:	2½ C.	3 C.	2⅔ C.	2⅔ C.	3 C.
Comments:		Color markings fade a bit.			Very foamy. Discard first boiling water. Rinse, use fresh water.

Cooking Chart

Type of Bean:	Anasazi Beans	Flageolets	China Yellow Beans	French Navy Beans
Amount:	1 C. dried	1 C. dried	1 C. dried	1 C. dried
Approx. Cooking Time:	50 minutes	60 minutes	40 minutes	30 minutes
Approx. Yield:	2¼ C.	2¼ C.	2¼ C.	2½ C.
Comments:	Markings fade after soaking and cooking. Bean turns pale pink.	Some color fades.	Very tender. Good for purées.	Very soft. Skins slip off. Good for purées. Silky texture.

Fresh Snap Beans

There are several varieties:

- Green—most common, usually stringless.
- Yellow or wax—popular in the East and Southern states.
- Italian Romano—broader and flatter, in green or yellow. Need stringing.
- Purple pods—similar in flavor to green snap beans. However, color is purple or green mottled with purple and the color fades after cooking.
- Haricot vert or French bean—long, very thin, young bean. Cut off tip before cooking.

Time of cooking varies with variety. They should be cooked, steamed or sautéed quickly to retain flavor and texture. Approx. Yield: 1 lb. serves 4.

Sweet Orange Peppers Stuffed
with Calypso Beans

SERVES 8 TO 10

These charming and dramatic hybrid beans taste as good as they look. They are tossed in a cilantro/cumin vinaigrette along with hot Jalapeño pepper Monterey Jack cheese, and tiny bits of pepperoni, then ladled into sweet orange peppers. They make a most colorful presentation for a buffet.

Peppers

8–10 orange sweet peppers (yellow or
   red can also be used, but use
   thick-walled Dutch peppers only)

Preheat the oven to broil. Cut off a thin slice from the bottoms of the peppers so that they will stand upright. Slice off about ½ inch from the top stem and cut out the seeds and ribs from the pepper interiors. Lay the peppers on their sides and slip them under the broiler, turning occasionally to char the surface skin all over. Do not overcook or the peppers will collapse. Slip them into a paper bag for 5 minutes, then scrape off the charred skin and set the peppers aside.

Beans

1½ C. dried calypso beans, soaked and
   drained (see NOTE)
1 small onion
1 small carrot
1 small stalk celery

1 bay leaf
2 sprigs thyme
3 sprigs parsley
Salt to taste

To a 3-quart saucepan, add the beans, onion, carrot and celery stalk. Tie the bay leaf, thyme and parsley together with a string and add to the pot. Add tepid water to cover the beans by 2 inches. Bring to a boil, skim the surface foam, cover and lower the heat. Simmer for about 25 minutes or until the beans are tender but maintain their shape. Lift out and discard the vegetables and the herb bouquet. Drain and rinse the beans in tepid water. Season with salt. Gently mix the beans with the cilantro vinaigrette (see below) while still warm.

Cilantro Vinaigrette
MAKES ⅔ CUP

¼ C. white wine vinegar
1 tsp. coarse-grain mustard
Salt and freshly ground black pepper
   to taste
⅛ tsp. ground cumin

1 small clove garlic, finely minced
   (½ tsp.)
⅓ C. olive oil
¼ C. coarsely chopped fresh cilantro

The

Versatile

Grain

and the

Elegant

Bean

462

In a small bowl, whisk together the vinegar, mustard, salt, pepper, cumin and garlic. Whisk in the olive oil and cilantro.

¾ C. ¼-in. cubes Monterey Jack cheese with Jalapeño peppers (about 4 ozs.)	½ C. finely diced pepperoni sausage (about 2 ozs.) Lettuce leaves (optional)

When the beans have reached room temperature, gently stir in the diced cheese and pepperoni and fill each pepper. Place the pepper on a lettuce leaf if you wish and serve at room temperature.

If you wish, you may prepare and stuff the peppers well ahead of time. Just wrap them in plastic wrap and refrigerate them, but bring them to room temperature before serving.

NOTE: You may substitute ¾ cup dried black beans and ¾ cup dried small white beans, cooked separately, for the 1½ cups dried calypso beans.

Flageolets with Celery Root, Roasted Red Peppers and Tarragon Vinaigrette

SERVES 4

Crisp celery root, smoky red peppers and the slim, elegant flageolet beans are perfumed with just a hint of tarragon in this warm salad.

Tarragon Vinaigrette

2 Tbs. red wine vinegar	½ tsp. dried tarragon, crumbled
1 Tbs. lemon juice	¼ C. olive oil
1 Tbs. Dijon-style mustard	1 Tbs. finely minced fresh parsley
Few drops Tabasco sauce	
Salt and freshly ground black pepper to taste	

In a small bowl, whisk together the first seven ingredients. Gradually whisk in the olive oil, then stir in the parsley. Set aside while preparing the salad.

Salad

½ lb. celery root (knob celery)	1 C. drained, cooked, dried flageolets (see Chart, page 461)
1 large sweet red pepper, roasted, skinned and seeded	8–10 leaves *frisée* (curled escarole)
2 thin scallions, sliced thinly on the diagonal (½ C.)	Minced parsley (optional)

Peel the celery root and cut into matchstick-thin pieces, either by hand or with an extra-fine julienne blade of a food processor. Put into a strainer and set the strainer in a large bowl. Pour boiling water over the celery root, blanch for 30 seconds, then drain and put into a large bowl.

Cut the roasted red peppers into very thin strips and add them to the bowl. Then add the scallions and the cooked beans and pour the vinaigrette over the vegetables. Toss gently to mix, cover and keep at room temperature for at least 4 hours or longer if you wish.

To serve, line four individual plates with the *frisée* leaves. Taste the beans for additional seasoning, then spoon equal amounts of the salad over the *frisée*. Sprinkle with minced parsley if you wish.

Purée of China Yellow Beans and Saffron Wrapped with Grilled Eggplant Slices

SERVES 4 TO 6

Golden, silky-textured, mellow-flavored bean purée teased with saffron is wrapped with thinly sliced eggplant, then quickly sautéed. It's an elegant side dish for roast leg of lamb or grilled lamb chops, or serve alone as an appetizer.

Bean Purée

4 C. unsalted chicken stock
1 C. dried China yellow beans, or white marrow beans, soaked and drained
1 large clove garlic
1 small bay leaf
1 whole small red dried hot chile such as Japonés

Small pinch saffron threads
1 whole clove
Salt and freshly ground black pepper to taste
2 Tbs. butter

In a 3-quart saucepan, bring the chicken stock and beans to a boil. Lower the heat, add the garlic, bay leaf, hot chile, saffron and whole clove. Cover and with the lid slightly ajar, simmer for 40 to 45 minutes (marrow beans will take longer—see Chart, pages 460–461) or until the beans are very soft. Lift out and discard the bay leaf, whole clove and the hot chile. Drain the beans and discard the liquid. Purée the beans and garlic in the bowl of a food processor along with the salt, pepper and butter. Cover and chill the purée until needed. It can be made the day before if you wish.

The

Versatile

Grain

and the

Elegant

Bean

464

Eggplant

½ C. olive oil
1½ lbs. long-shaped eggplant
Coarse salt and freshly ground black
    pepper to taste

2 Tbs. finely minced fresh chives
Small lemon wedges

Preheat the oven to 325°F. Line two cookie sheets with aluminum foil and brush with some of the olive oil. Cut off the stem end of the eggplant, then cut off thin slices from both sides and discard. Lay the eggplant on its side and cut horizontally into twelve ⅛-inch thick slices with a sharp chef's knife. Lay the slices on the prepared pans and brush both sides liberally with the remaining oil. Sprinkle lightly with coarse salt and pepper and bake for 10 to 12 minutes. Removing the slices carefully with a spatula, place two slices on a sheet of waxed paper. Cover with another piece of waxed paper and place two more slices of the eggplant on that piece of waxed paper. Repeat with the remaining eggplant. Then slip the pile on a plate, cover with plastic wrap and place in the refrigerator until ready to use. This can also be done the day before if you wish.

To assemble, put 1 heaping tablespoon of bean purée on the wider side of each slice of eggplant and roll it up. Place the rolls in a nonstick skillet and sauté over low heat for a few minutes on each side until golden, turning once carefully. Serve with a sprinkling of chives and small wedges of lemon.

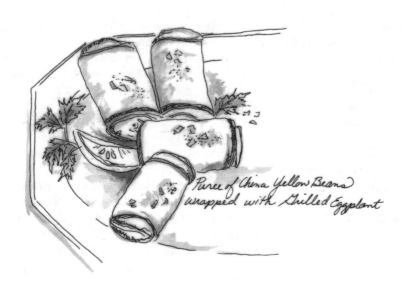

Puree of China Yellow Beans
wrapped with Grilled Eggplant

Cream of Flageolet Soup with Lemon and Fresh Herbs

SERVES 6 TO 8

We tend to think of bean soups as hearty and heavy winter fare. This one belies the cliché. It's light and brightly flavored, and a soup that you can serve hot or chilled.

5 Tbs. butter
1 small leek with 1-in. of green part, finely sliced (about ½ C.)
1 medium-large onion, coarsely chopped (1 C.)
2 stalks celery, finely sliced (about 1 C.)
6 C. unsalted Chicken Stock, preferably homemade (see page 171)
1 C. dried flageolets, soaked and drained
1 bay leaf
2 large cloves garlic

Salt
¼ C. milk
¼ C. light cream
1 egg yolk
Peel of ½ large lemon, finely minced (1 tsp.)
3 Tbs. lemon juice
Coarsely chopped mixed fresh herbs: 2 Tbs. parsley, 1 Tbs. basil, 2 Tbs. summer savory, 1 tsp. tarragon
Freshly ground black pepper to taste
Few grindings fresh nutmeg
Paper-thin slices lemon

In a heavy 4-quart Dutch oven, melt 3 tablespoons of the butter, add the leeks, onions and celery and sauté over low heat, stirring occasionally, until the vegetables are soft but not brown, about 6 to 8 minutes. Add the chicken stock, flageolets, bay leaf and garlic and bring to a boil. Then lower the heat to a simmer. With the pot lid slightly ajar, cook for 1 hour, 15 minutes, until the beans are very tender. Add salt during the last 5 minutes of cooking. Remove and discard the bay leaf and strain the soup into a bowl. Reserve the stock.

Purée the beans and vegetables in the bowl of a food processor along with a ladleful of stock and blend until smooth. Return this mixture to the Dutch oven. To the same unwashed food processor, add the milk, cream, egg yolk and remaining butter, cut into small pieces. Add the remaining warm stock and process until well mixed. Add this to the bean/vegetable purée and bring slowly to a simmer. Cook over low heat for 5 to 10 minutes, stirring occasionally until hot. Remove from the heat and stir in the lemon peel, lemon juice, chopped herbs, salt, pepper and nutmeg. Serve hot and float a paper-thin slice of lemon on the surface of each serving for garnish.

The

Versatile

Grain

and the

Elegant

Bean

466

Senate Navy Bean Soup with Ham

SERVES 8 TO 10

The story goes this way: Senator Everett Dirksen of Illinois, a well-known bean lover, upon finding no bean soup on the Senate restaurant menu, introduced a resolution that, while the Senate was in session, no day might pass without his favorite comfort food on the bill of fare. Hence, the name.

- 2 C. dried white pea beans or navy beans, soaked and drained
- 3 qts. water
- 3 sprigs thyme
- 1 bay leaf
- 3 cloves garlic, finely minced (about 1 Tbs.)
- 2 large stalks celery, finely chopped (1 C.)
- 1 large onion, finely chopped (1 C.)

- 1 C. cubed, peeled potatoes (about ½ lb.)
- Salt
- ¼ C. milk
- 1½ C. bite-size pieces lean baked ham (about ½ lb.) or 1 lb. meaty ham bone or ham hock (see NOTE)
- Freshly ground black pepper to taste
- ¼ C. finely minced fresh parsley

In a 7- or 8-quart stockpot or heavy Dutch oven, combine the beans with the water. Tie the thyme and bay leaf together with string and add to the pot along with the garlic, celery and onions. Bring to a boil, skim any foam then lower the heat and simmer, covered, for 45 to 60 minutes, or until the beans are tender.

Meanwhile, boil the potatoes in salted water for about 20 minutes, then drain and set aside. Lift out and discard the thyme and bay leaf bundle. Add the milk to the saucepan with the potatoes, then scoop out two ladles full of beans and add them. Mash with a potato masher, then return this rough purée to the pot along with the ham. Season with salt and pepper and continue to simmer for 30 minutes more. Stir in the parsley and simmer for 5 minutes before serving. Taste to adjust the seasoning.

NOTE: We have used trimmed, bite-size pieces of lean ham rather than a meaty ham bone or ham hock in order to cut down on the fat content and still be true to the taste of a classic recipe. If you wish to use a ham bone or ham hock, add it to the beans and water before adding the herbs and vegetables. Then remove the bone, returning any lean meat to the pot toward the end of cooking.

Portuguese Caldo Verde with
Cannellini Beans

SERVES 8

On a vacation trip through northern Portugal, we became addicted to this hearty peasant soup, so much so that we bought some Portuguese cabbage seeds (see NOTE) to grow in our garden, giving us a steady supply of leaves solely for this soup. Collard greens or kale are two green, leafy vegetables that approximate the flavor of Portuguese cabbage.

¾ lb. garlic sausage such as linguiça, or kielbasa

¼ C. olive oil

1 large sweet Spanish onion, coarsely chopped (about 1½ C.)

2 cloves garlic, finely minced (2 tsps.)

4 medium potatoes (about 1½ lbs.), peeled, cut into chunks and placed in a bowl of cold water (see NOTE)

8 C. Chicken Stock, preferably homemade (see page 171)

12 C. trimmed and coarsely shredded collard greens, kale or Portuguese cabbage

2 C. cooked dried cannellini beans (see Chart, page 460)

¾ tsp. salt or to taste

¼ tsp. freshly ground black pepper or to taste

Pierce the sausage, cover with water in a saucepan and bring to a boil. Then lower the heat and simmer for 5 minutes to remove excess fat. Drain, discard the water, slice the sausage into ¾-inch slices and reserve.

In a 7-quart Dutch oven, heat the oil, add the onions and garlic and stir, sautéeing for 2 to 3 minutes. Drain and add the potatoes, stirring, and cook for 1 to 2 minutes. Add the stock and bring to a boil, then lower the heat and simmer for 15 to 20 minutes.

Crush the potatoes lightly in the pot using a potato masher. Add the shredded greens and simmer for 15 minutes more. Add the cooked beans and reserved sausage and season with salt and pepper. Serve hot. The soup can be prepared a day or 2 in advance. Like most hearty soups or stews, the flavors intensify with time.

NOTES: Portuguese cabbage seeds are available through Le Jardin du Gourmet, West Danville, VT 05873.

Baking potatoes should not be used. They disintegrate too easily rather than maintaining their shape when lightly crushed.

The

Versatile

Grain

and the

Elegant

Bean

468

Settlemanale Pasta e Fagioli

SERVES 6

This dish, eaten weekly in Naples, was also a favorite of the colorful late mayor of New York City, Fiorello La Guardia. He, along with millions of other Italian-Americans, called it by its dialect name: *pasta fazool.* Our recipe was handed down to us by an Italian friend who claimed that it goes back at least a thousand years!

1½ C. dried small white beans or navy beans, soaked and drained
½ C. olive oil
10 C. water
3 large cloves garlic, cut into quarters
1 large onion
1 sprig rosemary
2 sprigs oregano
6 sprigs flat leaf parsley
1 bay leaf

1 small red dried hot chile such as Japonés
6 ozs. tubular pasta such as tubetti, ditalini or small elbows
1½ Tbs. tomato paste
Salt and freshly ground black pepper to taste
2 Tbs. finely minced fresh basil
Grated Parmesan cheese

Add the beans to a 7-quart heavy pot along with the olive oil. Add the water, garlic and onion and bring to a boil. Skim off any foam and lower the heat. Tie the rosemary, oregano, parsley, bay leaf and hot chile together with a string and add to the pot. Cover and simmer with the lid slightly ajar, for 1 hour, 15 minutes, or until the beans are tender.

Meanwhile, cook the pasta in boiling salted water, drain and set aside. When the beans are cooked, remove the onion and the herb bouquet with a slotted spoon and discard them. Stir in the tomato paste and cooked pasta, season to taste with salt and pepper and simmer until hot. Sprinkle with minced basil and serve, passing grated Parmesan cheese at the table along with a pepper mill.

Minestrone for a Crowd

There is no region of Italy that does not have some version of this hearty soup, perfect for a crowd. In the North, the Milanese replace the pasta with short grain rice. In Tuscany, they use Roman or cranberry beans. In Genoa, they add a basil pesto. We, in turn, have added some beef, making it a complete meal in itself.

2 Tbs. olive oil	¼ tsp. hot pepper flakes
1 large onion, finely chopped (1 C.)	1 Tbs. finely minced fresh oregano
2–3 cloves garlic, finely minced (1½ Tbs.)	(or 1 tsp. dried oregano)
	2 sprigs rosemary, leaves only
1½ lbs. beef shank, bone in, and cut into thick slices	Salt and freshly ground black pepper to taste
3 qts. water	1 C. green string beans, diagonally cut into ½-in.-lengths (about ¼ lb.)
2½ C. peeled tomatoes (about ¾ lb.), cut into 1-in. pieces, or 1-lb. can Italian plum tomatoes	2 C. ¾-in. slices unpeeled zucchini (about 1 lb.)
2½ C. coarsely chopped cabbage (about ½ lb.)	2 C. cooked cannellini beans (see Chart, page 460)
2–3 stalks celery, coarsely chopped (1 C.)	4 ozs. small tubular pasta such as tubetti or small elbow macaroni, cooked and drained
2 medium carrots, coarsely chopped (1 C.)	¼ C. finely minced flat leaf parsley
2 medium potatoes, peeled and cut into ½-in. cubes (1 C.)	Grated Parmesan cheese

Heat the olive oil in a 7-quart heavy pot and sauté the onions and garlic, stirring, until soft but not brown. Add the beef bones and cook until the meat loses its color, turning the pieces over while cooking. Add the water and bring to a boil. Skim any foam from the surface. Then lower the heat and simmer, covered, for 1 hour.

Lift out the bones with tongs, cut the meat into cubes and return to the pot, discarding the bones. Add the tomatoes and cabbage and simmer for 15 minutes. Stir in the celery, carrots, potatoes, hot pepper flakes, oregano, rosemary, salt and pepper. Continue to simmer for an additional 15 minutes. Add the remaining ingredients except for the parsley and cheese and continue to cook for 10 to 15 minutes or until the string beans and zucchini are tender and crisp. Then stir in the parsley. Serve hot and sprinkle Parmesan cheese over the soup at the table.

The

Versatile

Grain

and the

Elegant

Bean

470

Ribollitta:
A Tuscan Bean Soup

SERVES 8 TO 10

The literal meaning of this thick rustic peasant soup is "reboiled," and according to old Catholic custom it was prepared on "meatless Friday," to reappear a day or two later with enhanced flavors. It was then layered between toasted dry bread, onion rings and grated Parmesan cheese and baked in the oven. Prepare the soup and toasts several days in advance and finish the dish just before serving.

Soup

1 C. dried Great Northern beans or cannellini beans, soaked and drained
¼ C. olive oil
3 large cloves garlic, finely minced (about 1 Tbs.)
1 large onion, coarsely chopped (⅔ C.)
2 medium stalks celery, coarsely chopped (⅔ C.)
2 medium carrots, coarsely chopped (1 C.)
2½ C. peeled waxy potatoes, cut into ½-in. cubes (1 lb.)
14-oz. can Italian plum tomatoes, plus liquid

1 tsp. tomato paste
5 C. Chicken Stock, preferably homemade (see page 171)
3 large basil leaves, shredded
2 Tbs. coarsely chopped fresh parsley
¼ tsp. hot pepper flakes
Salt and freshly ground black pepper to taste
3 C. trimmed, shredded kale (¼ lb.)
6 C. trimmed, shredded Swiss chard (½ lb.)
½ head small cabbage (¾ lb.), shredded (6 C.)

Cook the beans in water to cover by about 2 inches, until tender, about 45 minutes, adding salt the last 5 minutes of cooking. Keep the beans in their cooking liquid and set aside.

In a 7-quart heavy Dutch oven, heat the olive oil and add the garlic and onions. Sauté over medium low heat for 2 minutes, stirring occasionally. Add the celery and carrots and cook for 2 to 3 minutes more. Then stir in the potatoes, tomatoes, tomato paste, chicken stock, basil, parsley, hot pepper flakes, salt and pepper. Drain the beans and reserve the liquid. There should be 3 cups of liquid. If not, add water to make 3 cups. Purée half the beans with half the liquid in the bowl of a food processor and add to the pot with the remaining bean liquid. Stir in the kale, Swiss chard and cabbage and bring the soup to the boil. Then, lower the heat and simmer, covered, for 15 minutes. Add the remaining beans and cook for 5 minutes more. Cool and refrigerate for up to 3 days, until ready to reheat.

Herbed Garlic Toast

6 Tbs. olive oil
2 large cloves garlic, crushed
6 sprigs fresh thyme, coarsely cut

16 ½-in.-thick slices good Italian peasant bread

In a small heavy saucepan, heat the olive oil, add the garlic and thyme and cook just until the garlic begins to color. Cool and strain into a cup, discarding the garlic and thyme. Preheat the oven to 350°F. and brush the herbed oil on both sides of the bread, using a pastry brush. Place on a cookie sheet in one layer and bake, turning once until the toasts are golden and crisp. Watch carefully so they don't burn. Cool and keep in an airtight box until ready to use.

Garnishes

¾ C. grated Parmesan cheese
1 medium onion, thinly sliced and separated into rings

Olive oil for drizzling over surface (optional)

About 45 minutes before serving, preheat the oven to 350°F. Arrange a layer of toast on the bottom of a large, deep oven-to-table casserole and sprinkle with one quarter of the cheese. Then spoon the soup over this layer and place the onion rings on top. Add another layer of toast and the rest of the Parmesan cheese. Cover and bake for 30 minutes. Remove the cover and continue to bake 15 minutes longer, until the cheese is crusty and golden. Serve hot in individual soup bowls. Lift off a piece of toast and place it on the bottom of the serving bowl, then spoon the soup over the toast and serve with an additional drizzle of olive oil if you wish.

The

Versatile

Grain

and the

Elegant

Bean

472

French Navy Bean Purée with
Nutmeg and Seared Salmon Scallops
with Sorrel and Green Peppercorns

SERVES 6

Roundly plump, silky-textured French navy beans are particularly suited to purées that are delicately flavored. Paired with quickly seared salmon scallops and a sauce with the tartly sour flavor of fresh sorrel and the sharp bite of green peppercorns, it makes for a most elegant first course.

Bean Purée
MAKES ABOUT 3½ CUPS

2 C. dried French navy beans or white marrow beans, soaked and drained
1 whole large carrot
1 whole medium onion, stuck with 2 whole cloves
3 cloves garlic, coarsely chopped (about 1 Tbs.)

4 sprigs flat leaf parsley
4 sprigs thyme
1 bay leaf
2 Tbs. soft butter
⅓ C. heavy cream
Salt and freshly ground black pepper to taste
¼ tsp. freshly grated nutmeg

To a 3-quart saucepan, add the beans and water to cover by 2 inches. Add the carrot, onion and garlic. Tie the parsley, thyme and bay leaf together with string and add to the pot. Bring to a boil, then lower the heat and simmer with the pot lid slightly ajar, until the beans are very tender. If current crop French navy beans are used, the time should be about 30 minutes. If marrow beans are used, increase the cooking time to 1 hour, 15 minutes and check to see if additional water is needed so that the beans remain covered. Remove and discard the carrot, onion, herbs and bay leaf. Drain the beans, transfer to the bowl of a food processor, add the butter, cream, salt, pepper and nutmeg and process to a purée. Scrape the purée into an ovenproof dish and keep warm in a preheated low oven, or prepare a day in advance and then rewarm before serving.

Salmon and Sorrel Sauce

1¼ lbs. center-cut salmon fillet, frozen and then partly defrosted (see NOTE)
2 tsps. water-packed green peppercorns, rinsed and drained
Coarse salt to taste
1 Tbs. lemon juice

3 Tbs. butter
¼ lb. sorrel, center rib cut out and shredded finely in chiffonade (about 1½ C.)
⅓ C. heavy cream

One hour before cooking, dry the salmon with paper towels and slice the partially defrosted fish at an angle across the grain into ¼-inch-thick scallops. Place them in a single layer on a large plate. Crush the peppercorns in a small bowl, using the back of a wooden spoon. Add the salt and lemon juice to make a paste. Spread lightly on the salmon scallops. Cover with plastic wrap and refrigerate for 1 hour.

Add the butter to a large skillet and heat until bubbles form. Sear the scallops for about 1 minute on each side, then set aside on a plate. Add the sorrel to the same skillet and stir until wilted, about 30 seconds. Stir in the cream, lower the heat and cook for about 1 minute.

To serve, spoon the warm bean purée off to the side of a serving plate and arrange several salmon scallops in a fan shape around the purée. Then spoon the sorrel sauce over the salmon.

NOTE: When the salmon is to be quickly cooked, as in this recipe, it is best to be on the safe side and to freeze it first for 2 to 3 days. This is a technique that the Japanese also use for sushi, since salmon in the wild may occasionally harbor parasitic worms, sometimes found in several other salt- and freshwater fish as well.

Poached Monkfish with Flageolets and a Tomato Basil Coulis

SERVES 4

Nuggets of monkfish in a creamy sauce with intense flavor developed through reductions. Spiked with just a touch of fresh tomatoes and lots of finely shredded basil, it forms a glorious sauce for pale green flageolets.

Flageolets

1 C. dried flageolets, soaked and drained	2 sprigs thyme
1 small stalk celery with leaves	3 sprigs parsley
1 medium onion, stuck with 1 whole clove	1 bay leaf
1 large carrot, cut in half crossways	5 whole black peppercorns
	Salt to taste

To a 5-quart Dutch oven, add the beans, celery, onion, carrot and tepid water to cover all by 2 inches. Tie the thyme, parsley, bay leaf and peppercorns in a cheesecloth bag and add to the pot. Bring to a boil, then lower the heat, cover and simmer for about 50 minutes to 1 hour, or until the beans are tender.

Remove and discard all the vegetables and the cheesecloth bag. Season with salt and keep the beans in their liquid. The beans can be kept this way for 1 or 2 days,

The

Versatile

Grain

and the

Elegant

Bean

covered and refrigerated. Just before preparing the fish, drain them, returning half the liquid to the beans, and reheat slowly while the fish is being prepared.

Monkfish

1½ lbs. monkfish fillets
3 Tbs. butter
1 small stalk celery, finely chopped (⅓ C.)
1 small leek, white part only, finely minced (⅓ C.)
1 small carrot, finely chopped (¼ C.)
2 C. dry white wine
½ C. water
1 bay leaf

1–2 small cloves garlic, finely minced (2 tsps.)
2 large plum tomatoes, coarsely diced (¾ C.)
Salt and freshly ground black pepper to taste
½ C. heavy cream
¼ C. very fine chiffonade basil leaves
1 tsp. lemon juice

Pull off as much of the dark membrane from the monkfish as you are able to. Then cut the fillets into 1-inch pieces and set aside.

In a 2-quart saucepan, melt 1 tablespoon of the butter and sauté the celery, leeks and carrots, stirring frequently, for about 5 minutes, or until the vegetables are soft. Add the wine, water and bay leaf and bring to a boil. Simmer for 5 minutes, then add the fish. Simmer for 5 minutes more, or until the fish is barely cooked through. Lift the fish out with tongs and set aside on a plate. Strain the poaching liquid and return it to the saucepan, reducing it to 1 cup over high heat, about 8 minutes. Set the cup of stock aside.

In a 10-inch skillet, melt the 2 remaining tablespoons of butter. Add the garlic and sauté for 1 minute. Stir in the plum tomatoes and salt and pepper and sauté for 1 to 2 more minutes. Add the reserved cup of stock and bring to a boil. Then lower the heat and simmer for 5 minutes. Stir in the cream and simmer just until the sauce is hot. Add the reserved fish to the sauce and simmer for 1 minute. Stir in the basil and lemon juice. Place the beans on a platter and spoon the fish and sauce over the beans. Serve hot.

Anasazi Cowgirl Beans with Beef Short Ribs

SERVES 4

The anasazi bean lends itself to hearty fare and intense spices. "Cowboy" beans are usually cooked with lard, bacon or pork. Our gentler version, the "Cowgirl," is flavored with a small amount of beef.

1 C. dried anasazi beans or Jacob's Cattle beans, soaked and drained
1 qt. water
1 large onion, peeled
1 large carrot, cut in half
1 large stalk celery, cut in half
½ lb. short ribs of beef flanken, cut into pieces between the bones
Salt to taste, plus ½ tsp. (or to taste)
2 Tbs. olive oil

1 small onion, finely chopped (⅓ C.)
3 large cloves garlic, finely minced (1 Tbs.)
1 Tbs. chile powder
½ tsp. dried oregano, preferably Greek or Mexican
3 Tbs. tomato paste
¼ tsp. freshly ground black pepper or to taste

To a 3-quart saucepan, add the beans, water, onion, carrot, celery and beef ribs. Bring to a boil, skim foam from the surface and lower the heat. Cover and simmer for 45 to 50 minutes or until the beans are tender, adding salt the last 5 minutes of cooking. Remove the carrot, onion and celery with tongs and discard. Then drain the beans, reserving the liquid, and return the beans to the pot.

Meanwhile, heat the olive oil in a small skillet and sauté the onions and garlic over low heat until almost golden, about 5 to 8 minutes. Add the chile powder, oregano, tomato paste, ½ teaspoon salt and the pepper, plus 1 cup of the reserved bean liquid. Stir and simmer for 1 minute. When the beans are cooked, add this mixture to the beans and meat. Cover and simmer for 15 minutes more, stirring occasionally and checking to see if additional liquid is needed. The beans should be moist but not soupy. Taste for additional seasoning and serve hot.

The

Versatile

Grain

and the

Elegant

Bean

476

Puerto Rican White Beans with Calabaza and Aji

SERVES 6 TO 8

Mottled green skin and bright orange flesh distinguish calabaza, sometimes called West Indian or green pumpkin, from our American paler, more watery kind. Found in Hispanic markets, its closest substitute is the pale, beige-skinned butternut squash. *Ají* translates from the Spanish into chile, and it refers to many varieties of hot chiles. Any small, lantern-shaped chile would give this bean dish its authentic flavor.

1½ C. dried small white beans (pea beans), soaked and drained

6 C. water

1 Tbs. olive oil

⅓ C. diced slab bacon (2 ozs.)

¾ C. lean diced ham, preferably Serrano (4 ozs.)

2 cloves garlic, finely minced (1 tsp.)

1 large onion, coarsely chopped (1 C.)

1 small green pepper, finely diced (½ C.)

1 hot fresh chile, either lantern-shaped rocotillo or Scotch bonnet, stemmed, seeded and minced (see TIP)

½ tsp. dried oregano

¼ C. chicken stock

1 Tbs. tomato paste

4 C. peeled calabaza or butternut squash, seeded and cut into 1½-in. pieces (about 1½ lbs.)

1 tsp. salt or to taste

⅛ tsp. freshly ground black pepper or to taste

1 Tbs. coarsely chopped fresh cilantro

In a 5-quart Dutch oven, bring the beans and water to a boil, lower the heat and simmer for about 30 to 40 minutes, until the beans are almost tender. Meanwhile, heat the olive oil in a 10-inch skillet, and fry the bacon and ham over medium high heat, stirring frequently, for about 5 minutes. Then lower the heat, add the garlic, onions, green pepper and chile and sauté, stirring frequently, over medium low heat, for 10 to 12 minutes, until soft, but not browned. Add the oregano to the onion mixture while sautéing. Mix the chicken stock and tomato paste together and stir into the onions and peppers. Combine with the almost tender beans. Simmer the beans, uncovered, for 20 minutes. Add the calabaza, salt and pepper, and simmer, uncovered, for 40 minutes more or until the sauce has thickened a bit and the calabaza is tender but still holds its shape. Correct the seasoning and stir in the cilantro before serving. Serve with rice if you wish.

TIP: One hot chile can be too much for some people and not nearly enough for others. Therefore, contrary to your natural instincts to douse the heat with water, just dip a dampened finger in a bit of sugar and lick it to cool your palate.

Swedish Brown Beans and
Sweet and Sour Meatballs

SERVES 8

The Scandinavian immigrants brought these light brown–colored beans with them and planted them in their gardens in the New World. They are still a sentimental favorite of their descendants in Minnesota.

2 C. dried Swedish brown beans or
Great Northern beans, soaked and
drained
1½ tsps. salt or to taste
¾ tsp. freshly ground black pepper or
to taste

½ tsp. ground ginger
⅓ C. light corn syrup
⅓ C. apple cider vinegar
⅓ C. heavy cream

To a 5-quart nonstick Dutch oven, add the beans and tepid water to cover. Bring to a boil, then drain and rinse. Add fresh warm water to cover by about 2 inches and bring to a boil again. Lower the heat and simmer for 45 minutes or until the beans are tender. Meanwhile, in a small bowl, mix the salt, pepper, ginger, corn syrup, vinegar and cream and blend well. When the beans are cooked, drain them, reserving 1 cup of the liquid. Gently stir the sauce into the beans and simmer, uncovered, for 5 to 8 minutes. Add some additional reserved liquid to the beans if the sauce is too thick.

Meatballs

MAKES ABOUT 26

1 lb. lean ground beef, preferably
chuck
1 small onion, grated (2 Tbs.)
2 Tbs. finely minced fresh parsley,
plus extra for garnish
¼ C. whole grain bread crumbs, made
with rye or whole wheat bread

2 Tbs. tomato paste
1 egg, lightly beaten
Salt and freshly ground black pepper
to taste
1 Tbs. olive or canola oil

Put all the ingredients, except the parsley for garnish, into a bowl and knead with your hands or a wooden spoon until well mixed. Dampen your hands and form the mixture into small balls, about 1 tablespoon of the mixture for each one. Lay them over the surface of the beans. Cover and simmer for 10 minutes. Gently turn the meatballs over and simmer for 8 to 10 minutes more. Spoon into a shallow serving dish and serve hot, garnished with minced parsley.

The

Versatile

Grain

and the

Elegant

Bean

478

Baked Soldier Beans with Sage
and Italian Sausage

SERVES 6

A caramel splash of color in the shape of a soldier's silhouette distinguishes this heirloom bean. Here, they are simmered first with lots of fresh sage, touched with tomato, then baked with sweet and hot Italian sausage.

1½ C. dried Soldier Beans or cannellini beans, soaked and drained

3 Tbs. very coarsely chopped fresh sage leaves, plus sprig for garnish (optional)

¼ C. olive oil

2 C. tepid water

2 cloves garlic, cut into vertical slivers

1 large tomato, peeled and diced (¾ C.)

2 Tbs. tomato paste

Salt and freshly ground black pepper to taste

1 lb. Italian sausage: ¾ lb. sweet and ¼ lb. hot

To a 3-quart nonstick saucepan, add the beans, chopped sage, olive oil, water and garlic and bring to a boil. Lower the heat and simmer for 25 minutes. Stir in the tomatoes, tomato paste, salt and pepper and continue to simmer for 5 minutes.

While the beans are cooking, place the whole sausages in a skillet with water to cover. Pierce them with a knife in a few places and cook over medium high heat for 20 minutes. Drain and cut the sausages in half crosswise and set aside.

Preheat the oven to 350°F. and transfer the cooked beans and tomatoes to a 2½-quart shallow baking dish, preferably earthenware. Cover with foil and bake for 30 minutes, then uncover and stir the beans, adding a bit more water if necessary. Tuck in the sausages, return to the oven, and bake, uncovered, for about 25 to 30 minutes more or until most of the sauce has been absorbed by the beans. Serve hot.

Baked Steuben Yellow Eyes with
Apples, Ham and Mustard

SERVES 6

Even though there are those who say, "Don't mess around with tradition," this is a lighter version of the traditional famous Boston baked beans, which cook in the oven for hours and hours and which also contain lots of bacon. We have included another, longer-cooking, more traditional version on page 334.

1½ C. Steuben yellow-eye beans or
    Great Northern beans, soaked and
    drained
Salt to taste
  1 small onion, peeled and stuck with
    3 whole cloves
½-lb. piece smoked ham steak, cut into
    ½-in. pieces (about 1 C.)
  1 C. apple juice

  2 Tbs. coarse-grain mustard
1½ Tbs. dark brown sugar
  1 Tbs. ketchup
  1 tsp lemon juice
  ¼ tsp. freshly ground black pepper
3–4 drops Tabasco sauce
  1 tart green apple, peeled and thinly
    sliced (1 C.)

In a 3-quart saucepan, cook the beans with tepid water to cover by 2 inches, until the beans are tender, about 30 minutes (Great Northern beans take longer—see Chart, page 460). Add salt the last 5 minutes of cooking. Drain and reserve the liquid.

Preheat the oven to 350°F. Place the beans in a 2½-quart ovenproof casserole or bean pot. Tuck the onion in the center. In a small bowl, mix the remaining ingredients together, including the reserved bean liquid, and stir into the beans. Cover and bake for 30 minutes. Then uncover, stir gently and bake for 30 minutes more. Remove the onion and cloves and discard. Serve right from the casserole.

The

Versatile

Grain

and the

Elegant

Bean

480

Turnip, White Bean and
Sage Purée with Lemon

MAKES 2½ CUPS

Adelicate white bean purée with sage and lemon. Use it as a dip for cold, crisp raw vegetables, or as a side dish for poached salmon.

1 C. dried small white beans (navy beans or pea beans), soaked and drained
5 C. tepid water
1 small onion, peeled and stuck with 1 whole clove
1 small whole turnip, peeled
1 small carrot
1 small stalk celery
1 large whole garlic clove
1 small red whole dried chile, such as Japonés

5 sprigs parsley
Small bay leaf
2 Tbs. lemon juice
2 tsps. finely minced lemon peel
6 medium fresh sage leaves, minced finely, plus additional leaf for garnish
¼ C. olive oil
¼ C. finely minced red onion (½ small red onion)
Salt and freshly ground black pepper to taste

Put the beans in a deep saucepan or Dutch oven along with the water, onion, turnip, carrot, celery and garlic clove. Tie the chile, parsley and bay leaf in a cheesecloth bag and add to the pot. Bring to a boil, then cover and lower the heat. Simmer for about 40 to 60 minutes or until the beans are very soft. Remove and discard the onion, carrot, celery and the cheesecloth bag. Drain the beans, saving the turnip and the garlic.

Purée the beans, turnip and garlic in the bowl of a food processor until smooth. Transfer the mixture to a bowl and add the lemon juice, lemon peel, sage, olive oil and red onion. Taste for salt and pepper. Serve at room temperature with an additional sage leaf for garnish if you wish.

Jacob's Cattle Beans with Peeled Wheat Berries and Dried Cranberries

SERVES 8

This recipe comes from a suggestion originally made by Phil Teverow of Dean & DeLuca in New York. It's a most unusual grain and bean salad just perfect for a picnic or buffet. Nut-sweet walnuts and walnut oil, tiny bursts of tart, dried cranberries, peeled wheat berries and somewhat chestnut-flavored beans add up to a perfect partnership with cold chicken or pork.

1 C. dried Jacob's Cattle beans or anasazi beans, soaked and drained
Salt to taste
2¾ C. cooked peeled wheat berries (see page 230 for cooking instructions)
⅔ C. Dried Cranberries (see NOTE)
2 tsps. finely minced fresh rosemary

1 tsp. finely minced fresh sage
2 scallions, thinly sliced diagonally (½ C.)
Freshly ground black pepper to taste
5 Tbs. walnut oil
3 Tbs. raspberry vinegar
¼ C. coarsely broken, toasted walnuts

Cook the beans in water to cover by 2 or 3 inches, for about 30 to 35 minutes. Drain and add salt. (The cooked grains and beans can be prepared up to 3 days in advance if you refrigerate them after preparation.)

Place the beans and grains in a large bowl along with the dried cranberries, herbs and scallions. Season with salt and pepper. Spoon the walnut oil over the surface and gently mix to combine. Trickle the raspberry vinegar over the surface and gently mix again. Scatter the toasted walnuts on top. Let the flavors develop for 2 hours at room temperature before serving.

NOTE: Dried cranberries can be purchased in specialty stores, or you may try the following recipe below for making your own.

Dried Cranberries
MAKES 1½ CUPS

3 C. sugar
12-oz. package fresh cranberries

1½ C. water

Mix the ingredients together in a large nonstick saucepan and bring to a boil. Lower the heat and simmer for 20 to 25 minutes. Drain in a strainer, reserving the syrup. Preheat the oven to 300°F. and line a jelly roll pan with parchment paper. Spoon the berries on the paper, separating and spreading them out in a single layer. Bake for 30 minutes to dry them out, then store, tightly covered. The syrup can be boiled down for 10 minutes, cooled and stored for use over pancakes.

The

Versatile

Grain

and the

Elegant

Bean

482

Flageolets with Fresh Thyme

SERVES 8 TO 10

The traditional French accompaniment and the perfect partner for a roasted leg of lamb. Or for a regal change of pace, fill the center of a crown roast of lamb with these lovely pale green beans.

2 C. dried flageolets, soaked and drained
8 C. tepid water
1 large carrot, cut in half crosswise
1 large onion, stuck with 3 whole cloves
1 large stalk celery, cut in half crosswise
4 sprigs parsley
4 sprigs thyme
1 bay leaf
3–4 whole black peppercorns

2 Tbs. butter
3 large cloves garlic, finely minced (1 Tbs.)
2–3 large shallots, finely minced (2 Tbs.)
½ C. heavy cream
1 Tbs. fresh thyme leaves
1 large tomato (about ¼ lb.), peeled and diced (⅔ C.)
Salt and freshly ground black pepper to taste
1 Tbs. finely minced fresh parsley

Put the beans in a 5-quart Dutch oven, along with the tepid water. Bring to a boil. Place the next seven ingredients into a piece of cheesecloth and tie with a string for easy retrieval. Add to the pot, lower the heat and simmer, covered with the lid slightly ajar for about 45 minutes or until the beans are tender. Remember that older beans will take longer to cook, so check occasionally to see if additional boiling water is needed to keep them covered.

Lift out and discard the cheesecloth bundle. Drain the beans, reserving ⅔ cup of the liquid, and set them aside. In a large skillet, melt the butter and add the garlic and shallots. Stir and cook over medium heat until wilted. Add the cream, thyme leaves, diced tomato, salt and pepper. Simmer until hot, stirring occasionally, for about 3 minutes. Stir in the beans and simmer until hot. If the beans seem dry, add some of the reserved liquid, or if you have prepared them well in advance and then reheat them, add some additional liquid or more cream if you wish.

When ready to serve, transfer to a serving dish and sprinkle the minced parsley over the surface.

Flageolets Gratin with
Garlic and Gruyère

SERVES 6

The garlic disintegrates during cooking to mix with fresh tomatoes and prosciutto. Then a crunchy herbal cheese mixture tops the tender, flavorful beans. It's a very special treat with simply roasted poultry or grilled fish.

5 Tbs. olive oil
1 small onion, finely chopped (½ C.)
1 small carrot, finely diced (⅓ C.)
1 small stalk celery, finely diced (¼ C.)
5 whole cloves garlic
4 sprigs thyme, tied together
1 cup dried flageolets, soaked and drained
1 qt. tepid water

Salt to taste
Freshly ground black pepper to taste
3 large fresh plum tomatoes, diced (about 1 C.)
2 ozs. prosciutto, cut into ½-in. dice or strips (about ¼ C.)
¼ C. finely minced fresh parsley
1 C. fresh bread crumbs
⅓ C. grated Gruyère cheese

Heat 2 tablespoons of the olive oil in a 3-quart oven-to-table casserole. Add the onions, carrots, celery and garlic and cook over medium low heat for 5 minutes, stirring occasionally, until the vegetables are wilted but not brown. Add the thyme, flageolets and water and bring to a boil. Then lower the heat, cover with the lid slightly ajar and simmer for about 1 hour or until the beans are tender. Add salt the last 5 minutes of cooking. This part of the recipe may be prepared well in advance. Just keep the beans in their liquid.

When ready to bake, preheat the oven to 350°F. Remove the thyme bundle and discard. Season the beans with additional salt and add pepper. The liquid in which the beans have cooked should be thick and syrupy. If it is not, drain the beans, boil down the liquid for 5 to 10 minutes and return the beans to the casserole. Stir in the tomatoes, prosciutto and 1 tablespoon of the parsley.

In a small bowl, combine the remaining parsley with the bread crumbs, Gruyère cheese and the remaining olive oil. Spread this mixture evenly over the beans and bake, uncovered, for 30 to 40 minutes or until the top is evenly brown and bubbly around the edges.

The

Versatile

Grain

and the

Elegant

Bean

484

Fagioli all' Uccelletto:
Cannellini Beans with Sage, Garlic and Tomato

SERVES 6

This Tuscan specialty literally translates into "small-bird style" and the name is derived from a recipe for quail that is cooked with tomatoes, garlic and sage, the same ingredients used in this bean dish.

¼ C. olive oil
2 large cloves garlic, finely minced (1 Tbs.)
2–3 fresh plum tomatoes, diced, or 14-oz. can Italian plum tomatoes, drained and cut up (about 1 C.)
2 Tbs. coarsely chopped fresh sage leaves

¼ tsp. ground allspice
¼ tsp. black pepper
Salt to taste
3 C. drained, cooked, dried cannellini beans (see Chart page 460)
2 Tbs. finely minced fresh parsley

Heat the olive oil in a large 3- or 4-quart saucepan and sauté the garlic over medium heat, stirring for 1 minute. Do not let the garlic brown. Add the tomatoes, sage, seasonings, and beans. Simmer, uncovered, for 10 minutes, stirring occasionally. Taste and adjust the seasoning. Spoon into a serving dish, sprinkle with parsley, and serve hot.

Pan-Grilled Shrimp with White Beans, Arugula, Oranges and Red Onion

SERVES 6

Hot, tart, sweet and refreshing, marinated white beans sit on a bed of dark green, peppery arugula, which is cooled with icy oranges. Warm, pan-grilled shrimp are placed around the beans and paper-thin rings of red onion are scattered over the surface. A light summer dinner or luncheon salad supreme.

Mustard and Garlic Vinaigrette
MAKES ½ CUP

1 small clove garlic, finely minced (1 tsp.)
½ tsp. salt or to taste
¼ tsp. freshly ground black pepper

2 Tbs. lemon juice
1 Tbs. balsamic vinegar
2 tsps. coarse-grain mustard
6 Tbs. olive oil

The

Elegant

Bean

In a small bowl, whisk together the first six ingredients, then the olive oil until combined.

Beans

2½ C. drained, cooked, dried Great
Northern or cannellini beans (see
Chart, page 460)

Add ¼ cup of the vinaigrette to the cooked beans and set aside for several hours, or make them the day before. Set aside the remaining ¼ cup of vinaigrette for dressing the arugula (see below).

Oranges

3 large navel oranges, peeled and
cut into bite-size segments

1 Tbs. finely minced crystallized
ginger

Toss together and chill for several hours or overnight. Drain any juice that accumulates and add the juice to the remaining ¼ cup vinaigrette.

Shrimp

1 lb. medium shrimp (allow 6–7
shrimp per person)
2 Tbs. olive oil

¼ tsp. hot pepper flakes
1 clove garlic, finely minced (1 tsp.)

Peel and devein the shrimp and set aside in a platter. Heat the oil in a nonstick pan, add the hot pepper flakes and garlic and sauté for 1 minute. Remove from the heat, allow the bubbles to subside, then pour over the shrimp. Toss to coat and set aside to marinate for 15 minutes. Then heat a large, heavy iron skillet and pan grill the shrimp in a single layer, turning them once. Pan grill only until the shrimp are cooked through, about 2 minutes on each side.

9 C. loosely packed arugula leaves

1 small red onion, very thinly sliced
and separated into rings

Gently toss the arugula leaves in a bowl with the remaining vinaigrette and distribute among six large plates. Spoon 2 tablespoons of the beans in the center of each plate, tuck in the marinated orange/ginger segments and add the shrimp attractively around the beans. Scatter a few red onion rings over the surface.

The

Versatile

Grain

and the

Elegant

Bean

486

Mixed Beans

Moroccan Harira Soup with Harissa

SERVES 12 TO 14

Traditionally, this soup is eaten to break the Muslim fast of the holy month of Ramadan, announced by the firing of a cannon—probably meaning "Soup's on!" The soup is usually accompanied by dates and a pretzel-shaped yeast dough that has been fried, soaked in honey and dipped in sesame seeds. A sourdough starter, prepared 2 to 3 days in advance, is used to thicken the soup.

Starter
(Prepare 2 to 3 days in advance.)

½ C. all-purpose flour   ⅓ C. warm water

Mix the flour and water in a small nonmetal bowl, cover lightly with waxed paper and allow to ferment at room temperature in a warm place for 2 to 3 days. Stir it each morning with a wooden spoon.

Soup

2 Tbs. olive oil	3 Tbs. long grain brown rice
1–2 lamb shanks, trimmed (¾ lb.)	⅔ C. whole red lentils
1 large onion, coarsely chopped (about 1 C.)	5 fresh plum tomatoes or canned plum tomatoes
2 stalks celery with leaves, coarsely chopped (about ¾ C.)	1 Tbs. tomato paste
1 large carrot, coarsely chopped (about ¾ C.)	1 C. fresh parsley leaves
	½ C. fresh cilantro leaves
1 tsp. freshly ground black pepper	¼ C. water
½ tsp. ground cinnamon	2 tsps. salt or to taste
¼ tsp. ground allspice	1 C. drained, cooked chick-peas (see Chart, page 338) or canned chick-peas, rinsed and drained
Pinch saffron threads, crushed	
6–8 large chicken wings (about 1 lb.)	Lemon wedges
3 qts. water	Harissa Paste (optional—see NOTE)
3 Tbs. pearl barley, washed well	

Heat the oil over medium heat in a heavy 7-quart pot. Sear the lamb shank in the oil, then add the chopped onions, celery and carrots. Add the pepper, cinnamon, allspice and saffron and sauté, stirring occasionally, over medium low heat, until the vegetables are wilted. Add the chicken wings and water, raise the heat to medium and bring to a boil. Skim the foam from the surface and add the barley, rice and red lentils. Cover, lower the heat to simmer and cook for 50 minutes.

Lift out the chicken wings and the lamb shank and let the meats get cool enough to handle. Purée the tomatoes and tomato paste in the bowl of a food processor and add to the simmering soup. Then, in the same unwashed food processor, process the parsley, cilantro and ¼ cup of water and add to the soup. Stir in the salt and the cooked chick-peas and simmer for 10 minutes more. Meanwhile, remove the meat from the chicken wings and add to the soup. Then cut the lamb from the bone into bite-size pieces and add them as well. Add 2 tablespoons of the sourdough starter to the hot soup and stir occasionally to thicken the soup and to heat the meats.

Serve in large bowls with a wedge of lemon to be squeezed into the soup at the table and Harissa paste, if you like hot peppers.

NOTE: Harissa paste is imported from Tunisia and can be purchased in a tube in Middle Eastern and other specialty shops. If you wish to prepare your own, the recipe for this incendiary condiment follows.

Harissa Paste

1 oz. small red whole dried hot chile peppers such as Japonés, soaked in water to cover for 1 hour	½ tsp. caraway seeds
	2 cloves garlic
½ tsp. ground coriander	Salt to taste
1 tsp. ground cumin	Olive oil

Drain the chile peppers, discarding the water, and add all the ingredients except for the olive oil to a small spice mill and purée. Put the purée in a jar and float some olive oil on the surface. Refrigerate; it will keep well for 2 to 3 weeks. *Use sparingly.*

The

Versatile

Grain

and the

Elegant

Bean

488

Layered Tricolor Bean Terrine with
Roasted Orange Pepper Sauce

SERVES 10 TO 12

Don't be put off by the length of this recipe. It is prepared in several stages over 2 or 3 days. The three beans—black, white and green—form attractive layers when sliced. They're surrounded by a sprightly saffron-colored orange pepper sauce speckled with red pepper diamonds and studded with a few capers. The terrine will dazzle your guests and give the cook a real sense of accomplishment.

Black Bean Layer

⅔ C. dried black beans, soaked and drained
2½ C. tepid water
1 small onion, stuck with 1 whole clove

1 small stalk celery
1 small carrot
¼ tsp. ground cumin
⅛ tsp. hot pepper flakes
Salt to taste

In a 2-quart saucepan, combine all the ingredients except the salt. Bring to a boil, lower the heat and simmer until the beans are very tender, about 1 hour. Add the salt during the last 2 or 3 minutes of cooking. Lift out and discard the onion, celery and carrot. Keep the beans in their liquid and set aside.

White Bean Layer

⅔ C. dried white navy beans or Great Northern beans, soaked and drained
2½ C. tepid water
1 small onion, stuck with 1 whole clove
1 small stalk celery

1 small carrot
1 bay leaf
2 sprigs parsley
½ teaspoon dried Herbes de Provence
Salt to taste

In a 2-quart saucepan, combine all the ingredients except the salt and bring to a boil. Lower the heat and simmer 45 to 60 minutes, or until the beans are very tender, adding salt during the last few minutes of cooking. Lift out and discard the onion, celery, carrot, bay leaf and parsley and transfer the beans in their liquid to a bowl and reserve.

Green Split Pea Layer

⅔ C. dried green split peas (they do not need soaking)
2¼ C. tepid water
1 small onion
1 large clove garlic

1 small stalk celery
1 small carrot
½ tsp. dried oregano, preferably Greek
Salt and freshly ground black pepper to taste

In a 2-quart saucepan, bring all the ingredients except the salt and pepper to a boil. Lower the heat, cover and simmer for about 45 minutes or until the peas are tender and most of the liquid has been absorbed. Stir occasionally while cooking and season with salt and pepper at the end. Remove the onion, celery and carrot and discard. Transfer the split peas to a bowl and set aside.

The three kinds of beans may be prepared and refrigerated 1 day in advance. In fact, their flavor will improve.

Purées

6 eggs (2 eggs for each purée)	**6 Tbs. heavy cream (2 Tbs. for each purée)**

To make the purées, drain the beans well. In the bowl of a food processor, add 2 eggs and 2 tablespoons cream and process well. Add the black beans and process until a thick purée is formed. Spoon and scrape the purée out into a bowl, cover and refrigerate. Wash and dry the food processor and repeat with the white beans and the green split peas. Again, this step may be prepared a day in advance.

To bake the terrine, preheat the oven to 350°F. and boil a kettle of water. Butter a 1½-quart loaf pan, preferably Pyrex so that you can see the depth of each layer. Cut and trim two pieces of parchment paper, one to fit the bottom of the pan and one a bit larger to fit the top of the pan.

Butter both sides of the bottom piece of paper and press it into the bottom of the pan. Spoon the black bean purée into the prepared pan and smooth the surface evenly. Then spoon in the white bean purée across the width of the pan without disturbing the black layer. Then spoon the green purée over the white. Butter one side only of the top piece of parchment and lay it butter side down onto the green layer. Place the loaf pan into a larger pan with deep sides and pour enough boiling water into the larger pan to come halfway up the sides of the loaf pan. Bake for about 1 hour, 15 minutes. Then lift off the parchment and test the center with a thin knife blade. If it comes out clean, the terrine is done. If not, return it to the oven for an additional 5 to 10 minutes and retest. Remove the top piece of parchment and discard. Cool on a wire rack for 20 minutes.

Run the tip of a knife around the inside of the pan to free the top edge. Place a large serving platter over the pan and, holding both, flip the terrine over. Lift off the baking dish and wait 5 minutes before peeling off the parchment. When slicing, use a sharp knife dipped in water before cutting each slice.

Serve warm or at room temperature with the following sauce, which can also be made 1 or 2 days ahead of time.

The

Versatile

Grain

and the

Elegant

Bean

490

Roasted Orange Pepper Sauce
MAKES 1½ CUPS

3 large orange peppers
2 Tbs. olive oil
1 small onion
2 medium cloves garlic
½ tsp. crushed dried rosemary
1 Tbs. white wine vinegar
3 Tbs. dry white wine

½ C. chicken stock, plus 2 Tbs.
Small pinch saffron
½ tsp. salt or to taste
¼ tsp. freshly ground black pepper or
  to taste
½ sweet red pepper
Nonpareil capers

Char the orange peppers over an open flame on top of the stove or under a broiler. Wrap them in foil or a paper bag to steam for 5 to 10 minutes, then open the wrapping, cool them slightly and scrape off the charred skin. Remove the stem and seeds and discard. Rinse the peppers, blot dry, cut them into strips and set aside.

In an 8-inch skillet, heat the olive oil. Cut the onion and garlic into large, rough pieces and add to the oil. Sauté for 3 minutes over medium low heat, stirring frequently, until the onion is wilted. Stir the reserved peppers into the onion-garlic mixture, add the rosemary, and sauté, stirring occasionally for 5 minutes. Add the vinegar, raise the heat and cook, stirring, for 1 minute, until the vinegar evaporates. Add the wine and cook until that evaporates as well, stirring for about 2 minutes. Then lower the heat, stir in the ½ cup chicken stock and the saffron and simmer for 5 to 8 more minutes. Let the mixture cool slightly, season with salt and pepper and purée in the bowl of a food processor until the mixture is smooth. Add the remaining 2 tablespoons of chicken stock to dilute the sauce if too thick and blend. Adjust the seasoning, transfer to a bowl and set aside.

When ready to serve, place the sliced terrine on a large platter. Spoon the sauce around it. Decorate the sauce with red pepper cut into small diamond shapes and arrange them in clusters of three, with 1 caper in the center of the cluster.

Tri-Color Bean Terrine

Savory Ezekiel Pancakes with
Hot Pepper Jelly

MAKES ABOUT 24

Ezekiel 4:9 in the Bible reads: "Take wheat, barley, beans, lentils, millet and spelt, put them in one vessel and make them into bread for yourself . . ." To complete it, we might add: ". . . or pancakes." These savory treats feature an Ezekiel flour—now called Multi-blend—a combination of beans and grains as described in the Bible.

1 Tbs. all-purpose flour	1 Tbs. canola or olive oil
1 C. mixed bean and grain flour (Multi-blend—see NOTE)	1 C. milk
	2 scallions, thinly sliced (½ C.)
1 Tbs. baking powder	Oil for greasing griddle
1 Tbs. sugar	8-oz. jar jalapeño jelly (see NOTE)
1 scant tsp. salt or to taste	1 Tbs. water
1 egg, lightly beaten	

In a medium-size bowl, whisk together all the dry ingredients to combine well. In another bowl, whisk together the egg, oil and milk. Combine the egg mixture with the dry ingredients and stir in the scallions.

Preheat a nonstick griddle and lightly oil it. Drop 1 tablespoon of batter for each pancake onto the griddle and bake over medium heat until the edges are dry. Then flip over and bake on the other side. Keep warm in a preheated low oven until all are made. Melt the jalapeño jelly with 1 tablespoon of water until liquefied, and spoon over the pancakes. Serve warm.

NOTES: Multi-blend is a bean and whole grain product that is now distributed by Arrowhead Mills. It consists of pinto beans and lentils plus whole wheat, barley, millet and rye. It can be found in most natural food stores across the country.

The jalapeño jelly, too, can be purchased in most specialty shops. However, we've been making our own for many years. We pass our recipe on to you.

Jalapeño Jelly

1 large green pepper, seeded and stemmed and cut into tiny pieces	1⅓ C. sugar
	⅓ C. cider vinegar
1–2 large jalapeño chiles, stemmed, seeded and finely minced	3 Tbs. liquid pectin

Bring all the ingredients to a boil, except for the pectin. Boil for 20 minutes, then let stand for 10 to 15 minutes. Stir in the pectin and cook over medium heat for 1 minute, until the mixture gels. Cool. Then transfer to a tightly covered container and refrigerate. It will keep for up to a month.

If you wish to make a red jelly, use a sweet red pepper and a ripe red jalapeño to replace the green ones.

The

Versatile

Grain

and the

Elegant

Bean

492

Mixed Beans, Grains and Greens with Minted Yogurt Sauce

SERVES 6 TO 8

A budget-aware dinner in a dish with only a bit of diced lamb for interest and flavor. The minted yogurt sauce cools and completes it for total nourishment.

- 2 Tbs. olive oil
- 1 large clove garlic, finely minced (1½ tsps.)
- 1 large onion, finely chopped (1 C.)
- ½ lb. lean lamb, cut from leg, cut into ½-in. cubes
- ½ tsp. freshly ground black pepper
- Salt to taste
- Pinch hot pepper flakes
- 1 tsp. ground turmeric
- ¼ C. long grain brown rice
- ½ C. pearl barley, rinsed several times
- 3 C. Beef Stock, preferably homemade (see page 172)

- ½ C. dried green lentils
- 1 C. drained, cooked chick-peas (see Chart, page 338)
- 1 C. drained, cooked red kidney beans (see Chart, page 434)
- 4 C. shredded leaves fresh spinach or Swiss chard (leaves only)
- 2 large scallions, thinly sliced (½ C.)
- ½ C. finely minced fresh parsley
- ¼ C. minced fresh dill
- 1 C. plain yogurt
- 2 Tbs. finely minced fresh mint

In a nonstick 5-quart Dutch oven, heat the oil and add the garlic. Stir and sauté over medium heat for 60 seconds, then add the onions. Continue to sauté until the onions are wilted, stirring frequently. Add the cubed lamb and sprinkle with black pepper, salt, hot pepper flakes and turmeric. Cook, stirring, until the meat loses its color. Add the rice and barley and stir for 2 minutes. Add the stock and bring to a boil, then lower the heat. Stir once, cover and simmer over low heat for 20 minutes. Add the lentils and continue to cook for 15 minutes more. (Add more liquid if necessary.) Stir in the chickpeas and kidney beans and simmer for 5 to 10 minutes more or until all the liquid is absorbed.

In a small bowl, mix together the spinach, scallions, parsley and dill and stir into the pot. Cook, stirring, over low heat only until the herbs wilt. Transfer the mixture to a shallow oven-to-table casserole. Mix the yogurt and mint together and serve separately in a small bowl at the table.

Soupe au Pistou

SERVES 8

A French country favorite, generally made with vegetables harvested directly from the small summer garden behind the house, when the summer bounty is at its peak. The French generally use a bean called *coco* (related to the cranberry bean). A big bowl of this soup, along with a crusty whole grain bread, some ripe, succulent fruit and a wedge of cheese (plus a glass of wine)—close your eyes and you are whisked away to the French countryside.

¾ C. dried small white beans or navy beans, soaked and drained

3 qts. water

3 Tbs. Barth's Chicken Nutra Soup (see NOTE)

¼ C. boiling water

3 waxy potatoes, peeled and cut into 1-in. cubes (1 lb.)

5 medium ripe tomatoes, peeled and cut into cubes (4½–5 C.)

½ lb. yellow squash, cut into 1-in pieces

½ lb. zucchini, cut into 1-in. pieces

10-oz. package frozen large lima beans

½ lb. green string beans, cut in half diagonally

3 large cloves garlic

16 large fresh basil leaves

Pinch hot pepper flakes

3 Tbs. olive oil

2 ozs. capellini or vermicelli pasta, broken into 2-in. pieces

Salt and freshly ground black pepper to taste

Grated Parmesan cheese (optional)

In a 7-quart pot, bring the beans and water to a boil. Cover and simmer for 1 hour. Put the Barth's Chicken Nutra Soup in a small cup, add the boiling water and stir until dissolved. Stir it into the pot. Then add the potatoes and simmer for 15 minutes. Add the tomatoes, yellow squash, zucchini, lima and string beans and simmer for 20 minutes more.

Meanwhile, chop the garlic in the bowl of a food processor, then add the basil and hot pepper flakes and process again. Slowly add the olive oil through the feeding tube to make a thick sauce. Scrape out into a small bowl and set aside.

Add the pasta to the soup and continue to cook for about 3 to 5 minutes. Stir in the basil sauce, salt and pepper and serve hot. Top with a sprinkling of grated Parmesan cheese if you wish.

NOTE: Barth's Chicken Nutra Soup can be purchased at local health food stores. It contains no salt and therefore does not toughen the beans that are cooked with it. Thus we feel it is an acceptable substitute when 3 quarts of homemade chicken stock are not readily available.

The

Versatile

Grain

and the

Elegant

Bean

494

Mixed Beans, Grains and Mushroom Loaf
with Hot and Sweet Pepper Tomato Sauce

SERVES 8

A delicious alternative—meatless meat loaf with complete protein. It's filled with several kinds of grains and beans, vegetables, cheese and eggs, and most of it can be chopped or puréed in a food processor.

Butter for greasing loaf pan
Flour for dusting loaf pan
- 3 C. Chicken Stock, preferably homemade (see page 171)
- ¼ C. barley grits
- ¼ C. whole millet
- ¼ C. rolled oats
- ¼ C. fine bulgur
- 3 Tbs. olive oil
- 1 medium leek, white part only, thinly sliced (½ C.)
- 2 large scallions, thinly sliced (½ C.)
- 1 clove garlic, finely minced (1 tsp.)
- 1 stalk celery, finely minced (⅔ C.)
- 5 large mushrooms, coarsely chopped

Salt and freshly ground black pepper to taste
- ½ tsp. ground cumin
- ½ tsp. dried marjoram
- 1 tsp. pure ground chile powder
- ½ C. drained, cooked black beans (see Chart, page 315)
- ½ cup drained, cooked pinto beans (see Chart, page 425)
- 1 C. shredded sharp Cheddar cheese (about 4 oz.)
- 2 eggs, lightly beaten
- 2 Tbs. masa harina
- 2 Tbs. finely minced fresh cilantro
- 1 Tbs. butter, cut into small pieces

Butter and flour a 9 × 5 × 3-inch loaf pan and preheat the oven to 350°F. Bring the chicken stock to a boil in a 5-quart nonstick Dutch oven. Add the barley grits and the millet, cover and simmer for 15 minutes. Turn off the heat, stir in the oats and the bulgur and set the pot aside, covered, for 20 minutes.

In a 12-inch skillet, heat the oil and sauté the leeks, scallions and garlic for 2 minutes. Add the celery, mushrooms, salt and pepper and sauté for 3 minutes more. Stir in the cumin, marjoram and chile powder and cook for 2 minutes more. Purée the beans coarsely in the bowl of a food processor and add to the vegetables. Stir into the cooked grains in the pot. Add the cheese, eggs, masa harina and cilantro and beat well with a wooden spoon to combine the ingredients. Pack them into the prepared loaf pan. Dot the surface with butter and bake for 45 minutes. Meanwhile, prepare the sauce.

Hot and Sweet Pepper Tomato Sauce
MAKES 2¼ CUPS

- 3 sweet red peppers, stemmed and seeded
- 1 large tomato, peeled
- 1 large clove garlic, sliced
- 2 large shallots, coarsely chopped (⅓ C.)
- 1 jalapeño pepper, seeded and stemmed
- ¾ C. chicken stock
- ¼ C. dry vermouth or dry white wine
- Salt and freshly ground black pepper to taste

The

Elegant

Bean

In a 3-quart saucepan, combine all the ingredients. Simmer, covered, for 15 to 20 minutes or until the peppers are soft. Transfer to the bowl of a food processor and purée. Adjust the seasoning. Put the sauce in a serving dish or sauceboat to pass at the table.

When the loaf is finished, remove the pan and set it on a wire rack to cool for 10 minutes before inverting onto a serving dish. Slice the loaf at the table and pass the sauce separately.

NOTE: This sauce can also be used with chicken, fish, veal or lamb.

The

Versatile

Grain

and the

Elegant

Bean

496

A Taste of the Future

In a classic "chicken and egg" conundrum, we ask if the new and evolving interest in beans has been the reason that we have begun to notice that more and more varieties are reaching the marketplace? Or is the fact that newer and more exciting varieties are reaching the marketplace the reason that more of us are becoming interested in the culinary potential for legumes? For the fact is that there are new names that are surfacing, many of which are seen sporadically now and will probably reach the popular marketplace within the next few years.

As with grains like quinoa and amaranth, some of the "new" beans, such as the *Tepary bean,* have been around for a long time and are being rediscovered. Some have been popular in Asia and Africa but have never seen our shores. Others are being developed by botanists and scientists. Some are heirloom beans and others are hybrids, sort of "designer" beans, raised for special taste or beauty or other individual properties.

The beans that we've described in this short conclusion to our recipe section will give you just an example of what may be in store for the home cook within the next few years. We, as you, will be looking intensely at the shelves of our specialty shops to see if they do, indeed, appear—and remain by popular demand.

Tepary Beans
Phaseolus acutifolius

They resemble the Great Northern bean or the navy bean, but the color varies from white to brown. Tepary beans are grown as a minor food crop in arid areas such as Arizona and Guatemala, and though we include them as a "bean of the future," they were profusely cultivated by Mexican Indians near Tehuacán about 5,000 years ago. They reached Europe as an archaeological specimen in 1888, as a part of an exhibit of materials excavated from the Los Muertos prehistoric site in Arizona. They are quite drought-resistant and have generally been limited to regional dishes in the areas in which they grow. They have just begun to be distributed in a minor way.

The

Elegant

Bean

497

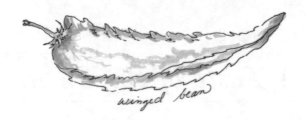

winged bean

Winged Beans
Psophocarpus tetrangonolobus

They go by the alias of the *goa bean,* named after one of the areas in which it has been cultivated. Until 1975, when it was uncovered and reported by the National Academy of Sciences' National Research Council, the bean was a virtually unknown, lanky vining plant. It had been grown almost exclusively for generations as a staple legume in tropical Southeast Asia, New Guinea, the Philippines and Ghana.

Upon its discovery, it was dubbed a "Supermarket on a Stalk," since it is exceedingly high in food value and every part of the plant is edible, except for the stalk. A decorative four-sided green pod flares from the center into rippled ridges on wings, and it is this immature pod that is the most popular edible part in the United States. It has been compared to a cross between the green bean and a cranberry bean. Supermarkets are now beginning to carry them in a limited fashion, and they are grown for this market in southern Florida, Hawaii and Puerto Rico.

The leaves of the plant are said to taste like spinach, and the flowers are sweetened by nectar and resemble mushrooms in flavor when they're sautéed. The immature seeds within the young pods taste like garden peas, and when they mature, they resemble soybeans, which are grown in the temperate zone rather than in tropical areas.

With much the same nutritional value and properties of soybeans, they can also be ground into flour for bread, pressed into oil or sprouted and turned into bean curd. The roots are not wasted either, and many varieties of winged beans produce tubers that are richer in protein than the potato, yam or cassava.

Given the proper marketing push and aggressive promotion, the winged bean may well become as common and accepted as the kiwi fruit, another unknown entity a short while back.

Nuñas

There's no doubt that the child in all of us just loves any grain or bean that promises that it will pop when heated. Just look at the success of popcorn. Nuñas, a New World bean, are also known as *"popping beans,"* and just like popcorn, they crack, swell and burst when heated, doubling in size and yielding a bean with a roasted nut flavor and a snack that is very high in fiber and protein with less oil than peanuts. Some say they have a sweet "Cracker Jack" flavor. Others describe them as tasting like peanuts.

The

Versatile

Grain

and the

Elegant

Bean

498

They thrive in the Andes mountains of Bolivia, Peru and Ecuador, and they range in color from purple to gold to cream, while some look like colorfully speckled miniature bird's eggs.

However, there appears to be a bit of a snag. They don't seem to act properly and pop at lower elevations. At Washington State University, Dr. Stephen Spaeth, a U.S. Department of Agriculture physiologist and research scientist, is trying to breed a strain that will flourish at lower altitudes. The beans are being grown experimentally in light- and climate-controlled greenhouses and it will probably take several years before it is understood just what the best conditions are for soil composition, hours of daylight, climate and elevation. All are thought to have some effect on the ability of the nuñas to pop. So it may be a while before nuñas become the new "movie food of the future."

A Brief Addendum . . .

Miguel de Cervantes, he of the delicious adventures of *Don Quixote* once wrote, "He that publishes a book runs a very great hazard, since nothing can be more impossible than to compose one that may secure the approbation of every reader." As the authors of this book, we have tried to impart to our readers not only our respect for the potential of the versatile grain and the elegant bean(s), but also our wonder at the vast range of recipes that can be achieved with them. We hope, of course, that there has been something for everyone and that new culinary doors have opened as a result.

Each time we come to the final pages of a book, the same feelings begin to surface, and we have the mixed sense of relief and of the loss of a friend who has been close to us for almost two years. And so, the easiest way to end is to, of course, just end. But this time, we have found the perfect farewell and we take leave with the words with which Louis Armstrong signed his letters:

"Red beans and ricely yours,"
Sheryl & Mel London

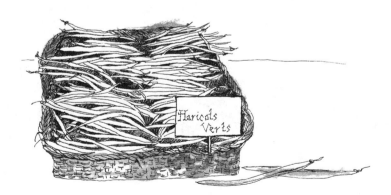

The

Versatile

Grain

and the

Elegant

Bean

500

Mail Order Sources . . .
and Other Product Information

With today's more nutritionally aware consumer has come the growth and expansion of product availability—especially in the area of whole grains and legumes. Many of the grain forms that once had to be located, then milled at home, are now on the shelves of the health food stores and specialty shops all across the country. We have even found some of them on display in supermarkets in towns as diverse as Henderson, North Carolina, and Gillette, Wyoming. On the other hand, some grains such as teff and amaranth and quinoa may not yet be available in your area, or your local market may not carry even the more common forms of grain such as rye flour or stone-ground cornmeal. In that case, the listings that follow may help, either through direct ordering by mail or by contacting the company or mill and asking about the nearest outlet for their products in your area. We have found most of the people with whom we are in contact are reliable, friendly, warm and quite giving of product information.

Arrowhead Mills
Box 2059
Hereford, TX 79045-2059
(806) 364-0730

Our old friend Frank Ford tells us that they now ship to supermarket chains and natural food stores all over the country, and their products run the gamut of grains—including teff, amaranth, blue corn, quinoa—and a good variety of legumes—including azuki beans, pinto beans, mung beans and lentils. They would be delighted to tell you which stores carry their products in your area, and in a case where you live in an isolated location, would accommodate you through mail order. Check your local health food store.

Balducci's
424 Avenue of the Americas
New York, NY 10011
(212) 673-2600

In addition to a large range of Italian specialties, they are now carrying many varieties of imported beans as well as grains and pastas. Retail and mail order sales.

Birkett Mills
P.O. Box 440
Penn Yan, NY 14527
(315) 536-3311

Stone-ground flours, buckwheat groats and flours and several grades of roasted buckwheat (kasha) from whole to find grind. Price list available for mail order.

Brumwell Flour Mill
328 East Second Street
Sumner, IA 50674
(319) 578-3207

Brumwell has been selling natural grain products since 1936 and they offer a range of grains that includes steel-cut oats, stone-ground cornmeal, as well as white, whole wheat, rye and corn flour. A price list is available on request.

Butte Creek Mill
Box 561
Eagle Point, OR 97524
(503) 826-3531

All their products are stone-ground using waterpower in a mill that has stood on the banks of the Little Butte Creek since 1872, and is the only operating gristmill in Oregon today. They sell a large variety of grains, including berries, rolled grains and stone-ground flours. Some can now be found in stores such as Dean & DeLuca in New York and in the Williams-Sonoma stores around the country (and even in Tokyo). Ask for their price list.

Callaway Gardens
Pine Mountain, GA 31822-2000
(404) 663-5100
To order: (800) 282-8181

Home of the excellent Speckled Heart Stone Ground Grits, available at their store, and in some airports (such as Atlanta) and also by mail order. Catalogue available.

Dean & DeLuca
560 Broadway
New York, NY 10012
(800) 221-7714
(Inside NYS) (212) 431-1691

They stock a large range of cooking utensils, grains, flours and legumes from all across the country and overseas, including arborio and basmati rice and legumes such as cannellini, pinto, azuki, fava and garbanzo beans. They are also a prime source of heirloom and hybrid beans. Their catalogue is available and their people quite knowledgeable if you call for information. Their store on lower Broadway in New York is well worth a visit if you're ever in the area.

Deer Valley Farm
RD #1
Guilford, NY 13780
(607) 764-8556

Organically grown grains, seeds, and stone-milled flour, including some of the hard-to-find varieties such as triticale. They also stock legumes. Ask for their price list.

Fall River Wild Rice
HC-01, Osprey Drive
Fall River Mills, CA 96028
(916) 336-5222

A fourteen-grower/member coooperative that sells only what the cooperative members produce. In addition to its wild rice, it also offers wild rice pancakes, one style with white flour and the other wheat-free. Write for further information and prices.

Falls Mills
Route 1, Box 44
Belvidere, TN 37306
(615) 469-7161

We've already mentioned that John and Jane Lovett's grits are our favorites. They're stone-ground in their water-powered mill, which dates back well over 100 years. In addition, they sell cornmeal, triticale, wheat and rye flours, buckwheat flour and rice flour. Price list on request.

Garden Spot Distributors
438 White Oak Road
New Holland, PA 17557
(Outside PA) (800) 829-5100
(Inside PA) (800) 292-9631

They are the exclusive Northeast distributors for all Shiloh brand products, including a large selection of grains, beans and herbs. They can give you information as to just which stores carry the products you're looking for, or they will ship by mail order. Write for complete catalogue.

Gray's Grist Mill
P.O. Box 422
Adamsville, RI 02801
(508) 636-6075

Another mill that is over 100 years old, and the last letter told us that Tim the Miller and his partner, Ralph Guild, are "still grinding their way into the hearts of millions!" They feature Jonny Cake Meal (their spelling) as well as stone-ground wheat and rye flours. Price list available.

Kenyon Corn Meal Company
Usquepaugh, RI 02892
(401) 783-4054

They feature Johnny Cake Corn Meal, ground by millstones at Kenyon's Grist Mill, dating back to 1886. They also offer yellow and white cornmeal, whole wheat, oat, buckwheat and graham flour plus miller's bran. Price list available.

King Arthur's Flour
(The Baker's Catalogue)
Rural Route 2, Box 56
Norwich, VT 05055
(800) 827-6836

Specializing mostly in excellent products for the home bread baker, including utensils and a range of flours such as 8-Grain, amaranth, rice flour, Cornell mix, teff and triticale flour. Catalogue available.

Los Chileros de Nuevo Mexico
P.O. Box 6215
Santa Fe, NM 87502
(505) 471-6967

An excellent resource for the lovers of Southwestern and Mexican cuisine. They feature hard-to-find items such as *chicos* (dried corn), *panocha* (sprouted whole wheat flour) and *atole* (roasted blue cornmeal cereal), as well as a variety of dried chiles, chile powder, corn husks, blue corn popcorn and hominy. Send for price list and order form.

Maskal Forages, Inc.
1318 Willow
Caldwell, ID 83605
(208) 454-3330

Teff grain (brown or ivory) and teff flour (brown or ivory). Maskal's products are beginning to appear in health food stores, but they also handle mail order. Send for price list.

Morgan's Mills
RD #2, Box 4602
Union, ME 04862
(207) 785-4900

The owners have resurrected the 185-year-old water-powered gristmill and they sell a range of flours—whole wheat, rye, barley, buckwheat, rice and millet—as well as cornmeal and corn flour and Jonny Cake Mix (their spelling).

New Hope Mills
RFD #2
Moravia, NY 13118
(315) 497-0783

Another of the old (1823) mills that uses waterpower for stone grinding their flour— bread, buckwheat, graham, pastry, rye and whole wheat—plus cornmeal, oat bran and buckwheat grits. Price list on request.

Old Mill of Guilford
1340 N.C. 68 North
Oak Ridge, NC 27310
(919) 643-4783

Listed in the National Registry of Historic Places, the Old Mill is not too far from Greensboro. Their company's products include whole wheat, rye and buckwheat flour plus cornmeal, grits, rolled oats, steel-cut oats, wheat bran and wheat germ. Price list on request.

Oriental Pastry & Grocery Co.
170-172 Atlantic Avenue
Brooklyn, NY 11201
(718) 875-7687

Syrian, Greek and Middle Eastern specialties, bulgur in four grades, assorted dried fruits, nuts, mixed spices, green-wheat and couscous plus legumes such as split, peeled favas. They also sell unusual pots for Middle Eastern dishes, including carved wooden *ma'amoul* molds. Retail sales or mail order catalogue available.

Phipps Ranch
P.O. Box 349
Pescadero, CA 94060
(415) 879-0787

One of the best resources for mail order beans. About sixty miles from San Francisco, the Phippses offer about forty varieties of beans, many of them heirloom and many grown on their ranch, with supply depending upon crop yields each year. Flageolet, anasazi, cranberry, Jacob's Cattle, Soldier, and scarlet runner are just a few that are for sale in their farm store or by mail order. Send for price list.

Pines Distributor's International, Inc.
P.O. Box 1107
1040 East Twenty-Third Street
Lawrence, KS 66044
(913) 841-6016

Dehydrated wheat grass products, all-vegetable seasoning. Catalogue available for mail order.

Purity Foods, Inc.
2871 West Jolly Road
Okemos, MI 48864-3547
(517) 351-9231

If their spelt products are not available in your local health food store, Purity will send information on just where you can buy their hulled berries, flour or organic pastas. They sell mail order only in case-size lots.

Quinoa Corporation
24248 Crenshaw Boulevard Suite 220
Torrance, CA 90505
(213) 530-8666

The distribution of quinoa has expanded to the point where it is now available in almost every health food store in the country. As a result, the distributors of Ancient Harvest Quinoa sell through mail order only in case quantities. If your local area does not carry quinoa, it can be ordered through their local distributor.

St. Maries Wild Rice
Box 293
St. Maries, ID 83861
(800) 225-9453
(208) 245-5835

Organically grown wild rice from the lakes of northern Idaho. The rice is grown, processed and marketed by St. Maries. Ask for their recipe pamphlet.

Shiloh Farms
P.O. Box 97
Benton County
Sulphur Springs, AR 72768-0097
(501) 298-9631 or 298-3359

One of the largest distributors of organic products, including grains and legumes. Most of their products are available in retail natural food stores, but they also mail order. Write for retail catalogue. (For the Northeast, Garden Spot is their distributor. See their listing in this section).

Stansel, Ellis
P.O. Box 206
Gueydan, LA 70542
(318) 536-6140

The only mail order source we know of for the superb Popcorn rice that Ellis grows (see page 158 for a description). When we asked Ellis and his wife, Grace, if they had any literature, Ellis gently replied, "I ain't got time for that fancy printin'—I only grow rice!" It's worth the trouble to order it. Send for his price list.

Vermont Bean Seed Company
RD # 1 Box 15
Whiting, VT 05778

Especially for gardeners! Vermont Bean Seed has the largest selection of heirloom bean seeds (as well as other varieties of legumes, vegetables, herbs and flower seeds), all of them untreated with chemicals—even their packages are recycled. Owner John Burke tells us "no new varieties are added until they are grown in our trial garden and passed by our taste tests." The catalogue is a modest $2.

Walnut Acres
Penns Creek, PA 17862
(800) 433-3998

One of the earliest organic farms, it was lauded by the *Last Whole Earth Catalog*, and it has become a valuable source for whole grains and for beans. The company's listing now includes specialty flours such as teff, amaranth, quinoa, several varieties of rice, as well as a large selection of legumes. Write or call for the catalogue.

Index

pilafs (cont.)
  whole buckwheat groats with lemon, red peppers and sweet marjoram, 53
  whole kasha with mixed dried fruit, walnuts and herbs, 55
pineapple oat bran muffins, 130–31
pink bean(s), 419–23
  albóndigas with, 422–23
  cooking chart for, 419
  and eggplant ragout with mustard-glazed garlic sausage, 420–21
  with fresh basil, tomato and black olives, 421
pinto beans, 424–32
  chili con carne with, 431–32
  cooking chart for, 425
  frijoles borachos con pico de gallo: drunken beans with tomato salsa, 430
  with mild chiles and pine nuts (quelites), 426–27
  mixed beans, grains and mushroom loaf with hot and sweet pepper tomato sauce, 495–96
  pintos "refritos," 432
  Provençale with yellow peppers and parsley, 429
  savory, Mexican grilled chicken breasts with chile paste and, 427–28
pistachios, Lebanese Easter cakes with semolina and (ma'amoul), 254–55
pistou, 494
pizza, rolled (whole wheat stromboli), 234–235
pizzoccheri: Italian buckwheat pasta with Swiss chard and potatoes, 58
plums, tea-poached, vanilla barley pudding with cinnamon and, 39
pod beans, 458–59
polenta, 4, 81–82
  basic, 99
  crostini with prosciutto di Parma and fresh basil, 100
  crostini with three cheeses, 101
  with goat's milk cheese (brynza) and garlic butter, Romanian (mamaliga), 103
  with Gorgonzola and roasted red peppers, 105
  with ground veal, sage and green peas, 102
  with "little birds," Bergamo-style, 104
Polish golobki: barley and mushroom–stuffed cabbage leaves with sour cream and dill sauce, 37
poor boy soup with red kidney beans and cabbage, 436

popcorn, 81, 84
popcorn rice, 158, 165
pork:
  baked chick-peas with country-style spareribs, 342
  chops, Dixie speckled butter beans with mustard greens and, 392–93
  garlic pepper, saffron rice with green peas, capers and, 187
  roasted tenderloin of, with orange Campari sauce and Brazilian-style black beans (féijão brasiliero), 324–25
  stew of chicken, whole hominy and (posole), 108–9
  triple wheat and apple terrine with herbs and spices, 234
  Vietnamese mung bean thread noodles with shrimp, fresh mint and, 396–97
  see also sausage
Portuguese dishes:
  broa: corn and wheat peasant bread, 276–77
  caldo verde with cannellini beans, 468
  manchoupa: pot roast and whole dried fava beans, 357–58
posole: stew of pork, chicken and whole hominy, 108–9
potato:
  and mung bean curry, 398–99
  oaties with Roquefort cheese, Yorkshire, 131
  teff and cheese biscuits, 213
pot roast and whole dried fava beans, Portuguese (manchoupa), 357–58
pressure cookers, 305–6
priest's soup: red lentils and rice, 371
prizewinner beans, 442, 443
  with lamb, tomatoes and fresh thyme (haricots d'agneau), 447
prosciutto di Parma, polenta crostini with fresh basil and, 100
Provençale dishes:
  appaloosa beans with yellow peppers and parsley, 429
  tapenade: puréed lentils with olives, anchovies and capers, 366
prune:
  and apple crumble with cognac, 137
  and peanut butter whole wheat cookies, 404–5
puddings:
  barley grits, orange and carrot, with raisins and toasted pecans, 40
  quinoa pasta, cheese and fruit, 152

rice (*cont.*)
  ground beef and yellow split pea bou-
    lettes with lemon and mint, 411
  and herb-stuffed baked tomatoes, 190
  lentils and crisp fried sweet onions (Le-
    banese *mejedrah*), 380–81
  lettuce and vegetable soup with saffron
    and (*minestra alla Milanese*), 182
  and mozzarella croquettes, Italian (*sup-
    pli al telefono*), 191
  old-fashioned fresh herbed tomato soup
    with, 183
  Persian saffron, mold with chicken, fruit
    and walnuts, 184
  pilafs, 177–79
  products, 159–61
  red lentils and (priest's soup), 371
  ring with mushrooms, hazelnuts and
    chicken liver, 186
  risottos, 173–76
  saffron, with garlic, pepper, pork, green
    peas and capers, 187
  steamed glutinous, rolls filled with
    shrimp, scallions and black sesame
    seeds, 181
  sweet, and azuki bean paste balls with
    plum wine sauce and Japanese green
    tea, 313
  types of, 157–59
  warm Wehani, salad with grapes, pine
    nuts and smoked turkey, 194
  washing, 180
  yellow, Cuban-style, with green peas,
    red pepper and black olives, 185
  see also wild rice
rice bran, 10, 159
rice flour, 161
  and raspberry flummery (Swedish *risen-
    gröt*), 195
rice noodles, 161
  seven vegetable, with chile and sesame
    sauce, 192–93
risengröt: Swedish raspberry and rice flour
  flummery, 195
rishta: Syrian lentils with noodles, onions
  and tomatoes, 380
risottos, 173–76
  with dried wild porcini mushrooms, 175
  Milanese: saffron and Parmesan cheese,
    174
  with shrimp, 176
  with spring vegetables, 175
  with tiny peas and prosciutto, 175
rivvels, 410
Roman beans, 297

Romanian dishes:
  cream of wheat, chive, parsley and to-
    mato dumplings, 237
  mamaliga: polenta with goat's milk
    cheese (brynza) and garlic butter, 103
roti with hot chiles, garlic and cilantro, 38
runner beans, 442–47
  cooking chart for, 443
  scarlet, 442, 443
  scarlet, baked with pasta, buttered bread
    crumbs and anchovies, gratin of 445–
    446
  sweet white, with *skordalia* sauce, 443–
    444
  white, 442, 443
  white, with fennel, olives and red pep-
    pers in lemon mint vinaigrette, 446
Russian dishes:
  beet, cabbage and tomato borscht with
    rye berries, 202
  buckwheat groats, garlic and sorrel soup
    with fresh herbs, 52
rye, 3, 6, 12, 197–208, 279
  and cabbage boards, Hungarian, 201
  and caraway flatbread wheels, Finnish,
    208
  cooking chart for, 200
  dark raisin pumpernickel bread, 206–7
  forms of, 198–99
  and red onion focaccia with thyme, 205–6
rye berries, 198
  beet, cabbage and tomato borscht with,
    202
  and parsley salad with Kalamata olives
    and Pecorino cheese, 204
  sweet and sour celery with, 203
rye grits, 198, 200

salad dressings, *see* vinaigrettes
salads, entrée:
  azuki bean, with cucumber, watercress
    and scallops in wasabi cream, 312
  fennel, endive and wild rice, with Gruy-
    ère cheese, 266
  French lentil and vegetable, with kiel-
    basa and chèvre, 369
  lingua di fuoco tonnato: Tongues of Fire
    beans with fresh grilled tuna, herbs
    and spinach, 350
  pan-grilled shrimp with white beans, aru-
    gula, oranges and red onion, 485–86
  poached mussels and red lentil, with
    herb and shallot vinaigrette, 376–77
  seafood and couscous, pescara with or-
    anges and red onions, 256–57

Index

527

Liquid and Dry Measure
Equivalencies

CUSTOMARY	METRIC
¼ teaspoon	1.25 milliliters
½ teaspoon	2.5 milliliters
1 teaspoon	5 milliliters
1 tablespoon	15 milliliters
1 fluid ounce	30 milliliters
¼ cup	60 milliliters
⅓ cup	80 milliliters
½ cup	120 milliliters
1 cup	240 milliliters
1 pint (2 cups)	480 milliliters
1 quart (4 cups, 32 ounces)	960 milliliters (.96 liters)
1 gallon (4 quarts)	3.84 liters
1 ounce (by weight)	28 grams
¼ pound (4 ounces)	114 grams
1 pound (16 ounces)	454 grams
2.2 pounds	1 kilogram (1000 grams)

Oven Temperature
Equivalencies

DESCRIPTION	°FAHRENHEIT	°CELSIUS
Cool	200	90
Very slow	250	120
Slow	300–325	150–160
Moderately slow	325–350	160–180
Moderate	350–375	180–190
Moderately hot	375–400	190–200
Hot	400–450	200–230
Very hot	450–500	230–260

About the Authors

MEL AND SHERYL LONDON are the authors of fourteen other books, including eight cookbooks, as well as books on subjects that range from travel to lifestyle, gardening and film and videotape career guides. Their *Fish Lovers' Cookbook* was First Prize winner in its category in the Tastemaker Awards.

As documentary filmmakers, Mel and Sheryl have worked in more than sixty countries on every continent, producing films for foundations and corporations on the environment, travel, energy, training, fund raising and health. Mel's documentary on aging and chronic disease was a nominee for the Academy Award and together they hold more than 250 other awards for their film work.

They make their home in New York's East Village, but create and test recipes at their house on Fire Island.